D1228304

TOUCHES OF SWEET HARMONY

TOUCHES OF SWEET HARMONY

Pythagorean Cosmology and Renaissance Poetics

by

S. K. Heninger, Jr.

THE HUNTINGTON LIBRARY · SAN MARINO, CALIFORNIA

Library of Congress
Card Number 73-78049

Designed by Mary Stoddard

Printed in the
United States of America
by Kingsport Press

Published with the assistance of the
Union Pacific Railroad Foundation Fund

TO MY MOTHER AND FATHER

CONTENTS

ILLUSTRATIONS

PREFACE

Quite early in my reading of renaissance literature I became aware that not only certain passages but even whole works would not submit to the terms of analysis then in vogue. *Paradise Lost* was openly denounced, while *The Faerie Queene* was relegated to a definitive edition, and no one even mentioned Sidney's *Arcadia.* Contemporary taste ran to the short rhetorical poem, so the lyrics of Wyatt and Donne were brought forth as the touchstones of literary excellence. Modern sensibility responded to physical stimulus and looked to literature for experience, so there was much talk about imagery and about the response of the reader.

Clearly we were passing by many of the most highly acclaimed and widely influential literary works with no more than a curt nod of dismissal. We were so busily engaged in finding examples to demonstrate and support our own critical theories that we were failing to recognize the masterpieces which have determined the English literary tradition. Our narrow concern with new criticism was cutting us off from the richest portion of our literary heritage.

In consequence, with confessed perversity, I began to consider other critical issues. I began to ask not what does this work mean today and what is my personal response to it, but rather what led the author to write in this way and what was an Elizabethan likely to have gotten from it. Many of my academic elders were asking the same questions, and there was a growing concern with the concept of natural order, for example, and with theories of indirect expression such as allegory. There were also searching efforts to reconstruct certain bodies of knowledge, such as the scientific and occult disciplines, the tenets of several religious sects, the history of various ideas, and the facts of historical events and movements. There has been a prodigious effort to learn as much as possible about the Elizabethan period, presumably with the intention of reading the literature within this context.

Now the barrier between us and Elizabethan literature is not so much a lack of information about the period (although we are far from fully informed), as a lack of sympathy with the modes of thought that then prevailed. Conditioned as we are by the assumptions of our scientific age, we cannot easily comprehend the produce of different modes of thought. Our thinking is permeated with the epistemology and ontology of physical science; it teaches us that we can know a thing only through our sense perception of it, and furthermore that the thing has no existence except these phenomena. Given our assumptions that we know a poem by its phenomena (i.e., its words), it is difficult for us to acquiesce in a reading process where meaning is located in predetermined absolutes and is conveyed by metaphor. It is difficult for us to accept *a priori* agreements between author and reader, agreements announced in advance by the genre of the work, by its title, and less overtly by its form. But a renaissance author expected us to read his work with certain presuppositions in mind, and he took pains to indicate what these presuppositions should be. He did not start from scratch. He did not assume that the reader's mind was a *tabula rasa* or that the experience of reading his work would be highly individual.

One astute critic has recently defined a method which he dubs "affective stylistics." Quite simply this method, in the critic's own words, "involves an analysis of the developing responses of the reader in relation to the words as they succeed one another in time."[1] I quarrel with this method only to the extent of pointing out that it largely predetermines the sort of reading it produces. Because of its grounding in subjectivism and phenomenalism, the interpretation is apt to be much more a reflection of the reader than of the author. But this is certainly one way of proceeding in criticism, and I admire the clarity and honesty of the critic in stating his postulates.

The method I have prepared for, however, approaches literature from the opposite direction. I have sought to reconstruct a doctrine which was prominent in the renaissance—indeed, as it was expressed in cosmology, it was the most forceful orthodox determinant of renaissance thought. The notion of a divinely ordered universe is one of our most ancient propositions, having emanated from the school of Pythagoras as early as the sixth century B.C. It was assim-

[1] Stanley E. Fish, "Literature in the Reader: Affective Stylistics," *New Literary History*, 2 (1970), 126–127.

ilated by Plato and thence by the Church Fathers, and after that it was a basic premise, stated or unstated, in most Western philosophy, religion, and science until the seventeenth century. The early renaissance humanists, and later the scientists, enthusiastically reaffirmed it. My effort has been to reconstruct the Pythagorean doctrine in all its ramifications. To this end, I have gathered a great deal of information from a wide variety of renaissance sources and have organized it under a few headings in Part II.

But my effort has been larger than merely to reconstruct a body of knowledge. I am interested not only in the subject matter of Pythagorean doctrine, but even more important, I have been concerned to throw light upon the modes of thought that it induced. The central belief in cosmos requires an acceptance of paradox (such as the coexistence of unity and multeity), of analogy (such as that between the four elements and the four bodily humors), and of mutability (that is, of two coordinate systems of time, one sequential and the other homogeneous). Ultimately my concern has been to theorize about the sort of poetics that would derive from such a doctrine, and Part III is the result of that speculation.

In other studies yet to be written, I hope to examine certain renaissance authors in the context of this poetics. Some, of course, used the tradition as a sounding board, and their work expresses their departure from it, even their refutation of it. The vitality of a literary work may well spring from the tension between the dominant world view and an author's individual interpretation of it in light of his own experience. But others adopted the tradition intact, and sought to exemplify it. Many renaissance authors, including some of the best, were eager proponents of the prevailing cosmology. With extraordinary optimism, they conceived of their works as autonomous art objects that imaged the perfection of the cosmos. They reproduced the infinite variety of the universe in their subject matter and the natural processes of the universe in their poetic techniques. They sought to create literary microcosmoi.

Needless to say, a poetics of this sort imposes certain demands upon the reader. While necessarily he must read discursively for the first time through the work, he must not stop with this phenomenalistic experience. From perception of the words in sequence, he is to proceed to a synthesis of the work as a whole. His ultimate aim is an overview of the totality, removed from the confines of time and space. Only when we look *sub specie aeternitatis* can we comprehend the full meaning of the work, can we see it as a literary microcosm.

Moreover, only when we have this totality in mind can we begin to read the work in any intensive fashion. The full dimension of any episode or any character or any image can be determined only by considering that part in relation to the whole. Therefore reading such a work consists in analyzing the multifarious particulars; but then, as a corollary process, we must relate each particular to the entirety of the work. Conversely, the totality must be brought to bear on every portion of it. In fact, by some sort of deductive process, the meaning of any portion must be derived from the whole.

This mode of reading, as I have suggested, comes to literature from a direction opposite to that of affective stylistics. According to that method, the meaning of the work lies in "the developing responses of the reader in relation to the words as they succeed one another in time." According to the poetics derived from Pythagorean cosmology, in contrast, the meaning of the work lies in the conception of the author, which he has expressed by means of actions, characters, and settings—that is, the work is a conceptual unity which has been made palpable to our senses through a verisimilar image of physical nature in all its multeity. Affective stylistics may be the critical method most successfully employed upon seventeenth-century literature, which reflects the growing empiricism and materialism of its era; but it does not cope successfully with the cosmic patterns of long works in the earlier English renaissance. Perhaps the best way to distinguish between the literary climate of Elizabethan England and that of the seventeenth century is to note the change between the cosmological assumptions which underlie Pythagorean poetics and those which underlie affective stylistics. This change, of course, is commonly called the scientific revolution.

What I have done in this study, then, is to reconstruct the conservative cosmology on the eve of the scientific revolution and the concomitant beliefs that sprang from it, including a poetics. I have been as orthodox, even retrospective, as possible in order to mark clearly the shift that occurred in the seventeenth century. I have exaggerated that shift in my efforts to delineate it distinctly; it began earlier and proceeded more gradually than my study might suggest. But the modern mind, implementing the scientific assumptions of our day, thinks in ways radically different from the renaissance mind. So I have worked to describe a body of knowledge and certain modes of thought which characterized the renaissance. And I emphasize the need of understanding the renaissance mind before we purport to read its literature. After all, literature is nothing more than someone's interpretation of his experience, a record of how he views the world.

Since Pythagorean cosmology was discredited by the scientific revolution, it will for the most part seem esoteric to us. Throughout this study I have felt as though I were swimming upstream against the current of our own cultural conditioning. I do not abide by the tenets of Pythagorean doctrine; but in order to understand the writings of those who did, it is important to shed our own equally delimiting assumptions. It is difficult for us to reason deductively, and we may never accept the validity of the syllogism. But the renaissance did. And we have little chance of entering the renaissance mind if we confine ourselves to the inductive process. For example, astrology is folly unless we accept the notion of cosmos, the premise that all things in the universe are interrelated; and metempsychosis is superstitious unless we recognize the *anima mundi*, the world soul from which the individual soul emerges and to which it returns. There is no empirical evidence to support either of these beliefs. But once the fact of cosmos is granted, then deductive logic prescribes that astrology and metempsychosis must obtain. The mental process of reasoning holds sway and brooks no contravention. I hereby warn my reader, though, that to follow this line of reasoning he must actively seek to relocate the point from which he is accustomed to view reality. The orientation of this study requires a point of view quite different from the familiar one.

I must issue also another warning. The tenets which the renaissance ascribed to Pythagoras and his school have been massively revised by modern scholars and in many instances rejected as unhistorical. Speaking factually, Pythagoras and his immediate disciples provided a small and elusive nucleus which later centuries lavishly surrounded with many strata of legends and ascriptions. The renaissance accepted this rich tradition with syncretistic zeal, and even elaborated it. But modern historians of philosophy have been more exacting. At the least they distinguish between Pythagoras himself, his early school (including Archytas and Philolaus), Plato and the early Academy, and Neopythagoreanism with its late classical forgeries. We should be aware of the discontinuity between Pythagoreanism as it flourished in the renaissance and as modern scholarship defines it.

In this same cautionary vein, I must call attention to a few words which I use in special (almost technical) senses. By the word "infinite" in this study I mean an all-inclusive and therefore unified totality, a summation of all the particulars and even alternatives. "Infinite" does not mean the indefinite without limit, a concept which was odious to the Pythagoreans. Consequently, even though it is limited, I say that the cosmos is infinite, meaning that it is an entity which exhausts and therefore subsumes the full range of multifarious possibilities. Again, by the word "multeity" I mean an aggregate of autonomous entities, in contrast to "unity." The more usual word in philosophical discussion today is "plurality." I prefer "multeity" in this study, however, not only because it has an archaic flavor, but also because it suggests a multitude of distinct and various items rather than merely a plural number. Finally, I use the terms "conceptual" and "physical" to designate two mutually exclusive areas of human experience. "Conceptual" pertains to an ontology where ultimate reality resides among ideas at some suprasensible level; "physical" pertains to an ontology where ultimate reality resides among the palpable objects of nature. The more familiar terms are "intelligible" and "sensible," which have been publicized by Plato. I do not wish to restrict my discussion to the Platonic system, however, and therefore I use the looser terms, "conceptual" and "physical." I might also note that my terms avoid the subjectivism of Plato's terms; "intelligible" and "sensible" depend upon a perceiving subject.

In my exposition the criterion of utility has been given precedence over gracefulness. My intent has been to display this rather esoteric doctrine as visibly as possible. I use frequent and extensive quotations, and often approach the frenetic eclectism of a commonplace book. I hope that I have satisfied without sating. Since utility has been my chief aim, I am also pleased to have found a large number of appropriate illustrations from renaissance books, and enormously grateful to the publications board of the Huntington Library for approving the full complement of plates. They have also generously allowed me lengthy footnotes of an enumerative sort, and I have often given a full list of authorities where one or two might suffice. But the extended bibliographical footnotes will show the limit of my own research, and I hope will provide a *terminus a quo* for those who wish to pursue a topic beyond that point.

I owe debts of gratitude to a large number of individuals and institutions, and I acknowledge these debts with joyous thanks for the helpfulness bounteously given. I have sharpened my argument by talking with many colleagues, including Stuart Curran, L. S.

Dembo, Daniel Donno, Elizabeth Story Donno, Madeline Doran, Helen Gardner, Karl Kroeber, Richard Rierdan, John T. Shawcross, Hallett Smith, John M. Steadman, Edward W. Tayler, James Thorpe, J. B. Trapp, Robert Westman—I count my blessings in the length of this list. In a category apart, I should like to recall my debt to Don C. Allen and Earl R. Wasserman, two mentors who to my sadness did not live to hold this book. I must also offer thanks to Robert Jordan and Joseph A. Wittreich, who read the completed typescript and made invaluable comments, and especially to Paul Oskar Kristeller, who read with flattering care. Less personally, though nonetheless deeply, I am grateful to the staffs of the Bodleian Library, the British Museum, the Cambridge University Library, the Duke University Library, the Folger Library, the John Rylands Library, the Warburg Institute, and most of all the Huntington Library. For financial support, I am indebted to the Duke University Research Council, the Graduate School of the University of Wisconsin (Madison), the John Simon Guggenheim Memorial Foundation, and the Huntington Library—*diutissime floreant!* For permission to reproduce material in their custody, I thank the Curators of the Bodleian Library (Plates 1, 2, 3, 4, 5, 6, 9, 10, 15, 16, 17, 18, 27, 30, 35), the Trustees of the British Museum (Plates 32, 44, 50), the Librarian of Duke University (Plates 21, 33, 39, 40, 48, 52), the Director of the Folger Library (Plates 29, 41, 42), and the Director of the Huntington Library (Plates 7, 8, 11, 12, 13, 14, 19, 20, 22, 23, 24, 25, 26, 28, 31, 34, 36, 37, 38, 43, 45, 46, 47, 49, 51). Finally, in the warmest terms I must thank Jane Evans, who dealt resolutely with a refractory typescript, Betty Leigh Merrell, who guided this book through the press with skillful and loving hands, and my wife, who performed the sort of yeoman service that no public acknowledgment can touch.

Pasadena, California
July, 1973

S. K. H.

PYTHAGOREANISM IN THE RENAISSANCE

I

Cosmology and Poetry: An Introduction

In the peroration of *The defence of poesie,* Philip Sidney dons the playful mask that he often assumes to cover his seriousness, and admonishes his reader to appreciate the powerful virtues of poetry. According to Sidney, we should believe the poet when he claims that he can make us immortal: "Thus doing, your soule shall be placed with *Dantes Beatrix,* or *Virgils Anchises.*" But if we deride poetry, Sidney threateningly jokes with only half a smile, we shall be doomed to dullness and lost in perdition:

> But if (fie of such a but) you bee borne so neare the dull-making *Cataract* of *Nilus,* that you cannot heare the Planet-like Musicke of *Poetrie;* if you have so earth-creeping a mind that it cannot lift it selfe up to looke to the skie of *Poetrie,* . . . [you] wil become such a mome, as to bee a *Momus* of *Poetrie.*[1]

Here Sidney is recalling from Cicero's *Somnium Scipionis* (v) a well-known passage devoted to the Pythagorean doctrine about the music of the spheres. We are not aware of the ever-present harmony in the heavens, Cicero explains, because our ears are deadened to the constant sound, just as those who dwell near the cataract of the Nile are accustomed to the deafening noise and therefore do not hear it. In Macrobius' commentary on the *Somnium Scipionis* this passage comes in for extensive exegesis, and innumerable other pedagogues repeat this strange bit of erudite lore. Much learning and a long-standing tradition are therefore compressed into Sidney's playful comment.[2]

Especially the phrase "the Planet-like Musicke of *Poetrie*" is fraught with recondite meaning. It implies not only that poetry is measured in quantity like music, but also that poetry should echo the cosmic order inherent in the music of the spheres. Just as each planet generates a note contributing to the harmony of the heavens to comprise an all-inclusive diapason which represents the cosmos in musical terms, so must the elements of a poem fit together to comprise a comprehensive whole which reflects the universal order. Only then will poetry reproduce the "Planet-like Musicke" that Macrobius so greatly admired, and that Sidney takes to be a reasonable expectation for a poem. To epitomize the rich tradition which Sidney assumes we recognize and accept, we might say that Pythagorean cosmology should determine poetic theory.

Sidney is not alone in his assumption that Pythagorean cosmology provides the proper patterns for beauty in our lives. In the final scene of *The Merchant of Venice*, after Antonio has proved his friendship for Bassanio and Bassanio has reciprocated in equal measure, after Bassanio has won Portia and Gratiano has paired with Nerissa, after Shylock has been thwarted and the Duke has confirmed justice in the realm, the happy couples converge on Belmont for the consummation of their triumph over selfishness. Portia and Nerissa have discarded the masculine disguise which circumstance forced upon them, and soon they will adopt the appropriate relationship to their husbands. We anticipate a scene like the wedding of Theseus and Hippolyta where all the lovers are decorously arranged in pairs, where we shall "find the concord of this discord" (*Midsummer Night's Dream*, V.i.60).

The scene opens with Lorenzo in the garden of Belmont alone with his lady, Jessica; and "the moon shines bright" (V.i.1), so it seems that Titania and Oberon have blessed this spot. The two lovers, stable in their relationship, look up to the shining sky and wittily recount sad tales of love in joyful celebration of their own happiness. While anticipating the arrival of the other lovers, Lorenzo leisurely contemplates the visible beauty of the scene and in a lengthy speech calls attention to the harmony which manifestly prevails in heaven:

> How sweet the moonlight sleeps upon this bank!
> Here will we sit and let the sounds of music
> Creep in our ears; soft stillness and the night
> Become the touches of sweet harmony.
> Sit, Jessica. Look how the floor of heaven
> Is thick inlaid with patines of bright gold;
> There's not the smallest orb which thou behold'st
> But in his motion like an angel sings,
> Still quiring to the young-ey'd cherubins.
>
> (V.i.54–62)

The passage is effective as physical description, setting a scene conducive to the satisfying close of the play. But it works even more effectively on the conceptual level, projecting a matrix of ideas wherein the plot can make its thematic statement. The Pythagorean doctrine about the music of the spheres provides a context within which moonlight and music and serenity and love are interrelated and underscore meaning. They are becoming (i. e., appropriate) to "the touches of sweet harmony" which pour upon the scene from the musical orbs. Through these touches of sweet harmony the heavenly music informs our lives with beauty. The Pythagorean cosmos is the source of beauty, the mold for beauty, the standard by which beauty is recognized.

Lorenzo continues his speech along just such a vein, applying the celestial music to the human condition. He extrapolates from the macrocosm to the microcosm:

> Such harmony is in immortal souls,
> But whilst this muddy vesture of decay
> Doth grossly close it in, we cannot hear it.
> (V.i.63–65)

As Lorenzo says, the heavenly harmony resides within the human soul, though we may not be aware of it. While Cicero gave a pagan reason for our inability to hear this celestial music (we are like those who live too near the cataracts of the Nile), Lorenzo offers a religious reason based upon man's fallen state: our senses are clogged by the grossness of our flesh. In this statement of *contemptus carnis*, Lorenzo conflates Christian doctrine with the older philosophical view of the dichotomy between body and soul. Despite its inaudibility, however, the harmony is nonetheless latent in our inmost being, bestowing immortality and allowing us to participate in the larger harmony of the universe. The thematic statement of the play attests to the importance of recognizing this harmony, and the plot demonstrates how to live in accord with it. The touches of sweet harmony fall upon us unstrained, like Portia's mercy, endowing our lives with music and concord and joy.

For the renaissance, art was intended to reflect and reveal these touches of sweet harmony which infuse our universe. In Sidney's words, poetry was to echo "the Planet-like Musicke" which makes palpable the divine consent of the empyrean. An esthetics was developed with the intention of making art an image of the cosmos. Art should embody the sempiternal beauty of the divine pattern, which might otherwise remain beyond our grasp.

The tradition of this esthetics can be traced back through the Florentine Platonists to St. Augustine and eventually to the Pythagorean doctrine recorded in Plato's *Timaeus* (47A-D). In that seminal discussion of our senses and their modes of perceiving, Timaeus insists that sight was bestowed on man so that we might observe the harmonious motions of the heavenly spheres, and by those celestial paradigms we might then regulate our own internal harmony. The sense of hearing, though slightly lower in the hierarchy of human faculties, was given us for a similar purpose. In consequence, poetry and music, the arts directed at hearing, bear the onus of expressing these orderly patterns in the heavens:

> It was for these same purposes that speech was ordained, and it makes the greatest contribution thereto; music too, in so far as it uses audible sound, was bestowed for the sake of harmony. And harmony, which has motions akin to the revolutions of the Soul within us, was given by the Muses to him who makes intelligent use of the Muses, not as an aid to irrational pleasure, as is now supposed, but as an auxiliary to the inner revolution of the Soul (47C-D).

In such an esthetics, there is a direct chain of relationships from the percipient through the art work to a concept of idealized nature and ultimately to the deity itself.

By reading the literary work, we become aware of truths embodied in the beauty of our natural surroundings, and thence we can extract the benign intentions and beneficent attributes of our world's creator. Sidney implies this elevating purpose for art when he says that an "earth-creeping . . . mind . . . cannot lift it selfe up to looke to the skie of *Poetrie*." Unless oriented upward toward the celestial realm, our minds are indifferent to art. Or perhaps, it is the function of art to direct our thoughts toward contemplation of the universe. In this didactic purpose, poetry becomes an adjunct to cosmology.

By cosmology I mean the composition of the universe, how our world is put together. It comprises our beliefs about the fundamental constituents of the environment. So actually, cosmology is an analysis of ultimate reality, what the Greeks called *φύσις* and what our forebears in English have ambiguously called "nature." Many different things have at one time or another been urged as the elemental components of reality. A few of the better known include atoms (both in classical times and in our own), the sense data of humans, the mental impressions of humans, bundles of energy, electronic fields, ideas in the Platonic sense, numbers as defined by the Pythagoreans, and basic qualities (such as hot, cold, moist, and dry). Cosmology consists in designating the intrinsic ingredients of reality and defining the interrelations between them.

There is in all cultures and in all periods—in every esthetics—a relationship between art and cosmology. Perforce there must be some relationship between an art work and the reality which it presumes to comment upon, otherwise the art work would be at best whimsy or fantasy—perhaps "an aid to irrational pleasure," to use Timaeus' phrase, but nothing more. Since art holds the mirror up to nature, it must necessarily deal with the data of nature, however that nature might be defined.[3] In this assumption, we have the reassuring voice of Philip Sidney: "There is no Art delivered unto mankind that hath not the workes of nature for his principall object."[4] The discipline of esthetics, in fact, might be defined as the attempt to determine the relationship between art and nature.

Even if the artist wishes to deny cause-and-effect and seeks to confirm prevalent disorder, he must maintain a relationship between his view of nature and his art. He must fashion an art work which embodies the principle of random occurrence. If like the dadaists and the surrealists he chooses to devise outlandish juxtapositions as a means of demonstrating the unreliability of our assumptions about ordinary things, his artifact still records a decision about ultimate reality. Surrealism makes fun of traditional cosmology; it takes preconceptions of how things are arranged and then deliberately contravenes them in a puckish manner. Dadaism is even more disturbing; it purposes to show outright that nothing has any connection with anything else. Both the dadaist and the surrealist reflect directly a reality which denies the dependability of causal relationships in our environment. Then we have the paradox of an art form which by its selection and arrangement rejects the notion of cosmology, the notion that our universe is a selection and arrangement of items chosen by some process from the infinite range of possibilities.

To take another example of an art movement which illuminates my point, we might look at cubism. When it became fashionable under the influence of early twentieth-century atomists to think of ultimate reality as a congeries of separate units subject to certain laws expressed by mathematical equations, then our artists likewise fragmented their interpretation of reality into discontinuous geometrical forms. Cubism is an attempt to correlate atomic theory with our everyday perception of things, an attempt to translate the ultimate reality posited by atomic physicists into terms which the layman can comprehend and confirm with his senses. A work of literature deriving from the same esthetics is Faulkner's *The Sound and the Fury* or *As I Lay Dying*, where subjective responses to fragmented reality are laid out piecemeal for the reader to synthesize into an integrated art work. The responsibility of the artist is merely to provide the discontinuous pieces.

But whatever reality the artist wishes to depict and whatever techniques he chooses as his means, art always pertains to the reality which it ventures to interpret, or else we would dismiss it as eccentric or trivial. Not even cubism or surrealism or dadaism is exempt from this condition. For those art forms to be effective, we must have an a priori agreement between artist and percipient about cause-and-effect sequences and about the arrangement of items in space and about the relentless progress of time. An art work presupposes certain interrelations (or the lack thereof) between things within the coordinates of space and time. It always presupposes a cosmology.

We must recognize too that art is not only a presentation of subject matter about reality, a discursive description of its content, but also an analysis of its form. If art is to be true to nature, it should reveal the structural dependence between the items of that nature which it reflects. Assumptions about time and space therefore determine not only the subject matter of an art work, but also the internal arrangement of its constituent parts. An art work, in fact, is an individual's attempt to record his perception of temporal and spatial relationships among the data of his experience, his attempt within the limits of the artifact to reproduce the content and the form of the universe as he perceives it.

An art work, then, is a description (entire or partial) of the artist's ultimate reality, comprising both subject matter and structure. We must now begin to sophisticate our inquiry, however, because this ultimate reality may be of two sorts. It might be conceptual or it might be physical. For some, like Plato, ultimate reality lies with the ideas or essences at some supra-sensible level where only the intellect might conceive it, though we can apply that knowledge to our mundane affairs. For others, like Aristotle, ultimate reality resides among the physical objects which our senses perceive, though by inductive reasoning we can abstract from these data a hypothesis which has universal application. The point to be made is that ultimate reality is posited by some in conceptual terms and by others in physical terms, and the two ontologies might tend toward a common ground between them—indeed, the thrust of each is necessarily in this direction—but they are in fact distinct and can never be reconciled as philosophical systems.

Moreover, as a further sophistication we must note that this ultimate reality might be objective or it might be subjective—that is, ultimate reality might remain a constant which is independent of and unaffected by any perceiving mind; or ultimate reality might be conditioned in varying degrees by the percipient himself. If we opt for an objective reality, our art will describe a permanent, unchanging nature, be it conceptual or physical, and it will deal with generalities. If we subscribe to a thoroughly subjective reality, our art will derive from an individual response to an undefined stimulus, be it intellectual or palpable, and it will record a unique human experience.[5]

These, of course, are extremes which we have posited, and few art works depend wholly upon one or the other possibility. Most draw in varying proportions upon both. But there are some art forms which strive to realize one or the other extreme. Abstract expressionism, for example, discounts completely the possibility of an objective reality. The result, however, is critical anarchy. There can be no community of response to abstract expressionism unless we postulate some collective unconscious such as Jung's and assume that the abstract patterns exhibited by the art work will activate some residual, archetypal patterns which we all share.[6] Otherwise, the response of each percipient to the art work will be unique and may not contain elements in common with the responses of other percipients. Conversely, purely representational art such as trompe-l'œil relies completely on an objective reality. It concentrates on appealing to the eye to the exclusion of all else. The eye is quickly satisfied, however, and our interest in trompe-l'œil soon wanes. Although art theories have developed and flourished at one pole or the other, it is rare as well as difficult—and perhaps rare because it is difficult—for an artist to assume a wholly objective or a wholly subjective reality. Most art works provide a somewhat subjective interpretation of an objective reality. Our literary heritage might be roughly categorized into neoclassical and romantic works, but there are very few pure examples of either.

Generally speaking, nonetheless, in our intellectual history we have usually recognized that we seem to have experience of two distinguishable sorts, one occurring in a realm of physical objects which we perceive with our senses and the other transpiring in a realm of abstract concepts which we contemplate with our minds. Plato was the first in recorded Western thought to formalize this dichotomy, which he did by postulating an unchanging world of absolute being and a transient world of continually becoming; and he interrelated the two halves of this reality by assuming that the physical objects in the world of becoming are replicas (albeit imperfect replicas) of the ideal essences in the world of being. Given such a dichotomization, however, we have difficulty in designating which kind of experience is real and which is only a projection of the other.

Indeed, a continuing problem in metaphysics, as far from solution today as ever, is to identify the limits of the physical realm and of the conceptual realm, and to describe the interaction between them. During the renaissance the familiar chain of being was an attempt to deal with this metaphysical problem. The physical realm comprised (in ascending order) stones, plants, and animals; the conceptual realm comprised (in descending order) God and the angels. And man was the nexus between them, holding the physical and the conceptual together in a single entity and providing a means of intercourse between them. Man is literally the crucial link in the chain. His superiority—what makes him lord of creation—is directly due to his ability to have experience at both the physical and the conceptual levels.

Likewise, art should be an attempt to interrelate the physical and the conceptual. It can be the record of man's wide scope of experience as he ranges the infinite continuum from the earth of plants to the footstool of God. Man surpasses the lower ranks of nature by virtue of his intelligence and his articulateness. And in a way he also holds superiority over the angels, who are confined to the spiritual realm and can operate in the physical realm only vicariously through influencing human agents. While the angels because of their noncorporeality are restricted to direct discourse and prohibited from artistic expression—even their dancing on a pin is highly questionable—the human artist through his artifact can render palpable the truths of God's empyrean. The art work, the produce of man's God-given reason, is in fact his highest achievement. And since speech is just below reason in the renaissance ranking of God's gifts, poetry is the highest achievement of man in art.

Others have already amply demonstrated that the notion of the great chain of natural order is a critical touchstone in our understanding of renaissance literature. It was a premise, stated or unstated, in the mind of every major poet from Dante to Pope. But I should like to extend this application of cosmology in criticism—extend it to the point of saying that every art work rests upon cosmological assumptions, and that we as critics must discover those assumptions before we presume to interpret the work. We must first ask, "What is the ultimate reality which this work is commenting upon; what ultimate reality serves as a referent for it?"

As an example of the wasteful confusion in criticism which results when a cosmology is not stipulated, we might look at the muddle surrounding what Aristotle intended when he said that poetry is imitation. This statement has been paraphrased by intelligent and well-intentioned critics to mean everything from A to Z. It has been used by some to exclude all but representational art, and by others to justify abstraction in art. Clearly, it is imperative to specify a cosmological framework before we talk about any theory of art as imitation. Imitating *what* ultimate reality? physical or conceptual? [7] Is this an objective or a subjective reality? Any attempt to understand Aristotle's statement without answering these questions is doomed to debilitating ambiguity and will gain few adherents.

Similarly, any attempt to devise a theory of allegory will be futile until a cosmological framework is specified. If one thing stands for another, as it does in allegory, which is original and which is projection? Which is real and which is image? Even the pastoral and tragedy and the novel as genres imply a cosmology, as do also the sonnet sequence and the ode and free verse. In fine, without specifying a cosmological framework it is fatuous to discuss any theory of symbol or of language or of style or of structure or of anything else that we as critics talk about, except perhaps the biographical facts pertaining to the author and the bibliographical facts pertaining to the text.

In our daily lives our cosmological suppositions underlie almost every choice of action and largely determine our life style. For example, we observe that the stars in the sky follow a regular course and the planets do not crash into one another. This is an empirical fact that we learn from observation. But we might explain the reality which lies behind this fact by several different assumptions. We might explain it in terms amenable to the Greeks and say that a demigod, Atlas, supports the heavens on his strong shoulders and protects us from celestial disarray.[8] Or we might explain it in terms amenable to the medieval Schoolmen and say that God's will keeps peace in heaven and generates *caritas*. Or we might explain it in terms most familiar to us as modern men and say that the force of gravity maintains a mechanical system and the attraction between two bodies is directly proportional to the product of their masses and inversely proportional to the square of the distance between them. The same phenomenon can be dealt with in quite different ways. We can explain it in terms of mythology or theology or physical science. And the scheme that we accept as truth—as ultimate reality—determines our own response to the universe and how we choose to live in it. Our cosmology determines whether we are euhemeristic pagans or faithful Christians or pragmatic scientists.

Just so, our cosmological presuppositions condition our theories of art. After all, art is only an attempt to sort through observed facts and arrange them in some sort of meaningful statement about our perception of the universe. We may view art as a palpable representation in accord with mythology, as a didactic extension of theology, or as an amusing alternative to the objectified nature of physical science. All of these esthetics—and probably others—are possible. We must decide, however, what cosmology is operative for any theory of art before we begin constructing its esthetics and applying it to individual works.

As critics, we must ask three questions as a preliminary to setting out, and two diametrically opposed answers are possible for each question. First, the ontological question: what is art? Is art an object, conceptual or physical, having an independent and immutable existence quite apart from any perceiving mind? or is it a subjective impression, intellectual or sensual, having no existence at all until it is perceived, and then having as many different existences as there are perceivers? For myself, I should like to work toward some theory of art as a happening, a dynamic event that transpires in the intermundum between the art object itself and the individual human percipient.[9] Second, the epistemological question: how do we know art? Do we best proceed to an understanding of it by conscious, rational analysis of our sense data? or by affective, emotional response to whatever appeals to us, a part or a whole? Even if we say by both, by rational analysis and by emotional response, we must ask which comes first, which is the more dependable, and which will be our final criterion. Third, the teleological question: what is the purpose of art? This question was especially important to Protestants in Elizabethan England, though Plato was also concerned about the effect of art on the commonwealth. Is art to influence human behavior, to make us better men, a moral aim? or is it entertainment, mere recreation, simple escapism? In his effort to elude the horns of this dilemma, Plato banished the poets from his republic. Horace, one of our most influential literary critics, wanted it both ways—poetry, he said, is to teach and to delight. But as he was interpreted by later moralists, the purpose of delighting was made subsidiary to the purpose of teaching, so that any pleasure in poetry is simply a ruse, an inducement to submit to instruction, a sugarcoating to the pill. These are the questions, it seems to me, that responsible critics must ask as a prolegomenon to their discipline, and I think they are best answered in the context of cosmology.

Cosmological assumptions, then, do condition our theories of art, and we must be aware of this. Proceeding now to practical criticism, we can say further that the cosmology of the artist conditions a particular art work, so that we must try to determine his perception of the universe before we attempt to analyze his art—his painting or musical composition or building or poem. An art work, being the artist's mirror of nature, must necessarily reflect that nature as the artist perceives it. Moreover, the artist not only uses cosmology for his subject matter—the art work is not only a narrative description of reality—but also the form of the art work reflects his perception of how the universe is put together. The organization of the art work, its structure, is an effective means of conveying the artist's view of how the basic constituents of reality are interrelated. The structure of a work contributes to its total statement, and may in some instances be a salient feature, a major means of making its statement.

To illustrate my point, I should like to offer two examples: Dante's *Divina commedia* and Eliot's *The Waste Land.* At first glance these two poems may appear to be wholly dissimilar. They are separated by a great distance in geography and in time, and their poetic statements are incompatible. But they also bear remarkable resemblances. Both poems anatomize the poet's home city —Florence in the first instance and London in the second. In each case the poet wanders through his community describing its deficiencies and seeking some sort of understanding and inner peace despite the prevalent evil, so his poem is at the same time an abrasive commentary on contemporary society and a spiritual progress.

Furthermore—and this is the point most pertinent here—each poem depends in large part upon its structure to convey its meaning. In Dante's day the prevalent cosmology was geocentric, with earth firmly fixed as the focal point of a finite, neatly ordered universe. And Dante writes a finite, neatly ordered poem. There is insistent evidence of careful arrangement: three books, 100 cantos, the terza rima, to mention merely the mechanical contrivances.

Moreover, the poem is finite. After traversing the inferno, purgatorio, and paradiso, we arrive at the presence of God, which is definitely the end of the line. There is no place farther to go. Dante has exhausted the possibilities of human experience, both in this world and the next. In contrast, Eliot's poem is a collection of fragments recounting subjective events, a loose and (seemingly) haphazard sequence of disconnected episodes. There are gaps between the episodes, no continuity except that provided by the reader as he responds to the succession of passionate vignettes paraded jerkily before his mind's eye. Furthermore, the poet could have continued with any number of other episodes; there is no apparent reason for him to have stopped where he did. *The Waste Land*, then, is a series of discrete fragments which must be interrelated by the reader and which could go on indefinitely. It reflects quite clearly the prevalent cosmology of Eliot's day: an infinite universe where motion is relative, where there are no fixed points, in which only the subjective response of the individual percipient gives any sense of order or of limit. In each instance, in the *Divina commedia* and in *The Waste Land*, the form of the work makes the clearest statement of its meaning. On this point, the two works are strikingly similar in poetic technique: the poet expresses his perception of reality most forcefully by means of the poem's structure. But of course the ultimate reality of Dante varies greatly from that of Eliot, and Dante's poetics, conditioned by his cosmology, is antithetical to the phantasmagoria of Eliot's *Waste Land*.

As a tenet of practical criticism, then, I hope to have established that determining an author's cosmology is prerequisite to understanding his work. Esthetic assumptions and the psychology behind them are conditioned largely by cosmological assumptions.[10] Once we discover the ultimate reality of the author, though, we can then deal with his art work as an interpretation of or a comment upon that reality. And we can proceed beyond subject matter to an inquiry into the techniques which he employs in his effort to present his view of reality. In sum, our final assessment should include an account of his thematic statement, which is static (*natura naturata*), and in addition an analysis of the process by which he makes this statement (*natura naturans*). In this way, we reveal the dynamics as well as the permanency of art.

Although it is immodestly hoped that this study will have implications for the consideration of any art form in relation to the cosmology which prevails at the time, I have narrowed my scope to an examination of poetics in relation to Pythagorean cosmology in the renaissance. It is especially interesting and valuable to study the relationship between cosmology and art in the renaissance because at this time our cosmological assumptions were being reviewed and revised as never before in our history. Preconceptions about reality were being challenged and replaced by another set of preconceptions. With the change in cosmology there was, of course, a correspondent change in art, and therefore the period is particularly instructive about the relationship between the two. One might define the renaissance, in fact, as this change in assumptions and the resultant efflorescence of scientific thought and artistic expression.[11]

Poetics provides a representative artistic mode, and in some ways is uniquely suitable for a study of the relation between cosmology and art. Literature is the artistic mode that utilizes words as its medium, and words have a dual citizenship, belonging to both the physical world and the conceptual world. It might be argued that sculpture and painting are wholly physical, while music is wholly conceptual, and therefore neither is representative. But without doubt a word conveys a physical datum but is itself a concept only.[12] Since words fit comfortably in either a physical or an intellectual universe—indeed, can be confined to neither—they are a peculiarly adaptable medium for artistic expression. Agrippa is unequivocal on this point:

> Words therefore are the fittest medium betwixt the speaker and the hearer, carrying with them not only the conception of the mind, but also the vertue [power] of the speaker with a certain efficacy unto the hearers, and this oftentimes with so great a power, that oftentimes they change not only the hearers, but also other bodies, and things that have no life.[13]

While we might not wish to go so far as Agrippa in assigning magical force to words, we should recognize that, especially in the renaissance, language was seen as the nexus between conceptualization and physicality, the means whereby the dictates of man's reason were translated into action. The word had something of the same divine imperative that Christ conveyed as λόγος. Renaissance poetics, then, occupies a venerated but nonetheless representative position in the history of esthetics. It produced a remarkable body of art.

I have focused on Pythagorean cosmology for the sake of convenience, because it is a distinct (although extensive and varied) set of beliefs. Even more important, however, it is a fully articulated cosmology that touched every field of human endeavor: ethics, theology, science, politics, art. Pythagorean doctrine was all-inclusive in its intention and all-permeative in actual effect, and in some fields it retained its potency until well into the modern period. The notion of cosmic order and its corollaries, perhaps better known as universal harmony, stemmed from the school of Pythagoras in the sixth century B.C. It flourished throughout the classical period (most notably in the Academy of Plato and in the Roman circle of Neoplatonists around Plotinus), cross-pollinated with Stoics and Peripatetics, scattered seed as far abroad as the Hermeticists and the Cabalists and the Syrian syncretists and St. Augustine, and came to full bloom in the renaissance. Its most ingenious and insistent advocate, strangely enough, was Johann Kepler, who like most partisans grew more vehement as it became clearer that his position was untenable. Pythagorean cosmology, though withered, did not die until the acceptance of Newtonian science and Humian philosophy. The physics of Newton reduced relationships in nature to mechanical laws to be determined empirically, and the skepticism of Hume denied any cause-and-effect relationships in the intellectual as well as the physical realm. In the meantime, however, the cosmic order first propounded by Pythagoras had provided the stimulus and the cohesion for the best Western thought through all the intervening centuries. And it must be mastered, I believe, if we wish to comprehend the art of those centuries.

At the same time that I point to the long history of Pythagorean cosmology, I wish to be clear that this study does not trace the chronological development of the concept of cosmic order or the influence of Pythagorean ideas on other systems of belief. Part II reconstructs a synoptic view of Pythagorean doctrine in renaissance Europe, and no more. It sets forth the traditional lore associated with Pythagoras, much of which modern scholarship discredits. Furthermore, it is scrupulously retrospective, ignoring the new forces for change. It is intentionally selective within its historical period, ignoring as much as possible the developments in philosophy and theology which encouraged inductive reasoning and neo-humanism, which in turn led to empiricism and the experimental method, which consequently produced the discoveries inaugurating a new science. Part II deals with orthodox beliefs only. It assembles the old-fashioned furniture of the reactionary mind, what by the mid-seventeenth century lay largely discarded in the attic of intellectual conservatism. Others have delineated the changeover from old to new, most notably, perhaps, A. O. Lovejoy in intellectual history, Alexandre Koyré in the history of astronomy, and Marjorie Hope Nicolson in literary criticism.

It is appropriate to note that others have also dealt with the subject of renaissance poetics in relation to cosmology. Hardin Craig's *Enchanted Glass* is a pioneer work in this field, clear-sighted and energetic, opening paths which have not yet been fully explored. Theodore Spencer in his germinal book, *Shakespeare and the Nature of Man*, took as a basic premise that cosmology conditions art, and he argued that the excellence of Elizabethan drama, the genre most expressive of conflict, derived directly from the tension between old beliefs and new. An interest in cosmology underpins the work of E. M. W. Tillyard, who felt compelled to publish separately his widely known *Elizabethan World Picture*. I hope that this study in a real sense extends these earlier investigations. My debt to these scholars and to many more unmentioned here will be obvious.

To be as orderly as possible, I begin with a summary of what the renaissance knew (or thought it knew) about Pythagoras and a rapid survey of the major materials available in the renaissance which purvey Pythagorean beliefs, a corpus remarkable for its variety as well as for its quantity. Bibliographical footnotes suggest the accessibility of these materials. Part II reconstructs the Pythagorean beliefs known in the renaissance grouped under a number of convenient headings. The doctrine was transmitted as a self-consistent body of thought, however, and knowledge of the whole is necessary for the full understanding of any particular tenet. Finally, Part III considers a few esthetic assumptions which derive directly from Pythagorean cosmology—that is, the poet is a creator acting in likeness of the godhead, metaphor depends upon correspondences between the various levels of creation, and the poem serves as a microcosm in literary form. Needless to say, it is the last for which the first was made, but also it is the last which must perforce remain inconclusive—not a set of facts, but rather open-ended essays which establish some artistic postulates and attempt a few critical applications.

Notes

[1] (William Ponsonby; London, 1595), K2.

[2] John Milton was also much interested in and susceptible to this tradition; his early attitude is clearly evidenced in his prolusion *De sphaerarum concentu*, and again in the "Nativity Ode" and in "At a Solemn Musick."

[3] For an analysis of various concepts of "nature" in relation to art, see Arthur O. Lovejoy, " 'Nature' as Aesthetic Norm," *Modern Langauge Notes*, 42 (1927), 444–450; also Harold S. Wilson, "Some Meanings of 'Nature' in Renaissance Literary Theory," *Journal of the History of Ideas*, 2 (1941), 430–

448. For a consideration of changing concepts of "nature" in various periods of Western thought, see R. G. Collingwood, *The Idea of Nature* (Oxford, 1945). For an historical study of how English poets thought of themselves vis-à-vis nature, see Meyer H. Abrams, *The Mirror and the Lamp* (Oxford Univ. Press, 1953).

[4] *Defence of poesie*, B4v. It should be noted that in this passage Sidney is using the word "art" in its literal sense of L. *ars*, "skill"; and among the arts he includes astronomy, geometry and arithmetic, music, natural and moral philosophy, law, history, grammar, rhetoric, logic, medicine, metaphysics—and also, of course, poetry.

[5] In the renaissance, critics were aware that art may induce only a subjective reality for the percipient. For example, Edward Norgate (d. 1650), an arbiter of Stuart taste, wrote a manual of painting in which he commented: "Landscape is nothing but Deceptive visions, a kind of cousning or cheating your owne Eyes, by our owne consent and assistance" (*Miniatura: or the Art of Limning*, ed. Martin Hardie [Oxford, 1919], p. 51).

[6] St. Augustine raised this possibility. "How do you explain," the master asks his docile pupil, "the fact that an ignorant crowd hisses off a flute-player letting out futile sounds, and on the other hand applauds one who plays well?" And he answers: "It is done by nature giving everyone a sense of hearing by which such things are judged" (*On Music*, tr. Robert C. Taliaferro [New York, 1947], p. 184). Cf. also *ibid.*, pp. 325–327.

[7] The different meanings of μίμησις as conceived by Plato and by Aristotle are painstakingly elucidated by Richard McKeon, "Literary Criticism and the Concept of Imitation in Antiquity," *Modern Philology*, 34 (1936), 1–35.

[8] Elizabethans were fully capable of interpreting the myth of Atlas as a rationalization. According to Thomas Cooper, for example, he was "the brother of Prometheus, who, as the Greekes suppose, did firste finde out the course of the starres, by an excellent imagination. Wherefore the Poets fained, that hee sustained the firmament with his shoulders" (*Thesaurus linguae Romanae & Britannicae* [London, 1584], Cccccccı).

[9] To be consistent with my thesis that esthetics depends upon cosmology, I should cite a modern metaphysician who has postulated that reality is a similar event which results from the interaction between an ultimate constituent of matter and a human mind; so see Bertrand Russell, "The Ultimate Constituents of Matter," an address delivered before the Philosophical Society of Manchester in February 1915, and printed in Russell, *Mysticism and Logic* (New York, 1957), pp. 120–139.

[10] Katherine E. Gilbert and Helmut Kuhn propose that a comprehensive cosmology was necessary before a concept of esthetics could develop, and they cite Pythagoreanism as a first example of an esthetic doctrine (*A History of Esthetics* [New York, 1939], pp. 3–10). The larger implications of my statement are sensitively considered from the twentieth-century perspective by Joseph Frank, *The Widening Gyre* (Rutgers Univ. Press, 1963), esp. chap. i, "Spatial Form in Modern Literature."

[11] For a provocative discussion of the interaction between humanism and empiricism in the renaissance, see Joan Gadol, "The Unity of the Renaissance: Humanism, Natural Science, and Art" in *From the Renaissance to the Counter-Reformation*, ed. Charles H. Carter (New York, 1965), pp. 29–55.

[12] For a patristic discussion of this statement, see Clement of Alexandria, *Stromateis* (VIII.viii), "The Method of Classifying Things and Names" in *The Ante-Nicene Fathers*, ed. Alexander Roberts and James Donaldson (New York, 1899), vol. pp. II, 564–565.

[13] *Three books of occult philosophy*, tr. John Freake (London, 1651), p. 152.

2

Pythagoras' School and Biography

In the development of Western philosophy as the renaissance saw it the sect of Pythagoras had played a definite and important role, a role much more important than is generally conceded today. For Ralph Cudworth, in fact, "*Pythagoras* was the most eminent of all the ancient Philosophers." [1] While such praise might be excessively generous—the myopic view of a Cambridge enthusiast in the mid-seventeenth century—there is no question about the reverence accorded Pythagoras and the long line of disciples that followed him down through antiquity. The two best known schools of classical philosophy, for the renaissance as for us, were the Academy of Plato and the Lyceum of Aristotle. The acknowledged prototype of philosophical schools, however, was the society for initiates which Pythagoras had founded at Croton in the late sixth century, known later as the Italic sect. Pythagoras stood behind Aristotle and Plato,[2] somewhat obscured by the mists of time, but clearly visible—certainly a more distinct personality and intellect than we discern from our modern vantage point.

Of these three giants of Greek philosophy, Aristotle was the least admired in the renaissance. For us, living in a post-Baconian world, Aristotelianism may suggest empirical observation and inductive reasoning. He may be invoked as the ancient exponent of modern science. But this view of Aristotle is contrary to what the renaissance knew best of his teaching. In the early renaissance, Aristotle retained his association with the medieval Schoolmen. He was primarily the logician and the moralist, author of the *Organon* and the *Ethica Nicomachea*. His work in the physical sciences was known, of course, and highly influential: the *Physica*, the *De caelo*, the *De generatione et corruptione*, the *Meteorologica*. But in a curious way, the high esteem in which these works were held made his natural treatises a bookish tradition in themselves; the very au-

Jamblichi Arithmetica
cum versione et notis
Samuelis Tennulii.
Ptolemæus.
Pythagoras.
Nicomachus.
Euclides.
ΑΡΙΘΜΟΙ
Aristoxenus.
Jamblichus.
Arnhemiæ apud Joh: Fridericum Hagium.

1. *Pythagoras in a group of colleagues*

Pythagoras holding a scroll inscribed ΑΡΙΘΜΟΙ ("numbers") stands amidst several of his cohorts. Aristoxenus, the musicologist who argued that the ear rather than the intellect should determine the consonant intervals between notes, plays upon a bass viol. Ptolemaeus, the eminent geographer and astronomer, takes astronomical readings with a Jacob's staff. Euclid, the geometer, measures distances on a terrestrial globe with a pair of compasses. Nicomachus, the arithmetician, leans forward attentively in the background. Iamblichus, the deferential biographer of Pythagoras, sits writing at a desk, perhaps recording the scene for posterity.

Iamblichus, *In Nicomachi Geraseni arithmeticam introductionem*, ed. Samuel Tennulius (Arnhem, 1668), frontispiece.

thority of Aristotle in such matters discouraged observation or experiment lest *the* Philosopher be proved wrong. This was the tradition that Bacon rejected and Glanvill denounced. It had, of course, already been forsaken by the practising scientists subsidized by commercial interests.[3]

Plato was, without doubt, the darling of the renaissance. In the early quattrocento several of the dialogues were rendered into Latin by various translators even before the Florentine Academy resurrected him in toto and enshrined him as their tutelary spirit. For centuries Plato's *Timaeus* had been the basic text for cosmology, passing over into both science and theology; his *Symposium*, adorned with Ficino's expansive commentary, provided a doctrine to guide moralist and love poet alike; his *Republic* was the touchstone for discussion of all public matters from government to education to art. Because of Plato's emphasis on mathematics in the Academy,[4] best publicized by the educational system prescribed for the *Republic* (522E ff.), he was seized upon by the empiricists who wished to justify measurement and was made the classical precedent for the new science.[5] As Henry Billingsley, a prominent citizen of London, proclaimed in his translation of Euclid:

> The wisest and best learned philosophers that have bene, as *Pithagoras, Timeus, Plato*, and their followers, found out & taught most pithely and purely, the secret and hidden knowledge of the nature and condicion of all thinges, by nombers, and by the proprieties and passions of them.[6]

Thomas Cooper, perhaps the most interesting Oxonian of the sixteenth century, spoke for his generation when he called Plato "the prince of all philosophiers (in wisedome, knowlage, vertue, and eloquence, far excedynge all other gentylles)." [7]

Through Plato's writings, especially the *Timaeus*, Pythagorean doctrine had entered the mainstream of Greek thought. It oversimplifies but slightly, in fact, to say that Socrates provided the method and the Pythagoreans the curriculum for Plato's Academy.[8] This is not to denigrate the achievement of Plato or to diminish his honor, but rather to place the Pythagorean school in better perspective. There is no doubt that much of Plato's teaching was a graft on the stock of Pythagorean doctrine.[9]

The regimen and the curriculum of the Pythagorean school were well known from a variety of authoritative sources, including Diogenes Laertius, Porphyry, Iamblichus, Ovid, Diodorus Siculus, Aulus Gellius, Apuleius, and Justinus.[10] Rather late in life, after syncretizing the wisdom of several disparate cultures—the Phoenicians, the Chaldeans, the Persians, the Hindus, the Arabians, the Jews, the Orphics, the Druids,[11] and especially the Egyptians—Pythagoras settled at Croton in Magna Graecia, where he founded a secret society open to both women and men. This society held out to its members the hope of divine perfection—in fact, each was dedicated to the release of his soul from its encumbering body, a purification to be effected through contemplation of the universal order revealed in nature. To achieve this purpose, Pythagoras offered instruction which began with mathematics, then proceeded to a study of physics and the investigation of primary principles, and finally promised knowledge of the deity.[12]

This progress to beatific vision by the long route through scientific study rather than the shortcut of irrational religious rapture became the *summum bonum* of the Pythagorean-Platonic doctrine. It is sketched by Urania in Spenser's *Teares of the Muses:*

> From hence wee mount aloft unto the skie,
> And looke into the Christall firmament:
> There we behold the heavens great *Hierarchie*,
> The Starres pure light, the Spheres swift movement,
> The Spirites and Intelligences fayre,
> And Angels waighting on th'Almighties chayre.
>
> And there with humble minde and high insight,
> Th'eternall Makers majestie wee viewe,
> His love, his truth, his glorie, and his might,
> And mercie more than mortall men can vew.
> O soveraigne Lord, O soveraigne happinesse
> To see thee, and thy mercie measurelesse.
>
> (ll. 505–516)

Experience of the deity was the ultimate aim of the Pythagorean sect, and therefore it became the fountainhead of a continuing strain of mysticism in Western thought. But because this experience was to be gained through study of nature, the sect was also the progenitor of systematic physical sciences. In the Pythagorean scheme, religion and science not only coexisted, but were mutually dependent. For this reason, the doctrine of Pythagoras was immensely reassuring to renaissance men who felt the forces of change dividing this world from the other.

As a means of preventing materialism in the society, Pythagoras deemed that all property was to be held communally, not individually. A prominent precept of the school was κοινὰ τὰ φίλων ἐιναι, *amicorum esse communia omnia*, "All is common among friends." [13] Another was φιλότης ἰσότης, *amicitia aequalitas*, "Friendship is equality," suggesting a prototypical democracy.[14] Devotion to friendship was a much publicized trait of Pythagoreans and gave rise to the well-known story of Damon and Pythias,[15] who according to the dictionary maker Thomas Cooper were "two Philosophers of Pythagoras hys secte, in the league of friendship being eache to other moste faithful." [16]

The regulations of the school were strict and severe. After careful selection, based upon physical as well as moral and intellectual criteria, the novices were admitted to a five-year probationary period, during which they were allowed to attend lectures but could not speak.[17] The reason for this restriction was given by Apuleius: "This was, I say, absolutely the first rudiment of wisdom, to learn to think, and unlearn to prate." [18] Clement of Alexandria offered a more mystical rationale for the imposition of silence: "That, abstracting themselves from the objects of sense, they might with the mind alone contemplate the Deity." [19] During the trial period of enforced silence, the novices were called *acousmatici*, "listeners." If successful, they passed into a more active phase of their instruction and were called *mathematici*, "students." These advanced members of the community were privileged to hear Pythagoras lecture in person, and were encouraged to search into the principles of things, not just to accept a statement without analysis. Pythagoras insisted upon oral transmission of his teachings and swore the initiated few to the utmost secrecy, so that neither he nor his immediate disciples left any writings.[20]

The daily routine at the school was prescribed by the master, and was austere but not unduly rigorous, allowing ample opportunity for meditation and study. The day began with a solitary walk in the woods in order to compose the soul, followed by a period of group study, followed in turn by physical exercise such as races and wrestling. After a modest noontime meal (no wine), they dealt as a community with community affairs. Late in the afternoon came another walk, but this time in pairs or parties to allow for discussion of what they had learned. After washing, they had supper in groups of no more than ten, performing ritual libations and of course observing the dietary laws of the sect, which forbade the eating of meat. After supper there were lectures, with the youngest reading and the eldest choosing the text. The day ended with another ritual libation and with the eldest leading the assemblage in recitation of the catechism known as the χρυσᾶ ἔπη, the *carmina aurea,* "the golden verses." [21] Retirement, though not necessarily sleep, followed immediately.

The discipline of the society was aimed at nurturing introspection. Memory was extolled and strengthened by exercises. Before going to sleep at night a Pythagorean recounted the events of the day, asking himself what he had accomplished, what he had done badly, and what he had left undone. In the morning before rising he tried to plan his next day in an orderly and productive fashion. Ausonius' Eclogue III is intended to be a character of the Pythagorean:

> A good wise person, such as hardly one
> Of many thousands to *Apollo* known,
> He his own judg strictly himself surveys,
> Nor minds the Noble's or the Common's ways:
> But, like the world it self, is smooth and round,
> In all his polisht frame no blemish found.
> He thinks how long *Cancer* the day extends,
> And *Capricorn* the night. Himself perpends
> In a just ballance, that no flaw there be,
> Nothing exuberant, but that all agree;
> Within that all be solid, nothing by
> A hollow sound betray vacuity.
> Nor suffer sleep to seize his eyes, before
> All acts of that long day he hath run o're;
> What things were mist, what done in time, what not;
> Why here respect, or reason there forgot;
> Why kept the worse opinion? when reliev'd
> A beggar; why with broken passion griev'd;
> What wish'd which had been better not desir'd;
> Why profit before honesty requir'd?
> If any by some speech or look offended,
> Why nature more than discipline attended?
> All words & deeds thus searcht from morn to night,
> He sorrows for the ill, rewards the right.[22]

The society assumed that wisdom and virtue begin with self-knowledge and the resultant self-control. The dictum *nosce teipsum,* it was later argued, originated among the Pythagoreans.[23]

Despite the emphasis placed upon introspection and individual virtue, there was nonetheless complete deference to the authority of Pythagoras. His way of life served as the model to be emulated and his teachings were unquestioned tenets. Each doctrine, in fact, was attributed to Pythagoras and carried the imprimatur αὐτὸς ἔφα, *Ipse dixit,* "He said it." As the late Roman miscellanist Aelianus recorded:

> Such as were present at his lectures, disputations, and reasonings gave great credit unto him, and beleeved his words which they esteemed equivalent, and countervaileable in truth, with *Apollos* Oracles.[24]

In the eyes of his followers, Pythagoras was raised above the level of mere mortal. As Aelianus intimated, he shared in the veracity of Pythian Apollo—in fact, his name derived from this august deity. And well Pythagoras deserved this veneration, as his biography (at least as it was legendized) reveals.

Most of what the renaissance knew of Pythagoras' life is mentioned in the narrow compass of this entry which Thomas Cooper prepared for his augmentation of Elyot's dictionary:

> *Pythagoras,* a man of excellente wytte, borne in an yle called *Samos,* whiche beinge subdued by Polycrates the tyraunte, Pythagoras forsoke his countrey and wente into Egypt and Babylonia, to lerne misticall sciences, and afterwarde came into Italy, where he continued the resydue of his lyfe. He was the first that named hym selfe a philosopher, where before men of great lernynge were called wise men: and bycause he wolde exchue the note of arrogance, whan one demanded of hym what he was, he sayde *Philosophus,* whiche signifyeth a lover of wysedome. He was in sharpnesse of wytte passyng all other, and founde the subtill conclusions and misteries of Arthemetike Musike and geometrye. Plato wondereth at his wisedome: his doctrine was dyvine, and commodyouse, the whiche he teachynge to other, injoyned them to kepe silence fyve yeres, and here hym dilygentely, er they demaunded of hym any question. He never wolde do sacrifice with any bloude, he wolde eate nothynge that had life, and lyved in a mervaylouse abstynence, and continence, and was in such auctoritie among his disciples, that whan in dispucions they maynteyned their opinion, if one demanded of them why it shuld be as they spake, thei wold aunswere onely *Ipse dixit, He* sayde so, meanynge Pythagoras, whiche aunswere was reputed as sufficient as if it had ben proved with an inevitable reason, so muche in estymation was he for his approved trouth and incomparable lernynge. He was noted to be expert in magike,

> and therfore it is written of hym, that nyghe to the citie of Tarentum, he behelde an oxe bytynge the toppes of beanes there growynge and treadinge it downe with his feete, wherfore he bade the herdsman to advyse his oxe, that he shulde absteyn frome grayne: the herde laughynge at hym, sayde, that he never lerned to speake as an oxe, but thou (sayde he) that semeste to have that experience therin, take myne offyce upon the. Forthwith Pythagoras went to the oxe, and layinge his mouthe to his eare, whispred some thynge of his art. A mervaylous thing, the oxe as yf he had ben taught, left eatynge of the corne, nor ever after touched any, but many yeres after mildely walked in the citie, & toke his meate only of them that wold give it hym.[25] Many lyke wonderfull thynges is written of hym, fynally his disciples, for their wysedome and temperaunce were alwayes had in great estimation. He was before the incarnation of Christe. 522. yeers.[26]

Early sources agree that Pythagoras' father was Mnesarchus, a gem engraver, and his most influential tutor was Pherecydes of Syros, an early cosmogonist with a mystical bent.[27] The birthplace of Pythagoras was disputed, like that of Homer, but he spent his childhood and youth in Samos and with this island he is invariably identified. Just as Aristotle is known as the Stagirite, Pythagoras is the Samian.

The dates of Pythagoras were a matter for argument which became a focal issue in one of the most acrimonious and pedantic squabbles of the late renaissance. Diogenes Laertius had recorded, "He flourished in the 60th Olympiad" (VIII.45)—i.e., 540–36 B.C. Caspar Peucer gave 495 B.C. as the year of Pythagoras' death,[28] and most learned contemporaries would have agreed that Pythagoras' life spanned roughly the last three-quarters of the sixth century.[29] The chronology digested from Iamblichus by Thomas Stanley represents a consensus:

> He was born about the third year of the fifty third Olympiad [566 B.C.]: That being eighteen years old, he heard *Thales* and others. Then he went to *Phoenicia*, thence into *Egypt*, where he staid twenty two years; afterwards at *Babylon* twelve years; then returned to *Samus*, being fifty six years old; and from thence went into *Italy*.[30]

In the last decade of the seventeenth century, the chronology of Pythagoras' life assumed an unwarranted importance in the notorious "battle of the books," because the dates (and therefore the authenticity) of Phalaris' epistles were pegged to it.[31] The most laborious sifting of the evidence, though, hardly improved upon Stanley's sketch.

Whatever the exact dates of Pythagoras, renaissance men saw him as living in a period of rather easy cultural exchange, like their own. Almost every eminent philosopher—Thales, Plato, Democritus—was reported to have had a youthful period of travel to other nations during which he assimilated foreign cultures and brought them home. Pythagoras was the example par excellence of such a syncretizer. Not only did he do it early, but he journeyed farther and assimilated more knowledge than anyone else. Jerome Turler, the professed authority on travelers, put Pythagoras at the top of the list in his chapter giving "Examples of Notable men that have traveilled," and his account of where Pythagoras went and what he accumulated is indicative of both the extent and the purpose of his wanderings:

> It is well knowne, y^t^ *Pythagoras* went first into *Egipt*, there to learne of the priestes of that cuntry the vertu of numbers, & the moste exquisite figures of *Geometrie*. From thence to *Babilon*, where of the *Chaldes* hee learned the course of the Planets, their stations, circuit, and effects, over these inferiour bodies. Then goynge backe into *Crete* how he came to *Lacedaemon*, to understand the most famous lawes which flourished at that time, made by *Lycurgus* and *Minos*. Lastlye, arrivinge in *Italie:* how hee remayned at the citie of *Croton* the space of twenty yeeres.[32]

The anonymous author of "A breefe conjecturall discourse, upon the hierographicall letters & caracters found upon fower fishes, taken neere Marstrand" imputed to Pythagoras an even wider range of knowledge. He began his preface with a mind-filling procession of esoteric lores which Pythagoras had mastered and transmitted to his pupils:

> *Pithagoras* the first instructer of the Greekes in misticall and profound Philosophie, and the earnest advoucher of *unum bonum* and *ens*, (who delivered unto his hearers the pith and substance of that knowledge and science that the *Egyptian* prophets, the *Assirian* Chaldes, the *Brittaine* Bards, the *French* Druids, the *Bactrian* Samanaei, the *Persian* Magi, the *Indian* Gimnosophists, *Anarcharsis* among the *Scithians*, in *Thracia* Zamolxis, and further East the Brachman Jewes did in his time and before professe. . . .[33]

The image of Pythagoras as exhaustive synthesizer of earlier cultures had basis in ancient authorities,[34] and learned men of the renaissance enthusiastically enhanced the evidence.[35]

Although tradition emphasized the secrecy of the Pythagorean sect and the oral transmission of its doctrine, Diogenes Laertius insisted that Pythagoras wrote at least three books: *On Education*, *On Statesmanship*, and *On Nature* (VIII.6–7). Iamblichus also spoke of voluminous works:

> This science, therefore, concerning intelligible natures and the Gods, Pythagoras delivers in his writings from a supernal origin. Afterwards, he teaches the whole of physics, and unfolds completely ethical philosophy and logic. He likewise delivers all-various disciplines, and the most excellent sciences. And in short there is nothing pertaining to human knowledge which is not accurately discussed in these writings.[36]

A corpus of Pythagoras' writings has been painstakingly reconstructed by later scholars,[37] but no extant work of any length can be seriously attributed directly to him. His teachings survive widely scattered in the published work of others.

As a natural result of ransacking other cultures for knowledge, Pythagoras was seen as a man of extraordinary wisdom. He was credited, in fact, with inventing several disciplines which lie at the center of Western culture. Although the "seven wise men" of Greece preceded him in point of time and although Thales was usually accorded the distinction of being the first to investigate nature,[38] Pythagoras had considerably more substance than any one of those tenuous personalities and received a lion's share of honor. It was unanimously agreed that he had coined the word "philosopher,"[39] many saw him as the father of Greek philosophy,[40] and all concurred that he was the most comprehensive of the pre-Socratics.

The variety of disciplines and discoveries traced back to Pythagoras is truly surprising. He holds pride of place in many different areas of learning. Thomas Stanley from his historical perspective declared:

> Practick [i.e., moral] Philosophy seems to have been the Invention of *Pythagoras;* for *Aristotle* affirms that he first undertook to discourse concerning Virtue; That *Socrates* is generally esteemed the Author thereof, perhaps is only because, as *Aristotle* adds, coming after him he discoursed better and more fully thereupon.[41]

By a slight extension, Pythagoras was praised as a law-giver: "They hold *Pythagoras* to be the Inventor of all Politick Discipline."[42] In the field of theoretical and applied science, Pythagoras through his preoccupation with numbers established arithmetic[43] and geometry[44] as systematic studies. Diogenes Laertius reported that Pythagoras "also discovered the musical intervals on the monochord" (VIII.II), and consequently he was credited with instituting musicology.[45] Because of his explanation of several celestial phenomena and because of his formulation of the first cosmology—he instituted, in fact, the word κόσμος[46]—Pythagoras was the progenitor of astronomy as a science.[47] These four disciplines—arithmetic, geometry, music, and astronomy—were the core of the curriculum in Plato's Academy and formed the *quadrivium* as Boethius transmitted it to the middle ages.[48] To be more specific about his astronomical theories, we should note that, according to some, Pythagoras had posited a spherical earth in a circular orbit about the sun[49] and an infinite universe,[50] two principles that were deferentially recalled by Copernicus and his followers. According to Pliny, Pythagoras was the earliest systematic botanist.[51] In theological matters, Pythagoras was the first to profess a deistic monotheism[52] and an immortal soul subjected to reward and punishment.[53] Because of such beliefs and his moral teachings, many saw Pythagoras as a proto-Christian.[54]

Today the best known fact about Pythagoras is the theorem which bears his name (Euclid, I.xlvii), that the square of the hypotenuse of a right-angled triangle is equal to the sum of the squares of the two sides ($c^2 = a^2 + b^2$). Discovery of this theorem was noted by Plutarch in order to relate the story of how Pythagoras sacrificed an ox to celebrate the occasion, a story that was oft repeated.[55] It was not the outstanding achievement of Pythagoras for the renaissance, however. Many other attributions took precedence. Far better known, for example, was the anecdote of how Pythagoras coined the word "philosopher." He chose to be called φιλόσοφος, "lover of wisdom," instead of the pretentious σοφός, "wise man," in use until his time. The *locus classicus* for this incident appears in Cicero's *Tusculanae disputationes* (V.3–4):

> [Pythagoras] came to Phliuns, a citie in Greece. And there, reasoned bothe learnedlye and largelye, with Leo the chyefe of the same towne. Whose wyt, and eloquence Leo wonderinge at, asked of him, in what arte he was mooste perfect. Whereunto, he aunswered, that he knewe no arte. But, that he was, a lover of wysedome [i.e., philosopher].[56]

The story was widely alluded to, and for many minds it gave evidence that Pythagoras was indeed the father of philosophy. The other notable coinage by Pythagoras was κόσμος, *mundus,* a word which, as Plutarch noted,[57] implied the beauty and order of the universe. In the *Gorgias,* Plato had taken pains to expound the significance of κόσμος:

> Now philosophers tell us, Callicles, that communion and friendship and orderliness and temperance and justice bind together heaven and earth and gods and men, and that this universe is therefore called Cosmos or order (507D–508A).[58]

In something of the same semantic vein, several memorable metaphors and aphorisms were attributed to Pythagoras. For example, when Leon Phliuntius asked how philosophers differed from other men, Pythagoras responded by comparing all mankind to the three separate groups that frequent the public games—contestants, venders, and spectators:

> Pithagoras aunswered, that the lyfe of man myght well be resembled, to that fayre, whych, wyth al pompe of playes, al Greece is wont to frequent, and solempnyse. For, like as there, some by the exercise of theyr bodyes, woulde assaye to winne some game, & crowne: and, some other, came thither, for the desyre to gayne, by byeng and sellynge, and also, there was a thirde sorte, farre passing al the rest, who sought neither game, nor gaynes, but came thither onelye to beholde, and see, what was done, and howe: so likewyse we comminge into this life, as it were into a great frequented fayre, or market, seke some for glory, and some for money. But very fewe, there are, which despisynge all other thinges, woulde studye the contemplation of nature. But these (he sayde) were they, whome he called the lovers of wisedome.[59]

In the same analytical mood, Pythagoras divided the life of man into four ages—a child, a youth, an adult, an old man—and he compared these ages to the four seasons,[60] thereby relating human experience to the natural cycle in a way that inspired poets down to Spenser's time.[61] With a comparably moral intention, a popular saw said that the choice at the crossroads between the path of virtue and the path of vice was like the letter Y (Greek *upsilon*), which was known as the Pythagorean letter.[62] Finally, speaking in the interest of public rather than private morality, Pythagoras was often quoted as having said:

> We ought to avoid with our utmost endeavour, and to amputate with Fire and Sword, and all other means from the Body, Sickness; from the Soul, Ignorance; from the Belly, Luxury; from a City, Sedition; from a Family, Discord; from all Things, Excess.[63]

Since so much gnomic wisdom had accrued to Pythagoras, it is not surprising to find that Walter Raleigh, among many, credited him with the much disputed dictum: "Man is the measure of all things."[64] Followers of Pythagoras for centuries maintained the tradition of *Ipse dixit.*

Because of his wide knowledge and extraordinary virtues, Pythagoras was endowed not unexpectedly with superhuman powers. His early biographers associated him with Pythian Apollo—indeed, his name asserted this association—and they claimed his descent from divinity. He was compared to Orpheus, exercising the same dominion over savage animals, except that what Orpheus accomplished by music Pythagoras achieved through words. Because of the purity of his life, Pythagoras alone of all men could hear the music of the spheres.[65] He was accorded the power of divination by a variety of means, including a magic mirror and a fortune-telling wheel,[66] and beginning with Porphyry (xxiii–xxix) a store of miracles was developed for him, such as those briefly recalled by Aelianus:

> This *Pythagoras* (as the rumor goeth) was seene in two severall places, namely in *Metapontio* and *Crotona*, in one present day, and in one instant houre. Besides that, he discovered his golden thigh in the *Olympiad.* Moreover he informed *Milo Crotoniata*, that hee was *Midas* the *Phrygian*, the sonne of *Gordius.* Furthermore hee plucked of the feathers of a white eagle which carried him, and as he passed over the floud *Cosa*, the streame spake unto him with an intelligible voice, calling him by his right name in this manner, *Salve Pythagora*, welcome *Pythagoras.*[67]

Such miracles gave Pythagoras a reputation for sorcery—as Thomas Cooper reports, "He was noted to be expert in magike"—and during the middle ages he kept company with other notable necromancers such as Vergil.

Pythagoras' dress and mien were appropriate to his lofty mind: "*Pythagoras Samius* was clothed in white apparel, and did weare uppon his head a crowne of Golde." [68] The fact of his golden thigh, visible proof of his near divinity, was recorded by Diogenes Laertius (VIII.II) and approvingly repeated by generations of later admirers in varying states of belief.[69] His demeanor, of course, was solemn and dignified. He maintained an even, unruffled disposition, subject to neither discernible joy nor sorrow. The image of Pythagoras as teacher, particularly as reconstructed by Ovid (*Metamorphoses*, XV.62–72), emphasizes his powers of persuasion (see Plate 2). Every aspect of Pythagoras contributed to his reputation for wisdom and piety.

Nonetheless, stemming from Lucian a defamatory tradition had developed which depicted Pythagoras as an inept and ridiculous egghead.[70] This caricature showed up in satire, of course, running the gamut from amused spoofing to angry denunciation. No philosopher was completely safe from such defamation of character—witness the parody of Socrates in Aristophanes' *Clouds*. In the case of Pythagoras, though, he usually appeared as a numskull gibbering about numbers or as a muddle-headed proponent of metempsychosis. In this pseudo-intellectual garb, for example, he serves as the butt of a skit devised by Mosca for the amusement of Volpone (I.ii.1–62).

Pythagoras' death occurred in Croton when a group of hostile townsfolk set fire to the house where the society was meeting, although other accounts of his death have been given.[71] He had a wife, Theano, several children, and a host of disciples.[72] Later eminent philosophers who were regularly seen in the direct line of Pythagoras include Empedocles, Parmenides, Zeno, Democritus, Socrates, and Plato.[73] Pythagoras' immediate influence as a practising philosopher and scientist continued to be felt, in fact, until far into the modern period. Writing in 1706 André Dacier, then probably the most distinguished classical scholar in France, offered a learned, if adulatory, opinion on Pythagoras' achievement:

> If we ought to measure the Glory of a Philosopher by the Duration of his Doctrine, and by the Extent of the Places that embrac'd it, nothing can equal that of *Pythagoras*, since most of his Opinions are at this Day literally follow'd in the greatest Part of the whole World: But this is not his highest Honour, for what is infinitely more glorious for him is this, that the two most excellent Men for Learning and Parts that *Greece* ever produc'd, *Socrates* and *Plato*, follow'd his Doctrine, and his Method of explaining it.[74]

In renaissance France, several academies were based explicitly on Pythagorean assumptions about number and harmony,[75] and Gulliver found in Laputa a full-blown Pythagorean society absurdly devoted to mathematics, astronomy, and music.

By the eighteenth century, which basked in the luminescence of the new science—"God said, 'Let Newton be, and there was Light!' "—the teachings of Pythagoras appeared impractical, a fit subject for satire. Science and religion were by then at odds, and any *modus vivendi* which attempted to encompass them both was bound to seem laughable. At the end of *Candide*, Pangloss as a disciple of Leibniz is still discoursing "du meilleur des Mondes possibles, de l'origine du mal, de la nature de l'âme, & de l'harmonie préétablie";[76] but his philosophy has been exposed as woefully inadequate to cope with a world which is far from the best in any list of possibilities. The modern age had begun.

In an earlier period, the serious-minded still strove to hear the music of the spheres, and renaissance poets, for sentimental as well as scientific reasons, were loath to relinquish that harmony for the monotonous whirrings of a great clock. Milton expressed the common regret at the passing of an age:

> How charming is divine Philosophy!
> Not harsh and crabbed, as dull fools suppose,
> But musical as is Apollo's lute,
> And a perpetual feast of nectar'd sweets,
> Where no crude surfeit reigns.
>
> (*Comus*, 476–480)[77]

The eighteenth century heeded Milton for his threatening theology, but largely ignored this softer strain. In the nineteenth century the more romantic of the poets attempted to recoup something of the lost sweetness of divine philosophy, but an aeolian harp is a poor substitute for Apollo's lyre.

During the renaissance, however, for one of the rare moments in history, science and ethics were incorporated into a single philosophical system, into the "divine Philosophy" of Pythagoras. Though science was subordinated to a higher purpose, it was nonetheless the essential first step in the *via humana*. For this reason, the Pythagorean doctrine appealed so strongly to the renaissance. Without diminishing the central importance of man or the possibility of his perfection, it urged the study of physics. It provided the humanists with a scientific orientation that Neoplatonism lacked, absorbed as it was in mysticism. Moreover, it provided a mathematical tradition of number, weight, and measure, a quantitative approach, that academic Aristotelianism lacked, absorbed as it was in qualitative analysis and logic. Pythagoras offered a mode of thought that kept man firmly in this world, but faced him in the direction of the next.[78] What more suitable authority could the renaissance resurrect from antiquity?

Notes

[1] *The true intellectual system of the universe* (London, 1678), p. 370.

[2] Photius preserves an anonymous life of Pythagoras which begins:

> It is said that Plato, being a pupil of Archytas, was the ninth in line to receive the doctrine of Pythagoras. Aristotle was the tenth in line.

> Excepit, inquit, docendi munere Pythagoram Plato nonus successor, Archytae senioris discipulus, decimus Aristoteles

(*Myriobiblon* [Rouen, 1653], col. 1314). When William Wotton entered the lists in the late seventeenth-century battle of the books, he began his argument by examining the doctrines of Pythagoras because that is where the history of learning started:

> In my Enquiries into the Progress of Learning . . . I shall begin with the Accounts which are given of the Learning of *Pythagoras,* rather than those of the more Ancient *Grecian* Sages [i.e., the Seven Wise Men]; because his School made a much greater Figure in the World, than any of those which preceded *Plato* and *Aristotle*

(*Reflections upon ancient and modern learning* [London, 1694], p. 91).

[3] I have necessarily oversimplified the status of Aristotle in the renaissance. For fuller treatment of the subject, see Paul O. Kristeller, "The Aristotelian Tradition" in *Renaissance Thought* [1955] (New York, 1961), pp. 24–47; and Kristeller, "Renaissance Aristotelianism," *Greek, Roman, and Byzantine Studies,* 6 (1965), 157–174.

[4] For a critique of mathematics in the Academy, see Nicomachus, *Introduction to Arithmetic,* tr. Martin Luther D'Ooge (New York, 1926), pp. 23–26.

[5] Jacques LeFèvre d'Etaples repeats a popular canard in the prefatory comment to his version of Boethian arithmetic:

> Plato in his Academy engraved this statement at the entrance: No one deficient in mathematics should enter here.

> Plato in suae Academiae vestibulo hoc insculpsit epigramma: Nemo huc mathematicae expers introeat

(*Introductio . . . in Arithmeticam . . . Boetii, pariter & Jordani,* in Gregor Reisch, *Margarita philosophica* [Basle, 1583], p. 1065). Cf. Robert Recorde, *The pathway to knowledg* (London, 1551), †1^{v}; and Gerard Johann Vossius, *De universae mathesios natura & constitutione liber* (Amsterdam, 1650), p. 18. In some instances, the saying is attributed to Pythagoras himself; cf. Humphrey Baker, *The well spring of science* (London, 1580), A4^{v}–A5; and Francis Meres, *Gods arithmeticke* (London, 1597), A2^{v}–A3. The ultimate literary source for this saying is Joannes Tzetzes, *Variarum historiarum liber* [viii.249], tr. Paulus Lacisius (Basle, 1546), p. 161. Oronce Finé, the influential professor of mathematics in the Collège de France, broadened Plato's insistence that the curriculum be based on mathematics:

> Rightly therefore Plato decreed that youths should first be taught numbers, without which, he concluded, neither private nor public affairs can be well

enough administered, demonstrating (just like Pythagoras) that all human affairs turn on the disposition of numbers themselves as well as on the harmony made from them.

> Merito igitur Plato, primùm numeros mandat pueros esse docendos: sine quibus nec privatas, nec publicas res, satis commodè administrari posse confessus est, omnia in ipsorum numerorum (veluti Pythagoras) cum dispositione, tum facta harmonia, mortalia versari demonstrans

(*Arithmetica practica* [Paris, 1542], fol. 3v). For a modern critique, see Harold Cherniss, "Plato as Mathematician," *Review of Metaphysics*, 4 (1951), 395–425.

[6] *The elements* (London, 1570), fol. 183.

[7] *Bibliotheca Eliotae* (London, 1548), Eee1v ["Plato"].

[8] The anonymous life of Pythagoras in Photius reports:

> Plato is said to have learned his speculative and physical philosophy from the Pythagoreans in Italy, and his ethical philosophy from Socrates. From the Eleatics, Zeno and Parmenides, he took his principles about logic. But all of these derived from the school of Pythagoras.

> Platonem à Pythagoreis in Italia Speculativam & Physicam aiunt, & à Socrate Ethicam didicisse: apud Zenonem vero, & Parmenidem Eleatas, fundamenta Logices jecisse, qui omnes è Pythagorae schola profecti sunt

(*Myriobiblon*, col. 1315). No less an authority than Proclus offered this opinion in his commentary on Plato's *Timaeus:*

> If, therefore, he [Plato] has any where mingled the Pythagoric and Socratic peculiarity, he appears to have done this in the present dialogue. For there are in it from the Pythagoric custom, elevation of conception, the intellectual, the divinely inspired, the suspending every thing from intelligibles, the bounding wholes in numbers, the indicating things mystically and symbolically, the anagogic, the transcending partial conceptions, and the enunciative or unfolding into light. But from the Socratic philanthropy, the sociable, the mild, the demonstrative, the contemplating beings through images, the ethical, and every thing of this kind

(*Proclus on the Timaeus of Plato*, tr. Thomas Taylor, 2 vols. [London, 1820], I.6–7). To garner an opinion from within the Church, we can cite St. Jerome:

> Plato, after establishing the Academy with its countless disciples and realizing the many shortcomings of his own system of teaching, went to Magna Graecia and there he studied the teachings of Pythagoras under Archytas of Tarentum and Timaeus of Locri. And he blended the elegance and charm of Socrates with Pythagoras' teachings

(*The Apology Against the Books of Rufinus* [III.xl], tr. John N. Hritzu [Catholic Univ. of America Press, 1965], p. 212). St. Augustine agreed:

> To the Socratic charm and precision which he had mastered in ethics, Plato joined the skill in the natural sciences which he had diligently acquired from the men I have mentioned [the Pythagoreans]. Then he added dialectic, which he believed to be either wisdom itself or at least an indispensable prerequisite for wisdom, and which would synthesize and determine those components

(*Answer to Skeptics* [III.xvii], tr. Denis J. Kavanagh, in *Writings of Saint Augustine* [New York, 1948], p. 213). Joannes Baptista Bernardus quotes Ficino to the effect that Plato gave preference to the Pythagorean doctrine before all others:

> Plato cum omnes philosophorum opiniones examinasset, Pythagoricam sectam tanquam verisimiliorem prae caeteris elegit. *Ficin. Platon. Theologiae lib.17.cap.4.*

(*Seminarium totius philosophiae Aristotelicae et Platonicae*, 2nd ed. [Lyons, 1599], II.721); cf. Ficino, *Opera omnia* (Basle, 1576), p. 386. Georg Horn, writing a history of philosophy in the mid-seventeenth century, cited other authorities on Plato's debt to Pythagoras:

> Nam illud in antiquorum scriptis observare pretium operae est, eos Platonicorum & Pythagoraeorum nomina saepe confundere. Quod propter sectarum harum convenientiam fieri, nemo non intelligit: & quia ex Pythagorae secretis pleraque emblemata sua hausit Plato. *Apuleius* Florid.15. *Plato, nihil ab hac secta vel paululum devius, Pythagorissat. Eusebius* lib. contra Hieroclem confut. libri primi: *Plato Pythagoricae praeter caeteros omnes disciplinae particeps factus est*

(*Historiae philosophiae libri septem* [Leyden, 1655], p. 187). The curriculum which Plato prescribes for the academy in his *Republic* (525A–530D) is most assuredly the Pythagorean quadrivium. For a modern review of the relationship between Plato and the Pythagoreans, see Cornelia J. de Vogel, *Pythagoras and Early Pythagoreanism* (Assen, 1966), pp. 192–207.

[9] A bit of ancient gossip, first recorded by Diogenes Laertius, intimated that Plato had purchased Pythagorean texts from Philolaus in order to plagiarize them:

> Down to the time of Philolaus it was not possible to acquire knowledge of any Pythagorean doctrine, and Philolaus alone brought out those three celebrated books which Plato sent a hundred minas to purchase (*Lives of Eminent Philosophers*, VIII.15).

Cf. also:

> [Philolaus] wrote one book, and it was this work which, according to Hermippus, some writer said that Plato the philosopher, when he went to Sicily to Dionysius's court, bought from Philolaus's relatives for the sum of forty Alexandrine minas of silver, from which also the *Timaeus* was transcribed (*ibid.*, VIII.85).

See also Iamblichus, *Life of Pythagoras* [xxxi], tr. Thomas Taylor (London, 1818), p. 142; Tzetzes, *Variarum historiarum liber* [XI.362], pp. 203–204; William Baldwyn, *A treatise of morall phylosophye* (London, 1550), F8; Joannes Jacobus Frisius, *Bibliotheca philosophorum classicorum authorum chronologica* (Zurich, 1592), fol. 15ᵛ; Thomas Stanley, *The history of philosophy*, 2nd ed. (London, 1687), p. 586; G. S. Kirk and J. E. Raven, *The Presocratic Philosophers* (Cambridge Univ. Press, 1962), p. 308; and W. K. C. Guthrie, *A History of Greek Philosophy*, 3 vols. (Cambridge Univ. Press, 1962), I.330.

[10] For accounts of Pythagoras' school, see Walter Burley, *Liber de vita et moribus philosophorum*, ed. Hermann Knust (Tübingen, 1886), pp. 70–72; Gerard Johann Vossius, *De philosophorum sectis liber* (The Hague, 1657), pp. 33–38; Stanley, *History of philosophy*, pp. 516–521; Joannes Scheffer, *De natura & constitutione philosophiae Italicae seu Pythagoricae liber singularis* (Upsala, 1664), esp. chaps. x–xiv; Theophilus Gale, *The court of the gentiles*, 2 parts (London, 1670), II.144–165; Abraham Grau, *Historia philosophica* (Franeker, 1674), pp. 153–169; André Dacier, *The Life of Pythagoras*, tr. anon. (London, 1707), pp. 23–27; J. F. Weidler, *Dissertatio historica de legibus cibariis et vestiariis Pythagorae* (Jena, 1711); C. E. Joecher, *De Pythagorae methodo philosophiam docendi* (Leipzig, 1741); William Enfield, *The History of Phi-*

losophy, 2 vols. (London, 1791), I.376–382; A. Ed. Chaignet, *Pythagore et la philosophie pythagoricienne*, 2 vols. (Paris, 1873), I.97–164; S. Ferrari, "La scuola e la filosofia pitagoriche," *Rivista italiana di filosofia*, 5 (1890), i.53–74, 184–212, 280–306; ii.59–79, 196–216; F. M. Cornford, "Mysticism and Science in the Pythagorean Tradition," *Classical Quarterly*, 16 (1922), 139 ff.; Hallie Watters, *Pythagorean Way of Life* (Adyar, 1926); Pierre Boyancé, "Sur la vie pythagoricienne," *Revue des études grecques*, 52 (1939), 36–50; Jean Mallinger, *Pythagore et les mystères* (Paris, 1944), chap. iii; and Eric T. Bell, *The Magic of Numbers* (New York, 1946), pp. 115–134.

[11] Although Pythagoras is regularly aligned with the other cultures in this list, his association with the Druids is less common; but see Joannes Bessarion, *In calumniatorem Platonis libri quatuor* et al. (Venice, 1516), fol. 3–3^{v}.

[12] In this aspiration toward divine perfection, the Pythagorean doctrine shared much with the Hermetic tradition; see Frances A. Yates, *Giordano Bruno and the Hermetic Tradition* (London, 1964), esp. pp. 4–5.

[13] Cf. Plato, *Phaedrus*, 279C; Plato, *Laws*, 739C; Cicero, *De officiis*, I.xvi; Diogenes Laertius, VIII.10; Porphyry, *De vita Pythagorae*, xxxiii; Iamblichus, *De vita Pythagorae*, xix; St. Jerome, *Against Rufinus* [III.xxxix], tr. Hritzu, (Catholic University of America Press, 1965), p. 211; Erasmus, *Praise of Follie*, tr. Thomas Chaloner, ed. C. H. Miller (EETS; Oxford Univ. Press, 1965), p. 69; Erasmus, *Adagiorum chiliades quatuor, et sesquicenturia* (Lyons, 1559), cols. 18–19; Richard Taverner, *Proverbes or adagies* (London, 1539), fol. 52^{v}–53; Joachim Zehner, ed., *Pythagorae fragmenta* (Leipzig, 1603), p. 70. For a modern analysis, see Edwin L. Minar, Jr., "Pythagorean Communism," *Transactions and Proceedings of the American Philological Association*, 75 (1944), 34–46.

[14] Cf. Diogenes Laertius, VIII.10; Porphyry, *De vita Pythagorae*, xxxiii; Iamblichus, *De vita Pythagorae*, xxix; St. Jerome, *Against Rufinus* [III. xxxix], tr. Hritzu, p. 211; Erasmus, *Adagia* (1559), cols. 19–20; Taverner, *Proverbes*, fol. 53; Zehner, *Pythagorae fragmenta*, p. 65. For the relevance of the tetrad to this gnomic saying, see Alastair Fowler, *Spenser and the Numbers of Time* (London, 1964), pp. 24–26.

[15] For representative accounts of this story, see Cicero, *De officiis*, III. x; Cicero, *Tusculanae disputationes*, V.xxii; Diodorus Siculus, *Bibliotheca*, X.iv.3–6; Porphyry, *De vita Pythagorae*, lx–lxi; and Baldwyn, *Morall phylosophye*, B6^{v}–B7.

[16] *Thesaurus linguae Romanae & Britannicae* (London, 1584), Eeeeeee4^{v}.

[17] The silence of the Pythagorean novice became proverbial; see Aulus Gellius, *Noctes Atticae*, I.x; Hugh of St. Victor, *Didascalicon* [III.iii], ed. Jerome Taylor (Columbia Univ. Press, 1961), pp. 86–87; Tzetzes, *Variarum historiarum liber*, [VII.116] p. 122, [VIII.187] p. 146; Andrea Alciati, *Emblemata* [XI. "Silentium"], ed. Claude Mignault (Antwerp, 1581), p. 64; Joannes ab Indagine, *Briefe introductions . . . unto the art of chiromancy*, tr. Fabian Withers (London, 1558), *2; Juan Luis Vives, *On Education*, tr. Foster Watson (Cambridge Univ. Press, 1913), p. 116; Stephen Gosson, *The schoole of abuse* (London, 1587), E6^{v}; and Robert Allot, *Wits theatre of the little world* (London, 1599), fol. 84.

[18] *The Florida* [xv], in *The Works of Apuleius* (London, 1872), p. 389.

[19] *Stromateis* [V.xi], p. 460.

[20] At a later time, however, his teachings were recorded; see p. 28, below. Thomas Digges joked about Pythagorean exclusiveness when he explained why he had not published his technical manuscripts: "By the example of my Father [Leonard Digges], Pythagoricallye I will contente my selfe *Per manus tradere*, and to communicate them onely wyth a fewe selecte friendes" (*Stratioticos* [London, 1579], a2).

[21] See pp. 259–262, below.

[22] Translated by Thomas Stanley, *History of philosophy*, p. 520. Translated also as "Virgils epigram of a good man" by George Chapman (*Poems*, ed. Phyllis B. Bartlett [New York, 1941], pp. 227–228). Cf. Ausonius' eclogue with the *Carmina aurea*, ll. 40–46 (quoted on p. 261, below). Ausonius' eclogue was often in the renaissance attributed to Vergil—e.g., by Jodocus Badius Ascensius and George Chapman (cf. Chapman, *Poems*, ed. Bartlett, p. 447).

[23] See Scheffer, *De natura . . . philosophiae Italicae*, pp. 67–73. See also pp. 263–265, below.

[24] *Registre of hystories*, tr. Abraham Fleming (London, 1576), fol. 62ᵛ. Cf. Heinrich Cornelius Agrippa, *Of the vanitie and uncertaintie of artes and sciences*, tr. James Sanford (London, 1569), fol. 4ᵛ.

[25] This incident is first reported by Porphyry, *De vita Pythagorae*, xxiv, and repeated by Iamblichus, *De vita Pythagorae*, xiii.

[26] Thomas Elyot, *Bibliotheca Eliotae* (London, 1545), Ee6–Ee6ᵛ ["Pythagoras"]. For ancient biographies of Pythagoras, see pp. 46–47, below. Later biographies of varying sorts include: Francesco Petrarca, *Rerum memorandarum, sive de viris illustribus libri quattuor* (Basle, 1563), pp. 329–330; Michael Neander, ed., *Anthologicum graecolatinum* (Basle, 1556); André Thevet, *Pourtraits et vies des hommes illustres* (Paris, 1584), fol. 50–51ᵛ; Zehner, *Pythagorae fragmenta*, pp. 39–47; Jean Jacques Boissard, *De divinatione et magicis praestigiis* (Oppenheim, 1616?), pp. 293–299; Horn, *Historiae philosophiae libri*, pp. 172 ff.; Stanley, *History of philosophy*, pp. 491–513; William Lloyd, *A chronological account of the life of Pythagoras* (London, 1699); Dacier, *Life of Pythagoras*, pp. 9–16; Christoforus Schrader, *Dissertatio prima de Pythagora, in quâ de eius ortu, praeceptoribus et peregrinationibus agitur* (Leipzig, 1708); Johann Jakob Brucker, *Historia critica philosophiae*, 2nd ed., 6 vols. (Leipzig, 1766–67), I.982–1100; Joannes Albertus Fabricius, *Bibliotheca Graeca*, 11 vols. (Hamburg, 1790–1808), I.750–776; Chaignet, *Pythagore*, I.23–96; Mallinger, *Pythagore et les mystères;* François Millepierres, *Pythagore fils d'Apollon* (Paris, 1953); Maria Timpanaro Cardini, ed., *Pitagorici testamonianze e frammenti*, 3 vols. (Florence, 1958–64), I.12–61; Ernst Bindel, *Pythagoras* (Stuttgart, 1962), pp. 23–89; and Rita Cuccioli Melloni, *Biografia di Pitagora* (Bologna, 1969). For a critical review of biographical materials, see Isidore Lévy, *Recherches sur les sources de la légende de Pythagore* (Paris, 1926); Robert Baccou, *Histoire de la science grecque de Thalès à Socrate* (Paris, 1951), pp. 87–102; and James A. Philip, *Pythagoras and Early Pythagoreanism* (Univ. of Toronto Press, 1966), pp. 8–23.

[27] See Kirk and Raven, *Presocratic Philosophers*, pp. 48–72.

[28] *Elementa doctrinae de circulis coelestibus, et primo motu* (Wittenberg, 1551), fol. A3ᵛ.

[29] Cf. Jacopo Filippo Foresti, *Supplementum chronicarum* (Venice, 1490), fol. 55; Thomas Lanquet, *Cooper's chronicle* (London, 1565), fol. 44ᵛ; Gulielmus Morellius, *Tabula compendiosa* (Basle, 1580), p. 151; Frisius, *Bibliotheca*, fol. 6ᵛ; John More, *A table from the beginning of the world to this day* (Cambridge, 1593), p. 59; Anthony Munday, *A briefe chronicle of the successe of times* (London, 1611), p. 21; and John Marsham, *Chronicus canon Ægyptiacus, Ebraicus, Graecus* (London, 1672), p. 264.

[30] *History of philosophy*, p. 492.

[31] Sir William Temple, the noble champion of the ancients, made Pythagoras a central figure in the "battle of the books." While the debate was at its fiercest in France, he fired the opening salvo in England with "An essay upon the ancient and modern learning," published in his *Miscellanea. The second part* (London, 1690). In this provocative essay Temple cited Pythagoras as the foremost guide who led the ancients to wisdom (pp. 11 ff.). Furthermore, Temple praised Aesop's *Fables* and Phalaris' *Epistles* as the best books in their kind and also the oldest; and he dated these authors as living in the time "of

Cyrus and *Pythagoras*" (p. 58). Actually, Epistle XXIII is addressed to Pythagoras, and in Epistle LXXIV Phalaris boasts that Pythagoras had spent five months with him.

When William Wotton challenged Temple in *Reflections upon ancient and modern learning* (London, 1694), his strategy was to compare systematically the ancient and the modern practitioners in each field of learning, of course to the detriment of the ancients. Aiming directly at Temple, Wotton began his attack by denigrating "The learning of Pythagoras" (chap. viii).

By the time Wotton's *Reflections* were printed in a second edition (London, 1697), Charles Boyle had published his edition of the letters of Phalaris (Oxford, 1695), claiming with Temple that they were some of the earliest writings in our culture, and incidentally in the preface being unjustifiably rude to Richard Bentley, the Royal Librarian. In consequence, to the second edition of Wotton's *Reflections*, Bentley appended "A Dissertation upon the Epistles of Phalaris, Themistocles, Socrates, Euripides, and Others; and the Fables of Æsop." The battle was now fully joined. By meticulous scholarship and impeccable argument, Bentley "demonstrated that the *Epistles* of *Phalaris* are Spurious, and that we have nothing now extant of *Æsop's* own composing" (pp. 5–6).

Boyle and his faction soon counterattacked with a massive assault entitled *Dr. Bentley's dissertations on the epistles of Phalaris, and the fables of Æsop, examined* (London, 1698). Nothing daunted, Bentley rallied with *A dissertation upon the epistles of Phalaris. With an answer to the objections of the Honourable Charles Boyle, Esquire* (London, 1699). And Bentley called in William Lloyd as an ally, who produced *A chronological account of the life of Pythagoras, and of other famous men his contemporaries* (London, 1699), a scholarly review of the ancient writings on Pythagoras with the intention of debunking Porphyry and Iamblichus as well as the Pythagoras legend. Many others now leapt into the fray, including Jonathan Swift with his malicious but delightful *Full and true account of the battel fought last friday, between the antient and the modern books in St. James's library* (London, 1704).

The battle lines, once drawn, were not easily dissolved because, as Wotton was well aware when he precipitated the controversy, there were far-reaching issues at stake, such as God's providence and human progress (see Wotton's *Reflections* [1694], "Preface," A6 ff.). In consequence, belligerent pens continued to write on both sides. The debate has been amply documented by A. Guthkelch, ed., *The Battle of the Books, by Jonathan Swift* (London, 1908), pp. ix–xxxv; and R. F. Jones, *Ancients and Moderns: A Study of the Background of the "Battle of the Books,"* Washington University Studies—New Series, Language and Literature, No. 6 (St. Louis, 1936).

The argument over Pythagoras' dates continued undiminished into the eighteenth century on both sides of the Channel; see Henry Dodwell, *Exercitationes duae: prima, De aetate Phalaridis; secunda, De aetate Pythagorae* (London, 1704); John Jackson, *Chronological Antiquities*, 3 vols. (London, 1742), II.372–375; De la Nauze, "Première dissertation sur Pythagore, où l'on fixe le tems auquel ce philosophe a vécu," *Histoire de l'académie royale des inscriptions et belles lettres*, 14 (1743), Part II, pp. 375–400; Nicolas Freret, "Observations sur la généalogie de Pythagore, et sur l'usage chronologique que l'on en a tiré pour determiner l'époque de la prise de Troye," *ibid.*, 14 (1743), Part II, pp. 401–447; Freret, "Recherches sur le tems auquel le philosophe Pythagore, fondateur de la secte Italique, peut avoir vécu," *ibid.*, 14 (1743), Part II, pp. 472–504; Richard Cumberland, "Circumstances Respecting the Philosopher Pythagoras," *Town and Country Magazine*, 21 (1789), 79–81, 116–119.

[32] *The Traveiler* [1575], ed. Denver E. Baughan (Gainesville, Fla., 1951), pp. 71–72.

[33] [STC 17650] (London, 1589), A2.

[34] Cf. Diogenes Laertius, VIII.3; Porphyry, *De vita Pythagorae,* vi–xii; Iamblichus, *De vita Pythagorae*, ii–iv, xxviii; Cicero, *De finibus,* V.50, 87; Apuleius, *Florida,* xv; Clement of Alexandria, *Stromateis,* I.xiv–xvi, V.iv–viii.

[35] For example, this is an extract from the "argument" preceding Chapter V, "Quid ex cuiusque gentis disciplinis in Italicam philosophiam eius conditor transsumserit," in Scheffer, *De natura . . . philosophiae Italicae:*

> Pythagoras à Phoenicibus accepit arithmeticam, & physicae quaedam. . . . ab Ægyptiis philosophia caetera, ut & mystica sacra, & notitiam de Deo uno, & geometriam, & arcana numerorum. . . . An & astronomiam? à Chaldaeis eam didicit, ut & rerum naturalium principia. . . . à Magis sacra magica, & divinationes. . . . Ab Hebraeis sacra, & interpretationes somniorum, & vaticinia, & ritus varios. Ab Arabibus divinationes ex thure . . . scientiamque auguralem. An & ab Orphicis quaedam hauserit. Ab Indis accepit explorationem animorum . . . (p. 19).

For other scholarly examination of Pythagoras' travels, see Stanley, *History of philosophy,* pp. 494–499; Gale, *Court of gentiles,* II.158–159; Temple, "Essay upon ancient and modern learning" in *Miscellanea* (1690), pp. 12–24; Johann Jacob Borsch, *Dissertatio historica de peregrinationibus Pythagorae* (Jena, 1692); Lloyd, *Account of life of Pythagoras,* pp. 5–7, 10–11; Dacier, *Life of Pythagoras,* pp. 12–15; Fabricius, *Bibliotheca Graeca,* I.756–758; Enfield, *History of Philosophy*, I.367–371; Pierre Sylvain Maréchal, *Voyages de Pythagore,* 6 vols. (Paris, 1799); Eduard Zeller, *A History of Greek Philosophy*, tr. S. F. Alleyne, 2 vols. (London, 1881), I.327–335. Although later scholars have rightly questioned the far-ranging travels of Pythagoras, the renaissance did not; see, for example, Alexander ab Alexandro, *Genialium dierum libri sex* (Paris, 1570), fol. 49^{v}–50.

[36] *Life of Pythagoras* [xxix], tr. Taylor, pp. 114–115.

[37] Cf. Conrad Gesner, *Bibliotheca universalis* (Zurich, 1545), fol. 574^{v}; Stanley, *History of philosophy*, pp. 511–512; Vossius, *De philosophorum sectis,* pp. 32–33; Theophilus Gale, *Philosophia generalis* (London, 1676), p. 186; Fabricius, *Bibliotheca Graeca,* I.779–787; and Chaignet, *Pythagore,* I.165–178.

[38] Cf. Aristotle, *Metaphysica,* 983b6; Plutarch,* "Opinions of Philosophers" [I.iii] in *The morals,* tr. Philemon Holland (London, 1603), p. 805; Polydore Vergil, *An abridgemente of the notable worke* [I.i–ii], tr. Thomas Langley (London, 1570), fol. 2, 4; Stanley, *History of philosophy,* "Preface," [*]–[*]^{v}; and Temple, "Essay upon ancient and modern learning" in *Miscellanea* (1690), pp. 10–12. [*The *De placitis philosophorum* is spurious in the canon of Plutarch, but the renaissance unhesitatingly ascribed it to him, and so shall I without further apology.]

[39] See pp. 29–30, below.

[40] "Pythagoras omnium Graeciae Philosophorum parens fuit" (Daniel Georg Morhof, *Polyhistor* [II.ii.7.1], 4th ed. [Lubeck, 1747], II.179). Cf. Diogenes Laertius, I.13; Filippo Beroaldo, *Symbola Pythagorae . . . moraliter explicata* (Paris, 1515), a3; Francesco Giorgio, *L'Harmonie du monde*, tr. Guy le Fèvre de la Boderie (Paris, 1579), p. 77; and Dacier, *Life of Pythagoras,* p. vi. René Rapin spoke for his age (as he intended to do) when he opined:

> In fine, *Pythagoras* had so extraordinary a genius for Philosophy, that all the other Philosophers have gloried to stick to his sentiments: *Socrates* and *Plato* have hardly any thing that is good but from him. And if we consider more narrowly, we shall even find that amongst all other Sects almost, there is somewhat of the Spirit of *Pythagoras* that bears rule

(*Reflexions upon ancient and modern philosophy,* tr. A. L. [London, 1678], pp. 8–9).

[41] *History of philosophy*, p. 541.

[42] *Ibid.*, p. 544. For Pythagoras' political philosophy and activity, see Iamblichus, *De vita Pythagorae*, xxvii; Petrarca, *Rerum memorandarum . . . libri*, p. 492; and Dacier, *Life of Pythagoras*, p. 88.

[43] "Isidorus vero .III. ethimologiarum dicit: Numeri disciplinam apud grecos primum Pythagoram nuncupant perscripsisse" (Burley, *De vita et moribus philosophorum*, p. 68). The reference to Isidore is *Etymologiae*, III.ii.1. Cf. Hugh of St. Victor, *Didascalicon* [III.ii], p. 83; Nicholas of Cusa, *De docta ignorantia*, I.xi; Gregor Reisch, *Margarita philosophica* [IV.ii], ed. Oronce Finé (Basle, 1535), p. 281; Joannes Martinus, *Arithmetica* (Paris, 1526), fol. 3; *Batman uppon Bartholome, his book De proprietatibus rerum* (London, 1582), fol. ¶5; Joannes Meursius, *Denarius pythagoricus* (Leyden, 1631), pp. 6–7; and Joannes Jonsius, *De scriptoribus historiae philosophicae libri IV* [III.xxxvi.11], 2nd ed. (Jena, 1716), p. 207. For modern opinions, see Zeller, *Greek Philosophy*, I.347; Sir Thomas Heath, *A History of Greek Mathematics*, 2 vols. (Oxford, 1921), I.65–66; Nicomachus, *Arithmetic*, tr. D'Ooge, pp. 18–19; and George Sarton, *A History of Science: Ancient Science Through the Golden Age of Greece* (Harvard Univ. Press, 1952), pp. 203 ff.

[44] Cf. Diodorus Siculus, *Bibliotheca*, X.vi.4; Diogenes Laertius, VIII.11; Iamblichus, *De vita Pythagorae*, xxix; Proclus, *Commentary on Euclid, Book I* in Ivor Thomas, *Greek Mathematics* (London, 1939), p. 149; Dacier, *Life of Pythagoras*, p. 80; and L. W. H. Hull, *The History and Philosophy of Science* (London, 1959), p. 25.

[45] "Hic Pytagoras, ut ait Boecius in primo musice, artis musice inventor fuisse apud grecos dicitur" (Burley, *De vita et moribus philosophorum*, p. 68). The reference to Boethius is *De musica*, I.x. Cf. Iamblichus, *De vita Pythagorae*, xxvi; Macrobius, *In somnium Scipionis*, II.1; Joannes Wallensis, *Florilegium* (Rome, 1655), p. 243; Chaucer, *Book of the Duchess*, 1167–69; and Reisch, *Margarita philosophica* [V.iv] (1535), pp. 346–347. Dacier gives an open-minded review of scholarship on Pythagoras' "Invention of harmonical Measures" (*Life of Pythagoras*, pp. 82–84). See also Sir John Hawkins, *A General History of the Science and Practice of Music*, 5 vols. (London, 1776), I.169, 174; Hans Oppermann, "Eine Pythagoraslegende," *Bonner Jahrbücher*, 130 (1925), 284–301; John Burnet, *Greek Philosophy: Part I, Thales to Plato* (London, 1928), pp. 45–49; and Edward A. Lippman, *Musical Thought in Ancient Greece* (Columbia Univ. Press, 1964), p. 6.

[46] See p. 30, below.

[47] Dacier lists the particular astronomical discoveries usually attributed to Pythagoras:

> He was the first that discover'd the Obliquity of the Zodiack, and who acknowledg'd that the Moon receiv'd all her Light from the Sun; that the Rainbow was only the Reflexion of the Light, and that the Evening-Star, which is call'd *Venus* and *Vesper*, was the same with the Morning-Star, call'd *Lucifer*, and *Phosphorus*, and he explain'd its Nature and its Course. . . . It appears that he was the first, who transporting to the Surface of the Earth the two Tropicks, and the two Polar Circles, divided that Surface into five Zones

(*Life of Pythagoras*, pp. 74–75). Cf. Plutarch, "Opin. of Phil." [II.xii] in *Morals*, tr. Holland, p. 820. See also J. L. E. Dreyer, *A History of Astronomy from Thales to Kepler*, 2nd ed. (New York, 1953), pp. 37–38; John Burnet, *Early Greek Philosophy*, 4th ed. (London, 1945), pp. 110–111; Theodor Gomperz, *Greek Thinkers*, tr. Laurie Magnus, 2 vols. (New York, 1908), I.110 ff.; Sarton, *History of Science*, pp. 212–213. Pierre Duhem began his monumental *Le système du monde* with "L'Astronomie pythagoricienne," 5 vols. (Paris, 1913–17).

[48] At the beginning of his *De musica*, Boethius declared:

> Among all men of ancient authority who flourished through the purer reason of the mind under the leadership of Pythagoras, it was considered manifestly certain that no one was to go forth in the study of philosophy unless excellence and nobility were investigated by means of a certain four-way path (quadrivium) which led to such knowledge

(Boethius, *The Principles of Music*, tr. Calvin M. Bower [typescript], opening sentence). Marshall Clagett echoes this statement: "Boethius appears to have been the first to use the Latin term *quadrivium* to embrace the four mathematical subjects long associated together by the Pythagoreans" (*Greek Science in Antiquity* [London, 1957], p. 150). See also Hugh of St. Victor, *Didascalicon* [III.iii], pp. 86–87; and Howard R. Patch, *The Tradition of Boethius* (Oxford Univ. Press, 1935), pp. 36–38.

[49] See Diogenes Laertius, VIII.48. "It is well known that the *Pythagoreans* held the Motion of the Earth about the Sun" (Henry More, *Conjectura cabbalistica* [London, 1653], p. 154). Cf. Martin Cortes, *The arte of navigation*, tr. Richard Eden (London, 1561), fol. 8; Vossius, *De philosophorum sectis*, pp. 39, 43–44; Edmund Halley as quoted by William Wotton, *Reflections* (1694), p. 277; and John Keill, *An Introduction to True Astronomy* (London, 1721), p. ix. Also see my article, "Pythagorean Cosmology and the Triumph of Heliocentrism" in *Le soleil à la renaissance* (Presses universitaires de Bruxelles, 1965), pp. 33–53.

[50] According to one tradition, Pythagoras had fancifully suggested that the world breathes, drawing in breath from an infinite void; see Aristotle, *Physica*, 203a1–203a16, 204a8–204a34, 213b24–213b27; and Plutarch, "Opin. of Phil." [II.ix, xiii] in *Morals*, tr. Holland, pp. 820, 821. Thomas Digges' famous diagram of an infinite heliocentric universe is drawn "according to the most auncient doctrine of the Pythagoreans" (see Plate 24); cf. Alexandre Koyré, *From the Closed World to the Infinite Universe* (Johns Hopkins Press, 1957), p. 37. See also Zeller, *Greek Philosophy*, I.466–468; and Burnet, *Early Greek Philosophy*, p. 108.

[51] *Historia naturalis*, XXV.13. Cf. Boissard, *De divinatione*, p. 297.

[52] Ralph Cudworth quoted St. Cyril: "*Pythagoras* held there was One God of the whole Universe, the Principle and Cause of all things, the Illuminator, Animator and Quickener of the Whole, and Original of Motion; from whom all things were derived, and brought out of Nonentity into Being" (*Intellectual system*, p. 377). The reference to St. Cyril is *Contra Julianum* [I] (Leipzig, 1696), p. 30. Cf. p. 229, n. 8, below. See also Cicero, *De natura deorum*, I.xi; Iamblichus, *De vita Pythagorae*, xxx; Pierre Bayle, *Dictionaire*, 2 vols. (Rotterdam, 1697), "Pythagoras," footnote N; and Enfield, *History of Philosophy*, I.393–395.

[53] "Listen to the principle that Pythagoras was first among the Greeks to discover: 'Souls are immortal and they pass from one body to another' " (St. Jerome, *Against Rufinus* [III.xxxix], tr. Hritzu, p. 211). Cf. Diogenes Laertius, VIII.14; Porphyry, *De vita Pythagorae*, xix; Plutarch, "Opin. of Phil." [IV.vii] in *Morals*, tr. Holland, p. 835; Burley, *De vita et moribus philosophorum*, p. 78; Baldwyn, *Morall phylosophye*, B8; Natalis Comes, *Mythologiae* (Padua, 1616), [iii, xx] p. 147, [x, "De Lethe fluvio"] pp. 537–538; Vossius, *De philosophorum sectis*, pp. 31–32; and Zeller, *Greek Philosophy*, I.481–487.

[54] For example, when Joannes Aurispa dedicated his Latin translation of Hierocles' *Commentarius in aurea carmina* (Padua, 1474) to Pope Nicholas V, he labeled it "an outstanding work, consonant with the Christian religion" (opusculum praestantissimum et religioni Christianae consentaneum, a2^{v}), and he claimed that "except for the miracles, it differs in little or nothing from the

Christian faith" (Parum enim aut nihil ubi miracula non fuerunt: a fide Christiana differt, a2).

[55] "No Pleasant Life According to Epicurus" in *Morals*, tr. Holland, p. 590. Cf. Cicero, *De natura deorum*, III.xxxvi; Vitruvius, *De architectura*, IX.preface. 6–7; Diogenes Laertius, VIII.12; Porphyry, *De vita Pythagorae*, xxxvi; Thevet, *Vies des hommes illustres*, fol. 50^{v}; Robert Norman, *The new attractive* (London, 1585), A2; Franciscus Junius, *Catalogus . . . architectorum, mechanicorum . . . aliorumque artificum* appended to *De pictura veterum libri tres* (Rotterdam, 1694), "Pythagoras"; and Dacier, *Life of Pythagoras*, pp. 81–82.

[56] *Those fyve questions*, tr. John Dolman (London, 1561), Z1^{v}. Cf. Diodorus Siculus, *Bibliotheca*, X.x.1; Diogenes Laertius, I.12, VIII.8; St. Augustine, *De civitate Dei*, VIII.ii; Isidore, *Etymologiae*, VIII.vi.2–3; Dante, *Il convivio*, III.xi.41–47; Petrarca, *Rerum memorandarum . . . libri*, p. 330; Reisch, *Margarita philosophica* [I.i] (1535), p. 2; Polydore Vergil, *Notable worke* [I.xiii], fol. 25; Hermannus Torrentinus, *Dictionarium poeticum* (Paris, 1550), "Pythagoras"; Baldwyn, *Morall phylosophye*, B4^{v}–B5; Louis LeRoy, *Of the interchangeable course, or variety of things*, tr. Robert Ashley (London, 1594), fol. 57^{v}; John Case, *Ancilla philosophiae* (Oxford, 1599), pp. 5–6; Gale, *Philosophia generalis*, pp. 1–2; Bentley, "Upon the Epistles of Phalaris" (1697), pp. 38–39; Pierre Bayle, *A General Dictionary*, tr. John Peter Bernard *et al.* (London, 1734–41), "Pythagoras," footnote A; and Fabricius, *Bibliotheca Graeca*, I.750.

[57] See pp. 146–147, below.

[58] Tr. Benjamin Jowett, *The Dialogues of Plato*, 4 vols. (Oxford, 1871), III.105. Cf. the note on this passage in *Gorgias*, ed. E. R. Dodds (Oxford, 1959), pp. 337–339, in which the "philosophers" are unequivocally identified as Pythagoreans.

[59] Cicero, *Those fyve questions*, tr. Dolman, Z1^{v}–Z2. Cf. Diogenes Laertius, VIII.8; Iamblichus, *De vita Pythagorae*, xii; Petrarca, *Rerum memorandarum . . . libri*, p. 330; Baldwyn, *Morall phylosophye*, B5–B6; Simon Robson, *The choice of change* (London, 1585) G4^{v}; Pierre de la Primaudaye, *The French academie*, tr. T. Bowes (London, 1586), pp. 38–39; LeRoy, *Interchangeable course*, fol. 57^{v}–58; and Dacier, *Life of Pythagoras*, pp. 14–15.

[60] See pp. 223–225, below.

[61] See my article, "The Implications of Form for *The Shepheardes Calender*," *Studies in the Renaissance*, 9 (1962), 309–321; and pp. 309–315, below.

[62] See pp. 269–272, below.

[63] Tr. Stanley, *History of philosophy*, p. 503. See p. 259, below.

[64] *The history of the world* [I.ii.5] (London, 1614), p. 31. Cf. Edward Forset, *A comparative discourse of the bodies natural and politique* (London, 1606), quoted by James Winny, ed., *The Frame of Order* (London, 1957), p. 89; Bernardus, *Seminarium totius philosophiae*, II.767; and Helkiah Crooke, *Microcosmographia* (London, 1615), p. 3. In the Pythagorean tradition, this dictum is simply another way of saying that man is a microcosm.

[65] "Pythagoras audivisse fertur, concentus coelestes. *Ficino in Plat. Phaedr. cap. 35.*" (Bernardus, *Seminarium totius philosophiae*, II.767). Cf. Porphyry, *De vita Pythagorae*, xxx; and Iamblichus, *De vita Pythagorae*, xv.

[66] See Fabricius, *Bibliotheca Graeca*, I.790–791. For the fortune-telling wheel, see p. 237, below, and Plate 46.

[67] *Registre of hystories*, fol. O4. Cf. *ibid.*, fol. F1^{v}; Ludovicus Caelius Rhodiginus, *Lectionum antiquarum libri XXX* (Basle, 1566), pp. 734–735; Bernardus, *Seminarium totius philosophiae*, II.768; Stanley, *History of philosophy*, pp. 505–506; and Dacier, *Life of Pythagoras*, pp. 69–71.

[68] Aelianus, *Registre of hystories*, fol. Kk2. Cf. Alexander ab Alexandro, *Genialium dierum libri*, fol. 289; Sigismundus Fridericus Dresigius, *De alba stola Pythagorae* (Leipzig, 1736).

[69] See Nicolaus Colding, *Dissertatio de Pythagora, eiusque femore aureo* (Copenhagen, 1702).

[70] See Don C. Allen, "The Double Journey of John Donne" in *A Tribute to George Coffin Taylor*, ed. Arnold Williams (Univ. of North Carolina Press, 1952), pp. 85–88.

[71] See Diogenes Laertius, VIII.39–40. Cf. Porphyry, *De vita Pythagorae*, liv–lvii; Marcus Junianus Justinus, *The historie*, tr. G. W. (London, 1606), fol. 77ᵛ; Bayle, *Dictionaire*, "Pythagoras," footnote P; Lloyd, *Account of life of Pythagoras*, pp. 17–18; and Dacier, *Life of Pythagoras*, pp. 93–95.

[72] See Diogenes Laertius, VIII.50–91; Iamblichus, *De vita Pythagorae*, xxxvi; Jonsius, *De scriptoribus historiae philosophicae*, I.xiv.3–5; Stanley, *History of philosophy*, pp. 513–515; Scheffer, *De natura . . . philosophiae Italicae*, pp. 169–180; Enfield, *History of Philosophy*, I.400 ff.; and Fabricius, *Bibliotheca Graeca*, I.772, 826–885.

[73] Cf. Alexander ab Alexandro, *Genialium dierum libri*, fol. 50; LeRoy, *Interchangeable course*, fol. 61; Gale, *Court of gentiles*, II.203–204; and Burnet, *Thales to Plato*, p. 64.

[74] *Life of Pythagoras*, p. 96. Modern evaluations of Pythagoras' contribution to Western civilization tend to hyperbole: "Pythagoras, undoubtedly one of the greatest names in the history of science . . ." (Sir Thomas Heath, *Aristarchus of Samos* [Oxford, 1913], p. 46); "[Pythagoras] is the founder of European culture in the western Mediterranean sphere" (Benjamin Farrington, *Greek Science* [London, 1953], p. 43); "This titanic spirit overshadows western civilization" (Bell, *Magic of Numbers*, p. 1); "Pythagoras of Samos, whose infleunce on the ideas, and thereby on the destiny, of the human race was probably greater than that of any single man before or after him . . ." (Arthur Koestler, *The Sleepwalkers* [London, 1959], p. 25). I have found only one dissenter: Otto Neugebauer, *The Exact Sciences in Antiquity*, 2nd ed. (Brown Univ. Press, 1957), pp. 148–149.

[75] See Frances A. Yates, *The French Academies of the Sixteenth Century* (London, 1947), esp. pp. 9, 52 ff., 248–249, 270, 274, 310, and 311; and Marie Boas, *The Scientific Renaissance, 1450–1630* (New York, 1962), p. 97.

[76] Voltaire, *Candide* [288], ed. André Morize (Paris, 1931), p. 220.

[77] William Rayner used this quotation on the title page of his edition of *The Commentary of Hierocles upon the Golden Verses of the Pythagoreans* (Norwich, 1797).

[78] My point is perfectly illustrated by the opening comments which Henry Billingsley makes to the Reader in his translation of Euclid, *Elements* (1570), [*]2.

3
Materials

There was no single, well-codified set of beliefs attributed to Pythagoras in the renaissance, no concise doctrine that neatly sets apart his school from all others. It is impossible to go to any one document, or even a few documents, for a thorough exposition of his philosophical system. Because Pythagoras had appeared so early and because his thought had ranged so widely, his ideas were diffused through several sects. Without exaggeration we can say that his teaching touched every major classical philosopher and Church Father. And during the renaissance it permeated almost every learned discipline. It provided, in fact, that unifying comprehensiveness that had produced the encyclopedia tradition in the late middle ages and gave to learning a large degree of coherence. The problem, then, is not to find sources for Pythagorean thought, but rather to identify those sources which are most distinctively Pythagorean and which had the greatest influence in disseminating Pythagoreanism in the renaissance. There is a large and varied assortment of materials from which to choose.

Comments here and there suggest that numerous biographies of Pythagoras had been written in the classical period,[1] but only four authoritative biographies survived: [2] 1) a detailed coverage in Diogenes Laertius, *De vitis, dogmatibus, et apophthegmatis clarorum philosophorum libri X*, dating from the late second or early third century A.D.; 2) a respectful account by Porphyry, *Liber de vita Pythagorae*, written in the mid-third century; 3) an even more reverential *Vita* by Iamblichus, written in the late third century; and 4) an anonymous biography preserved by Photius in his *Bibliotheca* (or *Myriobiblon*), which was compiled in the ninth century from earlier works.

In the bookish compendium of Diogenes Laertius, Pythagoras received conspicuous treatment as founder of the Italic school.[3] Drawing upon numerous earlier authorities, almost all of whom are now lost, Diogenes Laertius compiled a record of philosophic speculation to his own day, and duly recapitulated the biography and beliefs that had accrued to Pythagoras. There is a detailed account of his birth, his education and travels, and his previous incarnations

(VIII.1–5). There is a survey of Pythagoras' writings (6–9), and a brief enumeration of his wondrous qualities and feats (11–14), offered with as little interpretive comment as possible. The remainder of the discussion is then given over largely to Pythagorean precepts, with the *symbola* especially prominent. This is a balanced presentation of Pythagoras, with reports of several denigratory comments (e.g., 36–38, 41, 44–45), as well as the usual laudatory ascription of wisdom and probity. Diogenes Laertius followed his account of Pythagoras with an entry for Empedocles (VIII.51–77) and several other members of the Italic school, most notably Archytas, Alcmaeon, and Philolaus.

Porphyry (234–c.305), a disciple of Plotinus, prepared a *Pythagorae vita* which is brief and wholly laudatory, with emphasis on the wondrous acts and the transcendental doctrine.[4] Porphyry's attitude toward his subject is epitomized by this hyperbolic claim: "Never was more attributed to any man, nor was any more eminent" (xxviii). Pythagoras appears primarily as a teacher of morality and a practising exponent of virtue; in consequence, there is an extensive reference to the *Carmina aurea* (xxxviii) and a long list of *symbola* (xlii–xlv). Many of the miracles are narrated and much of the awesome nimbus reconstructed—his sympathy with animals (xxiii–xxv), his previous incarnation (xxvi), the golden thigh (xxviii), his control over inclement weather (xxix), his mastery of physiognomy (xiii, liv). Porphyry also expounds the religious views of Pythagoras (xxii, xli, xlvi), and with equal seriousness sets forth his theory of numbers (xlix–lii). To complete the exemplary image, the biographer records the belief in metempsychosis (xix, xlv), the use of music to calm aroused passions (xxx), and the abstinence from animate things in diet. Porphyry presents Pythagoras as an eminently acceptable authority on most aspects of human behavior, but not as a cosmologist or natural scientist.

Another *Pythagorae vita* was prepared by Iamblichus (c.250–c.330), who had studied with Porphyry.[5] This is, in fact, an expansion of the Pythagorean biography by Porphyry. Iamblichus writes in the exuberant spirit of hagiography and generously employs the epithet "divine." In the opening chapter he claims that Pythagoras received his doctrine from the gods themselves, and he approaches his subject with due reverence. After a detailed account of Pythagoras' birth, Iamblichus relates his travels: visits with Pherecydes, Anaximander, and Thales; sojourns with the Phoenicians, Egyptians, and Babylonians; a tour through Greece; and finally his arrival in Croton. His admirable beliefs and qualities are enumerated at length, and much attention is paid to the precepts and practices of the Pythagorean society. Iamblichus outpraises even Porphyry.

The fourth life of Pythagoras surviving from classical times is an anonymous vita included by Photius (c.820–891), Patriarch of Constantinople, in his wide-ranging *Myriobiblon* (item CCXLIX).[6] This biography, considerably shorter than any of the other three, is little more than a digest of the usual information about Pythagoras' doctrine. It does emphasize, however, the scientific aspect of Pythagoreanism, especially the theory of numbers and the orthodox geocentric cosmology.

Two medieval compendia in the tradition of Diogenes Laertius contain unusually full coverage of Pythagoras, his accomplishments and his teachings. Joannes Wallensis (fl. 1260–1283) prepared the *Florilegium de vita et dictis illustrium philosophorum* and Walter Burley (1275–1357) compiled the *Liber de vita et moribus philosophorum et poetarum*. Both of these works were early printed and went through several editions in the late fifteenth and early sixteenth centuries, though they then went out of fashion.[7]

Among post-classical authorities, the one most frequently cited for information about Pythagoras was the eleventh-century lexicographer Suda. In his Greek lexicon (¶231–236) Suda gave a résumé of Diogenes Laertius' account of Pythagoras, probably through a lost intermediary source, Hesychius of Miletus. Renaissance dictionary makers followed suit. All of those listed below, representing several nations, included an entry for "Pythagoras":

Ambrosius Calepinus (1435–1511), *Cornucopiae* (Reggio, 1502)

Hermannus Torrentinus (i.e., Van Beeck; c.1450–c.1520), *Elucidarius carminum et historiarum* (Deventer, 1498)

Carolus Stephanus (i.e., Estienne; 1504–1564), *De Latinis et Graecis nominibus* (Paris, 1536)

Thomas Elyot (c.1490–1546), *Bibliotheca Eliotae*, ed. Thomas Cooper (London, 1545).[8]

There was no dearth of biographical information about Pythagoras in the renaissance. Indeed, among philosophers only Plato and Aristotle received comparable attention.

The most important single vehicle of Pythagorean doctrine was Plato's *Timaeus*, amplified by Proclus' commentary on it.[9] This dialogue, which added Plato's authority to that of Pythagoras, came early in the development of Western thought and conditioned most cosmologies that followed it. The dialogue begins with the participation of several speakers, including Critias, who recounts the legend of Atlantis. But very soon the burden of discourse is turned over to Timaeus of Locri, "our best astronomer . . . [who] has made it his special task to learn about the nature of the Universe"; and he proceeds to render a monologue, as charged by Critias, "beginning with the origin of the Cosmos and ending with the generation of mankind" (27A). The renaissance considered Timaeus to be a Pythagorean, and most modern scholars concur.[10]

In his presentation, Timaeus begins by making the all-important distinction between a world of being, perceptible only to the intellect, and a world of becoming, perceptible to the senses. The "origin of the Cosmos" then becomes a problem of relationship between these two worlds: how did the physical world derive from the conceptual world? Timaeus posits a benign creator, a Maker and Father (*ποιητὴς καὶ πατήρ*; 28C), who fashioned an orderly universe as a projection of paradigms in the world of being. The creation is a *uni*verse because it is ordered. It is beautiful because the creator is good and the model is perfect. Although the space which the created universe fills is pre-existent, a pregnant void waiting to be realized, time did not begin until the moment of creation. At that moment, the sun and moon and other heavenly bodies were placed in the sky to mark the passage of time. The physical world, then, is an extension of the conceptual world into a time-space continuum, achieved by a godhead (*θεός*) that had both the idea and the power to execute it.

Descending toward specifics, Timaeus defines each of the four elements and propounds a concept of their interrelationship in a unified system, what the Pythagoreans called a tetrad or quaternion.[11] He proceeds to anthropomorphize this created object, this creature, endowing it with limited human characteristics and imbuing its body with a soul. The world-soul is constructed by mathematical proportions out of both physical and intellectual components, the incongruous parts being forced into combination by the godhead. Therefore this soul allows the body of the universe, which is physical, to participate in the non-corporeal realm. The soul's mathematical proportion, in fact, reproducing celestial harmony, makes the physical world consonant with the conceptual. Harmony expressed as mathematical ratios is therefore the controlling force in the cosmos, introducing into the time-space continuum the perfect order of the godhead's paradigm. Numerical relationships in such a system take precedence over all else; structure and form become salient over matter. Individual creatures to inhabit the physical world were made correspondent to the four elements so that the tetrad pattern could be realized even at this level of creation (see Plate 6), and a soul was given to each so that it might share in the cosmic harmony. Facing in the other direction toward physicality, the soul is subject to sensation, and the remainder of the *Timaeus* is given over to man's perception of the physical world and to his physical functions.

The doctrine of Plato's *Timaeus* was summarized in a short treatise entitled *De mundi anima*, attributed to Timaeus of Locri himself. This is now known to be a spurious text, dating from the Hellenistic period; but the renaissance thought it preceded Plato, accepted its validity, and paid it considerable attention.[12] Edward Sherburne, for example, appended "A Catalogue of the most Eminent Astronomers Ancient & Modern" to his translation of Manilius, and he included this entry:

> TIMAEUS LOCRUS, a *Pythagorean* Philosopher, wrote *de Naturâ Mundi;* from which piece *Plato* borrowed the greatest part of his Dialogue entituled *Timaeus*, in the beginning whereof he commends *Timaeus*, as most knowing and skilful in Astronomy.[13]

The *De mundi anima* is a shrewd digest of Plato's *Timaeus* and reinforces the Pythagorean tenets propounded in it.

Another text comparable in many ways to Timaeus of Locri's *De mundi anima* was the *De universi natura* attributed to Ocellus of Lucania, a historically identifiable disciple of Pythagoras.[14] Ocellus was antecedent to Plato, who reportedly obtained his work through Archytas, and he was held to be a strong influence on Aristotle in his views on generation and corruption. The treatise *De universi natura* was known in the 1st century B.C., and is probably a fabrication of shortly before that time. As a basic principle, it assumes an eternal unified cosmos, a monad, but one composed of the conventional four elements, which continuously transmute among themselves. There is a circuitous progression as fire condenses to air, air to water, and water to earth; but conversely, earth rarefies to water, water to air, and air to fire, so that despite the continuous mutation the net change is zero. Nature remains a constant, endlessly repeating this circular pattern. But the individual items of nature, including man, are imperfectly compounded of the four elements and are brought by change to a final dissolution.

This arrangement for constant change within a stable system underlies the concept which the Elizabethans called "mutability."

Many Pythagorean ideas are discussed in various treatises by Aristotle, who confronts the Pythagoreans with respect but often, as is his wont, controverts their doctrine as a starting point for developing his own theory. The most important passages where Aristotle cites the Pythagoreans (never, incidentally, Pythagoras himself) occur in the *De caelo* and the *Metaphysica*. In the *De caelo* (290b12–291a28), Aristotle reproduces the Pythagorean argument that the planets in their motion emit harmonious sounds, and of course refutes it. Later in the *De caelo*, Aristotle concerns himself with the Pythagorean belief "that the centre [of the universe] is occupied by fire, and that the earth is one of the stars, and creates night and day as it travels in a circle about the centre" (293a21–293a23)—an impeccable authority for the renaissance contention that Pythagoras had posited a heliocentric universe. In the *Metaphysica* Aristotle seems almost obsessed with Pythagorean thought, especially with the concept of number as the basic principle of the universe: "They assumed the elements (*στοιχεῖα*) of numbers to be the elements of everything, and the whole universe to be a proportion (*ἁρμονία*) or number (*ἀριθμός*)" (986a2–986a4).[15] Although Aristotle usually disagreed with the Pythagoreans, he was read so widely that he was himself a most successful disseminator of their beliefs.

The classical author who transmitted Pythagorean ideas to the largest number of readers, however, is probably Ovid. In the last book of his *Metamorphoses*,[16] as the culmination in his account of the illustrious Sabine and Latin history, Ovid describes the reign of Numa Pompilius, who succeeded to the Roman power after the death of Romulus. This noble man in his desire to rule well set out to learn "what is Nature's general law" (quae sit rerum natura; XV.6), and he went for this instruction to Croton, the city where Pythagoras conducted his school (see Plate 2).[17] Ovid presents Pythagoras as a teacher with wide and deep learning:

> He, though the gods were far away in the heavenly regions, still approached them with his thought, and what Nature denied to his mortal vision he feasted on with his mind's eye. And when he had surveyed all things by reason and wakeful diligence, he would give out to the public ear the things worthy of their learning and would teach the crowds, which listened in wonder-

2. *Numa Pompilius listening to Pythagoras in his school*

Pythagoras is seated while lecturing to his students. Numa stands at the back. The city of Croton is visible in the background at the left.

Ovid, *Metamorphoses* (Langelier; Paris, 1619), p. 438.

> ing silence to his words, the beginnings of the great universe, the causes of things and what their nature is: what God is, whence come the snows, what is the origin of lightning, whether it is Jupiter or the winds that thunder from the riven clouds, what causes the earth to quake, by what law the stars perform their courses, and whatever else is hidden from men's knowledge (XV.62–72).

From the mouth of Pythagoras comes a long lecture of 404 lines, such as those delivered in his school. He issues an extended injunction against eating animal flesh (75–142), and he exhorts his listeners to accept death fearlessly because the soul is immortal (153–175). In some of the most lyrical lines in the poem he describes the constant changes that Time brings:

> All things are in a state of flux, and everything is brought into being with a changing nature. Time itself flows on in constant

> motion, just like a river. For neither the river nor the swift hour can stop its course; but, as wave is pushed on by wave, and as each wave as it comes is both pressed on and itself presses the wave in front, so time both flees and follows and is ever new. For that which once existed is no more, and that which was not has come to be; and so the whole round of motion is gone through again (178–185).

As an epigraph to the longest passage on mutability in classical poetry, there appear the famous lines comparing the four ages of man to the four seasons (199–213), from spring with its "bright-coloured blossoms" through winter "with faltering step and shivering, its locks all gone or hoary." Time here (234) acquires his distinctive epithet, "the devourer" (tempus edax), and Age becomes "envious" (vetustas invidiosa). In a passage recalling Ocellus of Lucania (237–258), Pythagoras professes a concept of the four elements, each distinct and all undergoing continuous transmutation, but nonetheless joining together to form an eternal, imperishable nature: "All things in their sum total remain unchanged" (summa tamen omnia constant; 258). The emphasis, however, is on change, on metamorphosis, and Pythagoras gives a long and widely ranging list of "things which have assumed new forms" (419–420): the ages have passed from gold to iron, what was dry land is now part of the sea, slimy mud produces agile frogs, the phoenix in a cycle destroys and renews itself, nations rise and fall. Pythagoras' lecture ends where it began, with an injunction against killing animals lest we slay a body which shelters the soul of a kinsman.

After this instruction, Numa returns to his kingdom to reign wisely and peacefully. Pythagoras has been invoked as a mentor in physics, ethics, and politics. Most prominently, though, he appears as a prophet of mutability, supplying at the end of the work a rationale for Ovid's metamorphoses. As Arthur Golding explained in the epistle to the reader prefacing his translation: "The oration of Pithagoras implyes/A sum of all the former work." [18]

Another depiction of Pythagoras—though this time in a playful, even derisive, vein—occurs in several of Lucian's dialogues.[19] The *Ὄνειρος ἢ ἀλεκτρυών* is a dialogue between a cobbler and a cock, the present incarnation of Pythagoras. As the two strike up conversation, the cobbler is understandably inquisitive about the cock's ability to speak. By way of response, the cock asks: "Have you ever heard of a man named Pythagoras, the son of Mnesarchus, of Samos?" And the cobbler replies with pregnant scorn:

> You mean the sophist, the quack, who made laws against tasting meat and eating beans, banishing from the table the food that I for my part like best of all, and then trying to persuade people that before he became Pythagoras he was Euphorbus (Well-fed)? They say he was a conjurer and a miracle-monger (iv).

Such is the sort of denigratory information about Pythagoras, as well as the attitude toward him, which Lucian purveys. The Pythagorean doctrines are satirized even more extensively in the Βίων πρᾶσις, in which life-styles proposed by various philosophers are auctioned to the highest bidder. The exemplum of the Pythagorean sect is offered first; and when asked, "What does he know best?" the auctioneer replies: "Arithmetic, astronomy, charlatanry, geometry, music and quackery; you see in him a first-class soothsayer" (iii). Again in the Ἀναβιοῦντες ἢ ἁλιεύς, when the ancient philosophers rise from the dead to seek vengeance on Lucian for his calumny in the Βίων πρᾶσις, Pythagoras is present among the angry protesters (iv), though he is characteristically silent and allows Plato to do the talking. Lucian's representation of Pythagoras, however, is a scabrous anomaly, and cannot be considered a major factor in the dominant tradition.

The Pythagorean doctrine as it had evolved academically in classical times (cf. Plato, *Republic*, 522E ff.) was codified by Boethius and transmitted to the middle ages as the *quadrivium*.[20] These "four paths" to knowledge were four distinct disciplines—arithmetic, geometry, music, and astronomy. But they all depended upon the Pythagorean assumption that number is the basic principle in the universe and that relationships between items are determined by numerical ratios, thereby producing a structure of harmonious proportions.[21] The quadrivium became a staple of the medieval school and set the pattern for higher education in the early renaissance. It continued to exert influence even after the humanistic concern with classical texts, the *litterae humaniores*, established a new focus and dictated a new curriculum. Boethius wrote a textbook for each of the four disciplines in the quadrivium. His treatise on astronomy is lost, but his *De arithmetica*, *De geometria*, and *De musica* were admired in the early renaissance and soon printed.[22] Interest in Boethius rather quickly died, however, as renaissance practitioners of the Pythagorean disciplines made their own interpretation of the theory of numbers, developed their own hypotheses under the impetus of rationalism and empiricism, and wrote their own textbooks.

The arithmetical tradition through the time of Boethius had been sketched by Isidore of Seville:

> It is said that Pythagoras first among the Greeks wrote systematically about the discipline of numbers, and then it was set forth more extensively by Nicomachus. After that, Apuleius was the first to convey it to the Romans, and finally Boethius wrote on the subject.[23]

Standing behind Boethius, then, the most prominent exponent of Pythagorean mathematics is Nicomachus of Gerasa (fl. 100 A.D.), who set forth the fundamentals of number theory and described the properties of numbers in the traditional way. His major work is no longer extant,[24] nor is the Latin translation of it prepared by Apulieus. Boethius' *De arithmetica,* however, is conceded to be little more than an abbreviated version of this text, and consequently transmitted Nicomachus to later generations. Furthermore, Iamblichus prepared a commentary which was known in the renaissance.[25] A lesser work by Nicomachus, the *Arithmeticae libri duo,* was also known.[26]

A comparable mathematical text, of dubious origin though certainly belonging to antiquity, is the *Theologumena arithmetica,* which is sometimes attributed to Nicomachus and sometimes to Iamblichus.[27] Another ancient text which proffers much cogent matter is the *Expositio rerum mathematicarum ad legendum Platonem utilium* by Theon of Smyrna (fl. 120 A.D.), a work which as the title indicates compiles the specialized mathematical information necessary to read Plato.[28] In the Pythagorean school, an understanding of mathematics was a customary requisite for the study of philosophy, and these texts preserve the number theory as it was transmitted through the Platonists. In this same tradition, though of considerably later date than Boethius, is the *Arithmetica* of Jordanus Nemorarius (d. 1237). LeFèvre d'Etaples collected a corpus of these arithmetical texts and published them with commentary in 1496, a highly significant volume for renaissance mathematics.[29]

Geometry was given its first and almost final codification by Euclid, whose text has remained the basic authority to our own day.[30] Several portions of Euclid's text are essentially Pythagorean, the most evident being the definitions which open Books I, V, and VII, and the treatment of the regular solids in Book XIII. Furthermore, Proclus' commentary on Book I of Euclid has a decidedly

Pythagorean bias.[31] Boethius' *De geometria* is firmly in this tradition.[32]

Because of its development as a creative art capable of inducing pleasure or pain, as Boethius had noted, the specialized discipline of music could be set apart from the other mathematical disciplines and usually was. The classical work for Pythagorean music is the *Harmonices enchiridion* of Nicomachus,[33] which Boethius closely followed in his treatise *De musica*. In addition, later centuries provided the renaissance with many texts which offered instruction in orthodox harmonic theory, such as those by St. Augustine,[34] Martianus Capella,[35] Bede,[36] and Michael Psellus.[37]

There is no extant classical or medieval text on astronomy that can be claimed as unequivocally Pythagorean. In fact, by the fifth century B.C. the Pythagoreans were divided among themselves, some propounding a geocentric and others a heliocentric universe. The Pythagorean notion of cosmic harmony, however, underlay most discussions of astronomy, and the two textbooks most widely used in the early renaissance—Proclus' *De sphaera* and Sacrobosco's *De sphaera*—were fundamentally in the Pythagorean tradition as it had been transmitted by Ptolemaeus. The *De die natali*[38] of Censorinus (fl. 238 A.D.) is a practical summary of accepted beliefs based on geocentrism, while Macrobius' well-known *Commentarius in somnium Scipionis*,[39] written at the turn of the fifth century A.D. and continuously popular, gave utterance to many seminal ideas of a more expansive sort that found their way into later treatments of the subject.

The Pythagorean theory of numbers, though originally a way of organizing the intellectual world of pure forms, gave rise in practical affairs to a tradition of applied mathematics, to the implementation of arithmetic and geometry in arts and crafts. When translated into musical terms, it brought forth theories of harmony. When projected onto the heavens, it produced a beautifully proportioned cosmos. When imposed on human conduct, it resulted in ethical norms prescribing moderation and subservience to a natural order. Many writings which lay down a moral law purport to be the words of Pythagoras or his followers. These texts are the holy scriptures produced by advocates of Neopythagoreanism who during Hellenistic times broke the traditional oath of secrecy to plead their cause. The renaissance, though, accepted the texts as authentic without much concern for their date.

The foremost text among the moral writings associated with the Pythagoreans is the χρυσᾶ ἔπη, the *carmina aurea* or "Golden

Verses," ascribed to Pythagoras himself.[40] This poem of seventy-one hexameters preaches humility, patience, virtuous self-control, and piety. In some embryonic form it may well have been used as a catechism in Pythagoras' school. Certainly during the renaissance it was one of the most widely read poems in Greek, often being printed in schoolbooks as a text for learning the language.[41] In the fifth century Hierocles of Alexandria (fl. 430 A.D.) had prepared an extensive commentary for the *Carmina aurea*, interpreting it in a most pious way and making Pythagoras seem, at least to later generations, a near Christian. Joannes Aurispa (1369–1459), a papal secretary with a penchant for Greek manuscripts, very early translated Hierocles' commentary into Latin, thereby launching it into a career attracting considerable attention in certain circles throughout the renaissance.[42]

In addition to the *Carmina aurea*, several other collections of sentences were attributed to Pythagoreans. Sextus, a philosopher of the first century B.C. who established a school in Rome, had formulated a set of tenets that survived at least in part in a translation by Rufinus. They were accorded the permanence of print by the early sixteenth century.[43] Another set of sentences is attributed to Democrates, a shadowy figure perhaps of the first century B.C.[44] Democrates is given no more substance by being closely linked with Demophilus, who left both a collection of sentences and of similitudes.[45]

Serving much the same didactic intention as the sentences were several letters purported to be from Pythagoras, from members of his family, and from disciples. There was a letter from Pythagoras to Anaximenes, the philosopher of Miletus, and another to Hieron, the tyrant of Syracuse.[46] In 1695 someone under the name of Peter Grinau fabricated some letters from Pythagoras to the King of India, which he pretended to have translated into English.[47] There was a letter from Lysis of Tarentum,[48] a young disciple of Pythagoras, to another Pythagorean named Hipparchus, who is represented by a few fragments in Stobaeus' *Sententiae*. There were several letters from Pythagorean women: a set of three and another set of four from Theano, the wife of Pythagoras; a letter from Myia, the daughter of Theano and Pythagoras; and a letter from Melissa, a Samian woman.[49]

Moreover, in this category of ethical writings should be listed an assortment of Pythagorean fragments from various sources. Ethical and political fragments[50] were extracted from Stobaeus' *Sententiae*, a collection of ancient aphorisms put together in the fifth century. The French printer Henricus Stephanus published several fragments in his miscellany, *Poesis philosophica* (Geneva, 1573), garnered from St. Justin Martyr, Proclus, Sextus Empiricus, Diogenes Laertius, Plutarch, and Clement of Alexandria. A large collection was printed in Greek and translated into Latin by Joachim Zehner with the title *Pythagorae fragmenta, quae ad nostram aetatem pervenerunt* (Leipzig, 1603). An even larger collection, Greek text only, was printed by Conrad Rittershaus at the end of his edition of Porphyry's *De vita Pythagorae* (Altdorf, 1610). *Fragmenta metrica* and *Fragmenta prosaica* were included in an edition of Hierocles (London, 1654–55) prepared for school use, and Thomas Gale in the *Opuscula mythologica, ethica et physica* (Cambridge, 1671) published the Greek text and John North's Latin translation of five short prose essays first printed in Greek alone in Henricus Stephanus' edition of Diogenes Laertius, *De vitis . . . philosophorum* (Geneva, 1570).

A human exemplum of Pythagorean ethics was embodied in Apollonius of Tyana, whose life was legendized by Flavius Philostratus (c.170–c.245 A.D.).[51] Apollonius was a Neopythagorean sage and ascetic who lived approximately the same years as Jesus. His biography as recorded by Philostratus dwells upon his travels, his charismatic appeal to the populace, and his miraculous deeds, much in the manner of the late classical accounts of Pythagoras. The *De vita Apollonii Tyanei* was popular in ancient times and again in the renaissance, to the extent of raising Apollonius to near sanctity.[52] The legend of Apollonius lingers, so that John Keats wrote an ambitious poem about the encounter of this exemplary *philosophe* with a lamia in Corinth.

Finally and most important among the ethical materials are the *symbola*,[53] a large number of precepts expressed pithily as short sayings in the gnomic tradition best known through the emblem books. These *symbola* survived from antiquity in scattered sources. Diogenes Laertius lists seventeen (VIII.17; cf. VIII.34–35), and Porphyry in his life of Pythagoras mentions thirteen (xlii). Iamblichus in his *Protrepticae orationes ad philosophiam* enumerates no less than thirty-nine (xxi), and he repeats many of these in various paragraphs in his life of Pythagoras (esp. xviii, xxiii–xxiv). Plutarch often refers to specific *symbola* in his writings, the longest list (ten) appearing near the end of "The Education of Children" (xvii), but others appearing in "Table Talk" (VIII.vii, viii), in "Roman Questions" (xcv, cxii), in "Isis and Osiris" (x), and in "The Life of Numa" (xiv.3). In the *Deipnosophists* (X.lxxvii), Athenaeus lists six *symbola.* The Church Fathers were familiar with the *symbola:* Clement of Alexandria in his *Stromateis* (V.v) mines Iamblichus for nine *symbola,* St. Jerome in his *Apologia adversus libros Rufini* (III.xxxix) discusses eight taken from Porphyry, and in his *Contra Julianum* Cyril of Alexandria chooses eight of his own from Porphyry. Lists of *symbola* were provided in entries for Pythagoras by later compilers such as Suda and Walter Burley, and during the renaissance these distinctively Pythagorean dicta were given wide currency by many of the foremost scholars who wished to make the classics accessible to their contemporaries.[54]

Several oddments of an esoteric and occult sort had accrued to the name of Pythagoras over the centuries. A game of numbers bearing generic similarity to chess and learnedly called the *Rithmomachia* was known more commonly as the game of Pythagoras.[55] A question-answering device called "The Wheel of Pythagoras"[56] was enormously popular, and other fortune-telling schemes depending upon numbers and claiming the authority of Pythagoras were available to the credulous.[57] What we now know as the multiplication tables were also often attributed to Pythagoras.[58]

The renaissance, then, had a wealth of Pythagorean lore at its disposal. Not only were there ancient biographies of Pythagoras and accounts of his school, but there were adaptations and refutations by pagan philosophers such as Plato and Aristotle. There were literary treatments of Pythagoras' doctrine in works as widely read as Ovid's *Metamorphoses* and Lucian's *Dialogues.* There were "scientific" treatises dealing with the Pythagoreans' concept of nature and their theory of numbers, gloriously epitomized in the Boethian *quadrivium.* There were moral writings in a variety of didactic modes, but all compellingly pious, so that many Church Fathers—Clement, Jerome, Augustine, Cyril—had comfortably quoted Pythagoras with approving familiarity. There were incidental but oft-repeated legends and sayings and miraculous feats. From this welter of material Pythagoras emerged as a complex but fully realized personality. He possessed the wisdom of a philosopher, the perspicacity of a scientist, and the virtue of a Christian. Pythagoras, in fact, might well have typified idealized man as he was bodied forth by renaissance pedagogues and divines.

Late in the renaissance when scholars looked back upon the beliefs of their forebears, they composed histories of philosophy. They had gained a certain sagacity by dint of their rigorous study, and a certain perspective and even detachment. They wrote within a new framework of mental reference. The conflict in the past had been between religion and philosophy, both enterprises of the mind; but empiricism had now deflected the mind from focusing its reason on abstract concepts. Instead, the mind was now directed through the senses toward physicality. Reality no longer lay with ideal forms in Plato's world of being or with beatified souls in the Christian hereafter. Rather, reality had been shifted to the sense-perceptible world of Baconian science. Almost as a valedictory to that optimistic era when only the reconciliation of philosophy and religion was required for intellectual certainty, the most learned and sensitive men collected the precepts of the ancients. It is remarkable how many exhaustive histories of philosophy suddenly appeared across Europe in the mid-seventeenth century: Georg Horn, *Historiae philosophiae libri septem* (Leyden, 1655); Thomas Stanley, *The history of philosophy* (London, 1656–60); Gerard Johann Vossius, *De philosophia et philosophorum sectis libri II* (The Hague, 1658); Abraham Grau, *Historia philosophica* (Franeker, 1674); Theophilus Gale, *Philosophia generalis* (London, 1676). There was suddenly an attempt to recapitulate the past, to hold it captive, to preserve it. These historians wrote in the tradition of Diogenes Laertius, but with greater earnestness and more tender care. Their works are monuments of erudition. In each, the school of Pythagoras provides a major chapter.

Notes

[1] Among others, no less famous men than Aristotle, Democritus, Aristoxenus, Alexander Polyhistor, Nicomachus, and Plotinus reportedly wrote on this subject. See Gerard Johann Vossius, *De philosophorum sectis liber* (The Hague, 1657), p. 45; and A. Ed. Chaignet, *Pythagore et la philosophie pythagoricienne*, 2 vols. (Paris, 1873), I.9–15.

[2] Cf. Joannes Albertus Fabricius, *Bibliotheca Graeca*, 11 vols. (Hamburg, 1790–1808), I.763. For the most thorough critique of Pythagoras' historicity, see Cornelia J. de Vogel, *Pythagoras and Early Pythagoreanism* (Assen, 1966). For late seventeenth-century essays on this subject, see pp. 38–39, n. 31, above.

[3] The *editio princeps* of Diogenes Laertius was a Latin translation by Ambrogio Traversari of the order of Camaldoli printed by Georg Lauer in Rome, c.1472. The same translation was printed by Nicholas Jenson in Venice, 1475, and numerous other editions followed throughout the fifteenth and sixteenth centuries. The Greek text was first printed by the Froben press at Basle, 1533. Henricus Stephanus produced an important annotated edition at Geneva, 1570, which included the Greek text and Traversari's translation, as well as Willem Canter's Latin translation of several Pythagorean writings. Volume I of the first English translation, by several hands, was published by Edward Brewster in London, 1688; Volume II, which contains the section on Pythagoras, did not appear until 1696.

[4] Porphyry's life of Pythagoras, Greek text only, was edited by Conrad

Rittershaus and printed at Altdorf, 1610. A Latin translation by Giovanni Donato was printed at Milan, 1629. The Greek text with a parallel Latin translation by Lucas Holstenius was printed at Rome, 1630.

[5] An extensive Latin précis of Iamblichus' life of Pythagoras, prepared by Nicoló Scutelli, was printed in Rome, 1556. The Greek text with a parallel Latin translation by Johann Arcerius Theodoretus was printed at Heidelberg, 1598.

[6] The Greek text of Photius' *Myriobiblon* was edited by David Hoeschel and printed at Augsburg, 1601. A Latin translation by Andreas Schott was printed at Augsburg, 1606. Hoeschel's Greek text and Schott's Latin translation were printed together at Geneva, 1611. A Greek text of the anonymous *Vita Pythagorae* in Photius and a Latin translation by Lucas Holstenius were printed with Holstenius' edition of Porphyry's *De vita Pythagorae* at Rome, 1630.

[7] Joannes' *Florilegium* was printed at Venice, 1496; Lyons, 1511; and Strasbourg, 1518 (cf. A. G. Little, *The Grey Friars in Oxford* [Oxford, 1892], p. 146). I have used an edition printed at Rome, 1655, in which the section on Pythagoras appears pp. 234–252. Burley's *Liber* was first printed at Cologne, c.1470, and there are at least twenty incunables. I have used an edition printed at Strasbourg, 1516, in which the section on Pythagoras appears fol. $7–8^v$.

[8] With the exception of the last, these references cite first editions. The first edition of Elyot's *Bibliotheca* printed in 1538 does not contain a long entry on Pythagoras; the entry quoted on pp. 25–26, above, is an addition by Elyot's successor, Thomas Cooper. Each of these dictionaries went through several later editions and was kept in print throughout the sixteenth century.

[9] Throughout the middle ages the *Timaeus* was known only in a partial translation with an extensive commentary by Chalcidius (fl. 300 A.D.)—in fact, this was the only dialogue of Plato that enjoyed any currency in the middle ages. Chalcidius' Latin text, imperfectly rendering the first half of the *Timaeus,* was printed by Jodocus Badius Ascensius in Paris, 1520. Another notable edition was offered by Joannes Meursius, printed by Justus Colster in Leyden, 1617. In addition to Chalcidius, Cicero also had prepared a Latin version of the *Timaeus,* which was printed by Carolus Morellius in Paris, 1563. For the renaissance, however, Ficino's Latin translation of the *Timaeus* printed in his *Opera* of Plato (Laurentius Venetus; Florence, 1484), with commentary, was the more dependable and more usual version to read. A text in Greek only of Plato's *Omnia opera,* including the *Timaeus,* was published by the Aldine press in Venice, 1513. A separate Greek text of the *Timaeus* was published by Christopher Wechel in Paris, 1532. A French translation, *Le timée,* by Louis LeRoy, was printed by Michel Vascosan in Paris, 1551. An Italian translation, *Il timeo,* by Sebastiano Erizzo, was printed by Comin da Trino in Venice, 1558.

Proclus (410–485), the last of the great Neoplatonists in Athens, prepared an extensive and influential commentary on the *Timaeus* which emphasizes the microcosm-macrocosm analogy and nudges the Pythagorean-Platonic epistemology in the direction of idealism. Proclus' *Commentarii in Timaeum* was first printed in a Greek text with Plato's *Omnia opera* by Joannes Oporinus in Basle, 1534. Thomas Taylor translated it into English, printed in London, 1820. For a full summary, see Thomas Whittaker, *The Neo-Platonists,* 2nd ed. (Cambridge Univ. Press, 1928), pp. 264–295.

[10] "It seems probable that careful scrutiny would show that the science of Timaeus is, in the main, pretty much what might be expected from a progressive Pythagorean contemporary of Socrates, and that Plato has, at least, originated very little of it" (A. E. Taylor, *A Commentary on Plato's Timaeus* [Oxford, 1928], p. ix). Cf. R. G. Collingwood, *The Idea of Nature* (Oxford,

1945), p. 72. For a refutation of Taylor, however, see F. M. Cornford, *Plato's Cosmology* (London, 1937).

[11] See pp. 151–176, below.

[12] The *De mundi anima* was first published in a Latin translation by Giorgio Valla, printed by Simone Bevilaqua in Venice, 1498. The Greek text, with a Latin translation by Lodovico Nogarola, was printed by Hieronymus Scotus in Venice, 1555. The Greek text was printed also by Gulielmus Morellius in Paris, 1555; and in 1562 Morellius published an anonymous Latin translation to accompany his Greek text. An Italian translation by Dardi Bembo was printed in Venice, 1607. Thomas Stanley published his English translation in *The history of philosophy*, printed in London, 1660. See Fabricius, *Bibliotheca Graeca*, I.877–878; and Chaignet, *Pythagore*, I.180–181.

[13] Manilius, *The sphere*, tr. Sherburne (London, 1675), Appendix, p. 10.

[14] The Greek text of the *De universi natura* was first printed by Conrad Neobarius in Paris, 1539. A Latin translation by Gulielmus Christianus was published by the same printer in Paris, 1541. Later Latin translations were made by Joannes Boscius (Louvain, 1554), Lodovico Nogarola (Venice, 1559), and Carolus Emmanuel Vizzanius (Bologna, 1646). Thomas Taylor published his English translation in London, 1831. See Daniel Georg Morhof, *Polyhistor* [II.i.2.3], 4th ed. (Lubeck, 1747), II.13; Fabricius, *Bibliotheca Graeca*, I.855–859; Chaignet, *Pythagore*, I.181–183; and R. Harder, *Ocellus Lucanus* (Berlin, 1926).

[15] Note also *Metaphysica*, 985b23–990a32, 1080a37–1080b21, 1083b8–1085a2, 1090a16–1090a35, 1091a13–1091b15, 1092b8–1093a28.

[16] Ovid has been a perennial favorite since his own day, and was never more popular than in the renaissance. In consequence, a listing of early editions is superfluous.

Several renaissance editions of the *Metamorphoses* include commentaries that amplify the information about Pythagoras contained in Ovid's text, the most notable being those by Raphael Regius in Ovid, *Opera* (Venice, 1509), and by Georg Sabinus in Ovid, *Metamorphoses* (Cambridge, 1584). George Sandys in his English translation of the *Metamorphosis* (Oxford, 1632) has the most extensive commentary.

[17] Plutarch also in his "Life of Numa" emphasizes Numa's association with Pythagoras (viii.4–10, xi.1–2, xiv.2–3, xxii.2–4), though Plutarch here is less than deferential to the old philosopher.

[18] Ovid, *Metamorphoses*, tr. Golding [1567], ed. W. H. D. Rouse (London, 1961), "The Epistle," ll. 288–289. Note also "The Epistle," ll. 1–28.

[19] Lucian's *Dialogues* were first printed in a Greek text in Florence, 1496. They remained a popular work throughout the renaissance.

[20] Gregor Reisch explains the meaning of this term:

> This doctrine is called the *quadrivium* because there are four ways leading to a single goal: i.e., knowledge of quantity.
>
> Haec doctrina quadrivium appellata est: Sunt enim viae quatuor, ad unum finem (quantitatis scilicet noticiam) perducentes

(*Margarita philosophica* [Basle, 1583], p. 281). See p. 29, above.

[21] On this point, see Nicholas le Fèvre de la Boderie, "Les Sentiers de Sapience," in Francesco Giorgio, *L'Harmonie du monde* et al., tr. Guy le Fèvre de la Boderie (Paris, 1579), ẽ5–ẽ5ᵛ.

[22] The *De arithmetica*, *De geometria*, and *De musica* were printed in Boethius' *Opera* by Giovanni da Forlì in Venice, 1491–92. The *De arithmetica* had earlier been printed separately by Erhard Ratdolt in Augsburg, 1488. Another important edition was edited by Girard Ruffus and printed by Simon

Colinaeus in Paris, 1521. The *De arithmetica* and *De geometria* have not to my knowledge been translated into English. The *De musica* has been translated into English by Calvin M. Bower (unpublished Ph.D. dissertation, George Peabody College for Teachers, 1966), with a most informative introduction and notes.

The four disciplines of the *quadrivium* were set forth also by Michael Psellus (1018–1078), a Byzantine statesman and scholiast. A Greek text of his *Opus . . . in quattuor mathematicas disciplinas, arithmeticam, musicam, geometriam, & astronomiam* was printed in Venice, 1532. The Greek text with a Latin translation by Gulielmus Xylander was printed in Basle, 1556. An important Latin translation of the *De arithmetica, musica, geometria* by Elias Vinetus was printed in Paris, 1557.

[23] Numeri disciplinam apud Graecos primum Pythagoram autumant conscripsisse, ac deinde a Nicomacho diffusius esse dispositam; quam apud Latinos primus Apuleius, deinde Boetius transtulerunt (*Etymologiae,* III.ii).

Cf. Bede, "De arithmeticis numeris liber" in *Opera,* 8 vols. (Basle, 1563), I.98. For a scholarly account of the arithmetical tradition through the early middle ages, see Frank Egleston Robbins, "The Tradition of Greek Arithmology," *Classical Philology,* 16 (1921), 97–123. There are also, of course, many full-scale histories of mathematics, most of which start with the Pythagorean school —e.g., Sir Thomas Heath, *A History of Greek Mathematics,* 2 vols. (Oxford, 1921).

[24] But see Nicomachus, *Introduction to Arithmetic,* tr. Martin Luther D'Ooge (New York, 1926), p. 80.

[25] Iamblichus' *In Nicomachi Geraseni arithmeticam introductionem* was edited and translated into Latin by Samuel Tennulius and printed with the Greek text in Arnhem, 1668.

[26] The Greek text was printed by Christian Wechel in Paris, 1538. An English translation has been prepared by D'Ooge (see n. 24, above).

[27] The Greek text was printed by Christian Wechel in Paris, 1543. The title means, significantly, "Theology expressed in numbers."

[28] The Greek text with a Latin translation was edited by Ismael Bullialdus and printed in Paris, 1644.

[29] *In hoc opere contenta. Arithmetica* [*Jordani*] *decem libris demonstrata. Musica libris demonstrata quattuor. Epitome in libros arithmeticos divi Severini Boetii. Rithmimachiae ludus* (Paris, 1496). Consider also the volume compiled by Giorgio Valla, *De expetendis, et fugiendis rebus opus* (Venice, 1501); and another by LeFèvre d'Etaples, *Epitome compendiosaque introductio in libros arithmeticos . . . Boetii* et al. (Paris, 1503). For the arithmetical tradition as it appeared to a Dutch scholar of the mid-seventeenth century, see Gerard Johann Vossius, *De universae mathesios natura & constitutione liber* (Amsterdam, 1650), p. 40.

[30] Erhard Ratdolt first printed Euclid's *Elementa geometria* in a Latin version by Giovanni Campano of Novara in Venice, 1482. It has remained easily available in print ever since. The first English translation is a notable volume prepared by Henry Billingsley with an important preface by John Dee, printed in impressive folio by John Day in London, 1570. Another notable English edition, with indispensable commentary, has been prepared by Sir Thomas Heath, 3 vols. (Cambridge Univ. Press, 1908).

[31] Proclus' commentary was first printed in a Greek text edited by Simon Grynaeus with Euclid's *Elementa* by Johann Hervagius in Basle, 1533. A Latin version by Francesco Barozzi was published in Padua, 1560. An English version by Thomas Taylor was published in London, 1788–89.

[32] Additional scattered passages having to do with Pythagorean geometry

have been collected by Ivor Thomas, *Greek Mathematics* (London, 1939), pp. 172–225. See also Arturo Reghini, *Per la restituzione della geometria pitagorica* (Rome, 1936).

[33] The Greek text was edited by Joannes Meursius and included in *Aristoxenus. Nicomachus. Alypius. Auctores musices antiquissimi*, published by the Elzevir press in Leyden, 1616. A Latin translation by Marcus Meibom as well as the Greek text was printed in *Antiquae musicae auctores septem*, published by the Elzevir press in Amsterdam, 1652.

[34] In St. Augustine, *Omnia opera*, 10 vols. (Basle, 1528–29).

[35] *De nuptiis Philologiae et Mercurii*, Book IX, printed separately in Meibom, *Antiquae musicae auctores*.

[36] In Bede, *Opera* (1563), I.403–414.

[37] The Greek text in Psellus, *Opus . . . in quattuor mathematicas disciplinas* (1532), and a Latin translation in *Liber de quatuor mathematicis scientiis* (1556) by Gulielmus Xylander.

[38] The Latin text was first published as the initial item in a large collection edited by Filippo Beroaldo and printed by Benedict Hector in Bologna, 1497. It remained a popular treatise throughout the renaissance.

[39] The Latin text was first published by Nicholas Jenson in Venice, 1472. It remained in print with an accretion of notes throughout the renaissance.

[40] See Armand Delatte, "Un Discours sacré pythagoricien" in *Etudes sur la littérature pythagoricienne* (Paris, 1915), pp. 3–79.

[41] I have seen 147 texts of the *Carmina aurea*, in various languages, printed between 1474 and 1700. Moreover, I have accumulated bibliographical references to at least 90 additional printings of the text during the same period.

The text was first published in a Latin version by Joannes Aurispa dispersed in Aurispa's Latin translation of Hierocles' *Commentarius*, printed by Bartholomaeus de Val de Zoccho in Padua, 1474, with several later editions. The Greek text with a Latin parallel text was first printed by Aldus Pius Manutius in a collection of Greek texts for school use appended to Constantine Lascaris' *Erotemata* (Venice, 1494–95), with innumerable later editions. Outstanding translations into Latin were made by Ficino, first printed in his edition of *Iamblichus de mysteriis Ægyptiorum, Chaldaeorum, Assyriorum* et al. (Aldus; Venice, 1497); by Stephanus Niger, first printed in his *Elegantissimae è graeco authorum subditorum translationes* (Giovanni da Castellino; Milan, 1521); by Veit Amerbach, first printed in his edition of *Poemata Pythagorae et Phocylidis* (Craton Mylius; Strasbourg, 1539), with numerous later editions; by Jacobus Hertelius, first printed in his school text beginning with *Theognidis Megarensis sententiae elegiacae* et al. (Joannes Oporinus; Basle, 1561), with innumerable later editions including those taken over by Jean Crespin beginning in Geneva, 1569–70, and those taken over by Friedrich Sylburg beginning in Frankfurt, 1591, and those taken over by Ralph Winterton beginning in Cambridge, 1635; by Theodorus Marcilius, printed as *Aurea Pythagoreorum carmina* (Stephanus Prevosteau; Paris, 1585), designed to accompany Johann Curter's edition of Hierocles' *Commentarius* (Prevosteau; Paris, 1583); and by Joachim Zehner, first printed in *Pythagorae fragmenta* (Michael Lantzenberger; Leipzig, 1603).

Notable translations of the *Carmina aurea* into vernaculars include a French version by Jean Antoine de Baïf in *Etrènes de poézie fransoeze an vers mesurés* (Paris, 1574); another French version by Pierre Tamisier in his *Anthologie ou recueil des plus beaux epigrammes grecs* (Lyons, 1589); yet another French version by R. M. L. T. in *Les sages enseignemens . . . du philosophe Pythagoras, & du sage Sâlomon* (Rouen, 1602); an Italian version by Alessandro Adimari in *La Calliope* (Florence, 1641); another Italian version by Francesco Antonio Cappone in his *Liriche parafrasi* (Venice, 1670); two English versions by Thomas Stanley, one in his *Poems* (London, 1651), and the other in his *History of philosophy* (London, 1660); another English version by John Hall in his translation of Hierocles' *Upon the Golden Verses* (London, 1657); yet another English version by John Norris in his translation of Hierocles' *Upon the Golden Verses* (London, 1682); and yet another English version by Edmund Arwaker appended to his *Thoughts well employ'd*, 2nd ed. (London, 1697). A translation into Arabic and Latin was made by Johann Elichmann, appended to his edition of the *Tabula Cebetis* (Leyden, 1640).

The following textbooks illustrate the continuous use of the *Carmina aurea* in the schools:

Aldus Pius Manutius, *Rudimenta grammatices latinae linguae* (Venice, 1501)
Franciscus Tissardus, ed., *Liber gnomagyricus* (Paris, 1507)
Jacobus Musurus, ed., *Sententiae* (Paris, c.1510)
Hieronymus Aleander, ed., *Gnomologia* (Paris, 1512)
Eufrosino Bonini, ed., *Hesiodi opera* et al. (Florence, 1515)
Franciscus Taegius, ed., *Graecorum sapientum volumina* et al. (Pavia, 1516)
Scriptores aliquot gnomici (Froben; Basle, 1521)
Stephanus Niger, ed., *Elegantissimae è graeco authorum subditorum translationes* (Milan, 1521)
Ottomar Nachtigall, ed., *Moralia quaedam instituta* (Augsburg, 1523)
Caspar Ursinus Velius, ed., *Oratio dominica* et al. (Vienna, 1524)
Wolfgang Anemoecius, ed., *Phocylidis . . . praecepta* et al. (Augsburg, 1533)
Theognidis . . . sententiae elegiacae et al. (Paris, 1537)
Cebetis Thebani tabula. . . . Aurea carmina Pythagorae (Paris, 1537)
Hesiodi opera et al. (Junta; Florence, 1540)
Joachim Camerarius, ed., *Libellus scolasticus utilis* (Basle, 1551)
Claudius Monsellus, tr., *Sententiosa poetarum vetustissimorum . . . opera* (Paris, 1553)
Michael Neander, ed., *Liber aureus* (Basle, 1559)
Jacobus Hertelius, ed., *Theognidis Megarensis sententiae elegiacae* et al. (Basle, 1561)
Hieronymus Osius, ed., *Theognidis Megarensis sententiae elegiacae* et al. (Frankfurt, 1563)
Hesiodi Ascraei opera et dies. Aurea carmina Pythagorae (Plantin; Antwerp, 1564)
Henricus Stephanus, ed., *Poetae graeci principes* (Geneva, 1566)
Jean Crespin, ed., *Vetustissimorum authorum georgica, bucolica, & gnomica poemata* (Geneva, 1569–70)
Henricus Stephanus, ed., *Poesis philosophica* (Geneva, 1573)
Joannes Thomas Freigius, ed., *Graeca grammatica* (Nuremberg, 1580)
Friedrich Sylburg, ed., *Epicae elegiacaeque minorum poetarum gnomae* (Frankfurt, 1591)
Wolfgang Seber, ed., *Pythagorae, ac Phocylidis carmina* (Leipzig, 1622)
Ralph Winterton, ed., *Poetae minores graeci* (Cambridge, 1635)
Johann Vorst, ed., *Veterum poetarum graecorum poemata* (Frankfurt-am-der-Oder, 1692)

A particularly important edition of the *Carmina aurea* with a Latin translation was prepared by Johann Adam Schier and published in Leipzig, 1750.

[42] Hierocles' commentary on the *Carmina aurea* was first published in a Latin translation by Aurispa, printed by Bartholomaeus de Val de Zoccho in Padua, 1474. The Greek text with a Latin translation by Johann Curter was printed in Paris, 1583. A revised Greek text with a translation by Peter Needham was printed in Cambridge, 1709. An Italian translation by Dardi Bembo was printed in Venice, 1604. The first English translation was made

by John Hall and printed in London, 1657. There was another by John Norris, printed in London, 1682, and yet another by Nicholas Rowe(?), printed in London, 1707. A French translation by André Dacier was printed in Paris, 1706.

[43] They were edited by Laurentius Abstemius and first printed in *Sententiarum libellus* by Hieronymus Soncinus in Fano, 1502. They were often reprinted. The best edition appears in Thomas Gale, ed., *Opuscula mythologica, ethica et physica* (Cambridge, 1671). Thomas Taylor translated them into English and appended them to his translation of *Iamblichus' Life of Pythagoras* (London, 1818). For the extensive early bibliography, see Fabricius, *Bibliotheca Graeca*, I.870–874.

[44] The Greek text was printed by Henricus Stephanus in *Poesis philosophica* (Geneva, 1573). A Latin translation by Lucas Holstenius with the Greek text was printed in Rome, 1638. The best edition appears in Gale, *Opuscula mythologica*. An English translation by William Bridgman appears in his *Translations from the Greek* (London, 1804). For the early bibliography, see Fabricius, *Bibliotheca Graeca*, I.868–869.

[45] The *Sententiae* of Demophilus were translated by Lucas Holstenius and first printed with a Greek text in a volume with the sentences of Democrates in 1638 (see note 44, above). The best edition appears in Gale, *Opuscula mythologica*. Thomas Taylor translated them into English and appended them to his translation of *Sallust on the Gods and the World* (London, 1793). For the early bibliography, see Fabricius, *Bibliotheca Graeca*, I.868–869.

The *Similitudines* of Demophilus were published in Gale, *Opuscula mythologica*, in a parallel Greek text and Latin translation by Lucas Holstenius. An English translation by Bridgman appears in his *Translations from the Greek*.

[46] Diogenes Laertius had included the letter to Anaximenes in his account of Pythagoras (VIII.49–50), so that Greek and Latin texts were regularly printed with the *De vitis philosophorum*. The Greek text with a Latin translation by Joachim Camerarius was printed in *Delectae quaedam graecae epistolae* (Tübingen, 1540). The Latin translation by Ambrogio Traversari, taken from Diogenes Laertius, was printed in *Epistolarum laconicarum . . . farragines duae*, ed. Gilbert Cousin (Basle, 1554). Thomas Stanley printed his English version in *The history of philosophy* (1660), and Thomas Gale printed the Greek text and Thomas Aldobrandinus' Latin version (taken from Diogenes Laertius) in *Opuscula mythologica* (1671).

The Greek text of the letter to Hieron was printed in *Epistolae Basilii Magni* et al., ed. Aldus Pius Manutius (Venice, 1499). A Latin translation by Joachim Camerarius was printed in *Delectae quaedam graecae epistolae* (Tübingen, 1540). Another Latin version by Gilbert Cousin was printed in *Epistolarum laconicarum . . . farragines duae* (Basle, 1554). The Greek text and a Latin version by Joannes Arcerius was printed in Arcerius' edition of Iamblichus' *De vita Pythagorae* (Heidelberg, 1598). The Greek text and a Latin version by Jacobus Cuiacius (i.e., Cujas) were printed in *Epistolae graecanicae mutuae* (Geneva, 1606). Thomas Stanley printed his English version in *The history of philosophy* (1660), and John Savage printed another English version in *A Select Collection of Letters of the Antients* (London, 1703).

[47] *Being a transcript of several letters from Averroes. . . . Also several letters from Pythagoras to the King of India* (London, 1695).

[48] The Greek text was printed in *Epistolae Basilii Magni* et al., ed. Aldus Pius Manutius (Venice, 1499). A Latin version by Caspar Churrerius was printed in *Oratio Joannis Oecolampadii* (Hagenau, 1517). An anonymous

Latin version was printed in *Epistolarum laconicarum . . . farragines duae*, ed. Gilbert Cousin (Basle, 1554). The Greek text and a Latin version by Jacobus Cuiacius (i.e., Cujas) were printed in *Epistolae graecanicae mutuae* (Geneva, 1606).

[49] The Greek text of the set of three letters from Theano was printed in *Epistolae Basilii Magni* et al., ed. Aldus Pius Manutius (Venice, 1499). The Greek text and a Latin version by Joannes Arcerius were printed in Arcerius' edition of Iamblichus' *De vita Pythagorae* (Heidelberg, 1598). The Greek text and a Latin version by Eilhard Lubinus were printed in *Epistolae Apollonii Tyanei* et al. (Heidelberg, 1601). The Greek text and a Latin version by Jacobus Cuiacius (i.e., Cujas) were printed in *Epistolae graecanicae mutuae* (Geneva, 1606). John Toland published an English version of two letters in his *Collection of Several Pieces* (London, 1726). The Greek text (from a Vatican ms.) of the set of four letters from Theano, and a Latin version by Lucas Holstenius, were printed in Holstenius' edition of Porphyry's *De vita Pythagorae* (Rome, 1630). Myia's letter was printed with the three letters of Theano. A Latin version by Joachim Camerarius was printed in *Delectae quaedam graecae epistolae* (Tübingen, 1540). Melissa's letter was also printed with the three letters of Theano.

[50] The Greek text of 14 ethical fragments with a Latin translation by Willem Canter was appended to Aristotle's *De moribus ad Nicomachum libri decem*, ed. Theodorus Zuingerus (Basle, 1566); and also to Diogenes Laertius' *De vitis philosophorum*, ed. Henricus Stephanus (Geneva, 1570); and also to anon., ed., *Thesaurus philosophiae moralis* (Lyons, 1589).

The Greek text of 24 political fragments with a Latin translation by Jean de Sponde was appended to Aristotle's *Politicorum libri octo*, ed. Theodorus Zuingerus (Basle, 1582).

[51] A Latin translation of Philostratus' *De vita Apollonii Tyanei* by Alamanno Rinuccini was edited by Filippo Beroaldo and printed by Benedict Hector in Bologna, 1501, with numerous later editions. The Greek text followed by Rinuccini's Latin version was printed by the Aldine press in Venice, 1501–04. Rinuccini's Latin version emended by Frédéric Morel was printed with the Greek text in *Philostrati Lemnii opera* (Paris, 1608). An Italian version was prepared by Lodovico Dolce (Venice, 1549), and another by Francesco Baldelli (Florence, 1549). Blaise de Vigenère offered a French version in Paris, 1599 (a revised edition [Paris, 1611] is augmented with the valuable notes of Artus Thomas). An English translation of the first two books with extensive notes was published by Charles Blount in London, 1680. For bibliography, see Morhof, *Polyhistor* [II.i.2.5], II.15; and Fabricius, *Bibliotheca Graeca*, I.830.

[52] Hierocles of Bithynia (fl. 300 A.D.), an anti-Christian writer, had compared Philostratus' life of Apollonius to the life of Christ, with the intention of denigrating the latter. This attack on the uniqueness of Christianity brought forth a famous refutation from Eusebius. For a discussion of the relation between Pythagoreanism and Christianity with this as a starting point, see Ferdinand Christian Baur, *Apollonius von Tyana und Christus* (Tübingen, 1832).

[53] For a scholarly analysis of their intention and authenticity, see James A. Philip, *Pythagoras and Early Pythagoreanism* (Univ. of Toronto Press, 1966), pp. 134–150.

[54] Thirty-nine *symbola* without commentary were first printed in Ficino's Latin translation (from Iamblichus' *Protrepticae orationes ad philosophiam*) in Iamblichus' *De mysteriis Ægyptiorum, Chaldaeorum, Assyriorum* et al. (Aldus; Venice, 1497), frequently repeated. Within a few years Filippo Beroaldo selected eight *symbola* for thorough explication in a treatise entitled *Symbola Pythagorae moraliter explicata* (Bologna, c.1500), which

proved to be one of the most popular textbooks of the first quarter of the sixteenth century and was oft-reprinted, sometimes separately, more often in the *Opuscula varia* of Beroaldo. When Erasmus published his first collection of *Adagia* (Paris, 1500), he included nine *symbola* with brief one-sentence explanations, eventually augmented to thirty-six *symbola* with full explanations; and through this volume of ancient wisdom, the *symbola* received their widest circulation (see my article, "Pythagorean Symbola in Erasmus' *Adagia*," *Renaissance Quarterly*, 21 [1968], 162–165). Joannes Alexander Brassicanus chose eighteen *symbola* from Iamblichus, which he translated into Latin, annotated in terms of analogues and applications in classical literature, and published with his *Proverbiorum symmicta* (Vienna, 1529). Richard Taverner translated fifteen *symbola* into English from Erasmus before 1539 (date of the first extant—though not the first—edition), giving them a morally Christian interpretation in his oft-reprinted *Proverbes or adagies*. The most extensive compilation of *symbola* was prepared by Lilio Gregorio Giraldi, who gathered a group of sixty-one from all available sources and arranged for each a commentary comprising variant translations and explanations by all recognized authorities—published in *Libelli duo, in quorum altero aenigmata pleraque antiquorum, in altero Pythagorae symbola . . . sunt explicata* (Joannes Oporinus; Basle, 1551). When Nicoló Scutelli published a résumé of Iamblichus' life of Pythagoras (appended to his translation of Iamblichus' *De mysteriis* [Rome, 1556]), he included two lists of *symbola* in Latin: (1) nine *symbola* with no commentary (BB3–BB3^{v}), and (2) thirty *symbola* dispersed in a treatise entitled "Symbola Pythagorae" (GG1^{v}–HH1^{v}). Claude Mignault, editor of Andrea Alciati's *Emblemata*, prefaced his editions of Alciati with a "Syntagma de symbolis," and in some instances thirty-three Pythagorean *symbola* from Erasmus are inserted—e.g., Paris, 1601; Paris, 1602; Antwerp, 1608; Paris, 1618; and Padua, 1621. Joachim Zehner included ten *symbola*, mostly from Plutarch, in his *Pythagorae fragmenta* (Leipzig, 1603), quoting the standard authorities on each. The following year Carolus Boscardus arranged fifty-eight *symbola* according to pertinence in his *Ænigmata et griphi veterum ac recentium* (Douai, 1604). In his compendium of the occult, *De divinatione & magicis praestigiis* (Oppenheim, 1616?), Jean Jacques Boissard listed twenty-one *symbola*, taken over from Diogenes Laertius with a few added from Iamblichus. The *symbola* were again independently collected from all available sources and translated into English by Thomas Stanley in his *History of philosophy* (1660). The most extensive and imaginative commentary was prepared by Count Francesco Berni in *Moralitatis arcana ex Pytagorae symbolis* (Ferrara, 1669), elaborating Ficino's translation of the *symbola* from Iamblichus. Finally, a comprehensive list of *symbola* was assembled by André Dacier for his authoritative volume of Pythagorean texts, *La vie de Pythagore, ses symboles, ses vers dorez, & la vie d'Hierocles* (Paris, 1706), translated into English by Nicholas Rowe(?) and printed by Jacob Tonson in London, 1707.

[55] The *Rithmimachiae ludus* was first printed in a Latin version by Jacques LeFèvre d'Etaples at the end of his edition of mathematical texts, *Arithmetica* et al. (Paris, 1496). Claude de Boissière published a full French account in Paris, 1554, and a Latin version of it in Paris, 1556. Ralph Lever and William Fulwood published an English version in London, 1563. Francesco Barozzi published an Italian version in Venice, 1572. Gustavus Selenus (the pseudonym of August II, Duke of Braunschweig-Lüneberg) published a German version in Leipzig, 1616. See also David E. Smith, *Rara arithmetica* (Boston, 1908), p. 340. For a different game of numbers associated with Pythagoras, see Innocent Ringhieri, *Cento giuochi* (Bologna, 1551), fol. 55–56. More's Utopians play a game "not unlike chess" which is called "a battle

of numbers" in which one number plunders another (*Utopia*, ed. Edward Surtz, S. J., and J. H. Hexter in *The Complete Works of St. Thomas More* [Yale Univ. Press, 1965], p. 129).

[56] The "sphera Pythagorae" was ancient in origin and had survived in many manuscripts. It was first published as "la roüe de Pythagoras" by Gabriel du Preau at the end of Christophe de Cattan's *La géomance* (Paris, 1558), with several later editions. Cattan, along with "the wheele of Pythagoras," was translated by Francis Sparry and printed in London, 1591. In the late seventeenth century, "Pythagoras his wheel of fortune" as translated by Sparry was regularly printed with an ephemeral handbook entitled *The knowledge of things unknown* attributed to a fabulous author named Godfridus. A French version by le Sieur de Peruchio was printed as the last item in his collection, *La chiromance, la physionomie, et la géomance* (Paris, 1657). See p. 237, below, and Plate 46. See also Fabricius, *Bibliotheca Graeca*, I.790; David E. Smith, *Addenda to Rara Mathematica* (Boston, 1939), p. 42; and Charles Singer, *From Magic to Science* (New York, 1958), pp. 144–145.

[57] See *A brefe and plesaunte worke, and sience, of the phelosopher, Pictagoras. Wher in is declared the aunswer of questyons which there in be contained after the order of thys syence* [STC 20524] (William Copeland; London, 1560?); Jean de Meun, *Le plaisant jeu du dodechedron de fortune* (Paris, 1556), translated into English by Sir. W. B. (London, 1613); Heinrich Cornelius Agrippa, *Of the vanitie and uncertaintie of artes and sciences*, tr. James Sanford (London, 1569), fol. 26^{v}–27; John Heydon, *The Rosie Crucian infallible axiomata* (London, 1660); and G. Oliver, *The Pythagorean Triangle* (London, 1875).

[58] See, for example, Bede, *Opera* (1563), I.104; *Enneades arithmeticae* [Wing E3128] (London, 1684); Fabricius, *Bibliotheca Graeca*, I.790; and David E. Smith, *History of Mathematics*, 2 vols. (Boston, 1923), II.124–126.

PYTHAGOREAN DOCTRINE

I

Numbers

The primary tenet of Pythagorean doctrine—indeed, what gave it a unique orientation—was the belief that numbers are the ultimate constituents of reality.[1] By number, the Pythagoreans meant something quite special; they meant a form determined by an arrangement of points (see Plate 3). For example, four points determine a square number and eight points determine a cube number. But the number exists, independent of space, as an abstract concept. The number is pure form, uncreated and unchanging, nonphysical and atemporal. It remains a permanent entity in an intellectual realm. A number *can* be used to define a limited portion of space, of course, and it can even be used to impose shape upon matter. Then it receives physical extension into the time-space continuum and becomes perceptible to our senses as well as to our intellect. By number strictly speaking, however, the Pythagoreans meant form in the abstract, divorced from matter.

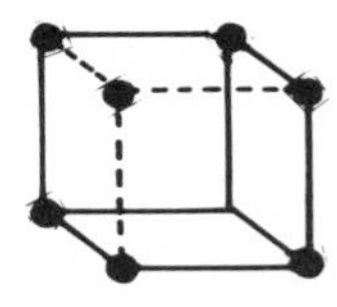

The early Pythagoreans, and perhaps Pythagoras himself, arrived at their theory of numbers in response to problems raised by other philosophers. In consequence, the Pythagorean theory of numbers is best approached through a rapid canvass of the earlier philosophical systems that the Pythagoreans wished to counter. Until the time of Pythagoras, those philosophers who thought about physics in other than mythological ways had each postulated a material substance as the ultimate constituent of reality. The philosophers of Ionia in the sixth century B.C. were materialists and each assumed a single self-existent element out of which all items of nature evolve and back to which they all return. Thales, the first investigator of physics, had postulated a substratum of water. Anaximander accepted the principle of a self-existent substratum, but identified it vaguely as an unlimited entity beyond sense perception. In the same tradition, Anaximenes argued that air is the basic substance, and that items of nature evolve from it

THEO.

tertios,quartos've,aut aliquot altiores cupis habere: id facies per ductionem primo-rum numerorum,vt in fine primæ regulæ deductum eſt. Ex his facile ſignari poterunt petenti,numeri omnes proportionales,tam maiores inæqualites, q̄ minores. ❡Infero vltimo ex dictis in hoc tractatu,in genere proportionum multiplicium, minimam pro portionem eſſe duplam,quæ prima eſt in illo genere:maximam vero reperire non eſt. in genere autem proportionum ſuperparticularium,ſeſquialtera(quæ dicitur prima) maxima cenſetur,minima vero ſignari non poteſt:in aliis tribus generibus proportio-num,nec maiores,nec minores in dato ſenſu poſſunt aſſignari. Corolla-rium non præter-mittẽdũ.

DE ACCEPTO SECVNDVM FIGVRAM NVMERO, tractatus tertius.

Vpereſt,duobus primis tractatibus expeditis,tertium ſubintre mus; in quo quatuor & viginti conſtituemus diffinita:quæ om nem numerum ſecundum figuram conſyderatũ, Laconica bre-uitate abſoluent. Id autẽ pro huius tractatus intellectione præ-notare oportet,omnem figuram eſſe linearem,planam,aut ſo-lidam. Linearem figuram eam eſſe dicimus,quæ ſolam dimen-ſionum obtinet longitudinem,& duobus intercipitur pũctis:vt eſt linea omnis finita & mathematice conſyderata. Planam figu ram eam appellamus, in qua præter longitudinem, ſola amplitudo habetur,& eædem lineis terminatæ inueniuntur:vt eſt quæq; ſuperficies,prout ſic conſyderatur. Solidam vero figuram eam ſignificamus,quæ limitatas longitudinem,amplitudinem,atq; craſ-ſitiem,ſibi vendicat dimenſiones:vt corpus de genere quantitatis. Is igitur numerus ſecundũ figuram ſumitur,qui analogice aliquam aliquáſve obtinet dimẽſiones. Nam, ſi cuiuſpiam numeri cunctæ vnitates recta via procedant, omnis talis,linearis nume-rus dicetur:ſi vero in longum,atque latum porrigantur monades,profunditate negle-cta,planus,ſuperficialis've numerus exprimetur: quòd ſi eius monades in longum,la-tum,& profundum dirigantur,ſolidi nuncupationem talis numerus obtinebit.

Linearis figura. Figura plana. Solida figura.

DIFFINITA.

❡Numerus linearis, eſt numerus qui ſuas omneis in eandem poſitio-nem porrigit vnitates. 1

❡Vt 2, 3, 4. & vt clarior omnibus ſit doctrina: omnes vnitates, omnéſque numeros per rotunda puncta deſignabimus. Nam ſi vnitas explicetur,id erit hoc pacto a •. ſi au tem binarium velis ſignificare, eo modo facies b ••. pari modo ſi ternarium linearem numerum deſcribas,hoc pacto per tria puncta deſignabis c •••. hac arte conſequen-ter procede. Quandam inter ſe obſeruant analogiam numerus linearis in arithmeti-ca,& linea in Geometria:ita vt quemadmodum in longum,quauis alia dimenſione ſe-cluſa,Geometrica linea porrigitur,ſic numetus linearis in ſolam dimenſionum exten-ditur longitudinem. ❡Harum generatio apprehenditur,ſi ab vnitate incœperis (quæ principium linearis numeri appellatur) & naturalem numerorum ſeriem per rotunda puncta ſignificaueris. Exemplum.

Naturalis ſeries numerorum linearum	•	••	•••	••••	•••••	••••••

❡Numerus planus, eſt numerus qui per ſuas vnitates deſcriptus, ſolas longitudinem, latitudinemq; obtinet dimenſiones. 2

•
d
• •

• •
e
• •

❡Vt 3, 4, 5. Nam ſi ternarium inſtar trianguli hoc pacto diſponas d:reperies illum nu merum vtriſque dimenſionibus gaudere, videlicet longitudine, atque latitudine: porri gitur enim à ſiniſtro in dextrum, & à deorſum in furſum, vt ſenſui patet. Eodem mo do ſi in longum, & latum, ad modum quadrati 4 deſcribatur, vt e: dicendus eſt nume-rus planus: aperte enim patet in ſignato numero duas inueniri dimenſiones, longitu-dinem ſcilicet, atque latitudinem. Conſimiliter dicendum eſt de 5, qui ſi in altum, &

3. *A representation of linear numbers, plane numbers, solid numbers, triangular numbers, and square numbers*

The paragraph marked 1 in the inner margin is devoted to linear numbers, and the successive linear numbers 1, 2, 3, 4, 5, and 6 are demonstrated in the text. The paragraph marked 2 in the inner margin is devoted to plane numbers, and the successive plane numbers 3, 4, and 5 are demonstrated in the outer margin. The paragraph marked 3 in

III 16

dextrum ſecundum ſuas vnitates diſtendatur, vt f:numeri plani nomen ſortietur. Hic autem quem numerum planum diffinimus, à plæriſque authoribus ſuperficialis numerus nuncupatur: quippe qui ſuperficiei ſimilis eſt, atque analogus. Et hic numerus planus, infinitas continet ſpecies: quarum prima eſt trigonus: ſecunda, tetragonus: tertia, pentagonus: & ita conſequenter. Sed de his inferius fiet ſermo. ¶Generatio omnium planorum incipit ab vnitate, ſolo binario excepto, nullum ſequentium numerorũ prætermittens: qui omnes, ſi ſecundum duas prænominatas dimenſiones protendantur, ipſorum propagatio omnibus reddetur aperta. Exemplum.

Linea naturalis planorũ numerorũ	1	3	4	5	6	7	8	9	10	11	12	13	14	15

3 ¶Numerus ſolidus, eſt numerus qui ſuapte natura omnem ſibi vendicat dimenſionem, vt puta longitudinem, latitudinem, atq; craſſitiem.

¶Exemplum 4, 5, 6. Vnde ſi quaternarij tres vnitates admodũ trianguli diſponas, cui deſuper vnitas locetur tanquam conus, ſeu vertex pyramidalis figuræ, vt g: inuenies 4 omni dimenſione gaudere, & per conſequẽs ſolidus numerus erit. Eodem modo ſi quatuor quinarij vnitates admodum quadrati deſcribãtur, & alia vnitas deſuper tanquam vertex ſituetur, vt h: non minus ſolidus numerus dicetur. Pari ratione dicendum eſt de ſenario: nam ſi quinq; eius vnitates ad ſimilitudinem pentagonalis figuræ ordinentur, & deſuper tanquam conus vnitas vna ponatur, vt i: ſolidus numerus erit. Numerus autem ſolidus, & corpus de genere quantitatis, in hoc conueniunt, vt per omnem porrigantur dimenſionem. ¶Solidi numeri generantur, capta naturali numerorum ſerie, ſi præter binariũ, & ternariũ, ab vnitate incipiendo, cũctos ſumpſeris numeros. Exẽplũ.

Linea naturalis ſolidorũ numerorum	1	4	5	6	7	8	9	10	11	12	13	14

4 ¶Numerus trigonus, eſt numerus planus tria cõtinens latera æqualia.

¶Vt 3, 6, 10. Nam ſi 3 triangulari diſtendatur interuallo, vt hic k, trigonus numerus appellabitur: vtpote quòd tribus conſtet lateribus æqualibus. Simili modo ſi 6 in tria æqualia latera porrigatur, vt hic l, numerus trigonus dicetur: nam quodlibet ipſius latus tres continet vnitates. Etiam vbi 10 in tres coſtas laterales profundatur, vt hic m: trigonus erit numerus. Dicitur etiam triangularis, quem trigonum numerum diffinimus. Nec prætereas omnium planorum numerorum, trigonum eſſe primum: ſicut in Geometria, omnium rectilinearum figurarum prima, triangulus appellatur. Duabus nanque vnitatibus, ſola linearis emanat figura: plana vero, ad minus tres exigit vnitates, ſicut & triangulus lineas tres: nam duabus lineis, ſaltem rectis, nulla geometrica intercipitur figura. ¶Generantur numeri trigoni naturali numerorum linea diſpoſita, ſi prioribus proxime ſequentes continuo addideris. Vnde ſi vnitati, quæ primus trigonus potentialiter appellatur, ſecundum adijcias numerum, videlicet binarium, conſurget 3, ſecundus trigonus. Et ſi 1, 2, 3 ſimul colligas: tertius trigonus procreabitur, ſcilicet 6. Pari modo ſi 1, 2, 3, 4 ſimul colligantur, quartus trigonus emanabit, videlicet 10. & hoc pacto conſequenter. Exemplum.

Naturalis linea numerorũ	1	2	3	4	5	6	7	8	9	10	11	12	13	14	15
Linea trigonalis	1	3	6	10	15	21	28	36	45	55	66	78	91	105	120

¶Hinc ſequitur omnem numerum trigonum ab vnitate totum eſſe, quota eius lateris fuerit aliqua vnitas pars aliquota.

5 ¶Numerus tetragonus, eſt numerus planus, quatuor æqualibus lateribus conſtans.

¶Vt 4, 9, 16. Si enim 4 quatuor angulis explicetur, vt n: dicendus eſt numerus tetragonus. Etiam ſi in quatuor æqualia latera, ad modum quadrati 9 diſtendatur, vt o: numeri tetragoni appellationem tenebit. Eſt conſimili arte dicendum de 16: qui ſi ad formam quadrati, in latera quatuor ęqualia dilatetur, vt p: non minus tetragonus nuncupabitur. Numerus autem tetragonus, alio nomine quadratus exprimitur: & hoc quia geometrico quadrato ſimilis eſt, & ſodalis. ¶Propagatio autem iſtorum numerorum habetur, ſi trigonalis lineæ quoſvis duos numeros trigonos ſibi inuicem collaterales cõ

the inner margin is devoted to solid numbers, and the successive solid numbers 4, 5, and 6 are demonstrated in the outer margin. The paragraph marked 4 in the inner margin is devoted to triangular numbers, and the successive triangular numbers 3, 6, and 10 are demonstrated in the outer margin. The paragraph marked 5 in the inner margin is devoted to square numbers, and the successive square numbers 4, 9, and 16 are demonstrated in the outer margin.

Joannes Martinus, *Arithmetica* (Paris, 1526), fol. 15ᵛ–16.

in a continual process of condensation and rarefaction. Finally, Heraclitus proposed that fire was the primordial element. Moreover, Heraclitus stated overtly what had heretofore been implicit only: all things continue in constant flux. This inevitable conclusion to Ionian materialism was troublesome, however, because it paved the way for incipient skepticism. Does that which is always in flux have any true identity? How can we know that which incessantly changes?

To answer these ontological and epistemological questions the Pythagoreans dichotomized reality into a realm of abstract concept and a realm of physicality. Timaeus begins his discourse with just this distinction. There is a permanent world of being and a transient world of becoming:

> What is that which is Existent always and has no Becoming? And what is that which is Becoming always and never is Existent? Now the one of these is apprehensible by thought with the aid of reasoning, since it is ever uniformly existent; whereas the other is an object of opinion with the aid of unreasoning sensation, since it becomes and perishes and is never really existent (*Timaeus*, 27D–28A).

The world of being is an intelligible world, perceptible only to the mind, the spirit, the soul. The world of becoming is a sensible world, perceptible to the senses, the body, the flesh. Since that which is becoming continually changes, it has no essence and cannot be known, and therefore is the object of opinion only. That which exists in the conceptual realm, however, is permanent, and therefore knowable through the exercise of reason.

Having established this dualistic framework for reality, Pythagoreans turned from the notion of a principal substance which had been assumed by the Ionian materialists and argued instead for nonsubstantial forms with a permanent existence in the conceptual realm which nonetheless are susceptible to temporary extension into the physical realm of space. In such a system, as Plutarch explains, every item of nature can be analyzed into two distinct components, a form which appeals to the intellect and matter which appeals to the senses:

> The very world and every part thereof is compounded of a substance intelligible or spirituall, and of a substance sensible or corporall: whereof the one hath furnished the thing that is made and engendred with forme and shape, the other with subject matter.[2]

This statement of Plutarch was echoed in the renaissance by many, often with emphasis on the dichotomy between the intelligible and the sensible. In his dialogues entitled *Of the knowledge whiche maketh a wise man*, Thomas Elyot offers the usual Platonic formulation of this dichotomy:

> Of all that whiche bereth the name of a thynge/there be two kyndes, one hath no bodye & is ever stedfast and permanent/the other hath a body, but it is ever moveable and uncertein. The first, bicause it may be understande only/it is called intelligible. The second, bicause it may be felt by sensis it is called Sensible. The way to know the fyrste is called raison, & the knowlege thereof is namid understanding. The way to know the .ii. is called Sense or feling/the knowlege therof is named Perceivinge.[3]

The forms, which reside in the realm of abstract concept, are intellectualized as numbers, as potential portions of space defined by an arrangement of points. Plato accepted this system of the Pythagoreans and adapted their theory of numbers as the foundation for his own famous theory of ideas.[4] Numbers, forms, ideas—the basic assumption is the same.[5] A formalist metaphysics replaces a materialistic system. Ultimate reality is located in an intellectual world of forms rather than a physical world of matter. Thereby the changes that undeniably occur in nature, as our senses attest, can be correlated with unchanging absolutes, and consequently can be submitted to rational analysis.

Aristotle in the *Metaphysica* (983b7–985b23) offers a lucid account of the development of materialism from Thales to Heraclitus and beyond to Empedocles, and this discussion eventuates in a critique of the Pythagorean doctrine that numbers rather than any substance are the ultimate constituents of physics:

> The so-called Pythagoreans applied themselves to mathematics, and were the first to develop this science; and through studying it they came to believe that its principles (ἀρχαί) are the principles of everything. And since *numbers* (ἀριθμοί) are by nature first among these principles, and they fancied that they could detect in numbers, to a greater extent than in fire and earth and water, many analogues of what is and comes into being . . . and since they saw further that the properties and ratios of the musical scales are based on numbers, and since it seemed clear that all other things have their whole nature modelled upon numbers, and that numbers are the ultimate things in the whole

> physical universe, they assumed the elements (στοιχεῖα) of numbers to be the elements of everything, and the whole universe to be a proportion (ἁρμονία) or number (ἀριθμός) (985b24–986a4).[6]

This passage is our most authoritative source for the Pythagorean theory of numbers. Not only does it designate numbers to be the principles (ἀρχαί) and elements (στοιχεῖα) of everything, but it indicates how the various items of nature can be interrelated to form a unified system. The conditions for cosmos are established. The items of nature are organized according to mathematical proportion or (the same thing) musical harmony. Relationships rather than qualities thereby become salient in any description of reality.

The numbers themselves, then, and their harmonious arrangement provide the appropriate subject for ontological and epistemological inquiry. They are presumed to be true, beautiful, and good, and they dictate direction in the pursuit of knowledge. They are the predetermined goals that we seek in our spiritual ascent toward experience of essential reality, of absolute truth, of the deity. As Thomas Stanley understood St. Justin Martyr, Pythagorean mathematics is a necessary preliminary to beatitude, "abstract[ing] the Soul from sensibles, preparing and adapting her for her intelligibles."[7] The contemplation of numbers provides a means of rising from the temporal world to participation in the divine, the ulterior motive for study in Pythagoras' school.[8] It is easy to see that an esthetics derived within this cosmology would expect an art work to reveal the harmony of numbers so that the percipient might have a suitable object for his contemplation as he sought to rise above the illusory world of physics in search of the real.

Conversely, from an opposite point of view, numbers were the paradigms in the mind of the creating godhead, as the *Timaeus* reports, and therefore they imprint their stamp on the mutable realm of nature. According to Theon of Smyrna, they are "the principle, fountain, and root of all things . . . that which before all things exists in the Divine mind; from which and out of which all things are digested into order."[9] This fecundity of numbers was a donnée transmitted from the classical world through the middle ages to the renaissance. As John Dee understood Boethius:

> All thinges (which from the very first originall being of thinges, have bene framed and made) do appeare to be Formed by the reason of Numbers. For this was the principall example or patterne in the minde of the Creator.[10]

In this way, the intellectual world of pure forms interacts with the physical world of generation and corruption—indeed, determines its constitution. At the same time, the constant flux undeniable in nature can be fitted into a scheme which eludes skepticism and submits to scientific investigation.

We must conclude that Pythagorean metaphysics is remarkably sophisticated. While it posits a dualism, a world of forms and a world of matter, it nonetheless effectively interrelates them. A number, in fact, leads an amphibious existence, so that when a mathematician draws a diagram, the figure should be considered conceptual as well as physical. Its ultimate reality still lies in the intellectual world beyond the senses, as Plato so carefully explains in the *Republic:*

> Although they use visible figures and argue about them, they are not thinking about these figures but of those things which the figures represent. . . . When they model or draw objects, . . . they use them in turn as images, endeavouring to see those absolute objects which cannot be seen otherwise than by thought (510D–E).[11]

The physical representation of number, however, is a legitimate means of rendering perceptible what might otherwise remain beyond human knowledge. For example, Plato had resorted to this expository method when he described the soul in numerical terms (*Timaeus*, 34C–37C), as Robert Recorde was well aware:

> This nomber also hath other prerogatives, above all naturalle thynges, for neither is there certaintie in any thyng without it, nother good agremente where it wanteth. Whereof no man can doubte, that hath been accustomed in the Bookes of *Plato, Aristotell,* and other aunciente Philosophers, where he shall see, how thei searche all secrete knowledge and hid misteries, by the aide of nomber. For not onely the constitution of the whole worlde, dooe thei referre to nomber, but also the composition of manne, yea and the verie substaunce of the soule. Of whiche thei professe to knowe no moare, then thei can by the benifite of nomber attaine.[12]

For a man like Recorde imbued with the scientific spirit, number is requisite to knowledge—"for neither is there certaintie in any thyng without it." Number is necessary to quantify the relationships between items and between events in a world to be described as a complex of mechanical forces. But even for Recorde, as for the scholars in Pythagoras' school at Croton, the study of nature was preparatory to understanding the ultimate reality of the empyrean. Number, then, is the means of bridging the physical and the conceptual worlds, of allowing intercourse between them. Echoing Porphyry (*De vita Pythagorae*, xlvii), Thomas Stanley says that Pythagoras "used the Mathematical Sciences" because numbers "are intermediate betwixt Corporeals and Incorporeals." [13] Numbers have existence in both worlds, embrace both worlds, allow interaction between both worlds.

The practical manner in which numbers interrelate the intellectual and the material is well demonstrated when the theory of numbers is used to explain how the extended universe was created. The generation of the physical world out of the conceptual world is described in a general way near the beginning of the *Timaeus* (31B–34B). A more specialized account of the creation in terms of number, however, is available in several sources and underlies most Pythagorean thought as an unstated premise. The conceptual world, being all-inclusive and permanent—that is, perfect—is of course a unit. In the technical parlance of Pythagorean mathematics, it is designated "the monad." The problem, quite simply, is how to explain the production of multeity out of this unity, how to explain the diversity of creation out of this undifferentiated atemporal abstraction (see Plates 4, 5, and 6).

The first step is recognition of a paradox: although unlimited and eternal, the monad, being a unit, is represented in the terms of Pythagorean number by a point, which of course has no dimension—indeed, has no existence except as a concept. As Gregor Reisch explains: "One is not a number, but the principle of number, just as a point is the principle of magnitude." [14] Yet a point can be given physical identity by being placed in relationships within a diagram, as Henry Billingsley made clear in his commentary on Euclid:

> A signe or point is of *Pithagoras* Scholars after this manner defined: *A poynt is an unitie which hath position.* Numbers are conceaved in mynde without any forme & figure, and therefore without matter wheron to receave figure, & consequently without place and position.[15]

But when a number is imposed upon space and fixed in position, it acquires extension; when number is impressed upon matter, it acquires physicality. Therefore, since the point as concept is correlative with the number 1, it assumes substance when it becomes

1 something—for example, 1 dot in a diagram, or 1 stone, or 1 tree, or 1 man. In this fashion, the monad, infinite and eternal though it may be, is placed in relationship to each item in nature.

Once the barrier between the conceptual world and the physical world is overcome by establishing the relationship between the monad and the number 1, the rest of multeity can be educed without difficulty. When the number 1 passes from the world of concept to the world of matter, it becomes extended and therefore divisible; 1 becomes capable of 2. Furthermore, two points, though having no dimension themselves, define by their relationship a line, which does have dimension  . From there, it is easy to arrive at an explanation for the three-dimensional universe. Three points define a surface  , and four a volume  .[16] Ecce! a time-space continuum springs from the abyss. The number 4, the final possibility of extension in our three-dimensional world, serves as an ideogram for the creation *in toto*. The tetrad, as we shall see, furnishes an elementary scheme for the extended universe, the skeletal diagram for cosmos.

Diogenes Laertius cites a lost source, Alexander Polyhistor, for his account of how Pythagoreans derived the extended universe from the conceptual monad:

> This principle (ἀρχή) of all things is the monad or unit; arising from this monad the undefined [i.e., unlimited[17]] dyad or two serves as material substratum to the monad, which is cause; from the monad and the undefined dyad spring numbers; from numbers, points; from points, lines; from lines, plane figures; from plane figures, solid figures; from solid figures, sensible bodies, the elements (στοιχεῖα) of which are four, fire, water, earth and air; these elements interchange and turn into one another completely, and combine to produce a universe, animate, intelligent, spherical (VIII.24–25).

Diogenes Laertius sees the monad as a first cause which acts upon latent matter, represented by the unlimited dyad. From this interaction spring the point, the line, the plane surface, and the solid—the four possibilities of physical extension. From solid figures Diogenes Laertius then derives sense-perceptible bodies, comprised of fire, water, earth, and air—the four possibilities within the system of elements. Again, we have a notion of cosmos conceived as a derivative of the number 4, and the physical universe is described as an organism composed of four elements.

MONAS PYTHAGORICA.

ESSENTIA	VERITAS	BONITAS
VNITAS	POTESTAS	PVLCHRITVDO
VIRTVS INSE PERMANES	VIRTVS COPVLANS	VIRTVS EXTRORSV FVSA

IN TOTO VNIVERSO.

Forma cui apparẽtia indefinita annectitur.	*Proportio & connexus extremorũ.*	*Materies cui gluten vel humor annexus.*	Principia.
Aequabilitas materiæ.	*Mediocritas Materialis glutinis.*	*Inæquabilitas siue asperitas materiæ.*	Coagulum Materiæ.
Perspicuitas formæ seu lux.	*Mediocritas apparentiæ in forma.*	*Opacitas formæ.*	Coagulum Formæ.
Proportio inæqualitatis minoris.	*Proportio æqualitatis.*	*Proportio maioris inæqualitatis.*	Coag. proportionis.
Aer.	*Aura.*	*Tellus.*	elemẽta. 1. cõp.
Ignis.	*aura.*	*Aqua.*	elem. 2. cõp.
Esse simplex.	*Esse determinatũ.*	*Esse commune.*	esse in rebus
Vita & vnitas.	*Compositio & ordo.*	*Multiplicitas & pulchritudo.*	Natura.
Mundus maior.	*Mundus minor.*	*Mundus minimus*	Mũdi species.

IN MVNDO MAIORE.

Continentia.	*Vincula et Spiritus*	*Contenta.*	
Cælum.	*Aether.*	*Sublunaris regio.*	partes coutinẽtes.
Lux.	*Splendor.*	*Lumen & color.*	dimanatio & influxus.
Formæ præsides.	*Spiritus.*	*qualitat. et corpora*	Partes mundo contentæ.
Animæ sublimes.	*Animæ mediæ & rationales.*	*Animæ infimi gradus.*	

4. *The Pythagorean monad proliferating by threes*

The Pythagorean monad, symbolized at the top by a refulgent sun, proceeds to generate the extended universe in the triad pattern of three items presented as two extremes conjoined by a mean. Each triad can be read across on the same line. The several triads are also arranged hier-

LIBER I.

IN MICROCOSMO HOMINE.			
Anima.	*Spiritus*	*Corpus.*	Partes maiores.
Anima rationalis.	*Anima irascibilis.*	*Anima cõcupiscibilis & vegetatrix.*	Anima.
Intellectus.	*Ratio.*	*Imaginatrix virtus.*	Anima rationalis.
Spiritus animalis.	*Spiritus vitalis.*	*Naturalis Spiritus*	Spiritus.
Humor aerius.	*Aura media.*	*Humor terreus.*	Elementa 1. & 2. compositionis.
Igneus humor.	*aura media.*	*Humor aqueus.*	
Viscera.	*Vasa.*	*Externæ corporis partes.*	Partes sensibiles.
Cerebrum et nerui	*Cor & arteriæ.*	*Hepar & venæ.*	
IN MVNDO POSTREMÆ COMPOSITIONIS.			
Notiones.	*Discursuum seminaria.*	*Sensibilia simulachra.*	Seminaria.
Metaphysica.	*Logica.*	*Physica.*	Fines
Secta Methodica.	*Secta Dogmatica.*	*Secta empeirica.*	Sectæ
Analogismus.	*Conuersio vtriusque.*	*Epilogismus.*	Instrumenta primaria.
Synthesis.	*Conuersio.*	*Analysis.*	Motus primarij.
Mens legum.	*Lex.*	*Vsus & historia.*	Principia Reipub.
Principes.	*Magistratus.*	*Populus.*	Partes Reipub.
Discursus Metaphysicus in longit.	*Discursus Logicus in altitudine.*	*Discursus Physicus in latitudine.*	Methodus.

archically from the highest level of creation to the lowest. Four categories are indicated: "in the universe at large," "in the macrocosm," "in the human microcosm," and "in the lowest world."

Cornelius Gemma, *De arte cyclognomica, tomi III* (Antwerp, 1569), pp. 66–67.

	1 MATERIEM, ceu ſubiectum vltimum.	2 QVALITATEM, vt vinculū ſpiritus.	3 SPIRITVM, vt vinculū animæ.	4 ANIMAM, vt totius præſidem formam.
IN MVNDO INTELLIGIBILI	*Lux intelligibilis in glutine materiali conſimili.*	*Qualitates intelligibiles.*	*Spiritus intelligibiles.*	*Intellectus puriſsimi.*
IN CAELESTIBVS	*Lux corporea cæleſtis & firmiſsimæ concretionis.*	*Cæleſtis calor ex luce perſpicua, & frigus cæleſte eiuſdem vinculū ex luce opaca vel inperſpicua.*	*Cæleſtis ſpiritus inferiorum gubernatores.*	*Intelligẽtiæ orbium cæleſtium gubernatrices.*
IN ÆTHEREIS	*Corpora ſplendida mediæ concretionis.*	*Calor æthereus, frigus æthereum.*	*Spiritusætherei.*	*Dæmones.*
IN SVBLVNARIBVS	*Corpora luminoſa infirmæ cõcretionis.*	*Calor elementaris & frigus illi oppoſitum.*	*Spiritus elementares.*	*Heroës.*
IN ANIMANTIBVS	*Corpora colorata concretionis polymorphæ.*	*Calor animãtis Hippocrati innatum calidum, huic frigus innatum opponitur.*	*Spiritus animæ ideas continens & rationes rerum agendarum, vel ante fœtus formationem.*	*Animæ.*
IN HOMINIS ANIMA	*Senſus, in quo obiecta ſenſibilia.*	*Imaginatio, in qua phantaſmata.*	*Ratio, in qua diſcurſuum ſeminaria comp. & diuiſ. rudimenta.*	*Mens, in qua notiones, καὶ κοιναὶ ἔννοιαι.*
IN REPVBLICA	*Corporeæ partes in republica, vt principatus, magiſtratus, populatus.*	*Legum, qualitatū, & circumſtantiarū velut nexus propiores.*	*Legum ritus et ceremoniæ, velut vincula.*	*Legum rationes velut animæ earundem.*

QVATERNIO PYTHAGORICVS PER MVNDI *ſeptenos ordines pari proportione diſtributus.*

5. *"The Pythagorean quaternion proportionally distributed throughout the seven levels of the world"*

The monad here has proliferated by fours, producing a chart wherein each of seven levels of creation (listed at the left-hand side) is analyzed into four parts, under the headings "matter," "quality," "spirit," and "soul." The levels of creation designated are 1)the intelligible world (perceptible only to the mind), 2)the visible heavens, 3)the atmosphere, 4)the sublunary world, 5)living creatures, 6)the soul of man, 7)the commonwealth.

Cornelius Gemma, *De arte cyclognomica, tomi III* (Antwerp, 1569), p. 34.

	Lux perſpicua cum humore æquabili.	*Lux perſpicua cum humore inæquabili.*	*Lux opaca in humore inæquabili.*	*Lux opaca in humore æquabili.*
	Calidum Humidum.	Calidum Siccum.	Frigidum Siccum.	Frigidum Humidum.
ELEMENTA COMMVNIA.	AER	IGNIS	TERRA	AQVA
ELEMENTA CAELESTIA.	Lux qualis in ♃ ♀	Lux qualis in ♂ ☉	Lux qualis in ♄ ☿	Lux qualis in ☾
ELEMENTA AETHEREA.	Splendor aut vehiculum aëreum.	Splendor aut vehiculum igneum.	Splendor aut vehiculum terreum.	Splendor aut vehiculum aqueum.
ELEMENTA SVBLVNARIA.	Lumen aëreum ex perſpicuo & æquabili.	Lumen aut ſubiectum igneum ex perſpicuo & inæquabili.	Lumẽ terreum ex opaco & inæquabili.	Lumen aqueũ ex opaco & æquabili.
HVMORES ET TEMPERAMENTA	Sanguis & ſanguineũ temperamentum.	Cholera & bilioſa craſis.	Atra bilis & craſis melancholica.	Pituita & craſis phlegmatica.
AETATES.	Pueritia. Pubertas. Adoleſcentia.	Iuuentus. Aetatis virilis exordia.	Senectus & ætas decrepita.	Virilis ætas. Senium.
ANNI TEMPORA.	Ver Galeno temperatum.	Aeſtas.	Autumnus Galeno inæqualis.	Hyems.
CARDINES MVNDI.	Meridies.	Ortus.	Septentrio.	Occaſus.
VENTI.	Auſter cum collateralibus.	Eurus.	Aquilo.	Zephyrus.
PARTES ANIMALIVM.	Caro, pulmones, medullæ.	Parenchymata, vt hepar, ſplen, cor.	Solidæ partes, vt oſſa, neruí, cartilag. venæ, arteriæ.	Cerebrum, adeps, ſtomachus, inteſtina.
PARTES VINI, OLEI ET SIMILIVM.	Flos { Vini. Olei.	Vinum feruentius aut oleum.	Fex { Vini. Olei.	Muſtum aut oleum quod iam concoqui pridem cæpit.
ANALOGIA accidentiũ cæterorũ prę-ſentim ſenſibilium. { Viſu Auditu Guſtu Olfactu Tactu.	*Aërea.* Aequabilia tenuia.	*Ignea* Tenuia leuia, ſed inæquabilia.	*Terrea* Craſſa & inæquabilia.	*Aquea* Craſſa, ſed æquabilia quæuis.

6. *The universe schematized according to the four elements*

This chart demonstrates various categories of creation analyzed in the quaternion or tetrad pattern established by the four elements (see pp. 166–174 and Plates 31–34). The categories are listed at the left-hand side: "the common elements," "the celestial elements," "the atmospheric elements," "the sublunary elements," "humours and temperaments," "the ages of man," "the seasons of the year," "the cardinal points," "the winds," "the parts of the body," "the parts of wine, oil, and similar things," "the correspondence of other qualities according to sense perception."

Cornelius Gemma, *De arte cyclognomica, tomi III* (Antwerp, 1569), p. 37.

This physical cosmos, of course, being temporal and finite, must have a limit. Strict reasoning in terms of Pythagorean mathematics places this limit at the number 10 according to a logical argument. Since the point, the line, the surface, and the volume exhaust the possibilities for the extension of number into space, the universe is composed of these numbers and no more. The limit of the universe, in other words, is determined by adding these numbers; and $1 + 2 + 3 + 4 = 10$. Moreover, since the decad exhausts the possibilities of physical extension, leaving nothing to be added, it is equivalent to perfection. To quote Aristotle, "The decad is considered to be a complete thing and to comprise the whole essential nature of the numerical system" (*Metaphysica*, 986a9–11). Therefore 10 is the perfect number in the physical world. As Thomas Stanley translated a well-known quotation from Proclus:

—Sacred Number springs
From th'uncorrupted Monad, and proceeds
To the Divine Tetractys, she who breeds
All; and assigns the proper bounds to all,
Whom we the pure immortal Decad call.[18]

By such reasoning, the tetrad and the decad acquired special significance for the Pythagoreans: 4 represented the extended universe and 10 its limit. But these numbers, as Robert Recorde insists, are merely modifications of the monad, the conceptual reservoir of all things:

> Unitie is of it self undivisible, and yet is it in al partes of the worlde, and in every thing. Yea, the worlde it self consisteth of unitie, is named of unitie [i.e., *uni*verse], was made by unitie, and is preserved by unitie.[19]

By explaining the diversity of created things in terms of number, the Pythagoreans succeeded in maintaining unity simultaneous with diversity: 10 and 4 are equivalents of each other and also of 1. Indeed, Pythagoreans made unity and multeity interchangeable, each deriving from the other.

The Pythagorean theory of numbers was dutifully expounded by Saluste du Bartas in his compendious *Devine weekes and workes.* In "The Columnes," the poet interprets the four mathematical disciplines of the quadrivium as they had been revealed on the pillars of Seth (according to cabalistic tradition, inscriptions on these pillars preserved the quadrivium when God destroyed the world by flood and flame). Du Bartas properly begins with arithmetic; and though he passes quickly over the details and therefore obscures some of the subtleties, he nonetheless touches upon the outstanding virtues of each digit and offers a reasonable explanation of how multeity proceeds from unity:

> Marke heere, what Figure stands for *One*, the right
> Roote of all Nomber; and of Infinite:
> Loves happines, the praise of Harmonie,
> Nurcerie of All, and end of *Polymnie:*
> No Nomber, but more then a Nomber yet;
> Potentially in all, and all in it.
> Now, note *Two's* Character, Ones heire aparant,
> As his First-borne; first Nomber, and the Parent
> Of Female [20] Payres. Heere now observe the *Three,*
> Th' eldest of Odds, Gods Nomber properly;
> Wherein, both Nomber and no-Nomber enter: [21]
> Heav'ns deerest Nomber, whose inclosed Center
> Doth equally from both extreames extend:
> The first that hath beginning, mid'st, and end.
> The (*Cubes*-base) *Foure;* a full and perfect summe,
> Whose added parts just unto Tenne doo come;
> Nomber of Gods great Name,[22] Seasons, Complexions,
> Windes, Elements, and cardinall Perfections.
>
> . . . .
>
> The *Tenne*, which doth all Nombers force combine:
> The *Tenne*, which makes, as *One* the *Point*, the *Line*.[23]

Du Bartas emphasizes the paradox of the monad: it is "no Nomber, but more then a Nomber yet;/Potentially in all, and all in it." It is a concept, and therefore noncorporeal, yet endlessly fecund. It inheres in each item of nature, yet holds the universe in a single continuum. The perpetuation of this paradox was the great achievement of Pythagorean cosmology.

The Pythagorean theory of numbers of course underlies each of the mathematical [24] disciplines, of which four had been differentiated: arithmetic, music, geometry, and astronomy. The particular intention of each of these is specified by Proclus:

> The whole science of Mathematicks, the *Pythagoreans* divided into four parts, attributing one to *Multitude*, another to *Magnitude*, and subdividing each of these into two. For Multitude either subsists by it self, or is consider'd with respect to another; Magnitude either stands still, or is moved. *Arithmetick* contemplates Multitude in it self: *Musick* with respect to another:

> *Geometry*, unmoveable magnitude; *Sphaerick* [i.e., astronomy], moveable.[25]

Proclus notes that two of the mathematical sciences—arithmetic and music—deal with number as *multitude* (that is, number as an aggregate of discrete units), while the other two—geometry and astronomy—deal with number as *magnitude* (that is, number as a continuous quantity). Arithmetic, then, is the simple study of multitudes at rest. Music is the study of relationships between multitudes, known as ratios, proportions, or harmonies. Geometry is the study of magnitudes (i.e., numbers with spatial extension—what we might call "forms") at rest. Astronomy, finally, is the study of forms in motion.

1. *Arithmetic*

Arithmetic, according to Isidore of Seville, "is the discipline which deals with quantity that can be counted considered only in relation to itself"; more simply, it "is the study of numbers."[26] Then Isidore, echoing Euclid (*Elements*, VII.definitions), proceeds to define "number" as "quantity composed of units"[27]—that is, multitude. These definitions were standard in all treatises of arithmetic until the early seventeenth century. Arithmetic thus interpreted permits seven basic operations: numeration, addition, subtraction, multiplication, division, progression, and the extraction of roots. Since it assumes that quantity is composed of units, however, it is incapable of dealing with any but whole numbers.[28]

There are two generic classifications of numbers: odds and evens.[29] Odd numbers do not submit to equal division—when an attempt is made to divide an odd number in half, a whole unit remains in the middle. Since odd numbers refuse to be divided, they have an integrity which suggests they are limited, capable of organization, productive of order. Even numbers, on the other hand, *can* be divided into two equal parts, and this ease of dissolution is construed as a lack of integrity and a penchant for divisiveness. An even number readily complies with further extension through division, and therefore is thought of as physical and unlimited. It generates discord and disorder wherever it exists. Consequently, odd numbers are associated with perfection and divinity and are masculine by virtue, while even numbers indicate defectiveness and physicality and are feminine.

The monad and the dyad are the archetypes of odd and even numbers, respectively, but they are not arithmetical numbers themselves. The monad contains the potential for all numbers, but this very inclusiveness disallows its being considered a number itself. It is the impetus behind number or the superior being above number. As Macrobius carefully explained:

> One is called *monas*, that is Unity, and is both male and female, odd and even, itself not a number, but the source and origin of numbers. This monad, the beginning and ending of all things, yet itself not knowing a beginning or ending, refers to the Supreme God.[30]

The monad, then, represents the unity of the conceptual world, while the dyad represents the idea of extension and therefore the divisibility of the physical world. The dyad, however, like the monad, is an abstraction rather than an aggregate of units. The first arithmetical number per se—that is, a "quantity composed of units"—is 3, whose physical extension is proved by the fact that it has a *terminus a quo* and a *terminus ad quem*, with something in between. In the words of St. Augustine, "There is a certain perfection in three because it is a whole: it has a beginning, middle, and end" (*De musica*, I.xii). Johann Reuchlin also extolls the virtue of 3: "The *Triad*, through its propensity to multiply, and communicate its goodness to all creatures, proceeds from power [i.e., potential] to operation, beholding with a perpetual intuition that faecundity of multitude which is in it." [31]

The distinctive qualities of odd and of even numbers were generally accorded metaphysical significance. Pierre de la Primaudaye cites Pythagoras as an authority who derived all creatures from the even and the odd, the former contributing the matter while the latter supplied the forms:

> In the first production of things, there were present the Even and the Odde: for the Even (according to the doctrine of those which doe philosophically discourse by numbers) and principally the binarie (or number of two) signifieth the matter, and the uneven or odde betokeneth the forme.[32]

While La Primaudaye only implies a value judgment that makes the odd superior to the even, Plutarch is explicit about Pythagoras' ethical application of odd and even numbers:

> *Pythagoras* affirmeth, that of the two first principles, Unitie was God, and the soveraigne good; which is the very nature of one,

7. *The "Typus arithmeticae"*

Arithmetic is personified as a noble lady holding a textbook in each hand. On her gown are inscribed two geometrical progressions, 1, 3, 9, 27 and 1, 2, 4, 8—the two legs of the lambda by which Plato had analyzed the soul in the *Timaeus* (see pp. 210–212). In the lower right corner sits Pythagoras before an abacus-like device which uses unit counters for performing arithmetical computations based on a decimal system. In the lower left corner Boethius employs pen and ink to work arithmetical problems using the notation of arabic numerals. The appearance of fractions on his board (½, ⅔) indicates an advance over simple Pythagorean arithmetic.

Gregor Reisch, *Margarita philosophica* (Freiburg, 1503), f1[v].

> and is Understanding it selfe: but the indefinite binarie, is the divell and evill, about which is the multitude materiall, and the visible world.[33]

Pythagorean arithmetic, according to Plutarch, assigned probity to 1 and corruptiveness to 2. No Elizabethan would have missed the numerical import of Una and Duessa in Book I of *The Faerie Queene*.

Arithmetic, like each of the disciplines in the quadrivium, had both a speculative and a practical side. The theory was articulated in a formal manner, as though it were philosophical discourse. The *arithmetica speculativa* consisted largely of defining number as quantity and demonstrating the various sorts of number differentiated by their forms; for example,

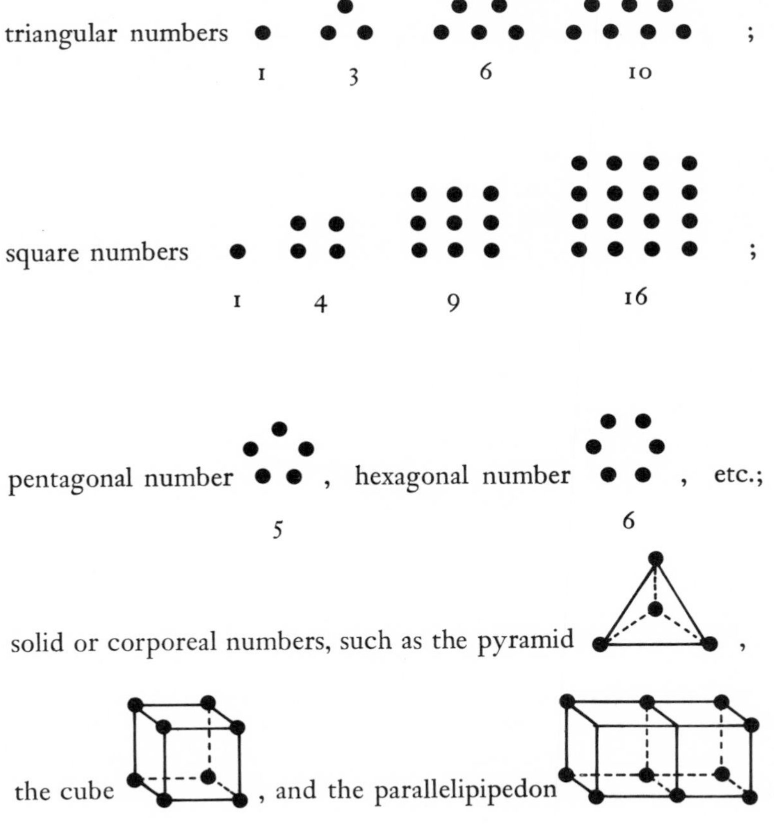

Also differentiated were three sorts of mathematical means:

4 is the *arithmetical* mean in the progression 2 : 4 : 6;
4 is the *geometrical* mean in the progression 2 : 4 : 8;
4 is the *harmonic* (or musical) mean in the progression 3 : 4 : 6.[34]

Often quite apart from the theory were instructions for the everyday application of arithmetic. Practical arithmetic or "algorism"[35] consisted of computation according to the seven basic operations (numeration, addition, subtraction, multiplication, division, progression, and the extraction of roots), and led in the renaissance to the development of algebra and logarithms.

In the sixteenth century the traditional arithmetic of Boethius rapidly receded before the demand for new ways of computation created by commerce and science. The theory of numbers had been devised to provide a framework within which the changes of the physical world would become orderly and knowable. It furnished a means of conceptualizing time and space. But as ultimate reality came to reside in the physical objects themselves, the concern of numbering turned from the exposition of immutable forms imposed on mutable matter—turned from an understanding of squares and cubes and perfect numbers—and sought instead a means of describing the physicality of objects randomly placed in nature. Number is then no longer an abstraction, but rather four yards or nine acres or five bushels. The shift from deduction to induction is well illustrated by Thomas Masterson in the dedicatory epistle to his *Third booke of arithmeticke:*

> Seeing God made, governeth, and maintaineth all things in number, weight and measure,[36] it is verie difficult for man to know any thing certainly concerning the celestiall spheres, or assuredly to speake and determine, of terrestriall and humane affaires, without that excellent gift of God the science of numbers.[37]

Empiricism is thereby justified—indeed, made a sine qua non for knowledge of any sort. Numbers become a key to open nature's cabinet, rather than being the contents of that cabinet. Arithmetic is degraded to an ancillary discipline—as Robert Recorde called his textbook, "the ground of artes," a preliminary to practical success in business and navigation and medicine and the other daily affairs of men. It is no longer the dominant discipline, that which sets forth the universal patterns. Numbers no longer shape reality.

2. *Music*

In narrow terms of the Pythagorean quadrivium, music was the science that dealt with relationships between multitudes (whole numbers), expressed as ratios or proportions.[38] Arithmetic, the prime discipline of the quadrivium, dealt with number as multitude considered without relationship to anything else: for example, 7 or 30 or 53. Music, however, dealt with multitudes considered in relation to one another: for example, a multitude 3 relates to a multitude 6 as 3 to 6, expressed as the ratio 3/6 or the proportion 1/2. Therefore the relationship of the multitude 3 to the multitude 6 is one half. As another example, the multitude 24 relates to the multitude 8 as 24/8 or 3/1; the multitude 24 is therefore a triple of the multitude 8. Multitudes could be expressed in the medium of sounds—that is, by musical notes—and their ratios were judged to be consonant or not, harmonious or not. The discipline of music was thereby translated from the world of pure concept into the world of sense perception.

Since music led a double life—sense-perceptible sounds as well as numerical ratios—it was subject to two different sets of esthetic criteria.[39] It could be judged by its appeal to the intellect or by its effect on the ear. Aristoxenus (fl. 380 B.C.), a student of Aristotle, argued that the notes of the scale should be determined finally by the ear, with an adjustment of the mathematical ratios to please that judge. A comparable adjustment in another medium is the enlargement of the lower portion of the columns in a Greek portico to accommodate the mass of the temple roof and thereby to gratify the eye. In this instance, also, sense is the arbiter of artistic proportion. The Pythagoreans, however, were strict constructionists, as Plutarch reports, and insisted on the mathematical purity of music:

> *Pythagoras* that grave and venerable personage, reproved all judgement of Musicke which is by the eare, for he said, that the intelligence and vertue thereof, was verie subtile & slender, and therefore he judged thereof, not by hearing, but by proportionall harmonie: and he thought it sufficient to proceed as farre as to Diapason, and there to stay the knowledge of Musicke.[40]

Such music apprehended by the intellect is the "unheard" music which Keats finds in the pastoral scene on the Grecian urn:

8. *The* "*Typus musicae*"
Music is personified as a richly dressed noblewoman holding a sheet inscribed with musical notes. In the lower right corner an unidentified ancient (surely Pythagoras) weighs hammers preparatory to performing the experiment of reproducing the musical scale as Macrobius reported Pythagoras to have heard it outside the blacksmiths' shop (see pp. 97–99). This man represents *musica theorica*. Other men, illustrating *musica practica*, play a variety of instruments.

Gregor Reisch, *Margarita philosophica* (Freiburg, 1503), h3.

Heard melodies are sweet, but those unheard
  Are sweeter: therefore, ye soft pipes, play on;
Not to the sensual ear, but, more endear'd,
  Pipe to the spirit ditties of no tone.
("Ode on a Grecian Urn," 11–14)

Keats transports us to a realm of pure art, where the ancient vase by its beauty and serenity transmutes human passions to abstract counters in philosophy. This was the aim also of Pythagorean music, as Dacier argues when he explains why Pythagoras insisted that music be criticized by the intellect alone:

> This in my Opinion was to shew that the Beauty of Music is independent of the Tune that strikes the Ear, and consists only in the Reason, in the Conformity, and in the Proportions of which the Understanding is the only Judge.[41]

Pythagoras directed music toward a reality of intellectual forms conceived as numbers; Aristoxenus adapted it for aural perception in a reality of physical experience. Although the contention between Pythagoras and Aristoxenus has continued down through the history of Western music, the Pythagorean tuning system has been the usual victor.

Even early discussions of music, however, consider it in the sense-perceptible state of sound as well as in the abstract state of numerical ratios, and later treatises on music invariably offer it as a practical art. Nonetheless, musical theory depends upon mathematical proportion, as the term "harmony" suggests,[42] and early definitions of music emphasize its quantitative basis. St. Augustine was interested in metrics (the measurement of poetry) and harmonics as sister arts; and to him, "music is the science of mensurating well."[43] Similarly for Isidore of Seville, "music is the skill of mensurating, consisting of sound and voice."[44] Boethius, being more consciously orthodox, insists upon the dual nature of music, noting that it is perceptible to the intellect as well as to the ear: "Harmonics is the study which uses the sense and the reason to investigate the distances between high and low sounds."[45] The Pythagorean tuning system, derived by manipulation of simple numerical ratios, is clearly the model for these definitions.

Within the mathematical discipline of music there are three types of proportion, as Archytas had differentiated them before the time of Plato.[46] There is arithmetical proportion, where each term in the progression differs from its immediate antecedent by a constant amount—for example: 2, 4, 6, 8, 10. . . . There is geometrical proportion, where each term in the progression differs from its immediate antecedent by a constant ratio—for example: 1, 2, 4, 8, 16. . . . And there is harmonic or musical proportion, where the terms in a progression are related by the ratio of the differences between adjacent terms—for example: 3, 4, 6 (see Plate 9). We are least familiar with the last, but Thomas Blundeville offers a lucid explanation of it:

> Musical proportion which requireth 3. numbers at the least, is when the first number hath the same proportion unto the third, which the difference betwixt the first and the second, hath to the difference which is betwixt the second and the third, as 3.4. and 6. for looke what proportion 3. hath to 6. which is *subdupla* [i.e., half], the same hath the difference betwixt 3. and 4. which is 1. to the difference betwixt 4. and 6. which is 2. for 1. to 2. is *Subdupla*, and this is called Musicall proportion.[47]

Today we would express this musical proportion by simple mathematical notation:

$$3 : 6 = (4 - 3) : (6 - 4) = 1 : 2$$

Mathematical problems involving these three types of proportion

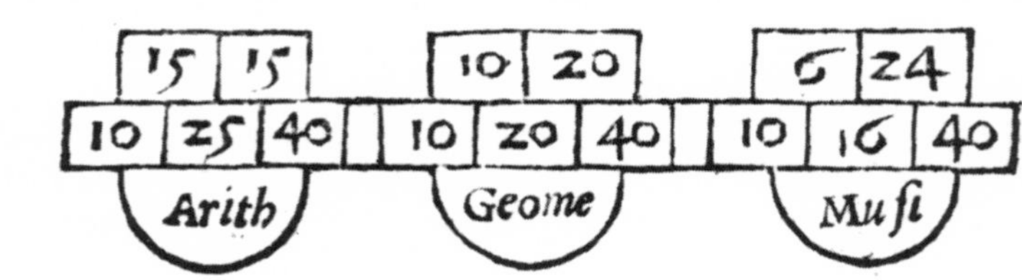

9. *The three kinds of proportion*

This illustration exemplifies the three kinds of mathematical proportion. There is an arithmetical proportion 10 : 25 : 40, where each term varies from the preceding term by a constant number, 15. There is a geometrical proportion 10 : 20 : 40, where each term varies from the preceding term by a constant ratio, 2, so that the differences between adjacent terms also reflect this ratio, such as 20 : 10. And there is a musical or harmonic proportion 10 : 16 : 40, where the third term, 40, has the same ratio to the first term, 10, as the difference between the third and second term, 24, has to the difference between the second and first term, 6; so that 40 : 10 = 24 : 6.

Boethius, "De arithmetica" in *Opera, quaę extant, omnia*, ed. Henricus Loritus Glareanus (Basle, 1546), p. 1056.

usually depended upon finding the mean between two terms, known as "the extremes." For example, what is the mean between 4 and 10 in an arithmetical progression? The answer: 7, so that the arithmetical series is 4 : 7 : 10. Or, what is the mean between 4 and 9 in a geometrical progression? The answer: 6, so that the geometrical series is 4 : 6 : 9. Or, what is the mean between 4 and 12 in a harmonic progression? The answer: 6, so that the harmonic series is 4 : 6 : 12.[48] Following this ancient example, the renaissance was aware of a variety of relationships between numbers.

The Pythagorean tuning system depends upon a special set of simple relationships between the four smallest integers—1, 2, 3, 4. It produces a scale of eight notes. To use technical terms, the "diapason" [49] comprises eight "tones." [50] The system is most easily demonstrated with a single string which can be stopped at any point by a moveable bridge, so that the notes are indicated as intervals on a single linear quantity. The concordant intervals of the scale, determined by mathematical reasoning alone, are then assumed to be the proportions between the component numbers of the perfect number 10, the decad.[51] The number 10 defines the limit of the physical universe [52] and therefore only proportions between its component parts can be considered as natural. Since 1 + 2 + 3 + 4 = 10, the possible proportions are 2 : 1, 3 : 1, 4 : 1, 3 : 2, and 4 : 3. The double proportion 2 : 1 clearly defines a diapason, which we may analyze as the prototypical unit in our mathematical continuum—as Plutarch comments, Pythagoras "thought it sufficient to proceed as farre as to Diapason, and there to stay the knowledge of Musicke." [53] The triple proportion 3 : 1 and the quadruple proportion 4 : 1 are simple multiples of the double proportion, and therefore should not intrude into its analysis. What is true of the prototypical diapason can later be extended to include other diapasons determined by the triple and quadruple proportions.

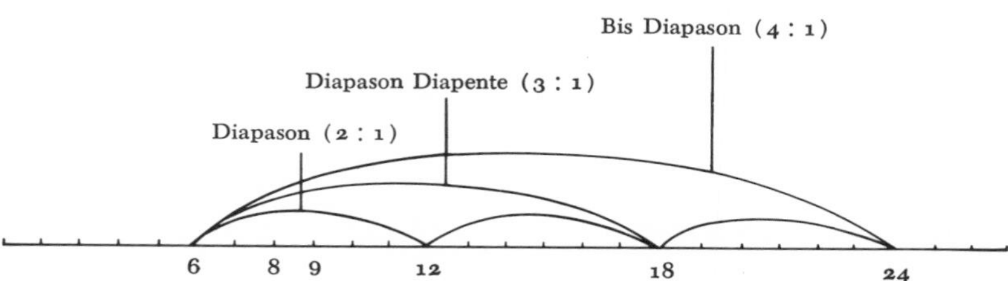

To analyze the diapason, then, we have only to deal with the proportions 2 : 1, 3 : 2, and 4 : 3. To place these in a continuum, a "harmony" on our monochord, we turn them into ratios with a common denominator—12/6, 9/6, and 8/6—and mark the resultant fixed intervals on the scale.

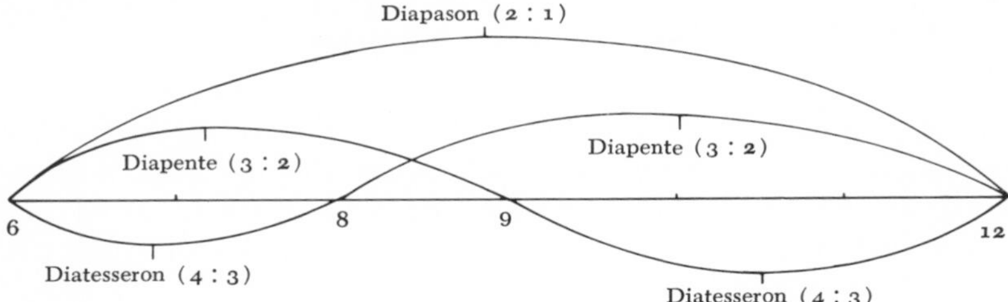

The ratio 12 : 6 is the proportion 2 : 1, the diapason itself. The ratio 9 : 6 and the ratio 12 : 8 are the proportion 3 : 2, the sesquialteral proportion (1½) determining the interval known as the *diapente*, the fifth. The ratio 8 : 6 and the ratio 12 : 9 are the proportion 4 : 3, the sesquitertial proportion (1⅓) determining the interval known as the *diatesseron*, the fourth. We now have in effect two intermeshed proportions, an arithmetical proportion 6 : 9 : 12 and a harmonic proportion 6 : 8 : 12. Furthermore, that mean which is sesquitertial to 6 is in a sesquialteral proportion with 12, and vice versa—that is, 8 is sesquitertial to 6 and in a sesquialteral proportion with 12, and 9 is sesquialteral to 6 and in a sesquitertial proportion with 12—so that the diapason is comprised of a diatesseron and a diapente, regardless of whether 8 or 9 is used as the mean.

The difference between the two possible means (9 — 8) therefore assumes central importance. The interval between the fourth and the fifth, determined by the ratio 9 : 8, the sesquioctaval proportion (1⅛), becomes the tone (see Plates 10 and 11). Using this interval of the tone as a measurement, we can then insert two notes between the point represented by 6 and the point represented by 8, thereby completing a segment of four notes in a concordant proportion. Similarly, we can insert two notes between the point represented by 9 and the point represented by 12, completing a second segment of four notes in a concordant proportion.

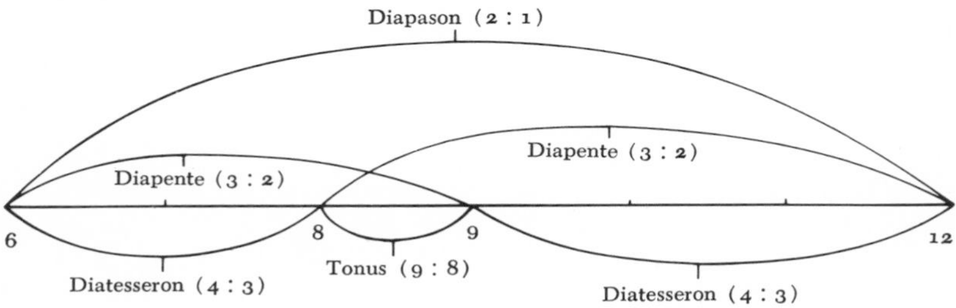

These two segments placed tandem finally produce the consonant diapason of eight notes.[54] The resultant scale has the following proportions:

1	$\frac{9}{8}$	$\frac{81}{64}$	$\frac{4}{3}$	$\frac{3}{2}$	$\frac{27}{16}$	$\frac{243}{128}$	$\frac{2}{1}$
6			8	9			12

This tuning system was known to the ancients and the renaissance as "the eight-stringed lyre of Pythagoras." [55]

Returning now to the two proportions which we earlier eliminated from consideration—3 : 1 and 4 : 1—we see that the triple proportion produces an interval of 18 on the scale, which is a diapason and a diapente; while the quadruple proportion produces an interval of 24, which is a double diapason. As Blundeville observes, "our Musitians doe make no more but 8. Musicall proportions in all," [56] and he gives this table to translate the mathematical proportion into the musical interval:

[2:1]	Dupla.	which are thus named	Diapason.
[3:1]	Tripla.		Diapason diapente.
[4:1]	Quadrupla.		Bis diapason.
[3:2]	Sesquialtera.		Diapente.
[4:3]	Sesquitertia.		Diatesseron.
[5:4]	Sesquiquarta.		Diatonus semitonus.
[8:3]	Dupla superbipartiens.		Diapason diatesseron.
[9:8]	Sesquioctava.		Tonus.

No matter how complicated a treatise on Pythagorean music may seem, it is based on these simple proportions involving whole numbers delimited by the decad.

In accordance with long-standing and widely-accepted tradition, Pythagoras had determined the proportions between the notes on the monochord when he passed a blacksmith's shop one day and heard the several smithies pounding in harmony. It is curious that the tradition should emphasize the fact that Pythagoras made this chance discovery by empirical observation. Equally curious, he verified it by experiment in the best spirit of modern science (although the experiment when actually performed does not give corroborative results). An account of the incident by Macrobius is a prominent source for the story in all its suspicious detail:

> [Pythagoras] realized that the sounds coming forth from the spheres were regulated by divine Reason, which is always present in the sky, but he had difficulty in determining the under-

10. *The diapason analyzed as whole numbers*

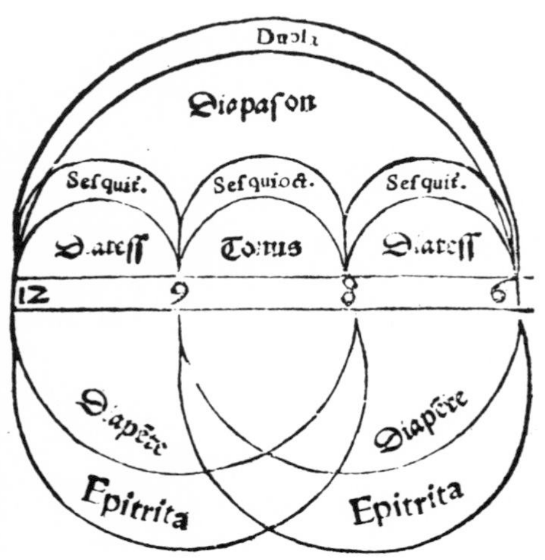

The diapason is derived mathematically from the ratios between the first four integers: 1, 2, 3, 4 (see pp. 95–97). The ratio 12 : 6 is equivalent to 2 : 1, the whole diapason, with a double (dupla) proportion. The ratios 12 : 9 and 8 : 6 are equivalent to 4 : 3, the diatesseron, with a 1⅓ (sesquitertial) proportion. The ratios 12 : 8 and 9 : 6 are equivalent to 3 : 2, the diapente, with a 1½ (epitrital) proportion. The ratio 9 : 8, the sesquioctaval proportion, determines a unit known as the "tone," two of which are then inserted between 12 and 9 and two more between 8 and 6, thereby making eight notes, an octave.

Boethius, "De musica" in *Opera, quae extant, omnia,* ed. Henricus Loritus Glareanus (Basle, 1546), p. 1070.

lying cause and in finding ways by which he might discover it. When he was weary of his long investigation of a problem so fundamental and yet so recondite, a chance occurrence presented him with what his deep thinking had overlooked.

He happened to pass the open shop of some blacksmiths who were beating a hot iron with hammers. The sound of the hammers striking in alternate and regular succession fell upon his ears with the higher note so attuned to the lower that each time the same musical interval returned, and always striking a concord. Here Pythagoras, seeing that his opportunity had been presented to him, ascertained with his eyes and hands what he had been searching for in his mind. He approached the smiths and stood over their work, carefully heeding the sounds that came forth from the blows of each. Thinking that the difference might be ascribed to the strength of the smiths he requested them to change hammers. Hereupon the difference in tones did not stay with the men but followed the hammers. Then he turned his whole attention to the study of their weights, and when he had recorded the difference in the weight of each, he had other hammers heavier or lighter than these made. Blows from these produced sounds that were not at all like those of the original hammers, and besides they did not harmonize. He then

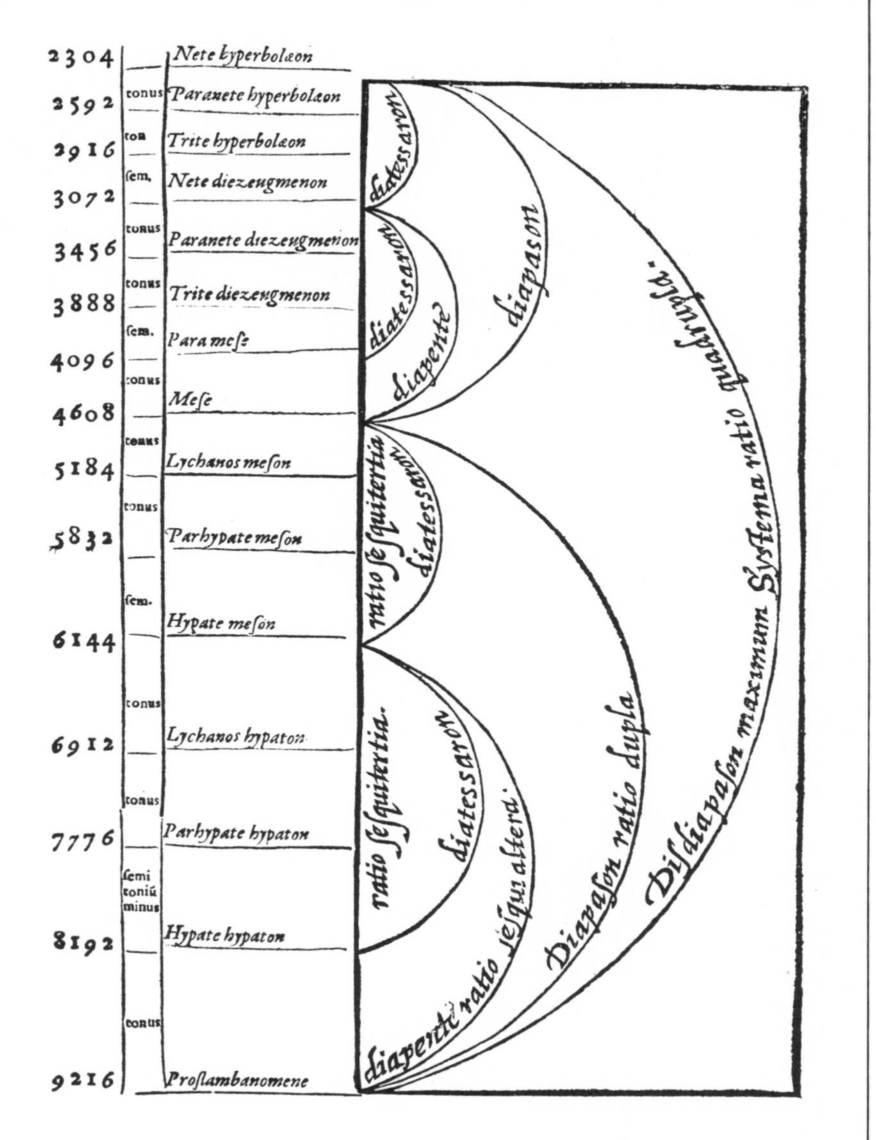

11. *"The harmonic system of fifteen chords in the diatonic mode"*

Morley provides an ample explanation of his diagram: "There be three things to be considered: the names, the numbers, and the distances. As for the names, you must note that they be all Nounes adjectives, the substantive of which is *chorda*, or a string [e.g., the lowest note is properly *proslambanomene chorda*]. . . . The numbers set on the left side, declare the habitude (which we call proportion) of one sound to another, as for example: the number set at the lowest note *Proslambanomene*, is *sesquioctave*, to that which is set before the next: and *sesquitertia* to that which is set at *Lychanos hypaton*, & so by consideration of these numbers, may be gathered the distance of the sound of the one from the other: as *sesquioctave* produceth one whole note. Then betwixt *Proslambanomene*, and *hypate hypaton*, is the distance of one whole note. Likewise *sesquitertia*, produceth a fourth: therefore *Proslambanomene* and *Lychanos hypaton* are a fourth, and so of others."

Thomas Morley, *A plaine and easie introduction to practicall musicke* (London, 1597), ¶ 2.

> concluded that harmony of tones was produced according to a proportion of the weights, and made a record of all the numerical relations of the various weights producing harmony.
>
> Next he directed his investigation from hammers to stringed instruments, and stretched intestines of sheep or sinews of oxen by attaching to them weights of the same proportions as those determined by the hammers. Again the concord came forth which had been assured by his earlier well-conceived experiment, but with a sweeter tone, as we might expect from the nature of the instruments. After discovering this great secret, Pythagoras chose the numbers from which consonant chords might be produced so that when stringed instruments had been adjusted with regard to these numbers, certain ones might be pitched to the tonics and others to other consonant notes, numerically harmonious.[57]

Pythagoras, as Porphyry had declared, was the sole mortal who could hear the music of the spheres.[58] By his analysis of the musical diapason, he made intelligible to fellow mortals the divine harmony of the universe (see Plate 12), thereby providing a celestial pattern for the ordering of human art.

Even more important, Pythagoras had shown how to set apart the diapason from the endless continuum of sound which stretches from immeasurable low to inexpressible high. Neither the diapason nor the tone admits a numerical mean of any sort—the mean between 2 and 1 and the mean between 9 and 8 are both irrational—so neither the diapason nor the tone can be divided into equal parts.[59] This fact allied them with odd numbers, indicating their limited and ordered nature. Pythagoras had demonstrated how to know this unit with its discrete parts and how to manipulate it for human ends. He had revealed a dependable relationship between the finite and the infinite, some manageable way of dealing with the infinite through knowledge of the finite. The diapason with its numerical ratios and its harmonies exposed in small to mortal comprehension the divinely proportioned structure of the universe.

Although Pythagoras was generally acknowledged to be the first to analyze the mathematical basis for musical harmony, other traditions about the origin of music were extant. Isidore cites several, starting with the legendary Tubal-cain in Genesis, iv.22:

> Moses says that the discoverer of the art of music was Tubal, who was from the line of Cain before the flood. The Greeks, however, say that Pythagoras came upon the origins of this art struck from the sound of hammers and from the extension of strings. Others hold that Linus the Theban and Zetus and Am-

> phion were the first to be distinguished in the musical art.[60]

The delightful art of music attracted a host of legendary devotés. The most thorough survey of music's earlier history from the Pythagorean point of view is given by Franchino Gafori.[61]

The celestial harmony permeates the universe, of course, modulating the items of nature and binding them together. Boethius speaks of three kinds of music, each reflective of the divine—*musica mundana*, *musica humana*, and *musica instrumentalis:*

> The first, the music of the universe, is especially to be studied in the combining of the elements and the variety of the seasons which are observed in the heavens. How indeed could the swift mechanism of the sky move silently in its course? . . . What human music is, anyone may understand by examining his own nature. For what is that which unites the incorporeal activity of the reason with the body, unless it be a certain mutual adaptation and as it were a tempering of low and high sounds into a single consonance? . . . The third kind of music is that which is described as residing in certain instruments. This is produced by tension, as in strings, or by blowing . . . or by some kind of percussion.[62]

Plato in the *Timaeus* had implied each of these kinds of music and had prepared for their interchangeableness. He had described the world-soul as a composite of numerical ratios (35A–36D), and likewise the lesser souls were created in a similar manner (41D). As Plutarch interpreted Plato, "The principall effect and efficacie of these numbers and proportions, which that great and sovereigne Creatour used, is the consonance, accord, and agreement of the soule in it selfe."[63] But the individual soul is concordant not only within itself, *musica humana;* but by repeating the pattern of the world-soul at large it participates in universal harmony, *musica mundana*. Donne recalls this doctrine at the beginning of his "Hymne to God my God, in my sicknesse":

> Since I am comming to that Holy roome,
> Where, with thy Quire of Saints for evermore,
> I shall be made thy Musique; As I come
> I tune the Instrument here at the dore,
> And what I must doe then, thinke here before.
> (ll. 1–5)

As the soul prepares to leave his body, Donne thinks of himself as a musical instrument which must be more finely tuned for his participation in the ideal melodies of God's symphony.

This assumption that the human soul is attuned to the *musica*

12. *Jubal visiting the blacksmiths' shop, and Pythagoras at his musical experiments*
In the upper-left corner, Jubal (i.e., Tubal) discovers the numerical ratios between the notes of the musical scale by visiting a blacksmiths' shop. Observe that the hammers are weighted by presumably appropriate whole numbers: 4, 6, 8, 9, 12, 16. In the upper-right corner Pythagoras verifies these ratios by using a set of bells, and again by using glasses filled with different amounts of water. In the lower-left corner Pythagoras confirms these numbers by using lengths of gut which are weighted to produce varying degrees of tension. In the lower-right corner Pythagoras and Philolaus repeat the experiment using pipes of varying length.
Franchino Gafori, *Theorica musice* (Milan, 1492), fol. b6.

mundana provides the basis for the microcosm-macrocosm analogy, so prevalent in the renaissance. By exercise of introspective reason —in Boethius' words, by examining our own nature—we might hopefully perceive our inner harmony and thence extrapolate outward to understanding of the universe, an expectation that gives purpose to the dictum *nosce teipsum*. Our best hope of hearing the music of the spheres, it seems, is to know the harmonious proportions in our own soul.

Conversely, since *musica mundana* is the pattern for *musica humana*, instrumental or vocal music which reproduces the universal harmony has a direct influence on the human soul. Plato himself had been explicit on this point:

> Harmony, which has motions akin to the revolutions of the Soul within us, was given by the Muses to him who makes intelligent use of the Muses, not as an aid to irrational pleasure, as is now supposed, but as an auxiliary to the inner revolution of the Soul, when it has lost its harmony, to assist in restoring it to order and concord with itself (*Timaeus*, 47D).[64]

Boethius therefore assigned to music an ethical as well as an epistemological function:

> Of the four mathematical disciplines, the others are concerned with the pursuit of truth, but music is related not only to speculation but to morality as well. Nothing is more characteristic of human nature than to be soothed by sweet modes and stirred up by their opposites.[65]

Music is capable of increasing or diminishing the passions of the human soul by affecting its harmony, and there are numerous examples of the emotional effects of music, Biblical as well as classical. David calmed the anguish of Saul by playing on the lyre and singing,[66] and Timotheus by his music aroused Alexander from feasting to warfare.[67] The source of this tradition for music's power is likely to have been Pythagoras' school made popular through Plato. Iamblichus reports that Pythagoras used music to cure both bodies and souls, and to assuage anger and other aberrations of the mind,[68] while Boethius recounts the well-known incident of how Pythagoras calmed a distraught Taurominian youth by means of a spondaic melody.[69]

The far-reaching effects of music were generally acknowledged and frequently acclaimed. Music provides a metaphor by which to represent the comprehensiveness and consonance of natural order. So great is its power and so pervasive its force that it performs the impossible and reconciles opposites in a single coordinated system. The diapason cannot be divided into equal parts; but as the monochord demonstrates, the extremes of the diapason (6 and 12) are made consonant in the harmonic mean (9), so that opposites are joined together in stable concord. For Boethius, this is the essential function of music, effected through the harmony of numbers:

> Not without cause is it said that all things, which consist of contraries, are conjoined and composed by a certain harmony. For harmony is the joining together of several things and the consent of contraries.[70]

Thomas Stanley, translating Theon of Smyrna, expands the co-adunating function of music:

> The *Pythagoreans* define Musick an apt composition of contraries, and an union of many, and consent of differents. For it not only co-ordinates rythms and modulation, but all manner of Systems. It's end is to unite, and aptly conjoyn. God is the reconciler of things discordant, and this is his chiefest work according to Music and Medicine, to reconcile enmities. In Musick, say they, consists the agreement of all things, and Aristocracy of the Universe. For, what is harmony in the world, in a City is good Government, in a Family Temperance.[71]

Here we see music as a universal force that organizes contraries and generates unity. We shall return to this theme in a later chapter on the cosmos.

3. *Geometry*

Geometry was defined as the study of numbers as magnitude (continuous quantity).[72] It was distinguished from the study of number as multitude (discrete units), which was the subject matter of arithmetic.[73] According to Gregor Reisch, "Geometry is the study of magnitude at rest, a contemplative description of the forms which makes clear the bounds of each form." [74] It deals, then, with the physical extension of numbers, with numbers having dimensions. A geometrical point corresponds to the number 1 in arithmetic (it is a 1 with position), a line corresponds to the number 2, a surface to the number 3, and a volume to the number 4. The data of geometry—the point, the line, the surface, and the volume—evolve from the monad, of course, as stages in an orderly process.[75]

Isidore of Seville has an informative passage "On the inventors of

13. *The "Typus geometriae"*
Geometry is personified as an elegant woman sitting at a table and using a compass to draw a complicated geometrical figure. At her left hand are various geometrical figures—a circle, a triangle, a square, an octogon—representing *geometria speculativa.* At her right hand are various other instruments representing *geometria practica.* Several men demonstrate the practice of geometry in actual measurement: two youths use a quadrant and a sphere (?) to take readings of the stars, another uses a yard to survey a plot of land, an older man uses a square in his carpentering, and a stonemason wields an enormous compass as he constructs vaulting in a building.
Gregor Reisch, *Margarita philosophica* (Basle, 1583), bb3.

geometry and its name" which must be quoted in full:

> It is said that the discipline of geometry was first discovered by the Egyptians. When the Nile overflowed and covered everyone's property with mire, the method of dividing the land according to lines and measures gave a name to the art of geometry. In time through the skillfulness of wise men the dimensions of the sea and even of the heavens and of the air were measured. Stimulated by such study they began to inquire after the size of the earth and the space of the sky: how much distance there is between the moon and the earth, and between the sun and the moon, and finally how far away the pole of the heaven itself might be. And so by this credible reasoning they indicated by the number of stades the very interstices of the spheres and the extent of the world. But since this discipline began as measurement of the land, it kept a name from its origin. For "geometry"

14. *A diagram of the "Pythagorean" theorem* (*Euclid, I.xlvii*)

The theorem that the square of the hypotenuse of a right triangle is equal to the sum of the squares of the two sides has been ascribed to Pythagoras since earliest times. Here the theorem is represented spatially by the use of geometrical figures depicting the smallest possible whole numbers which will exemplify it. The lines AB and BC form a right angle, and the line AC completes a triangle of which it is the hypotenuse. In the modern notation of algebra, the theorem would be stated: $(AB)^2 + (BC)^2 = (AC)^2$

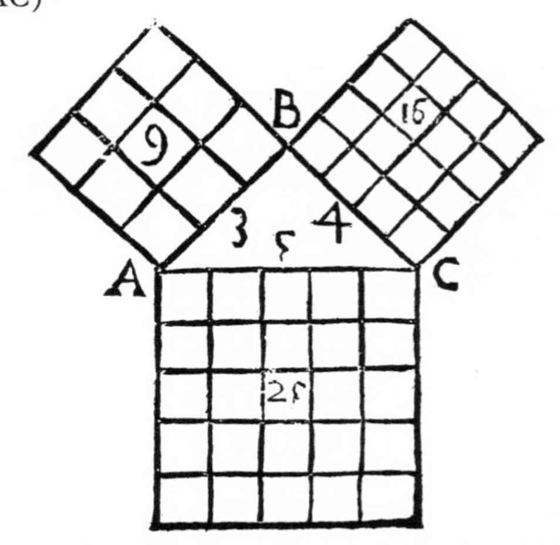

In this diagram:

$(AB) = 3$, and $(AB)^2 = 9$
$(BC) = 4$, and $(BC)^2 = 16$
$(AC) = 5$, and $(AC)^2 = 25$

Finally:

$3^2 + 4^2 = 5^2$
$9 + 16 = 25$

Perspicue probatum est.

Athanasius Kircher, *Arithmologia* (Rome, 1665), p. 299.

> is so named from "land" and from "measurement." In Greek, "land" is called γῆ and "measurement" is called μέτρα. This discipline therefore deals with lines, intervals, magnitudes, and figures, and with the dimensions and relations of figures.[76]

It was Pythagoras, all agreed, who systematized geometry and transported it from Egypt into Greece.

Like arithmetic and music, geometry was divided into two sorts: speculative and practical. Speculative geometry did little more than recapitulate Euclid, offering definitions and proving theorems. It expounded the unvarying characteristics of straight lines and angles, of plane figures such as circles, triangles, squares, and pentagons, and of solid figures such as pyramids, cubes, and cylinders. In contrast, practical geometry dealt with the techniques and instruments for actual measurement. It taught the means of measuring linear distance, of computing the area of circles and rectangles, and of calculating the volume of spheres and cubes and columns. It provided basic skills for such arts as surveying, carpentry, perspective, navigation, firing ordnance, and taking readings in astronomy.

A topos of particular interest in geometry was the "regular solids."[77] A regular solid is a three-dimensional form with all its faces equal and all its angles equal. As the ancients knew, there are only five: the cube, with square faces; the tetrahedron, the octohedron, and the icosahedron, with triangular faces; and the dodecahedron, with pentagonal faces. Pythagoras was credited with discovering the five regular solids,[78] and in the Pythagorean tradition each was associated with one of the four elements—the tetrahedron with fire, the octohedron with air, the cube with earth, and the icosahedron with water—while the dodecahedron was assigned to the heavens in their entirety, approximating a quintessence (see Plate 15).

The reasoning behind these assignments was not quite arbitrary; when the properties of the polyhedra are compared with the complexions of the elements, there is some empirical evidence to suggest a correlation, though admittedly of a selective sort. The cube is assigned to earth, as Kepler tells us, because "in the case of the cube its uprightness on a quadrate base conveys a certain impression of stability, which property also belongs to terrestrial matter."[79] The octohedron can be suspended by two opposite corners and spun as in a lathe, thereby representing "a certain image of mobility" suitable to air, the most mobile element. "The sharpness and thinness of the tetrahedron" suggests the complexion of fire; while "the globular form of the icosahedron," the figure with the largest number of faces, suggests "a water-drop." Finally, "the dodecahedron is left for the celestial form, having the same number of faces as the celestial zodiac has of signs; and it is shown to be the most capacious of all the figures, and accordingly the heavens embrace all things."

This lore, a strange mixture of mysticism and science typical of Pythagorean thought, was prominently displayed by Plato in the *Timaeus* (53C–55C), which became the *locus classicus* for its study, so that the regular solids were known also as the "Platonical bodies." Aristotle offered a snide critique in the *De caelo* (306b3–307b20), and Plutarch,[80] Diogenes Laertius,[81] and Stobaeus,[82] each duly re-

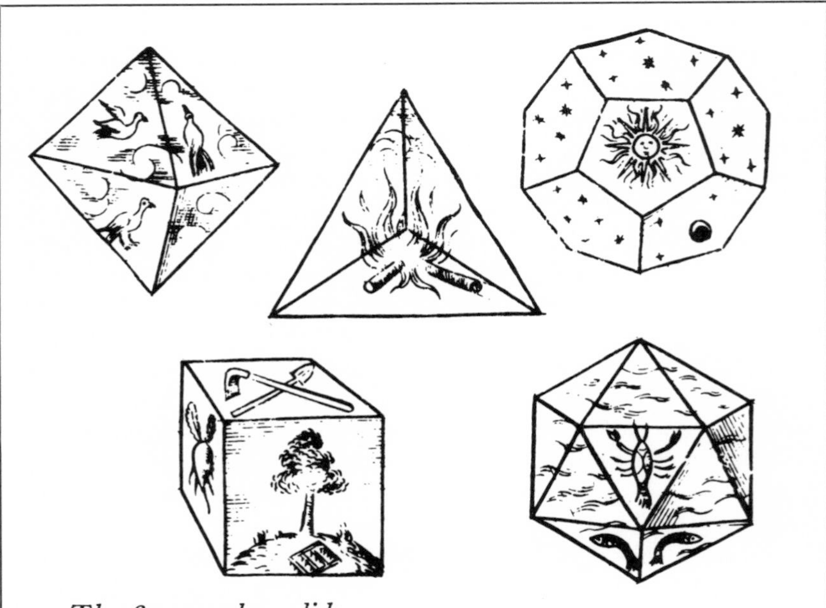

15. *The five regular solids*

Each of the five regular solids is pictorially identified with an appropriate element: the octohedron with air, the tetrahedron with fire, the cube with earth, and the icosahedron with water. The dodecahedron represents the universe at large, and therefore it displays the sun, the moon, and the stars of heaven.

Johann Kepler, *Harmonices mundi libri V* (Linz, 1619), p. 52.

corded in his compendium the correspondence between the elements and the "mundane figures." Euclid expounded them in a purely geometric way in the final book of his *Elementa*, showing how to construct them and proving that each can be inscribed in a sphere. A treatise by Hypsicles (fl. 160 A.D.), regularly printed as Books XIV and XV of Euclid, continued the geometry of the regular solids and demonstrated, among other things, how to inscribe them one inside another. During the Italian renaissance, concern with the regular solids was renewed by the painter Piero della Francesca, whose Latin treatise on the subject was translated into Italian by his friend Luca Paccioli, and was printed as the third and final section of the *Divina proportione* (Venice, 1509). In the sixteenth century Flussas (i.e., François de Foix, Comte de Candale; 1502–94) wrote an important treatise on the five regular polyhedra (first appended to the Latin version of Euclid printed in Paris, 1566),[83] and Thomas Digges adjoined to his father's *Pantometria* (London, 1571) "a *Mathematicall* treatise of the five regulare *Platonicall* bodies, and their *Metamorphosis* or transformation into five other equilater unifoorme solides Geometricall" (title page).

The regular solids as viewed by the renaissance are amply described by Henry Billingsley in his commentary on Euclid:

> These five solides now last defined, namely, a Cube, a Tetrahedron, an Octohedron, a Dodecahedron and an Icosahedron are called regular bodies. As in plaine superficieces, those are called regular figures, whose sides and angles are equal, as are equilater triangles, equilater pentagons, hexagons, & such lyke, so in solides such only are counted and called regular, which are comprehended under equal playne superficieces, which have equal sides and equal angles, as all these five foresayd have, as manifestly appeareth by their definitions, which were all geven by this proprietie of equalitie of their superficieces, which have also their sides and angles equall. And in all the course of nature there are no other bodies of this condition and perfection, but onely these five. Wherfore they have ever of the auncient Philosophers bene had in great estimation and admiration, and have bene thought worthy of much contemplacion, about which they have bestowed most diligent study and endevour to searche out the natures & properties of them. They are as it were the ende and perfection of all Geometry, for whose sake is written whatsoever is written in Geometry. They were (as men say) first invented by the most witty *Pithagoras* then afterward set forth by the

> divine *Plato*, and last of all mervelously taught and declared by the most excellent Philosopher *Euclide* in these bookes following, and ever since wonderfully embraced of all learned Philosophers. The knowledge of them containeth infinite secretes of nature. *Pithagoras*, *Timeus* and *Plato*, by them searched out the composition of the world, with the harmony and preservation therof, and applied these five solides to the simple partes therof, the Pyramis, or Tetrahedron they ascribed to the fire, for that it ascendeth upward according to the figure of the Pyramis. To the ayre they ascribed the Octohedron, for that through the subtle moisture which it hath, it extendeth it selfe every way to the one side, and to the other, accordyng as that figure doth. Unto the water they assigned the Ikosahedron, for that it is continually flowing and moving, and as it were makyng angles on every side according to that figure. And to the earth they attributed a Cube, as to a thing stable, firme and sure as the figure signifieth. Last of all a Dodecahedron, for that it is made of Pentagons, whose angles are more ample and large then the angles of the other bodies, and by that meanes draw more to roundnes, & to the forme and nature of a sphere, they assigned to a sphere, namely, to heaven. Who so will read *Plato* in his *Timeus*, shall read of these figures, and of their mutuall proportion, straunge matters, which here are not to be entreated of, this which is sayd, shall be sufficient for the knowledge of them, and for the declaration of their diffinitions.[84]

As Billingsley indicates, the regular solids by their identification with the four elements had a strong influence on cosmological speculation. They were, in fact, the archetypal numbers in the mind of the creator as Plato recounted creation in the *Timaeus*.

This kind of speculation culminated in the cosmological theories of Johann Kepler, who at the beginning of his career published a treatise, the *Mysterium cosmographicum* (Tübingen, 1596), arguing that the intervals between the planets are determined by the distances between spheres circumscribing the regular solids as they are placed concentrically (see Plates 16 and 17).[85] Kepler opens his "Preface to the Reader" with a statement of purpose:

> It is my intention, Reader, in this book to demonstrate that the Highest and Most Good Creator in the creation of this mobile world and the arrangement of the heavens had his eye on those five regular bodies, which have been most celebrated from the

> time of Pythagoras and Plato right down to our own day, and that to their nature He accommodated the number of heavenly spheres, their proportions, and the system of their motions.[86]

Near the end of his career, after a lifetime of working with empirical data, Kepler was still obsessed with the notion that the regular solids were the archetypal forms in the mind of the creator, and in the *Harmonices mundi libri V* (Linz, 1619) he expounded their characteristics and virtues at great length.[87]

Another topos of perennial fascination in geometry was the problem of squaring the circle.[88] It had been a subject of inquiry in Pythagoras' school, and Iamblichus reports the impiety and terrible fate of Hippasus, who drowned at sea for having revealed the secret of how to do it.[89] Among ancient mathematicians, Hippocrates of Chios and Archimedes were known to have studied the problem. Giovanni Campano of Novara (fl. 13th century) and Nicholas of Cusa (1401–64) revived interest in squaring the circle, while in the sixteenth century Charles de Bouelles, Oronce Finé, and Jean Borrel wrote important treatises on the subject.[90]

In essence, the problem of squaring the circle is a geometrical formulation of the incongruity between the world of concept and the world of matter. As a geometrical figure, a circle has certain properties which set it apart from all other forms: it has no beginning or end, every point on its circumference is equidistant from the center, and its circumference considered as linear distance encloses a maximum area.[91] It, like the point and the monad, represents unified perfection, and therefore infinity and eternity and deity. The circle emblematizes the conceptual world. God Himself had long been described as a circle (with center everywhere and circumference nowhere[92]). In contrast to the circle, the square has a finite number of sides. Moreover, in Pythagorean terms the square is the number 4, which in turn represents the physical universe because a minimum of four points is required for three-dimensional extension. The square emblematizes the material world.[93] Any attempt to change a circle to a square therefore involves reducing the infinite to the finite, involves transmuting the divine to the physical, as Donne was well aware:

> Eternall God, (for whom who ever dare
> Seeke new expressions, doe the Circle square,
> And thrust into strait corners of poore wit
> Thee, who are cornerlesse and infinite). . . .[94]

16. *The five regular solids inscribed in spheres*

Each of the five regular solids is inscribed in a sphere preparatory to use in Kepler's "mysterium cosmographicum" (see Plate 17).

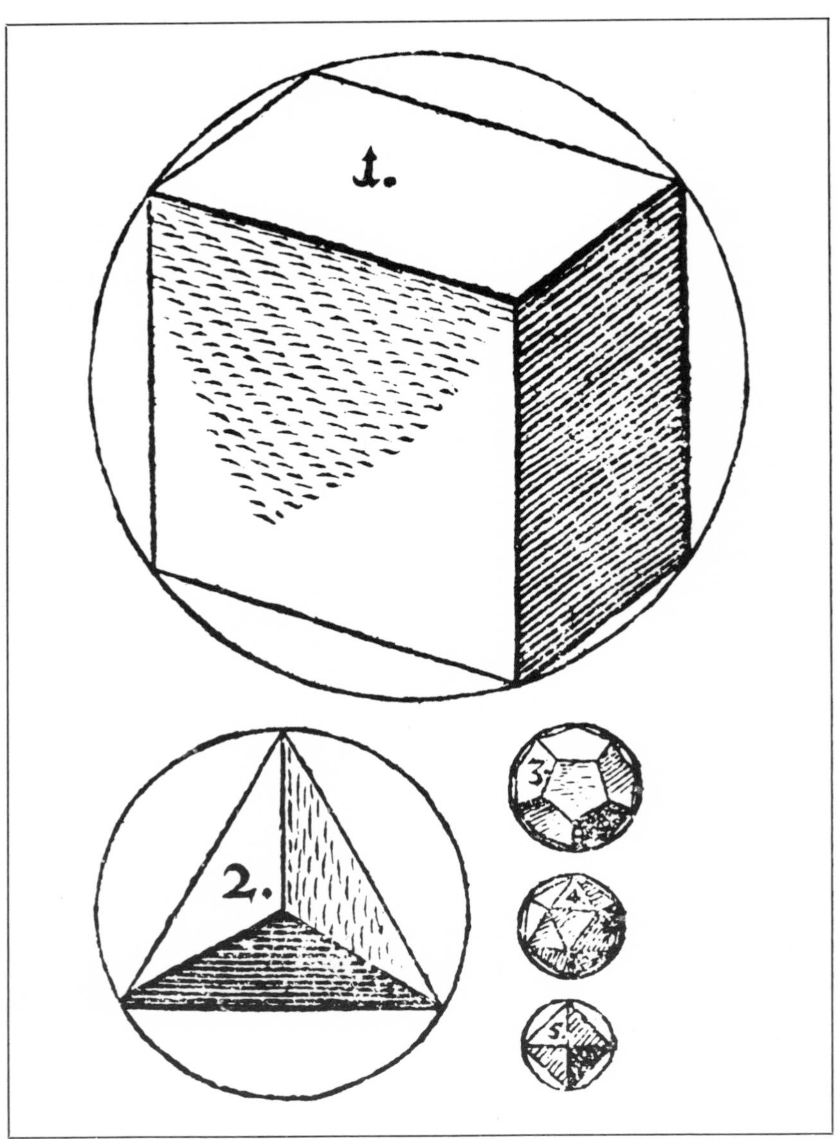

Johann Kepler, *Harmonices mundi libri V* (Linz, 1619), p. 180.

17. *Kepler's* mysterium cosmographicum, *his "key to the universe"*

By Kepler's reasoning, there are six planets circling the sun with five interplanetary intervals because there are only five regular solids for use in the cosmic structure. The diagram shows how the intervals between planetary orbits are determined by the five regular solids circumscribed successively around the planetary spheres in a heliocentric universe (cf. Book II, pp. 59–60). The orbit of Venus is determined by a sphere circumscribing an octohedron which in turn circumscribes the sphere of Mercury. The orbit of the Earth and its attendant Moon is determined by a sphere circumscribing an icosahedron which in turn circumscribes the sphere of Venus. The orbit of Mars is determined by a sphere circumscribing a dodecahdron which in turn circumscribes the sphere of the Earth. The orbit of Jupiter is determined by a sphere circumscribing a tetrahedron which in turn circumscribes the sphere of Mars. Finally, the orbit of Saturn is determined by a sphere circumscribing a cube which in turn circumscribes the sphere of Jupiter. For each planet, Kepler calculated the distance for its median orbit, although its *aphelion* and *perihelion* are shown as well. The path of the Sun according to Tycho Brahe is also indicated.

The intervals between the planets calculated from observational data are sufficiently close to the intervals determined by this geometric construction for Kepler to have thought that he had discovered the esoteric first principle of the universe, his "mysterium cosmographicum."

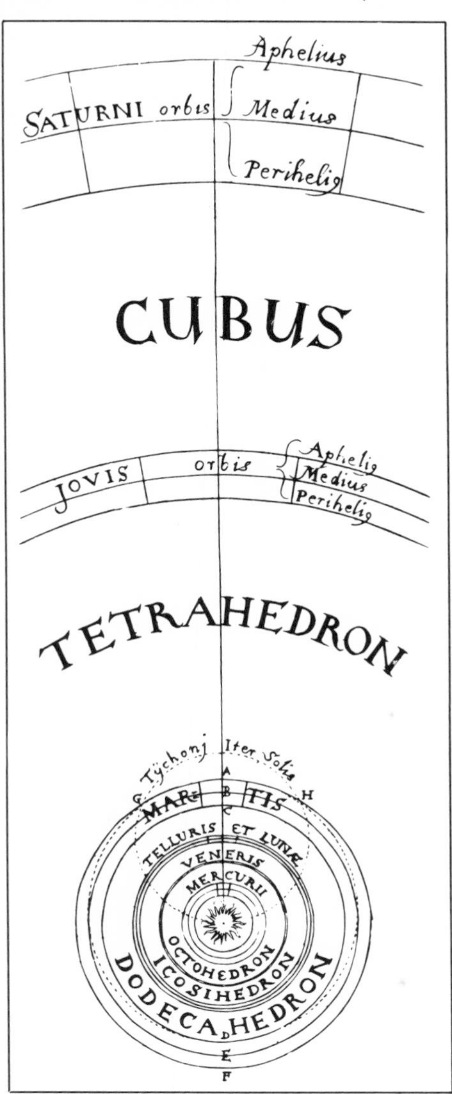

Johann Kepler, *Harmonices mundi libri V* (Linz, 1619), Book V opposite p. 186.

Donne did not dare constrict the circular perfection of God within the narrow confines of human understanding. Conversely, any attempt to circularize a square—for example, by increasing its sides an infinite number of times—becomes an effort to make continuous what is discontinuous, an effort to raise the physical to the level of perfection.[95] The problem of squaring the circle, then, crosses the boundary between the abstract conceptual world and the measurable time-space continuum. The coordinate problem of circularizing the square intends the same translation across the incongruity between sense-data and intellect, but in the opposite direction, where physicality etherealizes to concept. Solid geometry presented the same problem advanced one degree in sophistication, of course, when it attempted the cubifying of the sphere.[96]

The esoteric meaning of the squared circle is clearly explained by the diagram (see Plate 18) on the title page of Michael Maier's alchemical treatise, *De circulo physico, quadrato: hoc est, auro* (Oppenheim, 1616). The four basic qualities—dry, cold, moist, warm—are placed at the corners of a square. By their interaction, however, they produce the four elements: earth, water, air, fire. These four elements in this tetrad arrangement[97] comprise the cosmos, and hence a unity, represented by the inscribing circle. The ideogram, which relates the finite to perfection, is more explicit than any paraphrase can be.

By the sixteenth century, geometry had given over almost entirely to utility and most textbooks on the subject were little more than instructional manuals. In its original intention, however, geometry was meant to lead the soul above the mundane, as Proclus peevishly reminds us:

> The geometry deserving study is that which, at each theorem, sets up a platform for further ascent and lifts the soul on high, instead of allowing it to descend among sensible objects and so fulfill the common needs of mortal men.[98]

Study of the geometrical figures supposedly raises the soul to perusal of the eternal forms, so that, for instance, it can understand the work of God as geometer and perceive the cosmic significance of the regular solids. Even more rewarding, geometrical study can lead to comprehension of that ultimate, all-inclusive figure: God as a circle with center everywhere and circumference nowhere—the terminal point, incidentally, of Dante's journey in the *Divina commedia*. Here the infinite and the atemporal, otherwise inexpressible, is made intelligible through the terms of geometry. More and more

18. *The squared circle of Rosicrucian medicine*

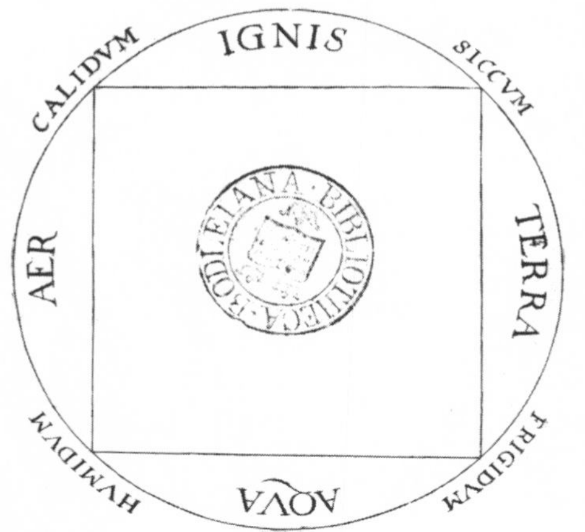

The four basic qualities—dry, cold, moist, hot—are arranged as the corners of a square, with contrary qualities diagonally across from one another. The elements, which arise from neighboring qualities—for example, hot and dry produce fire—are arranged around the sides of the square. Since the resultant four elements—fire, earth, water, air—comprise the universe, a unity, they are circumscribed by a circle to indicate the perfection of this arrangement. Thereby the circle and the square are made interchangeable; the circle is squared. To interpret this figure in medical terms, health derives from the perfect balance of the four humours correspondent to the four elements. The circular device within the square is a stamp from the Bodleian Library.

Michael Maier, *De circulo physico, quadrato: hoc est auro* (Oppenheim, 1616), title page.

frequently, though, renaissance men directed their eyes toward visible forms, eventuating in the new codification of geometry by Descartes.

4. *Astronomy*

By orthodox definition the discipline of astronomy was devoted to the study of forms in motion. In the words of Gregor Reisch, "Astronomy is the proper law and rule which covers the magnitudes and motions of bodies, so that we might comprehend the heavenly bodies, the spheres, and the stars." [99] Like geometry, astronomy dealt with forms—that is, with number as magnitude, continuous quantity, rather than as multitude, an aggregate of discrete units. Unlike geometry, however, astronomy dealt with forms in motion, not at rest. Like music, it was concerned with relationships, but between

19. *The "Typus astronomiae"*

Astronomy is personified as a handsome female figure who directs Ptolemaeus in the use of the quadrant as he takes readings of the moon and stars. In the lower left corner is an armillary sphere.

Gregor Reisch, *Margarita philosophica* (Freiburg, 1503), 18ᵛ.

mobile rather than static quantities. On the speculative level, astronomy was expected to devise a concept whereby all the items of nature, from lowest stone through highest planet, could fit into a scheme of universal order. This abstraction, which reduced the multeity of nature's creatures to the unity of an all-inclusive archetypal pattern, involved forms and their interrelationships in space as they changed position. Astronomy became therefore the most complex discipline in the quadrivium.

On the practical level, astronomy was charged with describing in their actual movements all of the observed phenomena of the universe. It was an empirical science concerned with measurements of space and time, and often employed for prognostication. It produced tables for the rising and setting of the stars, and provided the basis for such applied arts as geography, navigation, and astrology.

As always in the Pythagorean system, astronomy presupposed that there is free intercourse between the world of concept and the world of matter. Observation of physical nature leads us to perception of a divine plan, as Plato asserts to insure the teaching of astronomy in his ideal commonwealth:

> Those broideries yonder in the heaven, forasmuch as they are broidered on a visible ground, are rightly held to be the most beautiful and perfect of visible things, but they are nevertheless far inferior to those that are true, far inferior to those revolutions which absolute speed and absolute slowness, in true number and in all true forms, accomplish relatively to each other, carrying their contents with them—which can indeed be grasped by reason and intelligence, but not by sight.[100]

For Plato, there is a conceptual world beyond the heavens that are visible. And though the visible heavens are the most beautiful of created things, they are nevertheless inferior to the absolute perfection of the essential ideas. The truth of that invisible but ultimately real world may be perceived only by exercise of the reason, working from sense data of the heavenly bodies through mental activity until the soul is involved. This *aperçu* is the proper aim of astronomy.

We can also work in the opposite direction, by deductive reasoning rather than inductive. Once the orderly plan is established, either by observation or by revelation, we can rationally posit the phenomena necessary to complete the scheme, even to the point of postulating unseen or future events.[101] Not only does everything have its place in the cosmic operation, but it has its a priori cause and its subsequent effect—at least when the universe is considered as a multitude of parts subject to passing time. The universe can also be considered as an idea in the mind of its creator, of course, in which case it is atemporal as well as indivisible and unlimited.

Time began, in fact, when the creator gave physical extension to his archetypal idea. In terms of geometry, the other discipline that dealt with forms, this occurred when the monad proceeded to evolve the point, the line, the surface, and the solid. In terms of astronomy, this occurred when the godhead created the items of nature and placed them in regular motion. Plato in the *Timaeus* is careful to explain this point:

> As He set in order the Heaven, of that Eternity which abides in unity He made an eternal image, moving according to number, even that which we have named Time. . . . The sun and moon and five other stars, which bear the appellation of "planets," came into existence for the determining and preserving of the numbers of Time (37E–38C).

Pythagorean astronomy, then, was the study of these physical forms in motion, and essentially a study of time. It measured the orbits of the planets, not only their positions in space but also the distance each travelled in how much time. Speusippus, a purported student of Plato who had preserved a list of his definitions, quotes these epithets for time: "the motion of the sun, the measurement of its advance." [102]

Because the heavenly bodies return to their points of origin in a cyclical pattern, however, it is possible to abstract a scheme of natural order independent of durational time. It is possible to reconstruct the archetype in the mind of the creator. Thereby an absolute can be posited even in the presence of palpable mutability. Again, the temporal is related to the eternal and the finite to the infinite. Later, when Greek cosmology was taken over by the Church Fathers, it was easy to syncretize Plato's demiurge and Aristotle's unmoved mover with the Christian conception of God, the creator and the physical as well as spiritual support of our world.

In his *Fowre Hymnes* Spenser gives a full statement of this astronomical tradition in all its multifarious richness. As an apogee in his ascent from earthly experience to celestial knowledge, the poet in the last hymn, "An Hymne of Heavenly Beautie," recapitulates his progress and invites his reader to follow:

Beginning then below, with th'easie vew
Of this base world, subject to fleshly eye,
From thence to mount aloft by order dew,
To contemplation of th'immortall sky. . . .
(ll. 22–25)

He directs attention to "this wyde *universe*" with its "endlesse kinds of creatures" (lines 31–32), but then pushes upward from earth through the other elements—water, air, and fire—until our eyes rest upon the heavens, "that mightie shining christall wall,/Wherewith he hath encompassed this All" (lines 41–42). Focusing on this view, the poet singles out the sun and moon from the other "glistring stars more thicke then grasse" (line 53) and gives them special praise. But beyond the visible spheres of the planets and fixed stars are the conceptual heavens which, to use Plato's phrase, revolve "in true number and in all true forms":

For farre above these heavens which here we see,
Be others farre exceeding these in light,
Not bounded, not corrupt, as these same bee,
But infinite in largenesse and in hight,
Unmoving, uncorrupt, and spotlesse bright,
That need no Sunne t'illuminate their spheres,
But their owne native light farre passing theirs.

And as these heavens still by degrees arize,
Untill they come to their first Movers bound,
That in his mightie compasse doth comprize,
And carrie all the rest with him around,
So those likewise doe by degrees redound,
And rise more faire, till they at last arive
To the most faire, whereto they all do strive.
(ll. 64–77)

These unseen spheres, equivalent to Keats' "unheard" melodies of music, rise to the absolute perfection of the godhead. Line 72 identifies him as the "first Mover," analogous in the conceptual world to the *primum mobile* in the visible world, an Aristotelian definition of deity. The next stanza adds Platonism to the mix—the suprasensory heaven is more fair than that "where those *Idees* on hie/Enraunged be, which *Plato* so admyred" (lines 82–83). The next stanzas complete the synthesis and Christianize it by adding the Powers, Potentates, Dominations, Cherubim and Seraphim of the angelic hierarchies "which attend/On Gods owne person" (lines

97–98). Spenser has led us to the bounds of sense perception, encompassing the endless variety of creation en route, and has given us a glimpse even byond that limit into the empyrean, which can be apprehended by the intellect alone, if at all. He successfully performs the role of poet *vates* as he attempts this essay in *astronomia speculativa*.

There is little doubt that the early Pythagoreans had accepted a universe of homocentric spheres with the earth at its center.[103] The hypothesis of geocentrism is the most likely starting place for cosmological speculation and fully accords with the simple arithmetic, music, and geometry of the Pythagorean school. Photius ascribes to them a quite specific cosmology:

> Pythagoreans assert that there are twelve spheres in the heavens above. The first and most remote from the center is the firmament where, as Aristotle says, reside the highest god and the other deities endowed with intelligence; or, according to Plato, it is the locale of the ideas. Next follow the seven planets: Saturn, Jupiter, Mars, Venus, Mercury, the Sun, and the Moon. After the planets come fire, then air, which is followed by water, and finally earth, which is the lowest of all. The firmament is the moving force of the twelve spheres. And they say that whatever is closer to it is that much more durable and better, but what is farther away is not so durable. Down through the sphere of the Moon, this order is maintained; but below the Moon there is very little order. Necessarily, therefore, our planet contains all evil things, since it serves as the sink of the whole universe. It is the inevitable cesspool for those things which settle in the lowest place.[104]

This in its essentials is the cosmology adopted by Plato, Aristotle, and Ptolemaeus. The popular poem by Manilius (fl. I A.D.), the *Astronomicon*, also proceeds from these assumptions, and for centuries the quadrivium transmitted this *imago mundi* to later generations. We have no treatise *De astronomia* from Boethius—did he compose one, which is lost? was the discipline of astronomy in such disarray that he declined to write a textbook for it? was the *Almagest* of Ptolemaeus thought to be adequate? But the other two residual authorities most popular through the sixteenth century—Proclus and Sacrobosco—began their textbooks on astronomy with the Pythagorean assumptions of concentric planetary spheres which surround a stationary earth and which in turn are enclosed by a sphere of fixed stars.

20. *"The most ancient system of the universe, common to Pythagoras, Ptolemy, and several others"*

In his historical discourse "Of the Cosmical System," Sherburne gives an ample description of this diagram: "In this System the Terraqueous Globe is seated in the midst or Centre; about it, the Elementary Region; next above that, the *Moon;* then *Mercury;* next above him, *Venus;* the Sun, as Moderator of all, being placed, as in a Throne in the midst of the Planets, environed not only by the three foregoing, called the Inferiour, but by *Mars* likewise, *Jupiter,* and *Saturn,* called the Superiour Planets. Above Saturn is the Sphere of the Fixed Stars, called Ἀπλάνη, i.e. *Aplane,* or Unerring; by some, the Firmament. . . . And this was the first *Pythagorean* System, embraced by *Archimedes,* the *Chaldeans, Aristotle, Cicero, Livy, Ptolemy, Alphonsus, Purbachius,* and the greatest part of Astronomers, until the time of *Maginus* and *Clavius.*"

Manilius, *The sphere,* tr. Edward Sherburne (London, 1675), Part II, p. 130.

Despite the fact that Copernicus published his corrective *De revolutionibus orbium coelestium* in 1543, it would be wrong to assume that Pythagorean astronomy was soon abandoned for the Copernican heliocentric universe. Tycho Brahe, the most distinguished astronomer of the late sixteenth century, made at most a minor adjustment of it, and over a century later a polymath as learned and famous as Athanasius Kircher was still arguing for a stationary earth: "I have placed the Earth absolutely immobile in the middle of the Universe. . . . Therefore I have completely rejected the Copernican system."[105] The arts also were markedly reluctant to relinquish the venerable cosmology of the past, expressed in various metaphors such as the cosmic dance which organized the items of nature in patterns of rhythmic movement, or the golden chain whose links since Homer's time represented the ordered hierarchies that bind our earth in a firm relationship to heaven. Praise of the "vast chain of being" echoed down the corridors of poetic tradition at least until the end of Pope's career.

The orthodox image of the universe prevalent in the renaissance is fully articulated by Plate 21, which appears in a text of Aristotle's *De caelo* prepared by Johann Eck for students at the University of Ingolstadt and printed at Augsburg in 1519. As we might expect, it is a composite image, but the Pythagorean features are salient. In the center we see the familiar arrangement of the elements in the spatial relationship of concentric spheres: earth in the very middle, then, ranging outwards, water, air, and fire. Next are the spheres of the seven planets in accepted order from the Moon, through Mercury, Venus, the Sun, Mars, and Jupiter to Saturn.[106] Then the *firmamentum stellatum*, "the sphere of fixed stars," which contains the signs of the zodiac;[107] followed by the [*firmamentum*] *christallinum*, "the cristalline sphere" (added to bring the celestial spheres up to the necessary number 10); and finally the *primum mobile*, "the first mover," which is bounded by the *empireum immotum*, "the immobile empyrean"—which should stretch out indefinitely, of course, but here is crudely confined by the borders of the diagram.

To stress that this is a physical representation, a time-space continuum, the period of revolution is indicated at the right for each of the celestial spheres. The sphere of the Moon, for example, turns in 28 days; that of Mercury in 1 year, and of Mars in 2 years; the sphere of fixed stars in 1,000 years, and the cristalline sphere in the enormously long time of 49,000 years. These spheres rotate from west to east—that is, from the right-hand side of the diagram out of

21. *The universe in its entirety as a Ptolemaic astronomer would describe it*

Starting from the center, the diagram includes the four elements, the seven planets, the sphere of fixed stars, the cristalline sphere, the *primum mobile,* and the empyrean. The period of revolution is given for each planet as well as the musical note it plays. The label in the upper left announces: "the eight-chorded lyre of Pythagoras, with earth playing the lowest note."

Aristotle, *Libri de caelo. IIII.* et al., ed. Johann Eck (Augsburg, 1519), fol. 29[v].

the page toward the left-hand side (observe that south is at the top and north at the bottom, upside-down to the customary way of orienting a map today). In notable contrast, though, the *primum mobile* rotates in the opposite direction, from east to west, and its period of revolution is only 24 hours, to account for the diurnal rotation of the heavens.

This diagram, however, represents not just physical reality, but also the intellectual concept of *musica mundana*. On the left-hand side, printed within each sphere, is the musical note which that planet supposedly plays in the universal harmony—*hypate* for the Moon, *parhypate* for Mercury, *lychanos* for Venus, and so on. In the upper left corner within a box a label unmistakably identifies the scheme as "the eight-chorded lyre of Pythagoras, with earth playing the lowest note." This portion of the diagram, of course, is intended to demonstrate the music of the spheres, with each planet contributing its individual but complementary note to the total consort. This is conceptual reality; in fact, everyone agreed that human ears, being imperfect, could not hear this celestial music. And to validate the noncorporeality of this idea, in the upper right corner of the diagram a little angel appears. This "assisting intelligence" places his helping hand on the outermost sphere and applies motion to the *primum mobile*, whence this motion is transferred by friction down through the other spheres.[108] This angel serves as an entrepreneur, providing a bridge between the abstract and the concrete. Though he resides in the empyrean, in the infinite and eternal, he turns the *primum mobile*, the finite and temporal. Thereby he transmutes God's will into physical fact.

Such was the Pythagorean universe in its initial form. And in this context Pythagoras was credited with other important astronomical discoveries that continued in favor longer than geocentrism. He of course realized that the earth is a sphere,[109] a conclusion that he may have reached empirically from observation of eclipses or deductively from the geometrical fact that the sphere is the most "perfect" of solid forms and therefore the proper shape for the center of a beneficent deity's creation.[110] He taught that the planets are likewise spherical bodies moving in uniform circular orbits, a tenet that persisted until Kepler actually plotted the orbit of Mars from observational data. According to Pliny (*Historia naturalis*, II.vi), Pythagoras was the first to propose that the evening star, Vesper, and the morning star, Lucifer, are the same—i.e., the planet Venus—thereby inferring a circular movement of the heavens. According to Diogenes Laertius (VIII.27), Pythagoras was aware that the moon shines only by light reflected from the sun; and according to Plutarch, Pythagoreans explained that an eclipse of the moon is due to the interpolation of the earth between it and the sun.[111] Plutarch records also that Pythagoras prescribed the obliquity of the zodiac [112] —that is, the oblique path of the sun as it goes around the earth, beginning on the equator at the time of the vernal equinox, rising to the Tropic of Cancer at the summer solstice, crossing the equator on the other side of the earth at the autumnal equinox, dropping to the Tropic of Capricorn at the winter solstice, and continuing back around to its starting place in a year's time, thereby causing the seasonal changes (see Plate 22). Furthermore, Pythagoras recognized, if he did not actually delineate, the concomitant five climatic zones, which remain standard to the present day.[113] Such formulations bespeak a sharp eye and a quick mind for scientific hypothesis.

An aberrant item that belongs in any discussion of Pythagorean astronomy is a belief most frequently designated as "the plurality of worlds." [114] Several ancient philosophers—most notably Anaximander, Heraclitus, Democritus, and Epicurus—were credited with speculation that there exist other worlds comparable to our earth which are inhabited by creatures more or less recognizable to us. Plutarch ascribes such a belief to the Pythagoreans:

> *Heraclydes* [of Pontus] and the *Pythagoreans* hold, that every Star is a world by it selfe, conteining an earth, an aire, and a skie, in an infinit celestiall nature; and these opinions goe current in the verses of *Orpheus*, for they make of every Starre a world.[115]

Later Plutarch reports that the Pythagoreans believed the moon specifically to be an *altera terra:*

> The *Pythagoreans* affirme, that the Moone appeareth terrestriall, for that she is inhabited round about, like as the earth wherein we are, and peopled as it were with the greatest living creatures, and the fairest plants; and those creatures within her, be fifteene times stronger and more puissant than those with us, and the same yeeld foorth no excrements, and the day there, is in that proportion so much longer.[116]

Plato argues that there can be only one created universe (*Timaeus*, 31A–B), Aristotle states flatly that our world is the only one (*De caelo*, 276a18–279b4), and Pliny calls the plurality of worlds a foolish notion (*Historia naturalis*, II.i). Nevertheless, the possibility is so seductive to the imagination that a wide variety of thinkers

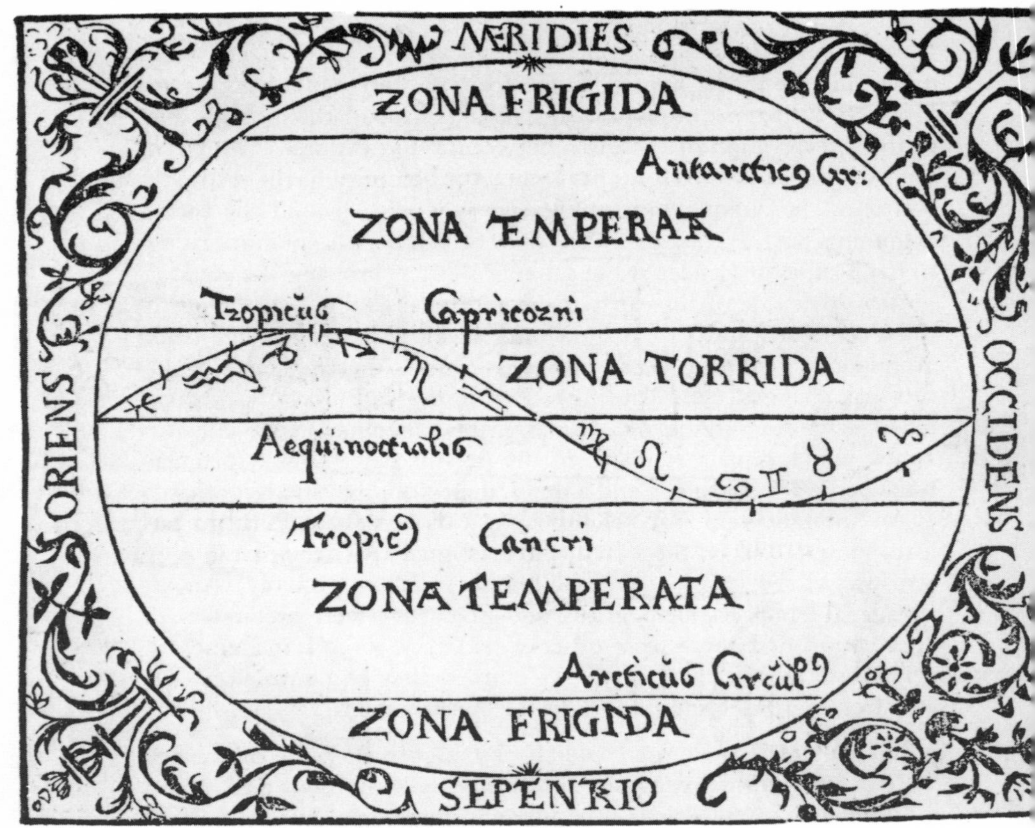

22. *The obliquity of the zodiac*

This is a crude attempt to depict the globe on a flat surface, with south at the top, north at the bottom, east on the left, and west on the right. The equator runs across the middle of the diagram, with the Tropic of Capricorn above it and the Tropic of Cancer below it. The Antarctic Circle and the Arctic Circle are also indicated. These two Tropics and two Circles define five climatic zones: a torrid zone centering on the equator, flanked by two temperate zones, which in turn are enclosed by two frigid zones.

The zodiac is marked by a sine curve showing the path of the sun in its annual journey. Starting at the right (the west), the sun at the beginning of a new year is on the equator for the vernal equinox, when it enters the sign of Aries. It proceeds to the Tropic of Cancer for the summer solstice. It crosses the equator at the autumnal equinox, when it enters the sign of Libra. It touches the Tropic of Capricorn for the winter solstice, and then continues to its point of origin at the left (the east). The sun, of course, travels from east to west in its *daily* journey; but this diagram shows the *annual* journey of the sun, which runs from west to east.

Peter Apian, *Cosmographicus liber*, ed. Gemma Frisius (Antwerp, 1533), fol. 6.

continued to titillate themselves with the fantasy. Especially in the seventeenth century, when the idea was compounded with the concept of the noble savage, the argument grew enthusiastic and a spate of books resulted.[117] The possibility of other worlds held out hope to the perennial band of those who seek utopias.[118]

Although the earliest cosmology of the Pythagoreans placed the earth in a fixed position at the center of the universe, already by the fifth century B.C. there were some within the school who argued that the earth moved in orbit about another center. This theory is attributed to Hicetas of Syracuse, or more usually to Philolaus of Croton. In its initial form, the system proposed a central fire, called variously the "watch-tower of Zeus" and "the hearth of the world," about which the earth turns.[119] To bring the total of heavenly bodies to the perfect number 10, proponents of this system theorized that a "counter-earth" revolves around the central fire in a position exactly opposite to the earth, and therefore is unseen by us.[120] Aristotle gives an ample account of this system (*De caelo*, 293a18–293b6), which Simplicius in his commentary elucidates even further:

> In the centre of the universe they say there is fire, and round the centre moves the counter-earth, being itself an earth, and called the counter-earth because it is opposite this earth of ours; and after the counter-earth comes our earth, which also moves around the centre; and after the earth comes the moon; for so Aristotle records in his work *On the Pythagoreans*.[121] The earth, being one of the stars and moving around the centre, makes day and night in accordance with its position relative to the sun. The counter-earth, as it moves around the centre following our earth, is invisible to us because the bulk of the earth is always in the way. . . . For on their assumption that the decad is the perfect number, they wished to bring the number of bodies revolving in a circle also up to ten. And so, Aristotle says, positing the sphere of the fixed stars as one, the planets as seven, and then this earth of ours, they completed the decad with the counter-earth. So Aristotle expounded the Pythagoreans' views; but the more genuine members of the school regard fire at the centre as the creative force which gives life to the whole earth from the centre and warms its cold parts; and so some call it the "Tower of Zeus," as Aristotle recorded in *On the Pythagoreans*, others the "Guard-house of Zeus," as he says here, others again the "Throne of Zeus," as other authorities tell us.[122]

Plutarch in a less pedantic vein gives the gist of Philolaic astronomy in his pandect of philosophical thought, *De placitis philosophorum:*

> *Philolaus* the Pythagorean saith, that fire is the middle, as being the hearth of the world, in the second place he raungeth the Earth of the Antipodes [i.e., the counter-earth]: and in the third, this wherein wee inhabit, which lieth opposite unto that counter earth, and turneth about it: which is the reason (quoth he) that those who dwell there, are not seene by the inhabitants heere.[123]

The name of Philolaus was inextricably linked with the argument for a moveable earth.[124] It should be noted, however, that his universe was still finite, bounded by the customary sphere of fixed stars.

In time the central fire of this system was identified with the sun, so that later generations attributed a genuinely heliocentric cosmology to the Pythagoreans.[125] The names associated with this sun-centered universe, in addition to Hicetas and Philolaus, are Heraclides of Pontus and Aristarchus of Samos, all of whom were Pythagoreans in the eyes of renaissance historians. These authorities, in the renaissance view, had argued for a spherical earth rotating on its own axis and revolving about the sun, the essentials of the Copernican theory.

In fact, in his preface to the *De revolutionibus orbium coelestium* Copernicus prudently cites these ancient philosophers as precedent for his own proposal, and even quotes a pertinent passage from Plutarch:

> I took upon myself the task of re-reading the books of all the philosophers which I could obtain, to seek out whether any one had ever conjectured that the motions of the spheres of the universe were other than they supposed who taught mathematics in the schools. And I found first that, according to Cicero,[126] Nicetas had thought the earth was moved. Then later I discovered according to Plutarch that certain others had held the same opinion; and in order that this passage may be available to all, I wish to write it down here:
>
> "But while some say the earth stands still, Philolaus the Pythagorean held that it is moved about the element of fire in an oblique circle, after the same manner of motion that the sun and moon have. Heraclides of Pontus and Ecphantus the Pythagorean assign a motion to the earth, not progressive, but after the manner of a wheel being carried on its own axis. Thus the earth, they say, turns itself upon its own center from west to east."[127]

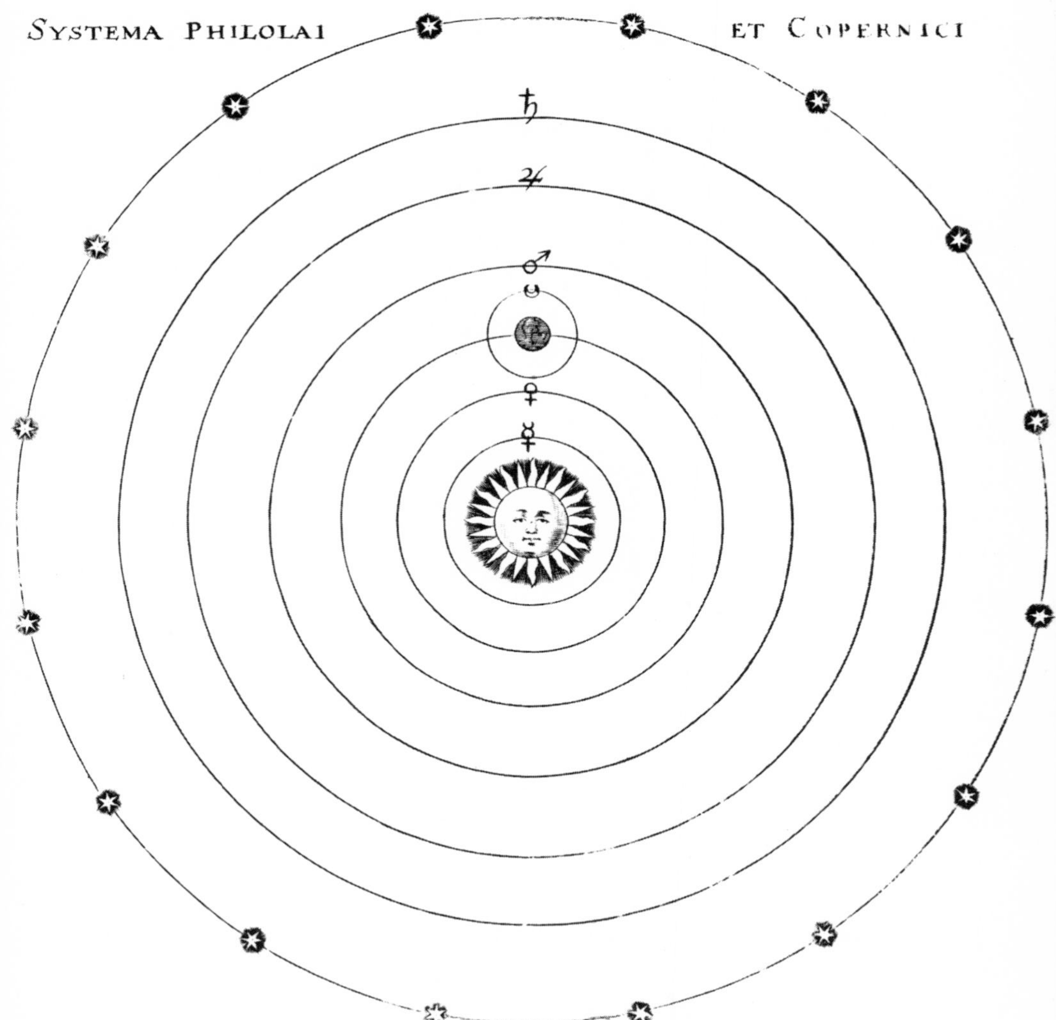

23. *"The system of Philolaus and Copernicus"*
As he does for Plate 20, Sherburne provides a description of this diagram: "In this System, we may perceive the *Sun* placed in the Centre of the World; next above him, *Mercury*, finishing his Course in the space of eighty dayes, or thereabouts; then *Venus*, making her Revolution in nine Moneths time; above her, the *Earth*, with the Elementary Sphere, in the Annual Orb, which it runs through in 365. days and half, by a Motion from West to East; that is in the same Circle, wherein the *Egyptian* and *Ptolemaick* System place the Sun. Besides which Annual Motion, *Copernicus* assigns to the Earth a Diurnal Revolution, in which it turns about its own Centre and Axis, inclined in the Plane of the Ecliptick, in the space of 24. hours, from West to East: The *Moon* by a Menstrual Revolution being carried about the *Earth*, as in an *Epicicle; Mars* running about the Sun, as the Centre of the Universe in two years; *Jupiter* above him in twelve; and *Saturn* in thirty. The Sphere of the Fixed Stars being distant by so vast an Interval from the Sphere of *Saturn*, that the Annual Orb, in which the Earth moves, appears, in respect to it, no other than a Point."
Manilius, *The sphere*, tr. Edward Sherburne (London, 1675), Part II, p. 133.

> When from this, therefore, I had conceived its possibility, I myself also began to meditate upon the mobility of the earth.[128]

Copernicus in his hypothesis kept most features of the orthodox Pythagorean cosmology: a spherical earth, circular orbits for the planets, a finite universe bounded by a sphere of fixed stars (see Plate 23). His innovations were few, little more than internal adjustments that latter-day Pythagoreans had already suggested.[129] Edward Sherburne, in fact, in his review of world systems (added as an appendix to his translation of Manilius) disallowed any claim to originality that Copernicus might have. His statement represents the attitude toward Copernicus that prevailed among the learned in the late seventeenth century:

> We come now to the most celebrious, and at this day most generally received Mundane System, from it's Reviver, called the Copernican, but owing it's original to the *Samian* and *Italick* School, as being proposed and asserted, in the one, by *Philolaus*, of *Crotona*, in the other, by *Aristarchus Samius*, both *Pythagoreans*, whence it is called the second *Pythagorick* System, as differing from the former before described; that, fixing the Earth immoveable in the midst of the world; this, on the contrary giving to the Earth, not only a diurnal Motion about its Axis, but also an Annual, about the Sun, as the centre of the Universe.[130]

The followers of Copernicus saw him in the role of revivalist rather than revolutionary, and in company with Copernicus himself they acknowledged the debt to Pythagorean astronomers.[131] Like those illustrious forebears, Copernicus placed the sun at the center to simplify mathematical computations. His overriding aim was to provide an orderly hypothesis that would accord with the Pythagorean notion of universal harmony while at the same time avoiding the complexity of Ptolemaeus' equants, eccentrics, and epicycles. His thrust was to return astronomy to the Pythagorean simplicity of whole numbers and modest geometrical forms.

The real break with the past did not occur until the bolder astronomers argued for an infinite universe with the stars not equidistant from the earth like ornaments stuck on the underside of a spherical heaven, but rather scattered at various distances through measureless space. Thomas Digges (fl. 1570–95) was one of the first to venture such a proposal (see Plate 24), though even he claimed the authority of the Pythagoreans as a precedent.[132] Kepler

A perfit description of the Cælestiall Orbes,

according to the most auncient doctrine of the Pythagoreans. &c.

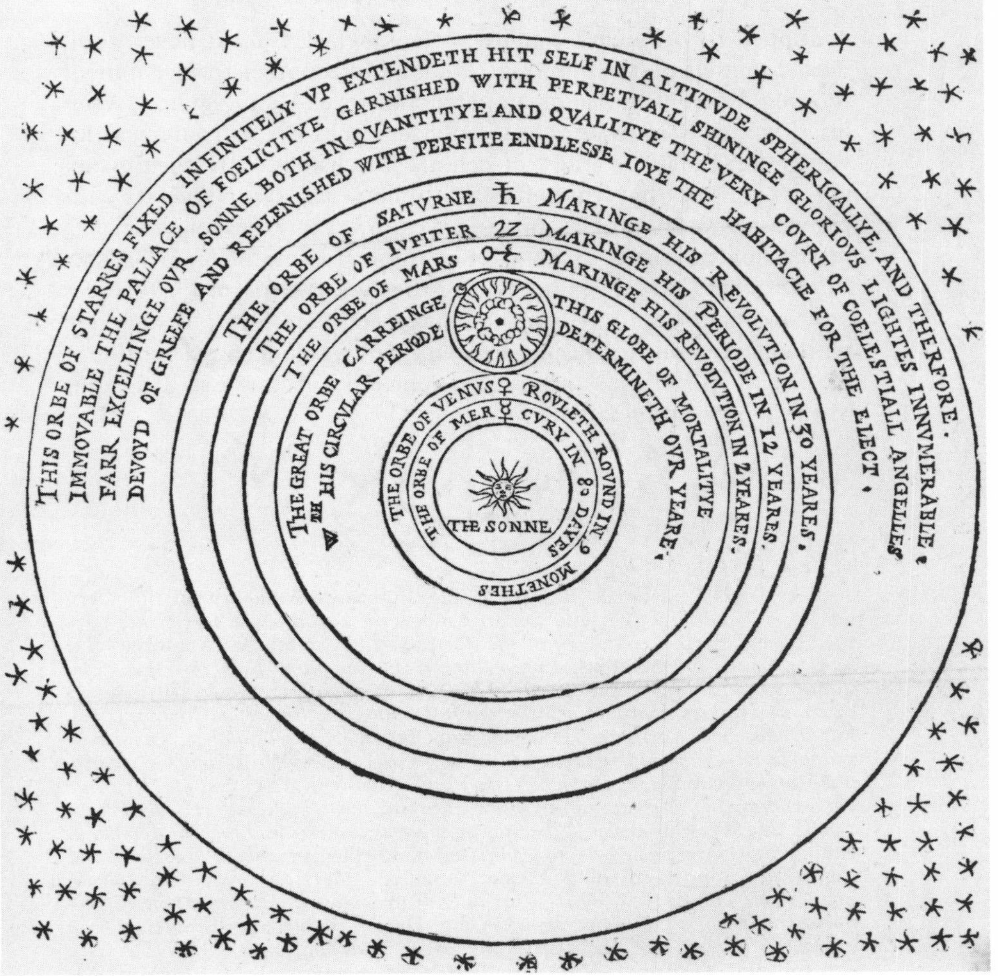

24. *A heliocentric universe*

In this diagram Thomas Digges purveys the Copernican theory of a heliocentric universe, but he calls upon "the most auncient doctrine of the Pythagoreans" for supportive authority. Six planetary spheres are centered on the sun, and the period of revolution for each planet is indicated. The moon is properly positioned in orbit about the earth. The empyrean stretches infinitely beyond the planetary spheres with the stars not fixed in one sphere, but scattered throughout space at varying distances from the finite universe. In effect, the sphere of fixed stars has been expanded to infinity, so that it thereby becomes the empyrean.

Thomas Digges, "A perfit description of the caelestiall orbes" in Leonard Digges, *A prognostication everlastinge* (London, 1576), fol. 43.

continued to propound a finite cosmos, while Galileo never committed himself on the question. The first astronomer to free himself thoroughly from Pythagorean convictions was Isaac Newton. After his *Principia mathematica* was published in 1687, astronomical investigation became a study of celestial mechanics, only then escaping its immemorial commitment to universal harmony. At that point astronomy left the quadrivium forever and became a science in the modern sense. Natural philosophy became phenomenalistic. *Physics* could no longer be used in the Greek sense of "nature"; it now meant the study of quantifiable mechanical laws. Reality lay without question in the physical world. The conceptual world, at most, was an artificial construct, a subjective abstraction, a figment of the human imagination.

Notes

[1] For original materials displaying the Pythagorean theory of numbers, see pp. 23–54, above. Cf. also Sextus Empiricus, *Against the Logicians*, I.93–109; Sextus Empiricus, *Against the Professors*, IV.2–10; St. Augustine, *De musica*, I.ix–xii; Macrobius, *Commentarius in somnium Scipionis*, I.v; Cassiodorus, *Institutiones*, II.iii.21–vii.4; Isidore, *Etymologiae*, Book III; Joannes de Muris (fl. 14th century), *Arithmeticae speculativae libri duo* (Mainz, 1538). For renaissance works, see Luca Paccioli, *Summa de arithmetica, geometria, proportioni, & proportionalita* (Venice, 1494); Gregor Reisch, *Margarita philosophica* (Freiburg, 1503), f1v-p2; Jacques LeFèvre d'Etaples, ed., *Epitome compendiosaque introductio in libros arithmeticos . . . Boetii* et al. (Paris, 1503); Charles de Bouelles, *Liber de duodecim numeris* in *Liber de intellectu* et al. (Paris, 1510), fol. 148v–171; Heinrich Cornelius Agrippa, *Three books of occult philosophy*, tr. John Freake (London, 1651), pp. 170–225; Nicoló Scutelli, *De vita & secta Pythagorae flosculi* in *Iamblichus de mysteriis Ægyptiorum* (Rome, 1556), pp. 52–67; John Dee, "Mathematicall praeface" to Euclid. *The elements*, tr. Henry Billingsley (London, 1570), [*]1-T4v (see also fol. 183); Gulielmus Morellius, *Tabula compendiosa* (Basle, 1580), p. 152; Francesco Patrizi, *De rerum natura libri II. priores. Alter de spacio physico. Alter de spacio mathematico* (Ferrara, 1587), esp. fol. 18–24; Guillaume Saluste du Bartas, *Devine weekes and workes*, tr. Joshua Sylvester (London, 1605), pp. 472–495; Robert Fludd, *Utriusque cosmi . . . historia*, 4 vols. (Oppenheim, 1617–19), esp. II.5–8, III.19–57; Joannes Meursius, *Denarius pythagoricus* (Leyden, 1631); Hugh Sempill, *De mathematicis disciplinis libri duodecim* (Antwerp, 1635), passim; John Heydon, *The Rosie Crucian infallible axiomata* (London, 1660). For secondary materials, see Gerard Johann Vossius, *De universae mathesios natura & constitutione liber* (Amsterdam, 1650), passim; Thomas Stanley, *The history of philosophy*, 2nd ed. (London, 1687), pp. 522 ff.; Joannes Franciscus Buddeus, *Compendium historiae philosophicae* (Halle, 1731), pp. 97–100; Thomas Taylor, *Theoretic Arithmetic* (London, 1816); *ibid.*, tr., *Iamblichus' Life of Pythagoras* (London, 1818), pp. 306–318; A. Ed. Chaignet, *Pythagore et la philosophie pythagoricienne*, 2 vols. (Paris, 1873), II.1–74, 96–128; Gaston Milhaud, *Les philosophes géomètres de la Grèce*,

2nd ed. (Paris, 1934), pp. 79–122, 309–326; Theodor Gomperz, *Greek Thinkers*, tr. Laurie Magnus, 2 vols. (New York, 1908), I.103–108; Sir Thomas Heath, *A History of Greek Mathematics*, 2 vols. (Oxford, 1921), I.65–117; Erich Frank, *Plato und die sogenannten Pythagoreer* [1923] (Darmstadt, 1962), pp. 219 ff.; John Burnet, *Greek Philosophy: Part I, Thales to Plato* (London, 1928), pp. 52–54; Nicomachus, *Introduction to Arithmetic*, tr. Martin Luther D'Ooge (New York, 1926), esp. pp. 16–45, 111–123; Léon Robin, *Greek Thought and the Origins of the Scientific Spirit* (New York, 1928), pp. 56–62; Sir Thomas Heath, *A Manual of Greek Mathematics* [1931] (Dover Publications, 1963), pp. 36 ff.; Harold Cherniss, *Aristotle's Criticism of Presocratic Philosophy* (Johns Hopkins Press, 1935), pp. 223–226, 237–242, 386–392; Edward W. Strong, *Procedures and Metaphysics* (Univ. of California Press, 1936), pp. 19–46; Vincent F. Hopper, *Medieval Number Symbolism* (Columbia Univ. Press, 1938), esp. pp. 33–49; R. G. Collingwood, *The Idea of Nature* (Oxford, 1945), pp. 50–52; Paul-Henri Michel, *De Pythagore à Euclide* (Paris, 1950), esp. pp. 295–328; W. P. D. Wightman, *The Growth of Scientific Ideas* (Yale Univ. Press, 1951), pp. 19–28; Robert Baccou, *Histoire de la science grecque de Thalès à Socrate* (Paris, 1951), pp. 103–134; L. W. H. Hull, *History and Philosophy of Science* (London, 1959), pp. 22–31; Alastair Fowler, *Spenser and the Numbers of Time* (London, 1964), esp. pp. 3–50; James A. Philip, *Pythagoras and Early Pythagoreanism* (Univ. of Toronto Press, 1966), pp. 76–109; Jacob Klein, *Greek Mathematical Thought and the Origin of Algebra*, tr. Eva Brann (Massachusetts Institute of Technology Press, 1968), esp. pp. 63–79; Edward A. Maziarz and Thomas Greenwood, *Greek Mathematical Philosophy* (New York, 1968), pp. 10–48; Christopher Butler, "Numerological Thought" in *Silent Poetry*, ed. Alastair Fowler (London, 1970), pp. 1–31; Christopher Butler, *Number Symbolism* (New York, 1970), pp. 1–21.

[2] "A Commentarie of the Creation of the Soule, which Plato describeth in his booke *Timaeus*" in *The morals*, tr. Philemon Holland (London, 1603), p. 1031.

[3] *Of the knowledge whiche maketh a wise man* [1533], ed. Edwin J. Howard (Oxford, Ohio, 1946), fol. 32–32ᵛ. For a similar argument in the same tradition, see Annibale Romei, *The courtiers academie*, tr. J. Kepers (London, 1598), pp. 6–8.

[4] On the derivation of Platonic ideas from Pythagorean numbers, see Aristotle, *Metaphysica*, 987a29–987b34; Ralph Cudworth, *The True Intellectual System of the Universe* [I.iv.21], 3 vols. (London, 1845), II.41–42; William Enfield, *The History of Philosophy*, 2 vols. (London, 1791), I.384; W. D. Ross, *Plato's Theory of Ideas* (Oxford, 1951), esp. pp. 13–14, 176–205, 216–220; John Elof Boodin, "The Discovery of Form" in *Roots of Scientific Thought*, ed. Philip P. Wiener and Aaron Noland (New York, 1957), pp. 57 ff.; Walter Burkert, *Weisheit und Wissenschaft: Studien zu Pythagoras, Philolaos und Platon* (Nuremberg, 1962), pp. 14–26, 74–85; Cornelia J. de Vogel, *Pythagoras and Early Pythagoreanism* (Assen, 1966), pp. 202–207; and Maziarz and Greenwood, *Greek Mathematical Philosophy*, pp. 132–143.

[5] Plutarch's definition of "idea" is germane here: "*Idea* is a bodilesse substance, which of it selfe hath no subsistence, but giveth figure and forme unto shapelesse matters, and becommeth the very cause that bringeth them into shew and evidence" ("Opinions of Philosophers" [I.x] in *Morals*, tr. Holland [1603], p. 813).

[6] Plutarch offers pretty much the same information (*De placitis philosophorum*, I.iii).

[7] *History of philosophy*, p. 522.

[8] See André Dacier, *The Life of Pythagoras*, tr. anon. (London, 1707), pp. 29–31.

[9] Quoted by Stanley, *History of philosophy*, p. 523.

[10] "Mathematicall praeface" to Euclid, *Elements*, tr. Billingsley, [*] 1.

[11] Cf. Porphyry, *De vita Pythagorae*, xlix.

[12] *The whetstone of witte* (London, 1557), b1–b1^{v}.

[13] *History of philosophy*, p. 522. At the beginning of his "Mathematicall praeface" to Billingsley's translation of Euclid, John Dee went to great lengths to make clear the intermediate role of number:

> All thinges which are, & have beyng, are found under a triple diversitie generall. For, either, they are demed Supernaturall, Naturall, or, of a third being. Thinges Supernaturall, are immateriall, simple, indivisible, incorruptible, & unchangeable. Things Naturall, are materiall, compounded, divisible, corruptible, and chaungeable. Things Supernaturall, are, of the minde onely, comprehended: Things Naturall, of the sense exterior, ar hable to be perceived. In thinges Naturall, probabilitie and conjecture hath place: But in things Supernaturall, chief demonstration, & most sure Science [i.e., knowledge] is to be had. By which properties & comparasons of these two, more easily may be described, the state, condition, nature and property of those things, which, we before termed of a third being: which, by a peculiar name also, are called *Thynges Mathematicall*. For, these, beyng (in a maner) middle, betwene thinges supernaturall and naturall: are not so absolute and excellent, as thinges supernatural: Nor yet so base and grosse, as thinges naturall: But are thinges immateriall: and neverthelesse, by materiall things hable somewhat to be signified. And though their particular Images, by Art, are aggregable and divisible: yet the generall *Formes*, notwithstandyng, are constant, unchaungeable, untransformable, and incorruptible. Neither of the sense, can they, at any tyme, be perceived or judged. Nor yet, for all that, in the royall mynde of man, first conceived. But, surmountyng the imperfection of conjecture, weenyng and opinion: and commyng short of high intellectuall conception, are the Mercurial fruite of *Dianoeticall* discourse, in perfect imagination subsistyng ([*]3^{v}).

[14] Unitas autem non est numerus, sed principium numeri: sicut magnitudinis punctum (*Margarita philosophica* [IV.iii] [Basle, 1583], p. 282). Cf. Euclid, *Elements*, tr. Billingsley, fol. 183^{v}; and Charles de Bouelles, *Geometria* (Paris, 1542), p. 5.

[15] *Elements*, tr. Billingsley, fol. 1.

[16] For ancient authorities on the creation of line, plane, and volume from the monad, see Plato, *Timaeus*, 32B; Aristotle, *De caelo*, 268a7–268a28; Aristotle, *De anima*, 404b18–404b24; Philo Judaeus, *On the Creation*, xlix; Nicomachus, *Arithmetic* [II.vii], tr. D'Ooge, pp. 239–240; Theon of Smyrna, *Expositio rerum mathematicarum ad legendum Platonem utilium*, tr. Ismael Bullialdus (Paris, 1644), p. 174; Sextus Empiricus, *Outlines of Pyrrhonism*, III.152–154; Sextus Empiricus, *Against the Physicists*, II.270–284; Sextus Empiricus, *Against the Professors*, IV.4–5; Proclus, *In primum Euclidis elementorum librum commentariorum . . . liber IV*, ed. Francesco Barozzi (Padua, 1560), pp. 56–57; Hierocles, *Upon the Golden Verses of Pythagoras*, tr. John Hall (London, 1657), p. 126; and Photius, *Myriobiblon* (Rouen, 1653), col. 1315. For renaissance authorities, see Johann Reuchlin, *De arte cabalistica libri tres*, translated in Stanley, *History of philosophy*, p. 574; Joannes Martinus, *Arithmetica* (Paris, 1526), fol. 15^{v}; Ludovicus Caelius Rhodiginus, *Lectionum antiquarum libri XXX* [xxii.15] (Basle, 1566), p. 857; Francesco Giorgio, *De harmonia mundi totius cantica tria*, 2nd ed. (Paris, 1545), fol. 40; Patrizi, *De rerum natura*, II.18–20; Joannes Jacobus Frisius, *Bibliotheca philosophorum classicorum authorum chronologica* (Zurich,

1592), fol. 6^v; Jean Jacques Boissard, *De divinatione et magicis praestigiis* (Oppenheim, 1616?), p. 295; Robert Fludd, *Mosaicall philosophy* (London, 1659), p. 73. Note also Donne, *Second Anniversarie*, lines 131–136. For modern authorities, see Eduard Zeller, *A History of Greek Philosophy*, tr. S. F. Alleyne, 2 vols. (London, 1881), I.434–436; G. S. Kirk and J. E. Raven, *The Presocratic Philosophers* (Cambridge Univ. Press, 1962), pp. 253–256; and W. K. C. Guthrie, *A History of Greek Philosophy*, 3 vols. (Cambridge Univ. Press, 1962), I.259–262.

[17] The dyad is "undefined" or "unlimited" because, unlike an odd number, it can be divided into equal parts an infinite number of times.

[18] *History of philosophy*, p. 512. For other statements of this basic tenet of Pythagoreanism, see Philo Judaeus, *On the Creation*, xlvii; Plutarch, "Opin. of Phil." [I.iii] in *Morals*, tr. Holland (1603), p. 806; *Theologumena arithmetica* in *Greek Mathematics*, tr. Ivor Thomas (London, 1939), p. 81; Martianus Capella, *De nuptiis Philologiae et Mercurii*, VII.[734]; St. Augustine, *De musica*, I.xii; Photius, *Myriobiblon*, "Pythagoras"; Rhodiginus, *Lectionum antiquarum libri*, p. 857; Reuchlin, *De arte cabalistica*, tr. Stanley, *History of philosophy*, p. 574; Henricus Stephanus, ed., *Poesis philosophica* (Geneva, 1573), pp. 118–119; Johann Kepler, *Harmonices mundi libri V* (Linz, 1619), Book III, pp. 4–7; Athanasius Kircher, *Musurgia universalis*, 2 vols. (Rome, 1650), I.534; Henry More, *Conjectura cabbalistica* (London, 1653), pp. 153–154; Hierocles, *Commentarius in aurea Pythagoreorum carmina*, 2 vols. (London, 1654–55), I.xvi–xvii; Kircher, *Arithmologia* (Rome, 1665), p. 260; Cudworth, *Intellectual System* (1845) [I.iv.20], II.14–15. For further explanation of the tetractys, see pp. 151–156, below.

[19] *Whetstone of witte*, A1^v. For an exposition of how 4, 7, and 10 relate to 1, see Joachim Camerarius, *Appendix problematum* (Geneva, 1596), p. 62.

[20] Two was the number of woman; see p. 86, below.

[21] I.e., $2 + 1 = 3$.

[22] I.e., the tetragrammaton.

[23] *Devine weekes and workes*, tr. Sylvester (1605), pp. 472–473. Cf. du Bartas, *Works*, ed. Urban T. Holmes, Jr. *et al.*, 3 vols. (Univ. of North Carolina Press, 1940), III.174–176.

[24] The term *mathematics* was associated particularly with the Pythagoreans; cf. Heath, *History of Greek Mathematics*, I.10–11. It comes from μανθάνειν, "to learn," and implies an epistemology best known to us through Plato's doctrine of knowledge as recollection. The study of mathematics, strictly speaking, is the recollection of the numbers which inhere in the human mind through its participation in the *anima mundi*. The study of mathematics is no more than the bringing into consciousness of the innate numbers which inform our being. Cf. Philolaus, fragment 11 in Kathleen Freeman, *Ancilla to the Pre-Socratic Philosophers* (Oxford, 1948), p. 75; Proclus, *Commentary on Euclid I*, cited by Stanley, *History of philosophy*, p. 522; Vossius, *De universae mathesios natura*, pp. 1–2; and St. Jerome, *The Apology Against the Books of Rufinus*, tr. John N. Hritzu (Catholic Univ. of America Press, 1965), p. 212.

[25] *Commentary on Euclid I*, quoted by Stanley, *History of philosophy*, p. 522.

[26] Arithmetica est disciplina quantitatis numerabilis secundum se. . . . Arithmetica est disciplina numerorum (*Etymologiae*, III.i).

For materials on Pythagorean arithmetic in addition to those cited on p. 132, n. 1, see Giorgio Valla, *De expetendis, et fugiendis rebus opus* (Venice, 1501), b2–e5^v; Gaspar Lax, *Arithmetica speculativa* (Paris, 1515); Pedro Sanchez Cirvelo, *Cursus quattuor mathematicarum artium liberalium* (Alcalá, 1516); Joannes Martinus, *Arithmetica* (Paris, 1526); Oronce Finé, *Protomathesis* (Paris, 1532), fol. 1–47; Franciscus Maurolycus, *Arithmeti-*

corum libri duo appended *to Opuscula mathematica* (Venice, 1575); Tommaso Garzoni, *La piazza universale di tutte le professioni del mondo* (Venice, 1586), pp. 130, 146, and *passim;* Fludd, *Utriusque cosmi . . . historia*, II.42–60; Thomas, *Greek Mathematics*, pp. 67–141; B. L. van der Waerden, "Die Arithmetik der Pythagoreer," *Mathematische Annalen*, 120 (1948), 127–153, 676–700; and Burkert, *Weisheit und Wissenschaft*, pp. 404–423.

[27] Numerus autem est multitudo ex unitatibus constituta (*Etymologiae*, III.iii).

[28] The Pythagoreans, like renaissance mathematicians, were aware of incommensurable (or irrational) number; cf. Heath, *History of Greek Mathematics*, I.90–91, 154–157; Heath, *Manual of Greek Mathematics*, pp. 54–55, 105–106; and Thomas, *Greek Mathematics*, pp. 215–217, 223–225. Of course, it was a serious embarrassment, even threat, to their arithmetic. The theorem specifically associated with Pythagoras' name (Euclid, I.xlvii) deals with this problem (cf. Thomas, *Greek Mathematics*, pp. 179–185). Book X of Euclid's *Elements* is concerned largely with incommensurability (cf. Euclid, *Elements*, tr. Billingsley, fol. 228–228ᵛ).

[29] Cf. Aristotle, *Metaphysica*, 986a18–986a23; Nicomachus, *Arithmetic* [I.vii], tr. D'Ooge, pp. 190–191; St. Augustine, *De musica*, I.xii; and Euclid, *Elements*, tr. Billingsley, fol. 184–184ᵛ.

[30] *Commentary on the Dream of Scipio* [I.vi.7–8], tr. William H. Stahl (Columbia Univ. Press, 1952), pp. 100–101. Cf. Ralph Cudworth, *The true intellectual system of the universe* (London, 1678), pp. 371–373.

[31] *De arte cabalistica*, tr. Stanley, *History of philosophy*, p. 572. Cf. Plate 4.

[32] Pierre de la Primaudaye, *The third volume of the French academie*, tr. R. Dolman (London, 1601), p. 174.

[33] "Opin. of Phil." [I.vii] in *Morals*, tr. Holland (1603), p. 812.

[34] For explanation of these three sorts of proportion, see pp. 93–94, below.

[35] A corruption of "al-Khwārizmī," author of the first arithmetical treatise translated from the Arabic.

[36] An allusion to Wisdom, xi.21; see p. 206, below. Diogenes Laertius reports that Pythagoras "according to Aristoxenus the musician, was the first to introduce weights and measures into Greece" (VIII.14).

[37] (London, 1595), A2ᵛ.

[38] For materials on Pythagorean music in addition to those cited on p. 55 and p. 32 n. 1, see Marsilio Ficino, "De rationibus musicae" in *Supplementum Ficinianum*, ed. Paul O. Kristeller, 2 vols. (Florence, 1937), I.51–56; Franchino Gafori, *Theorica musice* (Milan, 1492); Jacques LeFèvre d'Etaples, "Elementa musicalia" in *Arithmetica* [*Jordani*] *decem libris demonstrata* et al. (Paris, 1496), f1–h6ᵛ; Valla, *De Expetendis . . . rebus*, e6–m8; Ludovicus Folianus, *Musica theorica* (Venice, 1529); Henricus Glareanus, *Dodecachordon* (Basle, 1547); Gioseffo Zarlino, *Le istitutione harmoniche* (Venice, 1558); Franciscus Maurolycus, "Musicae traditiones" in *Opuscula mathematica* (Venice, 1575), pp. 145–160; John Dowland, "Other necessary observations belonging to the lute" in Robert Dowland, *Varietie of lute-lessons* (London, 1610), D2–D3; Fludd, *Utriusque cosmi . . . historia*, II.130–136, 164–171; Kepler, *Harmonice mundi*, esp. Book III, pp. 3–4, 55; Marin Mersenne, *L'Harmonie universelle* (Paris, 1627), *passim;* Kircher, *Musurgia universalis*, esp. Book III; Stanley, *History of philosophy*, pp. 530–535; Johann Heinrich Alsted, *Templum musicum: or The musical synopsis*, tr. John Birchensha (London, 1664); Johann Jakob Brucker, *Historia critica philosophiae*, 2nd ed., 6 vols. (Leipzig, 1766–67), I.1056–1060; Sir John Hawkins, *A General History of the Science and Practice of Music*, 5 vols. (London, 1776), I.39–45, 99, 169–180, 200–208, 308–334; Chaignet, *Pythagore*, II.128–140; Frank, *Plato und die sogenannten Pythagoreer*, pp. 150 ff.; John Burnet, *Early Greek Philosophy*, 4th ed. (London, 1945), pp. 45–49; J. Murray Barbour, "The Persistence of the Pythagorean

Tuning System," *Scripta Mathematica*, 1 (1932–33), 286–304; F. M. Cornford, *Plato's Cosmology* (London, 1937), pp. 66–72; James Hutton, "Some English Poems in Praise of Music" in *English Miscellany, II*, ed. Mario Praz (Rome, 1951), pp. 1–63; Claude V. Palisca, "Scientific Empiricism in Musical Thought" in Stephen Toulmin *et al.*, *Seventeenth-Century Science and the Arts* (Princeton Univ. Press, 1961), pp. 91–137; John Hollander, *The Untuning of the Sky* (Princeton Univ. Press, 1961), esp. pp. 20–31; Kirk and Raven, *Presocratic Philosophers*, pp. 229–231; Gretchen L. Finney, *Musical Backgrounds for English Literature: 1580–1650* (Rutgers Univ. Press, 1962), esp. chap. ii; Burkert, *Weisheit und Wissenschaft*, pp. 348–364; Richard L. Crocker, "Pythagorean Mathematics and Music," *Journal of Aesthetics and Art Criticism*, 22 (1963–64), 189–198, 325–335; and Edward A. Lippman, *Musical Thought in Ancient Greece* (Columbia Univ. Press, 1964), pp. 1–44.

[39] A good discussion of this point is given by Bede at the beginning of his treatise "Musica theorica" in *Opera*, 8 vols. (Basle, 1563), I.403–406.

[40] "Of musicke" in *Morals*, tr. Holland (1603), p. 1261.

[41] *Life of Pythagoras*, p. 84.

[42] Gr. ἁρμονία is literally the means by which things are joined together to form a continuum—for example, the joints between a ship's planks—so that a part is always considered in relation to the whole. In Greek music, it should be remembered, two or more notes were never played simultaneously to produce what we call a "chord"; notes were always played in sequence. See Hollander, *Untuning of Sky*, pp. 26–27; and Guthrie, *History of Greek Philosophy*, I.220.

[43] *On Music*, tr. Robert C. Taliaferro (New York, 1947), p. 172.

[44] Musica est peritia modulationis sono cantuque consistens (*Etymologiae*, III.xv).

[45] Harmonica est facultas differentias acutorum et gravium sonorum sensu ac ratione perpendens (*De musica*, V.i).

[46] See Freeman, *Ancilla to Pre-Socratic Philosophers*, pp. 79–80. Cf. Nicomachus, *Arithmetic* [II.xxii–xxv], tr. D'Ooge, pp. 266–276; Boethius, *De arithmetica*, II.1; Boethius, *De musica*, II.xii; and Gafori, *Theorica musice*, e8ᵛ–f2.

[47] *Exercises* (London, 1594), fol. 22. Cf. Reisch, *Margarita philosophica* [IV.xxii] (1583), p. 294; Recorde, *Whetstone of witte*, B1–B1ᵛ; and Thomas Morley, *A plaine and easie introduction to practicall musicke* (London, 1597), *3.

[48] For the common way of calculating the harmonic mean, see Isidore, *Etymologiae*, III.xxiii ("De numeris musicis").

[49] Gr. διαπασῶν from δία "through" + πασῶν (genitive plural of πᾶς), "all," meaning "the total extent of a continuum."

[50] Gr. τόνος, literally "that by which a sinew (or the like) is stretched"—hence, the pitch of sound.

[51] Cf. Theon of Smyrna quoted by Stanley, *History of philosophy*, p. 533; and Sextus Empiricus, *Against the Logicians*, I.94–98 (quoted *ibid.*, p. 550).

[52] See p. 84, above.

[53] Quoted p. 91, above.

[54] See Nicomachus, *Harmonices enchiridion*, v–vi; Plutarch, "A Commentarie of the Creation of the Soule" in *Morals*, tr. Holland (1603), p. 1039; *ibid.*, "Of musicke," p. 1255; Iamblichus, *De vita Pythagorae*, xxvi; Boethius, *De musica*, I.viii, x; Martianus Capella, *De nuptiis Philologiae et Mercurii*, II.[107–108]; Macrobius, *Commentarius in somnium Scipionis*, II.i.14–25; Isidore, *Etymologiae*, III.xxiii; Gafori, *Theorica musice*, f2–f4; and Reisch, *Margarita philosophica* [V.viii–x] (1583), pp. 350–353.

[55] See Plate 21. See also Valla, *De expetendis . . . rebus*, e8ᵛ; Dee, "Mathematicall praeface" in Euclid, *Elements*, tr. Billingsley, b2ᵛ; William Ingpen,

The secrets of numbers (London, 1624), pp. 51–52; Vossius, *De universae mathesios natura*, pp. 84–85. This tuning system is inscribed on a tablet beside Pythagoras in Raphael's "School of Athens" in the Vatican (reproduced in a detail in Rudolf Wittkower, *Architectural Principles in the Age of Humanism* [London, 1949], facing p. 109).

[56] *Exercises*, fol. 22^{v}–23.

[57] *Commentary on the Dream of Scipio*, [II.i.8–13], tr. Stahl, pp. 186–187. The bibliography on this incident of Pythagoras in the blacksmiths' shop is extensive; for representative accounts, see Nicomachus, *Harmonices enchiridion*, vi; Iamblichus, *De vita Pythagorae*, xxvi; Boethius, *De musica*, I.x; Joannes Wallensis, *Florilegium* (Rome, 1655), pp. 243 ff.; Maurolycus, "Musicae traditiones" in *Opuscula mathematica*, K2; and Stanley, *History of philosophy*, p. 532. See also Vossius, *De universae mathesios natura*, p. 84; Kircher, *Musurgia universalis*, pp. 346–352; Dacier, *Life of Pythagoras*, pp. 82–84; Hawkins, *History of Music*, I.29–36; Enfield, *History of Philosophy*, I.385–386; and John M. Steadman, "The 'Inharmonious Blacksmith': Spenser and the Pythagorean Legend," *Publications of the Modern Language Association*, 79 (1964), 664–665.

[58] *De vita Pythagorae*, xxx. Cf. Iamblichus, *De vita Pythagorae*, xv.

[59] To state the general proposition in Euclidean terms, no rational number can be a mean between n and $n+1$.

> [60] Moyses dicit repertorem musicae artis fuisse Tubal, qui fuit de stirpe Cain ante diluvium. Graeci vero Pythagoram dicunt huius artis invenisse primordia ex malleorum sonitu et cordarum extensione percussa. Alii Linum Thebaeum et Zetum et Amphion in musica arte primos claruisse ferunt (*Etymologiae*, III.xvi). See Plate 12.

[61] *Theorica musice*, a1–a7. See also John Case, *Apologia musices* (Oxford, 1588), pp. 1–2; Andreas Ornithoparcus, *Micrologus*, tr. John Dowland (London, 1609), p. 5; and Fludd, *Utriusque cosmi . . . historia*, II.165.

> [62] Et primum ea quae est mundana in his maxime perspicienda est quae in ipso coelo, vel compage elementorum, vel temporum varietate visuntur. Qui enim fieri potest, ut tam velox coeli machina tacito silentique cursu moveatur? . . . Humanam vero musicam, quisquis in sese ipsum descendit, intelligit. Quid est enim quod illam incorpoream rationis vivacitatem corpori misceat, nisi quaedam coaptatio, et veluti gravium leviumque vocum, quasi unam consonantiam efficiens, temperatio? . . . Tertia est musica, quae in quibusdam consistere dicitur instrumentis. Haec vero administratur, aut intentione, ut nervis, aut spiritu . . . aut percussione (*De musica*, I.ii).

Boethius' classification of music into these three sorts was long-lived. Cf. Gafori, *Theorica musice*, $a7^{v}$–$b2^{v}$; Reisch, *Margarita philosophica* [V.v] (1583), pp. 347–348; Zarlino, *Le istitutione harmoniche*, I.vi–vii; Case, *Apologia musices*, p. 6; Ornithoparcus, *Micrologus*, tr. Dowland, $B2^{v}$–$C1^{v}$; and Mersenne, *L'Harmonie universelle*, pp. 57, 67–93. See also David S. Chamberlain, "Philosophy of Music in the *Consolatio* of Boethius," *Speculum*, 45 (1970), 80–97.

[63] Plutarch, "A Commentarie of the Creation of the Soule" in *Morals*, tr. Holland (1603), p. 1047. For a discussion of Aristotle's important critique of the soul as harmony, see Cherniss, *Aristotle's Criticism*, pp. 322–326.

[64] Cf. Plato, *Republic*, 401D.

> [65] Unde fit, ut cum sint quatuor matheseos disciplinae, caeterae quidem ad investigationem veritatis laborent; musica vero non modo speculationi, verum etiam moralitati conjuncta sit. Nihil est enim tam proprium hu-

> manitati, quam remitti dulcibus modis astringique contrariis (*De musica*, I.i).

Cf. Shakespeare, *Richard II*, V.v.41–63; and *Lear*, IV.vii.14–25. Shakespeare knew that "music oft hath such a charm/To make bad good and good provoke to harm" (*Measure for Measure*, IV.i.14–15).

66 Samuel, i.16.14–23. Cf. Bede, "Musica quadrata seu mensurata" in *Opera* (1563), I.418; and Isidore, *Etymologiae*, III.xvii.

67 The *locus classicus* for this incident is Suda, *Lexicon graecum*, "Timotheus." Cf. E. K.'s gloss to Spenser, *October*, 27.

68 *De vita Pythagorae*, xv, xxv. Cf. Porphyry, *De vita Pythagorae*, xxx; Juan Luis Vives, *On Education*, tr. Foster Watson (Cambridge Univ. Press, 1913), p. 205; Joannes Baptista Bernardus, *Seminarium totius philosophiae Aristotelicae et Platonicae*, 2nd ed. (Lyons, 1599), II.642. See also Stanley, *History of philosophy*, pp. 533–534; and Frances A. Yates, *The French Academies of the Sixteenth Century* (London, 1947), pp. 38–41. Lorenzo in a strongly Pythagorean passage of Shakespeare's *Merchant of Venice* comments:

> The man that hath no music in himself,
> Nor is not moved with concord of sweet sounds,
> Is fit for treasons, stratagems, and spoils.
> (V.i.83–85)

69 *De musica*, I.i. Cf. Celio Calcagnini, *Opera* (Basle, 1544), p. 330.

70 Non sine causa dictum est, omnia quae ex contrariis consisterent, harmonia quadam conjungi atque componi. Est enim harmonia, plurimorum adunatio, et dissentientium consensio (*De arithmetica*, II.xxxii).

71 *History of philosophy*, p. 530. The passage in Theon of Smyrna is *Expositio rerum mathematicarum* [I.i], tr. Bullialdus, pp. 15–16. Cf. Plato, *Symposium*, 187A–C.

72 For materials on Pythagorean geometry in addition to those cited on p. 132, n. 1. see Valla. *De expetendis . . . rebus*, m8ᵛ–bb1ᵛ; Carolus Bovillus [i.e., de Bouelles], "Geometrici introductorii libri VI" in LeFèvre d'Etaples, *Introductio in libros arithmeticos Boetii* et al. (1503); Finé, *Protomathesis*, fol. 49–99; De Bouelles, *Geometria* (Paris, 1542); Robert Recorde, *The pathway to knowledg* (London, 1551); Fludd, *Utriusque cosmi . . . historia*, II.80–122; George J. Allman, *Greek Geometry from Thales to Euclid* (Dublin, 1889), pp. 24–51; Heath, *History of Greek Mathematics*, I.141–169; and Thomas, *Greek Mathematics*, pp. 172–225.

73 Because arithmetic is confined to the use of whole numbers, it cannot solve problems which involve an irrational number. Geometry, however, working in the medium of continuous quantities, can deal with irrational number by means of constructed figures. It is likely, in fact, that the Pythagoreans developed geometry as a result of their inability to work with incommensurables using arithmetical operations alone. The "Pythagorean" theorem (Euclid, I.xlvii) solves by geometric construction what is beyond the province of simple arithmetic. Although today we usually think of the Pythagorean theorem in its algebraic formulation ($a^2 + b^2 = c^2$), the traditional statement of the theorem was a diagram which relates its proof to the smallest possible arithmetical numbers (see Plate 14).

74 Geometria est disciplina magnitudinis immobilis, formarumque descriptio contemplativa, per quam uniuscuiusque termini declarari solent (*Margarita philosophica* [1583], p. 390).

75 See pp. 78–79, above.

[76] *De inventoribus Geometriae et vocabulo eius.* Geometriae disciplina primum ab Aegyptiis reperta dicitur, quod, inundante Nilo et omnium possessionibus limo obductis, initium terrae dividendae per lineas et mensuras nomen arti dedit. Quae deinde longius acumine sapientium profecta et maris et caeli et aeris spatia metiuntur. Nam provocati studio sic coeperunt post terrae dimensionem et caeli spatia quaerere: quanto intervallo luna a terris, a luna sol ipse distaret, et usque ad verticem caeli quanta se mensura distenderet, sicque intervalla ipsa caeli orbisque ambitum per numerum stadiorum ratione probabili distinxerunt. Sed quia ex terrae dimensione haec disciplina coepit, ex initio sui et nomen servavit. Nam geometria de terra et de mensura nuncupata est. Terra enim Graece γῆ vocatur, μέτρα mensura. Huius disciplinae ars continet in se lineamenta, intervalla, magnitudines et figuras, et in figuris dimensiones et numeros (*Etymologiae,* III.x).

[77] In addition to other references cited in these paragraphs on the regular solids, see Timaeus of Locri, *De mundi anima,* tr. Stanley, *History of philosophy,* p. 568; Nemesius, *The nature of man,* tr. George Wither (London, 1636), pp. 246–247; Reisch, *Margarita philosophica* (1583), pp. 404–406; Charles de Bouelles, *Liber de mathematicis corporibus* in *Liber de intellectu* (Paris, 1510), fol. 185–192; *ibid.,* 192ᵛ–196ᵛ; Agrippa, *Occult philosophy,* tr. Freake, pp. 254–255; Finé, *Protomathesis,* M6ᵛ–N2ᵛ; Pietro Crinito, *De honesta disciplina* [XIII.10] (Basle, 1532), p. 206; Jean Cousin, *Livre de perspective* (Paris, 1560); Ingpen, *Secrets of numbers,* p. 93; Mersenne, *L'Harmonie universelle,* pp. 343–344; Stanley, *History of philosophy,* p. 550; Dacier, *Life of Pythagoras,* pp. 72–73; Joannes Albertus Fabricius, *Bibliotheca Graeca,* 11 vols. (Hamburg, 1790–1808), I.791; Zeller, *Greek Philosophy,* I.436–438; Leopold von Schroeder, *Pythagoras und die Inder* (Leipzig, 1884), pp. 59–66; Eva Sachs, *Die fünf Platonischen Körper* (Berlin, 1917); Heath, *History of Greek Mathematics,* I.158–162; A. E. Taylor, *A Commentary on Plato's Timaeus* (Oxford, 1928), pp. 358–378; Heath, *Manual of Greek Mathematics,* pp. 106–109; Thomas, *Greek Mathematics,* pp. 216–225, 467–479; S. Sambursky, *The Physical World of Late Antiquity* (London, 1962), pp. 29–34; Ernst Bindel, *Pythagoras* (Stuttgart, 1962), pp. 173–179; and Guthrie, *Greek Philosophy,* I.266–271.

[78] Proclus, *Commentary on Euclid, Book I* in Thomas, *Greek Mathematics,* p. 149. Cf. Francesco Barozzi, *Cosmographia* (Venice, 1585), h5ᵛ.

[79] I have translated all quotations in this paragraph from *Harmonices mundi libri V* (Linz, 1619), Book II, pp. 58–59.

[80] "Opin. of Phil." [II.vi] in *Morals,* tr. Holland (1603), p. 819.

[81] III.70.

[82] *Eclogae,* I.xxi.

[83] Translated by Billingsley as Book XVI of his Euclid, *Elements* (London, 1570).

[84] *Elements,* fol. 319ᵛ–320.

[85] But see Kircher, *Musurgia universalis,* II.376–379. Cf. also Andreas Cellarius, *Harmonia macrocosmica* (Amsterdam, 1661), p. 79; and John Heydon, *The harmony of the world* (London, 1662), pp. 75–76.

[86] Propositum est mihi, Lector, hoc libello demonstrare quòd Creator Optimus maximus, in creatione Mundi huius mobilis, & dispositione Coelorum, ad illa quinque regularia corpora, inde à Pythagora & Platone, ad nos usque celebratissima respexerit, atque ad illorum naturam coelorum numerum, proportiones, & motuum rationem accommodaverit (p. 6).

[87] Esp. Book I, pp. 2–22; Book II, pp. 57–60; and Book V, pp. 180–187. Cf. Kepler, *Epitome astronomiae Copernicanae* (Linz, 1618), pp. 457 ff. See also

Dietrich Mahnke, *Unendliche Sphäre und Allmittelpunkt* (Halle, 1937), pp. 129–144; Gerald Holton, "Johannes Kepler's Universe: Its Physics and Metaphysics," *American Journal of Physics*, 24 (1956), 340–351; Bindel, *Pythagoras*, pp. 185–198; and my article, "Pythagorean Cosmology and the Triumph of Heliocentrism" in *Le soleil à la renaissance* (Presses universitaires de Bruxelles, 1965), esp. pp. 44–52.

[88] For bibliography on this topic, see Conrad Gesner, *Pandectae* (Zurich, 1548), fol. 78; Fabianus Justinianus, *Index universalis* (Rome, 1612), p. 441; R. A. Peddie, *Subject Index of Books Published Before 1880* (London, 1933), "circle squaring"; *ibid*., Second Series (London, 1935), and Third Series (London, 1939). For secondary materials, see Guido Pancirolli, *The History of Many Memorable Things Lost* (London, 1715), pp. 377–383; Vossius, *De universae mathesios natura*, p. 72; Jean Etienne Montucla, *Histoire des recherches sur la quadrature du cercle* (Paris, 1754); Ernest W. Hobson, *"Squaring the Circle": A History of the Problem* (Cambridge Univ. Press, 1913); Heath, *History of Greek Mathematics*, I.220–235; and Marshall Clagett, *Greek Science in Antiquity* (London, 1957), pp. 183–184.

[89] *De vita Pythagorae*, xviii.

[90] The treatise of Giovanni Campano of Novara was edited by Luca Gaurico and first printed as *Tetragonismus idest circuli quadratura* (Venice, 1503); that of Nicholas of Cusa was edited by Johann Schoener and was first printed as *De quadratura circuli* (Nuremberg, 1533). The treatise of Charles de Bouelles is "Liber de circuli quadratura" in LeFèvre d'Etaples, *Introductio in libros arithmeticos Boetii* et al. (1503), fol. 85–87[v]; reprinted as an appendix to Gregor Reisch, *Margarita philosophica* (Strasbourg, 1515), and later editions. The work of Oronce Finé is *Quadratura circuli, tandem inventa & clarissimè demonstrata* et al. (Paris, 1544), and Jean Borrel's treatise is *De quadratura circuli libri duo* (Lyons, 1559).

[91] On these characteristics of the circle, see for a representative statement Agrippa, *Occult philosophy*, tr. Freake, p. 253.

[92] Michael Maier, the Rosicrucian, attributes this dictum to Pythagoras; cf. *De circulo physico, quadrato: hoc est, auro* (Oppenheim, 1616), p. 13. Sir Thomas Browne formulates it in Latin (Sphaera, cuius centrum ubique, circumferentia nullibi) and attributes it to Hermes Trismegistus (*Religio Medici* [I.x] *and Other Works*, ed. L. C. Martin [Oxford, 1964], p. 10). See Martin's note on this passage, *ibid*., pp. 290–291, where this definition of God is traced to a pseudo-Hermetic text of the twelfth century, *Liber XXIV philosophorum;* cf. Marie-Thérèse d'Alverny, "Appendix I" in *Catalogus translationum et commentariorum: Medieval and Renaissance Latin Translations and Commentaries, Volume I*, ed. Paul O. Kristeller (Catholic Univ. of America Press, 1960), p. 152. For a renaissance explanation of it, see Mersenne, *L'Harmonie universelle*, pp. 75–76; and Theophilus Gale, *Philosophia generalis* (London, 1676), pp. 41–42. For a modern treatment of it, see Mahnke, *Unendliche Sphäre*, pp. 173–175. For the statement of it which underlies renaissance thought, see Nicholas of Cusa as discussed by Ernst Cassirer, *The Individual and the Cosmos in Renaissance Philosophy*, tr. Mario Domandi (New York, 1964), pp. 27–28; cf. Wittkower, *Architectural Principles*, p. 25. For the many literary mutations of this motif, see Georges Poulet, *The Metamorphoses of the Circle*, tr. Carley Dawson and Elliott Coleman (Johns Hopkins Press, 1966). John Heydon, another professed Rosicrucian, depicted God geometrically as a triangle inscribed within a circle and defined Him as "the *Idea* of absolute perfection":

> Some antient Philosophers . . . have defined *God to be a Globe of Light, a Circle whose Centre is every where and Circumference no where*, by

> which description certainly nothing else can be meant, but that the Divine Essence is every where present with all those Adorable Attributes of Infinite and absolutely perfect Goodnesse, Knowledge, and Power

(*Harmony of world*, pp. 23–24).

[93] That the square emblematizes the material world and the circle emblematizes the spiritual world was carried over into human geometry (see p. 193, below). A famous drawing by Leonardo da Vinci shows a human figure inscribed within a square superimposed upon the same figure with outstretched limbs inscribed within a circle (reproduced, among many places, in Wittkower, *Architectural Principles*, facing p. 12). When the figure is considered in relation to the circle, his navel is the center of the diagram; when considered in relation to the square, his sexual organs fill the central position. The conclusion to be drawn from this visual image is obvious.

[94] With these lines Donne begins his ode "Upon the translation of the Psalmes by Sir *Philip Sydney*, and the Countesse of Pembroke his Sister."

[95] Nicholas of Cusa explains the dichotomy between the intelligible world and the sensible world in just these terms; cf. Cassirer, *Individual and Cosmos*, p. 22.

[96] See Carolus Bovillus (i.e., de Bouelles), "Liber cubicationis spherae" in LeFèvre d'Etaples, *Introductio in libros arithmeticos Boetii* et al. (1503), fol. 87v–89v; reprinted as an appendix to Gregor Reisch, *Margarita philosophica* (Strasbourg, 1515), and later editions.

[97] See discussion of the tetrad, pp. 158–176, below.

[98] *Commentary on Euclid, Book I* in Thomas, *Greek Mathematics*, pp. 175–177. Cf. Plato, *Republic*, 526D–527C; and Dee, "Mathematicall praeface" in Euclid, *Elements*, tr. Billingsley, a2v.

[99] Astronomia est recta lex & regula, suorum corporum magnitudines & motus considerans. Corpora autem superiora, coelos & astra intelligamus (*Margarita philosophica* [VII.ii] [1583], p. 460). Cf. Plato, *Republic*, 528D–E.

[100] *Republic*, 529C–D, quoted in Thomas, *Greek Mathematics*, p. 15.

[101] This is the mode of reasoning employed by those scientists of the last hundred years who "filled in" the periodic table of chemical elements.

[102] Tempus, solis motus, progressionis mensura (*Liber de Platonis definitionibus* in Iamblichus, *De mysteriis* et al., tr. Marsilio Ficino [Venice, 1497], V8). The date of the *Liber de Platonis definitionibus* is uncertain and may be quite late. The attribution of the text to Speusippus was made by Ficino. Formerly it had circulated under Plato's name.

[103] See Diogenes Laertius, VIII.25. Cf. Plates 20 and 21. For materials on Pythagorean geocentric astronomy in addition to those cited on p. 55, see Martianus Capella, *De nuptiis Philologiae et Mercurii*, Book VIII; Isidore of Seville, *Liber de responsione mundi & astrorum ordinatione* (Augsburg, 1472); Georg Peurbach, *Theoricae novae planetarum* (Nuremberg, 1474?); Jacques LeFèvre d'Etaples, *Introductorium astronomicum*, ed. Jodocus Clichtoveus (Paris, 1517); Franciscus Maurolycus, *Cosmographia* (Venice, 1543); Pontus de Tyard, *L'Univers* (Paris, 1557); Brucker, *Historia critica philosophiae*, I.1061–1063; Jean Sylvain Bailly, *Histoire de l'astronomie ancienne*, 2nd ed. (Paris, 1781), pp. 207–223; Sir George C. Lewis, *An Historical Survey of the Astronomy of the Ancients* (London, 1862), pp. 122–136; Pierre Duhem, *Le système du monde*, 5 vols. (Paris, 1913–17), I.5–27; Sir Thomas Heath, *Aristarchus of Samos* (Oxford, 1913), pp. 48–51; Baccou, *La science grecque*, pp. 125–134; B. L. van der Waerden, *Die Astronomie der Pythagoreer* (Amsterdam, 1951); Guthrie, *Greek Philosophy*, I.289–295; and Philip, *Early Pythagoreanism*, pp. 110–122.

[104] Asserunt insuper duodecim orbes in coelo esse, & primum quidem &

remotissimum firmamentum, ubi & summus Deus, caeterique intelligentia praediti Dii, ut vocat Aristoteles, aut secundum Platonem Ideae. Deinde septem planetae sequuntur, Saturni, Jovis, Martis, Veneris, Mercurii, Solis & Lunae, post planetas ignis, mox aër, quem sequitur aqua, omnibus ultima subest tellus. Duodecim orbium firmamentum causa est prima: & quanto quodque illi vicinius, tanto etiam firmius & melius esse aiunt & quae longius absunt, non ita firma sunt, & usque ad Lunam hic ordo servatur, infra Lunam minime. Necessarie vero omnia mala terra sustinet, quandoquidem instar fundi totum mundum sustinet, & receptaculum necessarium est eorum, quae in imo subsistunt

(*Myriobiblon* [1653], col. 1315). For the arrangement of the planets, cf. Plato, *Timaeus*, 38D.

[105] Statuimusque Terram omnino immobilem in medio Universi. . . . Copernicanum igitur omnino rejicimus (*Iter exstaticum coeleste*, 2nd ed. [Herbipolis, 1660], p. 39; cf. pp. 20–22). Cf. also Alexander Ross, the prominent English scholar, who in 1646 published *The new planet no planet* with this peevish subtitle: "Or, the earth no wandring star; except in the wandring heads of Galileans . . . and Copernicus his opinion, as erroneous, ridiculous, and impious, fully refuted."

[106] The names of the planets are in the genitive singular, because the nominative *orbis*, "sphere," is understood.

[107] In the diagram the designation *orbis signorum*, "the sphere of the zodiacal signs," appears above the *firmamentum stellatum* in a misleading fashion, though it applies to the *firmamentum stellatum*.

[108] Given the premise of a geocentric system such as this, the other nine celestial spheres make almost an entire revolution from east to west each day in keeping with the *primum mobile*, but not quite. Mercury, for example, makes 364/365 of a complete revolution from east to west each day, so that it has a net relative movement of 1/365 of a revolution in the opposite direction from west to east—thereby in effect making in 365 days (one year) a complete revolution from west to east. The Moon, to take another example, makes 27/28 of a complete revolution from east to west each day, so that it effectively completes a revolution from west to east in 28 days. And so on comparably for the other celestial spheres. The cristalline sphere, being nearest the *primum mobile*, is carried farthest by it, and therefore has the longest period of revolution in the opposite direction.

[109] Diogenes Laertius, VIII.25. See also Alexander Sardus, *De rerum inventoribus, libri duo* appended to *De moribus ac ritibus gentium lib. III* (Mainz, 1577), p. 15; and J. L. E. Dreyer, *History of the Planetary Systems from Thales to Kepler* (Cambridge Univ. Press, 1906), pp. 37–40.

[110] Cf. Plato, *Timaeus*, 33B.

[111] *De placitis philosophorum*, II.xxix.

[112] *Ibid.*, II.xii. Cf. Vossius, *De universae mathesios natura*, p. 149.

[113] Plutarch, *De placitis philosophorum*, II.xii, xxiii; III.xiv.

[114] For bibliography, see Fabricius, *Bibliotheca Graeca*, I.176–181.

[115] "Opin. of Phil." [II.xiii] in *Morals*, tr. Holland (1603), p. 821. Cf. Stobaeus, *Eclogae*, xxiv.

[116] "Opin. of Phil." [II.xxx] in *Morals*, tr. Holland (1603), p. 825.

[117] See Grant McColley, "The Seventeenth-Century Doctrine of a Plurality of Worlds," *Annals of Science*, 1 (1936), 385–430. See also Marjorie H. Nicolson, *A World in the Moon* (Northampton, Mass., 1936), *passim;* Arthur O. Lovejoy, *The Great Chain of Being* (Harvard Univ. Press, 1936), pp. 108–143; and Milton K. Munitz, "One Universe or Many?" *Journal of the History of Ideas*, 12 (1951), 231–255.

[118] Spenser points the way to undying optimism:

Why then should witlesse man so much misweene
That nothing is, but that which he hath seene?
What if within the Moones faire shining spheare?
What if in every other starre unseene
Of other worldes he happily should heare?
(*Faerie Queene,* II.proem.3.4–8)

[119] For other epithets applied to the central fire, see Stobaeus:

> In the middle at the center Philolaus places fire, which he calls the hearth of the universe, and the dwelling-place of Jove, and the mother of the gods, and the altar and the measure of nature.

> Philolaus ignem in medio ad centrum ponit, quem Universi larem vocat, Iovisque domicilium, ac deorum matrem, aramque & mensuram naturae

(*Eclogae* [I.xxi], tr. Willem Canter [Antwerp, 1575], p. 51).

[120] Cf. Aristotle, *Metaphysica,* 986a8–986a14.

[121] *On the Pythagoreans* is a lost work of Aristotle.

[122] Translated in Kirk and Raven, *Presocratic Philosophers,* pp. 259–260. The passage in Aristotle was widely known; see Dante, *Il convivio,* III.v.29–44, and Martin Cortes, *The arte of navigation,* tr. Richard Eden (London, 1561), fol. 8.

[123] "Opin. of Phil." [III.xi] in *Morals,* tr. Holland (1603), p. 830; cf. *ibid.,* III.xiii.

[124] "[Philolaus] was the first to declare that the earth moves in a circle" (Diogenes Laertius, VIII.85). For an imaginative modern analysis of Philolaus' system, see George B. Burch, "The Counter-Earth," *Osiris,* 11 (1954), 267–294.

[125] For materials on Pythagorean heliocentric astronomy, see Vossius, *De universae mathesios natura,* p. 150; Stanley, *History of philosophy,* pp. 536–537; Bailly, *L'Astronomie ancienne,* pp. 219–221, 446; Brucker, *Historia critica philosophiae,* I.1136–1140; Chaignet, *Pythagore,* I.213–254; Gomperz, *Greek Thinkers,* I.112–117; Heath, *Aristarchus,* pp. 94–120; Duhem, *Système du monde,* I.11–21; Heath, *History of Greek Mathematics,* I.162–165; Frank, *Plato und die sogenannten Pythagoreer,* pp. 207–209; Cherniss, *Aristotle's Criticism,* pp. 197–200, 393–397; Baccou, *Science grecque,* pp. 237–246; Antonie Pannekoek, *A History of Astronomy* (London, 1961), pp. 100–101; Stephen Toulmin and June Goodfield, *The Fabric of the Heavens* (London, 1961), pp. 72–74; Burkert, *Weisheit und Wissenschaft,* pp. 315–335; and Guthrie, *Greek Philosophy,* I.282–289.

[126] See *Academica priora,* xxxix. Cf. Diogenes Laertius, VIII.85.

[127] Plutarch, *De placitis philosophorum,* III.xiii.

[128] Fol. 3^{v}–4, translated in Dorothy Stimson, *The Gradual Acceptance of the Copernican Theory of the Universe* (Hanover, N.H., 1917), pp. 111–112.

[129] See my article, "Pythagorean Cosmology and Triumph of Heliocentrism," esp. pp. 39–43.

[130] Manilius, *The sphere,* tr. Sherburne (London, 1675), pp. 132–133.

[131] For examples of those who saw Copernicus as reviver of the Pythagorean system, see Johann Kepler, *Mysterium cosmographicum* (Tübingen, 1596), A1^{v}; Didacus à Stunica, "An Abstract . . ." in *Mathematical collections and translations,* tr. Thomas Salusbury, 2 vols. (London, 1661), I.468; Paolo Antonio Foscarini, "An Epistle . . ." in *ibid.,* I.473; Galileo Galilei, *Dialogue Concerning the Two Chief World Systems,* tr. Stillman Drake (Univ. of California Press, 1962), p. 341; Antonius Deusingius, *De vero systemate mundi dissertatio mathematica* (Amsterdam, 1643), pp. 4–5; Ismael Bullialdus, *Astronomia philolaica* (Paris, 1645), p. 16; Pierre Gassendi, *Institutio astronomica*

(Paris, 1647), pp. 155–156; Joseph Moxon, *A tutor to astronomie and geographie* (London, 1659), Appendix, pp. 23–24, 35; Kircher, *Iter exstaticum coeleste*, p. 38; and Stanley, *History of philosophy*, p. 537. The classic study of this thesis is E. A. Burtt, *The Metaphysical Foundations of Modern Physical Science* (New York, 1932), esp. pp. 37–44; see also Mahnke, *Unendliche Sphäre*, pp. 127–129; Thomas W. Africa, "Copernicus' Relation to Aristarchus and Pythagoras," *Isis*, 52 (1961), 403–409; and Edward Rosen, "Was Copernicus a Pythagorean?" *Isis*, 53 (1962), 504–509.

[132] See F. R. Johnson and S. V. Larkey, "Thomas Digges, the Copernican System, and the Idea of the Infinity of the Universe in 1576," *Huntington Library Bulletin*, 5 (1934), 69–117.

2

Cosmos

Next to the theory of numbers, the belief in cosmos is the tenet which has been most closely associated with the Pythagorean school from its beginning. The one follows directly from the other, of course. If numbers are the ultimate constituents of reality which served as archetypes in the mind of the creating deity, then the creation must be ordered according to number.[1] Since the divine plan was conceived and executed by a rational godhead, its physical extension will demonstrate pervasive reason through the forms and relationships that comprise its structure. The concept of cosmos was devised to express this doctrine, and credit for the concept was invariably given to Pythagoras.

Pythagoras, as we have seen, invented the word *κόσμος*.[2] By Plutarch's account: "*Pythagoras* was the first who called the Roundle that containeth and comprehendeth all, to wit, the World, *κόσμον*: for the orderly digestion observed therein."[3] Diogenes Laertius cites another authority, now lost, to give weight to his testimony about the origin of the word: "The same Author [Favorinus] also tells us, that this *Pythagoras* was the first that gave the name of *κόσμος* to the whole Circumference of the Universe, to signify the Ornamental structure of it."[4]

The meaning of the word *cosmos* is complex, as we might expect of so inclusive a term, and Plutarch and Diogenes Laertius each suggests a component part. Plutarch speaks of the "orderly digestion" which it signifies—that is, the way it organizes the endless variety of the world in a systematic arrangement. Diogenes Laertius stresses the "ornamental structure" implied by the word—not just orderly design, but also beauty. Photius insists upon the same enriched meaning for *cosmos:* "Pythagoras was the first to name the heaven *κόσμος*, because it is perfect, and is embellished with all living creatures and with beautiful signs."[5] The notions of regularity and gracefulness, then, were integral to the concept of cosmos, as the renaissance well knew. In his first chapter, "What is the world?" (Quid mundus), the author of a mid-sixteenth-century cosmography makes this assertion:

> For the first time Pythagoras called this universal boundary of all things κόσμος, from the harmonious mixing and indeed the most beautiful arrangement by which it was set forth by God, the supreme artisan. For κόσμος means the coagmentation of things, disposed beautifully and well-ordered.[6]

The conception of cosmos clearly intends an organic whole which incorporates all the items of nature in a single scheme that is both orderly and beautiful. It conveys the notion of *universe* in its literal sense—"all things turning in unison," from L. *unus*, "one" + *versus*, past participle of *vertere*, "to turn about." Finally, it operates on both the conceptual level as the universal plan in the mind of God and on the material level as a physical system controlling sense-perceived nature.

The notion of cosmos can be expressed in various ways, as we shall see. Generally speaking, however, it comes down to two dominant motifs, which are quite distinct though interrelated. In one motif, cosmos is the reconciliation of opposites, *concordia discors*, a reconciliation in which the items retain their autonomous identity though they function coordinately or harmoniously in a stable system. The other motif postulates cosmos as a unity arising out of a multeity, *e pluribus unum*, a condition which subjugates, even sublimates, the individual items, so that the parts exist only as components of a larger whole. The first motif, the reconciliation of opposites, we may regard as an arithmetical or a geometrical operation, where the quantities (multitudes or magnitudes) are considered *per se*, primarily in relation to themselves. The second motif, unity out of multeity, we may regard as a musical or an astronomical operation, where the quantities (stationary or mobile) are seen primarily in relation to one another. Nevertheless, though the two motifs can be distinguished one from the other, they are interrelated. For unity to arise from multeity and be stable, all the items of multeity—indeed, the infinity of possibilities—must be incorporated in the final summation, and therefore opposites must be reconciled in the resultant unity. Cosmos is all-inclusive, exhaustive. It submits to expression by two motifs, however, because either the whole or its parts may be stipulated as its ultimate being. Cosmos comprises both synthesis and analysis.

During the renaissance, as at most times in our intellectual history, the longing for order was so strong that the belief in cosmos persisted despite all evidence to the contrary. The orthodox cosmology retained adherents because it was customary and optimistic. The alternative, an infinite universe, is largely unknowable and unpredictable—it cannot be neatly ordered. A celestial system that surrounds earth with boundless space makes no provision for heaven. It provides no place where we can attach the golden chain, no watchtower for the eye of providence. It is chaos come again. Robert Recorde, probably the most advanced scientist in mid-sixteenth-century England, was acquainted with Copernicus' work and with the Pythagorean authorities on heliocentrism whom Copernicus cites; in his textbook on astronomy, in fact, Recorde makes one of the earliest references to the Copernican hypothesis. But Recorde continued to hold tenaciously to a geocentric universe: "As for the quietnes of the earth I neede not to spende anye tyme in prooving of it, syth that opinion is so firmelye fixed in moste mennes headdes, that they accompt it mere madnes to bring the question in doubt." [7] Almost a century later—after Tycho, after Kepler, even after Galileo—David Person (a "Gentleman" of "Loghlands in Scotland," says the title page of his *Varieties*) can yet assert with confidence: "The heaven doth rolle still about this earth, . . . which (whatsoever fond conceit *Copernicus* had concerning the motion of it) yet remaineth firme and immovable." [8] With reason—or otherwise—renaissance thinkers sought to preserve the comfortable notion of cosmos.

And with increasing insistence and ingenuity the dogma of cosmos was proclaimed. The science of astrology, which presupposes the interrelationship of all things in our world and especially the interaction of planets and humans, was never more widely or fervidly practised than it was in the late renaissance. The science of alchemy was developed to its highest level of sophistication, so that seven stages were delineated for the opus, corresponding to the successive psycho-religious states of the alchemist as he sought the perfection of a microcosm.[9] There was a spate of essays in hexaemeral literature, the traditional paraphrase of the Book of Genesis—to name a few of the most prominent: Pico della Mirandola's *Heptaplus*, Tasso's *Le sette giornate*, Saluste du Bartas' *La sepmaine*—all of which painstakingly explain creation to preserve its continuity and comprehensiveness as a chronicle of cosmos. In the face of strange new worlds, there were equally strange societies—the Rosicrucians and later the Freemasons come immediately to mind. But these new societies were dedicated to perpetuation of the old belief in an animistic universe expressed in symbols which are often esoteric to the point of requiring mystical faith. When a tradition is threatened, its most devoted advocates appear; and the more the tradition is venerated, the more ardent its apologists. So was it with the doctrine of cosmos.

In the renaissance the conception of cosmos, whether *concordia discors* or *e pluribus unum*, was articulated in a variety of ways. Many metaphors which had flourished from earliest times continued in use to convey the idea of universal order: the golden chain by which the earth depends from heaven, the providential eye of God the caretaker, the cosmic dance of the elements and planets, the angelic hierarchies or the cohorts of gnomes and sylphs and ondines and salamanders, the world as an organism with bodily parts and a soul, the sun in his annual journey through the signs of the zodiac, the eight-chorded lyre of Pythagoras. Moreover, poets were free to devise their own metaphors for cosmos—for example, Homer in the *Iliad* encompasses all of human experience within the orb of Achilles' shield (XVIII.478–608), and Spenser in *The Faerie Queene* projects the court of Gloriana as a framework wherein each knight can exemplify his partial virtue to be subsumed in the inclusive virtue of Prince Arthur. Reassurance that order and justice prevail is a constant need in human affairs, and therefore a perennial theme in literature.

The idea of cosmos was articulated with the greatest clarity, however, in terms of the quadrivial disciplines. It is not surprising, of course, that mathematics lent itself to the explication of universal order since both the quadrivium and the idea of cosmos derived from a common source, the Pythagorean theory of numbers. Cosmos in its essentials is a mathematical concept, a concern for parts and the integrated whole, a relation of the diverse finite to the unified infinite. Cosmos is therefore best expressed in terms of the four mathematical disciplines, and it is formulated with increasing degrees of sophistication as we proceed from arithmetic to music and geometry and finally to astronomy.

Since arithmetic is the study of quantity as an aggregate of units, the statement of cosmos in terms of arithmetic must consequently rely upon whole numbers. The number 1, indivisible and self-consistent, is representative of cosmos itself. The number 2, however, allows division and therefore the establishment of contraries. According to Aristotle, the Pythagoreans had delineated a series of ten contraries in corresponding pairs: "Limit and the Unlimited, Odd and Even, Unity and Plurality, Right and Left, Male and Female, Rest and Motion, Straight and Crooked, Light and Darkness, Good and Evil, Square and Oblong."[10] A pair of contraries placed in opposition, however, do not submit to synthesis. The simplest statement of cosmos, in fact, requires at least three terms to permit an organic relationship between component parts. Put another way, 3 is the first number with spatial dimension, since the number 2 produces only a line ________, which does not permit internal organization. Put still another way, 1 is the monad, which is the principle of number rather than a number itself; 2 is the dyad, which represents the potential for extension but is no number itself; 3, therefore, is the first number with beginning, middle, and end. Arithmetic had specified ways of ordering three numbers—in technical parlance, of placing a mean between two extremes.[11] A mean—whether arithmetical, geometrical, or harmonic—brought the two extremes into a systematic relationship. It reconciled two opposites.[12]

Because of this pattern of a mean between two extremes, it was generally assumed that pairs of contraries were necessary for cosmos. Ocellus of Lucania, for example, argues that three conditions are required for our extended universe to be coherent: the presence of passive matter, the presence of contrarieties, and the presence of active forms. He explains why the contrarieties are essential to order:

> The second thing which is necessary, is the existence of contrarieties, in order that mutations and changes in quality might be effected, matter for this purpose receiving passive qualities, and an aptitude to the participation of forms. Contrariety is also necessary, in order that powers, which are naturally mutually repugnant, may not finally vanquish, or be vanquished by, each other. But these powers are the hot and the cold, the dry and the moist.[13]

When Macrobius needed to explain this point, he cited the *Timaeus:*

> We know, according to Plato (that is, according to the sanctuary of truth itself), that those bodies alone are closely held together which have a mean interposed between extremes to create a strong bond.[14]

The number 3 represents cosmos because the middle term can be a mean relating two extremes, and therefore it is a model for the reconciliation of opposites. Louis LeRoy applies the pattern to the universe at large in a chapter entitled, "How all things in the world are tempered and conserved by unlike, and contrarie things":

> In like maner is the Earth, and every other thing in the world tempered and conserved by things of dislike and contrarie qualitie. It is not then without cause, that nature is so desirous of contraries, making of them, all decency, and beautie; not of things which are of like nature. This kind of tempering is the cause, that such things as before were divers and different, do accord and agree together, to establish, intertain, and embellish one an other, the contrarietie, becomming unitie; and the discord concord; the enmitie amitie; and contention covenant.[15]

Discord, then, or at least dissimilarity, is a necessary condition for cosmos, as the number 3 demonstrates.

The concept of cosmos was implied not only by the number 3, but it unfolded also from the number 4. Four is the first number to produce a solid figure, a pyramid with triangular sides.[16] It is the first number to generate a three-dimensional form, thereby exhausting the possibilities of physical extension in our world. As corroborative evidence that 4 is the number of cosmos, there are only four elements.

Moreover—and this is the clincher—4 is genetrix of the decad; the sum of its component parts equals 10. We are most likely to express this fact by an arithmetical equation: $1 + 2 + 3 + 4 = 10$. The Pythagoreans, however, expressed it by a figure composed of points. This figure—or, as the Pythagoreans would say, "number"—reveals the special relationship between the decad and the tetrad and the monad, how each flows to the others. It was called the τετρακτύς in Greek and the *quaternion* in Latin, and was treated with utmost reverence, as Plutarch reports:

> He [Pythagoras] thought that the Denarie or Ten, was the absolute nature and perfection of numbers; for that all men, as well Greeks as Barbarians, count untill ten, and when they be thither come, they returne backe againe unto unitie: over and besides hee said: That all the power of ten, consisted within fower, and in a quaternarie; the reason is this: that if a man begin at one, and reckon on still, numbring upright unto foure, he shall make up ten; surpasse he once the quaternarie, he is gone beyond the denarie . . . insomuch as number collected by unities, resteth in ten; but the force and puissance thereof lieth in foure. The Pythagoreans therefore were wont to sweare by

> the quaternarie or number of foure, which they held to be the greatest oath that they could take.[17]

Iamblichus concurs that the tetractys was the sacred symbol by which Pythagoreans sealed their oaths. Although out of deference they refrained from swearing by Pythagoras himself, they invoked the authority of the master by citing the symbol of cosmos which he had devised:

> I swear by him who the tetractys found
> Whence all our wisdom springs, and which contains
> Perennial Nature's fountain, cause, and root.[18]

Hierocles argues that by calling upon the tetractys a Pythagorean "enters into the very Foundation of Theology, and manifestly demonstrates that the Quaternion, or Number of Four, which is the Source of the Eternal Order of the World, is nothing else than God himself, who has created all things." [19] The tetractys was held in such reverence by so many, in fact, that syncretists attempted to associate it with the sacred symbols of other religions. Iamblichus early identified it with the oracle at Delphi (*De vita Pythagorae*, xviii), while Johann Reuchlin saw it as the tetragrammaton, J[e]h[o]v[a]h, the four-lettered name of God among the Hebrews.[20] Christian apologists soon noted that the tetractys is an equilateral triangle and used it as a symbol of the Trinity (see Plates 40 and 43).

Hierocles in his *Commentarius in carmina aurea* stresses the fundamental importance of the tetractys:

> In a word, all things are comprised in the QUATERNARY, Elements, Numbers, seasons of the Year, and ages of Life. Neither can you name any thing which does not depend upon the QUATERNARY as its root and foundation. For as we said before, the QUATERNARY is the Producer and Cause of the Universe, the intelligible God, and the Author of the heavenly and sensible Gods.[21]

Drawing from the same tradition as Hierocles, Theon of Smyrna enumerates ten categories of being which are organized according to a quadripartite system (incidentally, pointing out also the interdependence of the numbers 10 and 4):

Numbers: 1, 2, 3, 4.

Magnitudes: point, line, surface (i.e., triangle), solid (i.e., pyramid).

Simple Bodies: fire, air, water, earth.

Figures of Simple Bodies: pyramid, octahedron, icosahedron, cube.

Living Things: seed, growth in length, in breadth, in thickness.

Societies: man, village, city, nation.

Faculties: reason, knowledge, opinion, sensation.

Parts of the Living Creature: body and the three parts of soul.

Seasons of the Year: spring, summer, autumn, winter.

Ages: infancy, youth, manhood, old age.[22]

After such statements by Hierocles and Theon, it became fashionable to list sets of things governed by the number 4. Symphorien Champier, for example, a prolific polymath of Lyons in the early sixteenth century, applied the principle of the tetractys to the various fields of learning. In a chapter heading, he asserts: "In every discipline, according to the Platonists, there are four basic principles"; and then he documents this claim:

> There are four basic principles in metaphysics: essence, being, power, and motion. There are four in mathematics: the point, the line, the plane figure, and the solid. There are four in physics: the seminal power of nature, the natural burgeoning, the mature form, and the fully completed.[23]

In each instance, Champier progresses by steps from potential to actuality. William Lilly, a seventeenth-century English polymath, is even more expansive in his enthusiastic praise for the number 4, gathering together a long list of quadripartite sets:

> The Pythagorians call it the perpetuall fountain of nature: for there are four degrees in the scale of nature, *viz.* to be, to live, to be sensible, to understand. There are four motions in nature, *viz.* ascendent, descendent, going forward, circular. There are four Corners in the heaven, *viz.* rising, falling, the midle of the heaven, and the bottome of it. There are four Elements under Heaven, *viz.* Fire, Aire, Water, and Earth; according to these there are four triplicities in Heaven: There are four first qualities under the Heaven, *viz.* Cold, Heat, Driness, and Moystness, from these are the four Humours, Blood, Flegm, Choller, Melancholy. Also the year is divided into four parts, which are the Spring, Summer, Autumn, and Winter; also the wind is divided into Eastern, Western, Northern, and Southern. There are also four rivers of Paradise, and so many infernall.[24]

The Scale.

The name of God with four letters.	יהוה				In the Originall world, whence the Law of providence.
Four Triplicities or intelligible Hierarchies.	Seraphim. Cherubin. Thrones.	Dominations. Powers. Vertues.	Principalities. Archangels. Angels.	Innocents. Martyrs. Confeſſors.	In the Intellectual world, whence the fatall Law.
Four Angels ruling over the corners of the world.	מיכאל Michael.	רפאל Raphael.	גבריאל Gabriel.	אוריאל Uriel.	
Four rulers of the Elements.	שרפ Seraph.	כרוב Cherub.	תרשיש Tharſis.	אריאל Ariel.	
Four conſecrated Animals.	The Lion.	The Eagle.	Man.	A Calf.	
Four Triplicities of the tribes of Iſrael.	Dan. Aſſer. Nephtalin.	Jehuda. Iſachar. Zabulun.	Manaſſe. Benjamin. Ephraim.	Reuben Simeon. Gad.	
Four Triplicities of Apoſtles.	Mathias. Peter. Jacob the elder.	Simon. Bartholemew. Mathew.	John. Phillip. James the younger.	Thaddeus. Andrew. Thomas.	
Four Evangeliſts.	Mark.	John.	Mathew.	Luke	
Four Triplicities of Signs.	Aries. Leo. Sagittarius.	Gemini. Libra. Aquarius.	Cancer. Scorpius. Piſces.	Taurus. Virgo. Capricornus.	In the Celeſtiall world, where is the law of nature
The Stars, and Planets, related to the Elements.	Mars, and the Sun.	Jupiter, and Venus.	Saturn, and Mercury.	The fixt Stars, and the Moon.	
Four qualities of the Celeſtiall Elements.	Light.	Diaphanouſneſs.	Agility.	Solidity.	
Four Elements.	אש Fire.	רוח Ayre.	מים Water.	עפר Earth.	In the Elementary, where the Law of generation and corruption is.
Four qualities.	Heat.	Moyſture.	Cold.	Dryneſs.	
Four ſeaſons.	Summer.	Spring.	Winter.	Autumne.	
Four corners of the World.	The Eaſt.	The Weſt.	The North.	The South.	
Four perfect kinds of mixt bodies.	Animals.	Plants.	Metals.	Stones.	
Four kinds of Animals.	Walking.	Flying.	Swimming.	Creeping.	

25. *The "scale" of the number 4*
This table compiles the several systems based on the number 4, such as the four elements, the four basic qualities, and the four seasons. Those items in the same column are correspondents—for example, Michael is correspondent to fire, heat, and

What anſwer the Elements, in Plants.	Seeds.	Flowers.	Leaves.	Roots.	
What in Metals.	Gold, and Iron.	Copper, and Tin.	Quickſilver.	Lead, & Silver.	
What in ſtones.	Bright, and burning.	Light, and tranſparent.	Clear, and congealéd.	Heavy, & dark.	
Four Elements of man.	The Mind.	The Spirit.	The Soul.	The body.	In the leſſer world, *viz.* man, from whom is the Law of prudence.
Four powers of the Soul.	The Intellect.	Reaſon.	Phantaſy.	Senſe.	
Four Judiciary powers.	Faith.	Science.	Opinion.	Experience.	
Four morall vertues.	Juſtice.	Temperance.	Prudence.	Fortitude.	
The ſenſes anſwering to the Elements.	Sight.	Hearing.	Taſt, and ſmel.	Touch.	
Four Elements of mans body.	Spirit.	Fleſh.	Humours.	Bones.	
A four-fold ſpirit.	Animall.	Vitall.	Generative.	Naturall.	
Four humours.	Choller.	Blood.	Flegme.	Melancholly.	
Four Manners of complexion.	Violence.	Nimbleneſs.	Dulneſs.	Slowneſs.	
Four Princes of divels, offenſive in the Elements.	סמאל Samael.	עזאזל Azazel.	עזאל Azael.	מהזאל Mahazael.	In the infernall world, where is the Law of wrath, and puniſhment.
Four infernal Rivers.	Phlegeton.	Cocytus.	Styx.	Acheron.	
Four Princes of ſpirits, upon the the four angels of the world.	Oriens.	Paymon.	Egyn.	Amaymon.	

summer. The tetragrammaton at the top suggests the divine origin of these correspondences as well as the cosmic perfection of these quadripartite systems.

Heinrich Cornelius Agrippa, *Three books of occult philosophy*, tr. John Freake (London, 1651), pp. 186–187.

There is literally no limit to the number of systems based on the number 4. Plate 25 shows the list compiled by Heinrich Cornelius Agrippa, in a mood of credulousness rather than skepticism.[25]

Another number which represented cosmos in the arithmetical fashion is 12, which of course may be considered as merely a sophistication of 4.[26] Just as there are 4 seasons, for example, there are 12 months, each season comprising 3 months. Or there are the 12 signs of the zodiac.[27] But these configurations of the number 12 return upon themselves, perfecting a circle, and therefore we are now within the province of geometry rather than arithmetic. The number 12 was also represented by one of the five regular solids, the dodecahedron. While each of the other regular solids was identified with one of the four elements, this geometrical figure with twelve equal pentagonal faces was taken as a symbol of the universe in its entirety. Again, 12 was the number of cosmos.[28]

A visual depiction of how 12 represents cosmos is offered in Plate 26, an illustration for the chapter on "Time" in Bartholomaeus Anglicus' *De proprietatibus rerum* (Lyons, 1485).[29] Around the outer edge are the signs of the zodiac arranged in a circle. Next are the 12 months, each represented by an appropriate occupation, which continue in cycles without beginning or end. The indication that this is a diagram of cosmos comes most evidently in the circle at the center. There a lady with flowers sits beneath green trees and a gentleman sits beside a fire beneath barren trees. The two half circles clearly contrast, yet complement one another exactly, and together form a perfect circle. The number 12 has been reduced to a reconciliation of two opposites: female/summer and male/winter. Out of the multeity 12 comes the complete unit, one year, which integrates the disparate parts into a single whole.

The discipline of music, which by definition depends upon relationships between whole numbers, provides a natural expression of cosmos. The diapason is a precisely delineated unit composed of discrete parts which are harmoniously arranged in a fixed order. Each part expressly relates to every other part and makes a distinct contribution to the whole. Moreover, the diapason, which represents the 2 : 1 proportion, can be repeated an infinite number of times along the open-ended continuum of sound—the proportions 3 : 1, 4 : 1, 5 : 1 and so forth *ad infinitum* are possible—so music provides a convenient way of relating the finite to the infinite, or better yet, of knowing the infinite through the finite.

One mathematical fact makes music a particularly apt discipline to demonstrate the reconciliation of opposites. The diapason cannot

26. *The signs of the zodiac and the twelve months arranged in a cosmic pattern*

In the outermost circle are the signs of the zodiac. Next are the twelve months, each represented by an appropriate activity. In the middle, the hemisphere containing the female figure conjoins the hemisphere containing the male figure to suggest the same self-sufficient synthesis of two contraries symbolized by the alchemical hermaphrodite. For continued use of this diagram, see *The kalendayr of the shyppars* (Paris, 1503), h7^{v}, and later editions.

Bartholomaeus Anglicus, *De proprietatibus rerum* (Lyons, 1485), R5.

be evenly divided. It expresses the proportion 2 : 1, and no mathematical mean of any sort can be inserted between these two numbers. The diapason can, however, be divided by the interval of either the diatesseron (the harmonic mean, 8, inserted between 6 and 12) or the diapente (the arithmetical mean, 9, inserted between 6 and 12.) In either instance, the result, though comprised of unequal parts, is harmonious. In consequence, the diapason can be said to reconcile the inevitably dissimilar, and therefore music is a demonstration of cosmos.[30] Gafori, shown lecturing to students in the frontispiece to his *De harmonia musicorum instrumentorum opus* (Milan, 1518), makes the classic statement of this motif: *Harmonia est discordia concors.*

The concept of cosmos could also be expressed in the continuous quantities characteristic of geometry, as we have seen when the number 12 takes the form of a circle composed of the zodiacal signs or of the twelve months. In somewhat the same vein, the expression of cosmos was sometimes achieved by a rather simplistic juxtaposition of geometric forms, each with its own symbolic intention. The total statement is then a summation of finite parts, each adding its bit of meaning to the whole. Plate 27 is an example of this sort of cosmic geometry. The diagram, a composite of several geometrical figures, each with its individual meaning, is labeled "A Pythagorean Emblem of the Universe."

However, the configuration for cosmos which was most ingenious and most common—indeed, almost synonymous with the term—was the tetrad, a geometrical interpretation of the number 4. Basically, the scheme is an arrangement of two pairs of opposites in a stable system—for example, hot-cold and moist-dry, or fire-water and earth-air, or choleric-phlegmatic and melancholy-sanguine. To speak mathematically, we can make two extremes harmonious—that is, reconciled in a continuum—by placing a mean between them. Two sets of extremes, however, require two means to be reconciled, but then the system is thoroughly durable. Devising such a scheme for cosmos was recognized as a Pythagorean achievement of prime importance. Hierocles declared: "The chief of his [Pythagoras'] Precepts was the Knowledge of the Quaternion that created all things."[31] John Hall translated the last phrase as "the Creative *Tetrad*," and John Norris as "the *All-productive* Quaternary,"[32] with reference of course to the tetractys, the figure which related the monad to the limiting decad through the number 4.

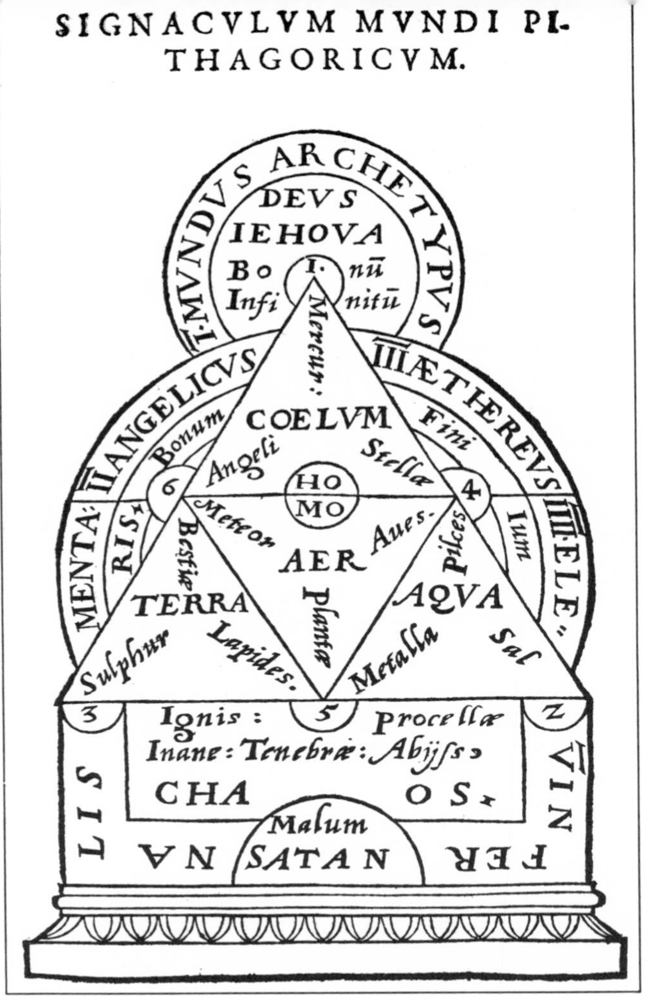

27. "*A Pythagorean emblem of the universe*"

Various geometrical forms with symbolic significance are conjoined in a cumulative fashion to produce a diagram of the universe in its entirety. At the top is a circle (I) representing the archetypal idea of the universe in the mind of Jehovah, Who is infinite and absolutely good. This archetypal idea is extended to a lower level of existence in the elementary world, represented by the lower circle, which is partly angelical (II) and partly etherial (III), but also partly composed of the four elements (IV). This world is good, but finite. The circle of the elementary world is further reduced to a triangle in the middle of the diagram, with mercury, salt, and sulphur (the three elements in the Paracelsan scheme) assigned to its corners. Disposed through the lower parts of this triangle are beasts, stones, atmospheric phenomena (meteora), birds, plants, metals, and fish. In a small circle at its center, reproducing the circular perfection of the macrocosm, rests man. The heavens, which contain the angels and the stars, occupy the portion of the triangle above him. At the very bottom of this diagram a rectangle represents the infernal region, which encompasses chaos and Satan. Chaos contains fire, storms, the void, darkness, and the abyss. Satan, represented by a half-circle to show his enormous deviation from the perfection which he once possessed, is absolutely evil, in contrast to the goodness of Jehovah.

Helisaeus Roslinus, *De opere dei creationis seu de mundo hypotheses* (Frankfurt, 1597), A1^{v}.

As we have noted, 4 is the proper number for cosmos because it is the first number with three-dimensional extension; geometrically speaking, it is the smallest number by which the full range of physical extension can be represented. The plainest verbal statement of the tetrad was also a commonplace: "All things are born from hot, cold, moist, and dry." [33] The intent, quite simply, was to arrange these four basic qualities in such a way as to explain the generation of the four elements—to demonstrate the autonomous existence of the elements and yet to allow their transmutation one into another. The four elements were regularly depicted in a physical context, of course, as stratified layers in an Aristotelian system, with earth, the absolutely heavy, at the bottom, then water and air, and fire, the absolutely light, at the top (see Plate 21). The tetrad, however, provides an arrangement of the elements to reveal the *conceptual* basis for their relationships. The tetrad is the simplest geometrical expression of the *idea* of cosmos.

Plato patiently explains the mathematics of the tetrad in the *Timaeus* (31B–32C). In the beginning, he says, God (θεός) started to construct the body (σῶμα) of the universe (πᾶν) from fire and earth—from fire to give his creation visibility and from earth to give it solidity and consequent tangibleness. But two items cannot maintain the cohesion necessary for cosmos without an intermediary to act as bonding agent:

> It is not possible that two things alone should be conjoined without a third; for there must needs be some intermediary bond to connect the two. And the fairest of bonds is that which most perfectly unites into one both itself and the things which it binds together; and to effect this in the fairest manner is the natural property of proportion (ἀναλογία). For whenever the middle term of any three numbers, cubic or square, is such that as the first term is to it, so is it to the last term,—and again, conversely, as the last term is to the middle, so is the middle to the first,—then the middle term becomes in turn the first and the last, while the first and last become in turn middle terms, and the necessary consequence will be that all the terms are interchangeable, and being interchangeable they all form a unity.

The mathematics of proportion are operative here. A mean is placed between two extremes to produce a conciliation of disparates.[34] This operation would suffice if only three terms were involved, if a plane figure were adequate to delineate the universe.

But of course it is necessary to organize four terms to justify its full-bodied extension as a solid with volume:

> Now if the body of the All had had to come into existence as a plane surface, having no depth, one middle term would have sufficed to bind together both itself and its fellow-terms; but now it is otherwise: for it behoved it to be solid of shape, and what brings solids into unison is never one middle term alone but always two. Thus it was that in the midst between fire and earth God set water and air, and having bestowed upon them so far as possible a like ratio (λόγος) one towards another—air being to water as fire to air, and water being to earth as air to water, —he joined together and constructed a Heaven (όυρανός) visible and tangible.

Between fire and earth—his starting materials, and incidentally the two extremes in the physical arrangement of elements—God placed two means, air and water. Two interlocking series of three terms each were consequently devised:

fire : air = air : water
air : water = water : earth
∴ fire : air = air : water = water : earth

In this way, as Bede explains in his "De natura rerum" (see Plate 28), the two extremes of fire and earth are reconciled in a four-part system. Plato concludes his exposition in the *Timaeus:*

> For these reasons and out of these materials, such in kind and four in number, the body of the Cosmos was harmonized (ὁμολογῆσαν) by proportion (ἀναλογία) and brought into existence. These conditions secured for it Amity (φιλίας), so that being united in identity with itself it became indissoluble by any agent other than Him who had bound it together.

Amity arises out of disparateness, stability out of diversity, and unity out of multeity. This synthesis is achieved, according to Plato, in a straightforward mathematical manner. The bonds between the elements are simple arithmetical means.

There was much more to the tetrad than that, however, more than a mere linear arrangement of the elements. What is needed, of course, is an arrangement whereby each element relates directly to every other element. As one would expect, the resultant system is considerably more complex, but still orderly and symmetrical. The next step in articulation of the tetrad is to ascribe the relationship

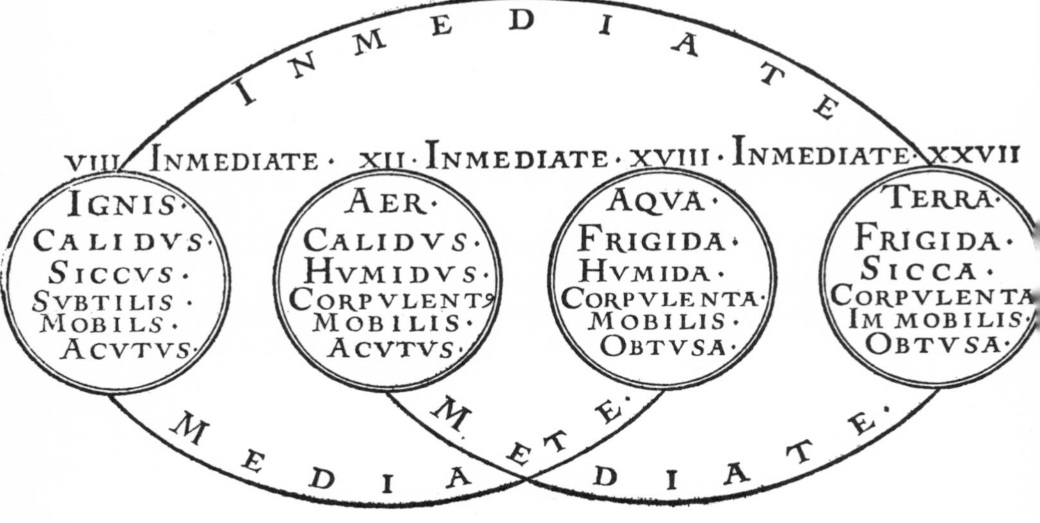

28. *The four elements arranged in arithmetical progression*

This diagram illustrates a passage which Bede cites from the *Timaeus* (32A-B, quoted on p. 160). Fire and earth, the physical extremes in the extended universe, are "inmediate"; they cannot be related by a mean. But fire and water are "mediate," and so are air and earth—that is, each pair can be related by a mean. By these two interlocking progressions with the resultant two means, the extremes of fire and earth, though "inmediate," can nonetheless be incorporated into a unified system.

The adjectives in each circle are qualities of that particular element; for example, fire is hot, dry, tenuous, mobile, and sharp.

The numbers above each element are more difficult to explain. The number 8 above fire is the cube of 2 (2 x 2 x 2), the limit of the even progression in the Platonic lambda (see pp. 210–211). The number 27 above earth is the cube of 3 (3 x 3 x 3), the limit of the odd progression in the Platonic lambda. Fire and earth, of course, are the two extremes in this arrangement. The number 12 above air represents a mean, derived by 2 x 2 x 3. The number 18 above water represents another mean, derived by 3 x 3 x 2.

Bede, "De natura rerum" in *Opera*, 8 vols. (Basle, 1563), II.5.

between adjacent elements not to mathematical proportion, but rather to the sharing of a common quality. For example, in the series *air* : *water* = *water* : *earth*, air and water share the quality "moist," while water and earth share the quality "cold." When the elements are plotted to demonstrate this sharing of qualities, a circular figure results. It is immediately apparent here that contraries are placed opposite one another in this scheme. In fact, every pair of schematic opposites is a pair of natural contraries as well: fire and water, earth and air, dry and moist, hot and cold. In consequence, between each pair of contraries there is an outward thrust which tends to disrupt the system—what Empedocles described as a primordial hate. By sharing qualities, however, the elements build up a force for stasis around the circumference of the figure—what Empedocles described as a primordial love. In this fashion, each element is held in a unified system and is related directly to every other element. For example, earth relates to water through the common quality "cold," to fire through the common quality "dry," and to air by being its opposite. This is *e pluribus unum*, as Spenser was aware:

EARTH
cold
dry
WATER
FIRE
moist
hot
AIR

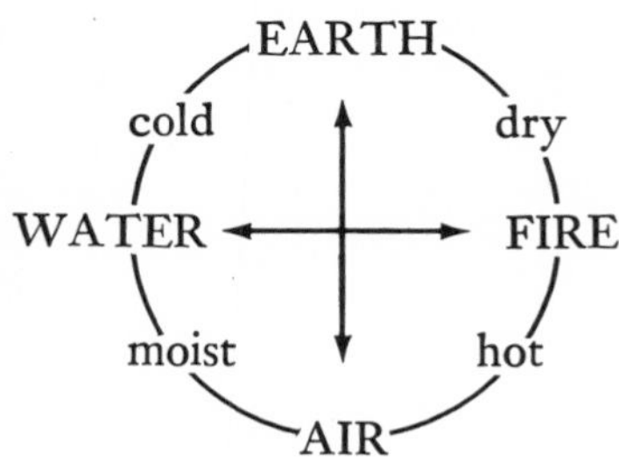

> . . . Water fights
> With Fire, and Aire with Earth approaching neere:
> Yet all are in one body, and as one appeare.
> (*Faerie Queene*, VII.vii.25.7–9)

Moreover, earth reconciles the opposites of water and fire, thereby producing *concordia discors*. In these terms, Manilius extolls the four elements:

> . . . All things they [the elements] compound,
> Applying Hot to Cold, to Humid Dry,
> To Heavy Light, which kind Discordancy
> The Matrimonial Bands of Nature knits.[35]

Edward Sherburne, the translator of Manilius, supplies a long marginal gloss on "kind Discordancy," citing Lactantius, Cassiodorus, Ovid, and the tetrachord of Orpheus.

Plate 29 is a simple illustration of the tetrad from a renaissance book, Agostino Nifo's commentary on Aristotle's *Meteorologica* (Venice, 1531). The four basic qualities are placed at the extremities of a cross to indicate their contrary relationships. The four elements are placed along the sides of the resultant square. The interaction of adjacent qualities to produce each element is indicated by the Latin verb, *constat*, "it stands in good order." A similar diagram, somewhat more finely articulated, appears in Oronce Finé's textbook of cosmography, *De sphaera mundi* (Paris, 1542) (see Plate 30). Notice that in these diagrams there is no such thing as physical space, dimensional space. Spatial arrangement is only apparent, not actual, an inevitable corruption when the idea is translated into visible terms. Space is designated only to represent a relationship between two portions of the concept. The diagram illustrates the *conceptual* reality of the four elements: their qualities, their mutual sympathies and antipathies, and their incorporation into a single stable system. In contrast, the spatial arrangement of the elements as a *physical* reality is illustrated in Plate 21.

Macrobius provides a representative discourse on the tetrad, remarkable for its clarity and completeness rather than for any originality. He begins quite properly with a critique of Plato:

> We know, according to Plato (that is, according to the sanctuary of truth itself), that those bodies alone are closely held together which have a mean interposed between extremes to create a strong bond. When that mean is doubled the extremes are bound not only firmly but even indissolubly. Now the number three is the first to have a mean between two extremes to bind it together, and the number four is the first of all numbers to have two means. Borrowing the means from this number the Creator of the universe bound the elements together with an unbreakable chain, as was affirmed in Plato's *Timaeus:* in no other way could the elements earth and fire, so opposed and repugnant to each other and spurning any communion of their natures, be mingled together and joined in so binding a union unless they were held together by the two means of air and water. For thus, in spite of the utter diversity of these elements, the Creator harmonized them so skillfully that they could be readily united.

But Macrobius expands upon Plato by inserting the four basic qualities as the bonds between adjacent elements:

29. *The tetrad deriving from the four basic qualities*
This diagram depicts the tetrad in its simplest form. At the four corners (marked A, B, C, D) the four basic qualities are placed, with contraries opposite one another—that is, with "hot" opposite "cold" and with "moist" opposite "dry." The opposition of contraries is indicated by the word *inconstat,* "it does not stand." Adjacent qualities interact to produce each of the four elements, placed between the qualities around a perimeter. For example, "hot" (A) and "moist" (B) interact to produce "air." This interaction is indicated by the word *constat,* "it does stand."

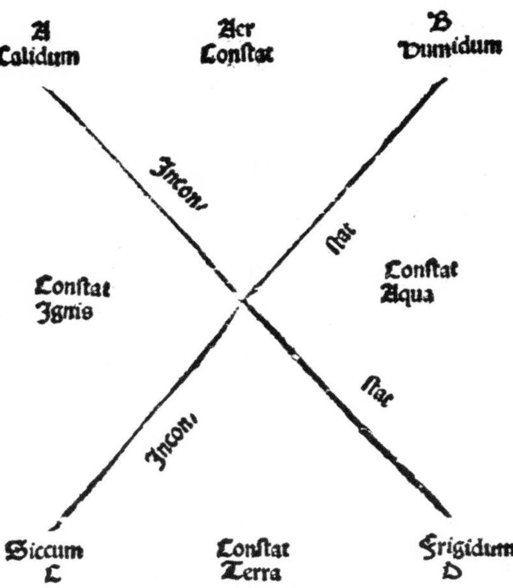

Agostino Nifo, *In libris Aristotelis meteorologicis commentaria* (Venice, 1531), fol. 3ᵛ.

---

30. *The tetrad of qualities and elements*
This diagram represents the tetrad in full development. It arranges the four elements in a conceptual scheme with fire at the top, water at the bottom, air on the right, and earth on the left. Each of these elements partakes of two among the four basic qualities: fire partakes of dryness and hotness, air of hotness and moistness, water of moistness and coldness, and earth of coldness and dryness, thereby completing the circle. For each element, one quality is dominant—i.e., *summa*—and one quality is recessive—i.e., *remissa;* for example, hotness is dominant in fire while dryness is recessive. Not only do elements partake of two qualities but, put another way, two adjacent qualities combine to form an element; for example, dryness and hotness combine to form fire, and this fact is indicated by the label, *combinatio possibilis.* But qualities that are opposite one another cannot combine—for example, dryness and moistness (the diagonal opposite of dryness) cannot combine—and this fact is indicated by the label, *combinatio impossibilis.* Similarly, an element can accord with its neighbor since they share a common quality, so that fire can accord with air, a compatibility that is labelled *simbolisantia.* But an element cannot agree with its opposite in the diagram—for example, fire cannot agree with water, a discord that is labelled *contraria.*

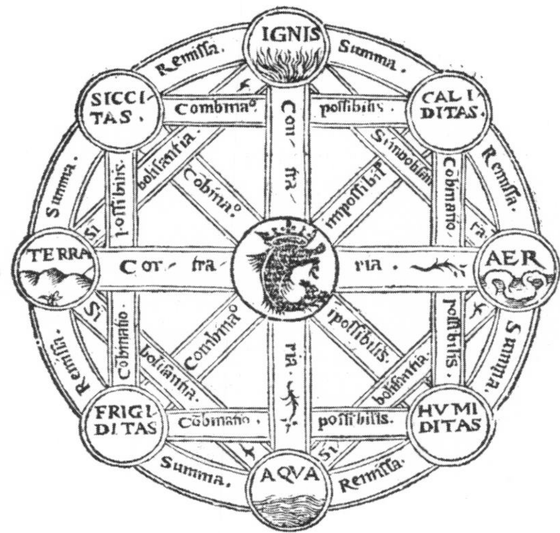

Oronce Finé, *De sphaera mundi* (Paris, 1542), fol. 2.

> To each of them [the elements] He gave two qualities, one of which was of such sort that each element would find this quality related and similar to itself in the element to which it adhered. Earth is dry and cold, and water cold and moist; but although these two elements are opposed, the dry to the wet, they have a common bond in their coldness. Air is moist and warm and, although opposed to water, the cold to the warm, nevertheless has the common bond of moisture. Moreover, fire, being hot and dry, spurns the moisture of the air, but yet adheres to it because of the warmth in both. And so it happens that each one of the elements appears to embrace the two elements bordering on each side of it by single qualities: water binds earth to itself by coldness, and air by moisture; air is allied to water by its moisture, and to fire by warmth; fire mingles with air because of its heat, and with earth because of its dryness; earth is compatible with fire because of its dryness, and with water because of its coldness. These different bonds would have no tenacity, however, if there were only two elements; if there were three the union would be but a weak one; but as there are four elements the bonds are unbreakable, since the two extremes are held together by two means.[36]

Like Plato, Macrobius emphasizes the stability of this system while at the same time it allows for an equitable transmutation among the elements.[37] With a similar purpose Milton in a hymn to God invokes the elements to join in the universal praise of creation:

> . . . Ye Elements the eldest birth
> Of Nature's Womb, that in quaternion run
> Perpetual Circle, multiform, and mix
> And nourish all things, let your ceaseless change
> Vary to our great Maker still new praise.
> (*Paradise Lost*, V.180–184)

The tetrad is an ingenious adaptation of Parmenidean stasis which, though permanent, still accommodates the flux insisted upon by Heraclitus. This is cosmos as dynamic equilibrium.

The tetrad as a mechanism of cosmos is operative at every level of creation and underlies every set of relationships between the items of nature. Hierocles is explicit on this point:

> The Tetrad cements al things that have any existence together, as the Elements, Numbers, Seasons of the year, and periods of Age. Neither are we to doubt that these flow not from the

31. *A tetrad interrelating the cosmoi of* mundus, annus, *and* homo

The world is comprised of the four elements, the year is comprised of the four seasons, and man is comprised of the four humours. At the top, fire, which partakes of the qualities dryness and hotness, is correspondent to summer and choler. On the right, air, which partakes of the qualities hotness and moistness, is correspondent to spring and blood. At the bottom, water, which partakes of the qualities moistness and coldness, is correspondent to winter and phlegm. On the left, earth, which partakes of the qualities coldness and dryness, is correspondent to autumn and black bile.

Isidore of Seville, *Liber de responsione mundi & astrorum ordinatione* (Augsburg, 1472), fol. b3[v].

> Tetrad as the root and spring: for the Tetrad, as we said before, is in the Creatour and cause of all things, the Intellectuall God, the Sonne of the Celestiall and Sensible God.[38]

Just as the four basic qualities interact to produce the four elements that comprise the world's body, they similarly produce the four humours that compose the body of man and make him a microcosm. Choler, for example, is hot and dry, blood is hot and moist, phlegm is moist and cold, black bile is cold and dry. In like fashion, the four qualities distinguish the four seasons which divide the year: summer is dry and hot, spring is hot and moist, winter is moist and cold, and autumn is cold and dry. The pattern of the tetrad is omnipresent, providing a common origin for all natural systems in the world, and thereby interrelating them. Isidore of Seville explains the exact correspondence between the cosmoi of the universe, the year, and man, for example, and an illustration in the first edition of his *Liber de responsione mundi* (Augsburg, 1472) makes abundantly clear the resultant complexity within this unity (see Plate 31). Late in the sixteenth century, Saluste du Bartas in "The Columnes" similarly describes "a foure-fold Consort in the humors, seasons, and Elements."[39]

A typical renaissance version of the tetrad which indicates these correspondences is provided by Johann Peyligk in the *Philosophiae naturalis compendium* (Leipzig, 1499) (see Plate 32).[40] At the corners are the four basic qualities. On the periphery of the tetrad the possible combinations of these qualities are indicated, while diagonally across the tetrad the impossibility of combinations is noted. The first combination, between hot and dry, produces fire, choler, summer, youth, and Subsolanus (the east wind). The second combination, between hot and moist, produces air, blood, spring, adolescence, and Auster (the south wind). The third combination, between moist and cold, produces water, phlegm, winter, old age, and Favonius (the west wind). The fourth combination, between cold and dry, produces earth, black bile, autumn, decrepitude, and Boreas (the north wind). The fifth combination, however, between dry and moist, is *impossibilis*, as is also the sixth combination between hot and cold. Such correspondences provide an inexhaustible reservoir of metaphors for poetry.

Lists of evident tetrads must have been an integral part of the Pythagorean doctrine from its inception. In extant writings, however—and we must remember that the early Pythagoreans were sworn to secrecy and oral communication—explicit delineation of

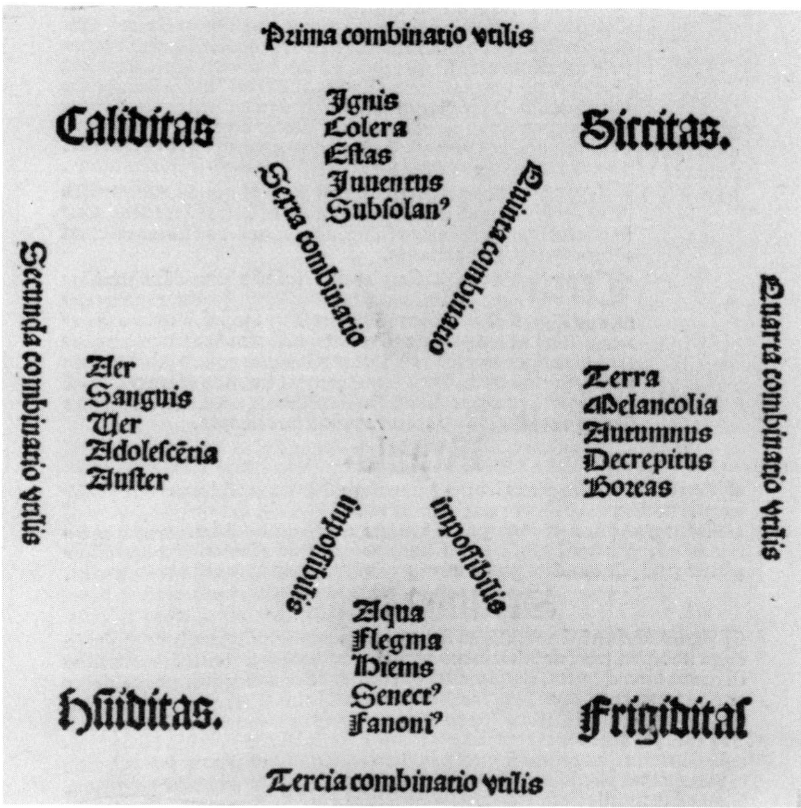

32. *A tetrad featuring the four basic qualities*

The four basic qualities—hotness, dryness, coldness, and moistness—are appropriately arranged as corners of a square. Each adjacent pair of qualities interacts to produce an element, and also one of the four humours, one of the four seasons, one of the four ages of man, and one of the four cardinal winds. Hotness and dryness at the top, for example, produce fire, yellow bile, summer, manhood, and the east wind Subsolanus. Dryness and coldness on the right produce earth, black bile, autumn, senility, and the north wind Boreas. Coldness and moistness at the bottom produce water, phlegm, winter, old age, and the west wind Favonius. Moistness and hotness on the left produce air, blood, summer, adolescence, and the south wind Auster. Thereby several quadripartite cosmoi are interrelated and made correspondent.

The interaction between dryness and moistness diagonally across the diagram, however, is a fifth combination which is not possible. Likewise, the interaction between hotness and coldness is "sexta combinatio impossibilis."

Johann Peyligk, *Philosophiae naturalis compendium* (Leipzig, 1499), fol. H1.

specific tetrads begins in the second century A.D. with the *Expositio rerum mathematicarum ad legendum Platonem utilium* by Theon of Smyrna, who explicated ten tetrads.[41] But from then on, the tetrad enjoyed a continuous and prolific tradition,[42] culminating for the renaissance in the elaborately diagrammed "Scale of the Number Four" in Agrippa's *De occulta philosophia,* which includes no less than thirty-one tetrads (see Plate 25).

Since the tetrad pattern is omnipresent, it was used in the renaissance to depict the first principle in many different fields of knowledge. As Pierre de la Primaudaye comments, "All the foundation of every deepe studie and invention, must be settled upon the number of fower, bicause it is the roote and beginning of all numbers."[43] In natural philosophy, the tetrad explained the arrangement of the four elements; in theology, it represented the symbiosis between Christ and the evangelists; in medicine, it balanced the four humours and differentiated the four ages of man; in psychology, it constituted the four faculties of the soul; in meteorology, it provided a wind rose (see Plate 33); in astrology, it organized the twelve signs of the zodiac into four seasons; and in alchemy, it showed how the philosophers' stone is the perfect center of the universe.[44]

The notion of the tetrad is often associated specifically with Empedocles, who was considered, even by himself, a Pythagorean. He designated four elements, giving them anthropomorphic identities to render them susceptible to love and hate. Diogenes Laertius, for instance, reports that Empedocles held these views:

> That there were four Elements of all things; *Fire, Water, Earth,* and *Air;* that Friendship and Concord united 'em together, and that Enmity and Discord kept 'em from Association. For thus he sings;
>
> *Jupiter* White, and *Juno* giving Life,
> Next Sooty *Pluto,* he the God Strife;
> And *Nestis* she that with corroding Tears
> Fills mortal Eyes, and still augments our Cares.
>
> Meaning thereby, that *Jupiter* is *Fire, Juno* the *Earth; Pluto* the *Air;* and *Nestis* the *Water:* which are always circling in continual changes, and never lye still, the Government and Interchangeable Order of all things being sempieternal.
>
> By Friendship all Things thus sometimes cement,
> Sometimes by Discord and Confusion rent.[45]

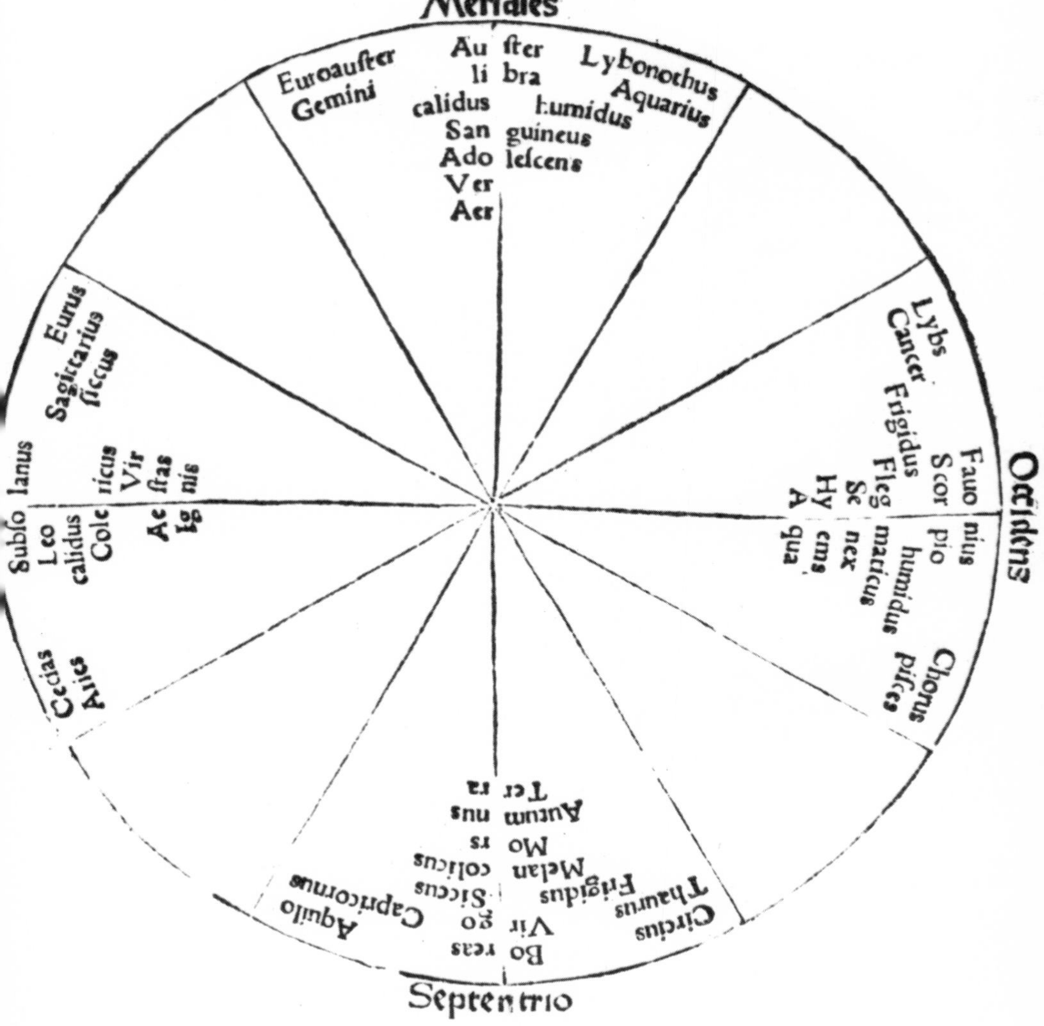

33. *A wind rose delineating the tetrad*

The basic intention of this diagram is to provide a wind rose of the winds which blow from the twelve points of the compass. In addition, it associates each of the four cardinal points of the compass with three signs of the zodiac, with two basic qualities, with one humour, with one age of man, with one season, and with one element. South at the top, for example, produces Euroauster (the southeast wind), Auster (the due south wind), and Lybonotus (the southwest wind). Each of these winds is associated with a sign of the zodiac: Gemini, Libra, and Aquarius, respectively. Furthermore, south is associated with hotness and moistness, with the bloody humour, with adolescence, with spring, and with air.

Aristotle, *Libri . . . meteororum .IIII.* et al., ed. Johann Eck (Augsburg, 1519), fol. 109v.

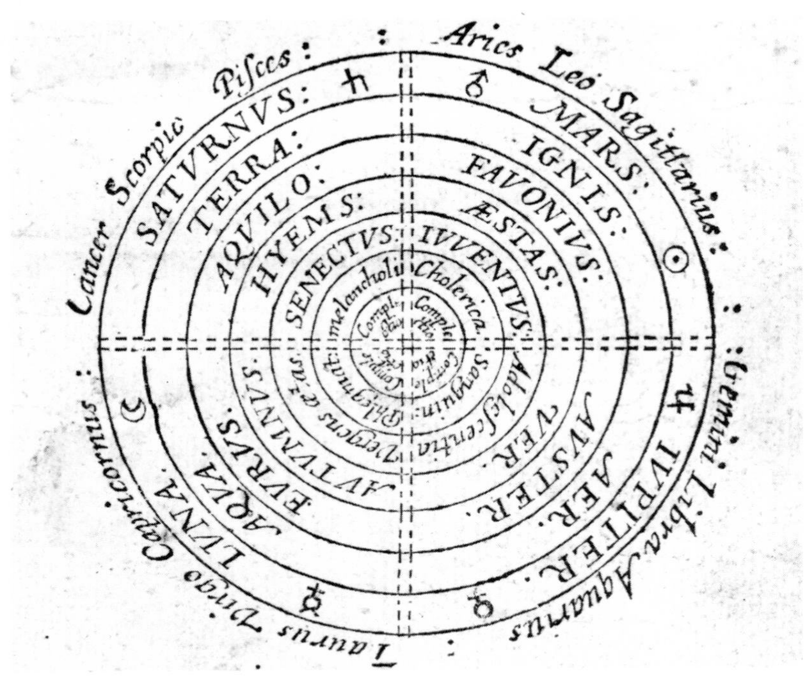

34. *A tetrad of humours, ages of man, seasons, winds, elements, planets, and zodiacal signs*

This diagram summarizes the information contained in Plates 29–33.

Robert Anton, *The philosophers satyrs* (London, 1616), title page.

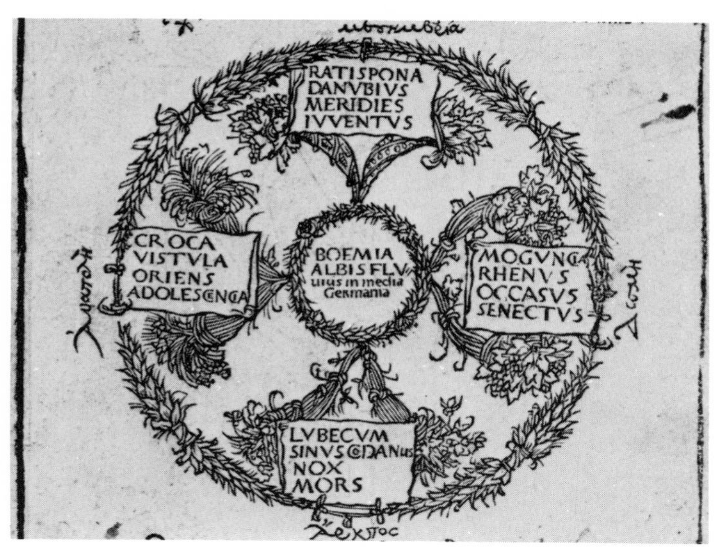

35. *A tetrad based on the four major cities in the geographical extremes of Germany*

The four major cities representing the south, west, north, and east of Germany are arranged opposite one another in a circle, and each city is associated with a body of water, a time of the day, and an age of man. Regensberg in the south (at top), for example, is associated with the Danube River, with noon, and with manhood. Mainz in the west (at right) is associated with the Rhine River, with sunset, and with old age. Lubeck in the north (at bottom) is associated with the Strait of Kattegat, night, and death. Cracow in the east (at left) is associated with the Vistula River, dawn, and adolescence. Furthermore, each city is identified by a particular crop, of which I can identify only two: grapes for Mainz and wheat for Cracow. In the center in its proper geographical position is Bohemia with the Elbe River. Finally, around the outside of the circle are the Greek names of the cardinal winds: Μεσημέρια, the south wind; Δισμή, the west wind; Ἄρκτο , the north wind; and Ἀνατολή, the east wind.

Conrad Celtis, *Quatuor libri amorum* (Nuremberg, 1502), title page.

Such an interpretation paved the way for poets to mythologize the elements (and so we find them, for instance, in the masques of Ben Jonson), and conversely to ascribe elemental qualities to the gods. La Primaudaye observes:

> The Poets, following his [Empedocles'] opinion, attributed the originall of things to etherian *Iupiter*, terrene *Pluto*, aërian *Iuno*, and to *Mestis* the beginning of the water, who (they said) nourished with her teares the rivers of the earth.[46]

We find a tetrad in this baroque form on the title page of George Sandys' translation of Ovid's *Metamorphosis* (Oxford, 1632) (see Plate 36). Although gods other than those designated by La Primaudaye may represent the elements, the intention of this visual image is the same as the verbal statement of the French encyclopedist. The splendid engraving in its four corners presents Jove as fire, Juno as air, Neptune as water, and Ceres as earth, with the pointed inscription: "All things take their origin from these" (Ex his oriuntur cuncta). An accompanying poem which gives "the minde of the frontispeece" begins:

> Fire, Aire, Earth, Water, all the Opposites
> That strove in *Chaos*, powrefull Love unites;
> And from their Discord drew this Harmonie,
> Which smiles in *Nature*.

The echoes of Empedocles are inescapable. With such a mixture of mythology, science, and aphoristic wisdom, the Pandora's box of iconography is opened.

One peculiar depiction of the tetrad deserves mention because of its strangeness and persistence. In the *Timaeus* Plato reports that the creating godhead first fashioned the gods and then turned over to them the task of fashioning the mortal creatures. Necessarily the gods populated the universe with creatures composed of the four elements:

> Imitating their own Maker, they borrowed from the Cosmos portions of fire and earth and water and air, as if meaning to pay them back, and the portions so taken they cemented together (43A).

In time, a tradition developed which associated each of the elements with a particular creature: fire with the salamander, air with the chameleon, water with the sturgeon, and earth with the mole or the camel. This tradition effloresced in the medieval bestiaries,[47] and continued to flourish in the renaissance. Milton, for example, play-

AD ÆTHERA VIRTUS
EX HIS
ORI—
DOCUIT QUE
OVID'S
METAMORPHOSIS.
Englished,
Mythologiz'd,
And
Represented
in figures
by
G. S.
MDCXXXII.
Francisco Clein Inv: Salamon Savery sculp:
formantur et
Amore
Sapientia
AFFIGIT HVMO DIVINÆ PARTICVLAM AVRÆ.
VNTVR
CVNCTA

36. *A tetrad of the four elements mythologized into deities*
In the upper-left corner is Jupiter representing fire, as the salamander indicates. In the upper-right corner is Juno with her peacock, and she traditionally represents air (in Greek, her name Ἥρα is an anagram for ἀήρ). In the lower-left corner is Ceres with a cornucopia and a bull representing earth. And in the lower-right corner is Neptune astride a sea-monster and representing water.
Ovid, *Metamorphosis,* tr. George Sandys (Oxford, 1632), title page.

ing the role of the pensive man, studies this lore by midnight oil and solemnly meditates upon

> . . . those Demons that are found
> In fire, air, flood, or under ground,
> Whose power hath a true consent
> With planet, or with element.
> ("Il Penseroso," 93–96)

Plate 37, the title page of an emblem-book entitled Μικροκόσμος, is a fine example of the sort of tetrad that Milton had in mind. Man, the microcosm, resides within a tetrad of four animals representing the four elements.[48] This arrangement, which incidentally makes man lord of creation, shows how he incorporates within himself the distinctive qualities of the four orders of lower animals.

A frequent metaphor for the tetrad is the cosmic dance, an orderly chorus wherein the four elements join hands and move in perpetual circle. La Primaudaye explicates the scientific basis of the metaphor:

> The elements are agreeable one to another, with their coupled qualities. . . . So that the fower elements are (as if each one of them had two hands, by which they held one another) as in a round daunce.[49]

Du Bartas expands the metaphor to its full dimension of lively and realistic detail:

> Water, as arm'd with moisture and with cold,
> The cold-dry Earth with her one hand doth hold;
> With th'other th'Aire: The Aire, as moist and warme,
> Holds Fire with one; Water with th'other arme:
> As Country Maydens in the Month of *May*
> Merrily sporting on a Holy-day,
> And lustie dauncing of a lively Round,
> About the May-pole, by the Bag-pipes sound;
> Hold hand in hand, so that the first is fast,
> By meanes of those betweene, unto the last.[50]

The cosmic dance has its *locus classicus* in an ancient text of impeccable authority. The detailed delineation of Achilles' shield in Book XVIII of the *Iliad*, a passage that George Chapman chose for individual translation and publication, is a pastiche of cosmic patterns, and it concludes with a description of a dancing scene (XVIII.590–605). Vulcan, the fabricator of this shield, has de-

37. *Man as microcosm, composed of four humours forming a tetrad in which the elements are represented by animals*

The roundness of the macrocosm is repeated in the roundness of the head of man, the microcosm. His bodily complexion of four humours is indicated by a tetrad of the four elements represented by animals: a chameleon for air, a salamander for fire, a mole for earth, and a sturgeon for water. Four winds blow from the four corners to reinforce the suggestion of completeness in small.

Μικροκόσμος *Parvus mundus* (Arnhem, c. 1609), title page.

picted on it "a dauncing maze," comparable (in the words of Chapman's translation) to "that in ages past/Which in brode Cnossus Daedalus did dresse/For Ariadne."[51] The scene is presented with graphic liveliness:

> There youthes and maids with beauties past compare
> Daunc't with commixed palms: the maids did weare
> Light silken robes, the youthes in coats were deckt
> Embroyderd faire, whose colours did reflect
> Glosses like oyle: the maides faire cronets wore,
> The youthes guilt swords in silver hangers bore:
> And these sometimes would in a circle meet
> Exceeding nimblie and with skilfull feet,
> Turning as round as doth a wheele new done,
> The wheelewright sitting trying how t'will runne.
> Then would they breake the ring and take their places
> As at the first.

Though Chapman may seem to be describing some contemporary masque, such as that in Act IV of Shakespeare's *Tempest,* he is in fact translating Homer rather closely.

Much in the spirit of this "dauncing maze" on Achilles' shield, actual ballets known in the renaissance as *danses figurées* attempted to display the order and beauty of the cosmic dance. These often informed a masque with their special meaning, as in Daniel's *Vision of the Twelve Goddesses.* In that royal pageant presented in 1604 by Queen Anne and her ladies, twelve dancers formed various figures which were "fram'd unto motions circular, square, triangular, with other proportions exceeding rare and full of variety," and they concluded by "casting themselves into a circle." The perfection of a circle is an appropriate resolution of the choral mutations which aim to glorify a "Temple of Peace . . . dedicated to unity and concord."[52] There is the inescapable sociological implication that each dancer by fulfilling her role contributes to the final order.

The metaphor of the cosmic dance conveyed a geometrical image of cosmos, but it included also the notion of music and recalled arithmetic by depending upon the whole number 4. It therefore drew upon arithmetic, music, and geometry for its referents while setting forth a cosmic theme. The most comprehensive representation of cosmos, however, was the concept of universal harmony—in its simplest form, the music of the spheres—and this concept embraced not only arithmetic, music, and geometry, but also astronomy. It was, in fact, the statement of cosmos to which each of the quadrivial sciences contributed coordinately.

The music of the spheres is one of our most complex traditions. It represents the concept of order as order prevails in the heavens, a divine plan that informs and controls our universe. It also provides the perfect pattern for art in any medium that purports to be true, the ideal of beauty in esthetics which provokes the most exquisite sensual response. It encompasses the full range of Pythagorean reality, from the highest celestial abstraction to the most affective of human experiences. Whenever that sweet harmony touches our lives, we are changed, improved, brought closer to divinity.

The music of the spheres is also one of our most ancient traditions. By Plato's time it had been fully formulated by the Pythagoreans, who treated it as a fundamental postulate in their science. In the last book of the *Republic* (616C–617B), recounting the famous vision of Er, Plato describes eight heavenly spheres whirling concentrically around the spindle of Necessity. On each sphere a siren sits, singing a single note of the diapason, and the eight together form a single harmony.[53] Aristotle, intentionally mistaking this doctrine as a statement of physical fact, denies the music of the spheres with obvious delight (*De caelo*, 290b12–291a27). But the idea nonetheless persisted because no other statement of cosmos conveyed its order and beauty with such imaginative completeness. The idea was soon articulated so finely that particular notes were assigned to the various spheres. With his usual attention to scientific preciseness, Pliny records:

> *Pythagoras* otherwhiles using the tearmes of musicke, calleth the space betweene the earth and the Moone a Tonus, saying, that from her to *Mercurie* is halfe a tone: and from him to *Venus* in manner the same space. But from her to the Sunne as much and halfe againe: but from the Sunne to *Mars* a Tonus, that is to say, as much as from the earth to the Moone. From him to *Iupiter* halfe a Tonus: likewise from him to *Saturne* halfe a Tonus: and so from thence to the Signifer Sphaere or Zodiake so much, and halfe again. Thus are composed seven tones, which harmonie they cal Diapason, that is to say, the Generalitie or whole state of concent and accord, which is perfect musicke.[54]

Plutarch similarly reports:

> Some attribute to the earth, the place of the musicall note Proslambanomenos: unto the moone Hypate: unto *Mercurie* and

> *Lucifer* Diatonos and Lichanos: the sunne they set upon Mese (they say) containing Diapason in the middes, distant from the earth one fifth or Diapente, and from the sphaere of the fixed starres a fourth, or Diatesseron.[55]

In this same vein, Nicomachus explains how the notes played by each planet received their names:

> From the motion of *Saturn,* which is the highest and furthest from us, the gravest sound in the diapason concord, is called *Hypate;* because ὕπατον signifieth *highest:* but from the Lunary, which is the lowest and nearest the earth, *neate;* for νέατον signifieth *lowest.* From those which are next these, *viz.* from the motion of *Jupiter* who is under *Saturn, parypate;* and of *Venus,* who is above the *Moon, paraneate.* Again, from the middle, which is the *Sun*'s motion, the fourth from each part, *mese,* which is distant by a diatessaron, in the Heptachord from both extreams according to the ancient way; as the Sun is the fourth from each extream of the seven Planets, being in the midst. Again, from those which are nearest the Sun on each side, from *Mars* who is placed betwixt *Jupiter* and the Sun, *Hypermese,* which is likewise termed *Lichanus,* and from *Mercury* who is placed betwixt *Venus* and the *Sun, Paramese.*[56]

The whole tradition is summed up by Macrobius at the beginning of Book II of his *Commentarius in somnium Scipionis* (esp. II.i.1–25, iv.1–10), and thereby it was transmitted to the middle ages.[57]

Very quickly the eight sirens that populate the spheres in Er's vision were conflated with the nine Muses of another tradition, so that soon the Muses presided over the celestial music. In his "Commentarie of the Creation of the Soule," Plutarch begins with a critique of Plato's theory and goes on to provide an accommodation for the discrepancy between eight sirens and nine Muses:

> [Plato] saith in his books of Common-wealth: That every one of the eight sphaeres hath a sirene sitting upon it, causing the same to turne about, and that ech one of them hath a severall and proper voice of their owne: but of altogether there is contempered a certeine harmonie. . . . But the more auncient sort have given unto us nine muses, to wit, eight as *Plato* himselfe saith, about the celestiall bodies, and the ninth about the terrestriall, called foorth from the rest to dulce and set them in repose, in stead of errour, trouble, and inequality.[58]

The earth, fixed at the center of the world, is called to play the lowest note in the universal harmony, thereby stabilizing the system and keeping the other bodies from wandering in error.

The entire system in its rich complexity is amply displayed in a woodcut illustrating Franchino Gafori's *Practica musice* (see Plate 38). Apollo at the top presides over a thoroughly musical universe. The planets are represented at the right by the appropriate god or goddess. A Muse also is assigned to each planetary sphere, with Thalia assigned to earth to provide a habitation for all nine. The note sounded by each planet and the intervals between planets (whether a full tone or a half tone) are carefully marked in every instance. This diagram should be compared to Plate 21, because it concentrates on the "eight-chorded lyre of Pythagoras."

The music of the spheres as heavenly harmony was easily generalized to a concept of universal harmony. To use Boethius' phrase, it became *musica mundana*. This is the interlocking complex of mathematical relationships that reaches throughout creation, binding together all the particulars of the universe from mute stones to the choirs of angels. There are extremes reconciled by means in the mode of arithmetic, harmonic proportions between disparate details in the mode of music, patterned configurations which organize dissimilar principles in the mode of geometry, and the regularized performance of moving parts in the mode of astronomy (see Plate 43).

The notion of universal harmony is implicit in Plato and even in Ptolemaeus, so that Plutarch can assert:

> *Pythagoras*, *Architas*, *Plato*, and all the rest of the old Philosophers doe hold that the motion of the whole world, together with the revolution of the starres, is not performed without Musicke: For they teach that God framed all things by harmonie.[59]

This is the assumption that Boethius articulates in the *De musica:*

> The music of the universe [*musica mundana*] is especially to be studied in the combining of the elements and the variety of the seasons which are observed in the heavens. How indeed could the swift mechanism of the sky move silently in its course? . . . Now unless a certain harmony united the differences and contrary powers of the four elements, how could they form a single body and mechanism? But all this diversity produces the variety of seasons and fruits, and thereby makes the year a unity.[60]

PRACTICA MVSICE FRANCHINI GAFORI LAVDENSIS.

MENTIS APOLLINEAE VIS HAS MOVET VNDIQVE MVSAS

APOLLO

EVPHROSINE

AGLAIA

THALIA

VRANIA · MESE · HYPERMIXOLYDIVS · CELVM STELLATVM

Tonus.

POLIHYMNIA · LYCHANOSMESON · MIXOLYDIVS · SATVRNVS

Tonus.

EVTERPE · PARHYPATEMESON · LYDIVS · IVPITER

Semitonium.

ERATHO · HYPATEMESON · PHRYGIVS · MARS

Tonus.

MELPOMENE · LYCHANOSHYPATON · DORIVS · SOL

Tonus.

TERPSICORE · PARHYPATEHYPATON · HYPOLYDIVS · VENVS

Semitonium.

CALIOPE · HYPATEHYPATON · HYPOPHRIGIVS · MERCVRIVS

tonus.

CLIO · PROSLAMBANOMENE · HYPODORIVS · LVNA

IGNIS · AER · AQVA · TERRA

THALIA

38. *The universe in its entirety arranged to demonstrate the music of the spheres*

Starting from the bottom, the diagram includes the four elements in spatial arrangement: *terra, aqua, aer, ignis.* Then rising in order are the spheres of the seven planets, and the sphere of fixed stars at the top, making a total of eight spheres in order to accommodate the eight musical notes of the diapason. The planets are labeled in the right-hand margin by both names and astronomical symbols, and are also indicated mythologically by the circular vignettes of the appropriate god or goddess. The intervals between planets are marked "tone" or "half-tone" in accordance with the statement of Pliny (*Historia naturalis,* II.xx; quoted p. 179). A musical mode for each planet is also indicated; for example, Mars plays in the Phrygian mode, Jupiter in the Lydian, and Saturn in the Mixolydian (cf. Pliny, *ibid.*). Each planet is also assigned a musical note, marked to the left of the three-headed dragon (which, though it doesn't have its tail in its mouth, symbolizes Time according to a passage from Macrobius' *Saturnalia**). Each celestial sphere is further identified with one of the Muses, depicted in the circular vignettes on the far left. To provide the necessary number of nine, earth is identified with Thalia at the bottom. Reigning over all, in the appropriate position of deity, is Apollo, attended by the three Graces and advertised by a banner which proclaims, "The power of the Apollonian mind completely controls these Muses." The intention is clear: each Muse, each note, each planet, though playing an individual part, contributes concordantly to a larger whole, represented in the single figure of Apollo.**

Franchino Gafori, *Practica Music*e (Milan, 1496), frontispiece.

* The heads of the dragon are those of a lion in front, representing the present, of a wolf on the left, representing the past, and of a dog on the right, representing the future; see Jean Seznec, *The Survival of the Pagan Gods,* tr. Barbara F. Sessions (New York, 1953), p. 120; and Erwin Panofsky, *Meaning in the Visual Arts* (New York, 1955), p. 158. For further discussion of Gafori's diagram, see Seznec, *ibid.*, pp. 140–142.

** In *The Enneads* Plotinus discusses "The One" as "the negation of plurality," and he reports: "The Pythagoreans found their indication in the symbol 'Apollo' (α = not; πολλῶν = of many) with its repudiation of the multiple" (tr. Stephen MacKenna, 3rd ed. [London, 1962], p. 408 [V.v.6]). For a repetition of this information, see Marsilio Ficino, *Théologie Platonicienne de l'immortalité des âmes* [IV.i], ed. Raymond Marcel, 2 vols. (Paris, 1964), pp. 154–155.

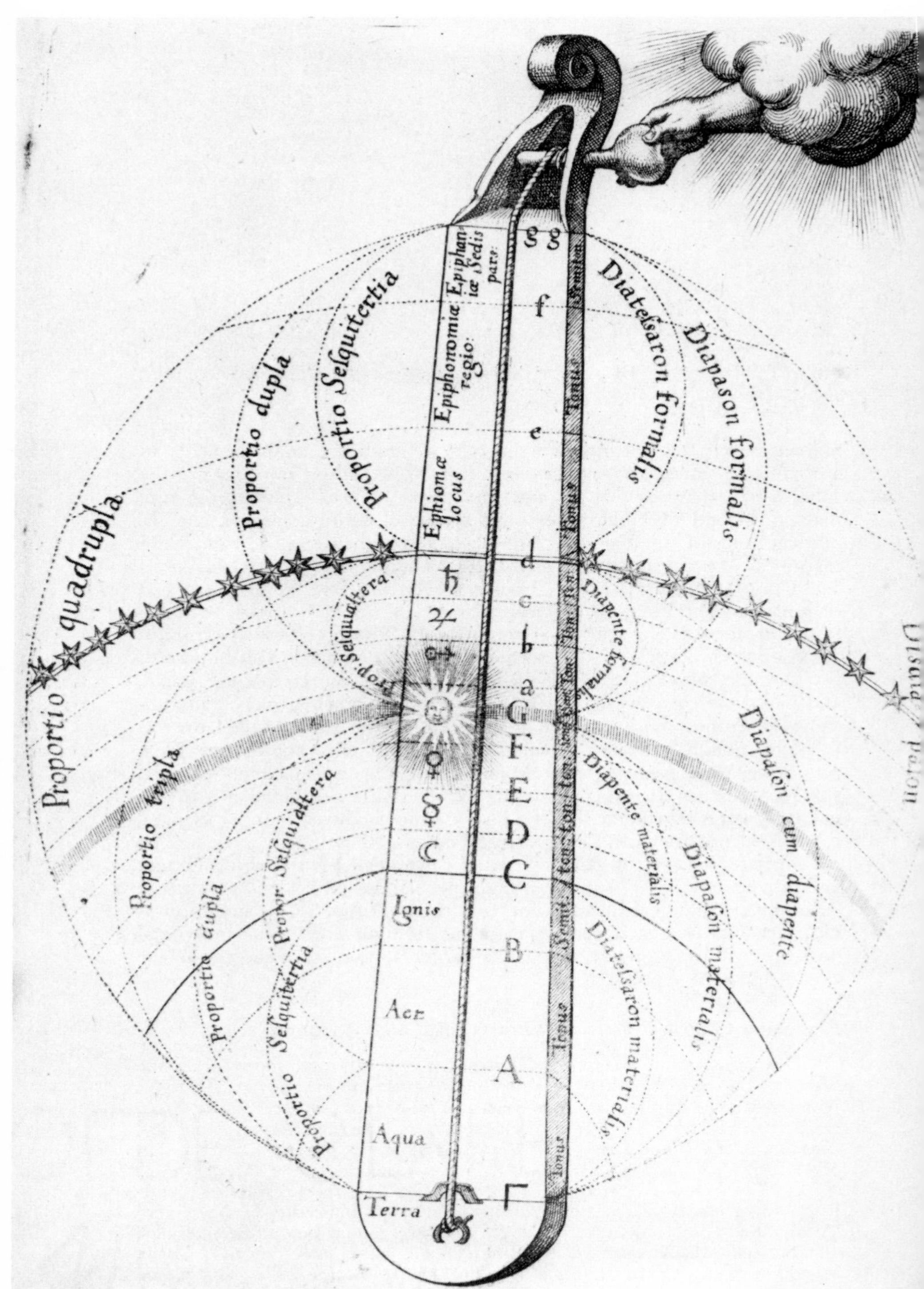

39. Musica mundana

39. Fludd gives the diagram this caption: "We set forth here quite precisely the monochord of the universe with its proportions, consonances, and intervals; and we show that its motive force is extra-mundane [i.e., a celestial hand]." The essential feature is a monochord stretching from the lowest to the highest in the universe, with the hand of God reaching from a cloud to tune it. There are fourteen intervals on the monochord which produce fifteen musical notes, corresponding to the "harmonic system of 15 chords" which, for example, Thomas Morley had described (see Plate 11). From the bottom, there are first the four elements (earth, water, air, and fire), then the seven planets (Moon, Mercury, Venus, Sun, Mars, Jupiter, Saturn), and the sphere of fixed stars, and finally the three angelic hierarchies (the place of the *ephioma*, the region of the *epiphonomia*, and part of the seat of the *epiphania*). The "material" diapason stretches from Earth to the sphere of the Sun; the "formal" (i.e., conceptual) diapason from the sphere of the Sun to the summit of the empyrean. These two taken together form a double diapason. Within each of these diapasons the fourth (diatesseron) and the fifth (diapente) are indicated. The "material" fourth stretches from the bottom through the four elements. The "material" fifth stretches from the sphere of fire to the sphere of the Sun. The "formal" fourth stretches from the sphere of the Sun to the sphere of fixed stars, including the planets Mars, Jupiter, and Saturn. The "formal" fifth stretches from the sphere of fixed stars through the empyrean. The appropriate musical notes are indicated by letters beside the monochord itself, and the intervals are marked as a full tone (*tonus*) or a halftone (*semitonus*). On the left are labeled the mathematical proportions —i.e., the sesquitertial proportion for the fourth, the sesquialteral proportion for the fifth, the double proportion for the diapason, the triple proportion for the diapason plus a fifth, and the quadruple proportion for the double diapason.

Robert Fludd, *Utriusque cosmi majoris scilicet et minoris metaphysica, physica atque technica historia*, 4 vols. (Oppenheim, 1617–19), I.90.

---

40. Fludd gives the diagram this caption: "A description of the universe according to the acceptable proportions of the monochord." At the top is a triangle representing the deity as the essence of trinal form. At the bottom is a circle representing the earth, the densest of substances. In between are two intersecting triangles. One triangle, labelled the *Pyramis Formalis* (the "Conceptual Pyramid"), has its base adjacent to the seat of deity and its apex on the earth. Its components, starting from the top and decreasing in magnitude, are "3. The highest and most formal region of the celestial empyrean inhabited by the highest hierarchy," "2. The middle region of the celestial empyrean assigned to the middle hierarchy," "1. The lowest region of the celestial empyrean appropriate to the lowest hierarchy," then the seven planets descending from Saturn through the Moon, and finally the four elements descending from fire to earth. The other triangle—not labeled, but surely the *Pyramis Materialis*—has the diameter of the earth as its base and its apex on the base of the *Pyramis Formalis*. Its components are in reverse order and of inverse magnitude relative to its counterpart, the *Pyramis Formalis*. Where the two triangles intersect is the *Sphaera aequalitatis* (the "circle of equality"), and there the relationship between materiality and conceptuality is in exact balance, an equal proportion. Significantly, the *Sphaera aequalitatis* coincides with the orbit of the Sun, which separates the *Diapason materialis* from the *Diapason formalis* in Plate 39.

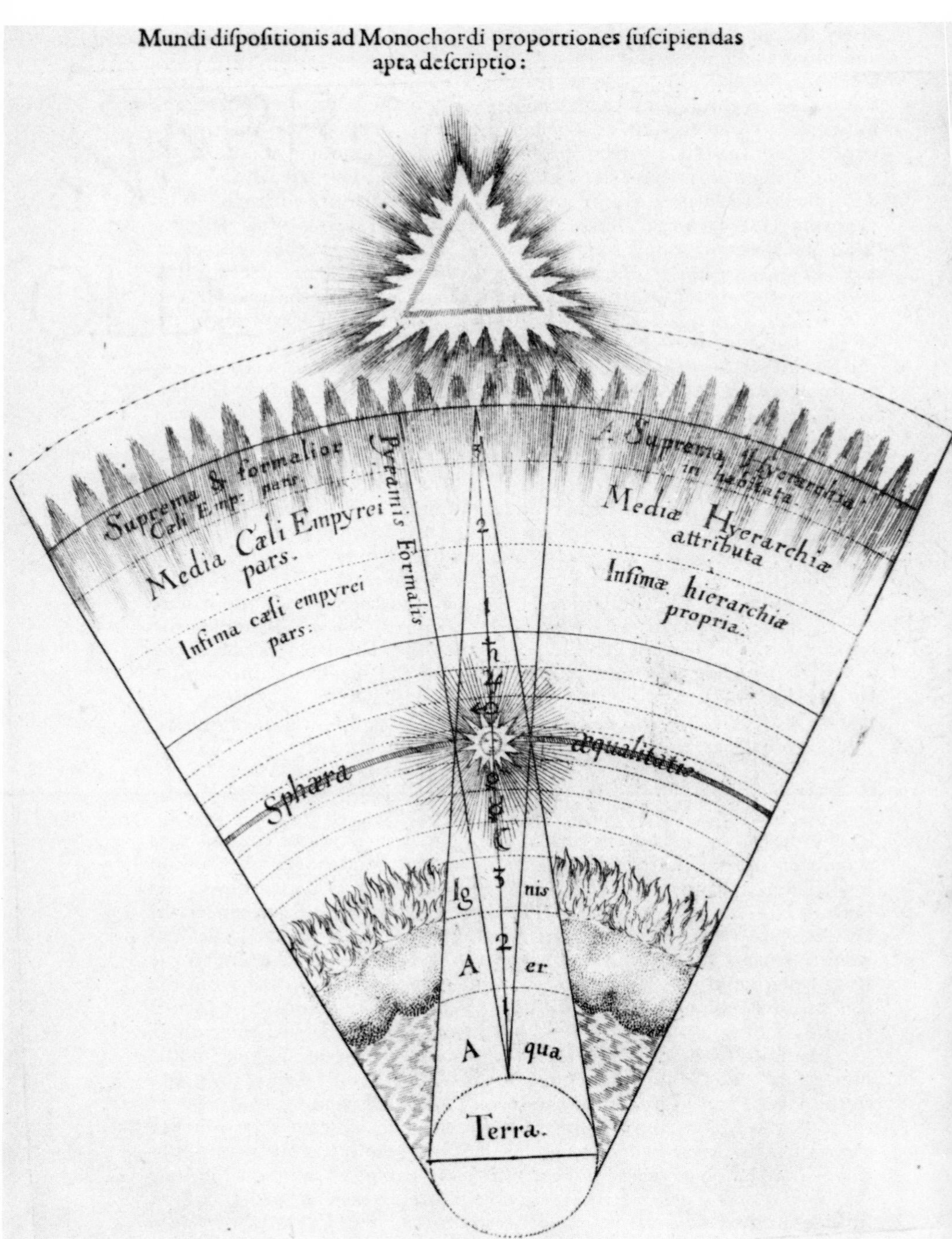

40. *A scheme of the universe showing geometrically by two intersecting triangles how materiality decreases as conceptuality increases, and vice versa*

Robert Fludd, *Utriusque cosmi majoris scilicet et minoris metaphysica, physica atque technica historia*, 4 vols. (Oppenheim, 1617–19), I.89.

This tradition served as an unexamined scientific premise for centuries. It also received exhaustive exposition in such renaissance works as Francesco Giorgio's *De harmonia mundi totius cantica tria* (Venice, 1525) and Antoine Mizauld's *Harmonia superioris naturae mundi et inferioris* (Paris, 1577). In the seventeenth century there was a continuing argument for universal harmony by renowned scientists such as Robert Fludd and Johann Kepler, and by ardent apologists such as Marin Mersenne, Athanasius Kircher, and John Heydon.[61]

Universal harmony as a musical paradigm of all creation is graphically depicted by Robert Fludd in Plate 39, which illustrates his *Utriusque cosmi majoris scilicet et minoris metaphysica, physica atque technica historia.* The categories of nature are arranged vertically on a monochord in rough correspondence to their physical stratification as perceived by our senses: the four elements at the bottom, then the eight heavenly spheres, and finally the three angelic hierarchies which comprise the empyrean. The diagram encompasses fifteen notes—two complete diapasons, one "material" and the other "formal." The sun sits appropriately in the middle, marking the highest note of the material diapason, which stretches upward from the lowest note played by earth. The sun also marks the beginning of the formal diapason, which stretches upward to the highest note of the monochord played by the seat of the Epiphanies. The implication, of course, is that both the "formal" and the "material" diapasons are tuned by the same harmonies. Plate 40 from the same text demonstrates how conceptuality increases and materiality decreases as one goes from bottom to top along the "universal monochord." The monochord stretches from absolute materiality to absolute conceptuality, and the ulterior intention of Pythagorean doctrine was to accomplish that ascent.

The *musica mundana* was repeated, of course, in the human body, producing there a responsive counterpart that Boethius called *musica humana.* This was the basis of the prevalent analogy between the microcosm of man and the macrocosm. The analogy was exact in every detail, both physical and intellectual. In Plate 41, for example, Fludd depicts the microcosmic harmony, which correlates closely with Plate 39; and in a diagram analogous to Plate 40, Fludd indicates how man increases in spirituality and decreases in sensuality as one ascends from the genitals to the head (see Plate 42). The ascent in this instance is introspective, though it follows a comparable route and arrives at the same celestial destination as the ascent through the physical universe. Conversely, the physical journey

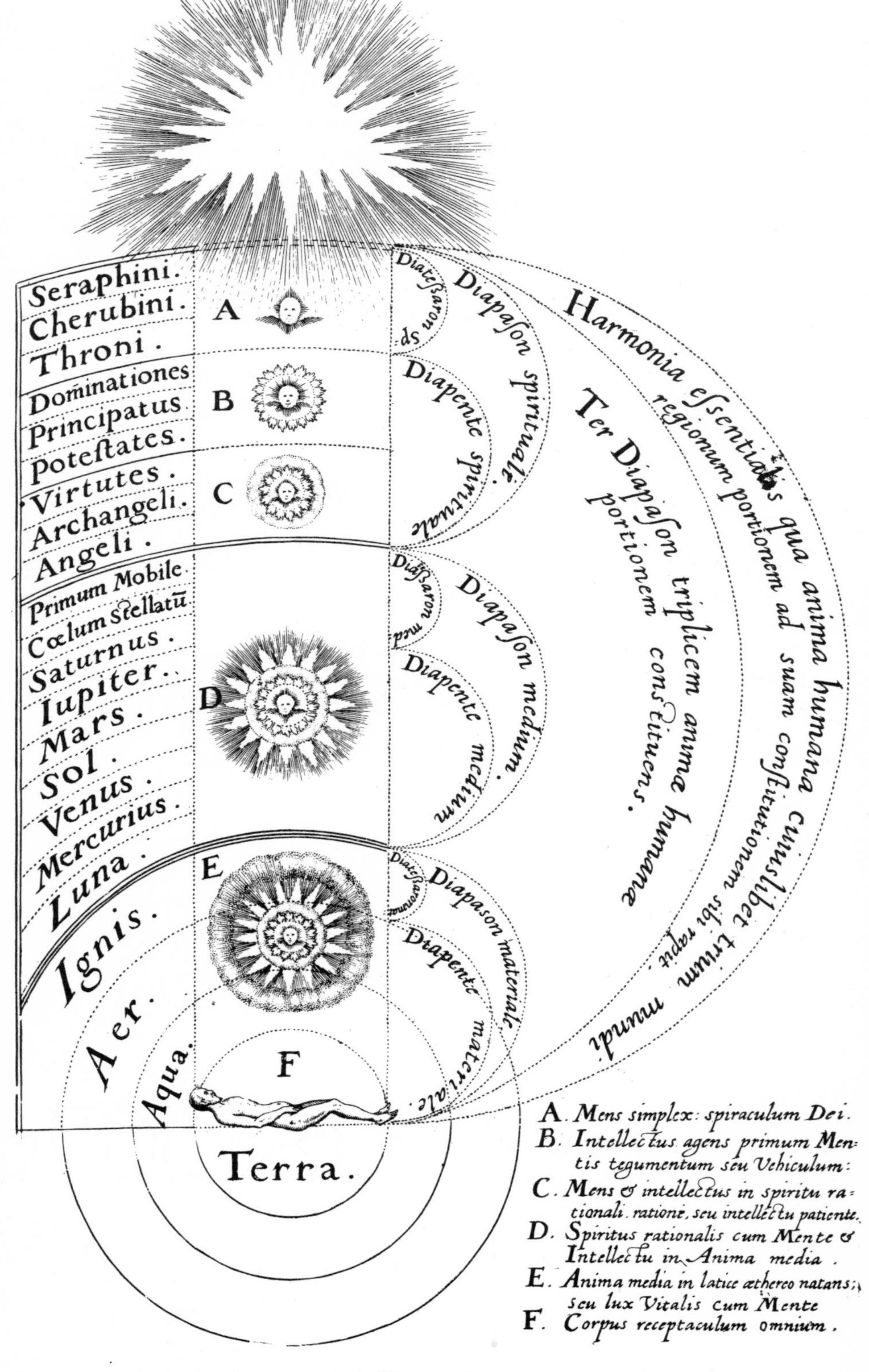

Seraphini.
Cherubini.
Throni.
Dominationes
Principatus.
Potestates.
Virtutes.
Archangeli.
Angeli.
Primum Mobile.
Cœlum Stellatū.
Saturnus.
Iupiter.
Mars.
Sol.
Venus.
Mercurius.
Luna.
Ignis.
Aer.
Aqua.
Terra.
A
B
C
D
E
F
Diatessaron sp.
Diapason spirituale.
Diapente spirituale
Diatessaron med.
Diapason medium.
Diapente medium
Diatessaron mat.
Diapason materiale
Diapente materiale
Harmonia essentialis qua anima humana cuiuslibet trium mundi regionum portionem ad suam constitutionem sibi rapit.
Ter Diapason triplicem anima humana portionem constituens.
A. Mens simplex: spiraculum Dei.
B. Intellectus agens primum Mentis tegumentum seu Vehiculum:
C. Mens & intellectus in spiritu rationali. ratione, seu intellectu patiente.
D. Spiritus rationalis cum Mente & Intellectu in Anima media.
E. Anima media in latice æthereo natans; seu lux Vitalis cum Mente
F. Corpus receptaculum omnium.

41. Musica humana (*cf. Plate 39*)

through the heavenly spheres, a favorite motif in literature from Cicero to Donne, is only a metaphor for the inward search for absolutes. Both quests have cosmic order as their goal, the one being objective and the other subjective. In poetry of the highest quality—such as Dante's *Divina commedia* and Spenser's *Fowre Hymnes*—the goal is achieved coordinately by both the objective and the subjective routes.

The notion of man as "a little world made cunningly," to use Donne's phrase,[62] is one of our most cherished and persistent metaphors. In duration it ranges all the way from Plato to Pope. In seriousness it ranges all the way from the tear-floods and sigh-tempests of Donne's Petrarchan lover to the mathematical science of "anthropography" solemnly defined by John Dee.[63] The microcosm-macrocosm analogy was early associated with Pythagoras, as Photius records in his entry for Pythagoras:

---

41. The harmonies of microcosmic man are set forth as three diapasons. There is a "material" diapason comprising the three elements above earth, a "middle" diapason comprising the nine heavenly spheres, and a "spiritual" diapason comprising the nine angelic hierarchies. At the side a label informs us: "Three times the diapason marking the threefold division of the human soul." Another label proclaims: "The essential harmony by which the human soul takes for its own arrangement the division of any cosmos, just so it has three parts." The numerical building blocks in this structure are 3 and 9, and the effective harmony is the ratio $\frac{9}{3}$. Fancifully, the diapason is determined by the proportion $\frac{3}{1}$; the diapente is marked as the proportion $\frac{2}{1}$ and the diatesseron as $\frac{3}{2}$. Decreasing degrees of spirituality are indicated by letters as the soul descends from the deity at the top to the human body at the bottom, and a table in the lower right identifies each step:

A. pure mind; the spirit of God
B. the intellect setting in motion the topmost portion or *primum mobile* of the mind
C. mind and intellect in the rational spirit, which allows reason or intellect
D. the rational spirit, with mind and intellect in the middle soul
E. the middle soul swimming in ethereal fluid; or the vital light within the mind
F. the body, which is the receptacle for all things

Robert Fludd, *Utriusque cosmi majoris scilicet et minoris metaphysica, physica atque technica historia*, 4 vols. (Oppenheim, 1617–19), III.93.

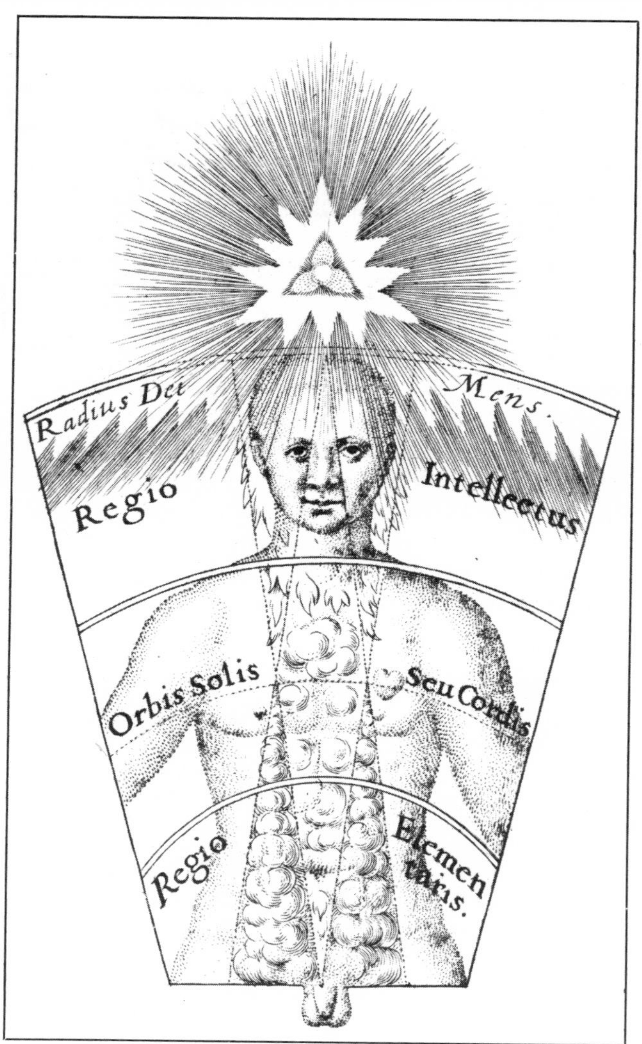

42. *A scheme of the microcosm showing geometrically by two intersecting triangles how sensuality decreases as spirituality increases, and vice versa* (*cf. Plate 40*)

The microcosm is stratified into three regions: 1) "the intellectual region," 2) a middle region through which runs "the sphere of the sun or heart," and 3) an "elemental region." At the top is the divine spirit, labeled "the light of God, the mind"; at the bottom are human genitals. The place of equilibrium between sensuality and spirituality is "the sphere of the sun or heart." Johann Reuchlin provides a moral gloss for the diagram: "As to intellect, man approaches nigh to God; as to inferior senses, he recedeth from God: Reason teaching us *what to imbrace*, when it converts it self to the mind, renders us blessed; when perverted by the senses, wretched" (*De arte cabalistica libri tres*, tr. Thomas Stanley, *The history of philosophy*, 2nd ed. [London, 1687], p. 574).

Robert Fludd, *Utriusque cosmi majoris scilicet et minoris metaphysica, physica atque technica historia*, 4 vols. (Oppenheim, 1617–19), III.83.

> Man is said to be a μικρόκοσμος (that is, a compendium of the universe) not because he consists of four elements like the other animals, even the lowest; but rather because he embodies all the qualities of the universe. There are in the world the gods, the four elements, animals, and plants, and man possesses all of these potencies. He has reason through a divine-like quality. Through the natural efficacy of the elements he has the ability to move, to grow, and to reproduce himself.[64]

Man held a central position in the chain of being, serving as nexus between the world of spirit and the world of matter. As such, he subsumed the virtues of the lower orders—the stones, plants, and animals—while at the same time he participated through his reason in the intellectual life of the empyrean. In keeping with the account of creation in Genesis, man is the summation of God's handiwork.[65]

It is difficult for us to appreciate the potency of this notion that man is a compendium of creation or to accept the literalness with which it was applied. It came to the renaissance out of the middle ages in a fully developed form:

> The body humayne is of the foure elementes y[e] which ben the erthe, the water, the ayre, and the fyre, so y[t] the flesshe answereth unto erthe, the blode unto the water, the wynde the ayre, and y[e] heete naturall unto the fyre. And know thou also . . . that the man is made unto the semblaunce of the worlde, for as the skye hath two grete lyghtes the whiche ben y[e] sonne and the moone. Also the man hath two lyghtis in his heed, the whiche ben the two eyen. And as the skye hath .vii. planettes, in lykewyse hath y[e] man .vii. partycyons in his heed. . . . And the hardnesse of the stones answereth unto the bones and unto the nayles. And unto the trees answereth the membres of his bodye. And unto the grasse the heres.[66]

In the tradition of popular medicine which grew from these assumptions, man had been apportioned around the zodiac so that each sign governed a particular member of his body. This lore also continued unabated from the middle ages into the renaissance, disseminated freely by such rudimentary almanacks as *The compost of Ptholomeus:*

> A man is a lytel World by hym selfe: for the lykenesse and symylytudes/that he hath of the great Worlde/Whiche is the aggregacion of the .ix. skyes [i.e., heavenly spheres] .iiii. ele-

> ments/and all thynges in them conteyned. Firste a man hath suche a lykenes in the firste mobyle [i.e., primum mobile]/that is the soveraygne skye/ and pryncipall parte of all the Worlde/ For lyke as in this firste mobyle the zodyake is devyded in .xii. partyes/that ben the .xii. Sygnes. So man is devyded in .xii. partyes/and holdeth of the sygnes every parte of his sygne. The sygnes ben these/Aries/Taurus/Gemini/Cancer/Leo/Virgo /Libra/Scorpio/Sagittarius/Capricornus/& Pisces. Of the Whiche /thre ben of the nature of fyre/that is Aries/Leo/and Sagittarius. And thre of nature of the ayre/Gemini/Libra/and Aquarius. And thre of the nature of Water/Cancer/Scorpio/and Pisces. And thre of the nature of the erth/Taurus/Virgo and Capricornus. The first is Aries that governeth the hede/& the face of man. Taurus the necke and the throte bole. Gemini the sholdres/the armes/and the handes. Cancer the breste/sydes/mylte/and lyghtes. Leo the stomake/the herte/and the backe. Virgo the bely and the entrayles. Libra the navyll/the graynes/& the partyes under the braunches. Scorpio the pryve partyes/the genytores/ the bladder: and the foundyment. Sagittarius the thyghes onely. Capricornus also the knees onely. Aquarius the legges from the knees to the heles & ankles. And Pisces hath the fete in his domynyon.[67]

For the renaissance, steeped in this lore, it was as evident that the microcosm epitomized the macrocosm, as it was that the earth stood stationary in the center of the universe. And the microcosm-macrocosm analogy carried the same authority. How else to interpret the holy scripture that man is created in the image of deity? Agrippa speaks for his era when he asserts:

> Seeing man is the most beautifull and perfectest work of God, and his Image, and also the lesser world; therefore he by a more perfect composition, and sweet Harmony, and more sublime dignity doth contain and maintain in himself all numbers, measures, weights, motions, Elements, and all other things which are of his composition; and in him as it were in the supreme workmanship, all things obtain a certain high condition, beyond the ordinary consonancy which they have in other compounds.[68]

In keeping with the hexaemeral tradition, man is the crowning achievement of creation, God's masterpiece, reproducing His image and encompassing in small the perfection of His workmanship. If the heavens declare His glory, man is the living example of it. In the words of Walter Raleigh, "Man . . . [is] an abstract or modell, or briefe Storie of the Universall: in whom God concluded the creation, and worke of the world, and whom he made the last and most excellent of his creatures." [69] John Swan echoes this commonplace sentiment: "He [man] was therefore the last, as the end of all the rest; the last in execution, but first in intention; the Map, Epitome, and Compendium of what was made before him." [70]

For Agrippa, as for his contemporaries, the similitude of the microcosm and the macrocosm was not an empty rhetorical figure of speech, but a physical fact, and he applied it with the rigor of a scientist:

> The measures of all the members [of the body] are proportionate, and consonant both to the parts of the world, and measures of the Archetype, and so agreeing, that there is no member in man which hath not correspondence with some sign, Star, intelligence, divine name, sometimes in God himself the Archetype.[71]

An entire geometry of the human body was developed to show its symmetry and proportion. The *locus classicus* for this doctrine is Vitruvius, who in his treatise *De architectura* laid down the basic tenet that an esthetically pleasing building "must have an exact proportion worked out after the fashion of the members of a finely-shaped human body" (III.i). Renaissance editions of Vitruvius flaunted diagrams which fitted the human form to geometrical figures, and in this vein Agrippa sets out the measurements in detail and provides illustrative woodcuts to show the body as it tends to the circle and to the square, with legs together and apart, with arms outstretched, raised, lowered.[72] It is in this sense, Raleigh says, that man is the measure of all things; and he cites Aristotle and Pythagoras as authorities.[73]

This model of perfection became the paradigm for beauty, and artisans strove to reproduce it in their work:

> From the very joynts of mans body all numbers, measures, proportions, and Harmonies were invented; Hence according to this measure of the body, they [the ancients] framed, and contrived their temples, pallaces, houses, Theaters; also their ships, engins, and every kind of Artifice, and every part and member of their edifices, and buildings, as columnes, chapiters of pillars, bases, buttresses, feet of pillars, and all of this kind.[74]

These are the humanistic esthetics employed by Alberti, Leonardo, Raphael, Dürer, Palladio, and the majority of artists who gave the renaissance a style which sets it apart from earlier periods and continues to draw admiration from later generations.[75] The dignity of renaissance art derives from an imitation of cosmos, that ordered and beautiful archetype which interrelates the diverse data of our experience through the application of harmony and proportion. Art, in fact, is a persuasive demonstration that our lives are patterned according to number, weight, and measure—according to the same dimensions as the universe.

Notes

[1] Nicomachus, following the Middle Platonists, makes this point with utmost clarity:

> All that has by nature with systematic method been arranged in the universe seems both in part and as a whole to have been determined and ordered in accordance with number, by the forethought and the mind of him that created all things; for the pattern was fixed like a preliminary sketch, by the domination of number preëxistent in the mind of the world-creating God, number conceptual only and immaterial in every way, but at the same time the true and the eternal essence, so that with reference to it, as to an artistic plan, should be created all these things, time, motion, the heavens, the stars, all sorts of revolutions

(*Introduction to Arithmetic* [I.vi], tr. Martin Luther D'Ooge [New York, 1926], p. 189).

[2] The Latin counterpart is *mundus;* cf. Pliny, *Historia naturalis*, II.iv; Robert Recorde, *The castle of knowledge* (London, 1556), p. 4; and Pierre de la Primaudaye, *The French academie*, tr. T. Bowes (London, 1586), *4^v and p. 179.

[3] "Opinions of Philosophers" [II.i] in *The morals*, tr. Philemon Holland (London, 1603), p. 818. Cf. St. Cyril, *Adversus libros athei Juliani* [II.xlvi] in Migne, *Patrologia Graeca*, Vol. 76, col. 571; André Dacier, *The Life of Pythagoras*, tr. anon. (London, 1707), p. 74; and Joannes Albertus Fabricius, *Bibliotheca Graeca*, 11 vols. (Hamburg, 1790–1808), I.750.

[4] *The lives, opinions, and remarkable sayings of the most famous ancient philosophers. . . . Made English by several hands* [VIII.48], 2 vols. (London, 1696), II.35.

[5] Primus Pythagoras coelum esse mundum (*κόσμον*) dixit, quia perfectum est, omnibusque animantibus ac signis pulchris decoratur (*Myriobiblon* [Rouen, 1653], col. 1318).

> [6] Primum autem omnium universam hanc circumscriptionem *κοσμον*, ex concinna digestione, ipsoque ordine pulcherrimo, quo à Deo summo opifice dispensatur, Pythagoras vocavit. Κοσμος enim rerum coagmentationem pulchrê, atque ordinate digestam sonat

(Rembertus Dodonaeus, *Cosmographica in astronomiam et geographiam isagoge* [Antwerp, 1548], A5). Cf. Joachim Camerarius, *Decuriae XXI* ΣΥΜΜΙΚΤΩΝ

ΠΡΟΒΛΗΜΑΤΩΝ (Geneva, 1594), pp. 308–309; Dacier, *Life of Pythagoras*, p. 74; and Fabricius, *Bibliotheca Graeca*, I.752–753. See p. 30, above.

[7] *Castle of knowledge*, pp. 164–165.

[8] (London, 1635), Book I, p. 8; cf. Book V, pp. 81–82.

[9] The outstanding study of this phenomenon is Carl G. Jung, *Psychology and Alchemy*, tr. R. F. C. Hull (New York, 1953).

[10] *Metaphysica*, 986a23–986a26. This list was often reproduced; for example, by Johann Reuchlin, *De arte cabalistica libri tres*, tr. Thomas Stanley, *The history of philosophy*, 2nd ed. (London, 1687), p. 572.

[11] See pp. 93–94, above.

[12] For a table which systematically reveals the universe as a system of two extremes joined by a mean, see Plate 4.

[13] *On the Nature of the Universe*, tr. Thomas Taylor (London, 1831), p. 12. There was also a source for *concordia discors* in the Heraclitean tradition; see Kathleen Freeman, *Ancilla to the Pre-Socratic Philosophers* (Oxford, 1948), pp. 25, 28 [items 8, 51].

[14] *Commentary on the Dream of Scipio* [I.vi.23], tr. William H. Stahl (Columbia Univ. Press, 1952), p. 104. For the reference in Plato, see p. 160, below.

[15] *Of the interchangeable course, or variety of things in the whole world*, tr. Robert Ashley (London, 1594), fol. 5ᵛ. Cf. John Norden, *Vicissitudo rerum* (London, 1600), esp. stanzas 82–100; cf. also Joannes Baptista Bernardus, *Seminarium totius philosophiae Aristotelicae et Platonicae*, 2nd ed. (Lyons, 1599), II.357; and G. S. Kirk and J. E. Raven, *The Presocratic Philosophers* (Cambridge Univ. Press, 1962), pp. 119–120.

[16] Those who are prone to think in the Pythagorean fashion would make much of the fact that the carbon atom is a tetrahedron—further evidence that 4 is of fundamental importance, since carbon is the basic unit of all life.

[17] "Opin. of Phil." [I.iii] in *Morals*, tr. Holland (1603), p. 806. Cf. F. M. Cornford, "Mysticism and Science in the Pythagorean Tradition," *Classical Quarterly*, 17 (1923), 1–5; and Kirk and Raven, *Presocratic Philosophers*, pp. 230–231. See also pp. 78–84, above, esp. n. 18.

[18] *Life of Pythagoras* [xxviii], tr. Thomas Taylor (London, 1818), p. 109; cf. also xxix.

[19] In Dacier, *Life of Pythagoras*, pp. 316–317.

[20] *De arte cabalistica*, tr. Stanley, *History of philosophy*, p. 572. Cf. Francesco Giorgio, *De harmonia mundi totius cantica tria*, 2nd ed. (Paris, 1545), fol. 56ᵛ, 148ᵛ; Heinrich Cornelius Agrippa, *Three books of occult philosophy*, tr. John Freake (London, 1651), p. 183; Ludovicus Caelius Rhodiginus, *Lectionum antiquarum libri XXX* (Basle, 1566), p. 857; Joannes Drusius, *Tetragrammaton* (Franeker, 1604), p. 8; Sir Thomas Browne, *Pseudodoxia epidemica* [IV.xii] in *Works*, ed. Geoffrey Keynes, 6 vols. (London, 1928–31), III.54; Godfridus Wendelinus, *Dissertatio epistolica, de tetractu Pythagorae, ad E. Puteanum* (Louvain, 1637); William Lilly, *Christian astrology* (London, 1647), p. 183; Ralph Cudworth, *The True Intellectual System of the Universe* [I.iv.20], 3 vols. (London, 1845), II.15–19; Dacier, *Life of Pythagoras*, pp. 32, 316; and Joannes Franciscus Buddeus, *Compendium historiae philosophicae* (Halle, 1731), p. 100.

[21] Tr. John Norris (London, 1682), p. 116. Erasmus makes fun of this notion; in answer to the question, "What engenders god and men?" Folly replies:

> It is evin that selie membre . . . whiche is the onely planter of mankynde. That, is the onely fountaine, whens all thynges receive life, a great deale sooner than from *Pythagoras Quaternion*

(*Praise of Follie*, tr. Thomas Chaloner, ed. C. H. Miller [EETS; Oxford Univ. Press, 1965], p. 15).

[22] This important passage from Theon's *Expositio rerum mathematicarum ad legendum Platonem utilium* is translated by F. M. Cornford, *Plato's Cosmology* (London, 1937), p. 70. For the Greek text, see Eduard Heller, ed. (Teubner; Leipzig, 1878), pp. 93–106. For a renaissance Latin translation, see Ismael Bullialdus, ed. (Paris, 1644), pp. 147–154. For another English translation, see Thomas Taylor, *Theoretic Arithmetic* (London, 1816), pp. 187–190. For the far-reaching significance of this passage, see pp. 328–332, below.

[23] In omni doctrina quattuor sunt elementa secundum platonicos. Caput. v.

> Quattuor apud methaphisicum sunt elementa: essentia : esse : virtus : & actio. Quattuor apud mathematicum: signum : linea : planum : atque profundum. Quattuor apud phisicum: seminaria naturae virtus : pullulatio naturalis : & adulta forma : atque compositum

(*Vocabularius . . . naturalis philosophiae* [Lyons, 1508], C3^{v}).

[24] *Christian astrology*, p. 183. Cf. also Agrippa, *Occult philosophy*, tr. Freake, pp. 183–187; Robert Fludd, *Demonstratio quaedam analytica* (Frankfurt-am-Main, 1621), tr. C. G. Jung and W. Pauli, *The Interpretation of Nature and the Psyche* (New York, 1955), pp. 226–236; and Leo Spitzer, *Classical and Christian Ideas of World Harmony* (Johns Hopkins Press, 1963), pp. 64–74.

[25] Cf. Plates 5 and 6. See also Plate 51.

[26] Joannes Goropius has a long passage unfolding the relationship of 12 to 4, and a marginal gloss explains: "The duodecad encompasses the idea of the entire universe" (Duodenarius totius mundi ideam complectitur) ("Hieroglyphica" in *Opera* [Antwerp, 1580], p. 154).

[27] See, for an example especially pertinent to this discussion, Thomas Hood, *The use of both the globes, celestiall, and terrestriall* (London, 1592), D8^{v}.

[28] See pp. 107–110, above. The number 12 continues to assert its cosmic connotation even today. Salvador Dali employed the symbolism of the dodecahedron in his "Sacrament of the Last Supper" (National Gallery of Art, Washington, D.C.), and Aldous Huxley in a contrary vein set up the solidarity meetings in his *Brave New World* for twelve participants in a circle.

[29] See also Plate 33.

[30] See the diagrams on pp. 95–96, above. See also John Burnet, *Early Greek Philosophy*, 4th ed. (London, 1945), p. 112.

[31] Translated by Dacier, *Life of Pythagoras*, p. 322.

[32] *Hierocles upon the Golden Verses of Pythagoras*, tr. Hall (London, 1657), p. 127; *Upon the Golden Verses*, tr. Norris, p. 117.

[33] Omnia ex calido, frigido, humido & sicco nasci (Gulielmus Morellius, *Tabula compendiosa* [Basle, 1580], p. 168). See Plate 36.

[34] See pp. 93–94, above.

[35] *The sphere*, tr. Edward Sherburne (London, 1675), p. 12.

[36] *Commentary on the Dream of Scipio* [I.vi.23–28], tr. Stahl, pp. 104–105. For other notably full explanations of the tetrad, see Aristotle, *De generatione et corruptione*, 330a30–331a6; Ocellus of Lucania, *Nature of Universe* [ii], tr. Taylor, pp. 12–18; Nemesius, *De natura hominis liber*, tr. Giorgio Valla (Lyons, 1538), pp. 66–77; Bartholomaeus Anglicus, *His booke De proprietatibus rerum*, ed. Stephen Batman (London, 1582), fols. 154, 165, 168–169; Gregor Reisch, *Margarita philosophica* (Basle, 1583), pp. 696–701; Charles de Bouelles, *Physicorum elementorum . . . libri decem* (Paris, 1512),

fol. 1; Symphorien Champier, *Symphonia Platonis cum Aristotele* (Paris, 1516), fols. 106 ff.; Godfridus, *The boke of knowledge of thynges unknowen* (London, c.1530), G1^v–H1^v; Agrippa, *Occult philosophy*, tr. Freake, pp. 6–7; Oronce Finé, *De sphaera mundi* (Paris, 1542), fol. 2; Franciscus Maurolycus, *Cosmographia* (Venice, 1543), fol. 14^v; John Dee, "Mathematicall praeface" in Euclid, *The elements*, tr. Henry Billingsley (London, 1570), *3–*4; Guillaume Saluste du Bartas, *Devine weekes and workes*, tr. Joshua Sylvester (London, 1605), pp. 39–40; Simon Girault, *Globe du monde* (Lengres, 1592), fol. 57–58; Norden, *Vicissitudo rerum*, D3; Thomas Walkington, *The optick glasse of humors* (London, 1607), fol. 38^v–40^v. In the library of Gonville and Caius College, Cambridge, there is a profusely illustrated eleventh- or twelfth-century manuscript entitled *Tractatus de quaternario*, suggesting that the tetrad tradition continued undiminished through the middle ages; cf. *A Descriptive Catalogue of the Manuscripts in the Library of Gonville and Caius College*, 2 vols. (Cambridge Univ. Press, 1907–08), no. 428. See also Charles Singer, *From Magic to Science* (New York, 1958), pp. 142–143; and Harry Bober, "In Principio: Creation before Time" in *Essays in Honor of Erwin Panofsky*, ed. Millard Meiss, 2 vols. (New York Univ. Press, 1961), I.13–28.

[37] Transmutation of the elements is probably best known from Aristotle's *De generatione et corruptione*, 331a7–333a16; cf. *De caelo*, 286a13–286a36, 312b7–313a13. In the *Timaeus* (49A–50A), however, Plato assumes that the elements change constantly, and Ocellus of Lucania in his *De universi natura* (esp. chap. ii) gives perhaps the most detailed description of how the elements mutate continually within the framework of an unbegotten and indestructible order. Ovid also has a passage on what changes the elements undergo (*Metamorphoses*, XV.237–251).

[38] *Upon the Golden Verses*, tr. Hall, p. 126.

[39] *Devine weekes and workes*, tr. Sylvester (1605), p. 494.

[40] See also Plates 33–35.

[41] See pp. 152–153, above, for Theon's list.

[42] For accounts well known in the renaissance, see Philo Judaeus, *De plantatione Noë*, 120 ff., and *De opificio mundi*, 48 ff.; Plutarch, "Opin. of Phil." [I.iii] in *Morals*, tr. Holland (1603), p. 661; Martianus Capella, *De nuptiis Philologiae et Mercurii*, II.106–107, VII.734; Hierocles, *Upon the Golden Verses*, tr. Hall, p. 126; and Isidore, *De natura rerum*, vii.4, xi.1–3. For renaissance examples, see Conrad Celtis, *Quatuor libri amorum* (Nuremberg, 1502), *passim* (see Plate 35); Charles de Bouelles, *Liber de duodecim numeris* in *Liber de intellectu* et al. (Paris, 1510), fol. 150^v–152; De Bouelles, *Liber de Sapiente* [1509] in *Individuum und Kosmos in der Philosophie der Renaissance*, ed. Ernst Cassirer (Leipzig, 1927), pp. 311–312; Jodocus Clichtoveus, *De mystica numerorum significatione opusculum* (Paris, 1513), fol. 8–9^v; Martin Cortes, *The arte of navigation*, tr. Richard Eden (London, 1561), fol. 28^v; Guillaume Postel, *Tabula aeternae ordinationis, quaternario . . . expositae* (Paris, c.1552); Philip Moore, *A fourtie yeres almanacke* (London, c.1566), a7^v; Cornelius Gemma, *De arte cyclognomica, tomi III* (Antwerp, 1569), p. 37 (see Plate 6); Du Bartas, *Devine weekes and workes*, tr. Sylvester (1605), pp. 52, 494; Pierre de la Primaudaye, *The third volume of the French academie*, tr. R. Dolman (London, 1601), pp. 177, 179 [a redaction of Hierocles]; John Davies of Hereford, *Microcosmos* [1603], ed. A. B. Grosart (London, 1877–78), pp. 30–32; Lilly, *Christian astrology*, p. 183; and Georg Horn, *Arca Mosis* (Leyden, 1668), p. 132. For modern studies of the origin of the tetrad tradition in the literature, see Armand Delatte, *Etudes sur la littérature pythagoricienne* (Paris, 1915), p. 255; and Paul Kucharski, *Etude sur la doctrine pythagoricienne de la tétrade* (Paris, 1952), pp. 18–26.

[43] *French academie*, p. 177.

[44] See my article, "Some Renaissance Versions of the Pythagorean Tetrad," *Studies in the Renaissance*, 8 (1961), esp. pp. 20–33.

[45] *Lives of ancient philosophers* [VIII.76] (1696), II.57. The same information is supplied by Plutarch, "Opin. of Phil." [I.iii] in *Morals*, tr. Holland (1603), pp. 807–808. Cf. Stanley, *History of philosophy*, pp. 580–581.

[46] *French academie*, pp. 50–51.

[47] See Florence McCullough, *Medieval Latin and French Bestiaries* (Univ. of North Carolina Press, 1960), p. 201. For an example in an historiated initial, see Bober, "In Principio," esp. I.26.

[48] A comparable tetrad appears also on the title page of Pliny, *The historie of the world*, tr. Philemon Holland (London, 1601), and another on the title page of Giovanni Battista Porta, *Natural magick* (London, 1658).

[49] *French academie*, p. 179.

[50] *Devine weekes and workes*, tr. Sylvester (1605), p. 42. For other treatments of the cosmic dance in Tudor literature, see E. M. W. Tillyard, *The Elizabethan World Picture* (London, 1943), pp. 94–99.

[51] *Achilles Shield* [1598], tr. Chapman, in *Chapman's Homer*, ed. Allardyce Nicoll, 2 vols. (New York, 1956), I.557. To place this passage in context, see pp. 379–381, below.

[52] Samuel Daniel, *Complete Works*, ed. A. B. Grosart, 5 vols. (London, 1885–96), III.194–195, 198–199.

[53] Cf. Milton, *Arcades*, 61–73.

[54] *Historie of world* [II.xx], tr. Holland, p. 14. For a diagram of this scheme, see Stanley, *History of philosophy*, p. 539.

[55] "A commentarie of the creation of the soule" in *Morals*, tr. Holland (1603), p. 1046.

[56] *Harmonices enchiridion* [III.iii], as translated in Stanley, *History of philosophy*, p. 531.

[57] For other notable authorities on the music of the spheres, see Censorinus, *De die natali*, xiii; Iamblichus, *De vita Pythagorae*, xv; Agrippa, *Occult philosophy*, tr. Freake, pp. 259–262; Milton, "De sphaerarum concentu"; Stanley, *History of philosophy*, pp. 531, 538; Edward Sherburne, tr., *The sphere* [of Manilius] (London, 1675), Appendix, p. 130; A. Ed. Chaignet, *Pythagore et la philosophie pythagoricienne*, 2 vols. (Paris, 1873), II.147–156; Théodore Reinach, "La musique des sphères," *Revue des études grecques*, 13 (1900), 432–449; Sir Thomas Heath, *Aristarchus of Samos* (Oxford, 1913), pp. 105–115; F. M. Cornford, "The Harmony of the Spheres" in *The Unwritten Philosophy and Other Essays* (Cambridge Univ. Press, 1950), pp. 14–27; Edward W. Naylor, *Shakespeare and Music*, 2nd ed. (London, 1931), pp. 147–158; Spitzer, *Ideas of World Harmony*, passim, esp. pp. 14–63; W. K. C. Guthrie, *A History of Greek Philosophy*, 3 vols. (Cambridge Univ. Press, 1962), I.295–301; James A. Philip, *Pythagoras and Early Pythagoreanism* (Univ. of Toronto Press, 1966), pp. 123–133; and Kathi Meyer-Baer, *Music of the Spheres and the Dance of Death* (Princeton Univ. Press, 1970).

[58] In *Morals*, tr. Holland (1603), p. 1046; cf. Porphyry, *De vita Pythagorae*, xxxi; Macrobius, *Commentarius in somnium Scipionis*, II.iii.1; Rhodiginus, *Lectionum antiquarum libri*, pp. 8 ff.; and Stanley, *History of philosophy*, p. 531.

[59] "Of musicke" [xliv] in *Morals*, tr. Holland (1603), p. 1263.

[60] Ea quae est mundana in his maxime perspicienda est quae in ipso coelo, vel compage elementorum, vel temporum varietate visuntur. Qui enim fieri potest, ut tam velox coeli machina tacito silentique cursu moveatur? . . . Jam vero quatuor elementorum diversitates contrariasque potentias, nisi quaedam harmonica conjungeret, qui fieri posset, ut in unum corpus ac machinam convenirent? Sed haec omnis diversitas ita et temporum

varietatem parit et fructuum, ut tamen unum anni corpus efficiat (*De musica*, I.ii).

[61] For Robert Fludd, see esp. *Utriusque cosmi . . . historia*, 4 vols. (Oppenheim, 1617–19), I.78–106. Cf. Daniel Georg Morhof, *Polyhistor* [II.i.2.6], 4th ed. (Lubeck, 1747), II.17–18. See also Peter J. Ammann, "The Musical Theory and Philosophy of Robert Fludd," *Journal of the Warburg and Courtauld Institutes*, 30 (1967), 198–227.

For Johann Kepler, see esp. *Harmonices mundi libri V* (Linz, 1619), Book V, pp. 192–243. See also D. P. Walker, "Kepler's Celestial Music," *Journal of the Warburg and Courtauld Institutes*, 30 (1967), 228–250.

For Marin Mersenne, see *Traité de l'harmonie universelle* (Paris, 1627).

For Athanasius Kircher, see *Musurgia universalis*, 2 vols. (Rome, 1650), esp. Book X.

For John Heydon, see *The harmony of the world* (London, 1662), esp. pp. 46–53.

[62] *Holy Sonnets*, V. The comparison of man to the macrocosm was so commonplace in the renaissance that a list of references to it would be supererogatory. It might be helpful, however, to cite a few of the more recherché books on the subject:

Francesco Giorgio, *De harmonia mundi totius cantica tria* (Venice, 1525), esp. Canticle I, Tone vi

Antoine Mizauld, *Harmonia coelestium corporum et humanorum* (Paris, 1555)

Joannes Pistorius, *Microcosmus, sive liber de proportione utriusque mundi* (Paris, 1607)

Rodrigues de Castro, *De meteoris microcosmi libri quatuor* (Florence, 1621)

Robert Fludd, *Philosophia sacra & vere Christiana, seu meteorologia cosmica* (Frankfurt, 1626)

Fortunius Licetus, *De mundi, & hominis analogia liber unus* (Udine, 1635)

Athanasius Kircher, *Musurgia universalis*, 2 vols. (Rome, 1650), esp. II.401–409

F. M. von Helmont, *The paradoxal discourses . . . concerning the macrocosm and microcosm*, tr. J. B. (London, 1685)

In seventeenth-century England *microcosmus* became a favorite term with authors and was frequently used as a title for a variety of works—for example, by John Davies of Hereford, Helkiah Crooke, Samuel Purchas, Peter Heylyn, John Earle, and Thomas Nabbes. In modern scholarship, the outstanding treatments of the subject include George P. Conger, *Theories of Macrocosms and Microcosms in the History of Philosophy* (Columbia Univ. Press, 1922); Ernst Cassirer, *Individuum und Kosmos in der Philosophie der Renaissance* (Leipzig, 1927); E. A. Grillot de Givry, *Witchcraft, Magic, and Alchemy*, tr. J. C. Locke (London, 1931), pp. 220–248; and Rudolf Allers, "Microcosmus," *Traditio*, 2 (1944), 319–407. One of the most useful for literary purposes is Chapter I in Marjorie Hope Nicolson's *The Breaking of the Circle* (Northwestern Univ. Press, 1950).

[63] In his "Mathematicall praeface" to Billingsley's translation of Euclid's *Elements*, Dee defines several different mathematical sciences, among which is "anthropographie," to be coordinate with astronomy and geography:

> Anthropographie, is the description of the Number, Measure, Waight, figure, Situation, and colour of every diverse thing, conteyned in the

> perfect body of MAN: with certain knowledge of the Symmetrie, figure, waight, Characterization, and due locall motion, of any parcell of the sayd body, assigned: and of Numbers, to the sayd parcell appertainyng (c4).

See pp. 264–265, below.

> [64] Dicitur homo μικρόκοσμος (id est mundi compendium) non quia quatuor, ut reliqua animalia etiam minima, constet elementis: verum quia omnes mundi virtutes continet. Nam sunt in mundo Dii, quatuor elementa, bruta, plantae. Has omnes potentias possidet homo, habet Rationem pro divina virtute, habet pro natura. Elementorum movendi vim, crescendi, suique similem productricem

(*Myriobiblon* [1653], col. 1318).

[65] Of the many renaissance statements to this effect, none is more noble than Pico della Mirandola's treatise, *De dignitate hominis*, a youthful statement intended as the general introduction to a wide-ranging analysis of human knowledge.

[66] Honoré d'Autun, *The lucydarye*, tr. Andrew Chertsey (London, c.1508), A4. To show the persistence of this physical comparison between man and nature, cf. Walter Raleigh, *The history of the world* [I.ii.5] (London, 1614), p. 30, where every detail is repeated. See also "Homo Microcosmus" in Henry Peacham, *Minerva Britanna* (London, 1612), p. 190; and Phineas Fletcher, *The purple island* (London, 1633), *passim*.

[67] (Robert Wyer; London, c.1532), c2–c2v. For similar information, cf. Godfridus, *The boke of knowledge of thynges unknowen* (Robert Wyer; London, c.1530), G4; and Erra Pater, *The pronostycacion for ever* (Robert Wyer; London, c.1540), A3v, A7. The ultimate source for this kitchen astrology is a French remnant of the middle ages, *Le kalendrier des bergers*. Cf. Plate 33.

[68] *Occult philosophy*, tr. Freake, p. 263.

[69] *History of world*, p. 30.

[70] *Speculum mundi* (Cambridge, 1635), p. 496.

[71] *Occult philosophy*, tr. Freake, p. 264.

[72] *Ibid.*, pp. 263–272. Cf. Fludd, *Utriusque cosmi . . . historia*, III.109–121.

[73] "*Homo est mensura omnium rerum*, saith *Aristotle* and *Pythagoras*" (*History of world*, p. 31). The reference to Aristotle is *Metaphysica*, 1053a36–1053a37. For attribution of the saying to Pythagoras, see p. 31, above.

[74] Agrippa, *Occult philosophy*, p. 263. Cf. Helkiah Crooke, *Microcosmographia* (London, 1615), p. 6.

[75] A particularly cogent study is Rudolf Wittkower, *Architectural Principles in the Age of Humanism* (London, 1949), esp. pp. 1–18, 24–28.

3

Concepts of Deity and of Time

Despite the difficulty in reconstructing a simple concept of deity which prevails in Pythagorean thought, there are certain religious attitudes and dicta ascribed to the Pythagoreans which the renaissance chose to emphasize. As we might expect, Pythagoreans defined the godhead in terms of number, so that he was equated with the monad, the all-inclusive unity from which the multeity of creation proceeded. Conversely, he was the self-consistent infinite which unified the multifarious items of nature and which by harmony tended to minimize differences between them. Stated simply, he was the progenitor and maintainer of cosmos. Translating this principle into moral law, Pythagoreans acknowledged that his ideas provided the archetypal forms determining our physical world, and therefore they must be the ideal patterns toward which we direct our aspiring thoughts and upon which we model our actions.[1]

Because of his numerical definition of God as the monad, Pythagoras was considered a proponent of monotheism, and by some the founder of monotheistic religion in Greece in opposition to the traditional pantheon.[2] Furthermore, since Judaism was the outstanding theology of the ancient world propounding a single deity, Pythagoras was often affiliated with Hebraic culture. Ficino, for instance, rummaging for half-remembered information, wrote: "St. Ambrose, if I recall correctly, showed that Pythagoras was born of a Jewish father."[3] In the Judeo-Christian tradition Moses is the chosen preceptor working in the service of an undisputed Jehovah, and therefore it was natural to assume that Pythagoras received his doctrine from Moses, as Pico della Mirandola suggests.[4] Henry More in the preface to his *Conjectura cabbalistica*, an interpretation of the first three chapters of Genesis, puts the case most strongly:

> For *Pythagoras* it is a thing incredible that he and his followers should make such a deal of doe with the mystery of Numbers, had he not been favoured with a sight of *Moses* his Creation of the world in six days.[5]

Pythagoras was therefore in the direct line of covenantal authority, and was so considered by the Church Fathers.[6] He is cited by St. Augustine and St. Jerome, to name only two, without a trace of embarrassment or discomfiture. The *Carmina aurea* attested to Pythagoras' piety, and the *Symbola* were clear evidence of his wisdom.

The basic text for reconstructing the Pythagorean concept of deity, at least as the renaissance knew it, is preserved by St. Justin Martyr (c.100–c.165), the early Christian apologist and one of the first in a long line of syncretists who sought to reconcile Christianity with pagan philosophy. In his *Exhortation to the Greeks*—translated into Latin, incidentally, by Giovanni Francesco Pico della Mirandola and printed at Strasbourg, 1506—Justin Martyr systematically canvasses Greek philosophers and poets for monotheistic beliefs, and he devotes a short chapter to Pythagoras (xix). He comments that Pythagoras "seems to have harbored thoughts about the unity of God, which may have been a profitable result of his sojourn in Egypt."[7] He notes also that Pythagoras "explained his own philosophical conclusions by means of mystical symbols," and he interprets the sanctification of the monad as an emblematic declaration of monotheism:

> He [Pythagoras] allegorically teaches that there is only one God when he states that unity is the first principle of all things and the cause of all good.

To support his argument that Pythagoras professed a single, omnipotent deity, Justin Martyr then gives what he claims to be a direct quotation from Pythagoras:

> God is one. And He is not, as some think, outside the world, but in it, for He is entirely in the whole circle looking over all generations. He is the blending agent of all ages; the executor of His own powers and deeds; the first cause of all things; the light in heaven; the Father of all; the mind and animating force of the universe; the motivating factor of all the heavenly bodies.

This quotation was repeated as authentic by St. Clement and by St. Cyril, and was thereby established prominently in patristic literature.[8] It was widely recalled during the renaissance.[9] According to Raphael Hythloday, the majority of Utopians affirmed just such a deity:

> The moste and the wysest parte . . . beleve that there is a certayne godlie powre unknowen, everlastinge, incomprehensible, inexplicable, farre above the capacitie and retche of mans witte, dispersed throughoute all the worlde, not in bignes, but in vertue and power. Him they call the father of al. To him alone they attribute the beginninges, the encreasinges, the procedinges, the chaunges and the endes of al thinges.[10]

Sir Thomas More here seems to extoll the ineffable permeative god of the Pythagoreans, the "Father of All," as Justin Martyr had recorded.

The primary postulate of the Pythagorean quotation recorded by Justin Martyr is, of course, that the supreme being is equivalent to the monad. He is infinite, omnipotent, eternal, conceptual—the monad placed in a religious frame of reference. Among the ranks of the pagan syncretists, Plutarch attributes to the Pythagoreans a similar belief: "*Pythagoras* affirmeth, that . . . unitie was God, and the soveraigne good." [11] The Pythagoreans were unquestionably monotheistic, though their definition of God is anything but concrete. Johann Reuchlin, the Christian cabalist who developed the theses of Pico della Mirandola, elaborates the statement of Plutarch, emphasizing the essential oneness of the Pythagorean deity:

> The divine Essence therefore, existent before Ævum and Age, (for it is the Age of Ages) the præexistent entity and unity of existence, substance, essence, nature, was by *Pythagoras* called ἓν *one*, by Parmenides ὄν *being*, both upon a like ground; because it is the super-essential Unite and Being, from which, and by which, and through which, and in which, and to which all things are, and are ordered and persist, and are contained, and are filled, and are converted.[12]

By this statement, God is a sempiternal essence. It is this conceptual quality of the Pythagorean deity, in fact, which most impressed Louis LeRoy: "Pythagoras was of opinion, that the first cause was not sensible, nor passible [i.e., changing]; but invisible, & incorruptible, and onely intelligible [i.e., perceptible to the intellect, not the senses]." [13]

A secondary postulate of utmost importance also emerges in the quotation from Justin Martyr: that the Pythagorean god is an immanent deity—"He is not, as some think, outside the world, but in it." Indeed, he permeates the entire creation, and in a real sense subsumes it in his own infinite being. He is "the mind and animating force of the universe." Those prone to think in Platonic contexts conceived the deity as the world-soul described in the *Timaeus*, the pervasive *anima mundi* that flows through all and binds all into one unity. Cicero reports that Pythagoras "supposed the Deity to be one soul, mixing with and pervading all nature." [14] Although Cicero refutes this view, the concept of deity as an inexhaustibly fecund spirit continued to typify the attitude associated with the Pythagorean doctrine. Representing Christian opinion, Lactantius ascribes to Pythagoras a similar definition of god: "a mind which commeateth, and is diffused through every part of the World, and through all Nature; from whom all animals that are produced receive life." [15]

In such a view, where god performs the unifying function of the *anima mundi*, his initial role is that of creator. The conclusive proof of his omnipotent divinity, in fact, is the ability to create a world, an ability shared by no other power on earth or in heaven. Another Pythagorean fragment preserved by Justin Martyr makes this point by eloquently challenging any pretender to divinity:

> If any one should say I am God, besides the only true God, let him create a World like this, and say this is my Work; but he ought not only to say this is my Work, but he must inhabit and fill the World he has created, for so has the true God done by this.[16]

But the responsibility of the deity does not stop with creation. He must supervise the operation of the *machina mundi* to insure its orderly continuance. Francesco Giorgio assigns to Pythagoras a definition of God which emphasizes this facet of His godhead:

> Pythagoras asserted that God is an admirable power, both the harmony and balance of the soul, its health and every good. Therefore, by His care and attention all things keep their order.[17]

Matter retains an inclination toward discord, so that chaos lurks as a perennial threat. But the benevolent watchfulness of God prevents such a castastrophe. This supervisory responsibility is known in the Christian scheme as "providence" (πρόνοια):

> The World is corruptible in its own nature, for it is sensible and corporeal; but it shall never be corrupted, by reason of the providence and preservation of God.[18]

Pythagoreans in a pagan milieu more likely called it "fate" (εἱμαρμένη)[19] or "necessity" (ἀνάγκη).[20] In any case, the stricture in the Pythagorean fragment that the deity "must inhabit and fill the World he has created" clearly points to a concept of god as an *anima mundi*, a continuous vivifying force.

As world-soul, then, the deity inhabits the world's body and gives it form as a soul should:

> For of the soule the bodie forme doth take:
> For soule is forme, and doth the bodie make.
> (Spenser, *Hymne of Beautie*, 132–133)

The deity informs the world's body through the imposition of cosmic harmonies, and creation may be expounded as the establishment of a mathematical cosmos out of chaos. No one carries this line of reasoning more logically to its extreme than does Andreas Cellarius, heir of the rich cosmographical tradition in seventeenth-century Holland, who writes with the *Timaeus* and with Hierocles[21] in mind:

> Since no body is able to exist without its own internal form, that is to say soul, from which it is acknowledged that its motion, properties, and effects derive, there are those who attribute a soul to the world also, composed ἐκ τ'αυτοῦ καὶ ἑτέρου, from the same and the other, and made as if a third nature, to which, containing in itself the ratios of harmonic numbers, that highly revered quaternion is accommodated, the sacred oath of Pythagoras, the fountain of eternal nature on account of the number 10 comprising the marvelous mystery, in which the preceding numbers both are always contained, unfolding themselves unto infinity, and also beginning again and again from unity they proceed to their multiplication.[22]

According to Cellarius, the creating godhead of the *Timaeus* works in strict Pythagorean fashion. He produces a soul by reconciling two opposites, the same and the other, and this soul imposes form on passive matter, determining its "motion, properties, and effects." The result is no less than a physical extension of the tetractys. Out of his infinite potential as the monad, the godhead generates the quaternion to serve as pattern for the world-soul. Imprinted on matter, the quaternion organizes chaos into the four elements, each distinct but all interrelated in a single system. Since the quaternion is "the fountain of eternal nature," it continues to realize its latency, producing the items of nature until it reaches the limit of the decad, 10, the number of perfection. Ten always contains the preceding numbers (1 + 2 + 3 + 4 = 10), as Cellarius says, so that the decad is the limit of the finite cosmos. But the decad, though finite, can be repeated indefinitely, and by this repetition can be extrapolated to infinity. We have, then, a limited unit—a quaternion, or a diapason, or a zodiac—which can be reproduced a limitless number of times, and thereby the finite becomes the integer of infinity, making infinity comprehensible. The creative process, in fact, is a metaphor for infinity, its ongoing vitality a means for understanding infinity.

As generator of these numerical forms which are realized in the physical universe, God appears as the supreme geometer, Blake's Ancient of Days with opened compasses at the ready. To give evidence of his power and mercy, he created the world according to number, weight, and measure (Book of Wisdom, xi.21), which is simply another way of saying that he ordained cosmos (see Plate 43). William Ingpen, a well-meaning Christian and self-professed Pythagorean in early seventeenth-century London, removed any disparity between the biblical and classical traditions:

> Whereas it is said, that *God had disposed all things according to number, waight, and measure,* what is signified unto us, but that when he created the world out of the lump before it had, he made it an harmonious body, containing number, order, beauty, and proportion, in all the parts thereof.[23]

God set limits, determined quantities, and constructed an artifact so that the heavens declare his glory and the firmament shows his handiwork.

Among pagan authors the *locus classicus* for this concept of a geometrizing deity is found, not surprisingly, in Plutarch. In his compendium of pedantic chit-chat, "Of Symposiaques" (VIII.2), Plutarch includes an item: "How *Plato* is to be understood, when he saith: that God continually is exercised in Geometry."[24] Although this statement is not found explicitly in Plato's writing, it is often implicit, most insistently in the *Timaeus,* and is customarily attributed to him. In a long passage drawing heavily upon Pythagorean doctrine, Plutarch explains what the statement means:

> Neither hath God by any other meanes framed and made the world, but onely by determining or making finit that matter which was infinit in it selfe, not in regard of quantitie, greatnesse, and multitude; but for that being as it was, inconstant,

> wandering, disorderly, and unperfect, our auncients were wont to call it infinit, that is to say, undetermined and unfinished: for the forme and figure is the terme or end of everything that is formed and shapen; the want whereof made it of itselfe to be shapelesse and disfigured: but after that numbers and proportions come to be imprinted upon the rude and formelesse matter, then being tied and bound (as it were) first with lines, and after lines, with superficies and profundities, it brought foorth the first kinds and differences of bodies, as the foundation and groundworke for the generation of aire, earth, water, and fire: for impossible it had beene, and absurd, that of matter so wandring, so errant, and disorderly, there should arise equalities of sides, and similitudes of angles, in those solide square bodies, which were called *Octaedra* and *Eicosaedra,* that is to saie, with eight and twentie bases: likewise in pyramidals and cubes, unlesse there had been some worke-man to limit, ordeine, and dispose everything Geometrically; thus a limit or terme being given unto that which was infinit; all things in this universall world, composed, ordered, and contempered accordingly in excellent manner, were first and made, and are made now every day; notwithstanding the said matter striveth and laboureth daily to returne unto her infinit estate, as very loth and refusing to be thus geometrized, that is to say, reduced to some finit and determinate limits.

Underlying this passage is the Pythagorean premise that reality is dichotomized into a conceptual world composed of ideal forms and a physical world of inchoate matter. Creation occurs as the forms are imposed upon the matter. Once more our understanding of ultimate principles depends upon relating the intellectual and the material, the infinite and the finite. The interaction of the two is here expressed in terms of Pythagorean geometry. The monad—limitless and unchanging—working through the point produces first the line, then plane surfaces ("superficies"), and finally volumes ("profundities"), thereby exhausting the possibilities of physical extension in our three-dimensional world. Next it brings forth the four basic qualities—hot, cold, moist, dry ("the first kinds and differences of bodies")—and from them generates the tetrad, which organizes the four elements ("aire, earth, water, and fire") in a stable system. The archetypal forms for the elements are of course the regular solids, the only perfect forms—the octahedron, icosahedron, pyramid, and cube. This universal order could not have been achieved without an omnipotent and rational deity—in Plu-

43. *Divine providence maintaining the cosmos*

tarch's words, "unlesse there had been some worke-man to limit, ordeine, and dispose everything Geometrically." Only by the ineluctable power of this supreme architect can a limit be imposed upon what would otherwise be chaotic. Even so, there is inherent in matter a tendency toward disruption, and consequently the godhead has the task not only of creating the cosmos but also of maintaining its determinate order.

This image of God as geometer translates the deity as *anima mundi* from the noncorporeal world of intellect to the extended world of physical objects. We detect here the two dominant concepts of deity in the Pythagorean tradition, both evident in the quotation preserved by Justin Martyr. One postulates the deity as an all-pervasive spirit that infuses the universe but is known only indirectly through its effects, a pantheistic numen that at most may be perceived as "something . . . whose dwelling is the light of setting suns." It leads to mysticism. The other, in strong contrast, postulates the deity as a workman setting about a concrete task, ordering the world according to mathematical measure, building with the tangible forms of the regular solids. It leads to empirical science, as we attempt to understand the deity through analyzing

---

43. At the top the beneficent deity is depicted as the eye of providence watching over creation from the center of a triangle symbolizing the trinity. This holy triangle is in turn the center of three superimposed triangles whose points signify the nine orders of angels. In the middle of the page is the universe, comprising our earth at the center, then the seven planetary spheres, next the sphere of fixed stars, and finally the *primum mobile*. The universe is winged to indicate that it is subject to the passage of time. Immediately above this cosmos two angels fly with accoutrements to proclaim that God created the universe according to measure, weight, and number (Book of Wisdom, xi.21). The angel on the left carries a ruler labeled *mensura* and a weight labeled *pondere*. The angel on the right carries a tablet labeled *numero* with the nine digits arranged in such a way that any row of three totals 15 when added together. In the landscape below, one philosopher discourses from a book which is illustrated with a five-pointed star and a six-pointed star, while another philosopher expounds the geometrical theorem traditionally associated with Pythagoras (see Plate 14). On a tablet in the foreground are inscribed the first four digits—1, 2, 3, 4—which represent the limit of extension in the physical world and define by their sum the perfect number 10 (see p. 84).

Athanasius Kircher, *Arithmologia* (Rome, 1665), title page.

his handiwork. Pythagoras, oddly enough, is the fountainhead for both these divergent trends in our philosophical development.

The simple interpretation of a geometrizing godhead saw him creating the universe out of familiar basic shapes. He used the cube, the pyramid, the icosahedron, and the octahedron to fashion the four elements, and he chose the dodecahedron, a form more nearly approximating the perfect figure of the sphere, to fashion the zodiac and the general layout of the heavens. In his "Opinions of Philosophers" (II.vi), Plutarch reports several views of how god had gone about the process of creation, including this doctrine of Pythagoras which, Plutarch says, Plato shared:

> *Pythagoras* affirmed, that of the five solid bodies, which are also called Mathematicall; the Cube (that is to say, a square bodie, with sixe faces) went to the making of the earth; of the pointed Pyramis, was made fire; of Octoedra or solide bodie with eight bases, the air; of Icosiedra with twentie sides, the water; of Dodecaedra with twelve faces, the supreame sphaere of the universall world.[25]

Here god constructs the universe from the well-known building blocks first identified by Pythagoras. Sir Thomas Browne applied this notion of a geometrizing god so simplistically that he reduced creation to a gridwork of "quincunxes," of interlocking tetrads—what he called a "Quincunciall Lozenge." [26]

A more sophisticated view, however, saw god working in the subtle and complicated mode of mathematical progressions and proportions and harmonic ratios. In such a discussion, simple numbers take on a dimension of complex meaning and they must be explicated with considerable care and sympathy. Plato had provided the license as well as the impetus for such modes of expression when in the *Timaeus* (34B–37C) he described how god (θεός) fashioned the world-soul (ψυχή). Knowledgeably within this context Macrobius explains how the number 7 contains the cryptic formula for the world-soul as Plato propounded it:

> It was by this number [7] first of all, indeed, that the World-Soul was begotten, as Plato's *Timaeus* has shown. With the monad located on the apex, two sets of three numbers each descended on either side, on one the even, on the other the odd: that is, after the monad we had on one side two, four, and eight, and on the other three, nine, and twenty-seven; and the mixture

> arising out of these seven numbers brought about the generation of the World-Soul at the behest of the Creator.[27]

At the behest of the creator, then, the world-soul is generated out of the monad as it extends to seven numbers. In one direction, the monad proceeds to 2, the first even number, which is represented by a straight line with two end points. This number 2 is then multiplied by itself to produce a square number, 4, represented by a plane surface, which in turn when placed in geometric progression (i.e., multiplied by 2) produces 8, a cube number and a volume. In another direction, the monad proceeds to 3, the first odd number. When 3 is multiplied by itself it produces 9, a square number, which in turn when placed in geometric progression (i.e., multiplied by 3) produces 27, a cube number. This formula, represented diagrammatically as Macrobius expounds it, is called the Platonic *lambda*, because the two progressions extending from the monad—the geometric progression of 2 and the other of 3—suggest the legs of the Greek letter Λ. It indicates how the monad can proceed through a geometric progression of even numbers until it reaches the limit of extension, the cube number 8, a volume having the three possible dimensions of length, breadth, and thickness. It indicates simultaneously how the monad can proceed through a geometric progression of odd numbers until it reaches the cube number 27, the limit of extension in that series. All of this is amply set forth by Macrobius,[28] who concludes:

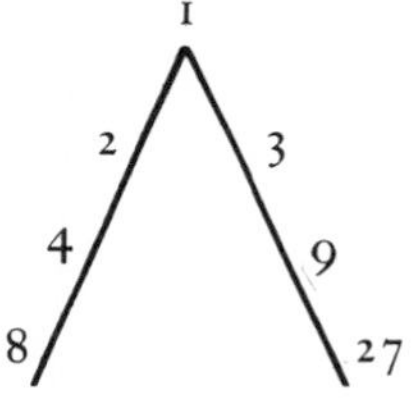

> Since the uneven numbers are considered masculine and the even feminine, God willed that the Soul which was to give birth to the universe should be born from the even and uneven, that is from the male and female; and that, since the Soul was destined to penetrate the solid universe, it should attain to those numbers representing solidity in either series.

Since the world-soul is that portion or that potential of the unified but limitless monad which can interact with matter, it is seen as an intermediary entity, "midway between the Being which is indivisible and remains always the same and the Being which is transient and divisible in bodies" (*Timaeus*, 35A). In his treatise "A commentarie of the creation of the soule, which Plato describeth in his booke *Timaeus*," Plutarch offers the most extensive commentary on the mystery of how a geometrizing god translates his complex archetypal ideas into physical facts.

Creation of our physical universe proceeded, then, as the harmonies of the world-soul were imprinted upon previously chaotic matter. Since the creator is benevolent—in the words of Justin Martyr, "the cause of all good"—this act is one of love, both φιλότης in the Empedoclean sense and *charitas* in the Christian sense. In his *Hymne of Love* Spenser recounts how the god of love ranged through the primordial disarray of strifeful elements, exercising his power to bring order and resultant beauty to the world:

> The earth, the ayre, the water, and the fyre,
> Then gan to raunge them selves in huge array,
> And with contrary forces to conspyre
> Each against other, by all meanes they may,
> Threatning their owne confusion and decay:
> Ayre hated earth, and water hated fyre,
> Till Love relented their rebellious yre.
>
> He then them tooke, and tempering goodly well
> Their contrary dislikes and loved meanes,
> Did place them all in order, and compell
> To keepe them selves within their sundrie raines,
> Together linkt with Adamantine chaines;
> Yet so, as that in every living wight
> They mixe themselves, and shew their kindly might.
>
> (ll. 78–91)[29]

The result is the pattern of the tetrad, with contraries reconciled through shared qualities ("loved meanes"). *Concordia discors* is established among the four elements and repeated in man, the microcosm. The same theme is proclaimed by Dryden in the well-known opening stanza of his "Song for St. Cecilia's Day," which begins with the confident lines—"From Harmony, from heav'nly Harmony/This universal Frame began"—and ends with the triumphant assertion—"Through all the Compass of the Notes it ran,/ The Diapason closing full in Man."

The wealth of tradition and weight of authority borne by such poetry is exemplified by this impassioned declaration from St. Clement:

> It [the musical voice of God] also composed the universe into melodious order, and tuned the discord of the elements to harmonious arrangement, so that the whole world might become harmony. It let loose the fluid ocean, and yet has prevented it

> from encroaching on the land. The earth, again, which had been in a state of commotion, it has established, and fixed the sea as its boundary. The violence of fire it has softened by the atmosphere, as the Dorian is blended with the Lydian strain; the harsh cold of the air it has moderated by the embrace of fire, harmoniously arranging these the extreme tones of the universe. . . . And He who is of David, and yet before him, the Word of God, despising the lyre and harp, which are but lifeless instruments, and having tuned by the Holy Spirit the universe, and especially man —who, composed of body and soul, is a universe in miniature— makes melody to God on this instrument of many tones.[30]

This passage is a joyful hallelujah from a pious man who feels the comfort of knowing where he belongs in the universal scheme. It is filled with contentment and optimism. It is also filled with certainty, a certainty that derives as much from reason as from faith. St. Clement has looked at his world and he sees order among its parts. Therefore he argues from this design that there is a beneficent deity who has arranged the four elements, in both the macrocosm and microcosm, so as to be most congenial to man. Christ as λόγος —the "Word of God" who as Jesus followed in the lineage of the great psalmist, David, and as Adam preceded him—has made this proclamation and has brought it all to pass. St. Clement's paean of praise with its "instrument of many tones" lies behind Robert Fludd's *monochordum mundanum* (see Plate 39). In Boethian terminology, it explains how the *musica humana* is attuned to the *musica mundana*, while being superior to *musica instrumentalis*, the music of "lifeless instruments" like the lyre and harp. It assumes a divinely-ordained universe, a cosmos, with correspondent patterns of order at all levels of existence. In a technical manner it demonstrates how man is created in the image of God, how man is a creature formed, if not confined, by the love of God.

The mystery of creation was devised as a metaphor to render tractable the enigma which lay at the center of Pythagorean metaphysics: the relationship between the limitless and the finite. There was recognition that each of these was a different order of being, one belonging to the conceptual world and the other to the material world: "Between a thing finite and a thing infinite there is no comparison, no proportion." [31] How, then, to cross the line of demarcation between them? How to bridge the discontinuity? The monad by definition is indivisible and all-inclusive. Being indivisible, how can it be fragmented to produce multiple parts? And since it is all-inclusive, where else might parts come from? This was the fundamental problem that Pythagorean philosophy in its multifarious branches attempted to solve: what is the relation between the unity which our minds *con*ceive and the multeity which our senses *per*ceive? The coadunating faculty of the imagination, to use a Coleridgean phrase, works toward a conception of the universe as a coordinated whole subsuming its disparate parts, a conception which can never be fully completed by mortal man. While in the opposite direction our senses compile a perception of data which remain separate entities, each of which is thoroughly knowable. By the mystery of creation, however, Pythagoreans explained how the unified infinite produced multiple parts: the monad generated the extended universe by working through the point to produce the line, the surface, and the volume; or the monad proliferated to the tetrad and thence the decad. Conversely, by the metaphor of creation the creator himself is rendered knowable. By analogy, the unknown is inferred from its known parts. The *sanctus sanctorum* is defined by patterns perceptible in the palpable portion of the cosmos. In this way, a relation is established between physical space, which is composed of finite parts, and conceptual infinity, which is noncorporeal. And this relation holds whether infinity be conceived as an abstract monad or a divine presence.

The mystery of creation was further elaborated to deal with problems of time as well as of space. The monad is not only free of spatial limitation, but also timeless—paradoxically, inclusive of all time and therefore out of time, atemporal. The creator himself is eternal, existing before his creation and continuing in existence even if his creation be destroyed. The monad in terms of time was known as αἰών in Greek and *aevum* in Latin—what we would translate as "eternity." In contrast, limited time—time as duration to be measured—was known as χρόνος and *tempus*.[32] It is important to distinguish between endless time and chronological time—indeed, only the latter can rightly be called "time," *tempus*, χρόνος.

When the metaphor of creation is explicated as a theory of time, we see that chronological time proceeds from eternity just as articulated space proceeds from infinity. *Tempus* began at the moment when (note the adverbial conjunction) the godhead gave physical extension to his archetypal idea. Andreas Cellarius makes the point quite clearly:

> God therefore is the Supreme Being, and the first Mathematicus, who created time and place, which eternity does not possess,

> and established the created world in time and place, defining by these limits his creation, so that thus it is set apart from its creator, who infinite and indeterminate in time and place wished to manifest his most glorious majesty by this act of separation.[33]

The creative act, says Cellarius, whereby a space-time continuum is set apart from the "infinite and indeterminate," is the most glorious demonstration of deity and the most praiseworthy. By the institution of time, moreover, the beneficent creator is able to establish order not merely as an immobile synopsis, a status quo, but as an ongoing process with the additional dimension of temporality. The three dimensions of our physical world are extended to yet a fourth dimension. The cosmos thereby becomes dynamic, vital, even organic, and subject to maturation and decay.

The changes brought by the passage of time, however, are not haphazard or incidental, but rather part of the four-dimensional scheme, phases in a predetermined cycle. Cosmos then is not just a pattern repeated horizontally and vertically in space, but also a kinesis repeated chronologically, both backward and forward, in time. The *De mundi anima* of Timaeus of Locri explains this controlled change as evidence of divine providence:

> God, being good, and seeing Matter receive Idæa [i.e., form], and become totally changed, yet disorderly, saw also it was needful to bring it into Order, and from indefinite transmutations, to fix it determinately, that bodies might have proportionate distinctions, and not receive promiscuous variations.[34]

Promiscuity, disorder, indefinite transmutations—these disrupt the pattern. These destroy the relationship between God's idea and matter, between the conceptual and the physical, the infinite and the finite, the ideal and the actual.

The *locus classicus* for this enormously sophisticated view of time is of course Plato's *Timaeus*. Immediately after describing the construction of the world-soul and its imposition upon receptive matter, Timaeus turns to an explanation of time. When the godhead surveyed his creation at this stage, Timaeus says, he was pleased, much as was Jehovah at the end of the first day in Genesis:

> When the Father (πατήρ) that engendered it perceived it in motion and alive, a thing of joy to the eternal gods, He too rejoiced; and being well-pleased He designed to make it resemble its Model still more closely (37C-D).

In pursuit of this aim, as a further stage of creation, the godhead extended his creature toward an approximation of eternity. In addition to physical extension into the three dimensions of space, he endowed his creature with the dimension of duration, what is called "time." He thereby provided for dynamic as well as synoptic development, and consequently more nearly reproduced the original, which is eternal as well as infinite:

> He planned to make a movable image of Eternity (αἰών) and, as He set in order the Heaven, of that Eternity which abides in unity He made an eternal image, moving according to number (ἀριθμός), even that which we have named Time (χρόνος). For simultaneously with the construction of the Heaven He contrived the production of days and nights and months and years, which existed not before the Heaven came into being. And these are all portions of Time (37D-E).

"Days and nights and months and years" are the units of time, the measurable parts of this near-facsimile of eternity which moves according to number. These are the finite coordinates for Plato's world of becoming, the termini within which the items of nature exist. As Timaeus continues, "Things which move in the world of Sense . . . [are] generated forms of Time, which imitates Eternity and circles around according to number" (38A).

Time proceeds, then, according to a predetermined pattern which is continuously repeated. In the words of Timaeus, it "circles around according to number." To mark this orderly passage of time, the godhead placed in the sky the heavenly bodies visible to man:

> As a consequence of this reasoning and design on the part of God, with a view to the generation of Time, the sun and moon and five other stars, which bear the appellation of "planets," came into existence for the determining and preserving of the numbers of Time (38C).[35]

This account of the generation and purpose of time is not incompatible with the account of creation in Genesis:

> And God said: Let there be lights in the firmament of heaven to divide the day from the night; and let them be for signs, and for seasons, and days and years (1:14–19).

Lucretius also ascribed the function of marking time to the heavenly bodies:

> It was the sun and moon, the watchmen of the world, . . . who taught men that the seasons of the year revolve and that there is a constant pattern in things and a constant sequence.[36]

These traditions coalesced, reinforcing one another, to eventuate during the renaissance in a prevailing concept of time as the image of eternity set before us by the revolutions of the sun and moon and planets. John Swan, a Cantabrigian during the student days of Milton, observes that "the starres . . . were appointed to be heavenly clocks, and remarkable [i.e., visible] measurers of time and the parts thereof." [37]

Elsewhere, Swan opens his hexaemeron with a definition of time which epitomizes the orthodox renaissance attitude toward it:

> *Time*, by whose revolutions we measure houres, dayes, weeks, moneths and yeares, is nothing else but (as it were) a certain space borrowed or set apart from *eternitie;* which shall at the last return to eternitie again: like the rivers, which have their first course from the seas; and by running on, there they arrive, and have their last: for before *Time* began, there was *Eternitie*, namely GOD; which was, which is, and which shall be for ever: without beginning or end, and yet the beginning and end of all things.[38]

Swan places time (*tempus*) in the context of eternity (*aevum*), and equates that with God, "the beginning and end of all things," the *alpha* and the *omega*, the end which is its own beginning. This motif became an aphoristic commonplace. Merged with the σῶμα-σῆμα dictum ("The body is a tomb" [39]), it permeates the title page of John Case's *Lapis philosophicus*, a collage where in one focal emblem a zodiac which contains a setting sun arches over a marble effigy reclining on a sepulchre (see Plate 44). The inscription reads: *Casus in occasum vergit; vivitque sepultus.* The translation of this is difficult, but without too much violence we might render it: "Like the course of the sun, the life of man comes to a close; but being entombed, he lives." At death, he returns to the bosom of his God. In the end, paradoxically, is *his* beginning. His short time on earth is exchanged for eternal life in heaven. As Donne says, "Death, thou shalt die," because eternity obliterates the dimension of time.

An important point in this theory of time which derives from the Pythagorean cosmogony is that it provides for change, clearly visible to the human eye, but it also postulates a permanent order, equally to be believed (if only through need) by the human mind.

LAPIS
PHILOSOPHICVS SEV
commentarius in 8 lib
phys: Aristot. in quo
arcana
Physiologiæ exa:
minentur
AVCTORE IO: CASO
in Medicina Doctore
Oxoniensi
EXCVDEBAT
JOSEPH9 BARNESI9
Oxoniæ
Casus in occasum vergit
VIVITQ: SEPVLTVS

44. *Ten emblems dealing with the condition of man* sub specie temporis

44. In the text (¶¶5[v]), Case provides this "Decastichon on the ten emblems of the title page" (begin in the lower-left corner and proceed clockwise):

> Behold man, a fish, a bird—chaos; behold the three seminal patterns of all creatures;
>
> Behold milk from the breast of Nature, flowers from her mouth, and limitless bounty from her horn of plenty;
>
> Behold the wheel of Fortune, her wallet, golden scepter, whip, and bridle;
>
> Behold the goddesses of Fate, the three who initiate, urge forward, and terminate;
>
> Behold the wings of Time, deer-hoofed, his scythe, his forelocks, his hours;
>
> Behold the horses of Phaëton as they journey around, and the Great and Little Bear;
>
> Behold the location in the heavens of the fixed stars, the signs of the zodiac, and the planets;
>
> Behold the vacuum (if it be a vacuum) which fills the heavenly sphere;
>
> Behold infinity; its terminus has wings lest its boundary be fixed;
>
> The last emblem shows the decline of life heading for its close in preparation for the grave.

In Primae Paginae Decem Imagines Decastichon.

En homo, piscis, avis, Chaos; en tria semina rerum.
En φύσις ubere lac, flores ore, omnia cornu.
En rota Fortunae, pera, sceptrum aurum, ultio, fraenum.
Fati Parca triplex en incipit, urget, & occat.
Alae cervipedes, falx, frons, en Temporis horae.
En cursu ut Phaëthontis equi moveantur & Arcti.
En locus in Coelo stellis signisque planetisque.
En vacuum (vacuum si quid sit) in orbe stat. Ecce
Infinitum; at habet, ne constet, Terminus alas.
Casus in Occasum vergens haec ante sepulchrum.

John Case, *Lapis philosophicus* (Oxford, 1599), title page.

It provides for the constant flux witnessed by Heraclitus and implied by the Milesian materialists, while at the same time it recognizes the argument of Parmenides that reality is both indivisible and homogeneous, a motionless unity. This cosmogony propounds a thesis that dominated renaissance concepts of time, a thesis expressed succinctly in the single word "mutability." There is continual change, the many writers on mutability readily confess; but in a controlled pattern, they firmly conclude. This is the statement of Spenser's *Mutabilitie Cantos.*

Sometimes mutability is analyzed into a two-phase cycle of "generation and corruption," to use the terms employed by Aristotle, and sometimes it is even more finely articulated as a quadripartite process known commonly as "the transmutation of the elements." Plutarch ascribes these thoughts to Pythagoras himself:

> *Pythagoras,* and as many as suppose matter to be passible [i.e., changeable], hold, that there is properly indeed Generation and Corruption: for they say that this is done by the alteration, mutation and resolution of the elements.[40]

But always mutability implies a relationship between chronological events and their summation in time—to borrow a phrase from music, a harmony between the parts to produce a whole.

Pessimists emphasize the fragmentation and lack of steadfastness in this theory of time, with its perpetual change.[41] They write lugubrious treatises *de vicissitudine rerum.* Optimists, however, note that change is necessary to complete the pattern. Only by change can the circle return to its point of origin. The wheel turns, admittedly, but still is forever still. And man, by prosecuting one complete cycle—be it the four seasons of one year or the four ages of a full life—participates in eternity by going through this pattern of eternity. Some, incorrigibly optimistic, draw comfort from the mere fact of change, from the expectation that change will bring improvement—the tradition of "This too shall pass."

Most, however, saw time as a regulated alteration of things, bringing sorrow and joy in turn. The nadir, in fact, is a necessary preliminary which must be "perfected" (in the literal sense of *perficere*) before the zenith can be achieved. One is necessary for the definition of the other; both are essential in completion of the whole. The emphasis here is on the cyclical nature of time, on how it returns upon itself. John Swan ventures into etymology, an uncommonly popular science in the seventeenth century, to show that the very word *annus* indicates a continuous circle of integrated parts:

> In Latine the yeare is called *Annus*, because we may say of it, *revolvitur ut annulus*. For as in a ring the parts touch one another, circularly joyning each to other; so also the yeare rolleth it self back again by the same steps that it ever went; whereupon it came to passe that the Egyptians, amongst other their hieroglyphicks, used to paint out the yeare like a snake winding her self as round as a ring, holding her tail in her mouth.[42]

When we look in Horapollo's *Hieroglyphica*, we find that his first emblem is indeed a serpent biting its own tail, signifying the *aevum*.[43] St. Jerome generalized this notion of cyclical time into a Pythagorean doctrine that all experience is merely a repetition of previous experience. According to him, Pythagoras taught "that after definite cycles of time, things which had once existed will again come into being; and that nothing in the world was thought to be new." [44]

No classical poet had been more eloquent than Ovid in his treatment of mutability. His most popular work, the *Metamorphoses*, is in fact a catalog of notable changes narrated in the mythological mode. The *Metamorphoses* opens with an account of creation in the Pythagorean vein, which, as the commentator Georg Sabinus notes, "is the first and most wondrous metamorphosis of all," since it transmutes that which is abstract into something concrete.[45] Sabinus also quotes a verse reminiscent of Pythagoras which he attributes to Orpheus on the authority of both Justin Martyr and St. Clement: "One is generated by itself; all else is created out of one." [46] This "One" is equivalent to Aristotle's unmoved mover.

Pythagoras himself appears in Book XV of the *Metamorphoses* and dominates the conclusion of the work. He delivers a characteristic lecture to Numa Pompilius, the newly chosen king of Rome, who has come to Croton for instruction in "Nature's general law" (XV.6). Ostensibly the theme of the lecture is an injunction against eating flesh, since an animal's body may well incorporate the soul of an ancestor. Incidental to this purpose, however, Pythagoras speaks movingly and memorably about the changes that time inevitably brings in human affairs:

> All things are in a state of flux, and everything is brought into being with a changing nature. Time itself flows on in constant motion, just like a river (XV.178–180).

But the cyclical pattern is maintained, "so the whole round of motion is gone through again" (XV.185).

The cyclical pattern for time appears in various forms which

Ovid delineates with care and which, he implies, are analogous. For example, the diurnal unit of time is composed of two parts, daylight and darkness: "You see how the spent nights speed on to dawn, and how the sun's bright rays succeed the darkness of the night" (XV.186–187).[47] The annual unit of time is composed of four parts: spring, summer, autumn, winter (XV.199–213). Our lives similarly progress through four ages (XV.214–236). The elements also undergo constant transmutation among themselves, all deriving from and returning to one another (XV.237–251). But the pattern is preserved: "All things in their sum total remain unchanged" (XV.258). And as John Swan comments, whatever the particular form of the pattern—one day, the year, etc.—it is subsumed in a greater whole:

> If we take seasons, dayes, and yeares together, it is no hard thing to see how the whole and parts are joyned. For *Tempus* is the whole: and *Annus* is *pars temporis:* and *Dies* is *pars anni.*[48]

The point to note is that time is a cosmos composed of days, seasons, and years; but at each level of articulation within this cosmos, the same pattern persists.

Louis LeRoy elaborates this idea to show a comprehensive network of cause-and-effect that reaches out to embrace our entire physical world. The system originates, in keeping with Pythagorean cosmogony, from the monad. Acting through the world-soul and using the sun as its agent, the monad effectively regulates the four basic qualities in their performance within the tetrad:

> From the superiour part of the world there descindeth a certaine vertue accompanied with light and heat, which some of them [astrologers and philosophers] do call the spirit or soule of the world. . . . The Sunne lightning all thinges with his beames doth give evident proofe therof, who rising and setting maketh the day and the night, by comming towards us, and going from us, causeth the yeres continually to be renewed, and by the obliquity or crookednes of the Zodiacke with the helpe of the twelve signes which are in it, doth distinguishe by his Solstices and Equinoxes, the fower seasons of the sommer and winter, of the spring and harvest: In the which consisteth the vicissitude of life and death, and the change of all thinges: by the mediation of the first qualities, hot and cold, drie and moist, being duely tempered for generation, and unproportionably distempered for corruption.[49]

To reduce LeRoy's statement to its Pythagorean assumptions, we may say that the sun, as symbol of the divine monad, controls the tetrad by tempering and distempering the basic qualities of hot, cold, dry, and moist. When properly mixed, they produce a burgeoning world of four elements and thence the extended universe. The pattern of time is marked by the sun in this universe in the customary forms: as the two-phase cosmos of day and night, as the four-phase cosmos of the seasons, and as the twelve-phase cosmos of the zodiac. When the basic qualities become disproportionate through loss of the sun's beneficent beams, however, the tetrad falters and the universe decays. But the regularity of the sun in its course assures that this corruption will verge into a fresh cycle of generation—it "causeth the yeres continually to be renewed." And this is the incessant and incontrovertible pattern of time, "in the which consisteth the vicissitude of life and death, and the change of all thinges."

One topos which appears in Pythagoras' lecture in the last book of the *Metamorphoses* received particular attention in the renaissance, becoming a commonplace at all levels of discourse, from hearthside platitude to courtly poetry of the highest pretention. By Ovid's account, Pythagoras inferred a similitude between the seasons of the year and the life of man: he asks rhetorically, "Do you not see the year assuming four aspects, in imitation of our own lifetime?" (XV.199–200). The ensuing passage is so richly poetic, and has proved such a prolific source of similes for later poets, that it must be quoted in full:

> Do you not see the year assuming four aspects, in imitation of our own lifetime? For in early spring it is tender and full of fresh life, just like a little child; at that time the herbage is bright, swelling with life, but as yet without strength and solidity, and fills the farmers with joyful expectation. Then all things are in bloom and the fertile fields run riot with their bright-coloured blossoms; but as yet there is no strength in the green foliage. After spring has passed, the year, grown more sturdy, passes into summer and becomes like a strong young man. For there is no hardier time than this, none more abounding in rich, warm life. Then autumn comes, with its first flush of youth gone, but ripe and mellow, midway in mood between youth and age, with sprinkled grey showing on the temples. And then comes aged winter, with faltering step and shivering, its locks all gone or hoary (XV.199–213).

Pythagoras draws from these observations a generalization about man: "Our own bodies also go through a ceaseless round of change" (XV.214–215). And after a glance at an emaciated Milon and a withered Helen, he concludes with an anguished apostrophe which contains an accusation: "O Time, thou great devourer (*tempus edax*), and thou, envious Age (*invidiosa vetustas*), together you destroy all things" (XV.234–235). Man at the end of his cycle, of course, perishes in death, as the pessimists gloomily assert:

> Summer succeeds the Spring; Autumn the Summer;
> The frosts of Winter the fall'n leaves of Autumn:
> All these and all fruits in them yearly fade,
> And every year return: but cursed man
> Shall never more renew his vanish'd face.
> (Chapman, *Byron's Tragedy*, V.iv.248–252)

But the seasons at the end of their annual cycle continue into a new year, repeating the pattern, rolling on interminably toward an approximation of eternity. The optimist draws his solace from knowing that man, by completing the four ages of his life, has prosecuted the pattern of time, the unit out of which eternity is compiled by endless repetition, and thereby has participated in eternity. His life is a microcosmic experience of eternity, incorporating the opposites set forth in the four seasons.

Diogenes Laertius also ascribes to Pythagoras this similitude between the four seasons and the ages of man:

> He distinguish'd the Life of Man thus: Childhood takes up Twenty Years, Youth Twenty, Manhood Twenty, and Old-age Twenty. These Ages he also compar'd to the Seasons of the Year, Childhood to the Spring, Youth to Summer, Manhood to Autumn, Old-age to Winter.[50]

By this similitude, the four seasons and the four ages of man become interchangeable cosmoi, each fulfilling the unit pattern of time. As such, they have produced verbal imagery in poetry and visual imagery in iconography of the most satisfying sort. To give but a single example of each—though examples are rife [51]—Colin Clout in the "December" eclogue, as E. K. pointedly tells us in the argument, "proportioneth his life to the foure seasons of the yeare." Using the same topos, but augmenting the verbal with visual imagery, Barthélemy Aneau in his *Picta poesis* (Lyons, 1552) offers an emblem which he entitles "The Undying Nature of Man" (see Plate 45). The accompanying hexastich reads:

> Spring, summer, autumn, winter—these are the four seasons as the years roll by in a cycle. Likewise man in his lifetime has four ages: he is first a child, then a youth, next an adult, and finally an old man—so that the cycle of human life, like the undying world, reveals to us that men are undying.[52]

This is the optimistic view of mutability. The emblem depicts a circle divided into four parts, each of which represents one of the seasons. The sun rises in spring, reaches its zenith in summer, sets in autumn, and is below the horizon in winter—as LeRoy observed, it "doth distinguishe by his Solstices and Equinoxes the fower seasons." In each quarter a man performs a chore suitable to the season amidst appropriate surroundings. At the bottom is an entombed corpse, symbolizing death, the finite end of man's life. But at the top, in the opposite position within the diagram, the deity sits enthroned, symbolizing eternity, the endless life promised the pious man. As John Swan proclaimed: "Before *Time* began, there was *Eternitie*, namely GOD . . . the beginning and end of all things." Time when extrapolated to eternity is tantamount to Him. This emblem, in effect, is an ideogram for time and was sometimes reduced to a simple abstract diagram, what Marvell concisely calls the "*Geometrick* yeer." [53] Lilio Gregorio Giraldi, for example, reports that "the ancient Greeks, when they wished to represent eternity, used this figure, as may be seen in old manuscripts to the present day." [54] The richness of this similitude between the seasons and the ages of man—its complexities and profundities—can perhaps be most fully realized in a tetrad, as in Plates 31–35. The tetrad could also be expanded, of course, to produce a diagram for time based on the twelve months and the signs of the zodiac, as in Plate 26.

Time, then, rolls in ever-recurring circles composed of two phases (day and night), four phases (the seasons), or twelve phases (the signs of the zodiac). This is the view of time presented *sub specie aeternitatis*. Time can also be viewed, however, in a stringently humanistic way from the vantage-point of the present moment. Rather than an objective notion of time as a process emanating from the monad and returning to it, man can hold a subjective notion of it obtained from his localized position in the time-space continuum. This view results in a linear definition of time rather than a cyclical pattern. It presumes a past reaching back to the moment of creation and a future stretching forward to the moment of

45. *An emblem entitled "The Undying Nature of Man"*

The emblem consists of a circle, representing eternity, divided into four quarters representing the seasons, the measurable parts of durational time. Taken together, the four quarters comprise a year, the basic unit of time. The sun is rising in the quarter for spring, at zenith in the quarter for summer, setting in the quarter for autumn, and absent in the quarter for winter. In each quarter there is vegetation appropriate to the season: ripening grain in spring, grain being harvested in summer, a tree with falling leaves in autumn, a bare tree in winter. In each a man pursues a suitable occupation: cultivating his grain, cutting his grain, picking fruit(?), retiring into a cave for the winter. Into each quarter a wind god blows, distributing flowers or leaves or hail(?) or cold blasts, and suggesting the omnipresence of the *anima mundi* (L. *anima*, soul = Gr. ἄνεμος, wind). At the bottom of the diagram a corpse rests in a grave, denoting that the end of man's cycle is death. But opposite, at the top, presiding over the whole is a resplendent Jove with thunderbolt and scepter, indicating not only that His providence is continual, but also that He is co-existent with eternity. The verses are translated on p. 225.

Barthélemy Aneau, *Picta poesis. Ut pictura poesis erit* (Lyons, 1552), p. 26.

world destruction. The present is but an instant, an infinitesimal portion of time, a point without dimension. During the renaissance there was intense awareness of the present as a point in time through which eternity enters our consciousness, streaming both backward into the past and forward into the future. Thomas Blundeville takes particular pains to be clear about this at the beginning of his discourse on time:

> I mind to speake here onely of that time which is a number measuring the mooving of the first mooveable, and of all other mutable thinges, which time had his beginning with the world, and shall ende with the same, and this time consisteth of two parts, that is first, and last, or rather before or after, successively following one another, and these two partes are knit together with a common bound called of the Latines *Nunc*, that is to say now, or at this present, which is the end of that which went before, and the beginning of that which followeth after, and therefore some doe devide time into three parts, that is, time past, time present, and time to come, but the time present is a moment indivisible, and is the beginning of time, even as a point or pricke is the beginning of all Magnitudes, & yet least part therof it selfe.[55]

The "now" is to time, then, as the point is to magnitude (which, like time, is a continuous quantity). This assumption divides the temporal continuum into three distinct parts: "time past, time present, and time to come." Such an analysis of time was reflected in demonology by the cryptic dictum: "Time is, time was, time is past." The brazen head constructed by necromancy could utter no truth more profound or more certain. The need to act at the right instant, while "time is," became a truism. But that instant, announced by the brazen head, is elusively short in duration, as Miles learns in Robert Greene's *Friar Bacon and Friar Bungay* (IV.i.53 ff.). Incidentally, it should be noted that time does not stretch *infinitely* back from the present, or *infinitely* forward. Logic dictates that if there were infinite time before the present, by definition there would be none left for a future.[56]

Following Pythagorean doctrine, the renaissance saw that time could be measured against two distinct sets of coordinates. At one level there is the atemporal monad, Plato's world of being, Aristotle's immutable αἰών,[57] the Judeo-Christian ageless Jehovah. At the other there is changeable multeity, Plato's world of becoming, Aristotle's palpable plenum, the Judeo-Christian valley of the shadow of death. Though man walks in this shadow, however, the way leads to eternal life in heaven because the two sets of coordinates are themselves synchronized. Pico della Mirandola offers to us the comfort of a deity which subsumes all in his goodness:

> The end of all things is the same as the beginning of all: one God, omnipotent and blessed, the best of all things which can exist or be thought of; hence the two appellations used by the Pythagoreans, One and Good. He is called one since He is the beginning of all things, just as unity is the beginning of all numbers, and good since He is the end, rest, and absolute felicity of all things.[58]

The omnipotent, benevolent deity has produced space and time in the image of an ideal model, thereby providing for man an earthly condition which is conducive to his perfection.

By acting in accord with this divine plan, man (particularly the poet) realizes his capacity for godlike experience.[59] In the act of love, for example, by imitating the cosmic pattern of completeness two lovers acquire something of the homogeneity of the monad. They achieve the timelessness of eternity, and the undifferentiated inclusiveness of infinity. They incorporate our entire time-space continuum. As Donne boasts, imperiously chiding that busy old fool, the sun:

> Love, all alike, no season knowes, nor clyme,
> Nor houres, dayes, moneths, which are the rags of time.
> . . . .
> She'is all States, and all Princes, I,
> Nothing else is.
>
> ("The Sunne Rising," 9–10, 21–22)

These lovers have reached the timeless state of God, whose "whole duration," Sir Thomas Browne declares, is "but one permanent point without succession, parts, flux, or division." [60] In such a way, man transcends his temporal limitation and fulfills the potential of his origin as an image of deity. To echo Marvell, he produces a world that seems enough, and makes the most of time.

Notes

[1] Cf. Plato, *Republic*, 500C. On this point, see Johann Tobias Wagner, *De ἀνόδῳ, seu adscensu hominis in Deum pythagorico* (Halle, 1710). For a comprehensive dissertation on the Pythagorean concept of deity, see Johann Bernhard Hassel, *Unum theologiae pythagoricae compendium* (Helmstadt, 1710).

[2] See, for example, Natalis Comes, *Mythologiae* [I.7], tr. Jean de Montlyard (Lyons, 1600), p. 16; and André Dacier, *The Life of Pythagoras,* tr. anon. (London, 1707), pp. 31–32.

[3] Ambrosius, si recte memini, Pythagoram patre Iudaeo natum ostendit (Marsilio Ficino, *Opera omnia* [Basle, 1576], p. 30). Ficino was trying to recall St. Ambrose, *Letters* [28 or 81], tr. Sister Mary Melchior Beyenka (New York, 1954), p. 454. Tommaso Campanella also recalled St. Ambrose's epistle which made Pythagoras of Jewish descent; cf. *The Defense of Galileo,* tr. Grant McColley (Northampton, Mass., 1938), p. 72.

[4] *Heptaplus,* tr. Douglas Carmichael, in Pico, *On the Dignity of Man* et al., tr. Charles Glenn Wallis (Indianapolis, 1965), p. 68.

[5] (London, 1653), B1. For early bibliography on Pythagoras' debt to Moses and other Jews, see Gerard Johann Vossius, *De philosophorum sectis liber* (The Hague, 1657), p. 30; Theophilus Gale, *Philosophia generalis* (London, 1676), pp. 169–173; Joannes Franciscus Buddeus, *Compendium historiae philosophicae* (Halle, 1731), pp. 92–93; and Joannes Albertus Fabricius, *Bibliotheca Graeca,* 11 vols. (Hamburg, 1790–1808), I.756–757, 764–765. See also Symphorien Champier, *Symphonia Platonis cum Aristotele* (Paris, 1516), fol. 165 ff.; and Isidore Lévy, *La légende de Pythagore de Grèce en Palestine* (Paris, 1927).

[6] See, for example, Eusebius, *Evangelica praeparatio,* IX–X, *passim.*

[7] *Exhortation to the Greeks* [xix] in *Writings of Saint Justin Martyr,* tr. Thomas B. Falls (New York, 1948), p. 396.

[8] St. Clement, *Exhortation to the Greeks* [vi], tr. G. W. Butterworth (London, 1919), p. 163.

St. Cyril, *Contra Julianum* [I.xxx] in *Opera,* tr. Wolfgang Musculus, 4 vols. (Basle, 1546), III.19. The Latin translation of the quotation in this volume is valuable for the phraseology, showing how the pagan dictum received Christian coloration in the transmission:

> Deus quidem unus, & ipse non, ut quidam suspicantur, extra mundi gubernationem, sed in ipso totus in toto circulo, omnes generationes considerat, contemperatio existens omnium seculorum, & lux suarum virtutum & operum, principium omnium, lumen in coelo, & pater omnium, mens et animatio omnium, circulorum omnium motio.

Cf. this renaissance Latin version with the modern translation in Migne, *Patrologia Graeca,* Vol. 76, col. 547.

[9] For examples, see Symphorien Champier, "Theologica Orphica" in *Vocabularius . . . naturalis philosophiae* (Lyons, 1508), bb4^v–5; Francesco Giorgio, *De harmonia mundi totius cantica tria,* 2nd ed. (Paris, 1545), fol. 7^v; Pontus de Tyard, *L'Univers* (Lyons, 1557), pp. 132–133; Joachim Zehner, ed., *Pythagorae fragmenta* (Leipzig, 1603), p. 67; Hierocles, *Commentarius in aurea Pythagoreorum carmina,* 2 vols. (London, 1654–55), I.xviii–xix; Thomas Stanley, *The history of philosophy,* 2nd ed. (London, 1687), p. 547; Ralph Cudworth, *The true intellectual system of the universe* (London, 1678), p. 377; Pierre Bayle, *Dictionaire,* 2 vols. (Rotterdam, 1697), "Pythagoras," footnote N; William Enfield, *The History of Philosophy,* 2 vols. (London, 1791), I.394.

[10] More, *Utopia,* tr. Ralph Robynson, ed. J. R. Lumby (Cambridge Univ. Press, 1879), pp. 143–144.

[11] "Opinions of Philosophers" [I.vii] in *The morals,* tr. Philemon Holland (London, 1603), p. 812.

[12] *De arte cabalistica libri tres,* tr. Thomas Stanley in *History of philosophy,* p. 571.

[13] *Of the interchangeable course, or variety of things in the whole world,*

tr. Robert Ashley (London, 1594), fol. 101. Actually, LeRoy is quoting Plutarch, "Life of Numa," viii.

[14] *The Nature of the Gods* [I.xi], tr. C. D. Yonge (London, 1868), p. 11.

[15] *The Divine Institutes* [I.v], tr. Stanley, *History of philosophy*, p. 547. Lactantius was echoed by numerous writers throughout the renaissance—e.g., Polydore Vergil, *An abridgemente of the notable worke*, tr. Thomas Langley (London, 1570), fol. 2; Giorgio, *De harmonia mundi* (1545), fol. 166; Ludovicus Caelius Rhodiginus, *Lectionum antiquarum libri XXX* (Basle, 1566), p. 836; Lilio Gregorio Giraldi, "Historiae deorum gentilium syntagma" in *Opera omnia* (Leyden, 1696), p. 9; and Fortunius Licetus, *De mundi, & hominis analogia liber unus* (Udine, 1635), p. 24.

[16] St. Justin Martyr, *The Monarchy or the Rule of God* [ii], tr. Dacier, *Life of Pythagoras*, p. ix. This fragment led a popular life in the renaissance, being often reprinted—e.g., Champier, "Theologica Orphica" in *Vocabularius*, bb5; Henricus Stephanus, ed., *Poesis philosophica* (Geneva, 1573), p. 118; Zehner, *Pythagorae fragmenta*, pp. 22–23, 60; Porphyry, *De vita Pythagorae*, ed. Conrad Rittershaus (Altdorf, 1610), ψ3; Hierocles, *Commentarius in aurea carmina* (1654–55), I.xix. See also Cornelia J. de Vogel, *Pythagoras and Early Pythagoreanism* (Assen, 1966), p. 201.

> [17] Pythagoras Jovem asserebat esse virtutem, & harmoniam, & animi temperamentum, sanitatem, omneque bonum: & ideo eius favore & iuvamento stare omnia

(*De harmonia mundi* [1545], fol. 64). Cf. Plato, *Timaeus*, 29D–30C.

[18] Stanley, *History of philosophy*, p. 550, who is actually quoting Plutarch, *De placitis philosophorum*, II.iv, who ascribes this statement to Pythagoras.

[19] Cf. Diogenes Laertius, VIII.27.

[20] Cf. Plutarch, *De placitis philosophorum*, I.xxv.

[21] See Hierocles' commentary on lines 45–48 of the *Carmina aurea* in Dacier, *Life of Pythagoras*, pp. 315–319.

> [22] Porrò cum Corpus nullum sine formâ sua interna, nempe anima, à qua motus, proprietates, & effecta ipsius proficisci in confesso est, consistere nequeat, sunt qui etiam Mundo Animam attribuant ἐκ τ'αυτοῦ καὶ ἑτέρου, ex *Eodem* & *Diverso* compositam, & quasi Naturam tertiam factam, cui in se harmonicorum numerorum rationes continenti accommodatur celeberrimus ille Quaternio, *Pythagorae* Sacramentum, sempiternae Naturae fons propter Denarium Numerum mysterium admirabile complectentem, in quo numeri precedentes, & se in infinitum explicantes semper finiuntur, & ab unitate iterum incipientes ad sui multiplicationem progrediuntur

(*Harmonia macrocosmica* [Amsterdam, 1661], pp. 79–80). In his *Utriusque cosmi . . . historia*, 4 vols. (Oppenheim, 1617–19), Robert Fludd includes a chapter entitled "De anima mundi, seu virtute divina ubique in mundo dispersa" (I.121–122).

[23] *The secrets of numbers* (London, 1624), p. 2.

[24] In *Morals*, tr. Holland (1603), pp. 767–768.

[25] In *Morals*, tr. Holland (1603), p. 819. See also pp. 107–113, above.

[26] *The garden of Cyrus* printed with *Pseudodoxia epidemica*, 4th ed. (London, 1658), esp. pp. 72–73.

[27] *Commentary on the Dream of Scipio* [I.vi], tr. Stahl, p. 109.

[28] *Ibid.* [II.ii], pp. 190–193. For a provocative discussion of the Platonic lambda in Giorgio and Milton, see Maren-Sofie Røstvig, *The Hidden Sense* (Oslo, 1963), pp. 43–58.

[29] In *Colin Clouts Come Home Againe*, Spenser offers a comparable passage

fitted to the hexaemeral tradition (lines 841–871), showing how the multifarious items of creation are taught by love to live in accord.

[30] St. Clement, "Exhortation to the Heathen" [i] in *The Ante-Nicene Fathers,* ed. Rev. Alexander Roberts and James Donaldson (New York, 1899), vol. II, p. 172.

[31] Hieremias Drexel, *The considerations of Drexelius upon eternitie,* tr. Ralph Winterton (Cambridge, 1636), p. 107.

[32] For the distinction between these terms, see Joachim Fortius Ringelberg, "Liber de tempore" in *Opera* (Lyons, 1531), pp. 441–442; Symphorien Champier, *Periarchon* (Lyons, 1533), pp. 5–6; Lilio Gregorio Giraldi, *De annis et mensibus, caeterisque temporum partibus . . . dissertatio* (Basle, 1541), pp. 1–2; and Fludd, *Utriusque cosmi . . . historia,* II.503–504.

[33]
> *Deus* igitur *Summus* est, & *Primus Mathematicus,* qui tempus & locum, quibus caret Æternitas, creavit, & in tempore atque loco Mundum Creatum constituit, his terminis Creaturam definiens, ut ita distingueretur à *Creatore* suo, qui infinitus & indeterminatus tempore & loco circumscribens *Gloriosissimam suam Majestatem* manifestare voluit

(*Harmonia macrocosmica,* p. 84).

[34] Translated by Stanley, *History of philosophy,* p. 566.

[35] The *De mundi anima* of Timaeus of Locri provides a useful gloss which reinforces for us the meaning of this passage:

> These are parts of Time called Periods, ordained by God together with the World: for before the World there were no Stars, and consequently neither year nor seasons, by which this generable World is commensurated. This time is the image of that which is ingenerate, called Eternity: for as this Universe was formed after the eternal examplar of the Ideal World, so was this Time ordained together with the World after its pattern, Eternity

(tr. Stanley, *History of philosophy,* p. 567).

[36] *On the Nature of the Universe* [V], tr. Ronald Latham (Harmondsworth, 1951), p. 215.

[37] *Speculum mundi* (Cambridge, 1635), p. 354.

[38] *Ibid.,* p. 45. Swan strongly echoes Macrobius' discussion of the monad: "This monad, the beginning and ending of all things, yet itself not knowing a beginning or ending, refers to the Supreme God" (*Commentary on the Dream of Scipio* [I.vi.8], tr. Stahl, pp. 100–101). And Macrobius continues to place the monad in the context of time: "It is also that Mind, sprung from the Supreme God, which, unaware of the changes of time, is always in one time, the present." Beside Swan and Macrobius, of course, stands the Revelation of St. John: "I am Alpha and Omega, the beginning and the ending, saith the Lord, which is, and which was, and which is to come, the Almighty" (i.8).

For similar definitions of time, see Pontus de Tyard, *Discours du temps, de l'an, et de ses parties* (Lyons, 1556); Michael Neander, *Physice* (Leipzig, 1585), p. 49; Hermann Witekind, *De sphaera mundi: et temporis ratione apud Christianos* (Newstadt, 1590), p. 289; and LeRoy, *Interchangeable course,* fol. 1^{v}.

[39] See p. 266, below.

[40] "Opin. of Phil." [I.xxiv] in *Morals,* tr. Holland (1603), p. 816.

[41] See George Williamson, "Mutability, Decay, and Seventeenth-Century Melancholy," *English Literary History,* 2 (1935), 121–150.

[42] *Speculum mundi,* pp. 361–362.

[43] Horapollo, *De sacris Ægyptiorum notis* (Paris, 1574), fol. 1.

[44] *The Apology Against the Books of Rufinus* [III.40], tr. John N. Hritzu (Catholic Univ. of America Press, 1965), p. 212. Actually, Jerome is quoting Porphyry, *De vita Pythagorae*, xix; cf. G. S. Kirk and J. E. Raven, *The Presocratic Philosophers* (Cambridge Univ. Press, 1962), p. 223. Porphyry adds that Pythagoras was the first to introduce these teachings into Greece, presumably from Egypt. Of course, the theory of recurrent world periods is more usually ascribed to the Stoics.

[45] Prima & maximè admiranda Metamorphosis est, rerum creatio (*Fabularum Ovidii interpretatio, ethica, physica, et historica* [Cambridge, 1584], p. 2).

[46] Unus est per se genitus, ab uno sunt quaecunque fabricata, omnia (*ibid.*, p. 3). The reference in St. Justin Martyr is *The Monarchy or the Rule of God* [ii], pp. 445–446. I cannot identify the reference in St. Clement.

[47] Hieremias Drexel provides a renaissance gloss on this motif:

> They [the ancients] have represented *Eternitie* by the *Sunne* and the *Moon*. The *Sunne* revives every day, although it seems every day to die, and to be buried. It alwayes riseth again, although every night it sets. The *Moon* also hath her increase after every wane. *Catullus* hath pretty verses to this purpose:
>
> The *Sunne* doth set; the *Sunne* doth rise again:
> The *day* doth close; the *day* doth break again.
> Once set our *Sunne*, again it riseth never:
> Once close our *day* of life, it's *night* for ever.

(*Considerations upon eternitie*, p. 9). The reference in Catullus is v.4–6. Cf. Giraldi, *De annis et mensibus*, p. 3. In occult traditions such as hieroglyphics and alchemy, the conjunction of sun and moon was a symbol used to designate eternity—e.g., Horapollo, *De sacris Ægyptiorum notis*, fol. 1. The motif is adapted to Christian use on the title page of the King James version of the Bible (London, 1611).

[48] *Speculum mundi*, p. 354.

[49] *Interchangeable course*, fol. 1^{v}–2.

[50] *The lives, opinions, and remarkable sayings of the most famous ancient philosophers. . . . Made English by several hands*, 2 vols. (London, 1696), II.7–8. For the same statement, see Diodorus Siculus, *Bibliotheca*, X.ix.5; Ovid, *Opera*, ed. Raphael Regius (Venice, 1509), fol. 157^{v}; Pietro Crinito, *De honesta disciplina* [V.ix] (Basle, 1532), p. 88; Levinus Lemnius, *Touchstone of complexions*, tr. Thomas Newton (London, 1565), fol. 30; and Pedro Mexia, *The foreste*, tr. Thomas Fortescue (London, 1571), M3.

[51] See Samuel C. Chew, *The Pilgrimage of Life* (Yale Univ. Press, 1962), pp. 154–160.

[52] Ver, Aestas, Autumnus, Hyems, Hae quattuor annis
Sunt tempestates, orbe volubilibus.
Quattuor aetates homo sic habet integer aevi.
Qui puer, hinc juvenis, mox vir, & inde senex.
Aeterno ut similis mundo revolutio vitae
Nos itidem aeternos arguat esse homines. (p. 26)

[53] "Upon the Death of the Lord *Hastings*," line 18.

[54] Antiqui quidem Graeci cum aevum ipsi effingere volebant, hac figura utebantur ut in vetustis adhuc codicibus datur videri (*De annis et mensibus*, p. 3).

[55] *Exercises* (London, 1594), fol. 167^{v}. In this passage Blundeville probably owes as much to Aristotle as to the Pythagorean-Platonic tradition; cf. *Physica*, 217b29–218a30.

[56] In the Pythagorean-Platonic system, the world had a definite beginning and will have a definite end. In the Aristotelian system, however, the world is ungenerated and indestructible. The usual Christian scheme attempts to hedge with the argument of *creatio ex nihilo*. According to this argument, only God has an existence prior to creation, and matter has no independent identity. Chaos is abstracted until it is no more than an abyss. There is ambiguity, then, about the mortality of the world, since it is an extension of God himself, innocent of any intermeddling with corruptible matter. In the quotation on p. 217, above, John Swan reflects some of this confusion, though his position is essentially Pythagorean. Sir Thomas Browne deals with the problem in *Religio Medici* [I.35, 45], ed. L. C. Martin (Oxford, 1964), pp. 34–35, 43.

[57] *De caelo*, 279a18–279a28.

[58] *Heptaplus* [VII.proem], tr. Carmichael, p. 148.

[59] Cf. for example Pico della Mirandola:

> If we are faithful like Moses, holiest theology will approach, and will inspire us with a twofold frenzy. We, raised up into the loftiest watch-tower of theology, from which, measuring with indivisible eternity the things that are, will be and shall have been, and looking at their primeval beauty, shall be prophets of Phoebus, his winged lovers, and finally, aroused with ineffable charity as with fire, placed outside of ourselves like burning Seraphim, filled with divinity, we shall now not be ourselves, but He himself who made us

(*Dignity of Man*, tr. Wallis, p. 14).

[60] *Religio Medici* [I.xi], ed. Martin, p. 11. Cogent here is Boethius' concept of eternity as *totum simul*.

4
Occult Sciences

The Pythagorean doctrine was a rational construct. Starting from certain postulates, it proceeded with unrelenting consistency to certain conclusions. From its theory of numbers came a dichotomization of reality into a conceptual realm and a physical realm, an intelligible world perceptible only to the mind and a palpable world perceptible only to the senses. The palpable world is material and, as our senses attest, mutable and multifarious. The intelligible world is incorporeal, and by definition is permanent, all-inclusive, and homogeneous. This unified infinite is given precedence because it is atemporal and unchanging. It is represented numerically by the monad. The world of physical nature, though a multitude of varied and variable items, is not, however, chaotic. Its multeity is carefully related to the unity of the monad by the theory of cosmos, so that the sensible world is made a derivative of the intelligible world. Pythagorean cosmogony explains in numerical terms how the monad through the point proceeded to generate a straight line (2 points), then a plane surface (3 points), and finally a volume (4 points). More expansively in the *Timaeus,* Plato explains how a creating godhead gave physical extension to his archetypal ideas by starting with two extremes, fire and earth, and then by placing two mathematical means between them made a stable system. In the act of creation, numerical ratios known as harmonies were established in our universe when the archetypal forms were imprinted upon inchoate matter, and they persist as cosmic patterns, perceptible to man in such microcosmic units as the tetradic arrangement of the four elements or the eight notes of the diapason or the twelve signs of the zodiac. By rational discourse, based upon empirical observation and careful logic, the Pythagoreans arrived at a conception of the universe as a structured system created and maintained by a beneficent deity. This system is characterized by a strict orderliness, wherein everything has its assigned place. Not only is there spatial order, so that cosmos is a synoptic condition, but also there is order maintained in a durational dimension by the measured passage of time, so that cosmos is a dynamic condition as well. Pythagorean metaphysics is as complete and coherent as Aristotle's, and it does almost as well as modern physics in explaining to us how the cold lifeless world of the atom relates to the world we perceive with our senses.

Nonetheless, although the Pythagorean doctrine is a rational construct, it produced some irrational offshoots and interacted with several alien doctrines of somewhat dubious respectability. Its theory of numbers could be irresponsibly applied in the service of arbitrary numerology, its reverence for the monad could be exaggerated into mysticism of the most speculative sort, and its belief in invisible forces could be perverted into elaborate methodologies for dealing with spirits. Most pervasively, its contention that everything is ordered and nothing is haphazard leads inexorably to a conclusion that all things and all actions—animate and inanimate—are interrelated. Each event of nature, no matter how far distant horizontally or vertically, affects our lives. Conversely, natural, even cosmic, events can be affected by what we do. In consequence, man has definite powers of a magical sort. If he can discover the occult means, he may control his universe. At the very least, by correct reading of the portents he may foretell its course.

But at the same time, on the constructive side, the belief in cosmos related the intelligible and the sensible worlds, and bestowed a unity on human experience which allowed a man—be he philosopher or scientist or theologian—to proceed with optimistic confidence that a beneficent deity presides over an ordered universe. White magic was far more common than black magic. The highly developed art of alchemy was an adjunct to religion, not its substitute or adversary. Faustus' progress as a rake took him down the broad highway to hell, but we must admire the purpose of his journey—he simply made the wrong turn after being maliciously misled onto a shortcut. At best, the occult sciences were seen as a mode of understanding the godhead and complying with his will, a means of transcending the mortal sphere of this world and expatiating in the perfection of the monad.[1] Of course, they also offered opportunity to satisfy petty curiosity, or even worse, sinful desires; and here the devil made profit from human credulity. But such is the ambiguity of the human condition, and the renaissance, most acutely of all ages, was aware of the need for moral choice. In any case, even the most esoteric subject in this chapter has its thread of reason which, no matter how finely spun and how tortuously unwound through the labyrinth of speculation, leads back to a thoroughly rational tenet.

From the earliest period Pythagoras was credited with divinatory powers.[2] He was associated with Pythian Apollo and thence with the Delphic oracle.[3] As evident in the *Carmina aurea*, he postulated the existence of spirits which thickly populate our environment and which, though invisible, have direct influence over us. According to Diogenes Laertius, Pythagoras taught:

> That all the Air was full of Souls; and that these were they who were thought to be *Demons* and *Heroes:* That by them Dreams were sent to Men, as also the signs of sickness and health. . . . To these also are attributed Lustrations, Propitiations, all sorts of Prophetic Divination, Omens and the like.[4]

Because of his extraordinary intelligence, coupled with his penchant for meditation, Pythagoras was often regarded as a seer in touch with these spirits, and perhaps as a necromancer who could control them. The tradition of *ipse dixit*, "The master said it," was applied here, and Pythagoras thereby became a prophet with authority in several divinatory sciences. Thomas Stanley offered some verses to this effect which he translated from the Byzantine polymath Joannes Tzetzes:

> *Pythagoras* Samian, *Mnesarchus* son,
> Not only knew what would by fate be done,
> But even for those who futures would perceive
> He of Prognosticks several Books did leave.[5]

Pythagoras' treatise on "Prognosticks" does not survive, if indeed it ever existed. But there was no question about the Pythagorean belief in divination. Iamblichus with his undeviating reverence provides a rationale for it:

> What things are agreeable to God, cannot be known, unless a man hear God himself, or the Gods, or acquire it by divine art. For this reason they diligently studied Divination, as being the only interpretation of the benevolence of the Gods. It is likewise an employment most suitable to those who believe there are Gods.[6]

In this context, divination is not damnable; rather it becomes a pious pursuit to ascertain the divine intention.

Diogenes Laertius reports that Pythagoras "us'd Divination by the observation of *Omens* and Flights of Birds only." [7] But Plutarch removes all restrictions on the procedures used by Pythagoras, noting that he "condemneth that onely which is wrought by sacrifices." [8] Many of the miraculous acts attributed to Pythagoras were intended to enhance his standing as a divinator, as Iamblichus suggests:

> When likewise he happened to be conversing with his familiars about birds, symbols, and prodigies, and was observing that all these are the messengers of the Gods, sent by them to those men who are truly dear to the Gods, he is said to have brought down an eagle that was flying over Olympia, and after gently stroking, to have dismissed it. Through these things, therefore, and other things similar to these, he demonstrated that he possessed the same dominion as Orpheus over savage animals, and that he allured and detained them by the power of voice proceeding from the mouth.[9]

Iamblichus associates Pythagoras with Orpheus in his affinity with and control over nature. It was generally agreed, however, that Pythagoras had learned the secrets of divination during his travels among the Chaldeans and Egyptians.[10]

Of the various fortune-telling devices ascribed to Pythagoras, the best known was his *sphera* or "wheel" (see Plate 46).[11] It is also one of the crudest methods of divination associated with Pythagoras. It consists of a circle comprising the 23 letters of the alphabet with a number between 2 and 28 assigned to each, and the numbers 1 to 30 divided (arbitrarily) into two groups. By a computation which combines a number chosen at random by the questioner, the number assigned on the wheel to the first letter of the questioner's name, and the number assigned to the day of the week in another fixed table, an answer of "yes" or "no" can be derived for any question. This "wheel of Pythagoras" is related to the wheel-of-fortune card in the Tarot,[12] and survives in the wheel of fortune which still spins at carnivals.

Because Pythagoras concerned himself with the physical characteristics of his students at Croton as well as their intellectual ability, he was regarded by many as the inventor of physiognomy. It is thoroughly in keeping with Pythagorean doctrine, of course, that external features reveal inner form—i.e., the soul. Iamblichus reports how Pythagoras used physiognomy to analyze prospective candidates for his school:

> He considered their presence and their gaite, and the whole motion of their body: and, physiognomizing them by the symptoms,

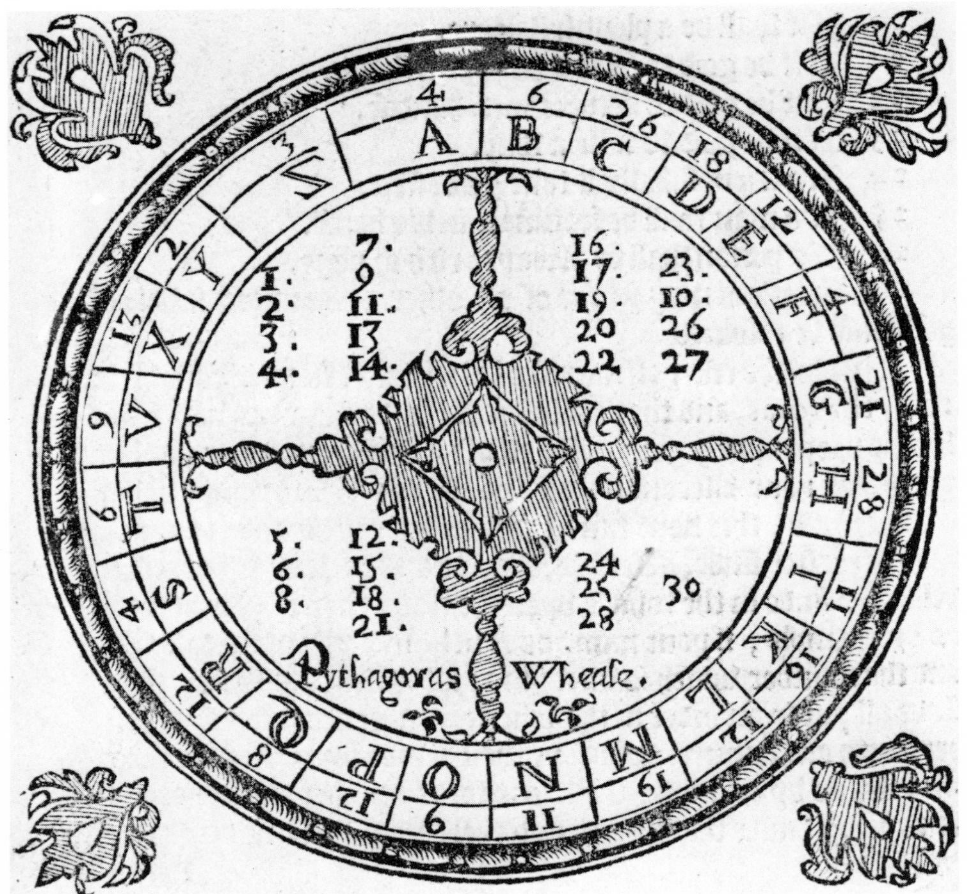

46. *The Wheel of Pythagoras*
This Wheel is an ingenuous device for answering questions. Instructions for obtaining a "yes" or a "no" to any question are given by Cattan:

> You must first of all choose a number, what you list at your discretion, as 10. 15. or 12. or anie other more or lesse, this done take the number of the day, as you shall hereafter finde, al set in order, and then take the number which ye finde in the wheele upon the fyrst letter of your name: as by example, if your name be *Anthony*, you must take *A*, and the number which is over him: all which things you shall finde all put in an order in the wheele, and gather al those numbers into one summe, which ye shall divide by 30, reserving the rest, as by example, if all your totall number doe amounte unto 134. divide that by 30. and there will fourteene remaine, which number ye must search in the wheele, and if you finde it in the upper halfe, your matter shall speede well, and if it be in the nether halfe, it shall be evill.

The numbers assigned to the days of the week are given in the following table:

sonday	munday	tuesday	wenesday	thursday	friday	satterday
106	52	52	102	31	68	45

It is worth noting that there are considerably more numbers in the "upper halfe" than in the "nether halfe," thus insuring the popularity of the Wheel.

Christophe de Cattan, *The geomancie*, tr. Francis Sparry (London, 1591), p. 238.

> he discovered by manifest signs the occult dispositions of their souls.[13]

Physiognomy developed as an independent science, and was ubiquitously popular throughout the renaissance. Perhaps the best known manuals for its practice were prepared by Bartholomaeus Cocles (1467–1504) and Joannes ab Indagine (fl. early 16th century).[14] Although it may be generally discredited today (not, incidentally, by some physiologists, who have provided an empirical basis for the science), its a priori assumption that the soul shaped the body was hardly questioned until the nineteenth century.

Pythagoras was also directly associated with the science of oneiromancy, the interpretation of dreams.[15] Within the framework of Pythagorean metaphysics, which dichotomizes reality into a conceptual world and a physical world, a dream is seen quite simply as an intrusion of the conceptual into the physical. A truth which would otherwise remain ineffable is thereby made conscious in the dreamer and rendered knowable. The deity often uses a dream or vision, in fact, as a means of communicating with man. A false dream sent by an evil-wisher to mislead is also possible, of course, and it is therefore important to evaluate whether a dream be truth or delusion. This tradition is not unique to Pythagoreanism—indeed, it is better known from the Homeric epics and from Biblical stories such as those of Joseph and of Daniel. There are also famous classical authorities on dreams, such as Artemidorus (fl. 138–179) and Synesius (378–431),[16] and Aristotle included a discussion on dreams in his *Parva naturalia*. Nevertheless, Pythagoras shared in this syncretic tradition for oneiromancy. Diogenes Laertius (VIII.32) notes that he fills the air with spirits, and these are the agents of informative dreams. Porphyry recalls that Pythagoras visited the Egyptians, the Arabians, the Chaldeans, and the Hebrews, and suggests that from them he gained expertise in the interpretation of dreams (*De vita Pythagorae*, xi). Pythagoras' high repute as a divinator was sufficient to qualify him as an adept in oneiromancy.

The identification of Pythagoras as an astrologer was tenuous, but nonetheless definite. Largely because of his sojourn among the Chaldeans and Egyptians, he acquired a reputation for prognostication based upon the stars. Thomas Stanley reports that Pythagoras was skilfull in judicial astrology, which meant primarily the casting of horoscopes, and he quotes Apuleius:

> The Caldaeans shewed him the Science of the Stars, the number of the Planets; their Stations, Revolutions, and the various effects of both in the Nativities of men.[17]

Auger Ferrier (1513–88), the contentious physician of Toulouse, wrote his most important astrological treatise "according to the Pythagorean doctrine." [18]

The divinatory science most distinctively Pythagorean is geomancy, a little-practised technique which is hardly known today except perhaps in the thoroughly debased form of tea-leaf reading. The word "geomancy" derives from the Greek γῆ, "earth" + μαντεία, "mode of divination." As the name suggests, it is the art of answering questions and foretelling the future by means of pebbles scattered in a free throw upon a flat surface, originally the earth. By reference to tables (see Plate 47), a divinator can then interpret the configurations that the pebbles have assumed when dropped. During the renaissance the more usual method was for the questioner to make dots and lines with ink on paper, which the geomancer then construed. Christophe de Cattan, a mid-sixteenth-century occultist in Geneva, provides a professional definition of the discipline:

> *Geomancie* is a Science and Art which consisteth of points, prickes, and lines, made in steade of the foure Elementes, and of the Starres and Planets of Heaven called, the Science of the earth, because in times past it was made on it, as we will hereafter declare. And thus every pricke signifieth a Starre, and every line an Element, and every figure the foure quarters of the Worlde.[19]

As Cattan expounds geomancy, it becomes an enormously complicated and sophisticated procedure, intimately linked with astrology. The rationale for it, however, is quite simply that nothing occurs by chance in our ordered universe and therefore the configuration of pebbles or points reflects the qualities of its maker. Moreover, the meaning assigned to a configuration in the tables is not arbitrary, but represents some innate significance of the form—i.e., number—which has been delineated. This science of geomancy, then, grows out of the Pythagorean theory that numbers are forms defined by points, and that numbers have inherent meanings assigned by the deity. Iamblichus opined that this is a higher type of divination:

> Instead of divination by the entrails of beasts, he [Pythagoras] delivered to him [Abaris] the art of prognosticating through numbers, conceiving that this was purer, more divine, and more adapted to the celestial numbers of the Gods.[20]

Figure.	Name.	Element	Planet.	Sign.
	Way *Iourney*	Water	☾	♌
	People *Congregation.*	Water	☾	♑
	Conjunction *An Aſſembling*	Aire	☿	♍
	A priſon *Bound*	The Earth	♄	♓
	Great fortune *Greater aid* *Safe-guard entering*	The Earth	☉	♒
	Leſſer fortune *Leſser aid* *Safe-guard going out*	Fire	☉	♉
	Obtaining *Comprehended within*	Aire	♃	♈
	Acquiſition *Comprehended without*	Fire	♀	♎
	Ioy *Laughing* *Healthy* *Bearded*	Aire	♃	♉
	Sadneſs *Damned* *Croſs*	Earth	♄	♏
	A Girle *Beautifull*	Watter	♀	♎
	A Boy *Yellow* *Beardleſs*	Fire	♂	♈
	White *Fair*	Water.	☿	♋
	Reddiſh *Red*	Fire	♂	□
	The head *The threſhold entring* *The upper threſhold*	Earth	☊	♍
	The Taile *The threſhold going out* *The lower threſhold*	Fire.	☋	♐

47. *A table of geomantical configurations*

The left-hand column depicts various configurations of points. The meaning of each is given in the next column. The last three columns indicate the element, the planet, and the zodiacal sign with which each configuration is associated. This data is then interpreted by a method akin to astrology to produce a prognostication.
Heinrich Cornelius Agrippa, *Three books of occult philosophy*, tr. John Freake (London, 1651), p. 310.

The originator of geomancy may well have been Eurytas, an early disciple of Pythagoras, who imitated the figures of living things with pebbles and then assigned the corresponding number to those things.[21] Credit for the invention of geomancy, however, usually redounded to Pythagoras himself.

The Pythagorean theory of numbers gave rise also to a large and diverse body of esoterica which dealt with the secondary meanings of numbers. Although never glorified as an autonomous and fully articulated science, it was put to a variety of uses under the name of arithmology or arithmomancy.[22] Since in the Pythagorean scheme the ultimate constituents of reality are numbers, it is a logical assumption that every real thing must have a corresponding number. Put another way, the creating godhead used numbers as his archetypal forms, and therefore the items of creation should be reducible to numbers. Agrippa makes the point with utmost succinctness: "*Pythagoras* . . . saith, that number is that by which all things consist, and distributes each vertue to each number."[23] A few simple, obvious examples were early educed in support of this argument. Four, for example, was seen as the number of justice because its form is a square with equal sides, and justice is defined as equality for all. Five was designated the number of marriage, because it is the sum of 2, the female number, and 3, the male number.

William Enfield in his sober *History of Philosophy* (2 vols. [London, 1791]) offers a sympathetic defense of arithmology:

> The most probable explanation of the Pythagoric doctrine of numbers is, that they were used as symbolical or emblematical representations of the first principles and forms of nature, and particularly of those eternal and immutable essences, to which Plato afterwards gave the appellation of Ideas. Not being able, or not chusing, to explain in simple language the abstract notions of principles and forms, Pythagoras seems to have made use of numbers, as geometricians make use of diagrams, to assist the conceptions of scholars. More particularly, conceiving some analogy between numbers and the Intelligent Forms which subsist in the divine mind, he made the former a symbol of the latter. As numbers proceed from unity, or the Monad, as a simple root, whence they branch out into various combinations, and assume new properties in their progress, so he conceived the different forms of nature to recede, at different distances, from their common source, the pure and simple essence of deity, and at every degree of distance to assume certain properties in some

measure analogous to those of number; and hence he concluded, that the origin of things, their emanation from the first being, and their subsequent progression through various orders, if not capable of a perfectly clear explanation, might however be illustrated by symbols and resemblances borrowed from numbers (I.384–385).

The actual practice of number symbolism, of course, quickly lost sight of this logical rationale, and arithmology proceeded to develop in irresponsible and fantastic ways. Already by the end of the sixteenth century Pierre de la Primaudaye with his Protestant literalness could complain about its obscurity:

> That all things consisted in numbers, and that there was need of the knowledge of them to conceive the sacred mysteries of God and nature; *Pythagoras, Plato* and all other Academicks have laboriously taught. But they have spoken so superstitiously and so obscurely concerning the mysteries in these numbers, that it seemed, they woulde even conceale them from those, who were devoted to the study of their doctrine.[24]

Agrippa in his skeptical mood had earlier denounced Pythagorean numerology for fostering the heretical belief "that the knowledge of all devine thinges is contained in numbers." [25] Robert Fludd, however, a consistent if perplexing mystic, attempted to apply the basic principle of arithmology, and assigned an object to each number based upon its visible form (see Plate 48). The excesses of partisan and even fanatic numerologists have brought this body of lore into disrepute, but we should heed the counsel of St. Augustine, who himself freely employed numbers as an expository device:

> We must not despise the science of numbers, which, in many passages of Holy Scripture, is found to be of eminent service to the careful interpreter. Neither has it been without reason numbered among God's praises, "Thou hast ordered all things in number, and measure and weight.[26]

Certainly the renaissance continued the well-established tradition of conveying meaning through number symbolism.

Because of their emphasis upon numbers and the resultant systems of numerology which they spawned, the Pythagoreans were claimed as allies by cabalists. Pythagoras' image as a Greek disciple of Moses had made easy the assimilation of Pythagoreanism by the cabala. As early as Philo Judaeus (c. 30 B.C.–c. 40 A.D.), Pythagorean nu-

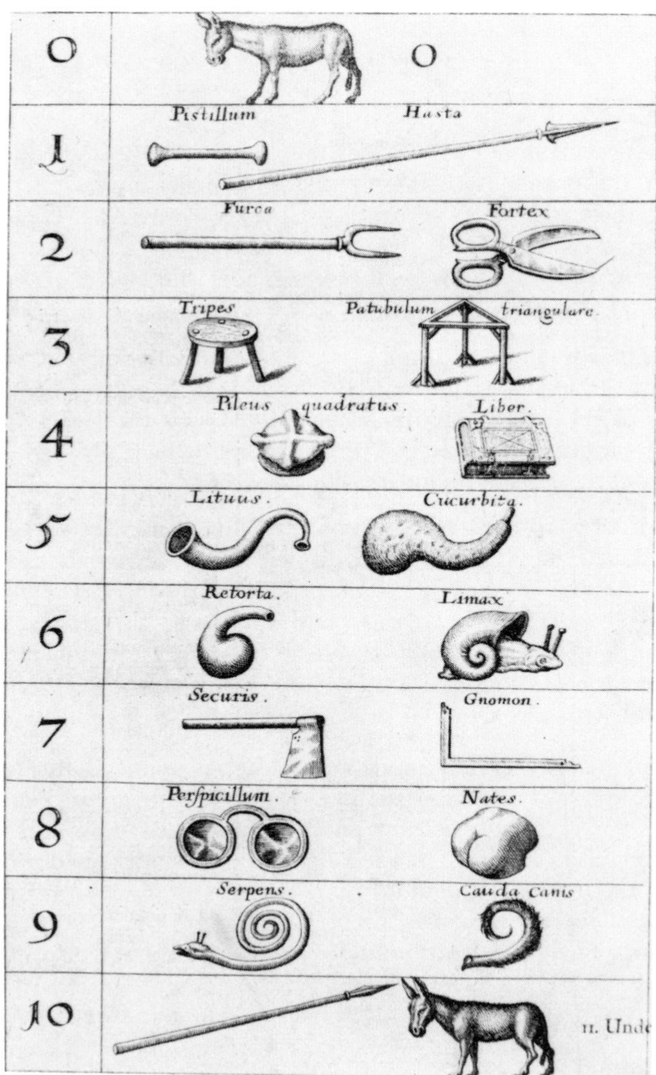

48. *A table entitled* Numerorum Descriptio

The nine integers and zero are here coordinated with certain natural shapes, suggesting an innate relationship between number and creature similar to the innate relationship which Adam revealed between words and creatures in Eden. An ass represents zero because, as the statement informs us at the top, an ass is worth nothing. For the other numbers, appearance is paramount in the designation of coordinates, and the physical similarity is obvious in each instance: 1 is like a pestle or a javelin; 2 is like a pitchfork or a pair of scissors; 3 is like a three-legged stool or a three-sided *patubulum*(?); 4 is like a square cap or a book; 5 is like a curved trumpet or a gourd; 6 is like a retort or a snail; 7 is like an axe or a carpenter's square; 8 is like a pair of spectacles or buttocks; 9 is like a snake or a dog's tail. The larger numbers can then be derived by combinations of these coordinates; for example, 10 is a javelin plus an ass.

Robert Fludd, *Utriusque cosmi majoris scilicet et minoris metaphysica, physica atque technica historia*, 4 vols. (Oppenheim, 1617–19), II.40.

merology had been employed to explicate the covert meaning of numbers in the book of Genesis, and this tradition for biblical exegesis through numbers had been continued by St. Augustine.[27] Cabalism was introduced into the mainstream of renaissance thought by Pico della Mirandola (1463–94), who published nine hundred theses attempting to bolster the truth of Christian revelation by supporting it with corroborative evidence from other doctrines.[28] The fusion of Pythagoreanism and the cabala with Christianity culminated in the work of Johann Reuchlin (1455–1522), an older contemporary of Pico who became the most distinguished Hebraist of the day. In his *De arte cabalistica libri tres* (Hagenau, 1517), Reuchlin sought to do for Pythagoras what Ficino had done for Plato and LeFèvre d'Etaples had done for Aristotle, as he professes in his dedicatory epistle to Pope Leo X:

> Most blessed Leo X, holiest priest of the Christian religion, the Italic philosophy which was introduced by Pythagoras, the father of its famous name, to the most distinguished men endowed with excellent minds, until the present has been obscured. For many years it has been victimized by the nasty barking of the sophists, and for a long time it has been buried in shadows and in darkness. . . .
>
> Therefore thinking that the Pythagorean doctrine alone has been unavailable to scholars, since it lies hidden and dispersed throughout the Laurentian Library, I decided that you would be in no way displeased if I brought to public attention those things which Pythagoras and the noble Pythagoreans are said to have believed. In that way, these teachings, hitherto unknown to the Latin people, may be read at your pleasure. Ficino has produced Plato for Italy, and LeFèvre d'Etaples has restored Aristotle for France. I, Reuchlin, will complete the trio and offer to the Germans Pythagoras reborn through my efforts and consecrated in your name. However, I could not do this without the cabala of the Hebrews, because the philosophy of Pythagoras took its beginning from the precepts of the cabalists. When in the time of our forefathers it was lost in Magna Graecia, it found another resting-place in the scriptures of the cabalists. Accordingly, almost all of these writings can be dug out of there. On that account, I have written this book *De arte cabalistica*, which is symbolic philosophy, so that the beliefs of the Pythagoreans might be better known to scholars.[29]

After Reuchlin, it was difficult to dissociate Pythagoreanism from cabalism, and Christianity wholly from either.[30]

With the cabala and with the hermetic tradition, Pythagorean doctrine shared an assumption that ultimate truths, the mysteries, were hidden from casual view.[31] Only after proper initiation and an extended educative program might a neophyte discern them. The cognoscenti, in fact, had the responsibility of protecting the truth from too-easy access and consequent abuse by the vulgar. Therefore they took to professing their tenets in a form which would be comprehensible only to the initiated. Iamblichus reports that Pythagoras adhered to this practice:

> He was also accustomed to pour forth sentences resembling oracles to his familiars in a symbolical manner, and which in the greatest brevity of words contained the most abundant and multifarious meaning, like the Pythian Apollo through certain oracles. . . . In others of a similar nature, the most divine Pythagoras has concealed the sparks of truth; depositing as in a treasury for those who are capable of being enkindled by them, and with a certain brevity of diction, an extension of theory most ample and difficult to be comprehended.[32]

Henry Reynolds, an early seventeenth-century theorist about poetry, cites Iamblichus and interprets one of the Pythagorean *symbola* as an expression of this doctrine. By the precept, "Give not readily thy right hand to every one," Reynolds claims,

> *Pythagoras* . . . advertiseth that wee ought not to communicate to unworthy mindes, and not the practized in the understanding of occulte doctrines, those misterious instructions that are only to bee opened (sayes he) and taught to sacred and sublime wits, and such as have beene a long time exercised and versed in them.[33]

To preserve their mysteries, the cabalists developed an elaborate system of symbolic numbers; the followers of Hermes Trismegistus displayed their beliefs through hieroglyphs; and Pythagoreans perpetuated the cryptic sentences known as the *symbola* of Pythagoras. Already by the second century St. Clement of Alexandria had lumped together the several interdependent modes which concealed their teachings from the merely curious and had analyzed their methods of knowledge.[34]

The development of this corpus of syncretic esoterica is sketched by Henri Estienne, sieur des Fossez, at the opening of his treatise dealing with "hieroglyphicks, symboles, emblemes, aenigmas, sentences, parables, reverses of medalls, armes, blazons, cimiers, cyphres and rebus" (title page):

> There is no doubt, but that after the Hebrewes, the Egyptians were the first that did most precisely addict themselves to all manner of Sciences; nor did they professe any one, which they esteemed more commendable, then that of *Hieroglyphicks*, which held the first rank among their secret Disciplines, whereof *Moses* had without doubt a perfect *Idea*, as the holy Scriptures testifie: From whence we gather, that he was absolutely perfect in all the learning of the Egyptians.
>
> *Philo* the Jew confirmes this more cleerly in the life of *Moses* which he hath written; where it is observed, that *Moses* had learned from the Doctors of Egypt, *Arithmetick*, *Geometry*, and *Musique*, as well practick as Theorick, together with this hidden Phylosophie, expressed by Characters, which they term *Hieroglyphicks*, that is to say, some marks and figures of living creatures, which they adored as Gods: Whence we prove the Antiquity of this Science, which had *Moses* for her most renowned Disciple.
>
> And *Pythagoras* (whose Master in this Science was *Ænopheus* of *Heliopolis*) transferred it into Greece, where he enrich'd it with many Symboles that beare his name.[35]

It was often stressed that Pythagorean teaching introduced the initiate to recondite knowledge which as a matter of policy had been concealed from the profane multitude. In the words of Cardinal Bessarion (c. 1395–1472), the Neoplatonist bibliophile whose manuscripts formed the nucleus for the library of St. Mark's in Venice, "Throughout their lives Pythagoreans kept concealed the secrets of the divine mysteries lest their doctrine circulate among strangers and less worthy men, a practice which seems to be similar to that evangelical injunction: 'Don't give sacred things to dogs, nor cast your pearls before swine.' "[36]

As a result of this need to conceal truth beneath a protective covering, a verbal statement functions as the knowable manifestation of the inner truth, a perceptible symbol without which truth would remain unknowable. The word therefore assumes an unwonted importance. Moreover, the word and the concept which it represents have an inherent, integral relationship, one which is not haphazard or alterable. When Pythagoras in his school was asked,

"What is the wisest thing?" he replied, "Number"; and he added, "But the next to this in wisdom, is that which gives names to things." [37] The fundamental significance attributed to words is evident also in the Hebraic tradition, where Adam's first task was to assign names to things in Eden, thereby giving them identity and making him lord of creation.[38] In the Academic tradition, the unique relation between a word and its meaning is explored by Plato in the *Cratylus* and enlarged by Isidore in the *Etymologiae*. In the Hermetic tradition the special role of words as visible symbols for hidden meanings was played by hieroglyphs. The easy coalescence of these various abstruse traditions is well demonstrated by Sir Thomas Browne, who proclaimed exultantly:

> I have often admired the mysticall way of *Pythagoras*, and the secret Magicke of numbers; Beware of Philosophy, is a precept not to be received in too large a sense; for in this masse of nature there is a set of things that carry in their front, though not in capitall letters, yet in stenography, and short Characters, something of Divinitie, which to wiser reasons serve as Luminaries in the abysse of knowledge.[39]

For Browne, the *medicus religiosus*, this lore had become the gist of philosophy, the very light of truth to guide us through the dark valley of ignorance.

Out of this esoteric mix in the renaissance developed the literary genre known as the emblem-book, wherein each emblem is a composite interaction between a symbolum, a hieroglyphic-like illustration, and an explanatory verse. An emblem comprises three modes of expression: a direct statement, a visual image, and a verbal image, each of which, be it noted, is simply a different demonstration of the same underlying truth, a different facet of the precious jewel which must be concealed in the head of a toad. A truth so conveyed in this triplex fashion is presumably more persuasive because it presents itself to the mind through several different, though cognate, channels of perception. Since Pythagoras on his travels through the Near East had assimilated the various beliefs of the Hebrews and the Egyptians, it was easy to see him as the syncretist who had brought together the wide range of materials which are fused in the emblem technique. Claude Mignault (1536–1606), the erudite Frenchman who edited Alciati, wrote an extensive introduction to the *Emblemata* in which he analyzes the broad variety of arcane materials that the emblem tradition amalgamates, and he emphasizes the prominent position that Pythagoras holds in it.[40]

49. *Three theists and three atheists disputing theology before the altar of Religion*

This neoclassical grouping states visually the argument of Cudworth's book, which advances the theosophical tradition over the atheistical systems. Representing the theists is Pythagoras backed by Socrates and Aristotle. Representing the atheists is Anaximander backed by Epicurus and Strato. A wreath blazoning "VICTORY" hangs over the heads of the theists. A torn wreath fluttering "CONFUSION" hangs over the heads of the atheists.

Ralph Cudworth, *The true intellectual system of the universe* (London, 1678), frontispiece.

In addition, Pythagoras was often assigned an assortment of other occult chores. As a priest of Apollo, he was capable of oracular utterance, such as "Know thyself" and "Nothing in excess." According to Pliny, he "was the first to compose a book on the properties of plants"[41]—presumably giving them names and fixing their virtues—and consequently had earned the reputation of a sorcerer. In a well-known twelfth-century treatise on alchemy, entitled the *Turba philosophorum*,[42] Pythagoras appears as the master of an academy devoted to the hermetic arts, and thereby he had earned the reputation of an alchemist. In the same occult vein, Pierre Bayle relates stories about his use of magic mirrors.[43] Pythagoras was regularly cast in the company of other enigmatic figures who had purveyed the mysterious, such as Hermes Trismegistus, Horapollo, Zoroaster, Orpheus, the Sibyls, Moses, and Solomon. He could easily be perverted into a personality fit to titillate the minds of those who need an alternative to reason and reality. Playing such a role, in Lyly's *Endymion* (IV.iii) he is summoned as an archetypal wizard who has mastered the magical lore of all nations.

This popular depiction of a philosopher, however, while viewed with deferential awe, is a far descent from the lofty place which the sage of Samos usually held in academic circles. More likely his closest associates included Ptolemaeus, Euclid, Nicomachus, Aristoxenus, and Iamblichus (see Plate 1), or Socrates and Aristotle (see Plate 49). In any company, though, even amongst the scoundrels who preyed on superstition, the presence of Pythagoras generated respect for his intelligence and reverence for his piety.

Notes

[1] The intelligent and educated attitude toward magic is propounded by Pico della Mirandola, *On the Dignity of Man*, tr. Charles Glenn Wallis (Indianapolis, 1965), pp. 26–29.

[2] The role of Pythagoras as *vates* is amply delineated by Pierre Mussard, *Historia deorum fatidicorum, vatum, sibyllarum, phoebadum, apud priscos illustrium* (Cologne, 1675), pp. 132–143.

[3] See, for example, Ludovicus Caelius Rhodiginus, *Lectionum antiquarum libri XXX* (Basle, 1566), p. 734.

[4] *The lives, opinions, and remarkable sayings of the most famous ancient philosophers. . . . Made English by several hands*, 2 vols. (London, 1696), II.22. Cf. Caspar Peucer, *Les devins* (Lyons, 1584), p. 339; Joannes Jacobus Frisius, *Bibliotheca philosophorum classicorum authorum chronologica* (Zurich, 1592), fol. 6^v; and Sir Thomas Browne, *Religio Medici* [I.xxxiii] *and Other Works*, ed. L. C. Martin (Oxford, 1964), p. 32.

On the authority of Cicero (*De divinatione*, xlv), "omens" (*omina*) are defined as prophecies by the voice of men (*HOMINes*), and are distinct from oracles, which are the voices of gods. Cf. André Dacier, *The Life of Pythagoras*, tr. anon. (London, 1707), p. 67.

[5] *The history of philosophy*, 2nd ed. (London, 1687), p. 512. Tzetzes' text in Latin is as follows:

> Pythagoras autem filius Mnesarchi Samii,
> Non solum praecognovit pulchrè ipse omnia,
> Sed & volentibus futura cognoscere,
> Praecognitionum reliquit varios libros.

(*Variarum historiarum liber* [II.56], tr. Paulus Lacisius [Basle, 1546], p. 36).

[6] *De vita Pythagorae*, xxviii, as translated by Stanley, *History of philosophy*, p. 548.

[7] *Lives of ancient philosophers* (1696), II.14.

[8] "Opinions of Philosophers" [V.i] in *The morals*, tr. Philemon Holland (London, 1603), p. 841.

[9] *Life of Pythagoras* [xiii], tr. Thomas Taylor (London, 1818), p. 41.

[10] See, for example, Christopher Heydon, *A defence of judiciall astrologie* (London, 1603), p. 278; Jean Jacques Boissard, *De divinatione et magicis praestigiis* (Oppenheim, 1616?), p. 296; Dacier, *Life of Pythagoras*, pp. 67–69.

[11] See also p. 58, above. For other examples not listed in n. 56, see Georg Pictorius, *De speciebus magiae ceremonialis in Pantopolion* (Basle, 1563), pp. 60–61; and Robert Fludd, *Utriusque cosmi . . . historia*, 4 vols. (Oppenheim, 1617–19), II.149–151.

[12] See A. E. Waite, *The Pictorial Key to the Tarot*, 2nd ed. (London, 1911), pp. 108–109.

[13] *De vita Pythagorae*, xx, as translated by Stanley, *History of philosophy*, p. 517. Cf. Rhodiginus, *Lectionum antiquarum libri*, p. 186; and Dacier, *Life of Pythagoras*, p. 23.

[14] The *editio princeps* of Cocles' *Chyromantiae ac physionomiae anastasis* was Bologna, 1504. The *editio princeps* of Joannes' *Introductiones apotelesmaticae elegantes, in chyromantiam, physiognomiam, astrologiam naturalem, complexiones hominum, naturas planetarum* was Strasbourg, 1522.

[15] The literature on oneiromancy is of course extensive. For early bibliography, see Conrad Gesner, *Pandectae* (Zurich, 1548), fol. 100^{v}, 105^{v} ff., and 217^{v}; and Nicolas Lenglet Dufresnoy, *Receuil de dissertations anciennes et nouvelles, sur les apparitions, les visions, et les songes* (Paris, 1751). A few of the more helpful volumes on dreams printed during the renaissance include Auger Ferrier, *Liber de somniis* (Lyons, 1549); Thomas Hill, *Interpretacion of dreames* (London, 1576); Fludd, *Utriusque cosmi . . . historia*, IV.28–36; and Thomas Tryon, *Pythagoras his mystick philosophy reviv'd* (London, 1691).

[16] Artemidorus' *De somniorum interpretatione libri quinque* was printed at Venice, 1518. It was translated into English by Robert Wood and printed in London, 1606.

Synesius' *De somniis* was translated into Latin by Marsilio Ficino and printed with Ficino's translation of Iamblichus' *De mysteriis Ægyptiorum, Chaldaeorum, Assyriorum*, et al., in Venice, 1497.

[17] *History of philosophy*, p. 548. The reference to Apuleius is *Florida*, xv. See also Gerard Johann Vossius, *De philosophorum sectis liber* (The Hague, 1657), pp. 4, 149. The single volume most useful in understanding astrology as practised in the renaissance is William Lilly, *Christian astrology* (London, 1647).

[18] *Liber de diebus decretoriis secundum pythagoricam doctrinam* (Lyons, 1549).

[19] *The geomancie of Maister Christopher Cattan*, tr. Francis Sparry (London, 1591), p. 1. This is the standard treatise on geomancy in the renaissance. The French text was first printed in Paris, 1558. Cf. also Fludd, *Utriusque cosmi . . . historia*, II.35–36, 143–146, 716–783; IV.37–46.

[20] *Life of Pythagoras* [xix], tr. Taylor, p. 68.

[21] G. S. Kirk and J. E. Raven, *The Presocratic Philosophers* (Cambridge Univ. Press, 1962), pp. 313–317.

[22] It is impossible here to present in detail the various systems of arithmology which appeared in the renaissance. They were mere offshoots—and often not respectable ones at that—from the Pythagorean doctrine. Nevertheless, several literary scholars have recently shown an intense interest in numerology, especially as an explicatory tool, and I should like to contribute modestly to the bibliography on this subject. For discussion of the theory of number symbolism as it derives from Pythagorean doctrine, see Vincent F. Hopper, *Medieval Number Symbolism* (Columbia Univ. Press, 1938), pp. 33–49; Ernst R. Curtius, *European Literature and the Latin Middle Ages* [1948], tr. Willard R. Trask (New York, 1953), pp. 501–509; W. D. Ross, *Plato's Theory of Ideas* (Oxford, 1951), esp. pp. 176–205, 216–224; Kirk and Raven, *Presocratic Philosophers*, pp. 248–250; and W. K. C. Guthrie, *A History of Greek Philosophy*, 3 vols. (Cambridge Univ. Press, 1962), I.301–306. For early bibliography on the subject, see Nicomachus, *Introduction to Arithmetic*, tr. Martin Luther D'Ooge (New York, 1926), pp. 90–91 (n. 8); Macrobius, *Commentary on the Dream of Scipio*, tr. William H. Stahl (Columbia Univ. Press, 1952), p. 95 (n. 2); Gesner, *Pandectae*, fol. 74^v; Hopper, *Medieval Number Symbolism*, pp. 213–232; and Christopher Butler, *Number Symbolism* (New York, 1970), pp. 180–181. The most important treatments of the subject for the renaissance were Bartholomaeus Anglicus, *De proprietatibus rerum* [XIX.cxvi–cxxv], tr. Stephen Batman as *Batman uppon Bartholome, his book De proprietatibus rerum* (London, 1582), fol. 412–414^v; Pico della Mirandola, *De adscriptis numero noningentis: dialeticis, moralibus, physicis . . .* (Rome, 1486), passim; Charles de Bouelles, *Liber de duodecim numeris* in *Liber de intellectu* et al. (Paris, 1510), fol. 148^v–171; Jodocus Clichtoveus, *De mystica numerorum significatione opusculum* (Paris, 1513); *Boetii Arithmetica . . . adjecto commentario, mysticam numerorum applicationem perstringente*, ed. Girard Ruffus (Paris, 1521); Francesco Giorgio, *De harmonia mundi totius cantica tria* (Venice, 1525), passim; Heinrich Cornelius Agrippa, *De occulta philosophia libri III* (Antwerp, 1531), esp. II.i–xv, xxi, xxiii; Pietro Bonghi, *Mysticae numerorum significationis liber* (Bergamo, 1585); Giordano Bruno, *De monade numero et figura liber* (Frankfurt, 1591); William Ingpen, *The secrets of numbers* (London, 1624); Joannes Meursius, *Denarius pythagoricus* (Leyden, 1631); John Heydon, *The Rosie Crucian infallible axiomata* (London, 1660); and Athanasius Kircher, *Arithmologia* (Rome, 1665). The best place for the modern reader to find a compilation of the various meanings of each number is Heinrich Cornelius Agrippa, *Three books of occult philosophy*, tr. John Freake (London, 1651), pp. 174–225. Later expositions of what each number means appear in Thomas Taylor, *Theoretic Arithmetic* (London, 1816), pp. 171–243; Armand Delatte, *Etudes sur la littérature pythagoricienne* (Paris, 1915), pp. 139 ff.; and Isidore Kozminsky, *Numbers, Their Meaning and Magic* (New York, 1927). For discussion of the practice of number symbolism in the renaissance, see Lynn Thorndike, *A History of Magic and Experimental Science*, 8 vols. (Columbia Univ. Press, 1923–1958), VI.437–465; Rudolf Allers, "Microcosmus," *Traditio*, 2 (1944), esp. pp. 370–383; C. A. Patrides, "The Numerological Approach to Cosmic Order During the English Renaissance," *Isis*, 49 (1958), 391–397; Maren-Sofie Røstvig, *The Hidden Sense* (Oslo, 1963), pp. 3–112; Alastair Fowler, *Spenser and the Numbers of Time* (London, 1964), esp. pp. 3–50, 237–257; Røstvig, "Renaissance Numerology: Acrostics or Criticism?" *Essays in Criticism*, 16 (1966), 6–21; George Boas, "Philosophies of Science in Florentine Platonism" in *Art, Science, and History in the Renaissance*, ed. Charles B. Singleton (Johns Hopkins Press, 1967), esp. pp. 242 ff.; Røstvig, "Structure as Prophecy" in *Silent Poetry*, ed. Alastair Fowler (London, 1970), pp. 32–72; and most important,

Christopher Butler, *Number Symbolism* (New York, 1970). For an instructive example of how numerical analysis can be applied to biblical (and therefore literary) exegesis, see Henry More, *Conjectura cabbalistica* (London, 1653), esp. pp. 22–33. For a sympathetic modern treatment of the subject, see Eric T. Bell, *Numerology* (New York, 1945).

[23] *Occult philosophy*, tr. Freake, p. 171.

[24] *The third volume of the French academie*, tr. R. Dolman (London, 1601), p. 59.

[25] *Of the vanitie and uncertaintie of artes and sciences*, tr. James Sanford (London, 1569), fol. 27.

[26] *City of God*, XI.xxx, quoted by Hopper, *Medieval Number Symbolism*, p. 78.

[27] Of invaluable help here is Butler, *Number Symbolism*, pp. 22–31.

[28] *De adscriptis numero noningentis: dialeticis, moralibus, physicis . . .* (Rome, 1486). On Pico as the syncretizer of Pythagorean numerology and the cabala, see Henry Reynolds, *Mythomystes* [1632] in J. E. Spingarn, *Critical Essays of the Seventeenth Century*, 3 vols. (Oxford Univ. Press, 1908–09), I.157–159.

> [29] Italica philosophia beatissime Leo decime religionis christianae Pontifex Maxime à Pythagora eius nominis parente primo, ad summos homines excellentibus ingeniis praeditos olim delata, perquam plurimis annis ingenti latratu sophistarum occiderat, tamdiu tenebris & densa nocte sepulta. . . .
>
> Quare cogitans sola studiosis Pythagorica defuisse, quae tamen sparsim in academia laurentiana delitescunt, credidi haud ingratum tibi futurum si & ea foro afferrem quae Pythagoras nobilesque Pythagorei sensisse dicuntur, ut tuo foelici numine legerentur latinis hactenus ignota. Italiae Marsilius Platonem edidit, Galliis Aristotelem Ja. Faber Stapulensis restauravit. Implebo numerum & Capnion ego germanis per me renascentem Pythagoram tuo nomini dicatum exhibebo. Id tamen absque hebraeorum Cabala fieri non potuit, eo quod Pythagorae philosophia de Cabalaeorum praeceptis initia duxit, quae patrum memoria discedens e magna Graecia rursus in Cabalistarum volumina incubuit. Eruenda igitur inde fuerant fere omnia. Quare de arte Cabalistica quae symbolica philosophia est scripsi, ut Pythagoreorum dogmata studiosis fierent notiora (A4–A4^{v}).

[30] Others known in the renaissance as cabalists include Raimond Lull, esp. for the *Opusculum . . . de auditu kabbalistico* (Paris, 1578), though this treatise is actually by Pietro Mainardi (c. 1500) and is spuriously attributed to Lull; Petrus Galatinus, a Franciscan who published *Opus de arcanis catholicae veritatis* (Basle, 1561), with the cabalistic works of Reuchlin appended; Joannes Pistorius, who edited a compendium of cabalistical writings entitled *Artis cabalisticae: hoc est, reconditae theologiae et philosophiae scriptorum . . . opus* (Basle, 1587); Hans Khunrath, an insatiable polymath who authored *Amphitheatrum sapientiae aeternae solius verae, Christiano-Kabalisticum, divinomagicum . . .* (Hanau, 1609); Robert Fludd, the London occultist whose most cabalistic work is the *Philosophia Moysaica* (Gouda, 1638); and Henry More, the Cambridge Platonist who offered in *Conjectura cabbalistica* (London, 1653) a threefold interpretation of the early chapters of Genesis. Later authorities especially useful to literary scholars are Johann Jakob Brucker, *Historia critica philosophiae*, 2nd ed., 6 vols. (Leipzig, 1766–67), II.916–1068; A. E. Waite, *The Doctrine and Literature of the Kabalah* (London, 1902); and Joseph L. Blau, *The Christian Interpretation of the Cabala in the Renaissance* (Columbia Univ. Press, 1944). The authoritative work on the subject is François Secret, *Les kabbalistes chrétiens de la renaissance* (Paris, 1964).

[31] See Pico della Mirandola, *Dignity of Man*, tr. Wallis, pp. 29–31.

[32] *Life of Pythagoras* [xxix], tr. Taylor, pp. 117–118.

[33] *Mythomystes* in Spingarn, *Critical Essays,* I.157–158.

[34] Cf. *Stromateis,* esp. V.iv–v. Sir Philip Sidney saw poetry as such a mode of discourse: "There are many misteries contained in *Poetrie,* which of purpose were written darkly, least by profane wits it should be abused" (*The defence of poesie* [London, 1595], K1ᵛ–K2). In this spirit, Spenser called *The Faerie Queene* "a darke conceit" ("A letter of the Authors," line 3).

[35] *The art of making devises,* tr. Thomas Blount (London, 1646), pp. 1–2. Estienne is echoing a tradition that goes as far back as Plutarch:

> The Aegyptians were very strict and precise, in not profaning their wisdome, nor publishing that learning of theirs which concerned the gods. And this the greatest Sages and most learned clerkes of all *Greece* do testifie, by name, *Solon, Thales, Plato, Eudoxus, Pythagoras,* & as some let not to say, *Lycurgus* himselfe; who all travelled of a deliberate purpose into *Aegypt,* for to confer with the priests of that country. For it is constantly held that *Eudoxus* was the auditour of *Chonupheus* the priest of *Memphis, Solon* of *Sonchis* the priest of *Sais, Pythagoras* of *Oenupheus* the priest of *Heliopolis.* And verily this *Pythagoras* last named, was highly esteemed among those men, like as him selfe had them in great admiration, in so much as he of all others seemed most to imitate their maner of mysticall speaking under covert words, & to involve his doctrine and sentences within figurative & aenigmaticall words: for the characters which are called Hieroglyphicks in *Aegypt,* be in maner all of them, like to these precepts of *Pythagoras:* Eat not upon a stoole or chaire; sit not over a bushell; Plant no date tree; Stirre not the fire in the house, nor rake into it with a sword

("Of Isis and Osiris" in *Morals,* tr. Holland [1603], p. 1291). The "precepts" quoted at the end by Plutarch are of course drawn from the familiar list of Pythagorean *symbola* (see pp. 272–277, below). For another authority who equates the *symbola* and hieroglyphs, see Pierre L'Anglois, *Discours des hieroglyphes Ægyptiens, emblemes, devises, et armoiries* (Paris, 1584), fol. 4ᵛ. Cf. also Athanasius Kircher, the greatest authority on hieroglyphs in the mid-seventeenth century: "Pythagoras, following the example of the Egyptians, teaches everything by means of *symbola*" (Pythagoras Aegyptios imitatus omnia per symbola docet; *Obeliscus Aegyptiacus* [Rome, 1666], p. 84).

[36]
> Secreta divinarum rerum, per omnem vitam occulta tenebant, ne quid ad exteros ac minus dignos homines exiret, quae res similis esse praecepto illi evangelico videtur, Nolite dare sacra canibus, nec projiciatis margaritas vestras ante porcos

(Joannes Bessarion, *In calumniatorem Platonis libri quatuor* [Venice, 1516], fol. 2ᵛ). Cf. Joannes Baptista Bernardus, *Seminarium totius philosophiae Aristotelicae et Platonicae,* 2nd ed. (Lyons, 1599), II.767.

[37] Iamblichus, *Life of Pythagoras* [xviii], tr. Taylor, p. 59.

[38] No one makes the point more clearly than Agrippa:

> *Adam* therefore that gave the first names to things, knowing the influencies of the Heavens, and properties of all things, gave them all names according to their natures, as it is written in *Genesis,* where God brought all things that he had created before *Adam,* that he should name them, and as he named any thing, so the name of it was, which names indeed contain in them wonderfull powers of the things signified

(*Occult philosophy,* tr. Freake, p. 153).

[39] *Religio Medici* [I.xii], ed. Martin, p. 12.

[40] Mignault's introduction, entitled "Syntagma de symbolis," first appeared

in the edition of Alciati's *Emblemata* published at Antwerp, 1574. There are, however, numerous later editions. Mignault's "Syntagma" has been translated and annotated in an unpublished M. A. thesis by Deirdre Malone Southall (University of North Carolina, 1967). For another discussion of the origin and development of literary symbols, see the introduction which Filippo Beroaldo prepared for his volume entitled *Symbola Pythagorae moraliter explicata*, first published in Bologna, c.1500.

[41] *Historia naturalis*, XXV.v. Cf. Peucer, *Les devins*, p. 243; and Boissard, *De divinatione*, p. 297.

[42] First printed in *Bibliothèque des philosophes*, 2 vols. (Paris, 1672–73); translated into English by A. E. Waite (London, 1896).

[43] *A General Dictionary*, tr. John Peter Bernard *et al*., 10 vols. (London, 1734–41), "Pythagoras," footnote L.

5

Moral Philosophy

The pattern of cosmos is intrinsic at all levels of creation, an effectual potency that informs the hierarchies of existence from the celestial spheres to microcosmic man and the grain of sand. Since it emanates from a beneficent deity, it is good as well as true and beautiful. Cosmos, however, though invariably *in potentia*, is not always realized as a physical state. The actuality of harmonious unity—of *concordia discors* and *e pluribus unum*—may be thwarted by deficiency of parts or by outright opposition. The result is evil, either relative or absolute. In consequence, man has a moral imperative to implement the latency of cosmos whenever possible. The institution and maintenance of natural order then becomes the fundamental objective of any moral code. By this line of reasoning, respect for order underlies the principles of behavior promulgated by the Pythagoreans.

According to Thomas Stanley in his impressive *History of philosophy*, "Practick [i.e., moral] Philosophy seems to have been the Invention of *Pythagoras*,"[1] and he cites Aristotle as his authority.[2] If this claim be exaggerated, it nonetheless contains the usual kernel of fact found in most legends. Pythagoras did depart from the direction of earlier thinkers. His overriding purpose, clearly enunciated, was to find and follow a moral way of life, a simple life in accord with the predetermined plan of our beneficent creator; and this intention set him apart from the rationalistic school of Miletus. For Pythagoras, morality dictated the *modus vivendi*. Reason and even science were employed by the Pythagoreans, but all disciplines were subjugated to ethical aims. To institutionalize this way of life, Pythagoras established his school in a formal way, a confined society with a catechism and a curriculum and a code of conduct governing every phase of human activity.

Pythagorean morality is defined most succinctly, as well as most characteristically, in a dictum ascribed to Pythagoras by Diogenes Laertius: "Virtue is harmony."[3] This metaphor places morality in the cosmic context of *musica mundana*, of universal harmony.

Virtue obtains when the individual properly assimilates to the whole, when each creature performs his preordained function, even when under duress. To quote Chaucer's preachy Clerk of Oxenford, "Every wight, in his degree,/Sholde be constant in adversitee" (*Clerk's Tale,* 1145–1146). Only then do members of a society—wives and husbands and all—live happily, and only then does the society prosper as a whole. Since God has structured His creation for our benefit ("for oure beste is al his governaunce"), the Clerk concludes, "Lat us thanne lyve in vertuous suffraunce" (lines 1161–1162). Richard Hooker 300 years later is still defending the Establishment by the same argument: "See wee not plainly that obedience of Creatures unto the Law of Nature is the stay of the whole World?" [4]

Since moral action consists in supporting the divine plan, the moral philosopher must first determine the outlines and contents of that plan. As André Dacier puts it, Pythagoras postulated an eternal law which binds all creatures to the deity:

> He believ'd there was an Eternal Law, and that this Law was only the immutable Virtue of God, who had created all things. In consequence of this Law, he imagin'd there was a divine Oath that preserv'd all things in the State and Order in which they had been created, and which by binding the Creator to his Creature, bound likewise the Creature to his Creator.[5]

In the Pythagorean system, the methodical study of nature is the starting place for discovering this eternal law. Science reveals the divine intention. Scientific investigation produces more and more facts which can be organized into a larger and larger scheme until the plan of the all-inclusive cosmos is detected. To be specific, construction of the tetractys, the divine oath of the Pythagoreans to which Dacier alludes, is the acme of profane knowledge.

Perception of this unity in the tetractys, of this corporate entity, becomes in its last stage a wholly intellectual experience. Though originating in sense perception of the physical universe, the final response of the percipient is knowledge of and participation in the purely intellectual world of the unchanging forms—in terms of the more familiar Platonic system, knowledge of and participation in the world of being where the ideas reside as permanent essences. This ascent from sensual experience to experience of a different order is the raison d'être of philosophy, as Porphyry claims:

> The scope [i.e., aim] of Philosophy is to free the mind, (the divine part of the soul) which is planted in us, and to set it at

> liberty, without which liberty none can learn or perceive any thing solid or true, by the help or benefit of sense: for the mind, according to him [Pythagoras], seeth all things, and hears all things: all things else are deaf and blind.[6]

The result of this disembodiment, to speak literally, is a sort of ecstasy in which the soul has direct access to the ideal essences. Affinity with these archetypes, in fact, is the impetus for learning, so that in the Pythagorean school science and religion are integrated in the common pursuit of absolute truth. St. Jerome quotes this dictum of Pythagoras: "Next to God, we must cherish truth, which alone makes man most like God."[7] Georg Horn in his history of philosophy presents a digest of the definitions of philosophy associated with several philosophers, and he cites this pursuit of abstract truth as the distinctive characteristic of the Pythagorean sect.[8]

Once truth is identified, a code of conduct to accord with it may be devised. Since the concept of cosmos is the ultimate verity, proper behavior must contribute to its order. Virtue is harmony within that inclusive system. The condition of harmony postulates a relationship between the whole and its individual parts, however, and therefore Pythagoreans differentiated two sorts of virtue, two spheres of conduct—the one, private; the other, public.[9]

Translated into terms of individual action, the respect for order is best expressed by the private virtue of self-control through self-knowledge, leading to temperance. According to Iamblichus, temperance was central to the Pythagorean ethic, in both theory and practice—temperance so severe that it verged on asceticism.[10] There were exhortations to paucity in speech, continence in diet, contempt of wealth (especially gold, which was worn only by harlots), and restraint from emotion (specifically anger and grief). Pythagoreans strove for a calmness of mind that we more frequently associate with the Stoics; but unlike the Stoics, Pythagoreans derived this inner peace from relentless introspection. It was not a passive acceptance of circumstance or a negative avoidance of tumult. It was synthesis rather than escape. The Pythagorean continually took stock of what he had done and what he must yet do. The art of memory was praised and developed, not suppressed. In consequence, temperance as a moral standard was an active choice, and moderation followed as a logical consequence. In other systems this moderation generated the motto "nothing in excess," it initiated a search for the *via media,* it encouraged observation of "the golden mean"

—a mathematical concept, incidentally, which itself smacks of Pythagoreanism.[11]

Translated into terms of the community, the respect for order is most obviously manifested by the public virtue of justice, which insures equity for all.[12] Temperance in personal morality is correspondent to justice in public affairs. Moderation is once more the aim. Pythagoras was again seen as an innovator here; according to Stanley, "They hold *Pythagoras* to be the Inventor of all Politick Discipline." [13] His teaching in this field is summarized in an oft-quoted apothegm best known in the Greek version recorded by St. Jerome.[14] Here is Thomas Stanley's translation of it:

> We must avoid with our utmost endeavour, and amputate with Fire and Sword, and by all other means, from the Body, Sickness; from the Soul, Ignorance; from the Belly, Luxury; from a City, Sedition; from a Family, Discord; from all things, Excess.[15]

Appropriately, there is posited a relationship between the individual and society at large, with an intermediate stop at family commitments. Perhaps old Gloucester has in mind this code of ethics when he laments the moral chaos in Lear's kingdom:

> Love cools, friendship falls off, brothers divide; in cities, mutinies; in countries, discord; in palaces, treason; and the bond crack'd 'twixt son and father (*Lear*, I.ii.101–104).

The gist of Pythagoras' apothegm, in the true Pythagorean spirit, is a demand for moderation in all things, so that societal organization remains stable. To exemplify the public virtue of justice and to exalt the resultant civil peace, a special character had been bestowed upon Numa Pompilius,[16] successor to Romulus as king of Rome and, according to Ovid,[17] sometime pupil of Pythagoras in Croton.

The moral philosophy of the Pythagoreans is codified in the hexameter lines of the χρυσὰ ἔπη, the *carmina aurea* or "Golden Verses," which probably in some rudimentary form served as a litany in the ceremonial life of the early school. This document, though without doubt a later fabrication, was the best-known text ascribed directly to Pythagoras.[18] It was taken to be his personal credo. The *Carmina aurea* received the widest possible circulation in the renaissance (see pp. 63–64, n. 41, above), being regularly appended, for example, to the grammars, both Greek and Latin, published by Aldus Pius Manutius.[19] It was often printed also with other gnomic works by early poets such as Theognis and Phocylides, and even with the works of Hesiod, Epictetus, and Cebes.[20] The earliest translation into English was made by Thomas Stanley and published in 1651 in his volume of *Poems.* It is a fairly faithful rendering of the customary Greek text:

First to immortal God thy duty pay,
Observe thy Vow, honour the Saints: obey
Thy Prince and Rulers, nor their Laws despise:
Thy Parents reverence, and neer allies:
Him that is first in Vertue make thy Friend,
And with observance his kind speech attend:
Nor (to thy power) for light faults cast him by,
Thy power is neighbour to necessity.
  These know, and with intentive care pursue;
But Anger, Sloth, and Luxury subdue.
In sight of others or thy self forbear
What's Ill; but of thy self stand most in fear.
Let Justice all thy words and actions sway,
Nor from the even course of reason stray;
For know that all men are to die ordain'd,
And riches are as quickly lost as gain'd.
Crosses that happen by divine decree
(If such thy Lot) bear not impatiently.
Yet seek to remedie with all thy Care
And think the just have not the greatest share.
'Mongst men discourses good and bad are spread,
Despise not those, nor be by these misled.
If any some notorious falshood say,
Thou the report with equal judgement weigh.
Let not mens smoother promises invite,
Nor rougher threats from just resolves thee fright.
If ought thou wouldst attempt, first ponder it,
Fools only inconsiderate acts Commit.
Nor do what afterward thou may'st repent,
First learn to know the thing on which th'art bent.
Thus thou a life shalt lead with joy repleat.
  Nor must thou care of outward health forget:
Such Temperance use in exercise and diet
As may preserve thee in a setled quiet.
Meats unprohibited, not curious, chuse,
Decline what any other may accuse:
The rash expence of vanity detest,

And sordidnesse: a Mean in all is best.
Hurt not thy self; act nought thou dost not weigh;
And every businesse of the following day
As soon as by the Morn awak'd dispose;
Nor suffer sleep at night thy Eyes to close
Till thrice that Diary thou hast orerun,
How slipt? what Deeds? what duty left undone?
Thus thy account summ'd up from first to last,
Grieve for the Ill, joy for what good hath past.
  These if thou studie, practise, and affect,
To sacred Vertue will thy steps direct.
Natures eternall Fountain [21] I attest,
Who did the soul with fourfold power invest.
Ere thou begin pray well thy work may end,
Then shall thy knowledge to all things extend
Divine and humane; where enlarg'd, restrain'd,
How nature is by generall likenesse chain'd.
Vain hope nor ignorance shall dim thy sight,
Then shalt thou see that haplesse men invite
Their Ills, to good (though present) Deaf and Blinde,
And few the cure of their Misfortunes finde;
This only is the fate that harms and rowls
Through miseries successive, humane souls.
Within is a continual hidden fight,
Which we to shun must study, not excite;
Good God! how little trouble should we know
If thou to all men wouldst their Genius show.
  But fear not thou; Men come of heav'nly Race,
Taught by diviner Nature what t'embrace,
Which if pursu'd, Thou all I nam'd shalt gain,
And keep thy soul cleer from thy Bodies stain;
In time of Pray'r and cleansing meats deny'd
Abstain from; Thy mindes rains let reason guide:
  Then rais'd to Heaven, thou from thy Bodie free,
  A deathlesse Saint, no more shalt mortal be.[22]

The aphoristic wisdom of the *Carmina aurea* and the careful couplets of Stanley's translation are unmistakable harbingers of Pope's didactic poetry. As a matter of fact, the *Carmina aurea* continued to enjoy considerable vogue in England with other English versions by John Hall, John Norris, Edmund Arwaker, and Nicholas Rowe.[23] Thomas Stanley, not satisfied with the translation published in his *Poems,* prepared a fresh version for his *History of philosophy.*[24]

In the fifth century A.D. Hierocles, a pious Neoplatonist of Alexandria, had written an extensive commentary on the *Carmina aurea,* expanding its morality in the direction of mysticism. About 1450 this commentary was rendered into Latin by Joannes Aurispa, apostolic secretary to Pope Nicholas V. Aurispa's translation was printed at Padua in 1474, and several later editions were published.[25] Hierocles also received other translations into Latin and the vernaculars (see p. 64–65, n. 42, above).

In his dedicatory epistle to Nicholas V prefacing his translation, Aurispa praises the Pope for his support of arts and letters, and notes that he has sent emissaries into all parts of the world to procure Greek and Latin manuscripts. Aurispa was on such a mission in Venice, he says, when he found Hierocles' commentary on the *Carmina aurea;* and though he was eighty years old at the time, he had never read anything of greater value. This literary pearl warrants so high an estimation because it contains a moral code consonant with the gospel: "Apart from miracles, it differs little if at all from the Christian faith." [26] With this benediction, the *Carmina aurea* was launched in the renaissance as one of those sanctified precursors of Christianity, a prominent item in the *prisca theologia.* Indeed, the title of Aurispa's translation of Hierocles advertises it as "an outstanding work thoroughly agreeable to the Christian religion." [27]

Humanists such as Erasmus, in the spirit of St. Clement of Alexandria, tended to conflate the gospel of Christianity and the doctrines of pagan philosophy. But others, and especially the Protestants, were more circumspect in defining the authority of each. William Baldwyn, for example, warns the reader in his *Treatise of morall phylosophye:*

> Thinke not (Lovyng Reader) that I allow Philosophie to be Scriptures Interpretour: but rather woulde have it as an handemayden, to perswade suche thinges as Scrypture dothe commaunde.

And he continues by noting:

> Morall Philosophie may wel be called y[t] parte of goddes lawe, whyche geveth commaundemente of outward behavyore.

But moral philosophy differs greatly from the gospel in the rewards which it can bestow:

> The gospell promyseth remission of sinnes, reconcilinge to God, and the gyfte of the holy goste, and of eternall lyfe, for Christes sake: whiche promise is reveled to us from above, not able to be comprehended by reason.[28]

Operative here is a difference in modes of apprehension as well as in rewards, however; for moral philosophy is a product of reason, whereas the truth of Christianity can be fully perceived by faith alone. Nonetheless, the morality of the *Carmina aurea* was acceptable to most Christians—in fact, was touted by many [29]—and the text continued to be taught in the schoolroom. The learned William Wotton (1666–1726), for example, at the age of six was reading St. John's Gospel in Latin, the Psalms in Hebrew, and the *Carmina aurea* in Greek.[30]

Because of their emphasis on introspection and individual morality, Pythagoreans were often credited with the dictum, "Know thyself." [31] It was widely known that *γνῶθι σαυτόν* had been inscribed over the entrance at Delphi; and probably Pythagoras' role as a priest of Apollo—sometimes Hyperborean Apollo himself—linked him with this Apollonian motto. Implicit in this dictum is acceptance of the microcosm-macrocosm analogy. By fully knowing himself, since he is a microcosm, the individual will have dependable knowledge of the macrocosm, and consequently can accommodate himself more readily to the divine plan. In his account of Pythagoras, Photius comments:

> Although it might seem easy, it is most difficult to know oneself. . . . In any case, the saying exhorts us to know what we are capable of. But *nosce teipsum* means no less than to know the nature of the entire universe, which, as God admonishes us, is not possible without philosophy.[32]

Pico della Mirandola adduced the interpretation of the dictum which held throughout the renaissance:

> That *γνῶθι σεαυτόν*, that is, know thyself, arouses us and urges us towards the knowledge of all nature, of which man's nature is the medium and, as it were, the union. For he who knows himself, knows all things in himself.[33]

In line with Pico, Guy du Faur de Pibrac (1529–84) observes in his overtly Pythagorean *Quadrains:*

> Who of Him-selfe hath perfect Knowledge gain'd,
> Ignoreth nothing that he ought to know.[34]

The anonymous author of *The golden cabinet of true treasure* gives the dictum a distinctly Christian interpretation, though nonetheless accordant with its classic intent:

> It behoveth him [man] to know himselfe: that is, he ought to be carefull for his soule, preparing her, to the knowledge of God his Creator, who framed him, after his owne Image, to the end that we may thereby as in a mirrour, contemplate on his invisible divinity, the efficient cause of all wisedome and goodnes. . . .
>
> To begin therefore to know God, we ought to have a knowledge of our selves, to understand what wee are, and to what ende wee were ordained.[35]

We may detect here a teleological argument: if man learns of God through knowledge of himself, his concept of God may be no more than an extrapolation of himself. But we need not fear the subjective fallacy. Since man is created in the image of the deity, any extrapolation that he makes from himself will likewise be in the image of deity. Applying the dictum "Know thyself" will therefore produce accurate knowledge of the universe. When the microcosm projects an image of the macrocosm from itself, it employs a dependable model, and therefore the projection will be correct. True, the macrocosm derives from the image of man; but that image in turn derives from God.

Sir John Davies, of course, wrote a lengthy and learned poetical treatise which he entitled portentously *Nosce teipsum.* Saluste du Bartas, however, an earlier poet-teacher from across the Channel, made the statement more briefly at the beginning of his discourse on the creation of man:

> Thear's under Sunne (as *Delphos* God did show)
> No better Knowledge then *Our selfe to Know:*
> Thear is no Theame more plentifull to scanne,
> Then is the glorious goodly frame of MAN:
> For in Man's self is Fire, Aire, Earth, and Sea,
> Man's (in a word) the World's Epitome.[36]

In accord with this reasoning—"The proper study of mankind is man," as Pope later put it in a nutshell—John Dee proposed a new mathematical discipline which he called "anthropography." This science of ἄνθρωπος was intended to correspond to sister sciences such as geography and cosmography. Dee counsels his reader:

> Remember the *Delphicall Oracle* NOSCE TEIPSUM (*Knowe thy selfe*) so long agoe pronounced: of so many a Philosopher repeated: and of the *Wisest* attempted: And then, you will perceave, how long agoe, you have bene called to the Schole, where this Arte might be learned.[37]

Sir Thomas Browne was a willing student of "anthropography." After announcing allegiance to Pythagoras and Hermes, he asserts that self-knowledge is man's greatest wisdom, and he laments: "Had he [man] read such a Lecture in Paradise as hee did at *Delphos,* we had better knowne our selves, nor had we stood in feare to know [God]." [38] This leads us back to the statement in *The golden cabinet of true treasure:* "To begin therefore to know God, we ought to have a knowledge of our selves." Self-knowledge becomes a means of religion and a basis for moral decision, as in Eden. The injunction "Know thyself" is sound advice in a moral code aimed at temperance and justice through self-control.

Tangential to moral philosophy are opinions concerning the human soul and its reward or punishment for good or bad behavior. The Pythagoreans postulated a world-soul as we know from the *Timaeus,* what came to be called the *anima mundi.* As a simplistic interpretation of the *Timaeus,* popularized by the Stoics, the individual human soul was thought to be a portion of the world-soul which temporarily inhabits a physical body. In the Pythagorean terms of Guy du Faur:

> Rightly to speake: what Man we call, and count
> It is a beamling of *Divinitie:*
> It is a dropling of th'*Eternall Fount:*
> It is a moatling hatcht of th'*Unitie.*[39]

Again in this doctrine we detect the perennial effort to relate the finite (the individual soul) and the infinite (the world-soul). The relationship of a particular human soul to the vast *anima mundi* was generally seen as a mystery, comparable to the relationship between the present moment and eternity. Just as time began when the creating godhead gave physical extension to his archetypal idea, so the human soul begins when it infuses a physical body. The human soul responds to sensible stimuli in our time-space continuum, yet paradoxically without interruption it partakes of the unified realm of pure spirit beyond the confines of space and time.[40] In fact, at death the individual soul returns to its abiding place in the spiritual world, reassimilated into the world-soul. As Plutarch reports: "*Pythagoras* and *Plato* affirme the Soule to be immortall; for in departing out of the bodie, it retireth to the Soule of the universall world, even to the nature which is of the same kinde." [41]

Particularly among Christians the descent of the soul into the body was seen as a debasement, a debilitating incarceration of the spiritual in the corporeal. In *The Merchant of Venice* after Lorenzo calls attention to the music of the spheres, he concludes:

> Such harmony is in immortal souls,
> But whilst this muddy vesture of decay
> Doth grossly close it in, we cannot hear it.
> (V.i.63–65)

To commemorate the degradation of the soul and to emphasize the difference between spirit and flesh, a pun was devised—σῶμα σῆμα—depending upon two Greek words: σῶμα, "body," and σῆμα, "tomb." [42] The body is a tomb for the soul. St. Clement quotes Philolaus to this effect: "The ancient theological writers and prophets also bear witness that the soul is yoked to the body as a punishment, and buried in it as in a tomb." [43] Donne uses the pun with the utmost economy:

> When bodies to their graves, soules from their graves remove.
> ("The Anniversarie," 20)

Though translated into English, the wordplay between σῶμα and σῆμα is still expected to strike our ears.

In a similar vein, St. Jerome had attributed to Pythagoras a definition of philosophy which likened the flesh to a prison for the soul: "Philosophy was a meditation on death, seeking daily to effect the freedom of the soul from the prison of the body." [44] And often the metaphor of body as tomb was conflated with the metaphor of body as prison. Guy du Faur, for example, anatomizes earthly existence in a series of such images:

> That which thou seest of Man, it is not Man:
> 'Tis but a Prison that him Captive keepes:
> 'Tis but a Toombe where Hee's interred (wan):
> 'Tis but the Cradle where a while he sleepes.[45]

In his encomium of reason, Robert Mason reflects the peculiarly Christian adaptation of this Pythagorean *bon mot:* "*Pithagoras* held opinion, that the Soule is a bodilesse and immortal substance, put into this bodie as into a prison for sin." [46]

The Pythagorean theory of the soul to this point is, generally speaking, compatible with Christianity. However, the formulators of Church dogma rejected other Pythagorean beliefs. Whereas in Christian doctrine the soul undergoes incarnation only once and suffers only one life on earth, the Pythagoreans postulated a progress for each soul through a series of incarnations. After the body dies, the individual soul is temporarily assimilated into the world-soul; but soon it is assigned to another body and sent on a journey through another life. Probably the best known tenet of the Pythagorean school, in fact, is this belief that the soul inhabits a series of bodies in a perpetual succession of reincarnations—what is known popularly, though somewhat affectedly, as *metempsychosis*.[47] Faustus, for example, in Marlowe's version of his legend, seeks to alleviate his anguish at the end by thinking upon "Pythagorean metempsychosis."

The most poetic as well as graphic description of this cycle is given in Plato's *Republic*, where Er describes what "he had seen in the world beyond" (614B). After passing a gateway where two judges separate the newly arrived souls—"the righteous journey to the right and upwards through the heaven . . . and the unjust . . . take the road to the left and downward" (614C)—Er arrives at a plain filled with souls where the three Fates sit on thrones. A marshall of Lachesis addresses the throng: "Souls that live for a day, now is the beginning of another cycle of mortal generation where birth is the beacon of death" (617D-E). Then the souls are allowed to choose lots for a new life, however ignorantly and foolishly, and are sent on their way, passing through the Plain of Oblivion and across the River of Forgetfulness. Finally, "after they had fallen asleep and it was the middle of the night, there was a sound of thunder and a quaking of the earth, and they were suddenly wafted thence, one this way, one that, upward to their birth like shooting stars" (621B). A new embodiment, the next phase in the continuing life of the soul, has begun.

As the soul is reborn in its succession of physical forms, on each occasion it is rewarded for virtue in its previous life and penalized for vice. If it lives well, it may eventually achieve such grace that it remains permanently exempt from earthly duty. If it has lived badly, however, it is punished by a next life lower on the scale of existence. Plato in the *Timaeus* is quite precise on this point:

> He that has lived his appointed time well shall return again to his abode in his native state, and shall gain a life that is blessed

> and congenial; but whoso has failed therein shall be changed into woman's nature at the second birth; and if, in that shape, he still refraineth not from wickedness he shall be changed every time, according to the nature of his wickedness, into some bestial form after the similitude of his own nature (42B-C).[48]

In this way, if the individual persists in evil, the soul might descend in its transmigrations right down the chain of being, so that, as Malvolio learnedly observes, "The soul of our grandam might haply inhabit a bird" (*Twelfth Night*, IV.ii.50–51). For this reason, of course, the Pythagorean sect refrained from eating anything animate, lest they violate the body currently inhabited by an ancestor.[49]

This belief in metempsychosis has a concomitant especially interesting for literary critics. Some authorities opine that transanimation may be no more than a concoction of the fabulists to make evident in this world the punishment for various sins, with the purpose of deterring men from evil. The *De anima mundi*, the paraphrase of Plato's *Timaeus* supposedly by Timaeus of Locri himself, concludes with this observation:

> As we cure Bodies with things unwholsome, when the wholesome agree not with them, so we restrain souls with fabulous relations, when they will not be led by the true. Let them then, since there is a necessity for it, talk of these strange punishments, as if souls did transmigrate, those of the effeminate into the bodies of Women, given up to ignominy; of Murtherers, into those of Beasts, for punishment; of the Lascivious, into the forms of Swine; of the leight, and temerarious into Birds; of the slothful, and idle, unlearned, and ignorant, into several kinds of Fishes.[50]

Such an assumption places Ovid's *Metamorphoses* much more clearly in the Pythagorean tradition and renders it a much more sophisticated work than a mere recital of wondrous transformations. The outward form after change simply makes palpable the preexistent psychological state of a character. For example, when Daphne's soft flesh turns into the harsh bark of a laurel tree, her rigid, unyielding nature is made visible, thereby revealing the condition of her soul. In similar fashion, her prayers to the river-god, her father, articulate in audible form her innermost wishes. Her narrative then becomes a parable which warns against such attitudes.

All authorities—pagan and Christian—agreed that Pythagoras had instituted this belief in the transmigration of souls, having adopted it from the Egyptians. Diogenes Laertius, as usual, records the consensus:

> He is also said to be the first who was of opinion, That the Soul exchang'd Habitations from one living Creature to another constrain'd thereto by a certain Wheel of Necessity.[51]

St. Jerome agrees:

> Listen to the principle that Pythagoras was first among the Greeks to discover: "Souls are immortal and they pass from one body to another." [52]

Pythagoras himself had undergone a succession of well-known incarnations—some said in order to support his own theory of metempsychosis.[53] Some, such as Erasmus, said that "he had been all thinges, a Philosopher, a man, a woman, a kynge, a private person, a fisshe, an horse, a frogge, yea (I wene) a sponge also." [54] The point is that Pythagoras had to exhaust human experience to achieve his consummate wisdom. An analogous case in Greek mythology is that of Tiresias, who at least had been both male and female.

One curious bit of Pythagorean lore employed the letter Y (Greek *upsilon*) to symbolize the moral choice between a life of virtue or of vice, a choice which a young man faces upon reaching adulthood. Y was, in fact, known as the Pythagorean letter. The classic translation of the symbol was made in terms of a road which suddenly bifurcates into a path on the left and a path on the right, so that the traveler must choose between two clearly distinct ways. Isidore of Seville attributes this symbol to Pythagoras and offers the usual interpretation of it:

> Pythagoras of Samos was the first to fashion the letter Y into a pattern of human life. The straight portion at the bottom signifies the first, uncertain age, which at that point has been given over to neither vices nor virtues. The bifurcation at the top, however, begins at adolescence. The path to the right is difficult, but it tends toward a blessed life. The path to the left is easier, but it leads to ruin and destruction. Persius has this to say about it:
>
> And the letter which led to the branches of the Samian Y
> Has shown you on the right side a rising pathway.[55]

Isidore is drawing upon a famous passage in Lactantius [56] as well as upon Persius. Prominent in this tradition are also Ausonius'

50. *Hercules at the crossroads of the letter Y (upsilon)*

Hercules, identified by his lionskin and club, presides at the point of decision between the difficult narrow path on the right and the easy wide path on the left. The inscription reads: *Litera Pythagorae, discrimine secta bicorni* ("The letter of Pythagoras, divided into two paths"), the first line of the ancient anonymous poem on the Pythagorean Y (see p. 271). The virtuous hero raises a cautionary hand as two youths approach the bifurcation.

Joannes Christianus Knauthius, ed., *Pythagorae carmen aureum* et al. (Strasbourg, 1720), frontispiece.

Eclogue II and some anonymous verses (often attributed to Vergil [57]) that had survived from the ancient world:

> The Pythagorick Letter two ways spread,
> Shows the two paths in which Mans life is led.
> The right hand track to sacred Virtue tends,
> Though steep and rough at first, in rest it ends;
> The other broad and smooth, but from its Crown,
> On rocks the Traveller is tumbled down.
> He who to Virtue by harsh toyls aspires,
> Subduing pains, worth and renown acquires:
> But who seeks slothful luxury, and flies,
> The labour of great acts, dishonour'd dies.[58]

The image is the commonplace one of the traveler at the crossroads. The narrative action of Stephen Hawes's *Pastime of Pleasure* begins with a dreamer who comes to a fork where he must choose between right and left, explicitly designated the contemplative and the active life (i.3 ff.). Sir Thomas Browne equates the two branches of the letter Y—in his phrase, the "bicornous element of Pythagoras"—with "the narrow door of Heaven, and the ample gates of Hell." [59]

The most famous wayfarer who faced the choice between a path of virtue and a path of ease was Hercules, a pagan rather than a Christian hero, but nevertheless a trueborn paragon in the renaissance. A fully elaborated account of his timely decision is reported by Xenophon, who heard it from Socrates, who had in turn heard it from the sophist Prodicus:

> *Hercules* having attained to that Stage of Life, when Man, being left to the Government of himself, seldom fails to give certain Indications, whether he will walk in the Paths of Virtue; or wander through all the Intricacies of Vice:—Perplexed, and undetermined what Course to pursue; retired into a Place where Silence, and Solitude might bestow on him that Tranquility and Leisure, so necessary for Deliberation. When, two Women, of more than ordinary Stature, came on towards him.[60]

One of the women is named Happiness—though her detractors call her Sensuality—and she typifies the vicious life; the other is forthrightly named Virtue, and she of course seeks to counter the blandishments of the seductress. The topos of Hercules at the crossroads became a favorite of iconographers and poets, who gave it an unblushingly Christian interpretation.[61] Its meaning, as well as its

Pythagorean connections, is well illustrated by Plate 50. The letter Y has remained an archetypal pattern in art until our own age, when Robert Frost has hesitated where "two roads diverged in a yellow wood." [62]

Much of the moral wisdom of Pythagoreanism was embodied in *sententiae* and epistles and ethical fragments ascribed to various latter-day Pythagoreans (see pp. 56–57, above). Even better known, however, were the Pythagorean *symbola,* gnomic statements having affinity with hieroglyphs and emblems. The esoteric tenets of the Pythagorean brotherhood, usually taboos, were stated cryptically, in such a way as to render them unintelligible to all but the initiated. A sacred truth was encapsulated in a metaphoric precept. By this means the secrecy of the brotherhood was preserved. Iamblichus explains the rationale for the use of *symbola:*

> The most ancient, and such as were contemporary with, and disciples to *Pythagoras,* did not compose their writings intelligible, in a common vulgar style, familiar to every one, as if they endeavoured to dictate things readily perceptible by the hearer, but consonant to the silence decreed by *Pythagoras,* concerning divine mysteries, which it was not lawful to speak of before those, who were not initiated; and therefore clouded both their mutual discourses and writings by Symbols; which, if not expounded by those that proposed them, by a regular interpretation, appear to the hearers like old wives proverbs, trivial and foolish; but being rightly explained, and instead of dark, rendred lucid and conspicuous to the vulgar, they discover an admirable sense, no less than the divine Oracle of Pythian *Apollo.*[63]

Filippo Beroaldo (1453–1505), the learned Bolognese who explicated several of the *symbola,* defines the term with a reverence comparable to that of Iamblichus:

> . . . the Symbola of Pythagoras—that is to say, certain disclosures and revelations of the mysteries of the holier doctrine in which the moral sentences and salutary precepts are contained, in which as in earthen vessels the precious treasure is enclosed.[64]

No wonder these maxims were exhumed by pedagogues of the renaissance. Backed by the authority of Pythagoras and bolstered by the piety of the *Carmina aurea,* they carried considerable moral weight.

Lists of the Pythagorean *symbola* had been preserved by several of the most respected moralists of the ancient world: Plutarch,

Porphyry, Iamblichus. Diogenes Laertius and Athenaeus had also recorded numerous *symbola;* and among the Church Fathers, St. Clement, St. Jerome, and St. Cyril had written on them (see pp. 57–58, above). The best-known collection, however, was that enumerated by Iamblichus in the *Protrepticae orationes ad philosophiam* (xxi), quoted here *in extenso* as translated by Thomas Stanley:

1. When you go to the Temple, worship, neither do nor say any thing concerning life.
2. If there be a Temple in your way, go not in, no not though you pass by the very doors.
3. Sacrifice and worship barefoot.
4. Decline high-ways, and take the foot-paths.
5. Abstain from the Melanure,[65] for it belongs to the Terrestrial gods.
6. Above all things, govern your tongue, when you follow the gods.
7. When the winds blow, worship the noise.
8. Cut not fire with a sword.
9. Turn away from thy self every edg.
10. Help a man to take up a burthen, but not to lay it down.
11. Put on the shoo first on the right foot, but the left foot first into the bason.
12. Discourse not of Pythagorean things without light.
13. Pass not over a pair of Scales.
14. Travelling from home, turn not back; for the Furies go back with you.
15. Urine not, being turned towards the Sun.
16. Wipe not a seat with a Torch.
17. A Cock keep, but not sacrifice; for it is consecreated to the Moon and the Sun.
18. Sit not upon a Choenix.[66]
19. Breed nothing that hath crooked talons.
20. Cut not in the way.[67]
21. Receive not a Swallow into your house.
22. Wear not a Ring.
23. Grave not the image of God on a Ring.
24. Look not in a glass by candle-light.

25. Concerning the gods, disbelieve nothing wonderful, nor concerning divine Doctrines.
26. Be not taken with immoderate laughter.
27. At a sacrifice, pare not your nails.
28. Lay not hold on every one readily with your right hand.
29. When you rise out of bed, disorder the coverlet, and deface the print.
30. Eat not the Heart.
31. Eat not the Brains.
32. Spit upon the cuttings of your hair, and the parings of your nails.
33. Receive not an Erythrine.[68]
34. Deface the print of a pot in the ashes.
35. Take not a woman that hath gold, to get children of her.
36. First honour the figure and steps, a figure and a Tribolus.[69]
37. Abstain from Beans.
38. Set Mallows,[70] but eat it not.
39. Abstain from living creatures.[71]

During the renaissance some of the most eminent scholars of the day disseminated the Pythagorean *symbola* with notable largesse. Ficino translated into Latin the thirty-nine *symbola* from Iamblichus and published them along with a Latin translation of the *Carmina aurea* in his edition of Iamblichus' *De mysteriis Ægyptiorum, Chaldaeorum, Assyriorum* et al. (Venice, 1497).[72] Pico della Mirandola discussed four *symbola* in the *De dignitate hominis,* and it is clear that he was familiar with the long list.[73] Filippo Beroaldo selected eight *symbola* from Iamblichus and offered an extensive analysis of their meaning in a treatise entitled *Symbola Pythagorae moraliter explicata* (Bologna, c.1500), which was often reprinted. About the same time, Erasmus published his first collection of adages—*Veterum maximeque insignium paroemiarum id est adagiorum collectanea* (Paris, 1500)—which included nine *symbola* taken from St. Jerome and Porphyry.[74] The Pythagorean *symbola,* in fact, served as a nucleus for Erasmus' *Adagia,* and by the time of the Froben edition in 1526 the number had grown to thirty-six, representing a variety of sources.[75] The Viennese humanist Joannes Alexander Brassicanus appended eighteen *symbola* from Iamblichus to his *Proverbiorum symmicta* (Vienna, 1529), and supplied ample commentary.[76] Sir Thomas Elyot translated Plutarch's *Education or bringinge up of children* (London, 1535?), including of course the ten *symbola* near the end.[77] Richard Taverner selected fifteen *symbola* from Erasmus and gave them an English translation in his *Proverbes or adagies* (London, 1539).[78] Lilio Gregorio Giraldi, the distinguished scholar from Ferrara, compiled an enormous list of sixty-one *symbola* from all sources and published them in a volume entitled *Libelli duo, in quorum altero aenigmata pleraque antiquorum, in altero Pythagorae symbola . . . sunt explicata* (Basle, 1551).[79] Edward Grant repeated five *symbola* in his adaptation of Plutarch, which he entitled *A president for parentes* (London, 1571).[80] In the prefatory material introducing his arrangement of Alciati's *Emblemata*, Claude Mignault provided a "Syntagma de symbolis," and in some editions inserted a section of thirty-three Pythagorean *symbola* from Erasmus.[81] The *symbola* were easily available in a variety of formats designed to appeal to everyone from schoolboys to courtiers.[82]

We should join with Sir Thomas Browne, though, in lamenting the vulgarization of ancient wisdom:

> Many Errors crept in and perverted the Doctrine of Pythagoras, whilst men received his Precepts [i.e., *symbola*] in a different sense from his intention; converting Metaphors into proprieties, and receiving as literal expressions, obscure and involved truths.[83]

As a matter of fact, interpretations of the *symbola* tended to go in divergent directions. On one side were the pragmatic moralists who applied the *symbola* as literal commandments, those to whom Browne objected. On the other were the mystics who went farther and farther in their search for recondite meanings. The result could be a welter of contradictions.

An example will illustrate the diversity of opinion which might accrue to any one *symbolum*—though admittedly this is a flagrant case. The most notorious of the Pythagorean *symbola* is the injunction, "Abstain from eating beans." Among the ancients, it appears in Diogenes Laertius, Plutarch, Porphyry, and Iamblichus. Diogenes Laertius has an extended passage explaining it, purportedly taken from a lost work by Aristotle:

> According to Aristotle in his work *On the Pythagoreans*, Pythagoras counselled abstinence from beans either because they are like the gates of Hades . . . as being alone unjointed, or because they are injurious, or because they are like the form of the universe, or because they belong to oligarchy, since they are used in election by lot (VIII.34).[84]

The possibilities here are sufficient to accommodate any bent of mind. Later commentators, however, were not so catholic. Cicero, for example, is sensible and unequivocal, as usual:

> Pythagoras laid it down as a rule, that his disciples should not eat beans, because this food is very flatulent, and contrary to that tranquility of mind which a truth-seeking spirit should possess.[85]

Aulus Gellius in his eclectic fashion quotes Cicero, Callimachus, Aristoxenus, and Empedocles. He seems to support the opinion of the last, however, that beans refer to the human testicles, and therefore they should not be eaten "because they are the cause of pregnancy and furnish the power for human generation." Applied morally, the *symbolum* is meant "to keep men, not from eating beans, but from excess in venery." [86] Plutarch in his interpretation is uncharacteristically brief:

> Intermeddle not in the affaires of State and government: for that in olde time men were woont to passe their voices by beanes, & so proceeded to the election of Magistrates.[87]

Erasmus gives an extravagantly learned analysis of the *symbolum*, assessing all of the previous authorities,[88] which Richard Taverner imperfectly summarizes:

> There be sondry interpretacions of thys symbole. But Plutarche and Cicero thynke beanes to be forbydden of Pythagoras, bycause they be wyndye and do ingender impure humours and for that cause provoke bodily lust.[89]

With such a wealth of respected tradition bearing upon him, Sir Thomas Browne was understandably testy in his own interpretation of why Pythagoras had enjoined his disciples from eating beans.[90]

In all fairness to the Pythagorean tradition, we should consider another *symbolum* which does not lend itself so readily to absurd interpretation. "Do not stir the fire with a sword" appears in almost every collection of Pythagorean *symbola*, in both the renaissance and the ancient period—it is, for example, first on the list compiled by Diogenes Laertius (VIII.17) and second on Porphyry's list (xlii). Plutarch gave the dictum its classic explication: "a caveat, not to provoke farther a man that is angrie." [91] Diogenes Laertius concurred with slight modification: "Don't stir the passion or the swelling pride of the great" (VIII.18). When St. Jerome agreed—"Do not irritate with reproachful words a soul that is angered" [92] —the meaning of the *symbolum* was fixed within narrow limits.

That meaning, of course, is highly intelligent and imaginative, a metaphor or allegory or emblem—a *symbolum.*

As an exemplar of their moral principles, late Pythagoreans devised a hero in the semihistorical person of Apollonius of Tyana. He incarnated the virtue and the piety extolled in the Pythagorean system, and his biography, composed by Flavius Philostratus about 217 A.D.,[93] gave much the same satisfaction as an epic. Factually, Apollonius was an ascetic and mystic who lived during the first century A.D. and traveled a good part of the known world. Fictionally, he fashioned his life after that of his master, Pythagoras, proving an adept in the occult and a model of probity. The general knowledge about him in the renaissance is digested by Thomas Cooper:

> In his infancie [he] so profited in learning, that being but a childe, he was a great Phylosopher, and followed the sect of Pythagoras, going alway in linnen, and never eating any thing that had life. And notwithstanding he was excellently learned in ye mysticall knowledge of Philosophie and naturall magike, yet to have knowledge, he went into Ægypt, Persia, Ethiope, and Indea, to learne of the Bragmanes, Gymnosophistes, and retourned into Greece and Rome, where he was had in great admiration, for the mervayles that he shewed. And at last, being above the age of 80. yeares, in a great assembly of people, was sodeinly conveighed away, no man knoweth how nor whether, as Philostratus, who writeth his life, saith.[94]

Despite his questionable credentials—indeed, despite the charges by some that he was a fabrication to discredit the miracle-working powers of Christ—Apollonius was widely regarded as a pagan analogue to Christian sainthood. He was therefore acceptable as a cynosure in the Christian firmament of shining examples. As Edward Grant had said about Apollonius' prototype, Pythagoras himself, "Here is example for yongmen to follow that woulde be perfecte men, and in time to come, profitable members in the common weale." [95] Gloriana's exemplary knights were intended to do no more.

Notes

[1] 2nd ed. (London, 1687), p. 541.

[2] The reference is to a work, the *Magna moralia*, spuriously attributed to Aristotle, though probably belonging to his earliest circle; cf. William Enfield, *The History of Philosophy*, 2 vols. (London, 1791), I.390.

[3] VIII.33. For an explication by Hieronymus Wolff, see Gulielmus Morellius,

Tabula compendiosa (Basle, 1580), p. 158. Note the definition of *harmony* on p. 137, n.42, above.

[4] *Of the lawes of ecclesiastical politie* [I.iii] (London, 1617), p. 7.

[5] *The Life of Pythagoras*, tr. anon. (London, 1707), p. 53.

[6] *De vita Pythagorae*, xlvi, as translated by Stanley, *History of philosophy*, p. 540. For Richard Crashaw's cogent interpretation of this ecstatic state, see his "Preface" to *Steps to the Temple* in *The Poems*, ed. L. C. Martin (Oxford, 1927), p. 75.

[7] *The Apology Against the Books of Rufinus* [III.xxxix], tr. John N. Hritzu (Catholic Univ. of America Press, 1965), p. 211.

[8] Pythagoras verò finem omnis Philosophiae censebat esse contemplationem & cognitionem veritatis (*Historiae philosophiae libri septem* [Leyden, 1655], p. 4). Cf. Aelianus, *A registre of hystories*, tr. Abraham Fleming (London, 1576), fol. Mm3[v].

[9] See Enfield, *History of Philosophy*, I.390–391.

[10] *De vita Pythagorae*, xvi, xxxi. Cf. Stanley, *History of philosophy*, pp. 518, 542–543; and A. Ed. Chaignet, *Pythagore et la philosophie pythagoricienne*, 2 vols. (Paris, 1873), II.210–213.

[11] Apropos here is a quatrain by Guy du Faur, translated by Joshua Sylvester and appended to his Du Bartas:

> *Vertue*, betweene the Two extremes that haunts;
> Betweene two-mickle and two-little sizes;
> Exceedes in nothing, and in nothing wants:
> Borrowes of none: but to it-selfe suffizes.

(*The quadrains*, stanza 26, appended to *Bartas: His devine weekes and workes*, tr. Sylvester [London, 1605], p. 681). Spenser's Medina in Book II of *The Faerie Queene*, with her sisters Perissa and Elissa, immediately comes to mind. Of course, the notion of virtue as a mean has been popularized by Aristotle.

[12] Cf. Iamblichus, *De vita Pythagorae*, xxx; and Dacier, *Life of Pythagoras*, pp. 87–88.

[13] *History of philosophy*, p. 544.

[14] *Against Rufinus* [III.xxxix], tr. Hritzu, pp. 210–211. See also Porphyry, *De vita Pythagorae*, xxii; Iamblichus, *De vita Pythagorae*, vii; Iamblichus, *De mysteriis* et al., tr. Ficino, X3[v]; Walter Burley, *Liber de vita et moribus philosophorum et poetarum* (Strasbourg, 1516), fol. 8; Hartmann Schedel, *Liber cronicarum* (Nuremberg, 1493), fol. 61[v]; Joachim Zehner, ed., *Pythagorae fragmenta* (Leipzig, 1603), pp. 70–71; Theophilus Gale, *The court of the gentiles*, 2 parts (London, 1670), II.171; and Dacier, *Life of Pythagoras*, p. 64.

[15] *History of philosophy*, p. 542.

[16] Cf. Plutarch, "Life of Numa" in *The lives of the noble Grecians and Romanes*, tr. Sir Thomas North (London, 1603), pp. 61 ff. See also Diodorus Siculus, *Bibliotheca*, VIII.14; and Joannes Albertus Fabricius, *Bibliotheca Graeca*, 11 vols. (Hamburg, 1790–1808), I.854. Pythagoras was himself an effective political leader in the cause of liberty and justice; cf. Stanley, *History of philosophy*, pp. 503–505.

[17] *Metamorphoses*, XV.1 ff.

[18] The authorship of the *Carmina aurea* was the occasion of much scholarly concern. St. Jerome led to speculation that Archippus or Lysis was the author (*Against Rufinus* [III.xxxix], tr. Hritzu, p. 210); cf. Stanley, *History of philosophy*, p. 512; and Dacier, *Life of Pythagoras*, p. 8. Pico della Mirandola proposed that Philolaus had composed the verses ("Preface" to *Heptaplus*, tr. Nicolas le Fèvre de la Boderie in Francesco Giorgio, *L'Harmonie du monde*, tr. Guy le Fèvre de la Boderie [Paris, 1579], p. 829); cf. Joannes Baptista Bernardus, *Seminarium totius philosophiae Aristotelicae et Platonicae*, 2nd

ed. (Lyons, 1599), II.768; and Daniel Georg Morhof, *Polyhistor* [I.vii.2.13; II.i.2.8], 4th ed. (Lubeck, 1747), I.1047, II.19. Fabricius argued in favor of Empedocles (*Bibliotheca Graeca*, I.794). Most, however, have agreed with Thomas Stanley that Pythagoras was progenitor of the sentiments expressed in the *Carmina aurea* even if one of his disciples did compose the actual verses (see Stanley, *Poems* [London, 1651], p. 81).

[19] As an appendix for his grammars, Manutius prepared an anthology of readings on which schoolchildren might practise their skill in languages. It contained several items to help with the difficult orthography, pronunciation, and typography of Greek, beginning with "De literis graecis ac diphthongis." Then came the readings themselves, chosen for their religious and moral instruction as well as their linguistic interest. The texts are in Greek with a Latin trot, in some editions printed between the lines of Greek and in others printed in a parallel column. They consist of the Lord's Prayer, the Ave Maria, the Salve Regina, the Apostle's Creed, St. John's "In principio," Pythagoras' *Carmina aurea*, and a poem of Phocylides. The moral teachings of Pythagoras not infrequently traveled in this company of high seriousness.

Manutius first published this anthology as an appendix to his edition of Constantine Lascaris' *Erotemata* (Venice, 1494–95), and it appeared with several later editions of Lascaris' grammar. It first appeared with Manutius' own Latin grammar in Venice, 1501, and was a regular feature of his grammars after that. The appendix was sometimes printed as a separate volume with the title of the first text, "De literis graecis ac diphthongis"—e.g., by Thomas Anshelm at Tübingen, 1512, and at Hagenau, 1519, and by Michel Vascosan at Paris, 1534.

In the mid-sixteenth century when the popularity of Manutius' anthology had waned, the *Carmina aurea* was kept on the desks of schoolboys by inclusion in another collection which well illustrates the continuity of renaissance textbooks. Joachim Camerarius published the *Libellus scolasticus utilis, et valde bonus* at the press of Joannes Oporinus in Basle, 1551, containing the Greek text only of moral poems by Theognis, Phocylides, Solon, Tyrtaeus, and others as well as the *Carmina aurea* of Pythagoras. Oporinus printed a second edition at Basle, 1555. This volume formed the basis for Michael Neander's collection, *Liber . . . aureus, planèque scholasticus*, which contained Latin translations and notes and commentaries, printed by Oporinus at Basle, 1559 (another edition by Johann Steinman in Leipzig, 1577). It also formed the basis for a smaller textbook prepared by Jacobus Hertelius with Latin translations, printed by Oporinus in Basle, 1561, and at least eighteen later editions (the latest that I have seen was printed in Breslau, 1692). The Hertelius volume was then taken over by Jean Crespin as the fourth part of his collection, *Vetustissimorum authorum georgica, bucolica, & gnomica poemata*, printed by Crespin at Geneva, 1568–70, with at least seven later editions (the latest that I have seen was printed in Geneva, 1639). The Hertelius volume was also taken over by Friedrich Sylburg for his collection, *Epicae elegiacaeque minorum poetarum gnomae, graece ac latine*, printed by Johann Wechel and Peter Fischer in Frankfurt, 1591, with at least nine later editions (the latest that I have seen was printed at Florence, 1766). Sylburg's text and translation was subsumed by Ralph Winterton for his collection, *Poetae minores graeci*, first printed by Thomas and John Buck and Roger Daniel in Cambridge, 1635, with at least eleven later editions (the latest that I have seen was printed in London, 1739). There is no doubt that the *Carmina aurea* was a common item in the schoolroom throughout the renaissance.

[20] Cf. Fabricius, *Bibliotheca Graeca*, I.704–709; and Douglas Young, ed., *Theognis, Pythagoras, Phocylides* (Leipzig, 1961), esp. pp. xx–xxv.

[21] I.e., the tetractys; see p. 152, above.

[22] Stanley, *Poems*, ed. Galbraith M. Crump (Oxford, 1962), pp. 68–70.

[23] In Hall, tr., *Hierocles upon the Golden Verses of Pythagoras* (London, 1657), a3^{v}–a6. In Norris, tr., *Hierocles upon the Golden Verses of the Pythagoreans* (London, 1682), b6–c2. In Arwaker, *Thoughts well employ'd*, 2nd ed. (London, 1697), A2–A4^{v}. In Dacier, *Life of Pythagoras*, L4–l†8.

[24] *The third and last volume* (London, 1660), Kk2–Kk2^{v}.

[25] Rome, 1475; Rome, 1493; Strasbourg, 1511; Basle, 1543; Lyons, 1551.

[26] Parum enim aut nihil ubi miracula non fuerunt: a fide Christiana differt (Hierocles, *In aureos versus Pythagorae opusculum*, tr. Aurispa [Padua, 1474], a2). See also Dacier, *Life of Pythagoras*, pp. xv–xvi.

[27] Opusculum praestantissimum et religioni Christianae consentaneum (*ibid.*, a2^{v}).

[28] (London, 1550), ¶v^{v}–¶vi.

[29] E.g., by Edmund Arwaker, "Rector of *Drumglass* in *Ireland*" (title page), who added "Pythagoras's Golden Verses made Christian" to the second edition of his *Thoughts well employ'd* (1697).

[30] See *Dictionary of National Biography*, "William Wotton."

[31] For an authoritative treatment of the Pythagorean tradition for this dictum, see Joannes Scheffer, *De natura & constitutione philosophiae Italicae seu Pythagoricae liber singularis* (Upsala, 1664), pp. 67–73.

> [32] Difficillimum est seipsum nosse, quamvis facile videatur; . . . Nos autem hortatur, ut quisque, quid possit, cognoscat. Sed nihil est aliud *Nosse se ipsum*, quam totius mundi naturam nosse, quod sine Philosophia fieri non potest, quodque Deus nos monet (*Myriobiblon* [Rouen, 1653], col. 1319).

[33] *On the Dignity of Man*, tr. Charles Glenn Wallis (Indianapolis, 1965), pp. 14–15.

[34] Stanza 10 in *Bartas: Devine weekes and workes*, tr. Sylvester (1605), p. 676.

[35] An anonymous French work translated by William Jewel (London, 1612), p. 70. Spenser puts the same sentiment into the mouth of the muse Urania:

> By knowledge wee do learne our selves to knowe,
> And what to man, and what to God wee owe.
> (*Teares of the Muses*, 503–504)

[36] *Devine weeks and workes*, tr. Sylvester (1605), p. 205. Cf. Guy du Faur, *Quadrains*, stanza 9, in *Bartas: Devine weekes and Workes*, tr. Sylvester (1605), p. 676.

[37] "Mathematicall praeface" in Euclid, *Elements*, tr. Henry Billingsley (London, 1570), C3. See pp. 199–200, n.63, above.

[38] *Religio Medici* [I.13], ed. L. C. Martin (Oxford, 1964), p. 12.

[39] *Quadrains*, stanza 13, in *Bartas: Devine weekes and workes*, p. 677. "Th' *Eternall Fount*" is of course the Pythagorean tetractys, which proceeds from unity (see p. 152, above).

[40] This paradox is expounded with especial clarity by Ficino in his *Theologia platonica* (III.ii). The passage is translated by Josephine L. Burroughs in Paul O. Kristeller, "Ficino and Pomponazzi on the Place of Man in the Universe," *Journal of the History of Ideas*, 5 (1944), 229–231.

[41] "Opinions of Philosophers" [IV.vii] in *The morals*, tr. Philemon Holland (London, 1603), p. 835. Cf. Porphyry, *De vita Pythagorae*, xix. Several conflicting definitions of the soul were attributed to the Pythagoreans; for a critique, see Chaignet, *Pythagore*, II.175–185.

[42] See Plato, *Cratylus*, 400C; Macrobius, *Commentary on the Dream of Scipio* [I.x.10, xi.1–3], tr. William H. Stahl (Columbia Univ. Press, 1952), pp. 128, 130; John Case, *Lapis philosophicus* (Oxford, 1599), title page (see Plate 44); Gale, *Court of gentiles*, II.167; Eric R. Dodds, *The Greeks and the*

Irrational (Univ. of California Press, 1951), pp. 148–152; and W. K. C. Guthrie, *A History of Greek Philosophy*, 3 vols. (Cambridge Univ. Press, 1962), I.311–312. The σῶμα-σῆμα pun is often associated with Orphism.

[43] *Stromateis*, III.iv, translated in Guthrie, *Greek Philosophy*, I.311.

[44] *Against Rufinus* [III.40], tr. Hritzu, p. 212. Cf. Plato, *Phaedo*, 62B; William Baldwyn, *A treatise of morall phylosophye* (London, 1550), B8; and Stanley, *History of philosophy*, p. 540.

[45] *Quadrains*, stanza 11, in *Bartas: Devine weekes and workes*, p. 676.

[46] *Reasons monarchie* (London, 1602), p. 7.

[47] The literature on metempsychosis, as one might expect, is extensive. For early bibliography on the subject, see Gerard Johann Vossius, *De philosophorum sectis liber* (The Hague, 1657), p. 31; Burckhard Gotthelf Struve, *Bibliotheca philosophica* (Jena, 1704), p. 93; and Fabricius, *Bibliotheca Graeca*, I.775–776. The following titles are particularly interesting with respect to the Pythagorean origin of the belief: Francesco Giorgio, *De harmonia mundi totius cantica tria*, 2nd ed. (Paris, 1545), fol. 107–108^v; Paganino Gaudenzio, *De Pythagoraea animarum transmigratione opusculum* (Pisa, 1641); Whitelocke Bulstrode, *An essay of transmigration, in defense of Pythagoras* (London, 1692); Willem van Irhoven, *De palingenesia veterum seu metempsychosi sic dicta pythagorica* (Amsterdam, 1733); Gottlieb Wernsdorf, *De metempsychosi veterum non figurate sed proprie intelligenda* (Wittenberg, 1741); Louis Rougier, *L'Origine astronomique de la croyance pythagoricienne en l'immortalité céleste des âmes* (Cairo, 1933); Alister Cameron, *The Pythagorean Background of the Theory of Recollection* (Menasha, Wis., 1938); Herbert S. Long, *A Study of the Doctrine of Metempsychosis in Greece from Pythagoras to Plato* (Princeton Univ. Press, 1948); and James A. Philip, *Pythagoras and Early Pythagoreanism* (Univ. of Toronto Press, 1966), pp. 151–171.

[48] For an interesting variant, see Georg Sabinus' commentary in his edition of Ovid, *Metamorphoses* (Cambridge, 1584), p. 604.

[49] This is the burden of Pythagoras' lecture to Numa Pompilius in Ovid, *Metamorphoses*, XV.72 ff. Cf. Plutarch, "On the eating of flesh"; Diogenes Laertius, VIII.12–13; Porphyry, *De vita Pythagorae*, vii; Photius, *Myriobiblon*, col. 1315; Vossius, *De philosophorum sectis*, pp. 40–41. For a modern critique of the Pythagorean prohibition against eating meat, see Guthrie, *Greek Philosophy*, I.187–191.

[50] Translated by Stanley, *History of philosophy*, p. 570. For a similar opinion, see Pico della Mirandola, *Heptaplus*, tr. Douglas Carmichael, in Pico, *Dignity of Man* et al., tr. Wallis, p. 123; Pierre de la Primaudaye, *The second part of the French academie*, tr. T. Bowes (London, 1605), pp. 509–510; and Dacier, *Life of Pythagoras*, pp. 44–48.

[51] *The lives, opinions, and remarkable sayings of the most famous ancient philosophers. . . . Made English by several hands* [VIII.14], 2 vols. (London, 1696), II.10–11. The "Wheel of Necessity" probably comes from Plato's vision of Er (*Republic*, 616C). Cf. Walter Burley, *Liber de vita et moribus philosophorum*, ed. Hermann Knust (Tübingen, 1886), p. 78; Natalis Comes, *Mythologiae* [III.xx; X."De Lethe fluvio"] (Padua, 1616), pp. 147, 537–528; Jean Jacques Boissard, *De divinatione et magicis praestigiis* (Oppenheim, 1616?), p. 297; Vossius, *De philosophorum sectis*, p. 31; Morhof, *Polyhistor* [II.i.2.7], II.18; Chaignet, *Pythagore*, II.175; Eduard Zeller, *A History of Greek Philosophy*, tr. S. F. Alleyne, 2 vols. (London, 1881), I.481–487; John Burnet, *Early Greek Philosophy*, 4th ed. (London, 1945), p. 43; and G. S. Kirk and J. E. Raven, *The Presocratic Philosophers* (Cambridge Univ. Press, 1962), pp. 222–223, 261–262.

[52] *Against Rufinus* [III.xxxix], tr. Hritzu, p. 211.

[53] For the longest list of incarnations see Diogenes Laertius, VIII.4–5. Cf.

Ovid, *Metamorphoses,* XV.160 ff.; St. Jerome, *Against Rufinus* [III.xl], tr. Hritzu, p. 212; Iamblichus, *De vita Pythagorae,* xiv; and Stanley, *History of philosophy,* pp. 553–554. Lucian had parodied this tradition in *The Dream,* where one of the speakers is Pythagoras reincarnated as a rooster; for a learned renaissance commentary, see Lucian, *Somnium seu Gallus* et al. (Basle, 1557), pp. 74 ff.

See also the "argument" by Georgius Cedrenus prefixed to the *Carmina aurea,* in Zehner, *Pythagorae fragmenta,* pp. 50–53.

[54] *Praise of Follie,* tr. Thomas Chaloner, ed. C. H. Miller (EETS; Oxford Univ. Press, 1965), p. 47. Nano makes much of this exotic tradition when he introduces Androgyne in Jonson's *Volpone* (II.i.6 ff).

> [55] Y litteram Pythagoras Samius ad exemplum vitae humanae primus formavit; cuius virgula subterior primam aetatem significat, incertam quippe et quae adhuc se nec vitiis nec virtutibus dedit. Bivium autem, quod superest, ab adolescentia incipit: cuius dextra pars ardua est, sed ad vitam beatam tendens: sinistra facilior, sed ad labem interitumque deducens. De qua sic Persius ait
>
> Et tibi qua Samios deduxit litera ramos,
> Surgentem dextro monstravit limite callem.

(*Etymologiae,* I.iii.7). The reference to Persius is *Satires,* III.56–57. Cf. Hugh of St. Victor, *Didascalicon* [III.ii], ed. Jerome Taylor (Columbia Univ. Press, 1961), p. 84; *A breefe conjecturall discourse . . .* [STC 17650] (London, 1589), preface; Jacobus Schallerus, *Ethica Pythagorica Y adornata* (Strasbourg, 1653); Horn, *Historiae philosophiae libri,* p. 369; Stanley, *History of philosophy,* p. 565; and Gale, *Court of gentiles,* II.167. See also Franz de Ruyt, "L'Idée du 'Bivium' et le symbole pythagoricien de la lettre Y," *Revue Belge de philologie et d'histoire,* 10 (1931), 137–144; and Franz Cumont, *Lux perpetua* (Paris, 1949), pp. 278–280. For an artifact (a mirror frame) constructed on this principle, see Joan Evans, *Pattern,* 2 vols. (Oxford, 1931), I.154–155 (plate 204). For an early bibliography on this symbol, see Enfield, *History of Philosophy,* I.399–400, note †.

[56] *The Divine Institutes* [VI.iii], tr. Sister Mary Frances McDonald (Catholic Univ. of America Press, 1964), p. 397. See also Joannes Cruceus, *Litera Pythagorae Y cum divina L. Lactantii Coelii Firmiani explanatione* (Lyons, 1536); and Stanley, *History of philosophy,* p. 565.

[57] George Chapman translated these lines as "Vergils epigram of this letter Y," in *Poems,* ed. Phyllis B. Bartlett (New York, 1941), p. 234; by all means, see notes on p. 449 (and p. 447). Cf. Cruceus, *Litera Pythagorae Y,* p. 7.

[58] Translated by Stanley, *History of philosophy,* p. 565. The Latin text was frequently printed—e.g., in Cruceus, *Litera Pythagorae Y,* p. 8; *Selectiora veterum authorum collectanea* (Paris, 1536), B3^{v}; Hieronymus Wolff, ed., *Epicteti enchiridion . . . Cebetis Thebani tabula* (Basle, 1561), p. 186; Zehner, *Pythagorae fragmenta,* p. 78; Conrad Rittershaus, ed., *Porphyrii de vita Pythagorae* (Altdorf, 1610), $\phi 3^{v}$–$\phi 4$. Cf. Pope, *Dunciad,* IV.151–152; and Chaignet, *Pythagore,* I.154.

[59] *Pseudodoxia epidemica* [V.xix] in *Works,* ed. Geoffrey Keynes, 6 vols. (London, 1928–31), III.135.

[60] Xenophon, *Memoirs of Socrates* [II.i], tr. Sarah Fielding (Bath, 1762), p. 93.

[61] Cf. Ludwig Volkmann, *Bilderschriften der Renaissance* (Leipzig, 1923), pp. 64, 108, 123; Erwin Panofsky, *Hercules am Scheidewege* (Leipzig, 1930), esp. pp. 64–68 and tafel XXXV; Hallett Smith, *Elizabethan Poetry* (Harvard Univ. Press, 1952), pp. 293–303; Guy de Tervarent, *Attributs et symboles*

dans l'art profane 1450–1600 (Geneva, 1958), cols. 412–413; and Samuel C. Chew, *The Pilgrimage of Life* (Yale Univ. Press, 1962), pp. 175–178, figures 130, 131.

[62] Connoisseurs of the modern occult will enjoy an historical novel by Grove Donner (i.e., Florence Harvey) entitled *The Stone of Destiny* (Los Angeles, 1938). It opens with the verses on "The Pythagoric Letter Y" quoted from Stanley's *History of philosophy*, and tells how the Stone of Destiny got from Tyre to the coronation chair in Westminster Abbey. Pythagoreans, migrating from Sicily, arrived in England, built Stonehenge, etc., etc.

[63] *Protrepticae orationes ad philosophiam*, xxi, and *De vita Pythagorae*, xxiii, translated by Stanley, *History of philosophy*, p. 557.

> [64] . . . Symbola Pythagorae, videlicet indicia quaedam & signa mysteriorum doctrinae sanctioris quibus sententiae morales atque salutaria documenta continentur. Quibus tanquam vasculis fictilibus thesaurus preciosus includitur

(*Symbola Pythagorae . . . moraliter explicata* [Paris, 1515], a4^{v}). Dacier further distinguishes a *symbolum:* "A Symbol has an Advantage over a Proverb, as being more concise and figurative, and containing a Moral more delicate and perfect" (*Life of Pythagoras*, p. xiii; cf. *ibid.*, pp. 97–98).

[65] A black-tailed fish.

[66] A measuring-basket.

[67] The meaning of this *symbolum* seems to be that since philosophy is a way of life, we should choose one which is integrated, not divisive.

[68] A sea-mullet.

[69] I.e., *triobolus*, a coin of little worth. The meaning of this *symbolum* seems to be that philosophy must be sought by steps through things of little material value.

[70] A common marsh plant.

[71] *History of philosophy*, p. 557. For another English translation of Iamblichus' *symbola*, see William Bridgman, *Translations from the Greek* (London, 1804), pp. 65–118.

[72] X3–X3^{v}.

[73] *Dignity of Man*, tr. Wallis, p. 15.

[74] b3^{v}.

[75] b2–b6. See my article, "Pythagorean Symbola in Erasmus' *Adagia*," *Renaissance Quarterly*, 21 (1968), 162–165.

[76] K3^{v}–L4^{v}.

[77] F2.

[78] Fol. 53^{v}–59.

[79] Pp. 86–181.

[80] H4^{v}.

[81] The first edition to contain the Pythagorean *symbola* that I have seen was printed by Jean Richier in Paris, 1601, with the *symbola* dispersed in Latin commentary, A3–B2. On Mignault's "Syntagma," see p. 248, above.

[82] For additional renaissance publications containing *symbola*, see pp. 66–67, n. 54, above. For later authorities on the Pythagorean *symbola*, see Christian Friedrich Dornfeld, *De symbolis Pythagorae dissertatio* (Leipzig, 1721); Johann Jakob Brucker, *Historia critica philosophiae*, 6 vols., 2nd ed. (Leipzig, 1766–67), I.1098–1100; Johann Conrad von Orelli, *Opuscula graecorum veterum sententiosa et moralia*, 2 vols. (Leipzig, 1819–21), I.60–70; Sebastian Franck, *De Pythagora eiusque symbolis disputatio* (Berlin, 1869); and Friedrich Boehm, *De symbolis pythagoreis* (Berlin, 1905).

[83] *Pseudodoxia epidemica* [I.iv], ed. Keynes, II.33.

[84] Cf. Diogenes Laertius, VIII.24.

[85] *On Divination* [I.xxx], tr. C. D. Yonge (London, 1868), p. 171.

[86] *Noctes Atticae*, IV.xi.1–10.

[87] "Of the nouriture and education of children" in *Morals*, tr. Holland (1603), p. 15. In the "Romane questions" [xcv], Plutarch gives a much more expansive explication of this *symbolum* (ibid., pp. 881–882).

[88] *Adagiorum chiliades quatuor, et sesquicenturia* (Lyons, 1559), cols. 23–24.

[89] *Proverbes or adagies* (London, 1539), fol. 55.

[90] *Pseudodoxia epidemica* [I.iv], ed. Keynes, II.33. For other learned discourses reviewing this *symbolum*, see Beroaldo, *Symbola Pythagorae explicata* (1515), c3ᵛ–c6; Giraldi, *Libelli duo*, pp. 102–108; Claude Mignault, ed., *Andreae Alciati V. C. emblemata* (Plantin; Antwerp, 1608), pp. 29–30; Vossius, *De philosophorum sectis*, pp. 42–43; Dacier, *Life of Pythagoras*, pp. 61–62; and Guthrie, *Greek Philosophy*, I.184–185.

[91] "Education of children" in *Morals*, tr. Holland (1603), p. 15.

[92] *Against Rufinus* [III.xxxix], tr. Hritzu, p. 211. For learned accounts of this *symbolum*, see Erasmus, *Adagia* (1559), col. 22; Beroaldo, *Symbola Pythagorae explicata* (1515), b6–c1ᵛ; Giraldi, *Libelli duo*, pp. 98–99; and Mignault, "Syntagma de symbolis" in *Alciati emblemata* (1608), p. 28.

[93] Cf. Lynn Thorndike, *A History of Magic and Experimental Science*, 8 vols. (Columbia Univ. Press, 1923–58), I.243. For early bibliography, see p. 66, n. 51, above. For other learned views on Apollonius, see Theophilus Gale, *The court of the gentiles, Part III* (London, 1677), pp. 66–67; and Brucker, *Historia critica philosophiae*, II.98–161.

[94] *Thesaurus linguae Romanae & Britannicae* (London, 1584), Bbbbbbb3. For a fuller treatment of Apollonius in the role of *vates*, see Pierre Mussard, *Historia deorum fatidicorum, vatum, sibyllarum, phoebadum, apud priscos illustrium* (Cologne, 1675), pp. 147–155.

[95] Plutarch, *A president for parentes*, tr. Grant (London, 1571), h8–h8ᵛ.

POETICS

I

Poet as Maker

Early in his *Defence of poesie* Philip Sidney appropriately sets out to define poetry and to explain the role of the poet. The most estimable title that Sidney can bestow upon him is this:

> The Greekes named him ποιητήν, which name, hath as the most excellent, gone through other languages, it commeth of this word ποιεῖν which is to make: wherin I know not whether by luck or wisedome, we Englishmen have met with the Greekes in calling him a Maker.[1]

The poet, Sidney says, is a maker, as the very etymology of the word indicates. Ποιεῖν means "to make," "to fashion," "to form." Other Elizabethan critics reiterate Sidney's definition of a poet, likewise offering his etymology of the word. William Webbe begins his *Discourse of English poetrie* (1586) with a similar statement:

> Poetrie, called in Greeke ποετρια beeing derived from the Verbe ποιέω, which signifieth in Latine *facere*, in English to make, may properly be defined the arte of making.[2]

George Puttenham opens his *Arte of English poesie* (1589) in much the same way:

> A Poet is as much to say as a maker. And our English name well conformes with the Greeke word: for of ποιεῖν to make, they call a maker *Poeta*.[3]

In the preface to his translation of Ariosto's *Orlando Furioso* (1591), Sir John Harington refers to the treatises of Sidney and Puttenham, noting that they have "christned [the poet] in English" with "the name of a Maker."[4] Like many other practising poets, Spenser regularly uses the verb "to make" meaning "to compose poetry";[5] and E. K. glosses *April*, line 19, with one eye glancing back at Chaucer, who similarly uses the verb in this customary sense, but also with the other eye on the new etymology for poet:

> to make) to rime and versifye. For in this word making, our olde Englishe Poetes were wont to comprehend all the skil of Poetrye, according to the Greeke woorde ποιεῖν, to make, whence commeth the name of Poets.

It seems as though E. K., Spenser, and Sidney had discussed this concept before 1579, the publication date for *The Shepheardes Calender*. In any case, it was known to George Chapman, who in the play *Chabot* parrots, as is his wont, with borrowed learning:

> ποιεῖν, which is, to make, to create, to invent matter that was never extant in nature; from whence also is the name and dignity of *poeta* (III.ii.10).

Even Ben Jonson, that harbinger of neoclassicism, is still declaiming in *Timber:* "A *Poet* is that, which by the Greeks is call'd . . . ὁ ποιητής, Maker, or a fainer . . . From the word ποιεῖν, which signifies to make or fayne." [6]

This chorus of critics echoing Sidney's etymology for "poet" is unprecedented in criticism and unmatched by any answering chorus from across the Channel, in either Italy or France. Sidney, in fact, is announcing a new poetic credo, eclectic and syncretic in its intention but distinctly English.[7] It had already been demonstrated by Spenser, the loudly acclaimed "new poet" of the recently published *Shepheardes Calender*, and was soon to be employed on a large scale by that robust generation of poets that burst upon the London scene in the late 1580s. Although this is not the only poetics which we find in Elizabethan England, it was the dominant poetics by the end of the sixteenth century, a compelling triumph in critical theory. It accounts for much of the best poetry—epic, dramatic, and lyric—in our language.

In a general way the word "poet" had been always associated with "making." Bartholomaeus Amantius, for example, had offered the following definition to his students in Cologne:

> Poeta dicitur factor, vel fictor, a Graeco verbo ποιέω, id est facio vel fingo.[8]

Here the word "poet" is made cognate with two Latin nouns, *factor* and *fictor*, from the verbs *facere* and *fingere*, respectively, both meaning "to make." There is, however, a distinction to be drawn between the two Latin verbs: *facere* has the connotation of forcing by application of external pressure, while *fingere* has the connotation of informing by the skillful manipulation of what is already present. Evidently, Amantius associates the poet with "making" in a vaguely generic way.

An important Italian critic, Cristoforo Landino (1424–1504), had actually derived "poet" from ποιειν in one of the discourses which preface his monumental edition of Dante. Landino was prominent among the philosophers and poets clustered around the Platonic Academy when Ficino was its greater light.[9] His best-known work was the *Disputationes Camaldulenses,* first published in Florence about 1480, the last two books of which contain an extensive allegorization of the *Aeneid.* Without doubt, Sidney was acquainted with Landino's moral interpretation of Vergil, and he also knew of the prefatory essays on poetry in the edition of Dante, since at the end of *The defence of poesie* he refers to the one entitled "Furore divino." Despite this approving reference to Landino in the *Defence,* Sidney's debt to him has been largely overlooked in the welter of borrowings which Sidney made from other Italian critics. Nonetheless, the magnitude of the debt is only suggested by this quotation from Landino's essay entitled "Che chosa sia poesia et poeta et della origine sua divina et antichissima":

> The Greeks said "poet" from this word *piin:* which is in the middle between "creating," which is appropriate to God when out of nothing he brings something forth into being, and "making," which is appropriate to men when in any art-form they compose out of matter and form. Therefore, although the figment of the poet is not completely out of nothing, yet it departs from "making" and comes very close to "creating."[10]

The issue raised here by Landino is crucial to any poetics: for the substance of his art, is the poet bound to the reality which our senses perceive in objectified nature, or does he have license (indeed, an imperative) to create new matter according to his own will? As Sidney formulated the question: can he who "is wrapped within the folde of the proposed subject, and takes not the free course of his own invention" properly be called a poet at all?[11] The poetics implied by Landino's statement, a poetics which hedges on this issue, is in fact very near that articulated by Sidney in his *Defence of poesie.*

But by the time Sidney wrote, Landino's discourses on poetry were a century old. And at least for his generation, it is Sidney who first gives prominence to the etymology of *poet* from ποιειν and builds a fully developed poetics upon it.[12] Boccaccio had expressly denied the derivation from "poio, pois," and turned instead to an old Greek word *poetes*, which he claimed to mean "elegant expression" (exquisita locutio).[13] Giraldi Cinthio (1504–73) had suggested that the name of "poet" signifies "maker" (facitore) because the poet fantasizes the wonderful and impossible—to use the Elizabethan term, "feigns"; but Cinthio does not investigate the etymology of the term.[14] Julius Caesar Scaliger (1484–1558), recognizing that "poet" is generally associated with "making," insists that it derives not from fiction-making (à fingendo), but from verse-making (à faciendo versu).[15] Scaliger defines the poet as a maker of verses, a metrician.

As though to short-circuit intervening criticism, Sidney for his definition of "poet" goes back to the Greeks. By his assertive citation of classical authority in this matter, Sidney seems specifically to be refuting Scaliger, whose *Poetice* was the outstanding pronouncement of the day on literary theory.[16] The poet, Sidney says, is not to be identified merely by his composing in verse. Many great prose writers have used poetic modes of expression, and in fact owe their popularity to the effectiveness of poetic utterance. In various passages of his *Defence of poesie* Sidney readily bestows Apollo's laurel upon Plato, Herodotus, Xenophon, Heliodorus, Aesop, and Plutarch, all of whom wrote in prose. Even Christ, when He spoke in parables, "vouchsafed to use the flowers" of poetry (*Defence of poesie*, F2^{v}). Sidney is unequivocal on this issue of whether verse is the essential criterion for poetry:

> Verse . . . [is] but an ornament and no cause to Poetrie, since there have bene many most excellent Poets that never versefied, and now swarme many versefiers that need never answere to the name of Poets (*Defence of poesie*, C2^{v}).

With firmness, with even an unwonted note of contention, Sidney is setting his own poetics apart from the theory then most widely accepted in academic circles. Much later in the *Defence* Sidney alludes to Scaliger by name in order to refute him, and vaguely adducing Aristotle repeats tersely: "One may be a *Poet* without versing, and a versefier without *Poetrie*" (*Defence of poesie*, F3^{v}). For Sidney the name "poet" does not designate simply a maker of verses; rather, it is a "high and incomparable" title, "the name above all names of learning" (*Defence of poesie*, B4, C1^{v}).

Sidney claims, of course, like Landino, that the poet is a maker in the sense of creating. He is an inventor who exercises his mental powers to produce a poem which exemplifies a "second nature" (*Defence of poesie*, C1^{v}). In his poem the poet orders the items of his creation and generates a universe which rivals Nature's for variety and which surpasses it in excellence, a golden world, a mirror of perfection. To quote again George Chapman, who speaks with characteristic excess, the poet "invent[s] matter that was never extant in nature." To the purist mind of Ben Jonson, this license to invent reduced the poet to the status of "a fainer," and thereby made him subject to the charges brought by Bacon that he lied. Such charges, of course, had long ago been made by Plato, who had banished poets from his commonwealth—but that is a familiar story.[17] What is noteworthy in this retelling of it is the rapid and predictable evolution of Sidney's poet as maker through a phase of poet as inventor and finally his demise as a faining liar. Sic transit gloria Apollinis.[18]

For Sidney, though, the name ποιητής is the term for poet which is "the most excellent." And he draws upon revered antiquity—"the Greekes"—for authority in using it. As we might expect, the Greeks whom Sidney had in mind were Plato and his followers. But the dialogue of Plato which had the greatest influence on Elizabethan poetics was not the *Phaedrus* with its theory of poetry as a madness granted by the Muses, a frenzy during which the inspired poet recounts the actions of past heroes for instruction of the young (245A). It was not the *Ion*, where the poetic fit is extolled to a *divinus furor* and the poet becomes an amanuensis for the gods, although certainly the divine inspiration of the poet was often enough asserted in the renaissance.[19] Nor was it the *Republic*, written by that other Plato who cast derogatory doubts upon the relationship between art and essential truth. To the consternation of every apologist for poetry, Plato in Book X of the *Republic* had reduced poetry to an imitation of physical objects that are in turn only imperfect replicas of the ideas, so that poetry is an imitation of an imitation; and therefore on these grounds, in addition to their scurrilous misrepresentation of the gods, poets are deemed meretricious.[20] Rather for his poetics Sidney was drawing upon Plato in his most strongly Pythagorean mood, when he wrote about creation in the *Timaeus*. The creating godhead in the Timaean cosmogony is designated a ποιητής, thereby making possible by reverse analogy a poetics wherein the poet is creator.

The *locus classicus* for the concept of poet as maker occurs early in Plato's *Timaeus*, the one dialogue that enjoyed a continuing reputation throughout the middle ages and renaissance. Timaeus, the astronomer from Pythagoras' Magna Graecia, relates at length how the creating deity, sometimes called δημιουργός and sometimes θεός, acted out of the fullness of his own benevolence to make our physical universe. Starting with the idea of his own perfection as a pattern, he gave physical extension to what would otherwise have remained an abstract concept, and generated the time-space continuum which we know as the universe—the *cosmos*, to use the technical term of the Pythagoreans. The word "universe," in fact, means "that which rolls as one," suggesting that creation, though diverse, reflects the oneness of its maker. Time began at the moment of this physical event, so that by the passage of measured time our universe is set apart from the eternity and the infinity that is the godhead. When Timaeus first mentions the creating deity in this cosmogony, he refers to him with two epithets: "the poet and father of this all" (ποιητὴς καὶ πατὴρ τοῦ παντός; *Timaeus*, 28C). The godhead, then, is a poet, a maker, the architect of cosmos. In the words of Cristoforo Landino, "God is the supreme poet, and the world is His poem." [21]

It is common for us, thinking in anthropomorphic images, to depict God as an artisan—a weaver, a potter, a painter.[22] In a well-known letter to St. Jerome, St. Augustine presents God as a musician who measures out the universe in consent with the rhythms of time:

> If a man who is skilled in composing a song knows what lengths to assign to what tones, so that the melody flows and progresses with beauty by a succession of slow and rapid tones, how much more true is it that God permits no periods of time in the birth and death of His creatures—periods which are like the words and syllables in the measure of this temporal life—to proceed either more quickly or more slowly than the recognized and well-defined law of rhythm requires, in this wonderful song of succeeding events.[23]

Here creation is a melody, "the wonderful song of succeeding events," the continuing *musica mundana* of Boethius; and God is the author of measured time, of harmony. To change the metaphor, if the world is seen as a stage, then God is a "Skilful Dramatist," as Ralph Cudworth calls Him.[24] In any case, regardless of what artisan is employed in the metaphor, that which is created becomes God's art. In the words of Sir Thomas Browne, uncommonly brief for the *medicus religiosus*, "Nature is the Art of God." [25] God, therefore, is a maker, a poet. And as poet, He began with a λόγος, a word or scheme or plan, according to both the Book of Genesis and the Gospel of John. The notion that God is a careful workman proceeding from an abstract plan was epitomized by Philippe du Plessis Mornay, whom Philip Sidney rendered as follows: "For, as the Craftsman maketh his worke by the patterne which he had erst conceyved in his mynde, which patterne is his inward word: so God made the World and all that is therein." [26]

This concept of God as maker working from preconceived forms was transferred undiminished and applied to the poet. Sidney, for example, goes on in his *Defence of poesie* to state flatly: "The skill of ech [poetic] Artificer standeth in that *Idea*, or fore conceit of the worke, and not in the worke it self." [27] In this theory of poetry, the poem is an analogous universe created by the poet. And the initial conceit in the mind of the poet bears the same relation to the poem as the archetypal idea residing in the godhead bears to the extended universe. Just as the godhead had the will and the power to give three-dimensional extension to an abstract form, thereby transforming an idea into a physical object and creating the time-space continuum which we inhabit, so the poet exercises his will and power to create his poem, thereby through characters, setting, and actions giving sense-perceptible verisimilitude to what otherwise would remain an ineffable concept. Furthermore, just as time did not begin until the moment of physical creation when the archetypal idea received three-dimensional extension, so also time in the created universe of the poem does not begin until the poet bodies forth his conceit through narrative. In each instance, the physical extension is secondary, ancillary, almost incidental; the essential is the idea, the conceit—"that unspeakable and everlasting bewtie to be seene by the eyes of the mind," as Sidney says in one of his more visionary moments (*Defence of poesie*, B4). Physical extension is necessary, however—the physical extension of both the created universe and of the poetic narrative—so that mere mortals, dependent upon sense perception, may comprehend the otherwise concealed abstraction. Else a great prince in prison lies.

In such a mode of poetry, the fore-conceit is "bodied forth" by the poet, to employ an expressive term from Shakespeare. In *A Midsummer Night's Dream*, Theseus speaks disparagingly of antique fables and fairy tales, but he nonetheless gives a classic description of the poet as maker:

> The poet's eye, in a fine frenzy rolling,
> Doth glance from heaven to earth, from earth to heaven;

And as imagination bodies forth
The forms of things unknown, the poet's pen
Turns them to shapes, and gives to airy nothing
A local habitation and a name.

(V.i.12–17)

Inspired by Plato's *divinus furor*, the poet surveys the plenitude of God's creation, from heaven to earth and back again. Excited by this experience, his imagination "*bodies forth*/The forms of things unknown"—makes particular, and therefore palpable, the Platonic ideas, which otherwise would remain for us ineffable and unknowable. The poet's pen turns abstract forms into concrete shapes; by means of characters, actions, and settings, he "gives to airy nothing/A local habitation and a name." In our terms, the poet physically extends his fore-conceit into our time-space continuum. In Sidney's terms, "It is that faining notable images of vertues, vices, or what els, with that delightfull teaching, which must be the right describing note to know a Poet by" (*Defence of poesie*, C3).

In the practice of poetry, the conceit may be "bodied forth" in a character. Spenser, for example, in the letter to Raleigh appended to *The Faerie Queene* speaks of "the knight of the Redcrosse, in whome I expresse Holynes . . . Sir Guyon, in whom I sette forth Temperaunce . . . Britomartis a Lady knight, in whome I picture Chastity." A conceit may likewise be bodied forth by an action. In *Romeo and Juliet*, for instance, the "misadventured piteous overthrows" of the young lovers (prologue, 7) visibly demonstrate that civil disorder brings woe but that even enemies are reconciled in the commune of grief. Finally, a conceit may be bodied forth by a setting. Arcadia, for example, represents an idyllic existence of timeless perfection, or the *locus amoenus* represents the temptation of the epic hero by sensual delights. Usually, however, the bodying forth depends upon all three constituents of narrative, upon characters, actions, and settings taken in conjunction.

In the poetics based upon this concept of poet as maker, the conceit is primary, though it might be designated by other labels.[28] George Gascoigne, a precursor of later poetry in this as in so much else, thought in terms of the rhetorical tradition and called it "invention." In his *Certayne notes of instruction concerning the making of verse or ryme in English* (1575), he offers this counsel:

> The first and most necessarie poynt that ever I founde meete to be considered in making of a delectable poeme is this, to grounde it upon some fine invention.

And he continues:

> I would have you stand most upon the excellencie of your Invention, and sticke not to studie deepely for some fine devise.[29]

For Gascoigne, the conceit is an "invention" [30] or a "device." Ben Jonson calls it the "fable," echoing Italian critics and heralding the use of "fable" by neoclassical critics as a synonym for Aristotelian "plot"; and in *Timber* he argues that a mere versifier does not merit the title of poet, but only he who creates fiction:

> Hee is call'd a *Poet*, not hee which writeth in measure only; but that fayneth and formeth a fable, and writes things like the Truth. For, the Fable and Fiction is (as it were) the forme and Soule of any Poeticall worke, or *Poeme*.[31]

Never does Jonson sound so much like a Platonist as when he talks about "Truth" and calls the conceit of a poem its "forme and Soule." Sidney himself calls it the "*Idea*, or fore conceit," unmistakably having in mind the term *idea* as Plato first had used it.

In understanding Sidney and Jonson, it is important to remember that *idea* in Greek means "form." And it is also important to remember that Plato's theory of ideas derived directly from the Pythagorean theory of numbers. Just as Plato argued that ultimate reality is a world of absolute being composed of essential ideas, so the Pythagoreans before him had argued that ultimate reality consists of numbers (see pp. 75, above). By number, of course, the Pythagoreans meant a form determined by an arrangement of points, an abstract concept of form independent of physical matter and therefore not subject to the mutability which time brings in the changeable world of nature (see pp. 71–74). Plato's ideas, then—which, remember, mean "forms"—are a development of Pythagorean numbers, and share their formal characteristics. In consequence, a poetics which places the skill of the artificer in his ability to devise conceits makes the idea or the form the preeminent feature of the poem.[32] The action, characters, and setting—the narrative—are mere externals, what is necessary to make palpable the conceit. Sidney has this advice for readers of poetry: "They shall use the narration but as an imaginative groundplat of a profitable invention" (*Defence of poesie*, G1^{v}). To understand a poem, then, a reader must survey the narrative as though it were a groundplat bodied forth by the poet's imagination, and thereby he will discern the basic plan, the fore-conceit, the formal idea which is the poem's raison d'être. And the skill of the poet must be judged first of all by his ability to devise this "*Idea*, or fore conceit," rather than by his facility in fabricating a fictional narrative wherein to embody this conceit.

In such a poetics, if logic is carried to an extreme conclusion, the form of a poem is its essence. Its structure is the core of its meaning. Criticism must dwell upon the disposition of its constituent elements—character relationships, the sequence of actions, the arrangement of scenes. In juxtaposition or in symmetrical placement they comment upon one another. The poem builds by comparisons and contrasts. By comparison, elements of one sort supplement one another to build toward a comprehensive theme. By contrast, they define one another, often one existing only as the opposite of the other and therefore depending upon the other for its significance—again, though by way of contrast rather than comparison, complementing one another in order to build toward a comprehensive theme.[33] Comparison works in a cumulative way, contrast by means of reconciling opposites. In either case, however, a large portion of the poem's meaning is conveyed through the relationships developed between its constituent parts. A large portion of the meaning is conveyed through structure, through form, through the idea that serves as the soul informing the flesh of the poem's narrative. The critic's challenge is to bare this soul.

Examples of such structuring are obvious and well known. By comparison, Gloucester supplements Lear; by contrast, Hotspur defines Prince Hal. By comparison, the war in heaven sets the pattern for Adam's moral struggle when paradise is lost; by contrast, the activities of *il penseroso* define the *modus vivendi* of *l'allegro*. By comparison, the house of Celia complements the house of Alma; by contrast, the house of Celia shows up the castle of Pride for what it really is. In each of these instances, much of the meaning is conveyed through the arrangement of characters or of actions or of settings. The structure of the work is itself a primary mode of discourse, and therefore a primary concern of the critic. By reading the groundplat of its structure, we may most readily discern the poet's invention, his fore-conceit, his controlling idea. Only then can we claim to have perceived his fiction. We must discover the poet at his making.

The concept of poet as maker was introduced into the mainstream of English literary theory by Sidney in his *Defence of poesie*, and was demonstrated for subsequent English authors by Spenser. Sidney and Spenser gave it the prominence that led to its widespread acceptance among the London literati. But the concept was inherent in the Pythagorean-Platonic tradition from the beginning:

the poet creates his poem in a way analogous to the creative act by which the Timaean godhead gave physical extension to his archetypal ideas. This assumption underlies medieval esthetics and continues into the renaissance. It is incipient, for example, in the poetics of Boccaccio, who confidently defined poetry as an imaginative act, a by-product of the poet's mental search for truth:

> Poetry . . . is a sort of fervid and exquisite invention, with fervid expression, in speech or writing, of that which the mind has invented. It proceeds from the bosom of God, and few, I find, are the souls in whom this gift is born; indeed so wonderful a gift it is that true poets have always been the rarest of men. This fervor of poesy is sublime in its effects: it impels the soul to a longing for utterance; it brings forth strange and unheard-of creations of the mind; it arranges these meditations in a fixed order, adorns the whole composition with unusual interweaving of words and thoughts; and thus it veils truth in a fair and fitting garment of fiction.[34]

According to Boccaccio, and others who hold this view, poetry as fiction has eternal verity for its touchstone. But the poet is not a simple seer, passively receiving a statement which he transparently transmits. Rather, he is a busy agent, gathering and sorting and evaluating and organizing the data of experience into a statement of truth. He is an active maker.

As Puttenham explains, repeating a commonplace of faculty psychology, the brain has as one of its chief functions the giving of unity and form to extraneous experience. In a passage in which he decries the depth of disesteem to which poetry had fallen, Puttenham chides the ignorant who view the inventions of poets as idle fantasies. He admits that "the evill and vicious disposition of the braine" may in some cases hinder sound judgment—an incoherent state to which the Greeks applied the term φανταστικός. But when the brain is "well affected," it acts to produce a single image which is beautiful as well as good and true:

> [When] well affected, [the brain is] not onely nothing disorderly or confused with any monstrous imaginations or conceits, but very formall, and in his much multiformitie *uniforme*, that is well proportioned, and so passing cleare, that by it as by a glasse or mirrour, are represented unto the soule all maner of bewtifull visions.[35]

The key word in Puttenham's statement is "formall." The brain is well organized, he says, in no way disorderly or confused with impossible fantasies. It is "very formall"—that is, literally, predisposed to generate forms. In fact, Puttenham insists, despite the multifarious diversity which it perceives, the brain composes the disparate data into a single comprehensive, yet harmonious, form—"in his much multiformitie [the brain is] *uniforme*, that is well proportioned." When this multeity is integrated into a unity, the brain becomes a mirror of perfection, a *speculum* reflecting to the soul the "bewtifull visions" of order and harmony and proportion. To use a Coleridgean phrase, the brain possesses a "coadunating faculty" which synthesizes the multifarious experiences of our daily lives into a vision of oneness. This vision, by virtue of its completeness, is true—truth in the abstract, intelligible to the soul. To see life whole is the aim of the true poet. Portrayal of this truth is his task.

While the concept of poetry as making came to dominate the literary scene in Elizabethan London, there were other theories which commanded respectful attention. Sidney himself defines at least two other distinct poetics; although the poetry of making is indeed "right" poetry, Sidney discusses also vatic poetry and "philosophical" (what we would call didactic) poetry. The role of the poet as maker is rendered more precise when placed in contrast to these alternative roles: the poet as *vates* and as purveyor of factual knowledge.

First, the concept of poet as maker must be differentiated from the concept of poet as *vates*, a prophet or seer who by epiphanic vision sees into the life of things. Sidney is careful to draw this distinction.[36] The poet as maker is filled with the *divinus furor*, perhaps, and benefits from the "heavenly instinct," as E. K. puts it in the argument to *October;* but he is an active formulator of his verse, looking to his own mind for ideas, working without dependence upon mystic revelation. The *vates*, in contrast, writes under immediate direction from the divine. He serves largely as an inspired persona, transmitting holy dicta to his fellowmen. The result is poetry that "imitate[s] the unconceiveable excellencies of God" (*Defence of poesie*, C1^{v}), and Sidney educes the Psalms of David as the prototype of vatic rhapsody. Sidney gives this type of poetry the pride of place in his list; it is "the chiefe both in antiquitie and excellencie." Because of its holiness, prophetic poetry is admired with reverence, genuine or pretended, but hardly analyzed. The *vates* snatches a grace which raises him above the reach of critics.

The poet as purveyor of factual knowledge produces the second type of poetry delineated by Sidney, didactic poetry, that which "deale[s] with matters Philosophicall" (*Defence of poesie*, C2). Examples are Vergil's *Georgics* and the poems of Lucretius, Manilius, and Lucan. This theory sees poetry as a basically representational art, as the recorder of objectified nature. Though this type of poet has the sensitivity to see beauty and the license to idealize through universalization, there is no doubt that the data of his imitation must be the objects of our physical world. Plato in Book X of the *Republic* had assumed that art is an imitation of sense-perceptible objects—and since they in turn are merely imperfect replicas of the unchanging essences in the world of permanent being, then art is twice removed from truth and beauty. According to Plato in this rationalistic argument, art is inferior to nature as an image of essential reality. For Aristotle, however, ultimate reality lies not in Plato's conceptual world of essences, but rather in the physical world perceived by our senses. In consequence, his doctrine of art as μίμησις relates art directly to the reality it comments upon. Aristotle makes art an immediate representation of objective truth and thereby rescues it from opprobrium. In the Aristotelian tradition, especially as it had been interpreted by Italian critics in the renaissance, art was intended to reproduce nature in facsimile—perhaps a universalized, even idealized, nature, but nonetheless visualized.[37] It was necessary that art be recognizable as a depiction of nature, as a faithful reproduction of natural shapes and colors and arrangements. Roger Ascham deals with imitation in this way:

> Imitation is a facultie to expresse livelie and perfitelie that example which ye go about to folow. And of it selfe it is large and wide: for all the workes of nature in a maner be examples for arte to folow.[38]

As we might say, art must be "true to life," verifiable by our own sense experience. As the artistic genre that uses words as its medium, poetry then becomes "a speaking picture."[39]

Examples of a poet being self-consciously imitative in this representational sense are fairly common in the renaissance, but none perhaps is more telling than a passage in *Venus and Adonis*. Shakespeare wishes to describe Adonis' horse when the animal sees a potential mate run from a grove of trees, and he compares his task to that of the painter who wishes to portray a steed that excels nature in perfection:

Look, when a painter would surpass the life,
In limning out a well-proportion'd steed,
His art with nature's workmanship at strife,
As if the dead the living should exceed;
  So did this horse excel a common one
  In shape, in courage, colour, pace and bone.
(ll. 289–294)

In this esthetics, art is superior to nature because it can remove those accidents which render nature imperfect. Shakespeare proposes to create an artificial horse which, though lifeless, will surpass living nature in excellence. After establishing this expectation, he gives over the next four lines to unabashed physical description of the horse, as though each literary epithet were a brush stroke in a painting:

Round-hoof'd, short-jointed, fetlocks shag and long,
Broad breast, full eye, small head, and nostril wide,
High crest, short ears, straight legs and passing strong,
Thin mane, thick tail, broad buttock, tender hide.
(ll. 295–298)

Shakespeare has come as close as possible to making his verse a speaking picture. He gives a verbal image in imitation of the visual image from a painter, which, he assumes, would be drawn from a living horse. Here is verbal image imitating visual image which in turn imitates physical object. Here is Shakespeare, the poet, being intentionally "imitative," extending Plato's chain yet one link farther, so that nature, which imitates the ideal essences, is imitated by a painting that in turn is imitated by a poem. A comparable passage, though much larger in extent, occurs in Book III of *The Faerie Queene* when Britomart gains entrance to the house of Busyrane and finds that the walls are covered by a series of tapestries depicting an assortment of Cupid's triumphs (III.xi.28–46).[40]

These passages, however, are aberrant moments in the poetry of Shakespeare and Spenser, and do not typify their usual poetic practice. The poets themselves were aware of writing in a different vein for the express purpose of vivid sensual description. Art that merely reproduces nature is of course difficult to justify: why the fabrication of art when nature itself is available for perusal? Why an artifact when the original lies so readily before us? Spenser knew also that art which imitates nature representationally may well lack beauty, that quality which informs the haphazard accidents of our experience and gives them coherence and meaning. In the *Fowre Hymnes* he refutes those who argue that beauty is external:

> How vainely then doe ydle wits invent,
> That beautie is nought else, but mixture made
> Of colours faire, and goodly temp'rament
> Of pure complexions, that shall quickly fade
> And passe away, like to a sommers shade,
> Or that it is but comely composition
> Of parts well measurd, with meet disposition.
> (*Hymne of Beautie*, 64–70)

The "inward mynd" cannot be moved to ascend the hierarchies of the *Fowre Hymnes* either by "the blossomes of the field" or by "faire pictures," even though in those pictures "we Nature see of Art/Exceld, in perfect limming every part" (*ibid.*, 78–84). Beauty, Spenser insists—and we should complete the Neoplatonic trio with goodness and truth—comes from the inner form of art and nature, not from "an outward shew of things, that onely seeme" (*ibid.*, 91).

In actual fact, poetry as mere imitation was recognized as a limited, inadequate mode, a dull or slavish mimicry, a counterfeiting. Sidney explicitly disparages the poet as mimetic artisan. The poet who purveys factual knowledge alone is "wrapped within the fold of the proposed subject, and takes not the course of his own invention." He is restricted in both subject matter and technique, like "the meaner sort of Painters, who counterfeyt onely such faces as are set before them" (*Defence of poesie*, C2). Therefore a definition of poetry as an imitation of objectified nature was inadequate and dissatisfying.

The third and best type of poetry, composed by the "right poets" according to Sidney, is that which derives from the poet who makes. Sidney reserves his fulsome praise for the poet as maker:

> These third be they which most properly do imitate to teach & delight: and to imitate, borrow nothing of what is, hath bin, or shall be, but range onely reined with learned discretion, into the divine consideration of what may be and should be (*Defence of poesie*, C2^{v}).

This passage is screamingly eclectic. To "imitate" suggests a basis in Aristotelian poetics.[41] "To teach and delight" intrudes the purpose of poetry as Horace had specified it. But "rang[ing] . . . into the divine consideration of what may be and should be" firmly places this poetics in a Platonic framework[42] where the mind transcends the transient world of becoming and expatiates among the archetypal ideas in the world of being.

The poet, in fact, "borrow[s] nothing of what is, hath bin, or shall be." Leaving that behind, the poet has available much more than the objects of physical nature as the suitable matter of his imitation. The entire conceptual world, as well as the physical, is open to him, and is indeed his proper purview. In its ranging, however, in its ascent to the conceptual level, the mind is "reined with learned discretion." The ascent is controlled and vigilant, not the irrational propulsion of mystic vision, the *via vaticina.* The poet as maker, then, has access to the widest possible range of subject matter—conceptual as well as physical, internal as well as external, subconscious as well as conscious. He is not limited to objects in nature like the mimetic poet. But in pursuit of this subject matter he must stay within the bounds of the rational; he may not employ the visionary tactics of the *vates* (though on occasion, as a literary device, he may purport to employ them).

George Puttenham was alert to the contretemps between the theory of poetry as making and the theory of poetry as imitation, and in his *Arte of English poesie* he respectfully acknowledges both. In the opening paragraph, in fact, Puttenham is at pains to distinguish the two poetics and then to reconcile them, no matter how tenuously. He begins in the familiar way, by calling the poet a maker and deriving an etymology of the name from the Greek verb ποιεῖν:

> A Poet is as much to say as a maker. And our English name well conformes with the Greeke word: for of ποιειν, to make, they call a maker *Poeta.*

He then draws the expected analogy between the poet as maker and God as creator of the universe: "Such as (by way of resemblance and reverently) we may say of God." But Puttenham is aware of Scholastic views on the creation and of learned reservations about the *Timaeus.* According to Timaeus' account, the creating deity imposed his archetypal idea on preexistent matter. But this scheme was unacceptable to later Christians, who argued that since God is infinite, there can exist nothing beyond His being. The notion of preexistent matter is an affront to His infinitude, a logical impossibility. Therefore, said the Schoolmen, God created the universe out of nothing, *ex nihilo,* or perhaps less wondrously (though more dangerously), out of Himself. Puttenham opts for the Scholastic account of creation over the Timaean:

> Such as (by way of resemblance and reverently) we may say of God; who without any travell to his divine imagination made all the world of nought, nor also by any paterne or mould, as the Platonicks with their Idees do phantastically suppose.

He then continues to amplify the analogy:

> Even so the very Poet makes and contrives out of his owne braine both the verse and matter of his poeme, and not by any foreine copie or example, as doth the translator, who therefore may well be sayd a versifier, but not a Poet. The premises considered, it giveth to the name and profession no smal dignitie and preheminence, above all other artificers, Scientificke or Mechanicall.

So much for the theory of poetry based upon the concept of the poet as maker, where a conceit in the mind of the poet is given physical extension by means of characters, actions, and settings. This capacity for spontaneous invention, Puttenham agrees with Sidney, raises the poet above all other artisans.

But Puttenham feels obliged to recognize also the rival theory of poetry based upon an interpretation of the Aristotelian doctrine of imitation. In point, objectified nature is the ultimate reality and therefore the only fit subject matter for art. Rather cautiously he introduces this mimetic theory of poetry which opposes the poet-as-maker theory:

> And neverthelesse, without any repugnancie at all, a Poet may in some sort be said a follower or imitator, because he can expresse the true and lively of every thing [which] is set before him, and which he taketh in hand to describe.

Puttenham hopes to reconcile the theory of poetry as creation from a conceit and the theory of poetry as imitation of physical nature, at first glance two poetics that are irreconcilable. He introduces the imitative poetics with a "neverthelesse," followed by a monitory "without any repugnancie at all." And he concludes by insisting:

> In that respect [a poet] is both a maker, and a counterfaitor: and Poesie an art not only of making, but also of imitation.

Puttenham is not explicit here. He does not develop his poetics to the full. But his intention is clear and the lines of his argument can be easily extrapolated to a conclusion. It is true that the poet as maker places ultimate reality in the Platonic world of being, using the ideas from that conceptual realm as the conceits for his poems. Contrariwise, it is true that the poet as imitator places ultimate reality in the physical world of objectified nature, limiting himself to representing his sense perceptions of those objects. But what if the poet uses his sense data for raw material, his subject matter, which he then organizes according to his conceit, which has the validity of a Platonic idea? Then he fulfills the prototype established by the Timaean creator: he takes preexistent matter, his sense data, and gives it coherence by conforming it to a preconceived idea. The poet thereby is both imitator and maker, as Puttenham says, and "Poesie an art not only of making, but also of imitation."

Puttenham is not merely being eclectic, drawing upon this or that tradition at one or another time. Rather he wishes, following Sidney, to derive a poetics which is syncretic, which amalgamates and assimilates, which subsumes all conceivable theories of poetry in one exhaustive discipline. He might not articulate the details of this poetics—in fact, he states that a poet is both maker and imitator without much elaboration. But his intention becomes clear when he lays out the possibilities by which the poet may proceed:

> This science [poetry] in his perfection can not grow but by some divine instinct—the Platonicks call it *furor;* or by excellencie of nature and complexion; or by great subtiltie of the spirits & wit; or by much experience and observation of the world, and course of kinde; or, peradventure, by all or most part of them.

Poetry may result from divine inspiration à la Plato, or from the spontaneous expression of superior natural qualities in the poet, or from the poet's active exercise of his intellect, or from the poet's sense impressions of objectified nature, or from a combination of some or all of these. The last possibility—"by all or most part of them"—caps the list, without doubt being the most desirable.

When the poet proceeds in this inclusive fashion, he embraces the full range of human experience, from perception of the smallest physical item to the most far-reaching spiritual speculation. In fact, he pushes the limit of human experience and approaches the infinitude of the godhead. It was a truism among defenders of Parnassus that poetry is a sacred art, and poets have often taken their office so seriously as to entertain delusions of infallibility. Literary theorists, alert to the damage from such delusions, damage from within as well as without the Heliconian pale, had necessarily taken pains to counter the charge that the practice of poetry bordered upon impiety. The discreditors of poetry scornfully decried those poetic makers who claimed to speak with divine authority.

But poets do seem to hold a place above their fellow men, whether they rise to that eminence because of an ability to comprehend a wider range of human experience or whether they reign there as creators in their own right, as makers of analogous universes using the medium of words. In his poem a poet does generate a world, projecting a time-space continuum from his own being. Therefore poets demonstrate creative powers beyond the capacity of ordinary mortals and rightly enjoy a superhuman status. Sidney did not think it "too sawcy a comparison, to ballance the highest point of mans wit, with the efficacie of nature"; [43] and recalling from Genesis that man is made in the likeness of God, Sidney asserts that man nowhere reveals his divine prototype more clearly than in the production of poetry. When the poet makes his poem, in fact, he repeats the holy act of creating Adam: "with the force of a divine breath, he bringeth things foorth surpassing her [nature's] doings." He thereby produces a "second nature" which is comparable to Eden, and with God's approbation he presides over "all the workes of that second nature" just as Adam presided over the hexaemeral wonders. Within the universe of his poem, the poet is both omnipotent creator and first citizen, as these two roles are interrelated in the sacred scriptures of Genesis. Admiration of the poet, therefore, "give[s] right honor to the heavenly maker of that maker." These are bold assertions on Sidney's part, verging on the impious, and eventually his puritan conscience pulls him up short. He quickly concludes that of course the destruction to man's virtue occasioned by the Fall precludes our achieving the potential of prelapsarian man: "Our erected wit maketh us know what perfection is, and yet our infected wil keepeth us from reaching unto it." In his efforts to emulate his heavenly maker, the mortal maker is hampered by original sin. But ah! "that first accursed fall of Adam"! Except for that, poets would verily incarnate the image in which man is made. Except for that, man could fully realize the divinity which reposes in the act of poetic creation.

In his veneration of poetry, as in most else, Puttenham follows Sidney. He readily agrees to the omnipotence of poets and forthrightly states that they are like "creating gods":

> It is therefore of Poets thus to be conceived, that if they be able to devise and make all these things of them selves, without any subject of veritie, that they be (by manner of speech) as creating

> gods. If they do it by instinct divine or naturall, then surely much favoured from above; if by their experience, then no doubt very wise men; if by any president or paterne layd before them, then truly the most excellent imitators & counterfaitors of all others (*Arte of English poesie*, C1^{v}).

Puttenham inserts a protective proviso: perhaps the statement that poets are like gods is only a manner of speaking. But whatever the poetic process—divine inspiration, inherent talent, breadth of experience, even the imitation of literary precedents—the poet is extolled. He accomplishes what we all long for, enjoying the best of both worlds. He achieves the special function of poetry, the relation of the actual to the ideal. He manages to incorporate the particular and the universal into the same admirable continuum.

Returning to Sidney's *Defence of poesie*, we find operative a similar assumption that the poet functions as both an Aristotelian imitator and a Platonic maker. Sidney argues, for example, that the poet, unlike other artisans, is not bound to reproduce his subject matter as he finds it, but rather can impose a new shape upon it, thereby creating his own conceits:

> That name of making is fit for him, considering, that where all other Arts retain themselves within their subject, and receive as it were their being from it. The *Poet* onely, bringeth his own stuffe, and doth not learn a Conceit out of a matter, but maketh matter for Conceit (*Defence of poesie*, F2^{v}).

The poet does not take his "being" from a predetermined discipline ("subject"), nor does he take his images from physical nature ("learn a Conceit out of a matter"); but rather he "bringeth his own stuffe"—presumably his own experiences—and out of that he produces his images ("maketh matter for a Conceit"). He is an Aristotelian of a modified sort when he uses his own experiences as the raw material for poetry, but he is primarily Platonic when he shapes these experiences not according to a predetermined subject but according to his own ideas. Again in an early passage central to the main thesis of the *Defence*, Sidney argues that objectified nature limits the creativity of other artisans, just as a script determines the performance of players; only the poet is free of such limitation:

> Only the Poet disdeining to be tied to any such subjection, lifted up with the vigor of his own invention, doth grow in effect into an other nature: in making things either better then

> nature bringeth foorth, or quite a new, formes such as never were in nature: as the *Heroes, Demigods, Cyclops, Chymeras, Furies,* and such like; so as he goeth hand in hand with nature, not enclosed within the narrow warrant of her gifts, but freely raunging within the Zodiack of his owne wit.[44]

By "the vigor of his own invention," the poet creates the universe of his poem, a golden world of what might be or should be rather than of what is. But nonetheless, "he goeth hand in hand with nature," so that objects of the physical world, as Aristotle would expect, are still his referents. While the invention is a Platonic idea or form, the "delivering foorth . . . is not wholly imaginative, as we are wont to say by them that build Castles in the aire" (*Defence of poesie,* C1). The golden world of the poets cannot be wholly fantastical, but must relate to the brazen world of nature. Art must be cogent to the reality which it presumes to interpret.

There is no denying that Sidney was writing fully cognizant of established trends in renaissance criticism. But even when he appears to be most overtly Aristotelian or Horatian, his argument is still based upon, or at least compatible with, the Timaean scheme of poetic creation. For example, the following statement is one of the best known passages of the *Defence* and is often quoted as Sidney's summary definition of poetry. As Sidney condescendingly comments, it is the "more ordinarie opening of" the poet:

> *Poesie* therefore, is an Art of *Imitation:* for so *Aristotle* termeth it in the word μίμησις, that is to say, a representing, counterfeiting, or figuring forth to speake Metaphorically. A speaking *Picture,* with this end to teach and delight.[45]

The poet, Sidney says, may produce representational art by imitating an objectified nature, by "representing [and] counterfeiting." But in addition, by "figuring forth" he gives physical extension to a conceit. Repeating the act of creation performed by the Timaean godhead, the poet, a similar maker, figures forth the preexistent concept in his mind. He does this in order to "speake Metaphorically"—literally, to speak in such a way as to transfer meaning from one level to another.

When Sidney says that "*Poesie* . . . [is a] figuring forth to speake Metaphorically," therefore, he means that the poet uses characters and actions in order to translate the abstract into the concrete.[46] As Sidney says later in the *Defence,* "The *Poets* persons and dooings are but pictures, what should be" (*Defence of poesie,*

G1–G1[v]); and again, "*Poesie* . . . should be εικαστικη, which some learned have defined figuring foorth good things."[47] Because of this ability to fictionalize, the poet is superior to the philosopher, who is confined to precepts, and also to the historian, who is restricted to specifics. By speaking metaphorically, the poet interconnects the realm of abstract generalities and the realm of concrete particulars. The result is "a speaking *Picture*," but of a more expansive sort than Horace and Plutarch had in mind. Sidney is using the critical cliché in the sense that he develops later in the essay when he calls the poet the "moderator" between the philosopher and the historian:

> Whatsoever the *Philosopher* saith should be done, he [the poet] gives a perfect picture of it by some one, by whom he presupposeth it was done, so as he coupleth the generall notion with the particuler example. A perfect picture I say, for hee yeeldeth to the powers of the minde an image of that whereof the *Philosopher* bestoweth but a wordish description.

If the precepts of the philosopher be not embodied in poetry, they remain ineffectual as platitudes; in Sidney's words, they "lie darke before the imaginative and judging power, if they be not illuminated or figured forth by the speaking picture of *Poesie*" (*Defence of poesie*, D1[v]–D2).

The "speaking picture" which the poet presents, then, is laid before the imaginative and judging power of the reader to be acted upon by his cognitive faculties. The depictive narration of the poet is three-dimensional and has duration in time. It is a kinetic embodiment of an otherwise lifeless datum, providing a full-bodied and synesthetic experience for the reader, producing a work of art which has the dynamics of physical event. And yet, because it incorporates the archetypal, it shares the stasis of eternal ideas. In Sidney's words, "The *Poets* persons and dooings are but pictures, what should be." The poem is an item which both transpires within time and yet is timeless. Keats's appreciation of the Grecian urn, although occurring in a later century, illustrates the principle with perfect clarity. In that remarkable ode on the constituents of ultimate reality, Keats demonstrates the proper response to "a speaking picture"—how the art object embodies an eternal idea and how the percipient must work back through its sense-perceptible data to those conceits which inform it. Keats uses the configurations of the urn as an imaginative groundplat whereby he discerns a profitable invention, which he finally formulates in a gnomic saying: "Beauty is truth, truth beauty."

This poetics of making dominated the work of Sidney and Spenser, and even Milton. Perhaps this is what we mean when we say that Milton culminates the renaissance tradition. Perhaps we could argue that metaphysical poetry is most clearly defined as a rejection of this poetics. Certainly Francis Bacon sneered at such poetry and scornfully called it "fained historie," a fabrication in the derogatory sense of being false. The Augustans, uneasy about confining art to a representation of imperfect nature, redefined μίμησις in the spirit of Horace so that once again it came to mean the imitation of other literature, especially the much respected classics. But those areas, though tangential to this study, lie outside its proper boundaries. We must reluctantly leave Milton and metaphysical poetry and eighteenth-century esthetics for other times in other places.

What remains to be done here is to offer an example of practical criticism in order to show how this theoretical reconstruction of a renaissance poetics enlarges for us the meaning of an Elizabethan poem. When a poem devised by a "maker" is read in this context, it should acquire fresh significance. There is no better example than *The Shepheardes Calender*, a depreciated masterpiece which in its own time was highly praised. Today we find Spenser's first published volume an embarrassment—it seems to be not so much an integrated poem as a jejune exercise in various literary fashions. Like Prufrock's mermaids, its shepherds no longer sing to us, except perhaps disconnectedly in their infrequent moments of romantic sentimentality. We are surprised to learn that it was an occasional poem, even a propagandistic effort by a youthful activist who dared to meddle in the highest affairs of state: the marriage of his Queen to a prince of France. We can account for very little of what goes on in *The Shepheardes Calender*, despite the accumulation of footnotes; indeed, we are aware of but a small portion of its intention and even less of its achievement. Yet, the poem earned Spenser an immediate reputation as "the new poet" and placed him at the center of a large circle of admirers, including the most astute poets and critics of the day.

To start with the most obvious, we should note that *The Shepheardes Calender* has a fore-conceit which is fully visible in its calendar form. The title page announces "Twelve eclogues proportionable to the twelve monethes," and this plan is relentlessly carried out. Furthermore, the twelve-part form is stressed by E. K., the poem's contemporary commentator. In the dedicatory epistle, E. K. discusses "the generall dryft and purpose" of these eclogues, though in keeping with the charade of secrecy he refuses to say much. He does state without equivocation, however, "that his [the poet's] unstayed yougth had long wandred in the common Labyrinth of Love, in which time to mitigate and allay the heate of his passion . . . he compiled these xii. Æglogues, which for that they be proportioned to the state of the xii. monethes, he termeth the *Shepheards Calendar.*" According to Sidney, "the skill of ech Artificer standeth in that *Idea,* or fore conceit of the worke"; therefore an assessment of Spenser's achievement as well as an understanding of the poem's meaning lies in an analysis of this familiar twelve-part scheme.

As we read *The Shepheardes Calender,* we are kept continually aware of the calendar form. In each eclogue, Spenser takes pains to associate the subject matter with its appropriate month in the pagan calendar—*February,* for example, deals with the theme of old age in an environment of coldness, appropriate to the last month of the dying year; while *March,* the first month of the new year, is given over to young men bantering about sex. In this natural description and in his representation of the calendar as the astronomers reported it, Spenser performs as an imitative poet, purveying factual knowledge. In the literary medium of words, he constructs a calendar that reproduces the succession of months observable in physical nature. We progress from January through each month in turn to December, completing a year, the annual unit of time comprising the twelve disparate months.

But in addition to the linear sequence of eclogues through twelve months, a straight-line movement, there is another pattern, a circular movement. This cyclical pattern, of course implicit in the calendar form from the start, becomes fully evident only at the end of *The Shepheardes Calender,* when we can view it in its entirety, as a whole. The *December* eclogue is unmistakably reminiscent of *January*—it likewise is an amorous complaint sung by Colin Clout, a fact which E. K. brings to our attention in the Argument for *December*; and it likewise shows the same metrical form, a six-line stanza of iambic pentameters rhyming a b a b c c. Moreover, *December* has exactly twice as many stanzas as *January*—24 against 12, a ratio of 2 : 1, a diapason. We are compelled to recognize a relationship, a similarity, between the final and the beginning eclogue. We have, of course, come full circle. The end of December leads to the beginning of a new year. We are returned to our point of origin, and unmistakably are brought to realize that in nature a new seasonal cycle will commence. This calendar form therefore includes both a linear progression through the twelve months and a circular movement which returns to a starting point and suggests endless continuation by means of repetition. For Spenser's contemporaries, the calendar form was an acknowledged ideogram of time, an emblem of the cosmos (see p. 156, above). In the expression of this idea, Spenser was offering a verbal version of a well-known visual image.

The idea that the calendar is an emblem of cosmos can be demonstrated most succinctly by examining an illustration for the chapter on time in Jean Corbichon's edition of Bartholomaeus Anglicus' *De proprietatibus rerum* printed at Lyons, 1485 (see Plate 26). This illustration was frequently reproduced—most cogently for our purposes, perhaps, in the numerous editions of *The kalendayr of shepheards*, the oft-reprinted perennial almanac which Richard Pynson had early imported into England from France and which E. K. calls to mind in his dedicatory epistle. In the diagram we have three concentric circles, each of which represents the cosmos in different terms. The outermost circle sets forth the signs of the zodiac, through which the sun travels in its annual journey. The twelve signs taken together make up a unit, the year, thereby implying the renaissance commonplace of unity out of multeity, *e pluribus unum*, or to say it slightly differently, *concordia discors*.

The point might be clearer if we arrange the twelve zodiacal signs into four seasons, each with its distinct but contrasting weather, so that the heat and dryness of summer are balanced by the coldness and moisture of winter, and the heat and moisture of spring are balanced by the cold and dryness of autumn. Such an arrangement is illustrated by a diagram from Robert Anton's *Philosophers satyrs* (see Plate 34). This work was published in 1616 and suggests the continuing efficacy of the tetrad tradition into the seventeenth century. The significance of the arrangement is best gained, however, from a woodcut appearing in a 1472 edition of Isidore of Seville's *Liber de responsione mundi & astrorum ordinatione*, printed in Augsburg (see Plate 31). This figure displays three analogous systems: the four elements arranged in two sets of opposing pairs to produce a cosmos, our earth, *mundus;* the four seasons arranged in two sets of opposing pairs to produce a cosmos, the year, *annus;* and the four humours arranged in two sets of opposing pairs to produce a cosmos, man, *homo*. The same tetrad pattern persists at all levels of creation—in elemental nature, in time, and in man. Or to say it another way, man is a microcosm, repeating the pattern of the universe in his humours and the pattern of the year in the four seasons of his life: infancy, youth, maturity, and old age. This pattern of a four-phase cosmos underlies the twelve signs of the zodiac in the outer circle of the diagram from Bartholomaeus' *De proprietatibus rerum.* The twelve signs can be arranged as four seasons and of course represent the single unit of one year (see Plate 33).

The middle circle of the diagram from Bartholomaeus reinforces this significance of the outer circle. Here we have the twelve months of the year represented by the twelve occupations of man appropriate to each one. January, for example (near the bottom to the right), is represented by a two-headed Janus-like figure at a festive board, February by a figure warming himself before the fire, March by a husbandman breaking up the thawing soil, April by a husbandman pruning his orchard, May by a courtier wooing his lady, June by a ploughman driving his team, and so on around to December when the hogs are killed. The twelve months, of course, like the signs of the zodiac, can be arranged as four seasons and fulfill the same cosmic pattern of the tetrad. The implication is that each month is differentiated by a distinct occupation, but taken all together they exhaust the possibilities of human experience and thereby represent the full life considered as a whole. We now can understand why writing twelve eclogues proportioned to the twelve months might be helpful to an unstayed youth who had long wandered in the labyrinth of love. It helps him see his youthful passion in relation to life in its entirety. It helps him see his maytime wooing in proper perspective: appropriate for his youth and contributing significantly to the whole, but only part of a larger entity.

Finally, in the diagram from Bartholomaeus we must look at the innermost circle, which is cut in half, presenting a two-phase rather than a four- or a twelve-phase cosmos. Here we have at the top a young woman holding flowers in a meadow beneath trees in leaf, and at the bottom a young man sitting in a barren field beside a fire beneath bare trees. The intended contrast is obvious. But that each half is a careful counterpart of the other is equally obvious, and the two halves taken together form a whole greater than the sum of its parts, a self-sufficient unit comprising male and female, winter and summer, barrenness and fertility, and so on *ad infinitum* through all conceivable pairs of opposites—a symbol of self-contained completeness which is best known perhaps in the form of the alchemical hermaphrodite.

The point, of course, is that this diagram, this ideogram of time, does reconcile opposites. It does make concord out of discord, and by exhausting the total of possibilities it does produce a unity out of multeity. It demonstrates a favorite renaissance dictum: *contraria coincidunt in natura uniali*, "Contraries coincide in unified nature." This pattern pertains at all levels of creation and can be represented in the twelve-phase cosmos of the zodiac or the months, in the four-phase cosmos of the seasons, or in the two-phase cosmos of the hermaphrodite.

Without any doubt this scheme—this cosmic pattern interrelating the four elements, the year, and man—was the fore-conceit in the mind of Spenser which he extended in *The Shepheardes Calender*, "these xii. Æglogues, which . . . he proportioned to the state of the xii. monethes." Spenser is explicit about this in the concluding eclogue, which E. K. neatly explicates in his argument for *December:*

> Weary of his former wayes, he [Colin] proportioneth his life to the foure seasons of the yeare, comparing hys youthe to the spring time, when he was fresh and free from loves follye. His manhoode to the sommer, which he sayth, was consumed with greate heate and excessive drought. . . . His riper yeares hee resembleth to an unseasonable harveste wherein the fruites fall ere they be rype. His latter age to winters chyll and frostie season, now drawing neare to his last ende.

Colin's life is anatomized according to the four elements and the four seasons. The cosmos of *homo* is shown to be correspondent to the cosmoi of *mundus* and *annus*.

Spenser reiterates his intention in an envoy. At the end of the twelve eclogues he announces officiously:

> Loe I have made a Calender for every yeare,
> That steele in strength, and time in durance shall outweare:
> And if I marked well the starres revolution,
> It shall continewe till the worlds dissolution.

Spenser claims to have made a calendar that is applicable to every year, to any unit of time, and therefore it is atemporal and will outlast steel. Indeed it will outwear time itself—it is an abstract pattern, a mere form without corruptible substance, an idea in Plato's world of being, a Pythagorean number.[48]

Spenser, a poet as maker, has taken a pattern in imitation of the divine archetype and imposed it upon the raw material of his own experience. His exhaustive depiction of human activity in its full variety month-by-month provides a speculum of life both as it is and as it should be. Like any good mirror, the poem often shows how far the actual falls short of the ideal. This is the intent of the satiric eclogues, which have an immediately practical purpose, as Spenser goes on to tell us in the envoy:

> Loe I have made a Calender . . .
> . . . .
> To teach the ruder shepheard how to feede his sheepe,
> And from the falsers fraud his folded flocke to keepe.
> (ll. 1–6)

The poem also shows life whole, however, made up of discrete parts, but accommodated to the seasonal cycle and accumulating to the annual unit of time. The poem reflects the integer of eternity. By completion of this pattern, this shepherd's calendar, the individual man participates in the cosmos and thereby transcends the time-bound world of mutable things. He achieves perfection (< L. *perficere*), literally a working through to an end which is not static but itself an ongoing process:

> . . . all things stedfastnes doe hate
> And changed be: yet being rightly wayd
> They are not changed from their first estate;
> But by their change their being doe dilate:
> And turning to themselves at length againe,
> Doe worke their owne perfection.
> (*Mutabilitie Cantos*, VII.vii.58.2–7)

Already in *The Shepheardes Calender* Spenser had framed the conception of time which he propounded so magnificently in the *Mutabilitie Cantos*.

This is the way that Alexander Pope read *The Shepheardes Calender*. Pope was himself the author of four eclogues corresponding to the four seasons—a truncated calendar form—accompanied by "A Discourse of Pastoral Poetry." In this tribute to and analysis of the venerated pastoral tradition, Pope extols Spenser's poem (with reservations, of course), and then with unerring directness pinpoints its claim to greatness:

> The addition he has made of a Calendar to his Eclogues, is very beautiful; since by this, besides the general moral of innocence and simplicity, which is common to other authors of Pastoral,

> he has one peculiar to himself; he compares human Life to the several Seasons, and at once exposes to his readers a view of the great and little worlds, in their various changes and aspects.[49]

This statement, this vision, is expressed through the form of the poem, through the arrangement of its twelve parts and their resultant totality.

By reproducing the divine pattern of cosmos, Spenser's poem—like the man who accords with cosmos—will also last forever. It too will have the perfection of an endlessly repeated finite but all-inclusive cycle. If Spenser has been accurate in observation of the divine model—if he has "marked well the starres revolution"—then his literary microcosm organizing the twelve months and twelve human occupations "shall continewe till the worlds dissolution." His artifact will hold valid as long as the created world itself survives. In the words of Yeats, it will be an "artifice of eternity." Such is the authority—and also the responsibility—of the poet as maker.

A poetics of "making" is not found among the sixteenth-century Italians,[50] who were obsessed with Aristotle's *Poetics*, nor among the French, who were devoted to μίμησις of a different sort. Sidney seems the most prominent in the renaissance to enunciate such a theory of poetry, seconded by Puttenham. It is Spenser, though, the "new poet" of *The Shepheardes Calender*, who instituted the practice of such poetics in England. And it is likely that Sidney formulated his own theory after reading *The Shepheardes Calender* and talking with Spenser. This theory of poetry, much more than the reformed English versifying according to quantitative meter, was the important topic for discussion among the members of the Areopagus. Probably it was the central subject of "The English Poet," the prose tract by Spenser which E. K. mentions in the argument for *October*, but which was never published. This loss has deprived us of Spenser's *biographia literaria*, but we can infer it from other materials.

In their poetics Spenser and Sidney (I shall say admittedly in a rash moment) achieved a synthesis which had been seriously attempted at least since the time of Aquinas—a synthesis of Platonic idealism and Aristotelian physics within a Christian context. In the Italian renaissance Pico had renewed the effort as a humanistic exercise when the actual texts of Plato had become available.[51] But St. Thomas failed, and Pico died before he succeeded. Sidney would say, however, that they had limited themselves to the restrictive discipline of philosophy. Poetry is a more flexible and more inclusive discipline, and therefore provides a better chance of success. Plato had placed ultimate reality in a suprasensible world of ideas, and by deduction a poet might bring down from this unchanging, noncorporeal world some notion of the permanent essences that reside there. In contrast, Aristotle had placed ultimate reality in the objects of physical nature, and by induction a poet might construct a universal statement from the facts of our environment.[52] These divergent opinions of wherein lies truth are irreconcilable as philosophical systems. But the poet can achieve a synthesis. It was the unique triumph of renaissance poetics to fuse these two concepts of ultimate reality, or at least to make them congruous.

Puttenham announces the synthesis in its most ingenuous form: "They [the poets] were the first observers of all naturall causes & effects in the things generable and corruptible, and from thence mounted up to search after the celestiall courses and influences, & yet penetrated further to know the divine essences" (*Arte of English poesie*, C3ᵛ). The voice of Aristotle is unmistakably echoed here in the phrase "things generable and corruptible," and that of Plato in the phrase "divine essences." The poet's description of reality, as Sidney argued, was not the limited factuality of history, nor the tenuous abstraction of philosophy; but rather it was an imitation of life which started with the imperfect and ephemeral brazen world and by poetic imagination transmuted this to a golden world of perfection. Whether the poet began with the unrelated experiences of actual life, and by the coadunating faculty of his imagination arrived at a timeless verity, or whether he started with the eternal ideas of Plato's world of being, and purveyed them in the sensible form of objective correlatives in the physical world, he was dealing with the same truth. Poetry was ποίησις, a fashioning of random data into a significant statement of universal relevance. It was μίμησις, the imitation not of apparent or of fragmentary, but of essential reality.

Notes

[1] *The defence of poesie* (William Ponsonby; London, 1595), B4. All of my references to Sidney's *Defence* are made to Ponsonby's edition; see n. 45, below.

[2] In G. Gregory Smith, ed., *Elizabethan Critical Essays*, 2 vols. (Oxford Univ. Press, 1904), I.230.

[3] Ed. Gladys D. Willcock and Alice Walker (Cambridge Univ. Press, 1936), p. 3 [C1].

[4] In Smith, *Elizabethan Critical Essays*, II.196.

[5] For examples in *The Shepheardes Calender* alone, see *January*, 66; *February*, 98; *April*, 19, 154; *June*, 82; *October*, 78; *December*, 6.

[6] *Timber: or, Discoveries* in *Ben Jonson*, ed. C. H. Herford and Percy and Evelyn Simpson, 11 vols. (Oxford, 1925–52), VIII.635.

[7] In *A History of Literary Criticism in the Italian Renaissance* (Univ. of Chicago Press, 1961), Bernard Weinberg surveys Italian critics who drew in any way upon Plato (pp. 250–348). Only two share views with Sidney: Giovanni Bernardino Fuscano (pp. 261–262) and Bernardino Tomitano (pp. 264–267). Fuscano seems to have been completely unknown to the Elizabethans. Tomitano's refutation of Aristotle was known to Roger Ascham (cf. *The scholemaster* [1570] in Smith, *Elizabethan Critical Essays*, I.21); but there is no evidence that he was known to any other Elizabethan critic.

Robert M. Durling demonstrates convincingly that Ariosto saw himself as the omnipotent manipulator of his material, and "this attitude of absolute control of an extremely complex work of art is an example of the analogy between the poem and the cosmos and between the artist and God" ("The Divine Analogy in Ariosto," *Modern Language Notes*, 78 [1963], 1). I have no doubt that this practice of Ariosto is what attracted Spenser to the *Orlando Furioso*, as Gabriel Harvey intimates in the third of the *Three proper, and wittie, familiar letters*. But Ariosto does not propound explicitly a concept of poetry as making, and Spenser is following his example rather than his precept, while Sidney seems to have been influenced in an even more subtle way. In any case, my concern is not to establish Sidney's priority in enunciating this poetics (he manifestly takes from others), but rather to indicate the exhilarating effect that it had on English poets when Sidney unfolded the possibilities.

In *The Artist as Creator* (Johns Hopkins Press, 1956), Milton C. Nahm explores the ramifications for esthetics when the artist is given absolute freedom to fabricate; see esp. pp. 63–83.

[8] Domenicus Nannus Mirabellius and Bartholomaeus Amantius, *Polyanthea* (Cologne, 1567), p. 776; cf. *ibid.*, p. 773. Cf. also Ludovicus Caelius Rhodiginus, *Antiquarum lectionum libri XVI* [IV.iv] (Venice, 1516), p. 162.

[9] The best account of this Florentine Platonist appears in Don C. Allen, *Mysteriously Meant* (Johns Hopkins Press, 1970), pp. 142–154.

Professor Paul O. Kristeller has called my attention to a weighty and cogent article which focuses on Landino: E. N. Tigerstedt, "The Poet as Creator: Origins of a Metaphor," *Comparative Literature Studies*, 5 (1968), 455–488.

> [10] Et e greci dixono poeta da questo verbo piin: elquale e in mezo tra creare che e proprio di dio quando di niente produce in essere alchuna chosa: Et fare che e de glhuomini in ciaschuna arte quando di materia et di forma compongono. Imperoche benche el figmento del poeta non sia altutto di niente pure si parte dal fare et al creare molto sappressa

(Dante, *Divina commedia*, with commentary of Cristoforo Landino [Florence, 1481], [*]8^{v}). The poetics of Landino had lingering effects on the Continent, most notably in Francesco Giorgio, *De harmonia mundi totius cantica tria* (Venice, 1525), and in the prefatory comments which Guy le Fèvre de la Boderie offered before his French translation of Giorgio, *L'Harmonie du monde* (Paris, 1579). See Maren-Sofie Røstvig, *The Hidden Sense* (Oslo, 1963), pp. 27–36; and Christopher Butler, *Number Symbolism* (New York, 1970), pp. 56–61.

[11] *Defence of poesie*, C2. Cf. also *ibid.*, D3–D3^{v}.

[12] Giovanni Bernardino Fuscano apparently gave this etymology in the *De la oratoria et poetica facolta* printed as an introduction to his *Stanze sovra la*

bellezza di Napoli (1531); see Weinberg, *Criticism in Italian Renaissance*, p. 262. It is unlikely, however, that Sidney knew this treatise, nor is there any evidence that any Elizabethan was aware of Fuscano. Neither the British Museum nor the Bibliothèque Nationale seems to have any of his works, nor is he listed by Mario E. Cosenza, *Dictionary of the Italian Humanists*, 6 vols. (Boston, 1962).

For other medieval and renaissance adaptations of this etymology, see Tigerstedt, "Poet as Creator," p. 468.

[13] *Genealogiae*, XIV.vii.

[14] Giovanni Battista Giraldi Cinthio, *Discorsi . . . intorno al comporre de i romanzi . . .* (Venice, 1554), p. 56. Cf. *ibid.*, tr. Henry L. Snuggs (Univ. of Kentucky Press, 1968), p. 50.

[15] *Poetices libri septem* [I.ii] (Lyons, 1561), p. 3.

[16] For an important article on Sidney's adaptation of Scaliger, see A. C. Hamilton, "Sidney's Idea of the 'Right Poet,'" *Comparative Literature*, 9 (1957), 51–59.

[17] The skeptical opinion about poets is perennial, as Agrippa well knew:

> All vertuouse men have dispised Poetrie, as the mother of lies, seeinge that the Poetes doo lie so monstrously: as them that have spente theire studie not to speake, nor write any good thinge: but with bodged verses to delite the eares of fooles, and to make a clatteringe noise with the craftie coveringe of fables, and disceitefullie to devise all thinges upon a matter of nothinge

(*Of the vanitie and uncertaintie of artes and sciences*, tr. James Sanford [London, 1569], fol. 12ᵛ).

[18] But the concept of poet as maker persists, and is evident even in the work of Alexander Pope (cf. Martin C. Battestin, "The Transforming Power: Nature and Art in Pope's Pastorals," *Eighteenth Century Studies*, 2 [1968–69], 183–204). Cf. also Anthony, Earl of Shaftesbury: "A *Poet* is indeed a second *Maker:* a just PROMETHEUS under JOVE. Like that Sovereign Artist or universal Plastick Nature, he forms *a Whole*, coherent and proportion'd in it-self" (*Characteristicks of Men, Manners, Opinions, Times*, 2nd ed., 3 vols. [London, 1714], I.207). The concept is prominent also in the work of W. B. Yeats, where it becomes a motif in the poetry itself; for example, in *Sailing to Byzantium* the poet becomes an artificial bird set upon a golden bough, himself his own "artifice of eternity." Recently the concept has been newly formulated by Susanne K. Langer, *Philosophy in a New Key*, 3rd ed. (Harvard Univ. Press, 1957), esp. p. 257.

[19] Sidney expressly eloigns himself from this theory:

> He [Plato] attributeth unto *Poesie*, more then my selfe do; namely, to be a verie inspiring of a divine force, farre above mans wit, as in the fore-named Dialogue is apparant

(*Defence of poesie*, H1-H1ᵛ).

[20] It is interesting to note that in his explaining away of Plato's banishment of poets Sidney does not try to answer Plato's primary objection, that poetry is no more than an imitation of nature, which is itself an imperfect replica of the world of being. Sidney addresses himself only to the poet's scurrility against the gods: "*Plato* found fault that the *Poettes* of his time, filled the worlde with wrong opinions of the Gods, making light tales of that unspotted essence." Sidney considers this no more than an abuse of poetry, however, and excuses poets on the grounds that they merely repeated the prevalent beliefs of their day: "The *Poets* did not induce such opinions, but did imitate those opinions alreadie induced" (*Defence of poesie*, G4ᵛ).

[21] Et e idio sommo poeta: et e el mondo suo poema (Dante, *Divina commedia*, with commentary of Landino, [*]8ᵛ).

[22] See Ernst R. Curtius, *European Literature and the Latin Middle Ages*, tr. Willard R. Trask (New York, 1953), pp. 544–546, where the topos *Deus artifex* is reconstructed.

[23] St. Augustine, *Letters* [166.xiii], tr. Sister Wilfrid Parsons, 5 vols. (New York, 1951–56), IV.19.

[24] *The true intellectual system of the universe* (London, 1678), p. 879. Cf. Plotinus, *Enneads*, III.ii.16.

[25] *Religio Medici* [I.xvi] in *Works*, ed. Geoffrey Keynes, 6 vols. (London, 1928–31), I.23. Browne elaborates this statement in a revealing way by arguing that far from being at variance with one another, nature and art manifest the same divine intention:

> Now Nature is not at variance with Art, nor Art with Nature, they being both servants of his Providence. Art is the perfection of Nature (I.xvi).

Browne is here reflecting an argument of Plotinus, who had posited a definite relationship between art and nature which frequently, directly or indirectly, conditioned later estheticians. Just as nature is the physical extension of the archetypal idea of intellectual beauty, says Plotinus, so art derives immediately from this same "reason-principle." Art is not an imitation of physical nature, then, as Plato had argued in the *Republic* and Aristotle had confirmed; but rather it is a cognate of that nature, both art and nature proceeding independently from the same source. In a passage dealing with "how the Beauty of the divine Intellect and of the Intellectual Cosmos may be revealed to contemplation," Plotinus offers a telling example to make his point:

> Suppose two blocks of stone lying side by side: one is unpatterned, quite untouched by art; the other has been minutely wrought by the craftsman's hands into some statue of god or man, a Grace or a Muse, or if a human being, not a portrait but a creation in which the sculptor's art has concentrated all loveliness.
>
> Now it must be seen that the stone thus brought under the artist's hand to the beauty of form is beautiful not as stone—for so the crude block would be as pleasant—but in virtue of the Form or Idea introduced by the art. This form is not in the material; it is in the designer before ever it enters the stone; and the artificer holds it not by his equipment of eyes and hands but by his participation in his art. The beauty, therefore, exists in a far higher state in the art

(*The Enneads* [V.viii.1], tr. Stephen MacKenna, 3rd ed. [London, 1962], p. 422). The beauty of the statue is not inherent in the stone, but comes rather from the form which the artist imposes upon the stone. Art, therefore, like nature, is a manifestation of intellectual beauty—indeed, a reproduction of that reason-principle more nearly perfect than nature and in a state accessible for human contemplation. For a comprehensive study of these counterparts, see Edward W. Tayler, *Nature and Art in Renaissance Literature* (Columbia Univ. Press, 1964).

[26] *The trewnesse of the Christian religion*, tr. Sidney [1587], in Sidney, *Complete Works*, ed. Albert Feuillerat, 4 vols. (Cambridge Univ. Press, 1912–26), III.328.

[27] *Defence of poesie*, C1. The term "idea" has had a continuous, though changing, use in art theory since the time of Plato; for an account of its transmutations, see Erwin Panofsky, *Idea*, tr. Joseph J. S. Peake (Univ. of

South Carolina Press, 1968). Sidney's use of the term "idea" is best glossed by a passage from Du Bartas which describes how God created this All out of Nothing:

> . . . Before th'All-working Word alone
> Made Nothing be Alls wombe and *Embryon*,
> Th'eternall Plot, th'*Idea* fore-conceaved,
> The wondrous Forme of all that Forme receaved,
> Did in the Work-mans spirit devinely lye,
> And, yer it was, the World was wondrously.

(Guillaume Saluste du Bartas, *Devine weekes and workes*, tr. Joshua Sylvester [London, 1605], p. 483).

28 Through continued usage, the term "conceit" has largely lost its literal meaning: "that which has been conceived through sexual intercourse." In the *Timaeus*, the creating godhead is both "poet and *father* of this all" (*Timaeus*, 28C), not only the mental but also the physical progenitor of the universe. The epithet "maker" also carries a connotation of sire as well as architect. On the conceit as a propagation in the mind analogous to sexual procreation in nature, see Jay L. Halio, "The Metaphor of Conception and Elizabethan Theories of the Imagination," *Neophilologus*, 50 (1966), 454–461; and Robert J. Bauer, "A Phenomenon of Epistemology in the Renaissance," *Journal of the History of Ideas*, 31 (1970), 281–288. See also Shakespeare, *Love's Labour's Lost*, IV.ii.62–67, where Holofernes uses sexual terms to explain the origin of the "forms" and "figures" that fill his mind. On the meaning of *concetto* in Italian renaissance art theory, see Panofsky, *Idea*, p. 66.

29 In Smith, *Elizabethan Critical Essays*, I.47, 48.

30 Sidney also uses "invention" in this sense. In the *Defence of poesie* he declares that artisans are limited by Nature, just as actors are confined by the script of a play; only the poet, he says, escapes such subjection, and "lifted up with the vigor of his own *invention*, doth grow in effect into an other nature" (B4^{v}). Shortly after, Sidney distinguishes three kinds of poetry: religious poetry, didactic poetry, and "right poetry." The poet of the second sort, says Sidney, "is wrapped within the folde of the proposed subject, and takes not the free course of his own *invention*" (C2). Again, Sidney observes, "The greatest part of Poets have apparelled their poeticall *inventions*, in that numbrous kind of writing which is called *vers*" (C2^{v}); and the poet "calleth the sweete *Muses* to inspire unto him a good *invention*" (G1). Most tellingly, Sidney admonishes his readers, "They shall use the narration [of a poem] but as an imaginative groundplat of a profitable *invention*" (G1^{v}). Sidney uses "invention" in this sense also in the opening sonnet of *Astrophel and Stella*, where we see him actively casting about for a fore-conceit before beginning to write his sequence. Carrying on in this line, Sir John Harington makes "invention" synonymous with "fiction": "I have named the two parts of Poetrie, namely invention or fiction and verse" (*Preface* [to Harington's translation of *Orlando Furioso*, 1591] in Smith, *Elizabethan Critical Essays*, II.204). "Invention" was used in this sense at least through the lifetime of Milton; Edward Phillips, for example, observes, "*Invention* be the grand part of a Poet, or *Maker*, and Verse the least" (Preface to *Theatrum poetarum* in J. E. Spingarn, *Critical Essays of the Seventeenth Century*, 3 vols. [Oxford Univ. Press, 1908–09], II.267).

See also Murray W. Bundy, "'Invention' and 'Imagination' in the Renaissance," *Journal of English and Germanic Philology*, 29 (1930), 535–545.

31 *Timber* in *Jonson*, ed. Herford and Simpson, VIII.635.

32 At the time of writing, I did not have available Alastair Fowler's important book, *Triumphal Forms: Structural Patterns in Elizabethan Poetry*

(Cambridge Univ. Press, 1970). In the field of critical analysis based on formal structure, Mr. Fowler clearly has the bit in his teeth and is running with it. But *festina lente.* While Mr. Fowler presents much useful information and provokes us into speculation along the right lines, he errs in his insistence on seeing numerical composition as an attempt at spatial organization. He has been led astray by his own proclivity towards iconography. In renaissance poetry, especially that of the Elizabethans, the intellectual signification of symbolic numbers heavily outweighs the visible image they present to the eye. The palpability of symbolic numbers in a poem is but a means to a far more serious end, and deciphering any code of number symbolism is but the first step in the process of intellectualizing its significance.

[33] In a passage with the marginal gloss, "Why God ordained the Night and Day alternately to succeed each other," Du Bartas explains the symbiosis between two halves of a perfect contrast:

> . . . because all pleasures waxe unpleasant,
> If without pawse we still possesse them present:
> And none can right discerne the sweets of Peace,
> That have not felt Warres irksome bitternes
> And Swannes seeme whiter if swart Crowes be by
> (For contraries each other best descrie)
> Th'Alls-Architect, alternately decreed
> That Night the Day, the Day should Night succeed.

(*Devine weekes and workes,* tr. Sylvester [1605], p. 19). See also pp. 390–391, below.

[34] Giovanni Boccaccio, *Genealogy of the Gods* [XIV.vii] in *Boccaccio on Poetry,* tr. Charles G. Osgood (Princeton Univ. Press, 1930), p. 39.

[35] Sig. D3^{v}. See also William Rossky, "Imagination in the English Renaissance: Psychology and Poetic," *Studies in the Renaissance,* 5 (1958), esp. 50–52, 61–62; and Baxter Hathaway, *The Age of Criticism: The Late Renaissance in Italy* (Cornell Univ. Press, 1962), pp. 316–328, 342–344.

[36] *Defence of poesie,* B3^{v}. For a similar definition of the poet as *vates,* see William Webbe, *A discourse of English poetrie* [1586] in Smith, *Elizabethan Critical Essays,* I.231–232.

[37] This is the focal passage in the *Poetics:*

> Since the poet, like the painter and other makers of images, is an imitator, the object of his imitation must always be represented in one of three ways: as it was or is, as it is said or thought to be, or as it ought to be (1460b).

[38] *The scholemaster* [1570] in Smith, *Elizabethan Critical Essays,* I.5.

[39] This phrase has had a noteworthy career in literary criticism; cf. Smith, *Elizabethan Critical Essays,* I.386–387; and Sir Philip Sidney, *An Apology for Poetry,* ed. Geoffrey Shepherd (London, 1965), p. 160. For an art historian's survey of the alliance between poetry and painting in the renaissance, see Rensselaer W. Lee, "*Ut pictura poesis:* The Humanistic Theory of Painting," *Art Bulletin,* 22 (1940), 197–269.

[40] A series of visual representations which comments obliquely on the main action has been a familiar motif in narrative ever since Aeneas perused the walls of Juno's temple immediately prior to his first meeting with Dido (*Aeneid,* I.453–493).

[41] The use of the verb "to imitate" suggests an Aristotelian reference here, but does not insist upon it in a narrow sense. The meaning of μίμησις was much debated by literary critics. For the conflicting theories in renaissance

Italy about "imitation" in art, many of them tinged with Platonic doctrine, see Hathaway, *Age of Criticism,* esp. pp. 23–64.

[42] This passage, with justification, has been referred to Aristotle, *Poetics,* 1451b, to which Sidney explicitly alludes in the *Defence of poesie* (D3). There Aristotle states:

> The poet's function is to describe, not the thing that has happened, but a kind of thing that might happen, i.e. what is possible as being probable or necessary.

Aristotle in this section of the *Poetics* is distinguishing between the historian, who "describes the thing that has been," and the poet, who describes "a kind of thing that might be," with the conclusion that "poetry is something more philosophic and of graver import than history." Sidney also comes to this conclusion at a later point in the *Defence of poesie.* In this passage, however, Sidney is at pains to show the superiority of the "right poet" over the didactic poet, and his thought is more profitably referred to Plato than to Aristotle, since he is talking about "the divine consideration" of an idea rather than about a universal in nature. A cogent *locus* in Plato occurs in the *Timaeus,* where Plato explicitly denies the value of art which imitates the created, and therefore changeable, items of physical nature:

> When the artificer (δημιουργός) of any object, in forming its shape (ἰδέα) and quality (δύναμις), keeps his gaze fixed on that which is uniform (i.e., unchanging; τὸ κατὰ ταὐτὰ ἔχον βλέπων ἀεί), using a model of this kind, that object, executed in this way, must of necessity be beautiful (καλόν); but whenever he gazes at that which has come into existence (τὸ γεγονός) and uses a created model (γεννητὸν παράδειγμα), the object thus executed is not beautiful (28A-B).

[43] *Defence of poesie,* C1-C1^{v}. To show the orthodoxy of Sidney's passage with respect to the Platonic tradition as he received it, we may refer his argument to Ficino, *Theologia platonica,* XIII.iii:

> Human arts produce by themselves whatever nature itself produces, as if we were not the slaves, but the rivals of nature. . . . Thus man imitates all the works of the divine nature, and perfects, corrects and improves the works of the lower nature. Therefore the power of man is almost similar to that of the divine nature, for man acts in this way through himself. Through his own wit and art he governs himself, without being bound by any limits of corporeal nature; and he imitates all the works of the higher nature

(tr. Josephine L. Burroughs in Paul O. Kristeller, "Ficino and Pomponazzi on the Place of Man in the Universe," *Journal of the History of Ideas,* 5 [1944], 233).

[44] *Defence of poesie,* B4^{v}–C1. The phrase "the Zodiack of his owne wit" is difficult to gloss because of its ambiguity. On the one hand it suggests a range of activity commensurate with the heavens and therefore divine, but yet it does impose the tightly defined circumference of a circle. This ambiguity, assuredly intended by Sidney, is best explicated in terms of the microcosm-macrocosm analogy. The poet's wit is a zodiac, a microcosmic pattern of *mundus, annus, homo* (see Plate 31). Therefore the poet's wit, though a finite pattern, relates to all the levels of creation, from the individual to the universal. By knowing himself through "freely raunging within the Zodiack of his owne wit," the poet grows infinite. The motif was prominent in Marcellus Palingenius, *Zodiacus vitae* (Venice, c.1531), a much used schoolbook translated into English by Barnabe Googe in 1565.

[45] *Defence of poesie*, C1ᵛ. The punctuation of this passage differs significantly in the edition of Henry Olney and in that of William Ponsonby, both printed in 1595. Throughout this study I have used the text of Ponsonby, which has a claim to be the authorized edition because Ponsonby was chosen as printer of the authorized edition of the *Arcadia* in 1598. The edition of Olney, however, re-groups the phrases by different punctuation:

> Poesie therefore is an arte of imitation, for so *Aristotle* termeth it in this word *Mimesis*, that is to say, a representing, counterfetting, or figuring foorth: to speake metaphorically, a speaking picture: with this end, to teach and delight (C2ᵛ).

In Olney's version, the modifier "to speake metaphorically" is adjoined to "a speaking picture," thereby becoming a dangling infinitive. I prefer the reading in Ponsonby's edition. That poetry is "a speaking picture" was a renaissance platitude, and would require no introductory modifier such as "to speake metaphorically."

Sidney's paragraph is in essence a digest of Scaliger, *Poetice*, I.i, though it significantly modifies Scaliger's argument.

[46] We tend to think of metaphor as a static rhetorical formulation, but the renaissance did not. Rather, the metaphor is an action. Richard Carew, for example, observes: "Our speech doth not consist only of wordes, but in a sorte even of deedes, as when wee expresse a matter by Metaphors" (*The excellency of the English tongue* [c.1595] in Smith, *Elizabethan Critical Essays*, II.288).

[47] *Defence of poesie*, G2. For the term εἰκαστική Sidney must have had in mind Plato, *Sophist*, 235D–236C, where the term φανταστική also occurs.

[48] The proper context for Spenser's envoy derives from the following passage in Plato's *Timaeus:*

> The vision of day and night and of months and circling years has created the art of number and has given us not only the notion of Time but also means of research into the nature of the Universe. From these we have procured Philosophy in all its range (47A-B).

Robert Recorde recalled this passage and used it to justify his own humanism and scientism in the face of the tradition for *contemptus mundi* which had developed from Cicero's *Somnium Scipionis:*

> When Scipio behelde oute of the high heavens the smallenes of the earth with the kingdomes in it, he coulde no lesse but esteeme the travaile of men moste vaine, which sustaine so muche grief with infinite daungers to get so small a corner of that lyttle balle. . . . Who soever therefore (by Scipions good admonishment) doth minde to avoide the name of vanitie, and wishe to attayne the name of a man, lette him contemne those trifelinge triumphes, and little esteeme that little lumpe of claye: but rather looke upwarde to the heavens, as nature hath taught him. . . . Yea let him think (as Plato with divers other philosophers dyd trulye affirme) that for this intent were eies geven unto men, that they might with them beholde the heavens: whiche is the theatre of Goddes mightye power, and the chiefe spectakle of al his divine workes. There are those visible creatures of God, by which many wise philosophers attained to the knowledge of his invisible power. . . . In that boke who rightly can reade, to all secrete knowledge it will him straighte leade

(*The castle of knowledge* [London, 1556], a4).

[49] Pope, *Works*, ed. William Warburton (London, 1751), I.43.

[50] Ariosto is an exception; see p. 317, n. 7, above.

[51] Pico queries with contentious rhetoric: "What good was it to treat of natural things with the Peripatetics, unless the academy of the Platonists was also summoned"? And he continues to give a résumé of efforts to reconcile the Platonists and the Aristotelians:

> I have proposed the concord of Plato and Aristotle, believed by many before now, but adequately proved by no one. Among the Latins, Boethius, who promised to prove it, is not found ever to have done what he always wished to do. Among the Greeks, Simplicius made the same declaration: would that he had fulfilled his promise. Augustine too wrote in his *Academica* that there have been many who have attempted to prove the same thing in their very subtle disputations, namely, that the philosophy of Plato and of Aristotle is the same. Again, John the Grammarian, although he says that Plato seems to differ from Aristotle only to those who do not understand what Plato says, nevertheless left no proof of this to posterity

(*On the Dignity of Man*, tr. Charles Glenn Wallis [Indianapolis, 1965], pp. 24–25). Pico's treatise *On Being and the One* is also an extant fragment of a projected work aimed at demonstrating "the concord of Plato and Aristotle." On the attempt at syncretistic fusion of Platonic and Aristotelian doctrines in the Florentine Academy, see Ernst Cassirer, *The Individual and the Cosmos in Renaissance Philosophy*, tr. Mario Domandi (New York, 1964), pp. 2–3; cf. also *ibid.*, pp. 15–19.

[52] See A. J. Smith, "Theory and Practice in Renaissance Poetry: Two Kinds of Imitation," *Bulletin of the John Rylands Library*, 47 (1964–65), 230–231.

2

Metaphor as Cosmic Correspondence

As an inevitable corollary to the theory of poetry as "making," the poet utilizes metaphor as his vehicle of expression. Emulating the divine creator, the poet gives extension in three-dimensional terms to ideas from the conceptual realm. The poetic maker thereby renders concrete and knowable what would otherwise remain tenuous and ineffable. His mode of discourse by genus is metaphorical—metaphorical in a literal sense, because it translates meaning from one level to another, from the conceptual to the physical.[1] The *modus operandi* of the poet as maker is to devise metaphors with the purpose of relating different orders of being and various levels of meaning. It is for this reason, Sidney argues, that the poet is the "moderator" between the philosopher and the historian; the poet "coupleth the generall notion with the particuler example."[2] The essence of making is the framing of metaphors.

A rationale for metaphor in this sense is explicit in Pythagorean cosmology and is implicit in much Judeo-Christian thought. Our universe is, in fact, a metaphor devised by God, an extension of His thought from the abstract to the concrete. Cosmos, as the Middle Platonists interpreted the *Timaeus*, is a palpable projection of archetypal ideas in the mind of the creating godhead. As the Psalmist sings, "The heavens declare the glory of God and the firmament sheweth His handiwork." For Calvin, nature is a mirror in which God is reflected (*Institutio Christianae religionis*, I.v.i). Du Bartas assimilates all these traditions in one grand assertion which assumes that somewhere in His creation God appeals to each of our senses in His eagerness to be intelligible to man:

> God, of himselfe incapable to sence,
> In's Works reveales him t'our intelligence:
> There-in our fingers feele, our nostrils smell,

Our Palats taste his vertues that excell:
He shewes him to our eyes, talkes to our eares,
In th'ord'red motions of the spangled Spheares.[3]

That which is beyond sense perception is rendered knowable by this translation of attributes into a sense-perceptible form, into the objects of nature. Such is the raison d'être of metaphor.

To border on esthetics, we may say that nature is God's art, and we can discern His attributes by reading the Book of Nature,[4] His great poem. By using nature as an imaginative groundplat, as Sidney would have put it, we can discover the profitable invention in the mind of God which underlies creation. Spenser gave poetic expression to the thought in *An Hymne of Heavenly Beautie:*

The meanes therefore which unto us is lent,
Him to behold, is on his workes to looke,
Which he hath made in beauty excellent,
And in the same, as in a brasen booke,
To read enregistred in every nooke
His goodnesse, which his beautie doth declare.
(ll. 127–132)

Sir Thomas Pope Blount, though writing late in the seventeenth century, meant just what he said when he asserted:

> Every Flower of the Field, every Fibre of a Plant, every Particle of an Insect, carries with it the Impress of its Maker, and can (if dully consider'd) read us Lectures of Ethicks or Divinity.[5]

These lectures implicit in nature interpret for us the metaphor of creation and interrelate the human and divine levels.

This is a persuasive argument, and sixteenth-century scientists used it as frequently as poets, though for a different purpose: to justify their empirical observations. The scientist reasoned that study of nature was a first step in the study of God, the ultimate reality that nature objectified. Science at this stage was a handmaiden to religion, not its competitor or adversary. The rationale for metaphor convinced even the Recordes and Dees and Diggeses of Tudor London.[6]

Such reasoning can easily lead to the notion that our universe taken as a whole, the cosmos, is not only a metaphor devised *by* God, but also a metaphor *for* God Himself. Its plenitude reflects His all-inclusiveness; its order reflects His omnipotence and goodness; its limitless duration reflects His immortality. Walter Raleigh begins his *History of the world* with just such a sweeping statement:

> God, whome the wisest men acknowledge to be a power uneffable, and vertue infinite, a light by abundant claritie invisible, an understanding which it selfe can onely comprehend, an essence eternall and spirituall, of absolute purenesse and simplicitie, was and is pleased to make himselfe knowne by the worke of the World: in the wonderfull magnitude whereof, (all which he imbraceth, filleth, and sustaineth) we behold the image of that glorie, which cannot bee measured, and withall that one, and yet universall nature, which cannot be defined. In the glorious lights of heaven, we perceive a shadow of his divine countenance, in his mercifull provision for all that live, his manifold goodnesse: And lastly, in creating and making existent the world universall by the absolute art of his owne word, his power and almightinesse.[7]

The world in its fullness is a revelation of God in His infinitude.

But the world is a finite, and therefore knowable, thing—and consequently an effective metaphor. It translates the ineffable into the sense-perceptible, and then allows the percipient to reverse the process. By comprehending this image of God, we comprehend the original from whence this image proceeded. Poets in particular must be capable of discerning the two levels which are integrated by God's metaphor, and therefore Puttenham claims that they were the first observers of nature:

> They were the first that entended to the observation of nature and her works, and specially of the Celestiall courses, by reason of the continuall motion of the heavens, searching after the first mover, and from thence by degrees comming to know and consider of the substances separate & abstract, which we call the divine intelligences or good Angels.[8]

By discovering the mysterious ways of "nature and her works," by treating the universe as a metaphor, we approach an understanding of the inscrutable ways of its progenitor.

The universe, then, is a metaphor created by God, translating His archetypal idea into a palpable form, and also a metaphor for God, providing us with a means of knowing Him. Proceeding by direct analogy, we conclude in consequence that the poem for the poet as maker must also perform these two functions. The poem is a metaphor by the poet and also a metaphor for the poet. In the renaissance, it was considered sufficient if the poem succeeded in the first aim, that of translating a conceit into effective utterance. Revelation of self was not a primary interest of most Elizabethans, who still felt comfortable enough ensconced in the old cosmology and were satisfied with typicality. Alienation of the individual from his community was not yet a widespread concern, at least in literature. The second aim, that of making the poem a metaphor for self, did assume increasing importance in later generations, however, and eventually became the credo of the romantic poets.[9]

In Pythagorean cosmology as it verged on esthetics, our universe taken as a whole is a metaphor for God which resolves the paradox of how He is both one and infinite. The holy infinitude is represented by the multifarious diversity of our world, of course; His creation exhausted the possible permutations and combinations of matter. Yet this diversity is not chaotic. Cosmic order organizes it into the oneness of a *uni*verse. Multeity is reduced to unity in this prototypical metaphor.

The means by which physical variety is reduced to conceptual consistency is a triumph of Pythagorean rationality. Yet the means is undeniably simple. The Timaean scheme of creation, in order to account for variety, devolves actually into a hierarchy of categories of existence. This hierarchy provides for variety on a vertical scale —what is most commonly known as the great chain of being. There are stones and plants and animals, to list the categories of physical nature in ascending order, and angels and God in the noncorporeal categories. But what is equally important, though less often recognized, there is also in the Timaean scheme express provision for variety on a horizontal scale. At each level of creation, within each link of the chain, there also is diversity. This articulation of the scheme is necessary to account for differences within each category, for the different kinds of stones and of plants and of animals and of angels.

Furthermore, in an ingenious way the horizontal scale of variety is interlocked with the vertical scale to provide a complex but coherent system. Each of the several ascending levels, from the lowest to the highest, conceptual as well as physical, is coordinated because the same pattern of variety obtains in each. The same arrangement of diverse items persists at each level of creation, so that the category of stones in its arrangement repeats the pattern of the category of plants, and the category of plants repeats the pattern of the category of animals, and so on up the chain of being to the all-subsuming deity, God Himself. By this scheme, a hierarchy is maintained on a vertical scale. But also each level directly and immediately relates to any other level because it shares a common pattern with that level, so that the lowest, stones, can relate without hindrance to God. Even more remarkable—and here the coadunating tendency appears at its strongest—each level directly and immediately relates to *all* other levels because of the common pattern. The result is symphysis. The common pattern is a unifying factor which incorporates all (see Plates 5, 6, 25, and 51). We have, then, both the multeity of a hierarchy and also the unity of an indiscriminate whole. Donne states the proposition with utmost succinctness: "God made this whole world in such an uniformity, such a correspondency, such a concinnity of parts, as that it was an Instrument, perfectly in tune" (see Plate 39).[10] This consistency of parts is the very source of universal harmony in its literal sense.

Each level of creation, then, shares a common pattern, and this common denominator allows the several levels in the hierarchy to be organized into a homogeneous system. Each level of creation can be expressed in terms of this common denominator, in the abstract terms of this pattern. In fact, all levels of creation can be reduced to this pattern, to this form without substance, to this Pythagorean number. This abstract of cosmos was represented for different purposes by several different numbers: e.g., 3, 8, 9, 10, 12, 24, 100.[11] Most often, though, and most logically, it was represented by the number 4, the tetrad (see pp. 160–174). The four basic qualities arranged as two pairs of opposites—hot and cold, and moist and dry—was the simplest and the most convincing pattern to demonstrate.[12] From this tetrad of qualities a tetrad of elements is readily derived, and from thence can be extrapolated the numerous tetrads required to explain the variety of items at every conceivable level of creation, whether physical or conceptual (see Plates 29–36). In this way the diversity of God's creation is arranged in a single system determined by number, so that cosmic harmony and proportion and order (to use a term each from music, geometry, and astronomy) are achieved. The paradox of God's infinitude and yet His oneness is resolved by palpable example which satisfies even the most meticulous of mathematical minds. The world becomes effective as an intelligible metaphor for God. As Reuchlin said, "The *Tetractys* is the *Divine mind* communicating."[13]

In such a scheme which posits various levels of creation with a common pattern persisting at each level, there is also the corollary assumption of an elaborate network of correspondences between the levels. An item holding a certain position on the horizontal scale

51.

Harmonia Mundi Sympathica, 10 Enneachordis totius naturæ Symphoniam exhibens.

Enneachordon I	Enneach. II	Enneach. III	Enneach. IV	Enneach. V	Enneach. VI	Enneach. VII	Enneach. VIII	Enneach. IX	Enneach. X
Mundus Archetyp. DEVS	*Mundus Sidereus* Cœl.Emp.	*Mundus Mineralis*	*Lapides*	*Plantæ*	*Arbores*	*Aquatilia*	*Volucria*	*Quadrupedia*	*Colores varij*
Seraphim	Firmamentum	Salia,ſtellę Minerales.	Aſtrites	Herbæ & Flor.ſtell.	Frutices Bacciferę	Piſces ſtellares	Gallina Pharaonis	Pardus	Diuerſi Colores
Cherubim	♄ Nete	Plumbum	Topazius	Helleborus	Cypreſſus	Tynnus	Bubo	Aſinus, Vrſus	Fuſcus
Troni	♃ Paranete	Æs	Amethiſtus	Betonica	Citrus	Acipenſer	Aquila	Elephas	Roſeus
Dominationes	♂ Parameſ.	Ferrum	Adamas	Abſynthiũ	Quercus	Pſyphias	Falco Accipiter	Lupus	Flammeus
Virtutes	☼ Meſe	Aurum	Pyropus	Heliotropium	Lotus, Laurus	Delphinus	Gallus	Leo	Aureus
Poteſtates	♀ Lichanos	Stannum	Beryllus	Satyrium	Myrtus	Truta	Cygnus Columba	Ceruus	Viridis
Principatus	☿ Parhypa.	Argentum Viuum	Achates Iaſp is	Pæonia	Maluſpunica	Caſtor	Pſittacus	Canis	Cæruleus
Archangeli	☽ Hypate	Argentum	Selenites Cryſtallus	Lunaria	Colutea	Oſtrea	Anates Anſeres	Ælurus	Candidus
Angeli	Ter.cũEle. Proslamb.	Sulphur	Magnes	Gramina	Frutices	Anguilla	Struthio camelus	Inſecta	Niger

Diapaſon Ditonus
Diapaſon cum Tono
Diapaſon
Heptachordon
Hexachordon
Diapente
Diateſſaron
Ditonus
Tonus

51. "*The sympathetic harmony of the world, demonstrating the symphony of all Nature in ten enneachords*"

The title of this book means "The Universal Work-of-the-Muses." In a chapter called, "Symphonismus Lapidum, Plantarum, Animalium cum Coelo," Kircher offers this diagram setting forth the 9-fold correspondences between ten distinct categories of existence: angels, heavenly spheres, metals, stones, plants, trees, water creatures, winged creatures, four-legged animals, and colors. The diagram when read up-and-down delineates the hierarchical stratification within any given category. The first column, for example, lists the nine orders of angels. When read across, the diagram designates the items which are correspondent in each of the ten categories. For example, cherubim are correspondent to Saturn, lead, the topaz, the hellebore, the cypress, the tunny-fish, the bittern, the ass and the bear, and black. Kircher sees the whole as a unified, harmonious system which reconciles opposites in musical terms of the diapason:

> So that we might better explain "sympathies" and "antipathies" in nature—or what is the same thing, consonance and dissonance—imagine 10 enneachords, all of which are perfectly concordant—that is, the first consists of nine chords and represents the harmonious steps of one diapason, and all the remaining enneachords are concordant with it. In consequence, all the chords, which are measured from the lowest note, sound in unison, just like *hypate, parhypate, lichanos mese,* etc., as appears in the following diagram.
>
> Et ut Sympathias & Antipathias, sive quod idem est consonum & dissonum in natura melius declaremus, imaginare 10 eneachorda, quae omnia in unisonum concordata sint, hoc est, primum 9 chordis constet, gradusque harmonicos unius diapason exprimat, juxta hoc vero reliqua omnia concordentur; id est omnes chordae, quae proslambanomenon referunt unisonum sonent, non secus hypate, parhypate, Lichanos Mese, ut in sequente schemate patet.

Athanasius Kircher, *Musurgia universalis,* 2 vols. (Rome, 1650), II.393.

within a given category will share an identity with an item holding a correspondent position within another category. Each item, in fact, must have its counterpart at each level in the hierarchy, else the common pattern would be violated, as Pico carefully explains, and cosmos destroyed.[14]

The result is a highly articulated network of correspondences which interrelates the various levels of creation, which interconnects the various orders of being and allows intercourse between them. A visual image best serves as the example to make the point precisely. Plate 31 demonstrates how the four elements derive from combinations of the four basic qualities, the standard tetrad configuration. It also demonstrates how each element is correspondent with other items in different categories—for instance, fire is correspondent with summer in the seasonal cycle and with the humour choler in the make-up of man; air is correspondent with spring and with the sanguine humour; and so on. A consequence of these correspondences, of course, is to interrelate the categories in which they appear, the categories of *mundus* (the elements), *annus* (the seasons), and *homo* (the humours). Finally, because these categories reveal the same common pattern, it is implied that they reveal the common pattern which persists throughout the cosmos. Any one category is an abstract in miniature of the whole. By knowing one, we can know the whole. Any one is a metaphor for any other one or for the whole.

This visual image was a renaissance commonplace, as Plates 32–35 testify. There the list of correspondent planes is augmented to include not only the elements, the seasons, and the bodily humours, but also the four ages of man, the cardinal winds, the signs of the zodiac, and the four dominant planets. And actually, the list of correspondent planes can be extended indefinitely—literally *ad infinitum.*

This visual image was re-presented as a verbal image by Spenser in *The Shepheardes Calender*, as discussed in the previous chapter. There Spenser geared man's life to the twelve months and to the four seasons, using words rather than spatial arrangement to demonstrate the correspondences. The way in which Spenser's verbal image works is precisely illustrated by *February*, which according to the argument "conteyneth a discourse of old age." E. K. goes on to note that "the matter very well accordeth with the season of the moneth, the yeare now drouping, and as it were, drawing to his last age." A year which draws to his last age is clearly a metaphor interfusing the categories of *annus* and *homo*. E. K. makes the comparison overt in the next sentence: "For as in this time of yeere, so then in our bodies there is a dry and withering cold." Having conflated man and the seasons in this interchangeable way, E. K. can next speak of "stormes of Fortune, and hoare frosts of Care," as though man's troubles are identical with intemperate winter weather. Spenser's point in the poem is inescapable: there is an indissoluble relationship between the category *homo* and the category *annus*. Of course, he thereby implies the relationship between man and the entire cosmos.

Within the all-inclusive metaphor which is our universe, then, there are innumerable partial metaphors which interrelate its parts and imply the whole. The best known of these—the one relied upon by Spenser in *The Shepheardes Calender*—is the analogy between macrocosm and microcosm, the metaphor that allows transfer of meaning between the great world of nature and the little world of man. This metaphor came to the renaissance fully developed by earlier authors. Alanus de Insulis, for example, one of the medieval writers best known to Spenser, instructs us through a personification named Nature:

> I am she who have fashioned the form and eminence of man into the likeness of the original mundane mechanism, that in him, as in a mirror of the world itself, combined nature may appear. For just as, of the four elements, the concordant discord, the single plurality, the dissonant consonance, the dissenting agreement, produce the structures of the palace of earth, so, of four ingredients the similar unsimilarity, the unequal equality, the unformed conformity, the separate identity, firmly erect the building of the human body. And those qualities which come together as mediators among the elements—these establish a firm peace among the four humors.[15]

The old *Kalendayr of shepheards*, the perennial almanac that E. K. mentions in his dedicatory epistle to Gabriel Harvey, delineates the metaphor in exact detail:

> Some shepeherdes saye that a man is a lytell worlde by hym selfe for the lykenesses and symylitudes that he hathe of the grete worlde whiche is the aggregacyon of the .ix. skyes .iiii. elementes and all thynges in them conteyned. Fyrste man hathe suche a lykenes in the fyrste mobyle y^{t} is the soverayne skye & pryncypall party of the grete worlde for lyke as in this fyrste mobyle the zodyake is devyded in .xii. partyes that ben the .xii. sygnes

> so man is devyded in .xii. partyes. . . . Of ye whiche thre ben of nature of fyre y^t^ is Aries leo & sagittarius & .iii. of nature of the ayre. Gemini libra & aquarius. And thre of the nature of water. Cancer scorpio and pisces. And thre of the nature of erth. Taurus virgo & capricornus.[16]

To show how this metaphor allowed easy transfer of information between various levels of creation, we need only look at the discussion of the cardinal winds in Du Bartas' *Devine weekes and workes:*

> In their effects I finde fower Tempraments,
> Foure Times, foure Ages, and foure Elements.
> Th'*East-wind* in working, followes properly
> Fire, Choller, Summer, and soft Infancie:
> That, which dries-up wild *Affrick* with his wing,
> Resembles Aire, Bloud, Youth, and lively Spring:
> That, which blowes moistly from the *Westerne* stage,
> Like Water, Phlegme, Winter, and heavie Age:
> That, which comes shiv'ring from cold Climates soly,
> Earth, withered Eld, Autumne, and Melancholy.[17]

The tetrad pattern persists in man as in the universe at large, so that by his *concordia discors* man is a microcosm. This metaphor held as an unquestioned premise until well into the seventeenth century. When William Harvey published his *De motu cordis* (London, 1628), he thought he was confirming it.

Examples of this metaphor in the renaissance lie like sands along the shore of the collective unconscious, but none is more concrete or precise than the diagram which fills the title page of Robert Fludd's *Utriusque cosmi . . . historia,* printed at Oppenheim in 1617 (see Plate 52). This visual image of the metaphor is intended to delineate its broad outlines and to intimate its details. The most striking feature of the diagram is the human figure with outstretched limbs inscribed within a circle in a representation of divine geometry (see pp. 193–194, above). This circle, his area, is labelled the microcosm, and its composition is clearly specified. Starting at the center, we have the four elements, indicated by the four humours to which they correspond: *melancholia,* correspondent to earth; *pituita,* or phlegm, correspondent to water; then *sanguis,* correspondent to air; and finally *cholera,* correspondent to fire. Then come the seven spheres of the planets. And the outermost limit of the microcosm is a sphere of fixed stars which contains the constellations designating the twelve signs of the zodiac, each of which controls a part of the body. Correspondent to this circle, which depicts the microcosm in its entirety, is an analogous circle depicting the macrocosm, attended by some obvious difficulties in the visual representation. The two circles, of course, should be congruous, not concentric; the microcosm is not a hole in the middle of the macrocosm.

But the evident difficulty of translating the conceptual into the physical does not seriously impair the statement of the metaphor. We see immediately the correspondence between the macrocosm and the microcosm, and this, more than their spatial arrangement, is the important point. In the macrocosm, as in the microcosm, there should come first the four elements, and they do, indicated by four spheres—though these four spheres are unlabelled because the engraver could not bring himself to situate the four elements so far removed from the geometric center of the diagram. Then come seven spheres for the planets and a final sphere of fixed stars, which firmly sets the limit of the macrocosm. Outside this is the empyrean, depicted in an imaginative way to suggest infinity; and in the upper right, to suggest its eternality, a strange creature representing Time, winged and hoofed and with an hourglass on his head, pulls a rope which rotates the finite universe below him. Microcosm and macrocosm are linked by analogy, a fact which is emphasized by their shared subjection to time. They are joined in the same mortal coil.

In Pythagorean cosmology, since the universe is a system of metaphors such as the microcosm-macrocosm analogy, the method of knowledge consists in the straightforward process of translating meaning from one level of being to another by use of these metaphors. George Herbert makes the point with the precision of a seventeenth-century scientist:

> Man is all symmetrie,
> Full of proportions, one limbe to another,
> And all to all the world besides;
> Each part may call the farthest brother,
> For head with foot hath private amitie,
> And both with moons and tides.
>
> Nothing hath got so farre
> But Man hath got and kept it as his prey;
> His eyes dismount the highest starre;
> He is in little all the sphere.
>
> ("Man," 13–22)

52. *The microcosm and the macrocosm*

As Herbert sees man, we are the tidy summation of the great world, our parts enjoying an internal harmony and at the same time corresponding to portions of external nature such as the stars and the tides. We are an ordered object shaped by cosmic patterns. But we are likewise ordered as a contemplative being. Subjectively, we are also a summation of the world, so that regardless of how distant a thing may be, "Man hath got and kept it as his prey." Our perception of visible phenomena encompasses the universe and thereby makes us an epitome of the macrocosmic sphere.

As a consequence, by following the injunction to know ourselves—*nosce teipsum* (see pp. 263–265, above)—we can learn about the universe, since the microcosm-macrocosm analogy allows for the exchange of knowledge between these two levels. And subsequently we can arrive at knowledge of the deity, since the universe is but a metaphor for God. That is the external route to perception of divine truth through the study of nature, the route first charted by Pythagoras. There is, of course, also an internal route, since the

---

52. Man the microcosm is shown to be exactly correspondent to the macrocosm of the created universe. The human figure inscribed within the circle labelled "microcosmus" extends from the center through the four elements (labelled appropriately by the correspondent humours: *melancholia* for earth, *pituita* for water, *sanguis* for air, and *cholera* for fire), and thence through the seven planetary spheres, terminating at the sphere of fixed stars. In that sphere the constellations are indicated by the signs of the zodiac, and each sign is referred to that member of the body which it controls. The macrocosm is delineated by an exactly comparable structure: four circles which represent the four elements (though unlabelled), then seven planetary spheres, and finally a sphere of fixed stars. In both the microcosm and the macrocosm the sun and moon shine simultaneously and constantly to show that the system is eternal. Separating the finite, created universe—i.e., the microcosm-macrocosm—from the empyrean is a coil of rope which is pulled by a winged and hoofed creature symbolizing Time. This action gives motion to the finite universe and subjects it to the effects of time. This strange emblem of Time is reminiscent of the angel turning the *primum mobile* in Eck's diagram (see Plate 21)—but here he is mythological and pagan rather than Christian, a debased Saturn from the Golden Age.

Robert Fludd, *Utriusque cosmi majoris scilicet et minoris metaphysica, physica atque technica historia*, 4 vols. (Oppenheim 1617–19), I.title page.

individual can relate directly to the deity through sharing the common pattern of cosmos—or, as Genesis expresses the sentiment, man is made in the likeness of God. By knowing himself, man can know the model in Whose image he was made. Whichever the route, notice that this perception of the deity is not a mystic flight into the unconscious or revelation by means of beatific vision. It is an ascent which is controlled and rational, intellectual rather than emotional, completely explicable rather than wondrous.

With such a theory of metaphor as a universal principle, it is easy to postulate several assumptions about the role of the poet. In one sense, his task is lightened by the presence—indeed, the omnipresence—of metaphors. He does not need to fabricate metaphors; they lie everywhere ready to his pen, perhaps even with embarrassing abundance. As Du Bartas observed:

> There's nothing precious in Sea, Earth, or Aire,
> But hath in Heav'n some like resemblance faire. . . .
> And sacred patternes, which to serve all Ages,
> Th'Almighty printed on Heav'ns ample stages.[18]

The job of "making" then becomes not so much a creation of something new, but rather a discovering of something already prescribed in God's book of nature. The creative act rests more in selecting the prefabricated metaphor which is most expressive, rather than in devising with uniqueness or even with novelty. For the poet, therefore, the framing of metaphors is an act of discovery and choice more than of creating *ex nihilo*.

But in another sense, the role of the poet is rendered more difficult. Since he acts in emulation of God, he is enjoined to adhere to divine truth. As Sidney says forthrightly, poetry is "not . . . an Art of lyes, but of true doctrine" (*Defence of poesie*, H1^{v}). The poet's poem, like God's book of nature, must be rigidly structured—and not only in form, but also in thought. His metaphors must satisfy the criterion of truthfulness according to the scheme which God promulgates in the universe. To maintain the truth of his metaphor—to insure that his poem is a genuine product of the imagination rather than of the irresponsible fantasy—the poet must necessarily observe the divinely ordained relationship between the physical world and the conceptual world. Just as the creating godhead translated his archetypal idea into our time-space continuum, so that Plato's world of becoming is a replica in another medium of his world of being (despite imperfections), so also the poet must make sure that his narrative accords with that essential reality which it purports to expound.

The poetic metaphor, in fine, to be valid must be reversible—that is, the reader must be able to translate it back across the border between concrete and conceptual. The meaning must be inherent in the metaphor, not casual or arbitrary. The ontology of the metaphor—what its truth is—is predetermined by cosmology; it is a given. The epistemology of the metaphor—how we are to deal with it—is also fixed by the system of cosmic correspondences which the heavenly maker deployed in the universe.

It is an easy inference, then, to see that the poet as maker contrives a poem which, like the universe, becomes an inclusive metaphor devised by its maker. The poem is a literary microcosm, a proposition we shall consider in the next chapter. Furthermore, within the framework of the total metaphor—what critics call (often without realizing what they are saying) the "universe" of the work—there must be a system of partial metaphors which reproduce the metaphoric system of God's great poem, so that art and nature coincide. In the witty words of Sidney, "The *Poet* . . . bringeth his own stuffe, and doth not learn a Conceit out of a matter, but maketh matter for a Conceit" (*Defence of poesie*, F2^{v}).

In the best of all possible poems, the partial metaphors achieve the same infinite variety that can be discerned in the macro-poem. Then poetry does indeed become divine, or at least performs a sacred function, because it reveals fully and without distortion the intent of God in His own grand design. The subject matter of the book of nature is then successfully paraphrased in the poem of a mortal poet. The poem becomes a valid prophecy of what should be had Adam not fallen, a dependable projection of that beauty which is unattainable to us except in art. It is on these grounds that Sidney most fulsomely praises David for the Psalms, which Sidney calls "his prophecie":

> For what else is the awaking his musical Instruments, the often and free chaunging of persons, his notable *Prosopopeias*, when he maketh you as it were see God comming in his majestie, his telling of the beasts joyfulnesse, and hils leaping, but a heavenly poesie, wherin almost he sheweth himselfe a passionate lover of that unspeakable and everlasting bewtie, to be seene by the eyes of the mind. (*Defence of poesie*, B4)

This license to frame metaphors in translation of the ineffable is what sets the poet above both the historian and the philosopher.

The poet, though, is enjoined to reproduce not only the subject matter of God's metaphor, but also its technique. Just as God extended his metaphor from one level of creation to another until it reached through all the orders of being, so the poet should devise an assemblage of analogies with the hope of providing a continuum of meaning from the highest to the lowest. His poem should be a network of active correspondences, so that much of its meaning is conveyed in the arrangement of its parts, in its structure. Metaphor in such a poetics becomes the major mode of discourse, and structure is itself a metaphor, revealing the divine plan in action. The poet reproduces the subject matter of God's metaphor, which is *natura naturata*; but by reproducing the technique of God's metaphor-making process, the poet simultaneously reveals *natura naturans*.

Such is the theory of metaphor as it evolves by reason out of Pythagorean cosmology. It is a difficult theory to implement in practice, and was never, to my knowledge, employed by any poet to the exclusion of other types of metaphor. Aristotle's theory of metaphor, be it noted, is much simpler: "A metaphor is a word with some other meaning which is transferred either from genus to species, or from species to genus, or from one species to another" (*Poetics*, 1457b)—a definition, incidentally, which emasculates metaphor and makes it a mere exercise in rhetoric.

Although no poet restricted his practice to the Pythagorean theory of metaphor, there were serious efforts to produce poems prominently demonstrating this poetics. An example is the long Latin work of Conrad Celtis, *Quatuor libri amorum,* published in Nuremberg, 1502. The title page displays an elegant tetrad which comprises the four cities at the geographical extremes of Germany, the four bodies of water which mark its boundaries, the four parts of the day, and the four ages of man (see Plate 35); and the work is organized according to this plan. Another example is the *Microcosme* of Maurice Scève published in Paris, 1562, and divided into three books. This long poem of exactly 3,000 lines (a number that Scève calls to our attention in an envoy which is an additional rhyming triplet) opens with this declaration:

Dieu, qui trine en un fus, triple es, et trois seras,
Et, comme tes Eleus nous eterniseras,
De ton divin Esprit enflamme mon courage
Pour descrire ton Homme, et louër ton ouvrage,

Ouvrage vrayement chef d'oeuvre de ta main:
A ton image fait et divin, et humain.

The Shepheardes Calender and *The Faerie Queene*, of course, also represent efforts to implement the Pythagorean theory of metaphor, and as works of art they are much more successful than the poem of Celtis or of Scève.

Although few poets attempted to reproduce the metaphor of God's creation *in toto*, most of them accepted the validity of this theory in principle and applied it in practice whenever opportune. Examples of application in the renaissance are common—more common than in any other period, a fact which suggests that this theory had a special hold upon renaissance poets. In this incidental use, the theory appears in poetry most visibly as a metaphor depending upon the cosmic correspondences. An item on one level of existence is described by comparing it with its correspondent item on another level of existence known to the reader. By this transfer of information from one level to another the poet explains the unknown by means of the known and fulfills the purpose of metaphor. Poets frequently employ a partial metaphor of this sort within the totality of God's inclusive metaphor. Often by this part, a poet implies the whole, so that by a single metaphor he activates the entire system of cosmic correspondences—a possibility to which the critic should be sensitive.

Pierre de la Primaudaye, who was incapable of originality, states the principle of partial metaphors in its conventional formulation and gives it a full exposition. For him, in fact, as for many literary theorists, the principle provided a rationale for all figurative expression; it was "the originall of allegoricall sense." [19] His primary purpose in this passage is to delineate "the division of the universall world," [20] and he begins by repeating from Pico the traditional three-layered structure comprised of the supra-sensible conceptual realm at the top, the quintessential but visible realm of the heavenly bodies in the middle, and the fully sensible realm of the four elements at the bottom:

> The learned and venerable antiquitie figureth, and maketh the universall world (to be) one, and threefold. . . . For there is the uppermost world of all, which Divines name, the Angelicall, and philosophers call the intellectuall world: which (as *Plato* saith) was never yet sufficiently praised. Then is there the celestiall world, or that of the spheres, which succeedeth and is next the

> first: and the third and last is the elementarie world which we inhabite, under the concavitie of the moone.

La Primaudaye meanders on to other matters, and after considerable discussion which points out the distinctive qualities of each realm and yet their interdependence, he gets to the point that is most germane to our discussion. He goes on to state how these three realms are integrated into a single system by the perfect correspondences between their parts. Furthermore, correspondent items within each realm enjoy a certain interchangeability, so their appellations can also be transferred from one realm to another. We can apply to a divine thing the name of the correspondent heavenly or earthly thing, and we can apply to an earthly thing the correspondent divine or heavenly name:

> Oftentimes to divine natures are attributed both celestiall and terrestriall surnames: when as sometimes they are figured by starres: sometimes by wheeles and beasts, and sometimes by elements: as we sometimes also appropriate divine and celestiall names to terrestriall natures.

And then La Primaudaye offers a full-scale explanation justifying the rationale behind this metaphoric practice:

> For even as the three worlds being girt and buckled with the bands of concord doe by reciprocall liberalitie, interchange their natures; the like doe they also by their appellations. And this is the principle from whence springeth and groweth the discipline of allegoricall sense. For it is certaine that the ancient fathers could not conveniently have represented one thing by other figures, but that they had first learned the secret amitie and affinitie of all nature. Otherwise there could be no reason, why they should represent this thing by this forme, and that by that, rather then otherwise. But having the knowledge of the universall world, and of every part thereof, and being inspired with the same spirit, that not onely knoweth all things, but did also make all things: they have oftentimes, and very fitly figured the natures of the one world, by that which they knew to be correspondent thereto in the others.

The poet is justified in using metaphorical language because of the network of correspondences in the universe. It is this reciprocity between levels of existence, in fact, which makes poetry possible, because words are not haphazard in their meaning. Rather, a name has been assigned to an item according to some causal principle which links the name with the inherent qualities of the item and with its place in the cosmic scheme. The name is a manifest sign of the item, its hieroglyph, making known its inner essence.[21] The effective use of language, therefore, depends upon knowledge of "the secret amitie and affinitie of all nature." Moreover, the reader can hope to understand the metaphors only if he shares with the poet this same cosmology: "The same knowledge, and the grace of the same spirit is requisite for those, who would understand, and directly interpret such significations and allegoricall meanings."

Being now on the subject of response to metaphor, La Primaudaye quite plausibly proceeds to posit a fourth world, the microcosm of man, which relates directly to each and all of the other three:

> Moreover besides these worlds, which we have already distinguished, there is also another, a fourth, wherein may likewise be found all that which subsisteth in the others. And this is man.[22]

La Primaudaye anatomizes man in order to show how his faculties provide him with a means of responding to metaphor at any level of creation throughout the chain of being:

> It is a common use in schooles to teach, that man is a little world, and that within him the bodie is composed of the elements, the reasonable soule is celestiall, the vegetable power common to men and plants, the sense common to brute beasts, the reason participated to Angels: and finally the image of God is therein seene & considered.

By being a microcosm, man is capable of response to a partial metaphor wherever it takes place. Moreover, since he is created in the likeness of God, he is capable of subsuming into a continuum his several responses at the various levels, just as God subsumes into Himself all the links of the great chain.[23] In consequence, at the same time that man perceives a partial metaphor at whatever level, he is capable of extrapolating from there to the inclusive metaphor of "the universall world," which is paradoxically "one, and threefold," like the deity. Man, therefore, acting in the image of the godhead, is the medium which gives consistency to the other three realms.[24] By his perception of metaphors he gives unity to the tripartite universe. By understanding metaphors as cosmic correspondence, we resolve the paradox of multeity in unity which is evident in a poem and in the universe. We thereby acquire a status equivalent to the poet and even to the creating deity, because like them we see their work as a whole, *sub specie aeternitatis.* In a sense, we rise above their status because their making—poem or cosmos—has no meaning until it is perceived by us. But here we are calling down vengeance upon our heads, since we are venturing into the dark areas of subjectivity as well as impiousness.

In his overall responsibility, to sum up, the poet labors under the injunction to purvey the eternal verities, to place the celestial values within the reach of his mortal readers. He bears the onus of making verbally carnate a truth that is otherwise tenuous and elusive. As Shakespeare said, the poet "gives to airy nothing/A local habitation and a name"; or as Milton put it rather more officiously, he should "justify the ways of God to men." The poet is charged to render the highest intelligible to the lower.

But in the actual writing of his poem, the poet is more often working in the opposite direction. Rather than bringing down from above, he is raising up from below. Philip Sidney states the proposition in dignified terms when he says that poetry, of all the arts, most readily produces the "knowledge to lift up the minde from the dungeon of the bodie, to the enjoying his owne divine essence." [25] As an immediate situation, the poet needs to explain something in the here-and-now. He needs to explain a particular and endow it with lasting significance. He wants to give ulterior meaning to what would otherwise remain an isolated datum. To elude the restrictive fragmentation of experience, he draws upon the accepted system of analogies in the universe and describes the item by means of a metaphor. By devising a comparison within the familiar framework of cosmic correspondences, he invokes the Pythagorean cosmos and gives his particular fact both a place in the total scheme and a meaning—"a local habitation and a name."

For example, when wishing to describe the duty of the king to maintain order in his society, the poet need only say that the king is a sun, and the reader automatically makes the transfer of knowledge from heaven to earth and back to heaven. The correspondence between king and sun is belabored by Du Bartas in a passage of 14 lines for which Sylvester supplied this marginal gloss: "The Sunne as Prince of the Celestiall lightes marcheth in the midst of the other sixe Planets which environ him." [26] From the fund of common knowledge, the reader knows that the sun has three planets on each side of him and that he benevolently regulates their motion. In his commentary on the description of the Sun's palace which opens

Book II of Ovid's *Metamorphoses,* George Sandys develops the metaphor in its full dimension:

> The Sunne is . . . a King of the other Starres, from whom they receave their honour: his courtiers, the Houres, Dayes, Months, Yeares, and Ages; the Spring, Summer, Autumne, and Winter: being not only their Lord and moderator, but their father; the measure and vicissitude of Time proceeding from his motion.[27]

The metaphor therefore allows the reader to conclude that the king should control those around him in the same natural, benevolent, and complete way in which the sun controls the planets. And if the metaphor is valid, the reader can then reverse its applicability and translate its meaning back from the mundane level to the celestial. The sun rules like a king.

Here the poet is working not only deductively, bringing the divine scheme into human consciousness, but also he is working inductively, bringing sense data to bear on heavenly truths. A priori the poet and reader concur that the sun maintains order in the heavens as God has decreed. Applying this pattern at the level of human affairs, the poet can consequently convey to the reader how the king should behave toward his subordinates. The sun-king metaphor allows the poet to explain the unknown to the reader (the king's duties) in terms of what the reader does know (the sun's duties). But then the reader leaves off his passive role as listener and assumes an active role as participant in the metaphor making. The reader proceeds to draw upon his own observation of the world, his own experience, and thereby inductively corroborates the poet's metaphor, incidentally affirming the cosmic correspondence.

Of course, the reader might have a set of experiences which deny the validity of the metaphor. He would then refuse to participate in the metaphor making, and would deny the validity of the poem. Or—a most interesting possibility—the poet might exploit this opportunity that the prefabricated metaphor offers, and say in effect: "I am employing this metaphor, this assumed correspondence, merely as an hypothesis; let's test its validity in the light of the following fictive action."

Shakespeare often enunciates cosmic correspondences and other conventional metaphors with this ambiguous intention. The metaphor is profitable, of course, as a direct statement of meaning since it is the common currency of the intellectual marketplace. But also the metaphor can serve the larger purpose of establishing a norm which is then to be analyzed and tested. The metaphor, a previously unquestioned premise, is set up like the proverbial straw man, and its presuppositions are debated and modified and sometimes denied. This is a cautious way of calling into question what have earlier been accepted as self-evident truths.

Early in *Troilus and Cressida* (I.iii.78–137), for example, Ulysses' long speech on "the specialty of rule" posits in absolute terms the need for authority in the community, and the rest of the play examines what happens in actual fact, since leaders are only mortal and therefore imperfect. Ulysses' speech places before us by familiar metaphors the concept of natural order, which the action of the play submits to ruthless analysis. Similarly in *Henry V* and in *Coriolanus* Shakespeare early proclaims a cliché of social organization—the Archbishop of Canterbury's speech on the beehive in *Henry V* (I.ii.183–206) and Menenius' speech on the body politic in *Coriolanus* (I.i.94–152). Having established an accepted norm by the use of metaphor, the playwright then proceeds to demonstrate the complexity of its meaning. In each of these instances the play can be seen as a bodying forth in dramatic dimension of the conceit contained in the cosmic metaphor, with all of its ramifications when realized in human terms.

Shakespeare most stringently tests the validity of a cosmic correspondence in *Richard II*, when in Act III he introduces the sun-king analogy at the dramatic climax of the play—Richard's return from Ireland. After his loss of power, Richard is repeatedly likened to the sun, with obvious irony—and with the equally obvious intention of calling the metaphor into doubt.[28] Shakespeare is asking if the comparison of the king and the sun is a viable hypothesis, and by the action of his play he provides a negative answer. In fact, anyone who relies on the validity of the metaphor, like Richard, is in for a hard time. By refuting the presuppositions of this metaphor, Shakespeare furthermore calls into question the whole scheme of cosmic order—its operation in human affairs, at least, if not its existence as a principle. There are no sun-kings in this world, he says. Both Richard and Bolingbroke when measured against the sun-king ideal are shown to be lamentably deficient in one way or another. No one can fill the role of God's vice-regent on earth. Perhaps the role itself is only a figment of the human imagination, devised by the naïve for the comfort of an anguished spirit or by the politically aggressive for manipulation in the struggle for power.

The sun-king analogy permeates *Richard II*, giving shape to the play. It is a soul which informs the visible body of the dramatic action. Conversely, transferring meaning from a lower to a higher level, we can say that the metaphor allows us to transcend the historical facts of the play and perceive their ulterior significance. The metaphor permits intercourse between the human and the cosmic, and thereby interrelates the two levels, allowing us to participate in a much broader frame of experience than the bare facts would allow. This metaphor makes the difference between a chronicle and a play—as Sidney would quickly point out, between history and poetry.

To bring up a sharply different use of metaphor, we might consider the opening lines of *The passionate mans pilgrimage* by Walter Raleigh:

> Give me my Scallop shell of quiet,
> My staffe of Faith to walke upon,
> My Scrip of Joy, Immortal diet,
> My bottle of salvation,
> My Gown of Glory, hope's true gage;
> And thus Ile take my pilgrimage.
>
> (ll. 1–6)

Raleigh is not using the metaphor of cosmic correspondences in this stanza, but rather metaphors derived from Christian symbols. The system of Christian symbols, of course, is just as conventional as the system of cosmic correspondences—that is, the poet is drawing upon the same sort of prefabricated metaphor accepted in advance by both poet and reader. So the *subject matter* of Raleigh's metaphors differs from the subject matter of metaphors depending upon cosmic correspondences, but the *method* of his metaphors does not. By using Christian symbols, Raleigh is attempting to transfer meaning from one level of existence to another. What the scallop shell of the pilgrim stands for in the conceptual Christian scheme is equated with the peace of mind which the mortal pilgrim seeks in this world.

What is particularly noteworthy in Raleigh's use of metaphor, however—and indeed what gives distinction to this opening—is the consistency with which the poet stays on the conceptual level. There is almost no physical content in this passage, nothing for the senses to perceive. As the poet prepares to make a pilgrimage, he collects about him those necessities for the journey: peace of mind, faith, joy, hope of salvation, hope of glory. The scallop shell has no physical qualities to make it an acceptable symbol of quiet; in fact, the roaring of a shell when held against the ear militates against the metaphor. But because the scallop shell designated a pilgrim to St. James of Compostella, it suggested the concept of peace acquired through penance. Similarly for the other items—the staff of faith, scrip of joy, bottle of salvation, and gown of glory—they are not conveyed as physical entities. There is no inherent physical relationship between the concept and its objective correlative—between salvation and a bottle, for example, or between joy and a food bag. The metaphors remain as concepts, constructs of the mind. Only the staff of faith ventures into the realm of physicality; the staff is a symbol of faith because, conceptually, faith supports the pilgrim on his difficult journey to heaven, just as, physically, a staff supports a traveler on the highway. This last metaphor functions on both the physical and the conceptual planes, and in consequence is the most expressive of the list.

But otherwise, Raleigh's metaphors are concepts with but the barest reference to objects. The poet barely ventures into physical experience. The result is an other-worldly, saintly ambiance which appeals to the reader's mind, activates his imagination so that it "represent[s] unto the soule all maner of bewtifull visions," as Puttenham said (see p. 297, above). The reader's soul, under the poet's guidance, "travels to the land of heaven" (line 10), and views a new Jerusalem. In this scene opened before the mind's eye, the laws of nature are suspended, so that there are "silver mountains" (line 11) and "milken hill[s]" (line 16); and equally wondrous, the corruption inherent in physical nature has been overcome. But this is a limited view of reality, avowedly a mystic vision, one that takes us away from our sense experience. It is an "O altitudo!" but not a *probatum est*.

To provide a sharp contrast to Raleigh's poem, we might profitably examine a passage from Marlowe's *Hero and Leander*, a work which is relentlessly natural to the point of being amoral. At the start, in fact, the poet says without equivocation:

> It lies not in our power to love, or hate,
> For will in us is over-rul'd by fate.
> (i.167–168)

Fate, the predetermined course of events, controls our lives. The story is therefore unrolled as one of these predetermined occurrences, an episode in the mindless workings of the universe. It is not a tragedy because the characters are never faced with any moral choices. There are no internal struggles in the souls of the lovers, no ulterior meanings in their actions or in their destinies, no philosophical intentions on the part of the poet. He keeps his poem consistently in this world. The point is well demonstrated by his use of metaphor, as for example when he describes the buskins of Hero when she first walks into the poem:

> Buskins of shels all silvered used she,
> And brancht with blushing corall to the knee;
> Where sparrowes pearcht, of hollow pearle and gold,
> Such as the world would woonder to behold:
> Those with sweet water oft her handmaid fils,
> Which as shee went would cherupe through the bils.
> (i.31–36)

This is metaphor, although submerged, because by associating Hero with sea creatures and sparrows it tells us something about her natural beauty and potential fecundity. And it also says something about the artifice which she has used to enhance her native endowments: the shells are silvered, the sparrows are made of pearl and gold, and they chirrup by an artificial device. But the point to make is that this comparison per se is between physical things only and stays on the physical plane. The buskins, and consequently Hero, are depicted as coordinates of sea animals and birds visually described. Everything here is unilaterally physical, where Marlowe of course intended his poem to remain.

Like Raleigh's *Pilgrimage*, Marlowe's *Hero and Leander* is kept on a single level by the use of metaphor. But the technique by which the poet bends metaphor to his purpose is different in each instance. Raleigh's metaphors are random associations—there is no reason, for example, why joy should be a scrip rather than a bottle, or why salvation should be a bottle rather than a scrip. By denying the relationship between the concept and its objective correlative, Raleigh minimizes the importance of the physical component of the metaphor and thereby minimizes the importance of physicality. The result is a poem that transpires almost wholly in the conceptual realm. In contrast, Marlowe achieves the unilateral physicality of his poem in a different manner, simply by ignoring any level other than the physical. His metaphors have no conceptual component. In neither case, then, is there "metaphor" in the special sense of the term as we have defined it within the coordinates of Pythagorean cosmology. There is little transfer of meaning from one level to another.

There is no denying the excellence of Raleigh's *Pilgrimage* or of

Marlowe's *Hero and Leander*. Each is a masterpiece in its own right. But each is a *tour de force*, an adroit accomplishment without the compelling conviction of truth. Both excite our interest, but we believe neither. In fact, we recognize that each in its own way is nothing more than wish fulfillment, a fantastical projection into a never-never land, a compensation laboriously devised to counteract what the author had actually experienced as reality. Poems like these bring down upon poetry the charge of feigning and lying. Neither offers a reality that we can verify by our own experience and therefore that we can accept as truth. Raleigh and Marlowe achieve success within their intended limits, but that is only partial success—perhaps art for art's sake.

Complete success in poetry depends upon the interfusion of physical and conceptual reality, so that the poetic statement is relevant in either context. Only the most consummate poets have consistently managed this feat, and yet this is the distinctive mark of the greatest poetry—indeed, the special function of poetry—to show the interdependence of conceptual and physical, of ideal and real, of divine and mundane. The poet is superior to the historian and to the philosopher, said Sidney—and to all other artisans—because he combines the particularity of fact with the permanence of essential truth.

For examples of this supreme metaphor which functions coordinately on both the physical and the conceptual level we turn of course to the supreme masters of the poetic art. A lesser artisan can achieve it on occasion, but very few can pull it off with any frequency or can sustain individual metaphors to any extent. Shakespeare's greatness lies in many virtues—his facility with words, his sense of the theatre, his insight into human nature, and numerous others. But certainly one of his sturdiest virtues is this power to create full-dimensional metaphors of the cosmic sort that we are looking for. Examples abound throughout his work. His sonnet sequence, in fact, is a tissue of them. But for the sake of continuity in this study, we might proceed from *Richard II* to look at another example of how Shakespeare used the sun-king analogy. In *Troilus and Cressida* Ulysses gives a now famous argument for the necessity of order in the commonwealth. The passage has been much discussed of late, but not yet fully appreciated because we have not yet recognized that the *technique* of dynamic metaphor contributes as much to the meaning of Shakespeare's analogy as does its subject matter.

In Ulysses' speech, the inclusive metaphor is a comparison between the ordered celestial spheres and the ranks of human society. As Ulysses asserts:

> The heavens themselves, the planets and this center,[29]
> Observe degree, priority, and place.
>
> (I.iii.85–86)

He then goes on to define the responsibilities of the king in terms of what the sun does. In emulation of Sol, who holds the mid-most position as number four among the seven heavenly planets, the king should exercise the strongest authority in the commonweal:

> And therefore is the glorious planet Sol
> In noble eminence enthroned and sphered
> Amidst the other, whose medicinable eye
> Corrects the ill aspects of planets evil,
> And posts like the commandment of a king,
> Sans check to good and bad.
>
> (I.iii.89–94)

The king is like the sun in his physical aspects of brilliance and power, and he sits in the midst of his courtiers as the sun sits in the middle of the planets. But this comparison is effective also because of its conceptual significance, because the sun represents the concepts of goodness, beauty, and truth in the Platonic tradition, the concepts of divinity and providence in the Christian tradition, and the concept of beneficent cosmic control in the Aristotelian tradition. For Ulysses, the comparison of king to sun explains the necessary but neglected social order in terms of the well-known relationships in the celestial realm. The microcosm of human society and the macrocosm of the celestial spheres are shown to be correspondent, interdependent. And this thematic statement is confirmed by the way in which metaphors function. The metaphor demonstrates by its own dynamics that meaning can be transferred from one level to another, that the heavenly and the mundane are interchangeable.

In the sun-king analogy the interchange between human and celestial is a premise of the metaphor. The cosmic correspondence is a foregone conclusion, an accepted statement of the subject. But metaphor can interrelate human and heavenly by its technique alone, without depending upon a subject matter which assumes the relationship in advance. This type of metaphor, the most difficult of all, is the forte of Spenser. In fact, he narrates *The Faerie Queene* as a series of such metaphors which interconnect with similar metaphors to provide a complex network of images that comment on one another. The result is a narrative which moves easily between our time-space continuum and the farthest reaches of abstract speculation. At different times it centers at various points along this all-inclusive progression, but it always implies the whole at least in latency, and thereby firmly interrelates the possible extremes of our experience and all the intervening possibilities as well. One example of Spenser's achievement must suffice for our present purpose.

In Book I of *The Faerie Queene* Archimago soon separates Red Crosse from Una. Then in Canto iv the knight's new-found ladylove, Duessa, leads him to the palace of Lucifera, a female figure embodying the cardinal sin of pride. As Duessa and Red Crosse travel along the road, the palace of Lucifera suddenly looms before them: "a goodly building, bravely garnished,/The house of mightie Prince it seemd to bee" (I.iv.2.6–7). This initial description of Lucifera's house is unabashedly complimentary, wholly approbative. At first glance the palace is a handsome building of impressive dimensions. But after traveling this far along the quest for holiness we know, even if Red Crosse doesn't, that appearances are deceptive. We are, in fact, warned here to be wary by the narrator's comment that the building "seemd to bee" as described; perhaps it *seemed* to be, but actually wasn't. For a reader with any experience of Spenser's method—indeed, for a reader with any sensitivity to poetry—it is clear that as the narrative proceeds we must distinguish between what the narrator describes and what is true in the situation. We must distinguish between appearance and actuality, between the visual image and its ulterior meaning. We must posit two levels, illusion (which is evanescent) and reality (which is permanent). Moreover—and this is the difficult part for both poet and reader—we must seek a relationship between these two levels. How do they impinge upon one another? How do they imply one another? It is the special function of metaphor to accomplish this interrelationship.

In Spenser's ontology, the level of illusion is the level of sense experience and the level of reality is the heavenly level. To comprehend Spenser properly, we must see that the human is coordinate with illusion. Therefore what the eye perceives as visual image or the ear perceives as aural image cannot be trusted, cannot be taken for attested truth.[30] The visual and aural elements of a metaphor, its physical component, must be regarded suspiciously and declared unreliable. The point is demonstrated with utmost clarity when

Red Crosse and Duessa arrive at the gates of Lucifera's palace and the edifice is described in considerable physical detail. Like an imitative poet who wishes to paint a picture, Spenser constructs a vivid visual image for the mind's eye:

> A stately Pallace built of squared bricke,
> Which cunningly was without morter laid,
> Whose wals were high, but nothing strong, nor thick,
> And golden foile all over them displaid,
> That purest skye with brightnesse they dismaid:
> High lifted up were many loftie towres,
> And goodly galleries farre over laid,
> Full of faire windowes, and delightfull bowres;
> And on the top a Diall told the timely howres.
>
> (I.iv.4.1–9)

But of course in this stanza Spenser is not merely following the dictum *ut pictura poesis*. He is not merely painting a picture, providing a representational image of an object. Relating the illusory to the real, the human to the heavenly, cannot be accomplished in that fashion. To take the visual image per se as the sum total of this stanza, or even as one of its major concerns, is to misread the poet. The visual image is itself illusory, and is clearly stated to be so.

For every detail in the physical description of Lucifera's palace, there is a proviso which calls its appearance into question. What the eye cannot perceive, if the truth be known, is more important than the visible facts. The walls, for example, are high, but in no wise strong or thick. This information, supplied by the poet though unavailable to our senses, causes us to revaluate our opinion of the architect who "cunningly" laid the brick without mortar. Bricks, even though to the eye they fit snugly together, require a bonding agent for strength. The word "cunningly" requires an ambiguous reading—at first glance it may seem a term of approval which lauds the architect's skill; but mature thought suggests a sinister meaning such as "deceptively." In similar fashion, the golden foil spread over the exterior of the palace makes it appealing to the senses; but sober judgment decrees that such gaudy display is inappropriate to a human habitat, which should not compete with the heavens for brightness. The many lofty towers in this context become shameful products of human haughtiness; or still worse, impious threats against heaven like the Tower of Babel. Even the goodly galleries extend so far that they are incipiently unstable, suggesting that the palace is built upon a shifting foundation of appearances, as Spenser specifies in the next stanza. In such a building, even fair windows and delightful bowers must be construed as seductive delusions.

Finally—and this is the most telling detail of all—this house of pride is surmounted by a sundial which marks the passing hours. This gorgeous edifice, despite its high walls and golden foil and lofty towers, is subject to time. In actuality, it is a paltry, mortal thing, certainly nothing of lasting value. By placing a clock as the copestone of his description, Spenser allows us to read Lucifera's palace as an icon for all that falls within time's jurisdiction. The edifice can well be interpreted as an emblem of the finite universe, of our time-space continuum. By simple transfer it can then be seen also as an emblem of the human body, the microcosm.[31] As we recall from the title page of Fludd's *Utriusque cosmi . . . historia* (Plate 52), the macrocosm and the microcosm are correspondent and both are bound together in time's control.

All along in his description, then, Spenser demonstrates the untrustworthiness of sense experience, of visual image. But yet it is by means of the visual image that we must come to know the ulterior truth; we must use the data of the physical level to arrive at the conceptual. It is here that assumptions about the validity of metaphor in Pythagorean cosmology become operative and provide a rationale for proceeding from the lower to the higher level. Just as the sense-perceptible world is a replica, although an imperfect one, of essential reality, so the sense-perceptible components of the metaphor are an image of its higher meaning. We can take a useful tip from Thomas Elyot, who in *The castel of health* repeats ancient advice about interpreting our sense impressions in the sublunary world of the four elements:

> It is to be remembred, that none of the sayd elementes be commonly sene or felt of mortal men, as they are in their originall being: but they, whiche by our senses be perceyved, be corupted with mutual mixture, and be rather erthy, watry, airy, and fyry, than absolutely erth, water, ayre, & fyre.[32]

To arrive at some notion of essential reality behind our daily experience, we take our perception of nature and remove from it the imperfections and accidents. That is the process by which we interpret God's metaphor, the universe, in order to discover first principles. Similarly, to interpret a poet's metaphor, to arrive at some notion of essential reality from perception of his metaphor, we must refine it of imperfections and accidents.

In sum, to see the enduring values behind Lucifera's deceptive facade we repair the inadequacies and errors in the plan of her palace. We recognize that even squared brick require mortar, that walls must be strong and thick as well as high, that gaudy display and aspiring thoughts and sensual pleasures do not last but are delusions in a mutable world. Sin, as we know from Dante as well as theologians, is simply the negative of some heavenly value; it has no existence in its own right, and in fact can be defined only as the absence of or the denial of something good. Pride, therefore, is simply the negative aspect of that virtue which in its positive manifestation would be called integrity or self-respect. The positive value, which is the real, is implied by the negative, confirmed by the opposite.[33] Spenser erects the palpable image of Lucifera's palace, then, to reflect by a mirror-like reversal what the mind should perceive on the conceptual level. In the speculum of the visual representation, the mind perceives the concept of pride as deceptive display; and by easy extrapolation, it goes on to perceive what should be, which is the mirror image of what is. The theory of metaphor permits this mental extrapolation from the human level to the heavenly. Though illusory, the human level is related to the real because the poet's metaphor shares validity with God's.

In the visit of Red Crosse to Lucifera's palace, Spenser implies what should be by *indirect* means, by offering its mirror image to the mind's eye. In another prominent passage of *The Faerie Queene,* however, in which again he uses a palace as an icon for the human body, he pursues a different method and presents what should be by *direct* means. The house of Alma in Book II is also a "goodly castle" (II.ix.10.3), but its walls, though built of earth not brick, are sturdy and repel attack. Canto ix of Book II opens with an authorial comment which makes us privy to the poet's intention, as so many opening stanzas do in *The Faerie Queene:*

> Of all Gods workes, which do this world adorne,
> There is no one more faire and excellent,
> Then is mans body both for powre and forme,
> Whiles it is kept in sober government;
> But none then it, more fowle and indecent,
> Distempred through misrule and passions bace:
> It growes a Monster, and incontinent
> Doth loose his dignitie and native grace.
> Behold, who list, both one and other in this place.
> (II.ix.1.1–9)

Spenser tells us unequivocally that the house of Alma, being a house in order, is a "faire and excellent" example of God's handiwork. But he teaches by negative as well as positive example, and he expects us to recall also at this point the "fowle and indecent" house of Lucifera. The house of Lucifera comments on the house of Alma, and like counterpoint, vice versa. "Behold, who list, both one and other in this place."

Of course, there is in the narrative an exact contrast to the house of Lucifera much closer to it than is the house of Alma. The house of Celia occurs in the same book of *The Faerie Queene* with the house of Lucifera, and in fact holds a place in Book I symmetrical with it. This edifice, like the house of Alma and unlike the house of Lucifera, is a positive model of what should be. It is well governed by Celia, who runs the household with wisdom, compassion, and joy (I.x.3). From Celia's rooftop Red Crosse sees a panoply of heavenly glory, whereas, by contrast, he sees in Lucifera's basement a hellish scene of human misery. The house of Lucifera and the house of Celia also comment upon one another.

Not only does Lucifera's palace have its *opposite* within the structure of Book I, but also it has a reiterative counterpart which precedes it and preconditions our response to it. The house of pride must be compared to the den of error in Canto i, the generic manifestation of evil that Red Crosse faces first. Just as "a broad high way . . ./All bare through peoples feet" (I.iv.2.8–9) leads to Lucifera's palace, so also "pathes and alleies wide,/With footing worne" (I.i.7.7–8) lead to Error's cave. This inviting road to evil recalls the path to the left in the Pythagorean letter Y (see pp. 269–272, above). Or here more immediately applicable is the familiar statement in Matthew: "Wide is the gate, and broad is the way, that leadeth to destruction, and many there be which go in thereat" (vii.13).

In the house of Lucifera, then, Spenser creates a metaphor for which there is no predetermined meaning dictated by the system of cosmic correspondences. The poet writes wholly within the context of his own subject matter. But the metaphor works—i.e., it conveys meaning to us—because we subscribe to the theory of metaphor within the Pythagorean cosmology. Our universe, which is God's metaphor, allows an interchange of meaning between various levels of existence; therefore the poet's metaphor, by maintaining the assumptions of God's metaphor, can similarly relate the human to the heavenly. In consequence, with this heady knowledge we can in company with Theseus' poet allow our eye to roll in a fine frenzy, glancing from earth to heaven and back again from heaven to earth in a continuous movement of interrelating and correlating the several levels of our experience. The speculum of the poet's metaphor, like the speculum of God's metaphor, allows us to see a double vision: the perfection of what should be as well as the inadequacy of what is.

Moreover, to clarify his intention in this metaphor depicting the habitat of pride, Spenser places it in a network of metaphors that reinforce or refute it—or perhaps better, reinforce it by refutation. The den of error with its path of easy access prepares us for Lucifera's palace, and helps us see its dangerous deceptiveness. The two metaphors provide corroborative evidence about evil. Conversely, the house of Celia placed symmetrically with the house of pride in the structure of Book I provides a positive statement of what should be and shows up Lucifera's palace for what it really is, a false facade. Spenser extends his network of metaphors so far that at the end of Book II the house of Alma is still commenting upon the house of pride. The house of Alma is correspondent in the total structure of *The Faerie Queene* with the house of Celia—it holds in Book II the same position that the house of Celia holds in Book I; and therefore it holds a relation to the house of pride analogous to that held by the house of Celia. But also the house of Alma has a direct structural relation with the house of pride itself. Just as the episode of Lucifera's palace comes early in Red Crosse's quest for holiness and depicts the human body in its fallen state, a proper theme for a book dealing with ethics in the framework of religion, so also the episode of Alma's palace comes late in Guyon's quest for temperance and depicts the human body in its well-tempered state, a proper theme for a book dealing with ethics in the framework of physical nature.

Spenser's universe in *The Faerie Queene,* quite evidently, has its own system of correspondences. Spenser, of course, is acting wholly in accord with the postulates of his poetics. He is making metaphors in order to transfer meaning from one level to another and thereby to relate the various levels of existence. And the technique of metaphor urges the reader to participate in this dynamic exercise in epistemology and instructs him how to go about it.

To conclude, the doctrine of metaphor as cosmic correspondence depends upon an orthodox view that our world is made up of separate but interrelated parts—that it is a *uni*verse. Moreover, it depends upon the assumption that each of these parts in its interior organization is analogous to each of the other parts, that a single pattern of order subsists throughout all levels of creation. In such a self-contained and coordinated arrangement, the poet can readily find a comparison by which to explain the unknown. Metaphors are strewn in great abundance about our feet, and the poet's particular talent lies in discovering them, his particular task in revealing them. When the notion of *uni*verse broke down in the seventeenth century, however, when the new scientists displaced the four elements from the center of our world and removed its finite boundaries, the poet could no longer rely upon natural metaphors. He no longer had a ready-made supply of incontrovertible comparisons. The poet then had to contrive his own comparisons, and a known by which to explain an unknown was hard to come by. This change in cosmology and epistemology had a profound effect upon poetics.[34] The demand that poets devise original metaphors, and the corollary that poets were now free to contrive their metaphors however they might choose, prompted Samuel Johnson's strong censure of the metaphysical poets: "Their thoughts are often new, but seldom natural. . . . The most heterogeneous ideas are yoked by violence together." [35] Although Dr. Johnson might not agree that he was being gothic in his orthodoxy, he was in fact bewailing the end of an era when ultimate reality lay comfortably nestled in a benign empyrean which was reassuringly knowable because of the efficacy of metaphors.

Notes

[1] Note *metaphor* < Gr. μετά "into the middle of" + φέρειν, "to carry" = L. *transferre*. Sir Thomas Browne illustrates how to use the word in a literal sense: "An horn is the Hieroglyphick of authority, power and dignity, and in this *Metaphor* is often used in Scripture" ("Of the picture of Moses with horns," *Pseudodoxia epidemica* [V.ix] in *Works*, ed. Geoffrey Keynes, 6 vols. [London, 1928–31], III.111–112; italics mine).

[2] Cf. *The defence of poesie* (William Ponsonby; London, 1595), D1^{v}.

[3] Guillaume Saluste du Bartas, *Devine weekes and workes*, tr. Joshua Sylvester (London, 1605), p. 6.

[4] The concept of nature as a book to be read by the questioning eyes of mortals is widespread and long-standing; cf. Ernst R. Curtius, *European Literature and the Latin Middle Ages*, tr. Willard R. Trask (New York, 1953), pp. 319–326. Ample documentation of this commonplace is provided by Georg Horn in a chapter with the heading "Mundus bibliotheca":

> Augustine (*De doctrina Christiana*, Book I) and Nicephorus (VIII.xl) report that when Antonius the Hermit was asked by a philosopher, "How might we know heavenly things, since there are no books about them," he replied: "This universal book of the world takes the place of a library, and always and everywhere it lies open to men."

> *August.* l.1 de doctrina Christiana & *Niceph.* l.8 c.40 referunt Antonium Eremitam à Philosopho interrogatum: quomodo res sublimes contemplare-

> tur, quum nullos libros haberet: respondisse: *Universum hunc mundi librum sibi Bibliothecae loco esse, hanc omni tempore & ubivis, homini praesto esse*

(*Historiae philosophiae libri septem* [Leyden, 1655], p. 333).

[5] *A natural history* (London, 1693), A4. Of course, Blount is only repeating what the Duke in *As You Like It* had already told us:

> And this our life, exempt from public haunt,
> Finds tongues in trees, books in the running brooks,
> Sermons in stones, and good in everything.
> (II.i.15–17)

[6] John Dee, for example, justified the study of astronomy by this argument:

> Now if you way well with your selfe but this litle parcell of frute *Astronomicall*, as concerning the bignesse, Distances of *Sonne*, *Mone*, *Sterry Sky*, and the huge massines of *Ha Rakia* [i.e., the firmament], will you not finde your Consciences moved, with the kingly Prophet, to sing the confession of Gods Glory, and say, *The Heavens declare the glory of God, and the Firmament (Ha Rakia) sheweth forth the workes of his handes*. And so forth, for those five first staves, of that kingly Psalme. Well, well, It is time for some to lay hold on wisedome, and to Judge truly of thinges: and not so to expound the Holy word, all by Allegories: as to Neglect the wisedome, powre and Goodnes of God, in, and by his Creatures, and Creation to be seen and learned. By parables and Analogies of whose natures and properties, the course of the Holy Scripture, also, declareth to us very many Mysteries. The whole Frame of Gods Creatures, (which is the whole world,) is to us, a bright glasse: from which, by reflexion, reboundeth to our knowledge and perceiverance, Beames, and Radiations: representing the Image of his Infinite goodnes, Omnipotency, and wisedome

("Mathematicall praeface" in Euclid, *The elements*, tr. Henry Billingsley [London, 1570], b2).

[7] (London, 1614), p. 1.

[8] *The arte of English poesie* (London, 1589), C2v. The notion that God can be perceived in the courses of the stars is an ancient precept, having behind it, as one of many, the authority of Plutarch. In his *De placitis philosophorum*, Plutarch includes a section entitled "From whence it came that Men had the notion of God," in which he deals with the visible heavens (with a quote from Euripides and an echo from Plato) as a metaphor for the deity:

> To consummate and accomplish the beautie of the world, there be the celestiall signes which appeare unto our eie; for the oblique circle of the Zodiake, is embelished with twelve divers and sundry images. [There follows a twelve-line poem describing the signs of the zodiac.] . . . Besides an innumerable sort of other configurations of starres, which God hath made in the like arches and rotundities of the world; whereupon Euripides wrote thus:
>
> The starrie splendour of the skie,
> which χρόνον some do call,
> The woondrous worke of that most wise
> Creatour, Lord of all.
>
> Thus then we apprehended heereby, the notion of God

("Opinions of Philosophers" [I.vi] in *The morals*, tr. Philemon Holland [London, 1603], p. 809). This notion became commonplace in the renaissance, as Du Bartas bears witness; cf. *Devine weekes and workes*, tr. Sylvester (1605), pp. 483–484. Cf. also the note on Spenser's envoy to *The Shepheardes Calender* (p. 323, n. 48, above) and Chapman's interpretation of Achilles' shield (pp. 379–381, below).

[9] See Meyer H. Abrams, *The Mirror and the Lamp* (Oxford Univ. Press, 1953), esp. pp. 21–26, 47–69, 226–244.

[10] "A Lent-Sermon Preached at White-hall, February 12. 1618" in *The Sermons*, ed. George R. Potter and Evelyn M. Simpson, 10 vols. (Univ. of California Press, 1953–62), II.170.

[11] See Plates 4, 26, 51. The number 10 and its multiples (especially its square 100) provide an abstract of cosmos because 10 is the number of perfection (see p. 84, above).

[12] As Plato noted in the *Timaeus*, the simplest stable system is comprised of two pairs of opposites joined by two shared means; see pp. 160–161, above.

[13] *De arte cabalistica libri tres*, tr. Thomas Stanley, in *The history of philosophy*, 2nd ed. (London, 1687), p. 571.

[14] In the "Second Proem" to his *Heptaplus*, Pico postulates that the universe is stratified into three orders of being: the elementary world (our habitation), the celestial world (the visible heavens), and the supercelestial world (the abode of the angels and God). Then he makes the point which is cogent to my argument:

> It should above all be observed, a fact on which our purpose almost wholly depends, that these three worlds are one world, not only because they are all related by one beginning and to the same end, or because regulated by appropriate numbers they are bound together both by a certain harmonious kinship of nature and by a regular series of ranks, but because whatever is in any of the worlds is at the same time contained in each, and there is no one of them in which is not to be found whatever is in each of the others. If we have understood him rightly, I believe that this was the opinion of Anaxagoras, as expounded by the Pythagoreans and the Platonists. Truly, whatever is in the lower world is also in the higher ones, but of better stamp; likewise, whatever is in the higher ones is also seen in the lowest, but in a degenerate condition and with a nature one might call adulterated

(tr. Douglas Carmichael, in Pico, *On the Dignity of Man*, tr. Charles Glenn Wallis [Indianapolis, 1965], p. 77).

[15] *De planctu naturae*, tr. Douglas M. Moffat (Yale Studies in English, 36; New York, 1908), Prose III, 72–84.

[16] *The Kalender of Shepherdes*, ed. H. Oskar Sommer (London, 1892), III.99–100. Cf. *The compost of Ptholomeus* (London, 1532?) [STC 20480], *c*2; Godfridus, *Boke of knowledge of thynges unknowen* (London, 1530?) [STC 11931], G4 ff.; and Erra Pater, *Pronostycacion for ever* (London, 1540?) [STC 10517], A3^v–A7^v. The statement was commonplace, to say the least.

[17] Tr. Sylvester (1605), p. 52.

[18] *Devine weekes and workes*, tr. Sylvester (1605), pp. 483–484.

[19] *The third volume of the French academie*, tr. R. Dolman (London, 1601), p. 67. In this passage La Primaudaye is doing little more than translating Pico della Mirandola's "Second Proem" to *Heptaplus*, tr. Carmichael, in Pico, *Dignity of Man*, tr. Wallis, pp. 75–79.

[20] *Ibid.*, p. 64. This tripartite division of the universe had become commonplace; it retained the basic characteristics of Aristotelian cosmology, but with a heavy overlay of occult associations gained by its transmission through the cabalistic tradition. For a similar division of the world, see Reuchlin, *De arte cabalistica*, tr. Stanley, *History of philosophy*, pp. 571–574; Heinrich Cornelius

Agrippa, *Three books of occult philosophy*, tr. John Freake (London, 1651), pp. 1–2; and Guy le Fèvre de la Boderie, tr., *L'Harmonie du monde* [of Francesco Giorgio] (Paris, 1579), ē6ᵛ (for reproduction of the diagram, cf. Maren-Sofie Røstvig, *The Hidden Sense* [Oslo, 1963], p. 47).

21 An observation by Agrippa is cogent here:

> The *Platonists* therefore say, that in this very voice, or word, or name framed, with its Articles, that the power of the thing as it were some kind of life, lies under the form of the signification

(*Occult philosophy*, tr. Freake, p. 153).

22 In 1635 La Primaudaye's statement was still a commonplace, as shown by John Swan's echo of it:

> Three worlds there are, and Mankinde is the fourth: The first is Elementarie; the second a Celestiall world; the third Angelicall; and the fourth is Man, the little world

(*Speculum mundi* [Cambridge, 1635], p. 496).

23 Nicholas of Cusa had made this point a central issue in his theology; cf. Ernst Cassirer, *The Individual and the Cosmos in Renaissance Philosophy*, tr. Mario Domandi (New York, 1964), pp. 40, 63–66. Pico della Mirandola stretched this line of argument to its permissible extreme within the limits of Christian orthodoxy. After God had created the superior and the inferior orders of being, Pico says, He created man as a nexus between and summation of the spiritual and physical realms:

> He took up man, a work of indeterminate form; and placing him at the midpoint of the world, He spoke to him as follows:
>
> "We have given to thee, Adam, no fixed seat, no form of thy very own, no gift peculiarly thine, that thou mayest feel as thine own, have as thine own, possess as thine own the seat, the form, the gifts which thou thyself shalt desire. A limited nature in other creatures is confined within the laws written down by Us. In conformity with thy free judgment, in whose hands I have placed thee, thou art confined by no bounds; and thou wilt fix limits of nature for thyself. I have placed thee at the center of the world, that from there thou mayest more conveniently look around and see whatsoever is in the world"

(*Dignity of Man*, tr. Wallis, pp. 4–5).

24 Using traditional physiology, Guy le Fèvre de la Boderie gives the standard explanation of how man incorporates within himself the three divisions of the universe:

> Each man is the summary and epitome of the great world divided into three equal parts. Similarly, man derives three principal levels or ranks from the natural or vegetable life, the vital or sensitive life, and the animal or mobile life—to wit, the liver, the heart, and the brain.
>
> Chacun homme est le sommaire & l'abregé du grand monde distingué en 3. mipartemens, ainsi que l'homme contient trois estages ou sieges principaux de la vie naturelle ou vegetable, vitale ou sensitive, & animale ou motive, à sçavoir le foye, le coeur & le cerveau

(Prefatory epistle to Giorgio, *L'Harmonie du monde*, tr. Le Fèvre, ā5ᵛ).

25 *Defence of poesie*, C3ᵛ. Cf. also: "Under what name so ever it [learning] come forth, or to what immediate end soever it be directed, the finall end is,

to lead and draw us to as high a perfection, as our degenerate soules made worse by their clay-lodgings, can be capable of" (*ibid.*, C3).

[26] *Devine weekes and workes*, tr. Sylvester (1605), p. 133.

[27] *Ovid's Metamorphosis*, tr. Sandys (Oxford, 1632), p. 65.

[28] See my article, "The Sun-King Analogy in *Richard II*," *Shakespeare Quarterly*, 11 (1960), 319–327.

[29] I.e., our planet, earth.

[30] After writing this passage, I realized that the words of St. Paul were in the back of my mind: "Eye hath not seen, nor ear heard . . . the things which God hath prepared for them that love him" (1 Corinthians 2:9). St. Paul's words rolled around also in the head of Robert Recorde (cf. *The castle of knowledge* [London, 1556], a7ᵛ) and of Shakespeare (cf. *Midsummer Night's Dream*, IV.i.216 ff., when Bottom reports on his connubial experience with Titania). The Biblical passage is very much germane to Spenser's poetics.

[31] At a high-point of the *Epithalamion*, culminating a passage which praises the mistress in terms reminiscent of *The Song of Songs*, Spenser again uses this simile of the human body as a "pallace fayre" (line 178). Cf. Du Bartas, *Devine weekes and workes*, tr. Sylvestor (1605), p. 206.

[32] (London, 1541), fol. 1ᵛ.

[33] Spenser's assumptions here are best discovered by reference to the Pythagorean-Platonic cosmology, especially as it has been analyzed by Cassirer:

> Plato's vision of the world is characterized by the sharp division he makes between the sensible and the intelligible world, i.e., between the world of appearances and the world of ideas. The two worlds, that of the 'visible' and that of the 'invisible,' that of the ὁρατόν, and that of the νοητόν, do not lie on the same plane and, therefore, admit of no immediate comparison. Rather, each is the complete opposite, the ἕτερον, of the other. Everything predicated of the one must be denied to the other. All the characteristics of the 'idea' may therefore be deduced antithetically from those of appearance. If continuous flux is characteristic of appearance, abiding permanence is proper to the idea

(*Individual and Cosmos*, p. 16).

[34] In "A Seventeenth-century Theory of Metaphysical Poetry," Joseph Mazzeo examines the treatises of several mid- to late-seventeenth-century critics —Gracián, Tesauro, Sforza-Pallavicino, Minozzi, and Pellegrini—who based a poetics on the *concetto*. In this poetics, the poet by exercise of his "wit" (*ingegno*) contrives a conceit that has the purpose, according to Sforza-Pallavicino, "to show how things which appear unconnected are really similar and to arouse thereby a certain sensation of wonder" (in Mazzeo, *Renaissance and Seventeenth-Century Studies* [Columbia Univ. Press, 1964], p. 33). This conceit, Mazzeo argues, then provides the "form" for the poem. In "Metaphysical Poetry and the Poetic of Correspondence," Mazzeo extends his study and concludes, "The theorists of the conceit envisaged the poet's universe as a complex system of universal analogical relationships which the poet expressed and revealed" (*ibid.*, p. 59). What differentiates the poetics of the *concetto* from the poetics of making is the stance vis-à-vis reality which the poet in each instance assumes. The poet as maker works on the premise that the various levels of creation share analogous patterns and therefore the objects of nature are obviously interrelated. The poet as contriver of conceits, however, must exercise his wit to reveal analogies, and then he chooses the least obvious in order to excite the greatest wonder. The poet as maker demonstrates cosmos; the poet as contriver of conceits insists upon cosmos as a logical postulate, though he educes the strongest possible evidence to the contrary. In devising this sort of conceit, there is an intellectual masochism comparable to

the religious masochism of Sir Thomas Browne, who "thinkes there be not impossibilities enough in Religion for an active faith" (*Religio Medici* [I.ix] in *Works*, ed. Keynes, I.13). Like the religious doctor, the *concettista* loses himself in a mystery and pushes his reason to the limit, where only *Certum est quia impossibile est*. The reason expires in an exclamation of exquisite anguish, "O altitudo!" In contrast, the poet as maker deals in contradictions and even paradoxes; but his intention is to show the reconciliation of opposites in accord with a familiar pattern which is fully visible wherever one looks in the universe—in elemental nature, in human nature, and in durational nature called "time." See also Eugenio Donato, "Tesauro's Poetics: Through the Looking Glass," *Modern Language Notes*, 78 (1963), 15–30.

[35] In the essay on Cowley, quoted here from *The Works of Samuel Johnson*, ed. Arthur Murray, 12 vols. (London, 1816), IX.20.

3
Poem as Literary Microcosm

The poet in the act of making gives physical extension to an idea by means of characters, actions, and settings. In emulation of the Timaean godhead, he creates a universe which bodies forth his fore-conceit. And just as the great world of nature is a metaphor *for* the creating deity as well as *by* him, so also the poem is a metaphor for as well as by the poet. The poet is the creator of his metaphor in the same sense that the deity is creator of the universe; he is immanent in it, so that the poem is a dynamic expression of the poet's being. By correspondence, then, the poet himself is a metaphor for the creating deity, occupying a place in the hierarchy of existence just a bit lower than God. Moreover, the metaphor of the poet (his poem) bears the same relation to the metaphor of God (the universe) as the two creators bear to one another—that is, the poem is but slightly lower than the universe in the hierarchy of existence and is otherwise a reproduction of it. In the vertical scale of variety, it is subordinate; but by the common pattern that persists among the horizontal levels in the hierarchy, it is analogous. In consequence, the poem like the physical universe must disclose the plenitude and comprehensiveness of its maker. The poem must possess the same inner ordered completeness and outer exhaustive completeness as the universe. Since the poet performs the role of a creating deity, his poem to be true must reproduce the cosmos. In the poetics of making, a poem should be a literary microcosm.

The theory of poet-as-maker using the cosmos as his pattern effectively nullifies Plato's objection to the artist as a mere imitator of imitations, the objection stated with such devastating unequivocality in the last book of the *Republic*. In the poetics of making, the artist no longer reproduces representationally the imperfect physical replicas of the Platonic ideas which appear in nature, repeating all of the flaws and by his own ineptness even exaggerating them. Instead, he goes for his model direct to the divine idea of cosmos. Poetry thereby becomes truer than life, a super-reality, a golden world, an Arcadian paradise, a reconstruction of perfection as it existed before the Fall, a replica refined of flaws. In the speculum tradition, of course, this image of perfection can be used in a positive way as a means of presenting the ideal, or in a negative way as a means of defining the deficiencies of the actual. In its most interesting use, we get a two-way reflection from the one mirror, seeing simultaneously in juxtaposition both what is and what should be.[1]

If his poem is to be a replica in small of the great world, and if the poet in its production is to follow the example of our heavenly maker, then he will begin with a λόγος, a *ratio*, a scheme or plan. To phrase it in terms of the Platonic tradition, as Sidney did, he will begin with an idea as his fore-conceit. Or to state it in terms of the Pythagorean tradition, which has focused our attention in this study, he will begin with a number, a form without substance (like a Platonic idea). The act of making then consists of imposing this form on the raw material of the poet's experience, thereby repeating the creative act of the Timaean godhead who imposed his archetypal idea on preexistent matter. The result is an art work which because of the efficacy of metaphor carries the weight of God's own truth.

Furthermore, just as nature is God's art, so the poem is the poet's nature. As Sidney says, "The Poet . . . lifted up with the vigor of his own invention, doth grow in effect into an other nature."[2] The nature created by the poet, in fact, exceeds in beauty the physical nature that our senses perceive because the poet can remove from his creation the imperfections inherent in matter and the accidents occasioned by time. In consequence, the poet's nature more nearly approximates the radical beauty of God's art. As Sidney concludes:

> Nature never set foorth the earth in so rich Tapistry as diverse Poets have done, neither with so pleasaunt rivers, fruitfull trees, sweete smelling flowers, nor whatsoever els may make the too much loved earth more lovely: her world is brasen, the Poets only deliver a golden (*Defence of poesie*, C1).

With more than a touch of *contemptus mundi*, Sidney turns his back on this "too much loved earth" and faces the golden world of Arcadia.

By this act of making, incidentally, the poet is also synthesizing the esthetics of Plato and that of Aristotle. The form for his poem comes from Plato's ultimate reality—it is an idea from the world of being; while the substance of his poem comes from Aristotle's ultimate reality—it is the data of objectified nature. By means of form, the poet places an inscrutable mystery within reach of our sense perception. In his subject matter, the poet selects and arranges random experience to give it lasting significance. The poet works deductively, bringing down celestial values from Plato's world of being. He also works inductively, transcending the mundane and arriving at conclusions that have universal validity. It is this very ability to do more than imitate, in fact, which for Sidney defines the "right poet." Like an Aristotelian, Sidney agrees that the poet must work with his sense impressions of physical nature (what Yeats in a black moment called "the foul rag-and-bone shop of the heart")—indeed, "there is no Art delivered unto mankind that hath not the workes of nature for his principall object." But the poet, alone among artisans, breaks out of such restriction for his artifact:

> Only the Poet disdeining to be tied to any such subjection, lifted up with the vigor of his own invention, doth grow in effect into an other nature: in making things either better then nature bringeth foorth, or quite anew, formes such as never were in nature: as the *Heroes*, *Demigods*, *Cyclops*, *Chymeras*, *Furies*, and such like; so as he goeth hand in hand with nature, not enclosed within the narrow warrant of her gifts, but freely raunging within the Zodiack of his owne wit.[3]

In this passage central to Sidney's poetics, we should read "invention" in its technical sense, almost synonymous with *fore-conceit* and *idea* (see p. 320, n. 30, above). By exercise of his imagination, the inventive faculty, the poet is able to escape to the empyrean of ideal forms. But even while expatiating freely within the zodiac of his wit, he must still go hand in hand with nature, keeping in touch with the physical realm. The poem is a place where the widest reaches of human experience converge. It is the common ground where we can lay the restless spirits of Plato and Aristotle in a single tomb. In this way the poet can create "for short time an endlesse moniment."[4]

There is no better example of a literary microcosm than Spenser's *Shepheardes Calender*, which I have already shown to be an emblem of the cosmos (see pp. 309–315). Those "twelve Æglogues proportionable to the twelve monethes" display the variety of

God's handiwork both by means of the climatic distinctions between the months and by means of the widely differing activities of the shepherds. Taken together the eclogues display the variety of God's handiwork in its totality and exhaust the possibilities of human activity, thereby achieving the paradoxical unity that belongs only to infinity. The all-inclusiveness of the poem is confirmed by the fact that twelve months complete the year, the basic unit of time.

Moreover, Spenser the creator of this microcosm is immanent in it, just as God permeates His universe. Through his persona, Colin Clout, the poet projects himself into his fictive world. *The Shepheardes Calender* is obviously a metaphor *for* Spenser as well as *by* him. It contains a large autobiographical element, drawing heavily upon Spenser's own circumstances in 1579 and his state of mind. The poem is a personal as well as a universal statement. Fortunately, Elizabethan punctuation allows the title to remain ambiguous as to number of shepherds, because the poem is both a shepherd'*s* calendar and a shepherd*s*' calendar.

The poem then is by this perfection a microcosm.[5] It shows the universe in all its variety and all its fullness, and it shows man's life in all its variety and all its fullness. As a consequence, we can distinguish at least three levels on which *The Shepheardes Calender* operates. Using the traditional tripartite stratification of the universal world which La Primaudaye outlined—the intellectual, the celestial, and the elementary (see pp. 341–342)—we can see that the poem represents all at once an archetypal idea in God's mind, a pattern discernible in the motion of the stars, and the facts of man's day-to-day existence. The poem, as an effective metaphor should, translates meaning from the intellectual empyrean to the visible spheres of the planets, and thence in turn to the terrestrial world which we inhabit. And of course the process is reversible, since this is a viable metaphor, and meaning is transferred in reverse from the elementary world to the celestial, and thence in turn to the intellectual. There is not only the variety on the horizontal level depicted by the emblematic calendar, but also the variety of the vertical scale. The great chain reaches down from heaven and links man in his proper place as the mediator between the conceptual and the physical. The poem has both the vertical and the horizontal amplitude of God's creation. For that reason, Spenser can make the grandiose claim for durability that he asserts in the envoy.

Spenser's intention in *The Shepheardes Calender* and his method of realizing it were not an aberrant incident in his career, not merely an academic exercise by an enthusiastic young poet who soon turned to other matters. The poetics of *The Shepheardes Calender* remained Spenser's artistic credo throughout his life, and the basic technique of that début continued to be his standard practice. Except in the case of a few anomalies when he was working in a clearly different idiom—*Mother Hubberds Tale* and *Colin Clouts Come Home Againe* are the prominent exceptions which prove my thesis—Spenser consistently sought to implement the poetics of making by framing his poem as a microcosm. Every one of his major poems has a structure—a form or idea—which must have been thought out in advance of verbal composition.

After *The Shepheardes Calender* comes *The Teares of the Muses*, a youthful effort so rigidly structured that it seems mechanical. Following an introductory passage in which the poet speaks as though preparing for a medieval dream allegory, each of the nine Muses laments in turn, completing a pattern of the perfect number 10 (1 + 9). This pattern of the total poem also is reproduced in each of its constituent parts; each Muse in her recitation is allotted nine stanzas plus one transition stanza, again making a total of 10. Finally, 10 parts each composed of 10 stanzas makes up a total of 100, the divine number, as Dante assumed we knew. The idea of this divine number is also given sense-perceptible form in another medium through expression in the visual image of the nine Muses under the direction of Apollo, a conventional depiction of cosmic harmony.[6] The Muses were readily correlated with the notes played by each planet in the music of the spheres (see Plate 38). In conclusion, *The Teares of the Muses*, like *The Shepheardes Calender*, is composed of discrete items representing the total variety of the universe; and just as infinity is greater than the accumulation of finite things, so also is the poem as a whole greater than the sum of its individual parts. The consort of the Muses in grief is greater than the seriatim presentation of their particular laments. The impact of *The Teares of the Muses* derives largely from our perception of its form and our response to the poetics that it implements. Its failure to please modern readers is due primarily to the current rejection of this poetics, which is the poem's raison d'être.

In the *Epithalamion* Spenser used the same poetics with considerably greater success.[7] In that poem there are twenty-four stanzas, and without being relentlessly mathematical even the most casual eye must see that the poem progresses from early one morning through the nuptial activities and the connubial night to the next dawn. Just as *The Shepheardes Calender* reconstructs the annual unit of time, the *Epithalamion* with equal effectiveness emblematizes time as a diurnal unit. The poem is, by Spenser's own declaration, "for short time an endlesse moniment" (line 433). The refrain at the end of each stanza marks the passing of each discrete part of this diurnal unit of time. The refrain comes like the striking of a clock to remind us that at each hour the day moves forward into a new phase of the marriage ceremony.

But the refrain comes for only 23 stanzas—there is no refrain for the last stanza because by then the poem and the poet have passed into an atemporal realm of perfection where life is not a chronological sequence of events but rather an unending, undifferentiated blissfulness. A comment on Genesis by St. Augustine is applicable here. He writes to his youthful companion Januarius:

> Read Genesis; you will find the seventh day without an evening, which signifies rest without end. . . . the last rest is eternal, and for this reason the eighth day will have eternal blessedness. . . . Thus the eighth shall be as the first, so that the first life may be restored to immortality.[8]

Another passage from St. Augustine is equally cogent to the *Epithalamion* as a whole: "Terrestrial things are subject to celestial, and their time circuits join together in harmonious succession for a poem of the universe." [9] Spenser clearly intends his epithalamium to be such a "poem of the universe," and the means to this end is the unabashed use of metaphor. Spenser's own marriage is generalized into the prototypical wedding day of all bridegrooms in all ages, and from that level another step in the series of metaphors carries us up to the abstract level of cosmic love. By its depiction of the diurnal unit of time, an orderly arrangement of both day and night, the poem becomes a knowable image of that harmony which reflects cosmic love. Thereby Spenser places himself in the same continuum with all other bridegrooms, and eventually with God, Who binds the universe with *caritas*. By loving, the poet realizes his potential as the image of the source of all love, and his poem becomes an icon of that benign order.

In the *Fowre Hymnes* Spenser uses yet another archetypal idea to give structure to his literary microcosm. The poem is patterned after the ascent, best known perhaps as the Platonic ascent from earthly to heavenly. There is a linear progression in the poem as we proceed from earthly love to its cause, earthly beauty, and thence from heavenly love to its cause, heavenly beauty. Or to map this ascent in terms of the deities to whom the hymn-like odes are addressed, we move from Cupid to Venus to Christ to God. There is a clear line of movement from the lowest to the highest; and when we finish the fourth hymn, we know that we have come to an end. There is no other place to go. We have exhausted the possibilities within this system, and a fifth hymn is unthinkable. God and Sapience reign over all.

Indeed, in their consummation of heavenly beauty, God and Sapience subsume and perfect the three earlier deities who have been glorified in the hymns. The fourth hymn, then, is the culmination of a linear progression. But it also produces an inclusive totality which assimilates the various discrete parts of the work into a greater whole—just as God resides at the top of the chain of being while at the same time He contains within Himself all the lower links of the chain. This scheme, which allows finite parts to relate to an infinite whole, was depicted also in the Pythagorean tradition as the tetrad (see pp. 160–166, above), and this is the pattern which Spenser has most immediately in mind for the *Fowre Hymnes*.

There are, of course, *four* hymns, to begin with an obvious fact. And these four parts are explicitly categorized, so that the poem falls into two halves: two hymns are earthly and two are heavenly. Moreover, each half contains a son-parent relationship—Cupid is the son of Venus, and Christ the son of God—so that while contrasted, the two halves are also coordinated by an identical pattern, the relationship between parent and child. The heavenly is the same as the earthly, though at a higher level. Furthermore, the line of demarcation between the earthly and the heavenly is blurred, even eradicated, because both Venus and Christ in their significance cross this border. Just as Christ descended into the flesh of man to make heavenly love known on earth (*Heavenly Love*, 134–140), so Venus reached above to the empyrean for the heavenly form imprinted on matter to give it beauty (*Beautie*, 43–56). The result is a quadripartite system which reconciles opposites by placing intermediaries between them. Cupid is reconciled with God through the intercession of Venus and Christ, and therefore is placed in a continuum with God. The pattern is the same as that educed by Bede to show that earth, the lowest element, is linked to fire, the highest element, through the intermediaries of water and air (see Plate 28). To use the mathematical terminology of Bede, Venus and Christ are the means between the extremes of Cupid and God.

The linear pattern of the *Fowre Hymnes* by a series of steps therefore arrives at a point where the individuality of the parts is lost in a whole which raises them to a conceptual level where time and space—and their individuality—are meaningless. The tetrad, like God, is an abstraction which cannot be reduced to discriminate parts. It is an indiscriminate abstraction. And while we can know its effects through sense perception, as we can know God's handiwork though not God himself, the tetrad per se cannot be reduced to physicality. It remains inviolably abstract. In consequence, in order to relate the infinite with the physical items perceived by our senses, the metaphor of creation has been devised. By that metaphor, meaning is translated from the conceptual to the physical.

In the Pythagorean tradition, the metaphor of creation is expressed in a mathematical way which shows how multeity proceeds from the monad (see pp. 204–214, above). We can also read Spenser's *Fowre Hymnes* in this way—that is, having read the poem from beginning to end as a discursive experience, we then contemplate the poem in its totality, *as* a totality, contemporaneous and nonspatial. Our view is not to consider the parts as they relate individually to one another, but rather to consider the whole as it relates to each part. We reverse the process, as it were, of the ascent, the linear progression up the steps toward godhead, and see instead how the divine is the source of the lower orders of existence. Johann Reuchlin—the gluttonous syncretist who ravenously digested the Homeric, the Pythagorean, the cabbalistic, the Christian, and anything else he could cram into his head—had presented the tetrad in its usual context, but mythologized in such a way as to provide a cogent gloss for Spenser's poem:

> From this *fountain of Eternal Nature* [the tetractys], floweth down the *Pythagorick* Number, One and Two, which from Eternity, in the fountain of the immense Ocean, was, shall be, or rather always is, plentiously streaming. This one was by the Ancients termed Ζεὺς, *Jupiter;* two, ἥρα, *Juno,* wife and sister to *Jupiter*, of whom *Homer:*
>
> *Golden-thron'd* Juno, *with eyes full of love,*
> *Beheld her spouse and brother, sacred* Jove,
> *Sitting on th'top of fount abounding* Ide.[10]
>
> In *Ida* (απὸ τοῦ ἰδεῖν, from *praescience*), *Jupiter* and *Juno* sat as *one* and *two,* in the streaming Idaea of the *Tetractys,* whence flow the principles of all things, *Form* and *Matter.*[11]

In the *Fowre Hymnes,* Spenser's God and Sapience similarly sit at the peak of the poem, "as *one* and *two,* in the streaming Idaea of the *Tetractys.*" God is of course one, the paradoxical unity that incorporates infinity, as the form of the *Fowre Hymnes* demonstrates. His consort, Sapience, is two, not only because she is a woman, but also because the apportionment of duties in heaven places her over the realm of created things: she "menageth the ever-moving sky,/ And in the same these lower creatures all" (*Heavenly Beautie*, 194–195). She governs the creation that proceeds from the one; she is, in fact, the plenum as Aristotle defined the term (lines 197–200). From her flows matter, as Reuchlin prescribed, just as form flows from God, and consequently "the principles of all things"—the first causes—are accounted for. From that marriage in heaven stems the cosmic harmony that encompasses form and matter. Within that context, Christ and Venus and Cupid are each seen in proper perspective at their appointed duties.

Like *The Shepheardes Calender*, then, *Fowre Hymnes* reveals a discursive progression through a series of discrete parts; but when this pattern is completed, a whole larger than the sum of those parts is perfected. This all-subsuming whole may have the circularity of the calendar or of the tetractys—the substance of the circle is secondary in importance to the form itself. The circular form—a nonverbal mode of discourse, be it noted—makes the clearest and fullest statement about the infinity and eternity which the poem wishes to eulogize as God.

The Faerie Queene derives from the same poetics as the other poems discussed here and displays the same cosmic patterns, though to deal with the matter fully requires another book. But for the present let me offer at least a sketch of my argument. The thesis, quite simply, is that the form of *The Faerie Queene* reproduces the structure of the cosmos and that its narrative reflects the fullness of the universe in all its variety and extremes. In short, *The Faerie Queene* is a literary microcosm, evident in both its form and its subject matter.

Without question, cosmic patterns abound in the poem. The ascent through a series of steps is metamorphosed into the quest, and especially the quest of Red Crosse has this form. The two-phase cosmos, best known as the daily unit of time comprising day and night, is embodied in Una and Duessa, who oppose, yet exactly complement, one another. The three-part cosmos wherein two opposites are reconciled by a shared mean is demonstrated by the castle of Medina in Book II. The four-phase cosmos, the tetrad, underlies Book IV, the legend of friendship. Cosmic patterns evidently structure various portions of the poem, providing a skeletal framework for this or that action in the plethora of episodes.

But there is one supreme pattern which incorporates all the lesser patterns and gives them consistency, and that of course is the twelve-part cosmos, the elaborated tetrad, the annual unit of time which organizes the twelve months and four seasons into a single ideogram (see Plate 26). This is the pattern that Spenser had imposed upon his data in *The Shepheardes Calender*. And as in that earlier publication, the title page of *The Faerie Queene* again proclaims: "Disposed into twelve bookes." Twelve is a useful number for determining the structure of a poem, as epic poets had realized for some time, because it breaks down into several factors: 1 and 2 and 3 and 4 and 6. In consequence, it allows a complex and varied arrangement of constituent parts. Spenser takes advantage of this opportunity to give his microcosm a range and diversity which is unequalled in English literature.[12]

Spenser constructs his cosmic pattern of twelve parts with full awareness of what he is doing. Each book of *The Faerie Queene* displays a single virtue—Book I, holiness; Book II, temperance; and so on, as we all know. And one knight bodies forth each virtue. But these are partial virtues, parts of a larger whole, qualities which together make up the good full life which Spenser depicts with the didactic intention of "fashion[ing] a gentleman or noble person in vertuous and gentle discipline," as he informs us in the letter to Raleigh which attended the publication of the first three books in 1590. The twelve partial virtues are to be subsumed in the inclusive virtue of magnificence, which is bodied forth by Prince Arthur. Magnificence is the unity which arises from the multeity of the partial virtues, and Prince Arthur rides through each book, saving each knight from destruction at the nadir of his fortunes and thereby preserving his virtue and assimilating it to the larger whole. As Spenser confides to Raleigh:

> Magnificence . . . is the perfection of all the rest, and conteineth in it them all, therefore in the whole course I mention the deedes of Arthure applyable to that vertue, which I write of in that booke.

When we read *The Faerie Queene* for the first time, it is necessarily a discursive experience and in consequence we think inductively. We gradually build up to Arthur's comprehensive virtue, magnificence, by adding partial virtue to partial virtue, by adding temperance to holiness, and then chastity, friendship, and so forth. But we should also see the poem as a whole, and then we can think deductively, applying Arthur's comprehensiveness to each individual book. And that is what Spenser invites us to do: "in the whole course" of the poem, he activates that twelfth-part of Arthur's magnificence which is applicable to the particular virtue being exemplified in any given book. In Book I, for example, Arthur appears in the context of holiness and acts as "heavenly grace," as Spenser explicitly interprets the allegory (I.viii.1.3). Arthur alone, in fact, without further ado could have completed the quest in each of the separate books. But Spenser unfolds Arthur into twelve subsidiary knights in order to exploit this opportunity for diversity. As Spenser says in the letter to Raleigh: "But of the xii. other vertues, I make xii. other knights the patrones, for the more variety of the history."

As Arthur rides through the projected twelve books of the poem, then, Spenser intended that he demonstrate twelve partial virtues. Furthermore, by perfecting that full range of possibilities Arthur exemplifies the comprehensive virtue of magnificence. Thereby he becomes a suitable consort for the fairy queen, the image of female perfectness. Just as Arthur's quest for Gloriana is the super-quest which surpasses the quest of Red Crosse and of Guyon and of all the other knights, so also the marriage of Arthur and Gloriana will surpass (yet include) all the other knight-lady matches in the poem. Their union will be announced and celebrated during the feast at Gloriana's court which Spenser promises as a conclusion to *The Faerie Queene.* The court of Gloriana quite obviously represents the largest possible whole, where the twelve knights will come together at the conclusion of the twelve books and where male and female are united in cosmic marriage.

In this final episode, Gloriana's latent perfection will be openly completed by the addition of her male counterpart. Even before this climactic moment, however, she represents an ideal toward which not only Arthur, but also each of the other knights strives. In the proem to Book I, Spenser beseeches the historical Elizabeth, his addressee, to inspire his efforts:

> . . . raise my thoughts too humble and too vile
> To thinke of that true glorious type of thine,
> The argument of mine afflicted stile.
>
> (I.proem.4.6–8)

In the spirit of typology, Spenser announces that Gloriana, the *type* of Elizabeth, is the argument of his invention. She is always present in the poem, if never completely visible in the portion which Spenser finished. Would she have appeared in full dress in Book

XII at her feast? I think so, though the depiction of such infinite goodness might have taxed the talent of even so consummate a poet as Spenser.[13] In any case, we get glimpses of her in the several other female characters who display various facets of her personality. Just as Arthur's wholeness is revealed to us through the subsidiary knights (Red Crosse, Guyon, and so forth), so also the complexity of Gloriana/Elizabeth is unfolded by characters such as Una, Belphoebe, Britomart, Mercilla, and perhaps even Radigund.

By identifying Elizabeth with Gloriana, Spenser paid his queen the most hyperbolic compliment, as she herself gratefully recognized. In the proem to Book VI of *The Faerie Queene*, where it is manifest that Elizabeth embodies in the physical realm the abstraction that Gloriana represents in the conceptual realm, Spenser bestows the ultimate in praise upon his sovereign:

> So from the Ocean all rivers spring,
> And tribute backe repay as to their King.
> Right so from you all goodly vertues well
> Into the rest, which round about you ring,
> Faire Lords and Ladies, which about you dwell.
> (VI.proem.7.4–8)

Elizabeth as Gloriana is the perfect unit which is infinity, *e pluribus unum*, ringed about with her twelve constituent knights who derive from her court and return to it, just as rivers rise from and return to the ocean, or as the moments of time rise from and return to eternity. She is a self-contained entity, revealing the cosmic pattern of twelve-in-one, demonstrating the paradox of *concordia discors* and representing the basic unit of time. Significantly her feast is an annual event, not only what is but what shall always be. It is a continuing process, *natura naturans* not *natura naturata*. For that reason none of her knights can settle down in complacency at the end of his quest—he simply starts over in the cyclical pattern by setting out again himself (our extrapolation) or by participating vicariously in the quest of a fellow knight which is analogous to his own quest (Spenser's extrapolation by means of the narrative). When seen within the totality of the poem, Gloriana's influence is all-pervasive and never-ending.

The form of *The Faerie Queene* as Spenser projected the finished poem makes this poetic statement incontrovertibly clear. There were to have been twelve books arranged to culminate in a feast at the court of Gloriana where her betrothal to Prince Arthur would certainly be celebrated. This conflation of male and female in perfect union is a poetic ideogram repeating the visual ideogram of the cosmos contained in the innermost circle of Plate 26. Moreover, each book is an analogous part of the same whole, and therefore should exhibit an analogous structure. This analogy of form is most evident in the parallel structure of Books I and II, but it holds for the other books also. Once Spenser has established the pattern, he expects us to apply it even in those books where it is not easily discernible. At the end of the letter to Raleigh, after explaining what virtue each knight exemplifies and after briefing us on the narrative-plot of each of the first three books, Spenser concludes:

> Thus much Sir, I have briefly overronne to direct your understanding to the wel-head of the History, that from thence gathering the whole intention of the conceit, ye may as in a handfull gripe al the discourse.

What Spenser intended for us to have, then, are twelve analogous parts, twelve analogous fictions, twelve analogous quests, which are laced together by the quest of Prince Arthur in search of Gloriana. The result is a *tout ensemble* which in its exhaustive entirety represents the good life to be emulated by the reader. Spenser knows that a narrative must be discursive, like the passage of time, like the journey of life. But he sees life whole. And the conceit of Gloriana as the wellspring of all goodly virtues extended into twelve analogous fictions allows us also to see human experience *sub specie aeternitatis*, to see it as an orderly arrangement of a diversified whole.

In devising his conceit of Gloriana, Spenser was working independent of any prefabricated system of metaphors, independent of cosmic correspondences and Christian symbol or even classical mythology. His ability to fashion this metaphor wholly in his own terms is the talent which has earned for Spenser the soubriquet "the poet's poet." As Coleridge would say, it is poetry of the pure imagination. As Coleridge did in fact say about *The Faerie Queene:*

> You will take especial note of the marvellous independence and true imaginative absence of all particular space or time in the Faery Queene. It is in the domains neither of history or geography; it is ignorant of all artificial boundary, all material obstacles; it is truly in land of Faery, that is, of mental space.[14]

Since the fairy queen is a metaphor of Spenser's own making, it is independent of restrictive referents. It is free from all extraneous restraints. It can include within its continuum the full spectrum of human experience, from the lowest physicality right through to the loftiest abstraction. Gloriana can represent—and often simultaneously—the aging woman who sat on England's throne as well as glory of the highest sort, heroic or spiritual. And by his metaphor Spenser carries us from mundane drabness to an exaltation that exceeds wonder and approaches knowledge.

So Spenser as a standard practice imposed an archetypal form on the data of his experience: the annual unit of time, the diurnal unit of time, the perfect number 10, the tetrad. Thereby he interrelated what might seem random, ordering it, rendering it understandable. And in the process, since his poem is a microcosm, he rendered knowable also the macro-world of the heavenly maker. In consequence, a great deal of the meaning in Spenser's poems is conveyed through the form, a nonverbal mode of discourse which conveys the ideas from the empyreal world of essences with the greatest directness and the least distortion.

Shakespeare also—at least the youthful Shakespeare—sometimes structured his work according to cosmic patterns. At the end of *Love's Labour's Lost* the secondary characters divide into two groups to sing a dialogue between the cuckoo and the owl. Don Armado, acting as majordomo, directs them: "This side is Hiems, Winter, this Ver, the Spring." Such a division reduces the year to its most rudimentary form, a pair of opposites; but nonetheless the full cycle of four seasons is implied. As I have argued elsewhere,[15] this abbreviated calendar provides the fore-conceit in Shakespeare's mind to which he gave durational extension in the dramatic action of the play. The plot similarly contrasts the springlike world of youthful love, especially as idealized by Navarre, with the wintry world of pain and death heralded by the arrival of Marcade. The cosmic patterning is reiterated in character groupings—for example, four young men and four young ladies to be arranged in suitable couples. Likewise in *A Midsummer Night's Dream* we have couples shuffled and reshuffled until "two of both kinds makes up four" (III.ii.438), a condition which applies to the mature love of Theseus and Hippolyta and Titania and Oberon as well as to the young love of the junior Athenians. Only when the opposites are reconciled and all of the couples are sorted out in appropriate pairs can the fairies dance at the wedding.

By strict rule the poet as maker conceived his poem as a microcosm. But within that larger whole he sometimes produced a *mini*-cosm—that is, by exhausting the range of possibilities within a limited system, he produced a miniature which embodies completeness. By organizing all of the possible constituent parts into a single scheme, he achieved a unity which imitates the *e pluribus unum* of the cosmos. Such is the case, for example, in Spenser's *Hymne in Honour of Love,* when the poet wishes to demonstrate that nothing can stand in the way of the man who serves Love as his god:

> Witnesse *Leander,* in the Euxine waves,
> And stout *Æneas* in the Trojane fyre,
> *Achilles* preassing through the Phrygian glaives,
> And *Orpheus* daring to provoke the yre
> Of damned fiends, to get his love retyre.
>
> (ll. 231–235)

By carefully citing an instance of heterosexual love, of filial love, of homosexual love, and of marital love, Spenser exhausts the possibilities. He proves his thesis in every category and thereby establishes it as a universal. He uses the same technique in Book I of *The Faerie Queene,* when the mount from which Red Crosse views the New Jerusalem is likened in turn to Mount Sinai, to the Mount of Olives, and to Mount Helicon (I.x.53–54), an instance from the Old Testament, from the New Testament, and from the classical tradition. The poet methodically puts together his metaphor—three parts which together achieve an exhaustive unity, thereby becoming the prototype of mountains, the idea of mountainness. In *Love's Labour's Lost* Shakespeare resorts to this technique when he wishes to display all of the characters in one category as a dramatic unit. He then writes what might be called a tetralogue: a passage of four lines in which one line is assigned to each of four characters. A passage of this type involving the young gentlemen occurs early in the first scene of the play (I.i.94–97). A comparable passage grouping the young ladies in relation to the young men occurs just after the masque of the Muscovites in the last scene, when identities have been mistaken and the couples are inappropriately paired:

> *Rosaline:* The King is my love sworn.
> *Princess:* And quick Berowne hath plighted faith to me.
> *Katherine:* And Longaville was for my service born.
> *Maria:* Dumain is mine, as sure as bark on tree.
>
> (V.ii.282–285)

Clearly what the playwright must do next is rearrange this disorder into cosmos; in the words of Theseus, we must "find the concord of this discord" (*Midsummer Night's Dream,* V.i.60).

Shakespeare and Spenser did not, of course, invent the notion that a poem may be a literary microcosm. Nor was it an invention of the renaissance. Although no evidence exists that the notion was enunciated as a theory in classical times, there are several unmistakable examples which appear prominently in our earliest poetry. For whatever reason, Greek and Roman poets did produce literary microcosms.

The most notable instance in classical poetry occurs early in our literary history, in Book XVIII of the *Iliad* when Hephaestus manufactures new armor for Achilles. The shield is composed of four metals—bronze, tin, gold, and silver—which are fused in a vat over a fire enflamed by twenty bellows. The shield has a threefold rim and is five layers thick. It is adorned at its inception with "the unwearied sun, and the moon at the full, and . . . all the constellations wherewith heaven is crowned" (lines 484–485), thereby becoming an icon of time—in Plato's words, "an image of eternity." Without doubt Homer intended to depict in small on Achilles' shield the amplitude of the great world in its timeless aspect, with its harmonies expressed as mathematical proportions between whole numbers.

Such certainly was the conclusion of George Chapman, who singled out this episode for special translation and separate publication. In 1598, the same year that saw the printing of Chapman's *Seaven bookes of the Iliades*, John Windet brought out Chapman's *Achilles shield*, with this note on the title page: "Translated as the other seven Bookes of Homer, out of his eighteenth booke of Iliades." In *Achilles shield*, Chapman does not render Homer into the clumsy rhymed fourteeners that lend such ponderous dignity to all his other renditions of "the first and best" [16] of authors. Instead, the translator uses rhymed iambic pentameter couplets, the metrics of *Hero and Leander*. The episode of Achilles' shield appears also of course in its proper place in Chapman's complete translation of the *Iliad* first published in 1611, and there it is given a wholly new rendition in rhymed fourteeners to accord with the rest of the translation. Clearly, Achilles' shield had special significance for Chapman.

What that significance entailed is stated openly by the translator. In the slim volume of *Achilles shield* Chapman offers a dedication to the Earl of Essex in which, echoing Spondanus, he praises this passage as a "more than Artificiall and no lesse than Divine Rapture." [17] By implication the poet, though blind, has seen into the life of things and from this heavenly vision has produced an image which is more than mere artifice (even in the good sense of being created by means of skill). Chapman goes on in his praise:

> For what is here prefigurde by our miraculous Artist but the universall world, which being so spatious and almost unmeasurable, one circlet of a Shield representes and imbraceth? In it heaven turnes, the starres shine, the earth is enflowred, the sea swelles and rageth, Citties are built—one in the happinesse and sweetnesse of peace, the other in open warre and the terrors of ambush &c. And all these so lively proposde as not without reason many in times past have believed that all these thinges have in them a kind of voluntarie motion.

Here is Homer "imitating," creating "a speaking picture." But the poet has taken as the object of his imitation not the physical world of nature, but rather the idea of cosmos. Chapman, still echoing Spondanus, insists that the passage is a literary microcosm. The authority of Eustathius, the twelfth-century commentator on Homer, is brought to bear on the interpretation of the text:

> The ground of his [Homer's] invention he [Spondanus] shews out of Eustathius, intending by the Orbiguitie of the Shield the roundnesse of the world; by the foure mettalles, the foure elementes, viz. by gold, fire, by brasse, earth for the hardnes, by Tinne, water for the softnes and inclination to fluxure, by silver, Aire for the grosnes and obscuritie of the mettal before it be refind. That which he cals ἄντυγα τρίπλακα μαρμαρέην he understands the Zodiack, which is said to be triple for the latitude it contains and shining by reason of the perpetual course of the Sun made in that circle.

If we read "invention" as we should, as an Elizabethan synonym for *fore-conceit* (see p. 320, n. 30), we see, like Chapman and Spondanus, that Homer began here with the idea of the tetrad as his conceit, which he then bodied forth in the images on Achilles' shield. The four elements are represented in the four distinct metals, and their confluence in a stable system is emblematized by the threefold rim, which is itself seen as a familiar cosmic emblem, the zodiac.

Of course, Chapman might well have proceeded to distinguish other cosmic patterns in Achilles' shield. There is the reconciliation of opposites in the contrasting images of the city at peace and the city at war (XVIII.490–540). There is the four-phase cycle of the seasons in the successive scenes of plowing, reaping, vintage, and cattle keeping (XVIII.541–589). Finally, there is the description of the "dauncing maze," to use Chapman's words, where "youthes and maids with beauties past compare/Daunc't with commixed palms." [18]

This is evidently the inclusive cosmic dance, incorporating both the male and female principles and producing "beauties past compare" (see pp. 176–178). The entire shield, in fact, as Chapman says, is a prefigurement of "the universall world." In consequence, the River Ocean which circles its circumference is "a christall wall,"[19] analogous to the cristalline sphere which sets our finite world apart from the empyrean. Such is the self-consistency of Achilles' shield, "an Homericall Poeme"[20] which Chapman sets apart from the rest of the Homeric universe.

In a direct literary line from Achilles' shield is Ovid's description of the doors to the Sun's palace, opening Book II of the *Metamorphoses*. There again are four materials and the four elements:

> The palace of the Sun stood high on lofty columns, bright with glittering gold and bronze that shone like fire. Gleaming ivory crowned the gables above; the double folding-doors were radiant with burnished silver. And the workmanship was more beautiful than the material. For upon the doors Mulciber had carved in relief the waters that enfold the central earth, the circle of the lands and the sky that overhangs the lands. . . . Above these scenes was placed a representation of the shining sky, six signs of the zodiac on the right-hand doors, and six signs on the left. (II.1–18)

When Arthur Golding translated this text, he took the liberty of inserting: "For there a perfect plat,/Had *Vulcane* drawne of all the worlde."[21] Actually, the *Metamorphoses* in its entirety can be considered a microcosm, beginning as it does with an account of creation and ending in the vision of a peaceful society when "Jupiter controls the heights of heaven and the kingdoms of the triformed universe; but the earth is under Augustus' sway" (XV.858–860). Within the time-space continuum between these two events, an abundance of incidents in a variety of cause-and-effect relationships demonstrate the full range of human action and emotion. Vergil's *Aeneid* has been read in a similar way. At least one ancient critic, Macrobius, saw the *Aeneid* as an image of the universe,[22] an opinion elaborated by Poliziano.[23]

There are examples of literary microcosms also in the Judeo-Christian tradition[24]—in the Holy Scriptures themselves, according to many, including Pico della Mirandola. That Italian syncretist, amalgamating Platonism and the cabala with Christian doctrine, saw the Pentateuch as an epitome of the macrocosm: "The scripture of Moses is the exact image of the world."[25] A particular passage which generated inordinate curiosity[26] is the description of the Tabernacle which God commanded Moses to build for His worship:

> Thou shalt make the tabernacle with ten curtains of fine twined linen, and blue, and purple, and scarlet: with cherubims of cunning work shalt thou make them. The length of one curtain shall be eight and twenty cubits, and the breadth of one curtain four cubits: and every one of the curtains shall have one measure. The five curtains shall be coupled together one to another; and other five curtains shall be coupled one to another (Exodus, xxvi.1–3).

This sort of prescription in precise quantities continues at some length, and does produce the impression that God is instructing Moses how to create according to specific dimensions with symbolic significance.

God Himself was credited with having created the universe according to dimensions with symbolic significance, and the Divine Geometer with distended compasses in hand was a familiar figure in iconography (see pp. 206–209). In fact, one of the most popular biblical quotations in the renaissance, first popular among the Neoplatonic syncretists and then among the new scientific rationalists as well, was a statement from the Book of Wisdom (xi.21): God created the universe according to number, weight, and measure.[27] When the analogy between God's universe and the poem as microcosm is carried to its logical extreme, the poem is expected to reproduce the geometrical proportions of the macrocosm, a feat appropriately achieved for the literal-minded only by poetic meter. In mimicry of his prototype, the poet must also create with diligent respect for quantity. As Philip Sidney observed, the oracles of Delphi and the Sibylline prophecies were expressed in metrical verse because "that same exquisite observing of number and measure in the words . . . did seeme to have some divine force in it" (*Defence of poesie*, B3^{v}).

Thomas Campion in his *Observations in the art of English poesie* (1602) succinctly makes the point that a poem must reiterate the universal harmony by means of poetic meter:

> The world is made by Simmetry and proportion, and is in that respect compared to Musick, and Musick to Poetry.[28]

To be harmonious, poetry must demonstrate the same mathematical exactness that God bestowed on His creation, the *musica mundana* of Boethius. In fact, Polydore Vergil, who wrote a lengthy treatise on the inventors of things, ascribed to poetic meter a divine origin:

> The beginner of meter was god, which proporcioned the world, with al the contentes of the same, with a certaine order, as it were a meter, for ther is none (as Pithagoras taughte) that doubteth, but that there is in thinges hevenly & yerthly a kinde of armony, and oneles it were governed with a formal concorde and discribed nombre, how coulde it longe continue? [29]

Our universe is a poem written in careful meter by the creative godhead, what is commonly known as the book of nature. Under such an assumption, God as poet and nature as poem are not arbitrary similes, but rather descriptive facts. To accord with these facts, the metrics, stanza form, and total structure of a man-made poem should therefore image the divinely-decreed orderliness of the cosmos.

Poetical composition by a mortal poet, then, should rightly repeat the universal harmony of numbers. This expectation was clearly enunciated by St. Augustine, the classic authority on poetic meter as numerical proportion. In the *De musica* he unequivocally declares: "A foot is divided into two harmonious parts and in this way delights the ear." [30] Moreover, this harmony must be repeated in the line: "A meter can only be a verse if it has two members harmoniously joined together." [31] According to the esthetics of St. Augustine, a poem is built up of units called "feet," each of which contains two parts harmoniously related, and of larger units called "verses" (or lines), each of which also contains two harmoniously related parts. Everywhere in the poem—in each foot and in each line—mathematical harmony should be evident. Proportion is the sine qua non of esthetics.[32] The principle is more easily enunciated in theory, of course, than applied in practice, and not surprisingly it seems to have been one of those things that the theorist proposes but the practitioner disposes. Nonetheless, the principle continued precariously as a premise for poetical composition,[33] so that most Elizabethan critics accepted it, some by tacit compliance and others by overt statement.

Samuel Daniel, for example, expressed the theory in its more modest latter-day formulation:

> All verse is but a frame of wordes, confinde within certaine measure; differing from the ordinarie speach, and introduced, the better to expresse mens conceipts, both for delight and memorie. Which frame of wordes consisting of *Rithmus* or *Metrum*, Number or Measure, are disposed into divers fashions, according to the humour of the Composer and the set of the time.[34]

Puttenham expounded the thesis at some length, giving it additional dimension by orienting it toward the disciplines of mathematics and theology:

> It is said by such as professe the Mathematicall sciences, that all things stand by proportion, and that without it nothing could stand to be good or beautiful. The Doctors of our Theologie to the same effect, but in other termes, say that God made the world by number, measure, and weight; some for weight say tune. . . . Poesie is a skill to speake & write harmonically: and verses or rime be a kind of Musicall utterance.[35]

In the same vein, Ben Jonson defined poetry as an art "expressing the life of man in fit measure, numbers, and harmony." [36] When Samuel Daniel rose to the defense of English meter, not so evidently quantitative as classical meters, he attempted to adjust its use of accent to the traditional expectation that verse be measured:

> As Greeke and Latine verse consists of the number and quantitie of sillables, so doth the English verse of measure and accent. And though it doth not strictly observe long and short sillables, yet it most religiously respects the accent: and as the short and the long make number, so the Acute and grave accent yeelde harmonie: And harmonie is likewise number, so that the English verse then hath number, measure and harmonie in the best proportion of Musike.[37]

A mind as large as Sidney's might define poetry so generously that any maker of fictions, whether he expressed himself in measured verses or in prose, was lauded as a poet.[38] But most critics were more circumspect in delimiting the poetic genre, and they reserved the title of poet for him who composed according to "number, weight, and measure." "Numbers" and "measures," in fact, became a synecdoche, almost a synonym, for poetry. While critics argued fiercely whether rhyme was essential to poetry, they rarely questioned the need for metrical arrangement.

As a prominent case in point, we might look at the concluding couplet of Marvell's commendatory poem addressed to Milton and printed with *Paradise Lost:*

> Thy verse created like thy theme sublime,
> In number, weight, and measure, needs not rime.

This is Marvell's highest praise for the poet who "assert[ed] eternal Providence," indeed a theme sublime. While absolving Milton of any blame for composing in blank verse, Marvell professes approval that he had complied with the rules of making. And even Sidney conceded that "the Senate of Poets hath chosen verse as their fittest raiment . . . , peasing [weighing] each sillable of eache word by just proportion, according to the dignitie of the subject." [39]

One of Sidney's arguments for the defence of poetry, in fact, is the commonplace assertion that "Speech next to Reason, be the greatest gift bestowed upon *Mortalitie*," and therefore poetry, "which doth most polish that blessing of speech," cannot be "praiseless." Sidney then analyzes how poetry brings speech to its highest polish:

> [Poetry] considereth each word not onely as a man may say by his forcible qualitie, but by his best measured quantity: carrying even in themselves a *Harmonie*, without perchance number, measure, order, proportion, be in our time growne odious (*Defence of poesie*, F3^{v}).

In Sidney's time, of course, the commitment to cosmic orderliness was beginning to weaken, and metrical experimentation—even flagrant violation of the rules—was soon to become an expected part of the virtuoso poet's performance. But Sidney still acknowledged the arithmetical proclivities of the divine metrician, and expected to find something of the same proportions in poetry.

The injunction that the artist create in emulation of the heavenly maker conditioned not only poetics, but also the esthetic assumptions behind other artistic media. The use of number, weight, and measure is particularly appropriate to architecture, which must use dimension of some sort, and not surprisingly we find among architects a tendency to proportion the building in accordance with the celestial harmony. The building in its structure reflects the arrangement of parts in the universe so that it becomes an architectural microcosm.[40]

The renaissance was well aware of classical precedent for buildings which reproduced cosmic patterns. Plutarch, for example, had offered this comment to explain the notable form of Vesta's temple in Rome:

> It was *Numa* that built the round temple of the goddesse *Vesta*, in which is kept the everlasting fire: meaning to represent not the forme of the earth, which they say is *Vesta*, but the figure of the whole world, in the middest whereof (according to the *Pythagorians* opinion) remaineth the proper seate and abiding place of fire, which they call *Vesta*, and name it the Unity.[41]

If Plutarch is correct, Numa Pompilius, the disciple of Pythagoras whom Ovid extolls in Book XV of the *Metamorphoses,* built the temple of Vesta as a sort of orrery to demonstrate the position of the central fire in the Pythagorean cosmos. In the seventeenth century, when heliocentrism became a viable alternative to geocentrism, Gerard Johann Vossius recalled Plutarch's observation and used it as the basis for including Numa among those ancients who placed the sun in the middle of the universe:

> As Plutarch records, Numa made the temple of Vesta (by which fire is represented) to be round, like an image of the world, in the middle of which there is that eternal fire, by which he meant the Sun.[42]

In a comparable vein Edward Sherburne, the translator of Manilius, recorded that the Circus Maximus in Rome was similarly intended as an architectural planetarium:

> The High Esteem, which the Antient *Romans* had for Astronomical Learning, appears even by their Publick Games in the *Circus Maximus;* whose Order and Disposition represented that of the Heavens. The *Circus* being of an *Elliptical* or *Oval* Figure; having twelve Gates or Entries resembling the twelve Signs of the Zodiack. In the Midst an *Obelisque,* as the *Sun:* On each side thereof three *Metae,* denoting the other Six Planets, which in their respective Courses mark out the several Intervals or Spaces, into which the Mundane System is divided. So that the *Circensian Games* seem not to have been so much, an Exercise of Charioting and Racing, as an *Astronomical Cursus;* wherein the People were not only delighted by the Exhibition of corporal Games, but had their Minds also instructed to apprehend the Course and Order of the Celestial Bodies, which in the Great *Circus* of the World are continually moving.[43]

An example of this sort of cosmic architecture in the Judeo-Christian tradition was developed from the fabulous temple which Solomon had constructed in Jerusalem, as Marin Mersenne reports.[44] Mersenne, like the other proponents of microcosmic architecture, was seeking to reassure those who were desperately looking for familiar forms as they felt their ordered universe dissolving into an incomprehensible physics without an ascertainable plan.

Given this context, it is not surprising to find that Tommaso Campanella laid out his utopian City of the Sun in a cosmic pattern with symbolic intentions:

> The greater part of the city is built upon a high hill, which rises from an extensive plain. . . . It is divided into seven rings or huge circles named from the seven planets, and the way from one to the other of these is by four streets and through four gates, that look towards the four points of the compass.[45]

It might be more surprising to realize that Michelangelo laid out his famed Medici Chapel as a tetrad, so that the figures on the tombs —the four river gods and the four statues representing divisions of the day—tie into the cycle of time and the cosmic form of the calendar.[46] And even more curious, Knole House, the home of Thomas Sackville, is faithfully reported to have contained "365 rooms corresponding to the days of the year, 52 staircases corresponding to the weeks of the year, and 7 courts corresponding to the days of the week." [47]

Since music is the discipline devoted to the exposition of proportion, it is wholly reasonable to expect that musical compositions reflect cosmic patterns.[48] In Boethian terms, the *musica instrumentalis* must be consonant with the *musica mundana*. A recent editor of a mass by Jacobus Obrecht (1452–1505), *Sub tuum presidium*, concludes: "It is a crystal-clear musico-mathematical cosmos, a number symphony, a cathedral in tone for Our Lady." [49] Dance as a visible performance of music likewise revealed cosmic configurations—it was, indeed, little more than a metaphor for cosmic order. To this end, Claude François Menestrier reconstructs a cogent bit of history about the ballet: "The origin of the use of dance and music in the cult comes from the opinion of the Pythagoreans who believed that God was a number and a harmony, and for that reason they honoured Him with measured cadences to show that they believed that He was." [50] By rendering palpable the *musica mundana*, God's art, instrumental music and the dance constituted an act of worship.

The discipline of music most clearly and directly echoes the celestial harmony, and therefore it is logical that other disciplines repeat its measures and proportions. St. Augustine had established the rhythms of music as the touchstone for poetical meters—in actuality, his *De musica* is first and foremost a prescription for metrics in poetry. Architecture also repeated the concordant modulations of music, as the treatise of Vitruvius had propounded. As a result, the imperative for harmony in an edifice was so strong that Mersenne argued this theorem: "L'Architecture & ses proportions sont semblables aux Consonances & aux concerts de la Musique."[51] The famed Italian architect Leone Battista Alberti (1404–72) was one among many who had put this theorem into practice.[52] Palladio (1508–80) carried it to its logical extreme.[53]

The rationale for a work of art (literary, architectural, or musical) as a microcosm had been fully expounded by St. Augustine in his *De musica*, probably the most important of all texts for understanding medieval esthetics. Augustine assumes that there are numbers in the soul, archetypal patterns, and the soul is pleased and judges favorably when sounds reiterate these numbers. A sympathetic vibration is produced, resulting in delight to the soul. As Boethius might have put it, the *musica instrumentalis* merges into *musica humana* which is in accord with *musica mundana*. The result is universal consent, with the listener placed in proper relation to both the physical and the conceptual realms: "Delight orders the soul" (VI.xi). In this experience, of course, ultimate reality for Augustine lies in the presence of God, the realm of the eternal and infinite, and therefore physical things are subordinated to conceptual things. A hierarchy is established, with the Timaean scheme of time as the criterion for ranking:

> But what are the higher things, if not those where the highest unchangeable undisturbed and eternal equality resides? Where there is no time, because there is no change, and from where times are made and ordered and changed, imitating eternity as they do when the turn of the heavens comes back to the same state, and the heavenly bodies to the same place, and in days and months and years and centuries and other revolutions of the stars obey the laws of equality, unity, and order. So terrestrial things are subject to celestial, and their time circuits join together in harmonious succession for a poem of the universe.[54]

This is what is meant by the "book of nature," by the universe being God's art. The "poem of the universe" is a second *verbum Dei*, equal in authority with the Holy Scriptures for declaring the glory of God and explaining His mysterious ways.[55] The book of nature is an inclusive metaphor, transferring meaning from the empyrean to our lowly habitation, interrelating the conceptual and physical realms.

In his own poem, the poet sought to reproduce God's poem of the universe. Through his use of metaphor, he sought to reveal the cosmic correspondences and thereby raise his reader to higher levels of understanding—perhaps even, as Spenser prays at the end of the *Mutabilitie Cantos*, to a vision of that great Sabbath when we shall perceive the cosmic forces that unify God and Nature and Change and Man. When the poet achieves this aim, he does indeed become a maker reproducing both the subject matter and the technique of our heavenly maker. He reveals to us by means of his artifact both *natura naturata* and *natura naturans*. As John Davies of Hereford says in the final stanza of *Microcosmos*, "*Time* flies away, these *Numbers* number *time*." By his act of making, the poet is both didactic and vatic.

But the very act of creating the poem is an experience that can be meaningful, especially to the poet. The very act of making is a process that brings new knowledge to the poet, a means of working through his own experience to a larger understanding of himself and his place in the universal scheme. It is *natura naturans* in the raw. In the words of Sidney, speaking as a practising poet, "We should exercise to know." Too often instead, Sidney laments, "We exercise as having knowne." When the poet treats the poem as a perfected action and the epistemological process has stopped, the result is often a too hasty leap to an unwarranted conclusion; as Sidney says, "So is our braine delivered of much matter, which never was begotten by knowledge." Such a poem containing statements unrelated to truth produces confusion for the poet and for his reader:

> For there being two principall parts, Matter to be expressed by words, and words to expresse the matter: In neither, wee use Art or imitation rightly. Our matter is, *Quodlibet*, indeed though wrongly performing, *Ovids* Verse. *Quicquid conabor dicere, Versus erit:* [56] never marshalling it into anie assured ranck, that almost the Readers cannot tell where to finde themselves (*Defence of poesie*, H3^{v}).

When the poetic art is improperly executed, the necessary relation between words and subject matter is not achieved. The poet's utterance does not properly express the conceptual truth which should inform it. Then the meaning of the poem is *quodlibet*, whatever anyone wishes to make of it. Critical anarchy ensues. Without order in a poem, reproducing the relationship between concept and thing as established by the universal metaphor of God's poem, the reader cannot ascertain his bearings in the welter of the narrative. What should be a microcosm degenerates into literary chaos.

These intentions on the part of the poet can be best understood in the context of cosmology. Only then can we see that the act of making reproduces the divine act of creation. We as readers must reconstruct the cosmology of the poet—his ontology and epistemology—to appreciate what he is doing. Only then can we properly interpret his art work. Only then can we read his "poem of the universe," his literary microcosm which reflects ultimate reality.

And having reconstructed this esthetic in the framework of cosmology, we must apply our new perception in the reading of poems derived from this poetics. We must realize that a poem, like the universe, is composed of discrete items, but from this multeity there evolves a unity. We must further realize that the part, being integrated with a whole, must be judged in relation to that whole. A part, in fact, acquires its meaning only when viewed in this relationship. An eclogue from *The Shepheardes Calender,* for example, has limited meaning in and of itself. It achieves its full meaning only when seen as part of a prototypical calendar.

Reading a poem of this sort, then, should not be a discursive experience for the reader. He is not dealing with a continuum of parts placed end to end in seamless sequence, but rather with a series of discrete parts each of which relates directly to the whole. The poem is not designed as a sequence of causes and effects. An item does not rise out of what goes before nor does it cause what follows. An eclogue in *The Shepheardes Calender* does not grow out of the precedent eclogue and does not prepare for the next one. Each part is discontinuous with its neighbors, and the arrangement of parts is prescribed by an abstract pattern, a whole to which each part must be referred for its interpretation. The meaning of an eclogue does not inhere within it, nor can its meaning be determined by reference to the equivalent part on each side.

Similarly, for a poem like *The Faerie Queene,* where the maker bodies forth his conceit in fictive narrative, the episodes are not meaningful as a chronological sequence of events linked by a chain of cause-and-effect. We cannot read *The Faerie Queene* as though it were a novel. Rather, each episode is referred directly to the abstract pattern represented by Gloriana's court—which in turn implies a whole composed of twelve parts, again a calendar form epitomized in the annual feast at which the twelve knights meet in triumph to celebrate the betrothal of Arthur and the fairy queen. We must keep that ideal constantly in mind and use it as a touchstone in evaluating any given passage.

Furthermore, this esthetic bears upon the concept of what is beautiful in art, as St. Augustine, echoing Plotinus, instructs us. Since the part, being integrated with the whole, must be judged in relation to the whole, it contributes to perfection. A part may not in itself be beautiful; but since it contributes to a beautiful whole, it shares in and partakes of beauty, and therefore is beautiful when viewed *sub specie totius*. The argument is similar to that for the *felix culpa:* although the fall of man was an evil act considered in isolation, it is an ultimate good when placed in the total pattern of eternal providence. The argument received formal statement in art theory in the notion of *chiaroscuro;* darkness is beautiful because it gives emphasis to light, and reality can be depicted by the use of only dark and light. In a similar pattern, Duessa is beautiful even when her ugliness is unflinchingly exposed in Canto viii—perhaps she is most beautiful then—because her seduction of Red Crosse is essential to the evocation of divine grace bodied forth by the coming of Prince Arthur.

Sidney comments on this principle as applied in practice by Homer: "Well may you see *Ulisses* in a storme and in other hard plights, but they are but exercises of patience & magnanimitie, to make them shine the more in the neare following prosperitie" (*Defence of poesie*, D4^{v}). By controlling his materials in this fashion, Sidney argues, the poet achieves an advantage over the historian, who is bound to facts, and Fortune is made the "well-wayting handmayd" to Poetry. To achieve his purpose of winning the reader's mind to goodness, the poet can exaggerate and rearrange the data. As Sidney says in another context, "Who seeth not the filthinesse of evill, wanteth a great foile to perceive the bewtie of vertue" (*Defence of poesie*, E4^{v}). In yet another context, Sidney cites a well-known verse of Ovid: *Ut lateat virtus, proximitate mali*, which Sidney (preserving the subjunctive) translates as, "that good lye hid, in nearnesse of the evill." [57]

Finally, this esthetic dictates the way we should read a poem. Of course, reading a poem for the first time is a discursive experience—necessarily we must begin with line one and methodically go through to the end. But this first reading is just a start—only a preliminary, hardly reading at all. At most it allows us to construct the abstract pattern of the poem in its totality; by working inductively, we arrive at a concept of the poem as a whole. Then we can begin to *really* read the poem. Having the totality in mind, we can understand within that comprehensive framework the significance of each of its constituent parts.[58] And at this point we no longer need to read the poem consecutively from beginning to end. Having the total pattern in mind, we can read any individual part and understand it in its full dimension by relating it to the whole in which it participates.

For example, having in mind all of Book I of *The Faerie Queene*, we can read about Red Crosse's descent into Lucifera's torture chamber or his ascent of Celia's mountain, and see that each is part of the abstract pattern known in Christian doctrine as the fortunate fall (though this in turn, as Milton knew, is geared to the seasonal cycle). Red Crosse's experience with Lucifera is the pride which goeth before that fall; his experience with Celia is the salvation which redeems that fall. Moreover, if we wish to relate these two incidents directly, we can see that they are both parts of the same whole—in fact, even symmetrical parts of the same pattern. They are opposite phases in a cycle which define one another by contrast.[59] Neither has meaning by itself alone, however—only in relation to the whole pattern, which comprises an integration of all the parts. Neither episode can be read in its full dimension until we have in mind all of Book I.

The same strictures about reading hold for all the poetry derived from the poetics of making in the renaissance. The wholeness of the poem takes priority over any of its parts or even the sum of its parts. The pattern is paramount. This assumption holds not only for *The Shepheardes Calender* and *The Faerie Queene*, though they perhaps are the two most salient examples. It holds also for Sidney's *Arcadia*, for many plays of Shakespeare (especially *Love's Labour's Lost* and *A Midsummer Night's Dream*), for Donne's *Anniversaries*, for Milton's *Paradise Lost*. It holds for Sidney's *Astrophel and Stella* and for most sonnet sequences that rise above mere concession to a fad; each sonnet must be read directly in relation to a totality abstracted from the sequence taken as a whole—perhaps to an idea of beauty embodied by the lady, an idea that holds the lover and nature in a single continuum with the cosmic deity. To anthologize sonnets from a sequence, choosing the sorrowful or the elated without due regard for their counterparts, is a barbarism comparable to printing "The Passionate Shepherd to His Love" without "The Nymph's Reply."

In sum, I am calling for a revised reading of much Elizabethan poetry, especially the best of it. Conditioned as we are by the prevalent esthetics of our own times, which assume that ultimate reality resides (if anywhere) among the objects of physical nature, we are insensitive to other possibilities. We are phenomenalists by default. We follow the words of a poem slavishly from start to finish, and think that we have *read* it. We shy away from re-reading, feeling as though a repeated confrontation with the work impairs its experiential spontaneity or destroys its organicism. But the poet as maker expects re-reading. On the first reading, according to his theory, each part cannot possibly be appreciated in its proper perspective.

Moreover, the poet as maker intends that his poem be finally abstracted into an idea, a pure form. Sidney said it twice: "The skill of ech Artificer standeth in that *Idea,* or fore conceit of the worke, and not in the worke it selfe," and "They [readers] shall use the narration but as an imaginative groundplat of a profitable invention" (*Defence of poesie,* C1 and G1^v). When the poem is abstracted to pure form, spatial and temporal relationships vanish. *Here* and *there* are meaningless except in relation to the whole pattern in which they inhere, and so are *then* and *now.* The poet does not want us to deal with his universe as though we were scientists accumulating data. As we all know, the product of inductive reasoning is never conclusive, and poetry should purvey truth. He expects us to arrive with him at cosmic truth.

And then quite independently we are to go one step farther and test the validity of this conclusion by applying it to its aliquot parts. This process presupposes successive readings of a poem, though not necessarily the entire poem. Once we perceive the totality, we can discriminate parts to which we apply that totality in any sequence. Once we understand the idea of Gloriana's court—indeed, only then—we can go back and appreciate the meaning of Red Crosse's union with Una, of Guyon's light-hearted escapade with Phaedria, of Scudamour's devotion to Amoret, of Marinell's need for Florimell, of Calidore's idyllic interlude with Pastorella. We can enjoy one or any number of these episodes, and we can determine the sequence of how they follow one another. Once we discern the comprehensive order of Spenser's universe, we can enjoy its wide variety in the quantity and in the sequence of our choice. Then *we* become the agents of metaphor. Then *we* begin to act as makers, imposing upon our own experience the forms devised by Spenser.

Notes

[1] For a discussion comparing the poem to a "perspective glass," see George Puttenham, *The arte of English poesie* (London, 1589), D3^v–D4. For the theory put into practice, see Spenser, *Faerie Queene,* VI.proem.5.

[2] *The defence of poesie* (William Ponsonby; London, 1595), B4^v.

[3] *Defence of poesie,* B4^v–C1. See pp. 306–307, above.

[4] Spenser, *Epithalamion,* 433.

[5] I use the word *perfection* as the Elizabethans did, in its literal sense from L. *perficere,* "to go through to the end." Cf. Spenser, *Mutabilitie Cantos,* VII.vii.58.7; and Guillaume Saluste du Bartas, *Devine weekes and workes,* tr. Joshua Sylvester (London, 1605), p. 117.

[6] Cf. Frances A. Yates, *The French Academies of the Sixteenth Century* (London, 1947), pp. 84–85. See also Gerald Snare, "The Muses on Poetry: Spenser's *The Teares of the Muses*," *Tulane Studies in English*, 17 (1969), 31–52.

[7] For an exhaustive analysis of number symbolism in the *Epithalamion*, see A. Kent Hieatt, *Short Time's Endless Monument* (Columbia Univ. Press, 1960).

[8] *Letters* [55], tr. Sister Wilfrid Parsons, 5 vols. (New York, 1951–56), I.274.

[9] *On Music*, tr. Robert C. Taliaferro (New York, 1947), p. 355. Here St. Augustine doubtless had in mind a suggestive passage from Plato's *Timaeus* (47A–C), quoted p. 323, n. 48, above. On the meaning of St. Augustine's phrase *carmen universitatis*, see E. N. Tigerstedt, "The Poet as Creator: Origins of a Metaphor," *Comparative Literature Studies*, 5 (1968), 465–468.

[10] *Iliad*, XIV.153–158. It is interesting to note how Reuchlin has perverted this passage from its original meaning. In Homer, Hera in this episode is angry at Zeus ("hateful was he to her heart"), not loving toward him.

[11] *De arte cabalistica libri tres*, tr. Thomas Stanley, in *The history of philosophy*, 2nd ed. (London, 1687), p. 573.

[12] In *Spenser and the Numbers of Time* (London, 1964), Alastair Fowler has attempted to read *The Faerie Queene* as "an astonishingly complex web of interlocking numerical patterns of many different kinds" (p. 4). While I accept most of his premises and admire his ingenuity, I do not usually agree with his conclusions. He has misapplied the principles of "numerical composition," to use the phrase of Ernst R. Curtius (*European Literature and the Latin Middle Ages*, tr. Willard R. Trask [New York, 1953], pp. 501 ff.). In his mania for counting lines, Fowler has in fact complicated what must remain simple, and consequently has obscured what should be obvious. And he has lost the most important point: that Gloriana's court provides the monad from which the individual quests proceed, and thereby holds each of the several books in the same continuum.

[13] We might deduce some hint about his technique of depicting Gloriana from his description of Nature in the *Mutabilitie Cantos*, esp. VII.vii.1–13.

[14] *Coleridge's Miscellaneous Criticism*, ed. Thomas M. Raysor (London, 1936), p. 36.

[15] "The Pattern of *Love's Labour's Lost*," *Shakespeare Studies*, Vol. VII, forthcoming.

[16] "Preface to the Reader," *The Iliads of Homer* [1611], tr. Chapman, in *Chapman's Homer*, ed. Allardyce Nicoll, 2 vols. (New York, 1956), I.14.

[17] *Chapman's Homer*, ed. Nicoll, I.543. Jean de Sponde (1557–95) published his edition of Homer in Basle, 1583.

[18] *Achilles shield*, in *Chapman's Homer*, ed. Nicoll, I.557.

[19] *Ibid.*, I.558.

[20] *Ibid.*, I.548.

[21] (London, 1575), fol. 17.

[22] Macrobius, *Saturnalia*, V.i.19, cited by Curtius, *European Literature*, p. 400. An elaborate structure for the *Aeneid* in terms of numerical composition has been worked out by George E. Duckworth, *Structural Patterns and Proportions in Vergil's Aeneid* (Univ. of Michigan Press, 1962).

[23] In *Manto* (1486), cited by Robert M. Durling, "The Divine Analogy in Ariosto," *Modern Language Notes*, 78 (1963), 4.

[24] This field has been productively explored by Maren-Sofie Røstvig. "Ars Aeterna: Renaissance Poetics and Theories of Divine Creation," *Mosaic*, 3 (1969–70), 40–61; and "Structure as Prophecy: The Influence of Biblical Exegesis upon Theories of Literary Structure," in *Silent Poetry*, ed. Alastair Fowler (London, 1970), pp. 32–72.

[25] "Second Proem" to *Heptaplus*, tr. Douglas Carmichael, in Pico, *On the Dignity of Man*, tr. Charles Glenn Wallis (Indianapolis, 1965), p. 79; cf. *ibid.*, pp. 70 ff.

[26] See, for example, *ibid.*, p. 76. The thesis that the tabernacle of Moses is an allegorical description of the whole world was first recorded by Clement of Alexandria (*Stromateis*, V.vi).

[27] Cristoforo Landino, for example, comments in an essay which prefaces his edition of Dante:

> God is the supreme poet, and the world is His poem. And indeed God arranged His creation, in the visible and in the invisible world, which are His "works," in number, measure, and weight. Whence the prophet said: God makes all things according to number, measure, and weight. So the poet composes his poem with number in the feet, with measure in short and long syllables, and with weight in the maxims and emotions.

> Et e idio sommo poeta: et e el mondo suo poema. Et chome idio dispone la creatura, in el visibile et invisibile mondo che e sua opera in numero Misura et Peso. Onde el propheta Deus omnia facit numero mensura et pondere. Chosi el poeta chol numero de piedi: Con la misura delle syllabe brievi et lunghe: et col pondo delle sententie et de glaffecti constituiscono ellor poema

(Dante, *Divina commedia*, with commentary of Landino [Florence, 1481], [*]8^{v}). See also Nicolas le Fèvre de la Boderie, "Les sentiers de sapience," in Francesco Giorgio, *L'Harmonie du monde*, tr. Guy le Fèvre de la Boderie (Paris, 1579), ē5; Giorgio, *ibid.*, pp. 343–344; and Henry Reynolds, *Mythomystes* [1632] in J. E. Spingarn, *Critical Essays of the Seventeenth Century*, 3 vols. (Oxford Univ. Press, 1908–09), I.157–159.

As an example from among the scientists, John Dee brings to a close his "Mathematicall praeface" to Billingsley's translation of Euclid with this statement:

> Unto God our Creator, let us all be thankefull: for that, *As he, of his Goodnes, by his Powre, and in his Wisedome, hath Created all thynges, in Number, Waight, and Measure:* So, to us, of hys great Mercy, he hath revealed Meanes, whereby, to atteyne the sufficient and necessary knowledge of the foresayd hys three principall Instrumentes: Which Meanes, I have abundantly proved unto you, to be the *Sciences* and *Artes Mathematicall*

(*Elements* [London, 1570], A4). See also the dedicatory epistle in Thomas Masterson, *Third booke of arithmeticke* (London, 1595), A2–A2^{v} (quoted p. 90, above); and Herbert Butterfield, *The Origins of Modern Science 1300–1800*, 2nd ed. (London, 1957), p. 90.

[28] In G. Gregory Smith, *Elizabethan Critical Essays*, 2 vols. (Oxford Univ. Press, 1904), II.329.

[29] *An abridgemente of the notable worke of Polidore Virgile*, tr. Thomas Langley (London, 1570), fol. 16^{v}.

[30] *On Music*, tr. Taliaferro, p. 298. The assumption that the poet is a creator reproducing the divine proportions and patterns underlies the entire *De musica*, but appears nowhere more explicitly than in VI.xii (tr. Taliaferro, p. 359).

[31] *Ibid.*, p. 321.

[32] Cf. *ibid.*, pp. 200–201.

[33] It is once again propounded, for example, by Bernardino Tomitano, *Quattro libri della lingua thoscana* (Padua, 1570), fol. 229–235.

[34] *A defence of ryme* [c.1603] in Daniel, *Poems and A Defence of Ryme*, ed. Arthur C. Sprague (London, 1950), p. 131.

[35] *Arte of English poesie*, K1. Cf. William Webbe, *A discourse of English poetrie* [1586], in Smith, *Elizabethan Critical Essays*, I.267.

[36] *Timber* in *Ben Jonson*, ed. C. H. Herford and Percy and Evelyn Simpson, 11 vols. (Oxford, 1925–52), VIII.635.

[37] *Defence of ryme*, p. 132.

[38] The question "Are prose fictions poems?" consumed the interest of many Italian critics; see Baxter Hathaway, *The Age of Criticism: The Late Renaissance in Italy* (Cornell Univ. Press, 1962), pp. 87–117.

[39] *Defence of poesie*, C3. Cf. also, "Hee [the poet] commeth to you with words set in delightfull proportion" (*ibid.*, E2).

[40] See Rudolf Wittkower, *Architectural Principles in the Age of Humanism* (London, 1949), esp. pp. 1–9, 24–28, 89–127; Otto von Simson, *The Gothic Cathedral* (New York, 1956), esp. pp. 3–50; and George Lesser, *Gothic Cathedrals and Sacred Geometry*, 2 vols. (London, 1957), esp. I.1–9.

It should be noted that a building which reproduces cosmic patterns might be put together in either of two different ways: in an arithmetical way—that is, it might be constructed of discrete parts, each of which has its own symbolic number and the sum of which might have symbolic value from numerology (cf. Plate 27); or it might be put together in a musical way—that is, the relationships between its parts are harmonious proportions and the edifice as a whole embodies the universal harmony. The arithmetical way seems to have been the common practice in the middle ages; see Elizabeth R. Sunderland, "Symbolic Numbers and Romanesque Church Plans," *Journal of the Society of Architectural Historians*, 18 (1959), 94–103. The musical way defines the distinctively renaissance style as instituted by Alberti.

[41] *The lives of the noble Grecians and Romanes*, tr. Sir Thomas North (London, 1603), p. 69 ["Numa"]. For a cosmology that places fire in the center of the universe see pp. 127–128, above.

> [42] Ac eapropter, ut Plutarchus tradit, templum Vestae, quo ignis significatur, rotundum fecit, ad mundi imaginem, in cuius medio esset ignis ille aeternus, quo repraesentabat Solem

(*De philosophorum sectis liber* [The Hague, 1657], p. 39).

[43] Manilius, *The sphere*, tr. Sherburne (London, 1675), fol. a1.

[44] *L'Harmonie universelle* (Paris, 1627), pp. 464–471.

[45] *Civitas solis, idea reipublicae platonicae* [1623], tr. T. W. Halliday, in *Famous Utopias of the Renaissance*, ed. Frederic R. White (New York, 1955), p. 158. It is likely that Campanella was influenced by the extensive layout of buildings which Tycho Brahe had constructed in a tetrad arrangement at Uraniborg; for a plan of the grounds, see Tycho, *Astronomiae instauratae mechanica* (Wandesburg, 1598), fol. H1^{v}.

[46] See Erwin Panofsky, *Studies in Iconology* [1939] (New York, 1962), pp. 205–208.

[47] Fowler, *Spenser and Numbers of Time*, p. 240; citing Victoria Sackville-West, *Knole and the Sackvilles* (London, 1958), p. 19. This inaccurate trivium is still duly repeated by guides at Knole House and appears in the first paragraph of the official guidebook published by the National Trust. It is manifestly a fabrication, however, since Knole House was built over a long period of time. The present structure dates largely from 1460–80, when the original house was owned by Thomas Bourchier, Archbishop of Canterbury, and from 1603–08, when the property was owned by Thomas Sackville. Clearly, the attribution of cosmic dimensions to Knole House is more a concession to wishful thinking than to fact. Nonetheless, the desire for such a construct is significant in itself, and obtrudes into the description of other famous buildings. For example, an early eighteenth-century Frenchman touring England visited the cathedral at Salisbury and observed that the townspeople "never fail to tell

those that come to see it, that it has as many Doors as there are Months, as many Windows as there are Days, and as many Pillars as there are Hours in the Year" (Henri Misson, *Memoirs and Observations in His Travels over England*, tr. John Ozell [London, 1719], pp. 281–282). For a discussion of other buildings in England constructed according to these principles, see Christopher Butler, *Number Symbolism* (New York, 1970), pp. 106–114.

[48] See pp. 95–97, above. See also Richard L. Crocker, "Pythagorean Mathematics and Music," *Journal of Aesthetics and Art Criticism*, 22 (1963–64), 189–198, 325–335.

[49] M. van Crevel in Obrecht, *Opera omnia*, Vol. VI (Amsterdam, 1959); quoted by Maren-Sofie Røstvig, *The Hidden Sense* (Oslo, 1963), pp. 21–22.

[50] *Des ballets anciens et modernes* (Paris, 1682), pp. 23–24; quoted by Yates, *French Academies*, p. 270. Cf. Yates, *ibid.*, pp. 60–62, 243, 248–249, 274, 300.

[51] *L'Harmonie universelle*, p. 464.

[52] "According to Alberti's well-known mathematical definition, based on Vitruvius, beauty consists in a rational integration of the proportions of all the parts of a building, in such a way that every part has its absolutely fixed size and shape, and nothing could be added or taken away without destroying the harmony of the whole" (Wittkower, *Architectural Principles*, pp. 6–7; cf. also pp. 29, 100–102). See Gretchen L. Finney, *Musical Backgrounds for English Literature: 1580–1650* (Rutgers Univ. Press, 1962), p. 35. See also Leo Spitzer, *Classical and Christian Ideas of World Harmony* (Johns Hopkins Press, 1963), pp. 125–126.

[53] See Wittkower, *Architectural Principles*, pp. 110–124.

[54] *On Music*, tr. Taliaferro, p. 355.

[55] No one made the point more concisely than Pierre de la Primaudaye:

> We must lay before our eyes two books which God hath given unto us to instruct us by, and to lead us to the knowledge of himselfe, namely the booke of nature, and the booke of his word

(*The second part of the French academie*, tr. T. Bowes [London, 1605], p. 12). Cf. also Sir Thomas Browne:

> There are two Books from whence I collect my Divinity; besides that written one of God, another of his servant Nature, that universal and publick Manuscript, that lies expans'd unto the Eyes of all: those that never saw him in the one, have discovered him in the other

(*Religio Medici* [I.xvi] in *Works*, ed. Geoffrey Keynes, 6 vols. [London, 1928–31], I.21).

[56] "Whatever I try to say, it will be verse." Sidney is recalling a line from *Tristia*, IV.x.26, though he changes it rather drastically for his own purpose.

[57] *Defence of poesie*, F3. The line alluded to in Ovid is *Ars amatoria*, II.662, though Sidney misquotes it for his own purpose.

[58] This state of mind is what Nicholas of Cusa called the *visio intellectualis;* cf. Ernst Cassirer, *The Individual and the Cosmos in Renaissance Philosophy*, tr. Mario Domandi (New York, 1964), pp. 13–14, 31–32. While writing this passage I was also recalling from afar Susanne K. Langer's *Philosophy in a New Key*, 3rd ed. (Harvard Univ. Press, 1957). Upon rereading it to confirm this debt, I am delighted to find a passage such as this: "The material of poetry is discursive, but the product—the artistic phenomenon—is not; its significance is purely implicit in the poem as a totality, as a form compounded of sound and suggestion, statement and reticence" (pp. 261–262).

[59] Spenser works similarly to produce a pattern by contrasts in the characters Belphoebe and Amoret; see C. S. Lewis, *Spenser's Images of Life*, ed. Alastair Fowler (Cambridge Univ. Press, 1967), pp. 45 ff.

LIST OF WORKS CITED

List of Works Cited

Abrams, Meyer H. *The Mirror and the Lamp.* Oxford Univ. Press, 1953.

Aelianus, Claudius. *A registre of hystories.* Translated by Abraham Fleming. London, 1576.

Africa, Thomas W. "Copernicus' Relation to Aristarchus and Pythagoras." *Isis* 52 (1961), 403–409.

Agrippa, Heinrich Cornelius. *De occulta philosophia libri III.* Antwerp, 1531.

———. *Three books of occult philosophy.* Translated by John Freake. London, 1651.

———. *Of the vanitie and uncertaintie of artes and sciences.* Translated by James Sanford. London, 1569.

Alanus de Insulis. *De planctu naturae.* Translated by Douglas M. Moffat. New York, 1908.

Alciati, Andrea. *Emblemata.* Edited by Claude Mignault. Antwerp, 1574.

———. *Emblemata.* Edited by Claude Mignault. Antwerp, 1581.

———. *Emblemata.* Edited by Claude Mignault. Antwerp, 1608.

Alexander ab Alexandro. *Genialium dierum libri sex.* Paris, 1570.

Allen, Don C. "The Double Journey of John Donne." In *A Tribute to George Coffin Taylor,* edited by Arnold Williams. Univ. of North Carolina Press, 1952.

———. *Mysteriously Meant.* Johns Hopkins Press, 1970.

Allers, Rudolf. "Microcosmos." *Traditio* 2 (1944), 319–407.

Allman, George J. *Greek Geometry from Thales to Euclid.* Dublin, 1889.

Allot, Robert. *Wits Theatre of the little world.* London, 1599.

Alsted, Johann Heinrich. *Templum musicum: or the musical synopsis.* Translated by John Birchensha. London, 1664.

Ambrose, St. *Letters.* Translated by Sister Mary Melchior Beyenka. New York, 1954.

Ammann, Peter J. "The Musical Theory and Philosophy of Robert Fludd." *Journal of the Warburg and Courtauld Institutes* 30 (1967), 198–227.

Aneau, Barthélemy. *Picta poesis*. Lyons, 1552.

Anton, Robert. *The philosophers satyrs*. London, 1616.

Apian, Peter. *Cosmographicus liber*. Edited by Gemma Frisius. Antwerp, 1533.

Apuleius. *The Florida*. In *The Works of Apuleius*. London, 1872.

Aristotle. *De anima*. Translated by R. D. Hicks. Cambridge Univ. Press, 1907.

———. *De caelo* et al. Edited by Johann Eck. Augsburg, 1519.

———. *De caelo*. Translated by W. K. C. Guthrie. Harvard Univ. Press, 1939.

———. *De generatione et corruptione* et al. Translated by E. S. Forster. Harvard Univ. Press, 1955.

———. *Metaphysica*. Translated by Hugh Tredennick. 2 vols. London, 1933–35.

———. *Parva naturalia* et al. Translated by W. S. Hett. Harvard Univ. Press, c.1955.

———. *Physica*. Translated by P. H. Wicksteed and F. M. Cornford. 2 vols. London, 1952.

———. *On Poetry and Style*. Translated by G. M. A. Grube. New York, 1958.

Artemidorus. *De somniorum interpretatione libri quinque*. Venice, 1518.

Arwaker, Edmund. *Thoughts well employ'd*. 2nd ed. London, 1967.

Athenaeus. *The Deipnosophists*. Translated by C. B. Gulick. 6 vols. London, 1927–41.

Augustine, St. *Omnia opera*. 10 vols. Basle, 1528–29.

———. *De civitate Dei*. Translated by G. E. McCracken. 7 vols. Harvard Univ. Press, 1957–60.

———. *Answer to Skeptics*. Translated by Denis J. Kavanagh. In *Writings of Saint Augustine*. New York, 1948, Vol. I.

———. *On Music*. Translated by Robert C. Taliaferro. In *Writings of Saint Augustine*. New York, 1947, Vol. II.

———. *Letters*. Translated by Sister Wilfrid Parsons. 5 vols. New York, 1951–56.

Ausonius. *Eclogues* et al. Translated by H. G. E. White. 2 vols. London, 1949–51.

Baccou, Robert. *Histoire de la science grecque de Thalès à Socrate*. Paris, 1951.

Bailly, Jean Sylvain. *Histoire de l'astronomie ancienne*. 2nd ed. Paris, 1781.

Baker, Humphrey. *The well spring of science*. London, 1580.

Baldwyn, William. *A treatise of morall phylosophye*. London, 1550.

Barbour, J. Murray. "The Persistence of the Pythagorean Tuning System." *Scripta Mathematica* 1 (1932–33), 286–304.

Barozzi, Francesco. *Cosmographia*. Venice, 1585.

Bartholomaeus Anglicus. *De proprietatibus rerum*. Lyons, 1485.

———. *His book De proprietatibus rerum.* Edited by Stephen Batman. London, 1582.

Battestin, Martin C. "The Transforming Power: Nature and Art in Pope's Pastorals." *Eighteenth Century Studies* 2 (1968–69), 183–204.

Bauer, Robert J. "A Phenomenon of Epistemology in the Renaissance." *Journal of the History of Ideas* 31 (1970), 281–288.

Baur, Ferdinand Christian. *Apollonius von Tyana und Christus.* Tübingen, 1832.

Bayle, Pierre. *Dictionaire.* 2 vols. Rotterdam, 1697.

———. *A General Dictionary.* Translated by John Peter Bernard *et al.* 10 vols. London, 1734–41.

Bede. *Opera.* 8 vols. Basle, 1563.

Bell, Eric T. *Numerology.* New York, 1945.

———. *The Magic of Numbers.* New York, 1946.

Bentley, Richard. "A Dissertation upon the Epistles of Phalaris, Themistocles, Socrates, Euripides, and Others." In William Wotton, *Reflections upon ancient and modern learning.* 2nd ed. London, 1697.

———. *A dissertation upon the epistles of Phalaris.* London, 1699.

Bernardus, Joannes Baptista. *Seminarium totius philosophiae Aristotelicae et Platonicae.* 2nd ed. Lyons, 1599.

Berni, Count Francesco. *Moralitatis arcana ex Pytagorae symbolis.* Ferrara, 1669.

Beroaldo, Filippo. *Symbola Pythagorae moraliter explicata.* Bologna, c.1500.

———. *Symbola Pythagorae . . . moraliter explicata.* Paris, 1515.

Bessarion, Joannes, Cardinal. *In calumniatorem Platonis libri quatuor* et al. Venice, 1516.

Bindel, Ernst. *Pythagoras.* Stuttgart, 1962.

Blau, Joseph L. *The Christian Interpretation of the Cabala in the Renaissance.* Columbia Univ. Press, 1944.

Blount, Sir Thomas Pope. *A natural history.* London, 1693.

Blundeville, Thomas. *Exercises.* London, 1594.

Boas, George. "Philosophies of Science in Florentine Platonism." In *Art, Science, and History in the Renaissance,* edited by Charles B. Singleton. Johns Hopkins Press, 1967.

Boas, Marie. *The Scientific Renaissance, 1450–1630.* New York, 1962.

Bober, Harry. "In Principio: Creation before Time." In *Essays in Honor of Erwin Panofsky,* edited by Millard Meiss. 2 vols. New York Univ. Press, 1961, I.13–28.

Boccaccio, Giovanni. *Boccaccio on Poetry.* Translated by Charles G. Osgood. Princeton Univ. Press, 1930.

Boehm, Friedrich. *De symbolis pythagoreis.* Berlin, 1905.

Boethius. *Opera, quae extant, omina.* Edited by Henricus Loritus Glareanus. Basle, 1546.

———. *De arithmetica.* In J.-P. Migne, *Patrologia Latina,* Vol. 63. Paris, 1882.

———. *Arithmetica . . . adjecto commentario, mysticam numerorum applicationem perstringente.* Edited by Girard Ruffus. Paris, 1521.

———. *De geometria.* In J.-P. Migne, *Patrologia Latina,* Vol. 63. Paris, 1882.

———. *De musica.* In J.-P. Migne, *Patrologia Latina,* Vol. 63. Paris, 1882.

———. *The Principles of Music.* Translated by Calvin M. Bower. Unpublished doctoral dissertation at George Peabody College for Teachers, 1966.

Boissard, Jean Jacques. *De divinatione et magicis praestigiis.* Oppenheim, 1616?.

Bonghi, Pietro. *Mysticae numerorum significationis liber.* Bergamo, 1585.

Borrel, Jean. *De quadratura circuli libri duo.* Lyons, 1559.

Borsch, Johann Jacob. *Dissertatio historica de peregrinationibus Pythagorae.* Jena, 1692.

Boscardus, Carolus. *Ænigmata et griphi veterum ac recentium.* Douai, 1604.

Boyancé, Pierre. "Sur la vie pythagoricienne." *Revue des études grecques* 52 (1939), 36–50.

Boyle, Charles. *Dr. Bentley's dissertations on the epistles of Phalaris, and the fables of Æsop, examined.* London, 1698.

———, ed. *Phalaris epistolae.* Oxford, 1695.

Brassicanus, Joannes Alexander. *Proverbiorum symmicta.* Vienna, 1529.

A breefe conjecturall discourse, upon the hierographicall letters & caracters found upon fower fishes, taken neere Marstrand [STC 17650]. London, 1589.

A brefe and plesaunte worke, and sience, of the phelosopher, Pictagoras [STC 20524]. London, 1560?

Bridgman, William. *Translations from the Greek.* London, 1804.

Browne, Sir Thomas. *Works.* Edited by Geoffrey Keynes. 6 vols. London, 1928–31.

———. *Religio Medici and Other Works.* Edited by L. C. Martin. Oxford, 1964.

———. *Pseudodoxia epidemica, The garden of Cyrus,* et al. 4th ed. London, 1658.

Brucker, Johann Jakob. *Historia critica philosophiae.* 2nd ed. 6 vols. Leipzig, 1766–67.

Bruno, Giordano. *De monade numero et figura liber.* Frankfurt, 1591.

Buddeus, Joannes Franciscus. *Compendium historiae philosophicae.* Halle, 1731.

Bullialdus, Ismael. *Astronomia philolaica.* Paris, 1645.

Bulstrode, Whitelocke. *An essay of transmigration, in defense of Pythagoras.* London, 1692.

Bundy, Murray W. " 'Invention' and 'Imagination' in the Renaissance." *Journal of English and Germanic Philology* 29 (1930), 535–545.

Burch, George B. "The Counter-Earth." *Osiris* 11 (1954), 267–294.

Burkert, Walter. *Weisheit und Wissenschaft: Studien zu Pythagoras, Philolaos und Platon.* Nuremberg, 1962.

Burley, Walter. *Liber de vita et moribus philosophorum et poetarum.* Strasbourg 1516.

———. *Liber de vita et moribus philosophorum.* Edited by Hermann Knust. Tübingen, 1886.

Burnet, John. *Greek Philosophy: Part I, Thales to Plato.* London, 1928.

———. *Early Greek Philosophy.* 4th ed. London, 1945.

Burtt, E. A. *The Metaphysical Foundations of Modern Physical Science.* New York, 1932.

Butler, Christopher. *Number Symbolism.* New York, 1970.

Butterfield, Herbert. *The Origins of Modern Science 1300–1800.* 2nd ed. London, 1957.

Calcagnini, Celio. *Opera.* Basle, 1544.

Calepinus, Ambrosius. *Cornucopiae.* Reggio, 1502.

Calvin, Jean. *Institutes of the Christian Religion.* Translated by F. L. Battles. 2 vols. Philadelphia, 1960.

Camerarius, Joachim. *Decuriae XXI.* ΣΥΜΜΙΚΤΩΝ ΠΡΟΒΛΗΜΑΤΩΝ. Geneva, 1594.

———. *Appendix problematum.* Geneva, 1596.

———. *Delectae quaedam graecae epistolae.* Tübingen, 1540.

Cameron, Alister. *The Pythagorean Background of the Theory of Recollection.* Menasha, Wis., 1938.

Campanella, Tommaso. *The Defense of Galileo.* Translated by Grant McColley, Northampton, Mass., 1938.

———. *Civitas solis, idea reipublicae platonicae* [1623]. Translated by T. W. Halliday. In *Famous Utopias of the Renaissance,* edited by Frederic R. White. New York, 1955.

Campano, Giovanni. *Tetragonismus idest circuli quadratura.* Edited by Luca Gaurico. Venice, 1503.

Campion, Thomas. *Observations in the art of English poesie* [1602]. In G. Gregory Smith, *Elizabethan Critical Essays.* 2 vols. Oxford Univ. Press, 1904.

Capparelli, Vincenzo. *La sapienza di Pitagora.* 2 vols. Padua, 1941–44.

Carew, Richard. *The excellency of the English tongue* [c. 1595]. In G. Gregory Smith, *Elizabethan Critical Essays.* 2 vols. Oxford Univ. Press, 1904.

Carpenter, Nan Cooke. *Music in the Medieval and Renaissance Universities.* Univ. of Oklahoma Press, 1958.

Case, John. *Apologia musices.* Oxford, 1588.

———. *Lapis philosophicus.* Oxford, 1599.

———. *Ancilla philosophiae.* Oxford, 1599.

Cassiodorus. *An Introduction to Divine and Human Readings.* Translated by Leslie W. Jones. Columbia Univ. Press, 1946.

Cassirer, Ernst. *Individuum und Kosmos in der Philosophie der Renaissance.* Leipzig, 1927.

———. *The Individual and the Cosmos in Renaissance Philosophy.* Translated by Mario Domandi. New York, 1964.

Cattan, Christophe de. *La géomance.* Paris, 1558.

———. *The geomancie.* Translated by Francis Sparry. London, 1591.

Cellarius, Andreas. *Harmonia macrocosmica.* Amsterdam, 1661.

Celtis, Conrad. *Quatuor libri amorum.* Nuremberg, 1502.

Censorinus. *De die natali* et al. Edited by Filippo Beroaldo. Bologna, 1497.

Chaignet, A. Ed. *Pythagore et la philosophie pythagoricienne.* 2 vols. Paris, 1873.

Chamberlain, David S. "Philosophy of Music in the *Consolatio* of Boethius." *Speculum* 45 (1970), 80–97.

Champier, Symphorien. *Vocabularius . . . naturalis philosophiae.* Lyons, 1508.

———. *Symphonia Platonis cum Aristotele.* Paris, 1516.

———. *Periarchon.* Lyons, 1533.

Chapman, George. *Poems.* Edited by Phyllis B. Bartlett. New York, 1941.

———. *Chapman's Homer.* Edited by Allardyce Nicoll. 2 vols. New York, 1956.

Chaucer, Geoffrey. *Poetical Works.* Edited by F. N. Robinson. Boston, 1933.

Cherniss, Harold. *Aristotle's Criticism of Presocratic Philosophy.* Johns Hopkins Press, 1935.

———. "Plato as Mathematician." *Review of Metaphysics* 4(1951), 395–425.

Chew, Samuel C. *The Pilgrimage of Life.* Yale Univ. Press, 1962.

Churrerius, Caspar, ed. *Oratio Joannis Oecolampadii* et al. Hagenau, 1517.

Cicero. *Academica.* Edited by J. S. Reid. London, 1885.

———. *De divinatione* et al. Translated by W. A. Falconer. Harvard Univ. Press, 1953.

———. *On Divination.* Translated by C. D. Yonge. London, 1868.

———. *De finibus bonorum et malorum.* Translated by H. Rackham. London, 1931.

———. *The Nature of the Gods.* Translated by C. D. Yonge. London, 1868.

———. *De officiis.* Translated by Walter Miller. London, 1928.

———. *Tusculanae disputationes.* Translated by J. E. King. Harvard Univ. Press, 1950.

———. *Those fyve questions* [Tusculan]. Translated by John Dolman. London, 1561.

Cirvelo, Pedro Sanchez. *Cursus quattuor mathematicarum artium liberalium.* Alcalá, 1516.

Clagett, Marshall. *Greek Science in Antiquity*. London, 1957.

Clement, St. *Stromateis* et al. In *The Ante-Nicene Fathers*, edited by Alexander Roberts and James Donaldson. New York, 1899. Vol. II.

———. *Exhortation to the Greeks*. Translated by G. W. Butterworth. London, 1919.

Clichtoveus, Jodocus. *De mystica numerorum significatione opusculum*. Paris, 1513.

Cocles, Bartholomaeus. *Chyromantiae ac physionomiae anastasis*. Bologna, 1504.

Colding, Nicolaus. *Dissertatio de Pythagora, eiusque femore aureo*. Copenhagen, 1702.

Coleridge, Samuel T. *Coleridge's Miscellaneous Criticism*. Edited by Thomas M. Raysor. London, 1936.

Collingwood, R. G. *The Idea of Nature*. Oxford, 1945.

Conger, George P. *Theories of Macrocosms and Microcosms in the History of Philosophy*. Columbia Univ. Press, 1922.

Cooper, Thomas. *Bibliotheca Eliotae*. London, 1545.

———. *Bibliotheca Eliotae*. London, 1548.

———. *Thesaurus linguae Romanae & Britannicae*. London, 1584.

Copernicus, Nicolaus. *De revolutionibus orbium coelestium, libri VI*. Nuremberg, 1543.

Cornford, F. M. "Mysticism and Science in the Pythagorean Tradition." *Classical Quarterly* 16 (1922), 139 ff.; 17 (1923), 1 ff.

———. *Plato's Cosmology*. London, 1937.

———. *The Unwritten Philosophy and Other Essays*. Cambridge Univ. Press, 1950.

Cortes, Martin. *The arte of navigation*. Translated by Richard Eden. London, 1561.

Cosenza, Mario E. *Dictionary of the Italian Humanists*. 6 vols. Boston, 1962.

Cousin, Gilbert, ed. *Epistolarum laconicarum . . . farragines duae*. Basle, 1554.

Cousin, Jean. *Livre de perspective*. Paris, 1560.

Craig, Hardin. *The Enchanted Glass*. Oxford Univ. Press, 1936.

Crashaw, Richard. *The Poems*. Edited by L. C. Martin. Oxford, 1927.

Crinito, Pietro. *De honesta disciplina*. Basle, 1532.

Crocker, Richard L. "Pythagorean Mathematics and Music." *Journal of Aesthetics and Art Criticism* 22 (1963–64), 189–198, 325–335.

Crooke, Helkiah. *Microcosmographia*. London, 1615.

Cruceus, Joannes. *Litera Pythagorae Y cum divina L. Lactantii Coelii Firmiani explanatione*. Lyons, 1536.

Cudworth, Ralph. *The true intellectual system of the universe*. London, 1678.

———. *The True Intellectual System of the Universe*. 3 vols. London, 1845.

Cuiacius, Jacobus, ed. *Epistolae graecanicae mutuae*. Geneva, 1606.

Cumberland, Richard. "Circumstances Respecting the Philosopher Pythagoras." *Town and Country Magazine* 21 (1789), 79–81, 116–119.

Cumont, Franz. *Lux perpetua*. Paris, 1949.

Curtius, Ernst R. *European Literature and the Latin Middle Ages*. Translated by Willard R. Trask. New York, 1953.

Cyril, St. *Contra Julianum*. In *Opera*. Translated by Wolfgang Musculus. 4 vols. Basle, 1546.

———. *Contra Julianum*. Leipzig, 1696.

———. *Adversus libros athei Juliani*. In J.-P. Migne, *Patrologia Graeca*, Vol. 76. Paris, 1872.

Dacier, André. *La vie de Pythagore, ses symboles, ses vers dorez, & la vie d'Hierocles*. Paris, 1706.

———. *The Life of Pythagoras*. Translator anonymous. London, 1707.

Daniel, Samuel. *Complete Works*. Edited by A. B. Grosart. 5 vols. London, 1885–96.

———. *Poems and A Defence of Ryme*. Edited by Arthur C. Sprague, London, 1950.

Dante. *Divina commedia*. Edited by Cristoforo Landino. Florence, 1481.

———. *Tutte le opere*. Edited by E. Moore. Oxford Univ. Press, 1897.

Davies, John, of Hereford. *Microcosmos* [1603]. Edited by A. B. Grosart. London, 1877–78.

De Bouelles, Charles. "Liber de circuli quadratura." In Jacques LeFèvre d'Etaples, *Introductio in libros arithmeticos Boetii* et al. Paris, 1503.

———. *Liber de sapiente* [1509]. In *Individuum und Kosmos in der Philosophie der Renaissance*, edited by Ernst Cassirer. Leipzig, 1927.

———. *Liber de intellectu. . . . Liber de duodecim numeris* et al. Paris, 1510.

———. *Physicorum elementorum . . . libri decem*. Paris, 1512.

———. *Geometria*. Paris, 1542.

De Castro, Rodrigues. *De meteoris microcosmi libri quatuor*. Florence, 1621.

Dee, John. "Mathematicall praeface." In Euclid, *The elements*. Translated by Henry Billingsley. London, 1570.

De la Nauze. "Première dissertation sur Pythagore, où l'on fixe le tems auquel ce philosophe vécu." *Histoire de l'académie royale des inscriptions et belles lettres* 14 (1743), Part II, pp. 375–400.

De la Primaudaye, Pierre. *The French academie*. Translated by T. Bowes. London, 1586.

———. *The second part of the French academie*. Translated by T. Bowes. London, 1605.

———. *The third volume of the French academie*. Translated by R. Dolman. London, 1601.

Delatte, Armand. *Etudes sur la littérature pythagoricienne*. Paris, 1915.

De Ruyt, Franz. "L'Idée du "Bivium' et le symbole pythagoricien de la lettre Y." *Revue Belge de philologie et d'histoire* 10 (1931), 137–144.

De Tervarent, Guy. *Attributs et symboles dans l'art profane 1450–1600.* 2 vols. Geneva, 1958–59.

Deusingius, Antonius. *De vero systemate mundi dissertatio mathematica.* Amsterdam, 1643.

De Vogel, Cornelia J. *Pythagoras and Early Pythagoreanism.* Assen, 1966.

Digges, Leonard, and Thomas Digges. *Pantometria.* London, 1571.

Digges, Thomas. "A perfit description of the caelestiall orbes." In Leonard Digges, *A prognostication everlastinge.* London, 1576.

———. *Stratioticos.* London, 1579.

Diodorus Siculus. *Bibliotheca.* Translated by C. H. Oldfather et al. 12 vols. London, 1946–67.

Diogenes Laertius. *Lives of Eminent Philosophers.* Translated by R. D. Hicks. 2 vols. Harvard Univ. Press, 1931–38.

———. *The lives, opinions, and remarkable sayings of the most famous ancient philosophers. . . . Made English by several hands.* 2 vols. London, 1696.

Dodds, Eric R. *The Greeks and the Irrational.* Univ. of California Press, 1951.

Dodonaeus, Rembertus. *Cosmographica in astronomiam et geographiam isagoge.* Antwerp, 1548.

Dodwell, Henry. *Exercitationes duae: prima, De aetate Phalaridis; secunda, De aetate Pythagorae.* London, 1704.

Donato, Eugenio. "Tesauro's Poetics: Through the Looking Glass." *Modern Language Notes* 78 (1963), 15–30.

Donne, John. *The Elegies and the Songs and Sonnets.* Edited by Helen Gardner. Oxford, 1965.

———. *The Anniversaries.* Edited by Frank Manley. Johns Hopkins Press, 1963.

———. *The Sermons.* Edited by George R. Potter and Evelyn M. Simpson, 10 vols. Univ. of California Press, 1953–62.

Dornfeld, Christian Friedrich. *De symbolis Pythagorae dissertatio.* Leipzig, 1721.

Dowland, Robert. *Varietie of lute-lessons.* London, 1610.

Dresigius, Sigismundus Fridericus. *De alba stola Pythagorae.* Leipzig, 1736.

Drexel, Hieremias. *The considerations of Drexelius upon eternitie.* Translated by Ralph Winterton. Cambridge, 1636.

Dreyer, J. L. E. *History of the Planetary Systems from Thales to Kepler.* Cambridge Univ. Press, 1906.

———. *A History of Astronomy from Thales to Kepler.* 2nd ed. New York, 1953.

Drusius, Joannes. *Tetragrammaton.* Franeker, 1604.

Duckworth, George E. *Structural Patterns and Proportions in Vergil's Aeneid.* Univ. of Michigan Press, 1962.

Du Faur, Guy. *The quadrains*. In Guillaume Saluste du Bartas, *Devine weekes and workes*. Translated by Joshua Sylvester. London, 1605.

Dufresnoy, Nicolas Lenglet. *Receuil de dissertations anciennes et nouvelles, sur les apparitions, les visions, et les songes*. Paris, 1751.

Duhem, Pierre. *Le système du monde*. 5 vols. Paris, 1913–17.

Durling, Robert M. "The Divine Analogy in Ariosto." *Modern Language Notes* 78 (1963), 1–14.

Elyot, Sir Thomas. *The castel of health*. London, 1541.

———. *Bibliotheca Eliotae*. Edited by Thomas Cooper. London, 1545.

———. *Bibliotheca Eliotae*. Edited by Thomas Cooper. London, 1548.

———. *Of the knowledge whiche maketh a wise man*. Edited by Edwin J. Howard. Oxford, Ohio, 1946.

Enfield, William. *The History of Philosophy*. 2 vols. London, 1791.

Enneades Arithmeticae [Wing E3128]. London, 1684.

Erasmus, Desiderius. *Veterum maximeque insignium paroemiarum id est adagiorum collectanea*. Paris, 1500.

———. *Adagiorum chiliades quatuor, et sesquicenturia*. Lyons, 1559.

———. *Praise of Follie*. Translated by Thomas Chaloner. Edited by C. H. Miller. EETS; Oxford Univ. Press, 1965.

Erra Pater. *The pronostycacion for ever*. Robert Wyer; London, c.1540.

Estienne, Henri, sieur des Fossez. *The art of making devises*. Translated by Thomas Blount. London, 1646.

Euclid. *Elementa geometrica, libris XV. . . . His accessit decimus sextus liber, de solidorum regularium sibi invicem inscriptorum collationibus*. Edited by François de Foix, Comte de Candale. Paris, 1566.

———. *The elements*. Translated by Henry Billingsley. London, 1570.

———. *The Thirteen Books of Euclid's Elements*. Edited by Sir Thomas Heath. 3 vols. Cambridge Univ. Press, 1908.

Eusebius, Pamphilius. *De evangelica praeparatione*. Translated by Georgius Trapezuntius. Venice, 1501.

Evans, Joan. *Patterns*. 2 vols. Oxford, 1931.

Fabricius, Joannes Albertus. *Bibliotheca Graeca*. 11 vols. Hamburg, 1790–1808.

Farrington, Benjamin. *Greek Science*. London, 1953.

Ferrari, S. "La scuola e la filosofia pitagoriche." *Rivista italiana di filosofia* 5 (1890), i.53–74, 184–212, 280–306; ii.59–79, 196–216.

Ferrier, Auger. *Liber de diebus decretoriis secundum pythagoricam doctrinam*. Lyons, 1549.

———. *Liber de somniis*. Lyons, 1549.

Ficino, Marsilio. *Opera omnia*. Basle, 1576.

———. *Théologie platonicienne de l'immortalité des âmes*. Edited by Raymond Marcel. 2 vols. Paris, 1964.

———. *Supplementum Ficinianum*. Edited by Paul O. Kristeller. 2 vols. Florence, 1937.

Finé, Oronce. *Protomathesis*. Paris, 1532.
———. *Arithmetica practica*. Paris, 1542.
———. *De sphaera mundi*. Paris, 1542.
———. *Quadratura circuli, tandem inventa & clarissimè demonstrata* et al. Paris, 1544.
———, ed. *Margarita philosophica* [by Gregor Reisch]. Basle, 1535.
Finney, Gretchen L. *Musical Backgrounds for English Literature: 1580–1650*. Rutgers Univ. Press, 1962.
Fletcher, Phineas. *The purple island*. London, 1633.
Fludd, Robert. *Utriusque cosmi majoris scilicet et minoris metaphysica, physica atque technica historia*. 4 vols. Oppenheim, 1617–19.
———. *Philosophia sacra & vere Christiana, seu meteorologia cosmica*. Frankfurt, 1626.
———. *Philosophia Moysaica*. Gouda, 1638.
———. *Mosaicall philosophy*. London, 1659.
Folianus, Ludovicus. *Musica theorica*. Venice, 1529.
Foresti, Jacopo Filippo. *Supplementum chronicarum*. Venice, 1490.
Fowler, Alastair. *Spenser and the Numbers of Time*. London, 1964.
———. *Triumphal Forms: Structural Patterns in Elizabethan Poetry*. Cambridge Univ. Press, 1970.
———, ed. *Silent Poetry*. London, 1970.
Franck, Sebastian. *De Pythagora eiusque symbolis disputatio*. Berlin, 1869.
Frank, Erich. *Plato und die sogenannten Pythagoreer* [1923]. Darmstadt, 1962.
Frank, Joseph. *The Widening Gyre*. Rutgers Univ. Press, 1963.
Freeman, Kathleen. *Ancilla to the Pre-Socratic Philosophers*. Oxford, 1948.
Freret, Nicolas. "Observations sur la généalogie de Pythagore." *Historie de l'académie royale des inscriptions et belles lettres* 14 (1743), Part II, pp. 401–447.
———. "Recherches sur le tems auquel le philosophe Pythagore . . . peut avoir vécu." *Histoire de l'académie royale des inscriptions et belles lettres* 14 (1743), Part II, pp. 472–504.
Frisius, Joannes Jacobus. *Bibliotheca philosophorum classicorum authorum chronologica*. Zurich, 1592.
Gadol, Joan. "The Unity of the Renaissance: Humanism, Natural Science, and Art." In *From the Renaissance to the Counter-Reformation*, edited by Charles H. Carter. New York, 1965.
Gafori, Franchino. *Theorica musice*. Milan, 1492.
———. *Practica musice*. Milan, 1496.
———. *De harmonia musicorum instrumentorum opus*. Milan, 1518.
Galatinus, Petrus. *Opus de arcanis catholicae veritatis*. Basle, 1561.
Gale, Theophilus. *The court of the gentiles*. 2 parts. London, 1670.
———. *The court of the gentiles, Part III*. London, 1677.
———. *Philosophia generalis*. London, 1676.

Gale, Thomas, ed. *Opuscula mythologica, ethica et physica*. Cambridge, 1671.

Galilei, Galileo. *Dialogue Concerning the Two Chief World Systems*. Translated by Stillman Drake. Univ. of California Press, 1962.

Garzoni, Tommaso. *La piazza universale di tutte le professioni del mondo*. Venice, 1586.

Gascoigne, George. *Certayne notes of instruction concerning the making of verse or ryme in English* [1575]. In G. Gregory Smith, *Elizabethan Critical Essays*. 2 vols. Oxford Univ. Press, 1904.

Gassendi, Pierre. *Institutio astronomica*. Paris, 1647.

Gaudenzio, Paganino. *De Pythagoraea animarum transmigratione opusculum*. Pisa, 1641.

Gellius, Aulus. *Noctes Atticae*. Translated by J. C. Rolge. 3 vols. London, 1927–28.

Gemma, Cornelius. *De arte cyclognomica, tomi III*. Antwerp, 1569.

Gesner, Conrad. *Bibliotheca universalis*. Zurich, 1545.

———. *Pandectae*. Zurich, 1548.

Gilbert, Katherine E., and Helmut Kuhn. *A History of Esthetics*. New York, 1939.

Giorgio, Francesco. *De harmonia mundi totius cantica tria*. Venice, 1525.

———. *De harmonia mundi totius cantica tria*. 2nd ed. Paris, 1545.

———. *L'Harmonie du monde* et al. Translated by Guy le Fèvre de la Boderie. Paris, 1579.

Giraldi, Lilio Gregorio. *De annis et mensibus, caeterisque temporum partibus . . . dissertatio*. Basle, 1541.

———. *Libelli duo, in quorum altero aenigmata pleraque antiquorum, in altero Pythagorae symbola . . . sunt explicata*. Basle, 1551.

———. "Historiae deorum gentilium syntagma." In *Opera omnia*. Leyden, 1696.

Giraldi Cinthio, Giovanni Battista. *Discorsi . . . intorno al comporre de i romanzi. . . .* Venice, 1554.

———. *On Romances*. Translated by H. L. Snuggs. Univ. of Kentucky Press, 1968.

Girault, Simon. *Globe du monde*. Lengres, 1592.

Glareanus, Henricus. *Dodecachordon*. Basle, 1547.

Godfridus. *The boke of knowledge of thynges unknowen*. Robert Wyer; London, c.1530.

Gomperz, Theodor. *Greek Thinkers*. Translated by Laurie Magnus. 2 vols. New York, 1908.

Goropius, Joannes. "Hieroglyphica." In *Opera*. Antwerp, 1580.

Gosson, Stephen. *The schoole of abuse*. London, 1587.

Grau, Abraham. *Historia philosophica*. Franeker, 1674.

Grillot de Givry, E. A. *Witchcraft, Magic, and Alchemy*. Translated by J. C. Locke. London, 1931.

Grinau, Peter, ed. *Being a transcript of several letters from Averroes.*

. . . *Also several letters from Pythagoras to the King of India.* London, 1695.

Guthkelch, A., ed. *The Battle of the Books, by Jonathan Swift.* London, 1908.

Guthrie, W. K. C. *A History of Greek Philosophy.* 3 vols. Cambridge Univ. Press, 1962.

Halio, Jay L. "The Metaphor of Conception and Elizabethan Theories of the Imagination." *Neophilologus* 50 (1966), 454–461.

Hamilton, A. C. "Sidney's Idea of the 'Right Poet.'" *Comparative Literature* 9 (1957), 51–59.

Harder, R. *Ocellus Lucanus.* Berlin, 1926.

Hassel, Johann Bernhard. *Unum theologiae pythagoricae compendium.* Helmstadt, 1710.

Hathaway, Baxter. *The Age of Criticism: The Late Renaissance in Italy.* Cornell Univ. Press, 1962.

Hawkins, Sir John. *A General History of the Science and Practice of Music.* 5 vols. London, 1776.

Heath, Sir Thomas. *Aristarchus of Samos.* Oxford, 1913.

———. *A History of Greek Mathematics.* 2 vols. Oxford, 1921.

———. *A Manual of Greek Mathematics* [1931]. Dover Publications, 1963.

Heninger, S. K., Jr. "The Sun-King Analogy in *Richard II.*" *Shakespeare Quarterly* 11 (1960), 319–327.

———. "Some Renaissance Versions of the Pythagorean Tetrad." *Studies in the Renaissance* 8 (1961), 7–35.

———. "The Implications of Form for *The Shepheardes Calender.*" *Studies in the Renaissance* 9 (1962), 309–321.

———. "Pythagorean Cosmology and the Triumph of Heliocentrism." In *Le soleil à la renaissance.* Presses universitaires de Bruxelles, 1965, pp. 33–53.

———. "Pythagorean Symbola in Erasmus' *Adagia.*" *Renaissance Quarterly* 21 (1968), 162–165.

———. "The Pattern of *Love's Labour's Lost.*" *Shakespeare Studies,* forthcoming.

Heydon, Christopher. *A defence of judiciall astrologie.* London, 1603.

Heydon, John. *The Rosie Crucian infallible axiomata.* London, 1660.

———. *The harmony of the world.* London, 1662.

Hieatt, A. Kent. *Short Time's Endless Monument.* Columbia Univ. Press, 1960.

Hierocles. *Commentarius in aurea Pythagoreorum carmina.* 2 vols. London, 1654–55.

———. *In aureos versus Pythagorae opusculum.* Translated by Joannes Aurispa. Padua, 1474.

———. *Upon the Golden Verses of Pythagoras.* Translated by John Hall. London, 1657.

———. *Upon the Golden Verses of the Pythagoreans.* Translated by John Norris. London, 1682.

———. *The Commentary of Hierocles upon the Golden Verses of the Pythagoreans.* Translated by William Rayner. Norwich, 1797.

Hill, Thomas. *Interpretacion of dreames.* London, 1576.

Hobson, Ernest W. "*Squaring the Circle*": *A History of the Problem.* Cambridge Univ. Press, 1913.

Hollander, John. *The Untuning of the Sky.* Princeton Univ. Press, 1961.

Holton, Gerald. "Johannes Kepler's Universe: Its Physics and Metaphysics." *American Journal of Physics* 24 (1956), 340–351.

Homer. *Iliad.* Translated by A. T. Murray. 2 vols. London, 1946.

———. *Odyssey.* Translated by A. T. Murray. 2 vols. London, 1946.

———. *Chapman's Homer.* Edited by Allardyce Nicoll. 2 vols. New York, 1956.

Honoré d'Autun. *The lucydarye.* Translated by Andrew Chertsey. London, c.1508.

Hood, Thomas. *The use of both the globes, celestiall and terrestriall.* London, 1592.

Hooker, Richard. *Of the lawes of ecclesiastical politie.* London, 1617.

Hopper, Vincent F. *Medieval Number Symbolism.* Columbia Univ. Press, 1938.

Horapollo. *De sacris Ægyptiorum notis.* Paris, 1574.

Horn, Georg. *Historiae philosophiae libri septem.* Leyden, 1655.

———. *Arca Mosis.* Leyden, 1668.

Hugh of St. Victor. *Didascalicon.* Edited by Jerome Taylor. Columbia Univ. Press, 1961.

Hull, L. W. H. *The History and Philosophy of Science.* London, 1959.

Hutton, James. "Some English Poems in Praise of Music." In *English Miscellany, II,* edited by Mario Praz. Rome, 1951.

Iamblichus, *De mysteriis Ægyptiorum, Chaldaeorum, Assyriorum* et al. Translated by Marsilio Ficino. Venice, 1497.

———. *De vita Pythagorica liber.* Edited by August Nauck. Amsterdam, 1965.

———. *Life of Pythagoras.* Translated by Thomas Taylor. London, 1818.

———. *Protrepticae orationes ad philosophiam.* Edited by Theophilus Kiessling. Leipzig, 1813.

———. *In Nicomachi Geraseni arithmeticam introductionem.* Edited by Samuel Tennulius. Arnhem, 1668.

Ingpen, William. *The secrets of numbers.* London, 1624.

Isidore of Seville. *Liber de responsione mundi & astrorum ordinatione.* Augsburg, 1472.

———. *Etymologiarum sive originum libri XX.* Edited by W. M. Lindsay. 2 vols. Oxford, 1911.

Jackson, John. *Chronological Antiquities.* 3 vols. London, 1742.

Jean de Meun. *Le plaisant jeu du dodechedron de fortune.* Paris, 1556.

Jerome, St. *The Apology Against the Books of Rufinus.* Translated by John N. Hritzu. Catholic Univ. of America Press, 1965.

Jewel, William, tr. *The golden cabinet of true treasure.* London, 1612.

Joannes ab Indagine. *Introductiones apotelesmaticae elegantes, in chyromantiam, physiognomiam, astrologiam naturalem, complexiones hominum, naturas planetarum.* Strasbourg, 1522.

———. *Briefe introductions . . . unto the art of chiromancy.* Translated by Fabian Withers. London, 1558.

Joannes de Muris. *Arithmeticae speculativae libri duo.* Mainz, 1538.

Joannes Wallensis. *Florilegium.* Rome, 1655.

Joecher, C. E. *De Pythagorae methodo philosophiam docendi.* Leipzig, 1741.

Johnson, F. R., and S. V. Larkey. "Thomas Digges, the Copernican System, and the Idea of the Infinity of the Universe in 1576." *Huntington Library Bulletin* 5 (1934), 69–117.

Johnson, Samuel. *The Works.* Edited by Arthur Murray. 12 vols. London, 1816.

Jones, R. F. *Ancients and Moderns: A Study of the Background of the "Battle of the Books."* St. Louis, 1936.

Jonsius, Joannes. *De scriptoribus historiae philosophicae libri IV.* 2nd ed. Jena, 1716.

Jonson, Ben. *Works.* Edited by C. H. Herford and Percy and Evelyn Simpson. 11 vols. Oxford, 1925–52.

Jordanus Nemorarius. *In hoc opera contenta. Arithmetica decem libris demonstrata* et al. Edited by Jacques LeFèvre d'Etaples. Paris, 1496.

Jung, Carl G. *Psychology and Alchemy.* Translated by R. F. C. Hull. New York, 1953.

——— and W. Pauli. *The Interpretation of Nature and the Psyche.* New York, 1955.

Junius, Franciscus. *Catalogus . . . architectorum, mechanicorum . . . aliorumque artificum,* appended to *De pictura veterum libri tres.* Rotterdam, 1694.

Justin Martyr, St. *Writings of Saint Justin Martyr.* Translated by Thomas B. Falls. New York, 1948.

Justinianus, Fabianus. *Index universalis.* Rome, 1612.

Justinus, Marcus Junianus. *The historie.* Translated by G. W. London, 1606.

The kalendayr of shyppars. Paris, 1503.

The Kalender of Shepherdes. Edited by H. Oskar Sommer. London, 1892.

Keill, John. *An Introduction to True Astronomy.* London, 1721.

Kepler, Johann. *Prodromus dissertationum cosmographicarum, continens mysterium cosmographicum.* Tübingen, 1596.

———. *Epitome astronomiae Copernicanae.* Linz, 1618.

———. *Harmonices mundi libri V*. Linz, 1619.

Khunrath, Hans. *Amphitheatrum sapientiae aeternae solius verae, Christiano-Kabalisticum, divino-magicum* . . . . Hanau, 1609.

Kircher, Athanasius. *Musurgia universalis*. 2 vols. Rome, 1650.

———. *Iter exstaticum coeleste*. 2nd ed. Herbipolis, 1660.

———. *Arithmologia*. Rome, 1665.

———. *Obeliscus Aegyptiacus*. Rome, 1666.

Kirk, G. S., and J. E. Raven. *The Presocratic Philosophers*. Cambridge Univ. Press, 1962.

Klein, Jacob. *Greek Mathematical Thought and the Origin of Algebra*. Translated by Eva Brann. Massachusetts Institute of Technology Press, 1968.

Knauthius, Joannes Christianus, ed. *Pythagorae carmen aureum* et al. Strasbourg, 1720.

Koestler, Arthur. *The Sleepwalkers*. London, 1959.

Koyré, Alexandre. *From the Closed World to the Infinite Universe*. Johns Hopkins Press, 1957.

Kozminsky, Isidore. *Numbers, Their Meaning and Magic*. New York, 1927.

Kristeller, Paul O. "Ficino and Pomponazzi on the Place of Man in the Universe." *Journal of the History of Ideas* 5 (1944), 220–242.

———. *Renaissance Thought* [1955]. New York, 1961.

———. "Renaissance Aristotelianism." *Greek, Roman, and Byzantine Studies* 6 (1965), 157–174

———, ed. *Supplementum Ficinianum*. 2 vols. Florence, 1937.

———, ed. *Catalogus translationum et commentariorum: Mediaeval and Renaissance Latin Translations and Commentaries, Volume I*. Catholic Univ. of America Press, 1960.

Kucharski, Paul. *Etude sur la doctrine pythagoricienne de la tétrade*. Paris, 1952.

Lactantius, Lucius Coelius. *The Divine Institutes*. Translated by Sister Mary Frances McDonald. Catholic Univ. of America Press, 1964.

Landino, Cristoforo, ed. *Divina commedia* [by Dante]. Florence, 1481.

Langer, Susanne K. *Philosophy in a New Key*. 3rd ed. Harvard Univ. Press, 1957.

L'Anglois, Pierre. *Discours des hieroglyphes Ægyptiens, emblemes, devises, et armoiries*. Paris, 1584.

Lanquet, Thomas. *Cooper's chronicle*. London, 1565.

Lascaris, Constantine. *Erotemata*. Venice, 1494–95.

Lax, Gaspar. *Arithmetica speculativa*. Paris, 1515.

Lee, Rensselaer W. "*Ut pictura poesis:* The Humanistic Theory of Painting." *Art Bulletin* 22 (1940), 197–269.

Le Fèvre de la Boderie, Guy, tr. *L'Harmonie du monde* [by Francesco Giorgio]. Paris, 1579.

Le Fèvre d'Etaples, Jacques. *Introductorium astronomicum*. Edited by Jodocus Clichtoveus. Paris, 1517.

———. *Introductio . . . in arithmeticam . . . Boetii, pariter & Jordani.* In Gregor Reisch, *Margarita philosophica.* Basle, 1583.

———, ed. *In hoc opere contenta. Arithmetica [Jordani Nemorarii] decem libris demonstrata. Musica libris demonstrata quattuor. Epitome in libros arithmeticos divi Severini Boetii. Rithmimachiae ludus.* Paris, 1496.

———, ed. *Epitome compendiosaque introductio in libros arithmeticos . . . Boetii* et al. Paris, 1503.

Lemnius, Levinus. *Touchstone of complexions.* Translated by Thomas Newton. London, 1565.

LeRoy, Louis. *Of the interchangeable course, or variety of things in the whole world.* Translated by Robert Ashley. London, 1594.

Lesser, George. *Gothic Cathedrals and Sacred Geometry.* 2 vols., London, 1957.

Lévy, Isidore. *Recherches sur les sources de la légende de Pythagore.* Paris, 1926.

———. *La légende de Pythagore de Grèce en Palestine.* Paris, 1927.

Lewis, C. S. *Spenser's Images of Life.* Edited by Alastair Fowler. Cambridge Univ. Press, 1967.

Lewis, Sir George C. *An Historical Survey of the Astronomy of the Ancients.* London, 1862.

Licetus, Fortunius. *De mundi, & hominis analogia liber unus.* Udine, 1635.

Lilly, William. *Christian astrology.* London, 1647.

Lippman, Edward A. *Musical Thought in Ancient Greece.* Columbia Univ. Press, 1964.

Little, A. G. *The Grey Friars in Oxford.* Oxford, 1892.

Lloyd, William. *A chronological account of the life of Pythagoras.* London, 1699.

Long, Herbert S. *A Study of the Doctrine of Metempsychosis in Greece from Pythagoras to Plato.* Princeton Univ. Press, 1948.

Lovejoy, Arthur O. "'Nature' as Aestheic Norm." *Modern Language Notes* 42 (1927), 444–450.

———. *The Great Chain of Being.* Harvard Univ. Press, 1936.

Lucian. *Dialogues.* Translated by A. M. Harmon. 7 vols. London, 1913– .

———. *Somnium seu Gallus* et al. Basle, 1557.

Lucretius. *On the Nature of the Universe.* Translated by Ronald Latham. Harmondsworth, 1951.

Lull, Raimond. *Opusculum . . . de auditu kabbalistico.* Paris, 1578.

McColley, Grant. "The Seventeenth-Century Doctrine of a Plurality of Worlds." *Annals of Science* 1 (1936), 385–430.

McCullough, Florence. *Medieval Latin and French Bestiaries.* Univ. of North Carolina Press, 1960.

McKeon, Richard. "Literary Criticism and the Concept of Imitation in Antiquity." *Modern Philology* 34 (1936), 1–35.

Macrobius. *Commentary on the Dream of Scipio.* Translated by William H. Stahl. Columbia Univ. Press, 1952.

———. *The Saturnalia.* Translated by P. V. Davies. Columbia Univ. Press, 1969.

Mahnke, Dietrich. *Unendliche Sphäre und Allmittelpunkt.* Halle, 1937.

Maier, Michael. *De circulo physico, quadrato: hoc est, auro.* Oppenheim, 1616.

Mallinger, Jean. *Pythagore et les mystères.* Paris, 1944.

Manilius. *Astronomicon.* Edited by A. E. Housman. 2nd ed. Cambridge Univ. Press, 1937.

———. *The sphere.* Translated by Edward Sherburne. London, 1675.

Maréchal, Pierre Sylvain. *Voyages de Pythagore.* 6 vols. Paris, 1799.

Marlowe, Christopher. *The Works.* Edited by C. F. Tucker Brooke. Oxford, 1910.

Marsham, John. *Chronicus canon Ægyptiacus, Ebraicus, Graecus.* London, 1672.

Martianus Capella. *De nuptiis Philologiae et Mercurii* et al. Edited by Adolf Dick. Stuttgart, 1969.

Martinus, Joannes. *Arithmetica.* Paris, 1526.

Mason, Robert. *Reasons monarchie.* London, 1602.

Masterson, Thomas. *Third booke of arithmeticke.* London, 1595.

Maurolycus, Franciscus. *Cosmographia.* Venice, 1543.

———. *Opuscula mathematica.* Venice, 1575.

Maziarz, Edward A., and Thomas Greenwood. *Greek Mathematical Philosophy.* New York, 1968.

Mazzeo, Joseph. *Renaissance and Seventeenth-Century Studies.* Columbia Univ. Press, 1964.

Meibom, Marcus, tr. and ed. *Antiquae musicae auctores septem.* Amsterdam, 1652.

Melloni, Rita Cuccioli. *Biografia di Pitagora.* Bologna, 1969.

Menestrier, Claude François. *Des ballets anciens et modernes.* Paris, 1862.

Meres, Francis. *Gods arithmeticke.* London, 1597.

Mersenne, Marin. *Traité de l'harmonie universelle.* Paris, 1627.

Meursius, Joannes. *Denarius pythagoricus.* Leyden, 1631.

———, ed. *Aristoxenus. Nicomachus. Alypius. Auctores musices antiquissimi.* Leyden, 1616.

Mexia, Pedro. *The foreste.* Translated by Thomas Fortescue. London, 1571.

Meyer-Baer, Kathi. *Music of the Spheres and the Dance of Death.* Princeton Univ. Press, 1970.

Michel, Paul-Henri. *De Pythagore à Euclide.* Paris, 1950.

Mignault, Claude, ed. *Andreae Alciati V. C. emblemata.* Antwerp, 1608.

Μικροκόσμος. *Parvus mundus.* Arnhem, c.1609.

Milhaud, Gaston. *Les philosophes géomètres de la Grèce.* 2nd ed. Paris, 1934.

Millepierres, François. *Pythagore fils d'Apollon.* Paris, 1953.
Milton, John. *Paradise Lost* et al. 2 vols. London, 1758.
Minar, Edwin L., Jr. "Pythagorean Communism." *Transactions and Proceedings of the American Philological Association* 75 (1944), 34–46.
Misson, Henri. *Memoirs and Observations in His Travels over England.* Translated by John Ozell. London, 1719.
Mizauld, Antoine. *Harmonia coelestium corporum et humanorum.* Paris, 1555.
———. *Harmonia superioris naturae mundi et inferioris.* Paris, 1577.
Montucla, Jean Etienne. *Histoire des recherches sur la quadrature du cercle.* Paris, 1754.
Moore, Philip. *A fourtie yeres almanacke.* London, c.1566.
More, Henry. *Conjectura cabbalistica.* London, 1653.
More, John. *A table from the beginning of the world to this day.* Cambridge, 1593.
More, Sir Thomas. *Utopia.* Edited by Edward Surtz, S. J., and J. H. Hexter. In *The Complete Works of St. Thomas More.* Yale Univ. Press, 1965.
———. *Utopia.* Translated by Ralph Robynson. Edited by J. R. Lumby. Cambridge Univ. Press, 1879.
Morellius, Gulielmus. *Tabula compendiosa.* Basle, 1580.
Morhof, Daniel Georg. *Polyhistor.* 4th ed. Lubeck, 1747.
Morley, Thomas. *A plaine and easie introduction to practicall musicke.* London, 1597.
Moxon, Joseph. *A tutor to astronomie and geographie.* London, 1659.
Munday, Anthony. *A briefe chronicle of the successe of times.* London, 1611.
Munitz, Milton K. "One Universe or Many?" *Journal of the History of Ideas* 12 (1951), 231–255.
Mussard, Pierre. *Historia deorum fatidicorum, vatum, sibyllarum, phoebadum, apud priscos illustrium.* Cologne, 1675.
Nahm, Milton C. *The Artist as Creator.* Johns Hopkins Press, 1956.
Nannus Mirabellius, Domenicus, and Bartholomaeus Amantius. *Polyanthea.* Cologne, 1567.
Natalis Comes. *Mythologiae.* Padua, 1616.
———. *Mythologiae.* Translated by Jean de Montlyard. Lyons, 1600.
Naylor, Edward W. *Shakespeare and Music.* 2nd ed. London, 1931.
Neander, Michael. *Physice.* Leipzig, 1585.
———, ed. *Anthologicum graecolatinum.* Basle, 1556.
Nemesius. *De natura hominis liber.* Translated by Giorgio Valla. Lyons, 1538.
———. *The nature of man.* Translated by George Wither. London, 1636.
Neugebauer, Otto. *The Exact Sciences in Antiquity.* 2nd ed. Brown Univ. Press, 1957.

Nicholas of Cusa. *De quadratura circuli.* Edited by Johann Schoener. Nuremberg, 1533.

———. *Of Learned Ignorance.* Translated by Germain Heron. London, 1954.

Nicolson, Marjorie H. *A World in the Moon.* Northampton, Mass., 1936.

———. *The Breaking of the Circle.* Northwestern Univ. Press, 1950.

Nicomachus. *Arithmeticae libri duo.* Paris, 1538.

———. *Introduction to Arithmetic.* Translated by Martin Luther D'Ooge. New York, 1926.

———. *Enchiridion harmonices.* In *Aristoxenus. Nicomachus. Alypius. Auctores musices antiquissimi.* Edited by Joannes Meursius. Leyden, 1616.

———. *Harmonices enchiridion.* In *Antiquae musicae auctores septem.* Translated and edited by Marcus Meibom. Amsterdam, 1652.

———. *Harmonices enchiridion.* In *Musici scriptores graeci.* Edited by Carolus Janus. Leipzig, 1895.

Nifo, Agostino. *In libris Aristotelis meteorologicis commentaria.* Venice, 1531.

Norden, John. *Vicissitudo rerum.* London, 1600.

Norgate, Edward. *Miniatura: or the Art of Limning.* Edited by Martin Hardie. Oxford, 1919.

Norman, Robert. *The new attractive.* London, 1585.

Ocellus of Lucania. *On the Nature of the Universe* et al. Translated by Thomas Taylor. London, 1831.

Oliver, G. *The Pythagorean Triangle.* London, 1875.

Oppermann, Hans. "Eine Pythagoraslegende." *Bonner Jahrbücher* 130 (1925), 284–301.

Orelli, Johann Conrad von. *Opuscula graecorum veterum sententiosa et moralia.* 2 vols. Leipzig, 1819–21.

Ornithoparcus, Andreas. *Micrologus.* Translated by John Dowland. London, 1609.

Ovid. *Opera.* Edited by Raphael Regius. Venice, 1509.

———. *Ars amatoria* et al. Translated by J. H. Mozley. Harvard Univ. Press, 1947.

———. *Metamorphoses.* Translated by Arthur Golding [1567]. Edited by W. H. D. Rouse. London, 1961.

———. *Metamorphoses.* Translated by Arthur Golding. London, 1575.

———. *Metamorphoses.* Edited by Georg Sabinus. Cambridge, 1584.

———. *Metamorphoses.* Paris, 1619.

———. *Metamorphosis.* Translated by George Sandys. Oxford, 1632.

———. *Metamorphoses.* Translated by F. J. Miller. 2 vols. London, 1960.

———. *Tristia* et al. Translated by A. L. Wheeler. London, 1924.

Pacioli, Luca. *Summa de arithmetica, geometria, proportioni & proportionalita.* Venice, 1494.

———. *De divina proportione.* Milan, 1956.

Palingenius, Marcellus. *Zodiacus vitae.* Venice, c.1531.

Palisca, Claude V. "Scientific Empiricism in Musical Thought." In Stephen Toulmin *et al., Seventeenth-Century Science and the Arts.* Princeton Univ. Press, 1961.

Pancirolli, Guido. *The History of Many Memorable Things Lost.* London, 1715.

Pannekoek, Antonie. *A History of Astronomy.* London, 1961.

Panofsky, Erwin. *Hercules am Scheidewege.* Leipzig, 1930.

———. *Idea.* Translated by Joseph J. S. Peake. Univ. of South Carolina Press, 1968.

———. *Studies in Iconology* [1939]. New York, 1962.

———. *Meaning in the Visual Arts.* New York, 1955.

Patch, Howard R. *The Tradition of Boethius.* Oxford Univ. Press, 1935.

Patrides, C. A. "The Numerological Approach to Cosmic Order During the English Renaissance." *Isis* 49 (1958), 391–397.

Patrizi, Francesco. *De rerum natura libri II. priores. Alter de spacio physico. Alter de spacio mathematico.* Ferrara, 1587.

Peacham, Henry. *Minerva Britanna.* London, 1612.

Peddie, R. A. *Subject Index of Books Published Before 1880.* London, 1933; Second Series (London, 1935); Third Series (London, 1939).

Persius. *Satires* et al. Translated by G. G. Ramsay. London, 1950.

Person, David. *Varieties.* London, 1635.

Peruchio, Le Sieur de. *La chiromance, la physionomie, et la géomance.* Paris, 1657.

Petrarca, Francesco. *Rerum memorandarum, sive de viris illustribus libri quattuor* et al. Basle, 1563.

Peucer, Caspar. *Elementa doctrinae de circulis coelestibus, et primo motu.* Wittenberg, 1551.

———. *Les devins.* Lyons, 1584.

Peurbach, Georg. *Theoricae novae planetarum.* Nuremberg, 1474?

Peyligk, Johann. *Philosophiae naturalis compendium.* Leipzig, 1499.

Philip, James A. *Pythagoras and Early Pythagoreanism.* Univ. of Toronto Press, 1966.

Philo Judaeus. *Works.* Translated by F. H. Colson *et al.* 10 vols. London, 1929–62.

Philostratus, Flavius. *The Life of Apollonius of Tyana.* Translated by F. C. Conybeare. 2 vols. London, 1948–50.

Photius. *Myriobiblon.* Rouen, 1653.

Pico della Mirandola, Giovanni. *De adscriptis numero noningentis: dialeticis, moralibus, physicis. . . .* Rome, 1486.

———. *On the Dignity of Man* et al. Translated by Charles Glenn Wallis. Indianapolis, 1965.

Pictorius, Georg. *De speciebus magiae ceremonialis.* In *Pantopolion.* Basle, 1563.

Pistorius, Joannes. *Artis cabalisticae: hoc est, reconditae theologiae et philosophiae scriptorum . . . opus*. Basle, 1587.
———. *Microcosmus, sive liber de proportione utriusque mundi*. Paris, 1607.
Plato. *Omnia opera*. Translated by Marsilio Ficino. Basle, 1546.
———. *The Dialogues*. Translated by Benjamin Jowett. 4 vols. Oxford, 1871.
———. *Timaeus Platonis, sive de universitate, interpretibus, M. Tullio Cicerone, & Chalcidio, una cum eius docta explanatione*. Paris, 1563.
———. *Gorgias*. Edited by E. R. Dodds. Oxford, 1959.
———. *Republic*. Translated by Paul Shorey. 2 vols. London, 1930–42.
———. *Theaetetus, Sophist*. Translated by H. N. Fowler. London, 1961.
———. *Timaeus* et al. Translated by R. G. Bury. London, 1952.
Pliny. *Historia naturalis*. Translated by H. Rackham *et al.* 10 vols. Harvard Univ. Press, 1949–62.
———. *The historie of the world*. Translated by Philemon Holland. London, 1601.
Plotinus. *The Enneads*. Translated by Stephen MacKenna. 3rd ed. London, 1962.
Plutarch. *The lives of the noble Grecians and Romanes*. Translated by Sir Thomas North. London, 1603.
———. *The morals*. Translated by Philemon Holland. London, 1603.
———. *The education or bringinge up of children*. Translated by Sir Thomas Elyot. London, 1535?
———. *A president for parentes*. Translated by Edward Grant. London, 1571.
Pope, Alexander. *Works*. Edited by William Warburton. London, 1751.
Porphyry. *De vita Pythagorae*. Edited by Conrad Rittershaus. Altdorf, 1610.
———. *De vita Pythagorae* et al. Edited by Augustus Nauck. Leipzig, 1886.
Porta, Giovanni Battista. *Natural magick*. London, 1658.
Postel, Guillaume. *Tabula aeternae ordinationis, quaternario . . . expositae*. Paris, c.1552.
Poulet, Georges. *The Metamorphoses of the Circle*. Translated by Carley Dawson and Elliott Coleman. Johns Hopkins Press, 1966.
Proclus. *De sphaera liber I* et al. Translated by Thomas Linacre. Basle, 1585.
———. *On the Timaeus of Plato*. Translated by Thomas Taylor. 2 vols. London, 1820.
———. *In primum Euclidis elementorum librum commentariorum . . . liber IV*. Edited by Francesco Barozzi. Padua, 1560.
———. *Commentary on Euclid, Book I*. In Ivor Thomas, *Greek Mathematics*. London, 1939.
Psellus, Michael. *Opus . . . in quattuor mathematicas disciplinas, arithmeticam, musicam, geometriam, & astronomiam*. Venice, 1532.

———. *Liber de quatuor mathematicis scientiis, arithmetica, musica, geometria, & astronomia.* Edited by Gulielmus Xylander. Basle, 1556.

———. *De arithmetica, musica, geometria.* Translated by Elias Vinetus. Paris, 1557.

Ptolemaeus (pseud.). *The compost of Ptholomaeus.* Robert Wyer; London, c.1532.

Puttenham, George. *The arte of English poesie.* London, 1589.

———. *The Arte of English Poesie.* Edited by Gladys D. Willcock and Alice Walker. Cambridge Univ. Press, 1936.

Raleigh, Walter. *The history of the world.* London, 1614.

Rapin, René. *Reflexions upon ancient and modern philosophy.* Translated by A. L. London, 1678.

Recorde, Robert. *The pathway to knowledg.* London, 1551.

———. *The castle of knowledge.* London, 1556.

———. *The whetstone of witte.* London, 1557.

Reghini, Arturo. *Per la restituzione della geometria pitagorica.* Rome, 1936.

Reinach, Théodore. "La musique des sphères." *Revue des études grecques* 13 (1900), 432–449.

Reisch, Gregor. *Margarita philosophica.* Freiburg, 1503.

———. *Margarita philosophica.* Strasbourg, 1515.

———. *Margarita philosophica.* Edited by Oronce Finé. Basle, 1535.

———. *Margarita philosophica.* Basle, 1583.

Reuchlin, Johann. *De arte cabalistica libri tres.* Hagenau, 1517.

———. *De arte cabalistica libri tres.* Translated by Thomas Stanley. In *The history of philosophy.* 2nd ed. London, 1687.

Reynolds, Henry. *Mythomystes* [1632]. In J. E. Spingarn, *Critical Essays of the Seventeenth Century.* 3 vols. Oxford Univ. Press, 1908–09, Vol. I.

Rhodiginus, Ludovicus Caelius. *Antiquarum lectionum libri XVI.* Venice, 1516.

———. *Lectionum antiquarum libri XXX.* Basle, 1566.

Ringelberg, Joachim Fortius. "Liber de tempore." In *Opera.* Lyons, 1531.

Ringhieri, Innocent. *Cento giuochi.* Bologna, 1551.

Ripley, George. *The compound of alchymy.* Edited by Ralph Rabbards. London, 1591.

Robbins, Frank Egleston. "The Tradition of Greek Arithmology." *Classical Philology* 16 (1921), 97–123.

Robin, Léon. *Greek Thought and the Origins of the Scientific Spirit.* New York, 1928.

Robson, Simon. *The choise of change.* London, 1585.

Romei, Annibale. *The courtiers academie.* Translated by J. Kepers. London, 1598.

Rosen, Edward. "Was Copernicus a Pythagorean?" *Isis* 53 (1962), 504–509.

Roslinus, Helisaeus. *De opere dei creationis seu de mundo hypotheses.* Frankfurt, 1597.
Ross, Alexander. *The new planet no planet.* London, 1646.
Ross, W. D. *Plato's Theory of Ideas.* Oxford, 1951.
Rossky, William. "Imagination in the English Renaissance: Psychology and Poetic." *Studies in the Renaissances* 5 (1958), 49–73.
Røstvig, Maren-Sofie. *The Hidden Sense.* Oslo, 1963.
———. "Renaissance Numerology: Acrostics or Criticism?" *Essays in Criticism* 16 (1966), 6–21.
———. "Ars Aeterna: Renaissance Poetics and Theories of Divine Creation." *Mosaic* 3 (1969–70), 40–61.
———. "Structure as Prophecy." In *Silent Poetry*, edited by Alastair Fowler. London, 1970.
Rougier, Louis. *L'Origine astronomique de la croyance pythagoricienne en l'immortalité céleste des âmes.* Cairo, 1933.
Russell, Bertrand. *Mysticism and Logic.* New York, 1957.
Sabinus, Georg. *Fabularum Ovidii interpretatio, ethica, physica, et historica.* Cambridge, 1584.
Sachs, Eva. *Die fünf Platonischen Körper.* Berlin, 1917.
Sacrobosco. *The Sphere of Sacrobosco and Its Commentators.* Edited by Lynn Thorndike. Univ. of Chicago Press, 1949.
Salusbury, Thomas, tr. *Mathematical collections and translations.* 2 vols. London, 1661.
Saluste du Bartas, Guillaume. *Devine weekes and workes.* Translated by Joshua Sylvester. London, 1605.
———. *Works.* Edited by Urban T. Holmes, Jr., *et al.* 3 vols.; Univ. of North Carolina Press, 1940.
Sambursky, S. *The Physical World of Late Antiquity.* London, 1962.
Sandys, George, tr. *Ovid's Metamorphosis.* Oxford, 1632.
Sardus, Alexander. *De rerum inventoribus, libri duo.* Appended to *De moribus ac ritibus gentium lib. III.* Mainz, 1577.
Sarton, George. *A History of Science: Ancient Science Through the Golden Age of Greece.* Harvard Univ. Press, 1952.
Savage, John. *A Select Collection of Letters of the Antients.* London, 1703.
Scaliger, Julius Caesar. *Poetices libri septem.* Lyons, 1561.
Scève, Maurice. *Oeuvres poétiques complètes.* Edited by Bertrand Guégan. Geneva, 1967.
Schallerus, Jacobus. *Ethica Pythagorica Y adornata.* Strasbourg, 1653.
Schedel, Hartmann. *Liber cronicarum.* Nuremberg, 1493.
Scheffer, Joannes. *De natura & constitutione philosophiae Italicae seu Pythagoricae liber singularis.* Upsala, 1664.
Schier, Johann Adam. *Pythagorae aurea carmina.* Leipzig, 1750.
Schrader, Christoforus. *Dissertatio prima de Pythagora, in quâ de eius ortu, praeceptoribus et peregrinationibus agitur.* Leipzig, 1708.
Schroeder, Leopold von. *Pythagoras und die Inder.* Leipzig, 1884.

Scutelli, Nicolò. "De vita & secta Pythagorae flosculi." In *Iamblichus de mysteriis Ægyptiorum*. Rome, 1556.

Secret, François. *Les kabbalistes chrétiens de la renaissance*. Paris, 1964.

Selectiora veterum authorum collectanea. Paris, 1536.

Sempill, Hugh. *De mathematicis disciplinis libri duodecim*. Antwerp, 1635.

Sextus Empiricus. *Works*. Translated by R. G. Bury. 4 vols. Harvard Univ. Press, 1933–49.

Seznec, Jean. *The Survival of the Pagan Gods*. Translated by Barbara F. Sessions. New York, 1953.

Shaftesbury, Anthony, Earl of. *Characteristicks of Men, Manners, Opinions, Times*. 2nd ed. 3 vols. London, 1714.

Shakespeare, William. *The Complete Works*. Edited by Peter Alexander. New York, 1952.

Sidney, Philip. *Complete Works*. Edited by Albert Feuillerat. 4 vols. Cambridge Univ. Press, 1912–26.

———. *The defence of poesie*. William Ponsonby; London, 1595.

———. *An Apology for Poetry*. Edited by Geoffrey Shepherd. London, 1965.

———. *The Poems*. Edited by W. A. Ringler, Jr. Oxford, 1962.

Simson, Otto von. *The Gothic Cathedral*. New York, 1956.

Singer, Charles. *From Magic to Science*. New York, 1958.

Smith, A. J. "Theory and Practice in Renaissance Poetry: Two Kinds of Imitation." *Bulletin of the John Rylands Library* 47 (1964–65), 212–243.

Smith, David E. *Rara arithmetica*. Boston, 1908.

———. *Addenda*. Boston, 1939.

———. *History of Mathematics*. 2 vols. Boston, 1923.

Smith, G. Gregory. *Elizabethan Critical Essays*. 2 vols. Oxford Univ. Press, 1904.

Smith, Hallett. *Elizabethan Poetry*. Harvard Univ. Press, 1952.

Snare, Gerald. "The Muses on Poetry: Spenser's *The Teares of the Muses*." *Tulane Studies in English* 17 (1969), 31–52.

Spencer, Theodore. *Shakespeare and the Nature of Man*. New York, 1942.

Spenser, Edmund. *The Works: A Variorum Edition*. Edited by Edwin Greenlaw *et al.* 10 vols. Johns Hopkins Press, 1932–57.

Speusippus. "Liber de Platonis definitionibus." In Iamblichus, *De mysteriis* et al. Translated by Marsilio Ficino. Venice, 1497.

Spingarn, J. E. *Critical Essays of the Seventeenth Century*. 3 vols. Oxford Univ. Press, 1908–09.

Spitzer, Leo. *Classical and Christian Ideas of World Harmony*. Johns Hopkins Press, 1963.

Stanley, Thomas. *Poems*. London, 1651.

———. *Poems*. Edited by Galbraith M. Crump. Oxford, 1962.

———. *The history of philosophy*. 2 vols. London, 1656–60.

———. *The history of philosophy*. 2nd ed. London, 1687.

Steadman, John M. "The 'Inharmonious Blacksmith': Spenser and the Pythagorean Legend," *Publications of the Modern Language Association* 79 (1964), 664–665.

Stephanus, Carolus. *De Latinis et Graecis nominibus*. Paris, 1536.

Stephanus, Henricus, ed. *Poesis philosophica*. Geneva, 1573.

Stimson, Dorothy. *The Gradual Acceptance of the Copernican Theory of the Universe*. Hanover, N.H., 1917.

Stobaeus. *Eclogae*. Translated by Willem Canter. Antwerp, 1575.

———. *Dicta poetarum quae apud Jo. Stobaeum exstant*. Edited by Hugo Grotius. Paris, 1623.

Strong, Edward W. *Procedures and Metaphysics*. Univ. of California Press, 1936.

Struve, Burckhard Gotthelf. *Bibliotheca philosophica*. Jena, 1704.

Suda. *Lexicon*. Edited by Ada Adler. 5 vols. Leipzig, 1928–38.

Sunderland, Elizabeth R. "Symbolic Numbers and Romanesque Church Plans." *Journal of the Society of Architectural Historians* 18 (1959), 94–103.

Swan, John. *Speculum mundi*. Cambridge, 1635.

Taverner, Richard. *Proverbes or adagies*. London, 1539.

Tayler, Edward W. *Nature and Art in Renaissance Literature*. Columbia Univ. Press, 1964.

Taylor, A. E. *A Commentary on Plato's Timaeus*. Oxford, 1928.

Taylor, Thomas. *Theoretic Arithmetic, in Three Books; containing . . . Theo of Smyrna, Nicomachus, Iamblichus, and Boetius*. London, 1816.

———, tr. *Iamblichus' Life of Pythagoras*. London, 1818.

———, tr. *Proclus on the Timaeus of Plato*. London, 1820.

———, tr. *Ocellus Lucanus on the Nature of the Universe* et al. London, 1831.

Temple, William. *Miscellanea. The second part*. London, 1690.

Theologumena arithmetica. Paris, 1543.

Theon of Smyrna. *Expositio rerum mathematicarum ad legendum Platonem utilium*. Translated by Ismael Bullialdus. Paris, 1644.

———. *Expositio rerum mathematicarum ad legendum Platonem utilium*. Edited by Eduard Heller. Leipzig, 1878.

Thesaurus philosophiae moralis. Lyons, 1589.

Thevet, André. *Pourtraits et vies des hommes illustres*. Paris, 1584.

Thomas, Ivor, ed. and tr. *Selections Illustrating the History of Greek Mathematics: From Thales to Euclid*. London, 1939.

Thorndike, Lynn. *A History of Magic and Experimental Science*. 8 vols. Columbia Univ. Press, 1923–58.

Tigerstedt, E. N. "The Poet as Creator: Origins of a Metaphor." *Comparative Literature Studies* 5 (1968), 455–488.

Tillyard, E. M. W. *The Elizabethan World Picture*. London, 1943.

Timpanaro Cardini, Maria, ed. *Pitagorici testimonianze e frammenti*. 3 vols. Florence, 1958–64.

Toland, John. *Collection of Several Pieces*. London, 1726.

Tomitano, Bernardino. *Quattro libri della lingua thoscana*. Padua, 1570.

Torrentinus, Hermannus. *Dictionarium poeticum*. Paris, 1550.

Toulmin, Stephen, and June Goodfield. *The Fabric of the Heavens*. London, 1961.

Tryon, Thomas. *Pythagoras his mystick philosophy reviv'd*. London, 1691.

Turba philosophorum. In *Bibliothèque des philosophes*. 2 vols. Paris, 1672–73.

The Turba Philosophorum or Assembly of the Sages. Translated by A. E. Waite. London, 1896.

Turler, Jerome. *The Traveiler* [1575]. Edited by Denver E. Baughan. Gainesville, Fla., 1951.

Tyard, Pontus de. *Discours du temps, de l'an, et de ses parties*. Lyons, 1556.

———. *L'Univers*. Paris, 1557.

Tzetzes, Joannes. *Variarum historiarum liber*. Translated by Paulus Lacisius. Basle, 1546.

Valla, Giorgio. *De expetendis, et fugiendis rebus opus*. Venice, 1501.

Van der Waerden, B. L. "Die Arithmetik der Pythagoreer." *Mathematische Annalen* 120 (1948), 127–153, 676–700.

———. *Die Astronomie der Pythagoreer*. Amsterdam, 1951.

Van Irhoven, Willem. *De palingenesia veterum seu metempsychosi sic dicta pythagorica*. Amsterdam, 1733.

Vergil, Polydore. *An abridgemente of the notable worke*. Translated by Thomas Langley. London, 1570.

Vitruvius. *De architectura*. Translated by Frank Granger. 2 vols. London, 1931–34.

Vives, Juan Luis. *On Education*. Translated by Foster Watson. Cambridge Univ. Press, 1913.

Volkmann, Ludwig. *Bilderschriften der Renaissance*. Leipzig, 1923.

Voltaire. *Candide*. Edited by André Morize. Paris, 1931.

Von Helmont, F. M. *The paradoxal discourses . . . concerning the macrocosm and microcosm*. Translated by J. B. London, 1685.

Vossius, Gerard Johann. *De universae mathesios natura & constitutione liber*. Amsterdam, 1650.

———. *De philosophorum sectis liber*. The Hague, 1657.

———. *De philosophia et philosophorum sectis libri II*. The Hague, 1658.

Wagner, Johann Tobias. *De ἀνόδῳ, seu adscensu hominis in Deum pythagorico*. Halle, 1710.

Waite, A. E. *The Doctrine and Literature of the Kabalah*. London, 1902.

———. *The Pictorial Key to the Tarot*. 2nd ed. London, 1911.

———, ed. *The Hermetic Museum, Restored and Enlarged*. 2 vols. London, 1893.

———, tr. *The Turba Philosophorum or Assembly of the Sages*. London, 1896.

Walker, D. P. "Kepler's Celestial Music," *Journal of the Warburg and Courtauld Institutes* 30 (1967), 228–250.

Walkington, Thomas. *The optick glasse of humors.* London, 1607.

Watters, Hallie. *Pythagorean Way of Life.* Adyar, 1926.

Webbe, William. *A discourse of English poetrie* [1586]. In G. Gregory Smith, *Elizabethan Critical Essays.* 2 vols. Oxford Univ. Press, 1904.

Weidler, J. F. *Dissertatio historica de legibus cibariis et vestiariis Pythagorae.* Jena, 1711.

Weinberg, Bernard. *A History of Literary Criticism in the Italian Renaissance.* Univ. of Chicago Press, 1961.

Wendelinus, Godfridus. *Dissertatio epistolica, de tetractu Pythagorae, ad E. Puteanum.* Louvain, 1637.

Wernsdorf, Gottlieb. *De metempsychosi veterum non figurate sed proprie intelligenda.* Wittenberg, 1741.

Whittaker, Thomas. *The Neo-Platonists.* 2nd ed. Cambridge Univ. Press, 1928.

Wiener, Philip P., and Aaron Noland, eds. *Roots of Scientific Thought.* New York, 1957.

Wightman, W. P. D. *The Growth of Scientific Ideas.* Yale Univ. Press, 1951.

Williamson, George. "Mutability, Decay, and Seventeenth-Century Melancholy." *English Literary History* 2 (1935), 121–150.

Wilson, Harold S. "Some Meanings of 'Nature' in Renaissance Literary Theory." *Journal of the History of Ideas* 2 (1941), 430–448.

Winny, James, ed. *The Frame of Order.* London, 1957.

Winterton, Ralph, ed. *Poetae minores graeci.* Cambridge, 1635.

Witekind, Hermann. *De sphaera mundi: et temporis ratione apud Christianos.* Newstadt, 1590.

Wittkower, Rudolph. *Architectural Principles in the Age of Humanism.* London, 1949.

Wolff, Hieronymus, ed. *Epicteti enchiridion . . . Cebetis Thebani tabula.* Basle, 1561.

Wotton, William. *Reflections upon ancient and modern learning.* London, 1694.

———. *Reflections upon ancient and modern learning.* 2nd ed. London, 1697.

Xenophon. *Memoirs of Socrates.* Translated by Sarah Fielding. Bath, 1762.

Yates, Frances A. *The French Academies of the Sixteenth Century.* London, 1947.

———. *Giordano Bruno and the Hermetic Tradition.* London, 1964.

Young, Douglas, ed. *Theognis, Pythagoras, Phocylidis.* Leipzig, 1961.

Zarlino, Gioseffo. *Le Istitutione harmoniche.* Venice, 1558.

Zehner, Joachim, ed. *Pythagorae fragmenta.* Leipzig, 1603.

Zeller, Eduard. *A History of Greek Philosophy.* Translated by S. F. Alleyne. 2 vols. London, 1881.

INDEX

TOUCHES OF SWEET HARMONY

Pythagorean Cosmology and Renaissance Poetics

by S. K. HENINGER, JR.

How sweetly sleeps the moonlight on this bank!
Here will we sit and let the sounds of music
Creep in our ears; soft stillness and the night
Become the touches of sweet harmony.
The Merchant of Venice

The notion of a harmonious universe is one of man's most cherished beliefs. It was taught by Pythagoras as early as the sixth century B.C., and remained a basic premise in Western philosophy, science, and art almost to our own day. This book demonstrates the pervasiveness of this concept in the renaissance. The theory of cosmos, expressed as universal harmony or as a tetrad, was prominent in the period and strongly conditioned its esthetics. Unless we understand this, much of the meaning and beauty of Elizabethan poetry will be lost.

The universe as conceived by Pythagoras was carefully constructed. Our earth stood fixed at the center. Ranging outward from it were the spheres of the planets, with the sun as the midmost of seven. Beyond them shone the stars, distributed around the underside of a single delimiting sphere. And outside all, secure in an unchanging empyrean, reigned a benevolent God. Throughout His creation the pattern of the tetrad persisted, so that there were four elements, four seasons, four humours, four ages of man. The traditional sciences taught in the universities—mathematics, music, geometry, and astronomy—derived from a study of these cosmic arrangements. To those who believed in it, the logic and symmetry of such a system brought welcome reassurance.

In this book the author recapitulates the extensive lore connected with Pythagoras. He recounts the legendary life of Pythagoras and describes his school at Croton, and he discusses the materials from which the renaissance drew its information about Pythagorean doctrine. The second section of the book reconstructs the many facets of this doctrine, while the final section shows its influence on renaissance poetics. Specifically, there are chapters which develop the assumptions that the poet is a maker acting in likeness of the creating godhead, that metaphor depends upon correspondences between the various levels of creation, and that the poem serves as a microcosm in literary form.

Finally, the author expresses his conviction that unless we accept the viability of a divinely-ordered universe, as did the sixteenth-century poet, we shall misinterpret much of the best writing in our language. Today's reader is predisposed to read in a different way. He is likely to follow the words of a poem from beginning to end and respond to these phenomena in an affective fashion, thinking that then he has read the work once and for all. But with a good deal of Elizabethan poetry, this first reading is just a preliminary. The reader must go further and consider the poem as a totality, a literary microcosm. Only then can he place each incident and each character and each metaphor in proper context, so that each part is integrally related to an inclusive whole. This totality in turn gives an added dimension of meaning to each of its constituent parts.

Professor Heninger's learning coupled with his warm enthusiasm is persuasive. He introduces the reader not only to Pythagoras but to a host of other classical, medieval, and renaissance figures—from Plato and Aristotle through St. Augustine and Macrobius down to Sidney and Spenser. For students in esthetics, in comparative literature, in the history of science and of philosophy, and in all related fields this book gathers together a wealth of information and shows its assimilation in renaissance thought. Equally important, it suggests fresh points of departure for further research and criticism.

S. K. Heninger, Jr., holds a Ph.D. degree from the Johns Hopkins University and has taught at Duke University and at the University of Wisconsin (Madison), where he was also Chairman of the English Department. He is currently Professor of English at the University of British Columbia. He has written *A Handbook of Renaissance Meteorology*, has edited the *Hekatompathia* of Thomas Watson and a volume of selections from the poetry of Edmund Spenser, and has contributed numerous articles and reviews to scholarly journals.